PRINCIPLES OF
MONEY, BANKING, AND FINANCIAL MARKETS

PRINCIPLES OF

MONEY, BANKING, AND FINANCIAL MARKETS

SIXTH EDITION

Lawrence S. Ritter
William L. Silber

BASIC BOOKS, INC., PUBLISHERS
NEW YORK

''. . . be careful in teaching,
for error in teaching amounts to deliberate sin.''

The *Mishnah*
Pirkei Avot, 4

Library of Congress Cataloging-in-Publication Data
Ritter, Lawrence S.
  Principles of money, banking, and financial
markets.

Includes bibliographies and index.
  1. Money. 2. Banks and banking. 3. Finance.
I. Silber, William L.   II. Title.
HG221.R536   1989   332   88–47759
ISBN 0–465–06350–0

Printed in the United States of America
Text Designed by Nancy Sugihara
Cover Design: Nancy Sugihara
Cover Photo: Robert Paftner/Comstock
89 90 91 92 RRD 9 8 7 6 5 4 3 2

For
Jonathan, *who likes to win*
Danny, *who likes his way*
Tammy, *who likes people*
and for
Steve *and* **Peter**
With Love

Acknowledgments

We are greatly indebted to our outstanding copy editor, Nina Gunzenhauser, who contributed immeasurably to the readability of this edition and to the preceding one as well. In addition, the first five editions of this book generated a number of communications from students and teachers. Some were favorable, others critical, but all helped us prepare this sixth edition. We would like to thank the following for taking the time and effort to help improve this revision (affiliations are those at the time the comments were received):

Burton Abrams, *University of Delaware*

Paul L. Altieri, *Central Connecticut State College*

Ernie Ankrim, *Pacific Lutheran University*

Eddie Ary, *Ouachita Baptist University*

William T. Baldwin, *Eastern Kentucky University*

John Bay, *University of Southern Maine*

Herbert Bernstein, *Drexel University*

W. Carl Biven, *Georgia Institute of Technology*

Deborah Black, *Hunter College of City University of New York*

Dwight M. Blood, *Brigham Young University*

Elbert V. Bowden, *Appalachian State University*

Robert C. Burton, *Frostburg State College*

Ralph T. Byrns, *Metropolitan State College*

John A. Carlson, *Purdue University*

Stephen Cecchetti, *Ohio State University*

Arthur D. Chesler, *Kentucky Wesleyan College*

Thomas C. Chiang, *Drexel University*

Dale Cloninger, *University of Houston at Clear Lake*

Bob Curl, *Northwest Nazarene College*

J. Kenneth Davies, *Brigham Young University*

Robert M. Domine, *University of Michigan*

James S. Earley, *University of California, Riverside*

William P. Field, Jr., *Nicholls State University*

Stanley Fischer, *Massachusetts Institute of Technology*

Ian Giddy, *Columbia University*

John B. Guerard, Jr., *University of Texas*

Satya P. Gupta, *Augsburg College*

Jerry W. Gustafson, *Beloit College*

Philip J. Hahn, *Youngstown State University*

Gabriel Hawawini, *INSEAD (The European Institute of Business), Fontainebleau, France*

Naphtali Hoffman, *Elmira College*

Robert S. Holbrook, *University of Michigan*

Mary Jaffier, *New York University*

Edward J. Kane, *Ohio State University*

Peter M. Kerr, *Southeast State College*

Jimmie King, Jr., *Tuskegee Institute*

Richard W. Kjetsaa, *Fairleigh Dickinson University*

Gregor Lazarcik, *State University of New York at Geneseo*

Marie Lobue, *University of New Orleans*

Darryl W. Lowry, *Roanoke College*

Morgan J. Lynge, *University of Illinois at Urbana*

John McArthur, *Claremont Graduate School*

John J. Merrick, *New York University*

vii

H. Brian Moehring, *University of the Redlands*

Robert L. Moore, *Harvard University*

Douglas W. Morrill, *Centenary College of Louisiana*

Alan Norton, *St. John Fisher College*

John A. Orr, *California State University at Chico*

Peter Parker, *Randolph-Macon College*

Braxton I. Patterson, *University of Wisconsin at Oshkosh*

Thomas J. Pierce, *California State University at San Bernardino*

Dean Popp, *San Diego State University*

Thomas P. Potiowsky, *Portland State University*

Alan Rabin, *University of Tennessee at Chattanooga*

Henry Rennie, *University of Toledo*

Deborah E. Robbins, *Wellesley College*

M. Richard Roseman, *California State University at Los Angeles*

David Sandberg, *Brigham Young University*

John M. Sapinsley, *Rhode Island College*

Donald J. Schilling, *University of Missouri*

Carole Scott, *West Georgia College*

Larry J. Sechrest, *University of Texas at Arlington*

Edward Shapiro, *University of Toledo*

Milton M. Shapiro, *California Polytechnic State University*

Thomas J. Shea, *Springfield College*

Cathy Sherman, *University of Texas*

William O. Shropshire, *Oglethorpe University*

Harinder Singh, *San Diego State University*

Theodore R. Snyder, Jr., *University of New England*

Milton H. Spencer, *Wayne State University*

Charles E. Staley, *State University of New York at Stony Brook*

H. Joe Story, *Pacific University*

Harry C. Symons, *Ursinus College*

Ronald L. Teigen, *University of Michigan*

John Thorkelson, *University of Connecticut*

Kenneth N. Townsend, *Hampden-Sydney College*

Dang Tran, *University of Baltimore*

Pearl S. Vogel, *Sacred Heart University*

Joan Walters, *Fairfield University*

Douglas A. Wion, *Lock Haven State College*

Stuart Wood, *Tulane University*

Notes to the Instructor

In preparing this sixth edition we were influenced primarily by the sweeping changes that have occurred in our monetary and financial system during the fifteen years since *Principles of Money, Banking, and Financial Markets* was first published. Although each of our previous five editions has kept pace with current developments, this sixth edition represents by far the most substantial overhaul of all. Improvements have been made in institutional and theoretical coverage as well as in pedagogical techniques; however, we still maintain the casual conversational style that has highlighted earlier editions.

The expanded theoretical coverage appears in Parts 1 and 4. In Part 1, which covers the basics, we have introduced two new chapters titled "Calculating Interest Rates" and "The Level of Interest Rates." The first of these chapters provides a systematic introduction to interest rate computations, while the second presents a concise supply-demand model explaining how the level of rates is determined. These chapters permit courses that focus on financial institutions and markets to sidestep entirely the extensive material on monetary theory. To accomodate those wishing to concentrate on theoretical issues, however, we have reorganized Part 4 to highlight the separate chapters dealing with *ISLM* analysis and aggregate supply-demand analysis. An entirely new chapter titled "Rational Expectations: Theory and Policy Implications" has been added for more advanced theoretical discussion.

Improved coverage of financial institutions and markets also comes in two forms. In Part 1 we present introductory material systematically in two chapters titled "Financial Instruments and Markets" and "Financial Institutions: Purposes and Profile." In Part 5 we have expanded coverage of financial markets with two entirely new chapters titled "Other Fixed Income Markets" and "Financial Futures and Options," and with an appendix on duration. In addition, existing material on the government securities market and on the stock market has been expanded into chapters that more fully reflect the structure and organization of those markets.

A number of pedagogical improvements also appear in this edition.

In addition to news clippings that have always been interspersed throughout the text, we have introduced discussion boxes dealing with "Reading the Financial News" and special topics of popular interest. A completely new chapter on "Careers in Banking and Financial Markets" has been added to provide perspective to students on how they might eventually apply some of the material covered during the semester. Finally, the book now ends with a Glossary, which we hope your students find useful.

These improvements in the coverage of the book have been mirrored in both the *Study Guide* by Gabriel Hawawini and the separate *Instructor's Manual with Test Bank* by Paul Warner and Gabriel Hawawini. For instructors, the test bank is available on Harper Test, a microcomputer test-generation system for Apple II and IBM PC computers. We think this entire package will permit you to tailor the course to meet the needs of your students.

The specific organization of the book reflects the way we would teach a course in Money and Banking or Financial Institutions and Markets. However, we realize that there are alternative ways to organize such a course, ways that would involve a different ordering of chapters. We have therefore written the book with the ideal of flexibility in mind. Although every instructor can best structure his or her own course, here are some illustrative examples of the ways this book can be adapted to different approaches.

Part 1 ("The Basics") forms the foundation for all future topics. Thus the chapters in Part 1 might all be assigned in the beginning of the course. Alternatively, each of the chapters in Part 1 can be used to initiate subsequent parts of the book. For example, Chapter 2 ("Money, the Economy, and Inflation") belongs with Part 3 ("The Art of Central Banking") or even with Part 4 ("Monetary Theory"); Chapter 3 ("Financial Instruments and Markets") goes with Part 5 ("Financial Markets and Interest Rates"); Chapter 4 ("Financial Institutions: Purposes and Profile") introduces Part 2 ("Intermediaries and Banks"); finally, Chapter 5 ("Calculating Interest Rates") and Chapter 6 ("The Level of Interest Rates") can be used to launch Part 4 ("Monetary Theory") or any other section, for that matter.

The two major types of course organization are (1) a financial institutions and markets and central banking emphasis, and (2) a monetary theory and policy emphasis. The ordering of the chapters as they appear in the table of contents reflects the first type of approach: financial institutions and markets and central banking. Even within each of these categories, it is possible to emphasize different subjects. Here are some suggestions:

1. *Financial institutions and markets and central banking:* After the basics in Part 1, Parts 2 and 3 present a comprehensive analysis of the business of financial intermediaries and the art of central banking. A limited amount of theory on the role of money in the economy is given in Chapters 1 and 2, and interest rates are introduced in Chapters 5 and 6, to provide the proper framework for the discussion of central banking.

   When the formal presentation of monetary theory begins in Part 4, it is possible to reduce the emphasis on theory by eliminating Chapters 21 and 22; these chapters construct and then apply *ISLM* analysis, but the rest of the book is written so that the omission of this material will not interrupt its continuity or intelligibility.

   In a course devoted exclusively to financial institutions and markets, it is possible to avoid formal monetary theory entirely by going directly to Part 5 ("Financial Markets and Interest Rates") after Part 1. For such courses, the overview of money in Chapters 1 and 2 and the framework for interest rate determination in Chapter 6 provide a more than adequate discussion of theoretical material.

   Many professors seem to prefer teaching Parts 1, 2, and 3 in sequence, then moving to Part 5 and possibly even 6 before backtracking to Part 4 ("Monetary Theory").

2. *Monetary theory and policy:* After Part 1 is completed, monetary theory can be introduced immediately by going directly to Part 4. One can then backtrack to Parts 2 and 3, which discuss financial institutions and central banking, and then continue with Part 5 ("Financial Markets and Interest Rates"). In fact, Chapters 28 and 33 ("The Structure of Interest Rates" and "Financial Futures and Options") could be brought into a theory-oriented course much earlier, right after Part 4.

3. *International aspects:* It is possible to put all of Part 6 ("International Finance") virtually anywhere one wishes, provided the basics in Part 1 have been covered. The international chapters, for example, could easily follow Part 3 ("The Art of Central Banking") or Part 4 ("Monetary Theory").

   We hope that you find both the new and continuing features of the book useful teaching devices. If you have any comments or suggestions for the next edition, we would appreciate hearing from you.

LSR
WLS

About the Authors

LAWRENCE S. RITTER is John M. Schiff Professor of Finance and Economics at the undergraduate and graduate Schools of Business of New York University. A former Chief of the Domestic Research Division of the Federal Reserve Bank of New York, he has served as a consultant to the U.S. Treasury, the Federal Deposit Insurance Corporation, the Board of Governors of the Federal Reserve System, the American Bankers Association, the Association of Reserve City Bankers, and the Garvin Guy-Butler Corporation. He has been the Editor of the *Journal of Finance* and is a past President of the American Finance Association. Professor Ritter is also the author of numerous articles in professional journals and of *The Glory of Their Times*, a best-selling book about the early days of baseball.

WILLIAM L. SILBER is Professor of Finance and Economics and Director, L. Glucksman Institute for Research in Securities Markets at the Graduate School of Business Administration at New York University. A former Senior Staff Economist with the President's Council of Economic Advisers and a former Senior Vice President at Lehman Brothers Kuhn Loeb, he has served as a consultant to the Board of Governors of the Federal Reserve System, the President's Commission on Financial Structure and Regulation, the U.S. Senate Committee on the Budget, the House Committee on Banking, Currency and Housing, the Justice Department, the Federal Reserve Bank of New York, the Federal Home Loan Bank Board, the National Commission on Electronic Funds Transfers, and the Department of Housing and Urban Development. He is an Associate Editor of the *Review of Economics and Statistics* and is the author of five books and numerous articles in professional journals.

Contents

PART 3   THE ART OF CENTRAL BANKING

PART 5   FINANCIAL MARKETS AND INTEREST RATES

PART 6   INTERNATIONAL FINANCE

PART I

THE BASICS

CHAPTER 1

Introducing Money

The lack of money is the root of all evil," said George Bernard Shaw. Although that may be something of an exaggeration, there have been numerous periods in history when it appeared to be more true than false. There have also been rather lengthy episodes when the opposite seemed true: when economic disruption apparently stemmed not from too little money, but from too *much* of it.

From this line of thought, the question naturally arises, what is the "right" amount of money? Not too little, not too much, but just right? And how can we go about getting it?

Actually those are fairly sophisticated questions requiring careful consideration to produce answers that stand the test of time. Although we will devote a fair amount of attention to the relationship between money and economic activity, a number of somewhat more fundamental issues spring to mind as well. For example, exactly what is this thing called money that has obsessed princes and paupers throughout the centuries? In the good old days money was gold, kept under lock and key until it was sent by ship or stagecoach to meet the payroll. Nowadays money is paper that we carry around until it is worn and frayed. Can these really be the same thing?

In truth, our discussion will have to extend far beyond the traditional confines of money if we want to understand the workings of our financial system. Financial institutions and markets have become so complex during the second half of the twentieth century that commercial banks are no longer the only financial institutions that matter and stocks and bonds no longer tell the entire story of how financial markets operate. The remaining chapters in Part 1 introduce the various sectors of our financial system as well as the basic tools for evaluating financial instruments. In this chapter we focus on the basics of money—the asset that despite modern complexities still lies at the heart of our financial system.

THE SUPPLY OF MONEY

What *is* money, anyway? And how much of it do we actually have?

Money is just what you think it is—what you spend when you want to buy something. The Indians used beads, Eskimos used fishhooks, and we use *currency* (coins and bills) and, most of all, *checking accounts.*

Money is used as (1) a means of payment, but it has other functions as well. It is also used as (2) a store of value, when people hold on to it, and (3) a standard of value (a unit of account), when people compare prices and thereby assess relative values. But most prominently money is what you can spend, a generally acceptable means of payment or medium of exchange that you can use to buy things or settle debts.

How large a money supply do we have? It amounted to $750 billion at the end of 1987, roughly $200 billion in the form of currency and about $550 billion in checkable deposits at banks and other financial institutions. This definition of money—currency outside banks plus checking accounts—is frequently called M1 (to distinguish it from two other definitions of money, M2 and M3, which we will get to in a moment). If you want to know what the money supply is *today,* add about 5 or 6 percent per annum to that figure since the end of 1987 and you probably won't be far off. Or you can check the *New York Times* or the *Wall Street Journal;* both newspapers list it every Friday.

Since currency and checking accounts are spendable at face value virtually anywhere, at any time, they are the most "liquid" assets a person can have. A liquid asset is something you can turn into the generally acceptable medium of exchange quickly without taking a loss, as compared with illiquid assets, which can be sold or liquidated on short notice only at a substantially lower price. Currency and checking accounts are the most liquid assets you can have (because they *are* the medium of exchange), but they are not the only liquid assets around. Savings deposits and government bonds are rather liquid, although you can't spend them directly. To spend them, you first have to exchange them for money. At the other extreme, real estate and vintage automobiles typically rank fairly low on the liquidity scale; if you have to sell quickly, you're likely to take a beating on the deal.

Thus liquidity is a continuum, ranging from currency and checkable deposits at the top of the scale to a variety of frozen assets at the bottom. As a result, what we call "money" is not a fixed and immutable thing, like what we call water (H_2O), but to a great extent is a matter of judgment; there are several different definitions of money, each of which drops one notch lower on the liquidity scale in drawing the line between "money" and "all other assets." Table 1 summarizes three different definitions of the money supply.

M1 refers to the most liquid of all assets, currency plus all types of checking accounts at financial institutions. Until the mid-1970s, commercial banks were the only financial institutions permitted to issue checking accounts (sometimes called demand deposits). Now, the so-called thrift or deposit-type institutions—savings banks, savings and loan associations, and credit unions—have entered the picture as well. However, most demand deposits are still in commercial banks.

In addition, as Table 1 indicates, other checkable deposits, such as negotiable order of withdrawal (NOW) accounts, are also considered part of M1. These interest-bearing checking accounts were made available to individuals and households during the 1970s as banks and thrifts circumvented the prohibition against paying interest on demand deposits. Since M1 is confined to these highly liquid assets, ones that can be used in an unrestricted way as a means of payment, it is the narrowest definition of money (as well as the most traditional one, by the way).

M2 drops a shade lower on the liquidity scale by adding assets that are most easily and most frequently transferred into checking accounts when a payment is about to be made. This category includes household savings accounts and small-denomination (under $100,000) time certificates of deposit (CDs). Unlike passbook savings accounts, CDs have a scheduled maturity date. If you want to withdraw your funds earlier, you suffer a substantial penalty by having to forfeit part of your accrued interest.

M2 also includes money market deposit accounts at banks and thrift institutions as well as shares in money market mutual funds. Actually, most money market deposit accounts and money market mutual fund shares carry limited check-writing privileges, so many people believe

TABLE 1
Three Definitions of the Money Supply
(End of 1987)

M1	Currency outside banks ($200 billion), plus demand deposits at banks ($285 billion), plus other checkable deposits at banks and at all thrift institutions ($260 billion), plus travelers' checks ($5 billion)	$750 billion
M2	Add small-denomination time deposits ($915 billion), plus money market deposit accounts ($525 billion) and passbook savings deposits ($415 billion) at all depository institutions, plus money market mutual funds shares ($220 billion), plus bank overnight repurchase agreements and Eurodollars ($75 billion)	2,900 billion
M3	Add large-denomination ($100,000 and over) time deposits at all depository institutions ($485 billion), plus bank long-term repurchase agreements	3,650 billion

SOURCE: *Federal Reserve Bulletin.*

NOTE: Money market mutual funds, money market deposit accounts, repurchase agreements, and Eurodollars are all explained and discussed in subsequent chapters.

they should really be listed in M1. However, the data as presently compiled include them in M2.

M3 adds primarily large-denomination ($100,000 and over) time CDs, most of which are held as short-term investments by business firms. We will discuss them further in Chapter 8.

So what is the money supply in the United States? Is it $750 billion (M1) or $3,650 billion (M3), or something in between? Each definition of money has its adherents, but by and large most economists prefer the narrow definition of the money supply—M1—because that and only that is generally acceptable as a means of payment. Once you go beyond currency and checking accounts, it is hard to find a logical place to stop, since many things (bonds, stocks, waterbeds) contain liquidity in varying degrees. Throughout this book, therefore, we will for the most part stick to the narrow definition of money: currency plus checkable deposits.[1]

[1]Which is not to say that M1 is a perfect measure of how much of the means of payment is in existence. As just one example of its shortcomings, notice that M1 does not include any estimate of existing bank "overdraft" facilities (which are arrangements that allow people to write checks—legally—even when they don't have enough

WHO DETERMINES OUR MONEY SUPPLY?

Why do we have $750 billion of money in the United States? Who, or what, determines how much there will be?

Regardless of what you may have heard, the amount of gold does *not* determine the money supply. Indeed, it has very little influence on it. In 1968 the last remaining link between the money supply and gold was severed when a law requiring 25 percent gold backing behind most of our currency was repealed. If that is all news to you, it is a good indication of just how unimportant the connection between gold and money has always been, at least in the past half-century.

Both currency and checking accounts can be increased (or decreased) without any relation to gold. Does that disturb you? Does it lead you to distrust the value of your money? Then send it to us. We'll be delighted to pay you ninety cents on the dollar, which should be a bargain if you believe all you read about a dollar being worth only sixty cents, or fifty cents, or whatever the latest figure may be.[2]

If gold is not the watchdog, then who (or what) does determine how much money we will have?

The monetary authority in most countries is called the central bank. A central bank does not deal directly with the public; it is rather a bank for banks, and it is responsible for the execution of national monetary policy. In the United States the central banking function is carried out by the Federal Reserve System, created by Congress in 1913. It consists of twelve district Federal Reserve banks, scattered throughout the country, and a Board of Governors in Washington. This hydra-headed monster, which some view as benign but others consider an ever lurking peril, possesses ultimate authority over the money supply.

As noted earlier, the money supply (M1) consists of currency and checking accounts. *Currency* is manufactured by money factories—the Bureau of Engraving and Printing and the Mint—and then shipped under heavy guard to the U.S. Treasury and the Federal Reserve for

---

in their checking accounts to cover them). These as well as other funds available for immediate payment are not included in M1 mainly because of the absence of reliable data on them.

[2]Actually, when you read that the dollar is worth only fifty cents you have a clue to why gold has little to do with the *value* of money, in addition to having little to do with determining the amount outstanding. Money is valuable only because you can buy things with it, like clothes and books and stereos. The value of a dollar is therefore determined by the prices of the things we buy. When people say a dollar is worth only fifty cents they mean that nowadays it takes a dollar to buy what fifty cents could have bought a few years ago (because prices have doubled).

further distribution. For the most part it enters circulation when people and business firms cash checks at their local banks. Thus it is the public that ultimately decides what proportion of the money supply will be in the form of currency, with the Federal Reserve banks wholesaling the necessary coins and paper to local banks. The Federal Reserve is not particularly concerned with the fraction of the money supply that is in one form or another, but rather with the *total* of checkable deposits plus currency.[3]

As Table 1 shows, most of the money supply (almost three-quarters of it) is in the form of checking accounts. These deposits come into being, as we will see in the next chapter, when banks extend credit—that is, when they make loans or buy securities. Checking deposits vanish, as silently as they came, when banks contract credit—when loans are repaid or banks sell securities. It is precisely here, through its ability to control bank behavior, that the Federal Reserve wields its primary authority over the money supply and thereby implements monetary policy.

This process of money creation by banks, and the execution of monetary policy by the Federal Reserve, will be introduced in the next chapter and discussed at great length in Chapters 13 through 18. But before we get into the details, we should back off for a moment and ask, why all the fuss? Why is money so important to begin with?

THE IMPORTANCE OF MONEY I: MONEY VERSUS BARTER

What good is money in the first place? To appreciate the importance of money in an economic system, it is instructive to speculate on what

---

[3]Just in case you're curious, here are some miscellaneous facts about coins and bills. Coins are manufactured by the U.S. Mint, which has production facilities in Philadelphia, Denver, and San Francisco. All bills are manufactured by the U.S. Bureau of Engraving and Printing in Washington, D.C. The largest denomination of currency now issued is the $100 bill; there used to be $500, $1,000, $5,000, and $10,000 bills in circulation, but printing them was discontinued in 1945. The average life of a $1 bill is about a year and a half, before it is torn or worn out, which is why the government tried to popularize the Susan B. Anthony dollar coins in 1979. Coins last much longer than bills. Banks send worn-out bills back to the Federal Reserve, which destroys them and then distributes newly printed bills in their place. With a population of 250 million, the $200 billion of coin and bills in circulation at the end of 1987 amounted to an average of $800 for each man, woman, and child in the country. Which means, if you stop to think about it, that there must be an awful lot of currency stashed away *somewhere*.

the economy might look like without it. In other words, why was money invented (by Sir John Money in 3016 B.C.)?

For one thing, without money individuals in the economy would have to devote more time to buying what they want and selling what they don't. In other words, people would have less time to work and play. A barter economy is one without a medium of exchange or a unit of account (the measuring-rod function of money). Let's see what it might be like to live in a barter economy.

Say you are a carpenter and agree to build a bookcase for your neighbor. Your friend happens to raise chickens and pays you with four dozen eggs. You decide to keep a dozen for yourself, so you now have three dozen to exchange for the rest of the week's groceries. All you must do is find a grocer who is short on eggs.

What's more, you have to remember that a loaf of bread exchanges for six eggs (it also exchanges for eleven books of matches or three boxes of crayons or one Yankee Yearbook, but never mind because you don't have any of these things to spare). And of course all the other items on the grocer's shelf have similar price tags. The tags are bigger than the items.

Along comes money and simplifies matters. Workers are paid in something called money, which they can then use to pay their bills and make their purchases. Money becomes the medium of exchange. We no longer need price tags giving rates of exchange between an item and everything else that might conceivably be exchanged for it. Instead, prices of goods and services are expressed in terms of money, a common denominator.

The most important thing about the medium of exchange is that everyone must be confident that it can be passed on, that it is generally acceptable in trade. Paradoxically, people will accept the medium of exchange only when they are certain that it can be passed on to someone else. One key characteristic is that the *uncertainty* over its value in trade must be very *low*. People will be more willing to accept the medium of exchange if they are certain of what it is worth in terms of things they really want. The uncertainty of barter transactions makes people wary of exchange. If I want to sell my house and buy a car and you want to do just the reverse, we might be able to strike a deal, except for the fact that you've got shifty eyes and are likely to sell me a lemon. Hence I don't make a deal; I'm uncertain about the value of the thing I'm being asked to accept in exchange. A medium of exchange, which is handled often in many transactions, becomes familiar to us all and can be checked carefully for fraud. Uncertainty in trading is thereby reduced to a minimum.

Closely related to the low-uncertainty-high-exchangeability requirement is the likelihood that the medium of exchange will not deteriorate in value. It must be a good store of value, or as soon as I accept the medium of exchange I'll try to get rid of it; otherwise it might be worth fewer and fewer goods and services tomorrow or the day after. Thus if price inflation gets out of hand and I have little confidence that the medium of exchange will hold its value, I'll be reluctant to accept it in exchange; in other words, it won't be the medium of exchange for very long. If that happens, we'll begin to slip back into barter.

The medium of exchange also usually serves as a unit of account. In other words, the prices of all other goods are expressed in terms of, say, dollars. Without such a unit of account, you'd have to remember the exchange ratios of soap for bread, knives for shirts, and bookcases for haircuts (and haircuts for soap). The unit of account reduces the information you have to carry around in your brain, freeing that limited space for creative speculation.

So money is a good thing. It frees people from spending too much time running around bartering goods and services and allows them to undertake other endeavors—production, relaxation, contemplation, and temptation.

It is important to emphasize, once again, that people use the medium of exchange—money—not because it has any intrinsic value but because it can be exchanged for things to eat, drink, wear, and play with. The *value* of a unit of money is determined, therefore, by the prices of each and every thing—more accurately, the average level of all prices. If prices go up, a unit of money (a dollar) is worth less because it will buy less; if prices go down—use your imagination—a dollar is worth more because it will buy more. Thus, the value of money varies inversely with the price level.

THE IMPORTANCE OF MONEY II: FINANCIAL INSTITUTIONS AND MARKETS

Money also contributes to economic development and growth, by stimulating both saving and investment and facilitating transfers of funds out of the hoards of savers and into the hands of borrowers who want to undertake investment projects but do not have enough of their own money to do so. Financial markets give savers a variety of ways to lend to borrowers, thereby increasing the volume of both saving and investment and encouraging economic growth.

People who save are often not the same people who can see and exploit profitable investment opportunities. In an economy without money, the only way people can invest (buy productive equipment) is by consuming less than their income (saving). Similarly, in an economy without money the only way people can save—that is, consume less than their income—is by acquiring real goods directly.

The introduction of money, however, permits separation of the act of investment from the act of saving: money makes it possible for a person to invest without first refraining from consumption (saving) and likewise makes it possible for a person to save without also investing. People can now invest who are not fortunate enough to have their own savings.

In a monetary economy, a person simply accumulates savings in cash (money is a store of value). Through financial markets, this surplus cash can be lent to a business firm borrowing the funds to invest in new equipment, equipment it might not have been able to buy if it did not have access to borrowed funds. Both the saver and the business firm are better off: the saver receives interest payments, and the business firm expects to earn a return over and above the interest cost. And the economy is also better off: the only way an economy can grow is by allocating part of its resources to the creation of new and better productive facilities.

In an advanced economy such as ours, this channeling of funds from savers to investors, through financial markets, reaches highly complex dimensions. A wide variety of financial instruments, such as stocks, bonds, and mortgages, are utilized as devices through which borrowers can gain access to the surplus funds of savers. Various markets specialize in trading one or another of these financial instruments.

And financial institutions have sprung up—such as commercial banks, savings banks, savings and loan associations, credit unions, insurance companies, mutual funds, and pension funds—that act as intermediaries in transferring funds from ultimate lenders to ultimate borrowers. Such financial intermediaries themselves borrow from saver-lenders and then turn around and lend the funds to borrower-investors. They mobilize the savings of many small savers and package them for sale to the highest bidders. In the process, again both ultimate saver-lenders and ultimate borrower-investors gain: savers have the added option of acquiring savings deposits or pension rights, which are less risky than individual stocks or bonds, and business-firm borrowers can tap large sums of money from a single source.

None of this would be possible were it not for the existence of money, the one financial asset that lies at the foundation of the whole superstructure.[4] But once we have this unique thing called money, we also have the problem of controlling it.

Uncontrolled, money may cause hyperinflation or disastrous depression and thereby cancel its blessings. If price inflation gets out of hand, for example, money ceases to be a reliable store of value and therefore becomes a less efficient medium of exchange. People become reluctant to accept cash in payment for goods and services, and when they do accept it, they try to get rid of it as soon as possible. As we noted above, the value of money is determined by the price level of the goods money is used to purchase. The higher the prices, the more dollars one has to give up to get real goods or buy services. Inflation (rising prices) reduces the value of money. Hyperinflation (prices rising at a fast and furious pace) reduces the value of money by a lot within a short time span. Hence people don't want to hold very much cash; they want to exchange it for goods or services as quickly as possible. Thus if money breaks down as a store of value, it starts to deteriorate as a medium of exchange as well, and we start to slip back into barter. People spend more time exchanging goods and less time producing, consuming, and enjoying them. Severe depression causes different but no less serious consequences.

So once we have money, the question constantly challenges us: *how much* of it should there be?

A PREVIEW

In the next chapter we spell out the relationship between money and economic activity and describe in simple terms how the Federal Reserve determines the appropriate money supply. That discussion is continued in greater detail in Part 3 of the book, which focuses on central banking, and in Part 4, dealing with monetary theory. The remaining chapters in Part 1 are devoted to an overview of our financial system, as well as basic analytic material crucial to money, banking, and financial markets. In addition, each of these chapters provides an introduction to subsequent sections of the book.

[4]Strictly speaking it is theoretically possible for transfers between savers and investors to occur within a barter framework. Thus credit arrangements could exist without money. But only the existence of money permits the complex and efficient channeling of funds between savers and investors.

Chapter 3 describes financial instruments, such as stocks and bonds, and the money and capital markets, thereby serving as an introduction to Part 5, which focuses on the operations and details of various financial markets.

Chapter 4 profiles the major financial institutions and thereby previews the material in Part 2, which concentrates on banks and other intermediaries.

The main introductory analytical material is presented in Chapters 5 and 6. The former focuses on what interest rates are, how to measure them, and alternative formulas for actual calculations. Chapter 6 examines interest rates from a different perspective: the forces that determine whether they are high or low. Thus, while Chapter 5 provides an understanding of the mechanics of interest rate calculations and therefore is relevant for just about everything in this book, Chapter 6 focuses on the underlying economics of interest rate determination and thereby corresponds to the theoretical analysis in Part 4 on monetary theory. Also, these analytical chapters will be helpful introductory material for Part 6, which concentrates on international finance.

SUMMARY

1. Money serves a number of functions in the economy. Perhaps the most important is its use as a medium of exchange. It also serves as a store of value and as a unit of account. In general, money is considered the most liquid asset, because it can be spent at face value virtually anywhere at any time.

2. The precise definition of the asset called money varies with the economic system. In the United States we have three definitions: M1, M2, and M3. Each represents a slightly different definition of liquidity and spendability. M1 is the narrowest and most popular definition: the sum of currency and all checkable deposits at banks and thrift institutions. This is the definition we use throughout the book unless we say otherwise.

3. Without money the economy would have to rely on the more cumbersome barter system to exchange goods and services. Only a primitive mechanism would exist for channeling savings into productive investments. The level of economic welfare would be lower on both counts.

4. Control over the money supply rests with the central bank. In the United States the central banking function is carried out by the Federal Reserve System.

Suggestions for Further Reading

An excellent summary of money in exchange systems is Chapter 2 of Mark J. Flannery and Dwight M. Jaffee, *The Economic Implications of an Electronic Monetary Transfer System* (Lexington, Mass.: Lexington Books, 1973). *Money, Information, and Uncertainty,* by Charles A. E. Goodhart (New York: Barnes & Noble, 1975), discusses the role of money with special emphasis on risk and uncertainty. Robert Clower's collection of essays, *Monetary Theory: Selected Readings* (New York: Penguin, 1970), focuses specifically on the foundations of money. His introduction is especially good.

If you want to step back a bit and view things from a broader perspective, we recommend Norman Angell, *The Story of Money* (New York: Frederick A. Stokes Co., 1929); and Paul Einzig, *Primitive Money,* 2d edition (New York: Oxford University Press, 1966). For a fascinating illustration of the need for money, and the functions it performs, read R. A. Radford, "The Economic Organization of a P.O.W. Camp," *Economica* (November 1945).

CHAPTER 2

Money, the Economy, and Inflation

Many people persist in thinking that money must somehow be based on gold, or maybe silver, or at least on *something* that has tangible physical substance. As we saw in Chapter 1, however, money is mostly an accounting phenomenon, reinforced by social convention and the legal power of government. There simply isn't any backing behind our currency, and demand deposits—which constitute most of our money—are nothing more than liabilities on the books of financial institutions.

How do such demand deposits come into existence? How does the central bank—the Federal Reserve ("the Fed")—regulate their amount? How does the Federal Reserve know how large the money supply should be, in the first place? Finally, just what is the relationship between the money supply, economic activity, and inflation?

We will devote this chapter to a preliminary exploration of such questions. Later in the book, especially in Parts 3 and 4, we will dig deeper into many of these same matters; meanwhile, the present chapter provides important background information intended to make much of the material in the intervening chapters more meaningful.

BANK RESERVES AND THE MONEY SUPPLY

Demand deposits come into being when banks extend credit—that is, when they make loans or buy securities. Checking accounts disappear when banks contract credit—when bank loans are repaid or banks sell securities. Here is how it works.

When a bank makes a loan to a consumer or business firm, it typically creates a checking account for the borrower's use. For example, when you borrow $1,000 from your friendly neighborhood bank, the bank will take your promissory note and give you a checking account in return. From the commercial bank's point of view, it has an additional $1,000 of assets (namely, your promissory note); this is matched by an additional $1,000 of liabilities (namely, your checking account). You could, of course, ask for $1,000 in $10 bills right then and there, stuff them in your pocket, and depart. But more likely you would be equally satisfied with the checking account, because by writing checks on it you can make payments just as well as with currency. The creation of this $1,000 in checking deposits means the money supply has increased by $1,000.

Similarly, when a bank buys a corporate or government bond, it pays for it by opening a checking account for the seller. Assume you are holding a $1,000 corporate or government bond in your investment portfolio, and you need cash. You might sell the bond to your local bank, which would then add $1,000 to your checking account. Once again, from the point of view of the bank, its assets (bonds) and liabilities (checking accounts) have gone up by $1,000. Just as by a bank loan, money has been created; the supply of money in the economy has increased by $1,000.

Conversely, when you repay a bank loan by giving the bank a check, the bank gives you back your promissory note and at the same time lowers your deposit balance. If a bank sells a bond to an individual, the same reduction in deposits occurs. The supply of money declines. To repeat: banks create money (checking accounts) when they lend or buy securities, and destroy money when their loans are repaid or they sell securities.

Can they do this without limit? Is there any control over their ability to create and destroy money? No they can't and yes there is, and that is where the Federal Reserve comes into the picture.

A bank cannot always expand its checking account liabilities by making loans or buying securities. Banks are required by the Federal Reserve to hold reserves against their checking account liabilities—the current requirement is reserves of about 12 percent against checking deposits. *These reserves must be held in the form of vault cash or as a deposit in their regional Federal Reserve Bank.* Therefore, only if a bank has "excess" reserves, reserves over and above its requirements, can it create new checking deposits by making loans and buying securities.

Once a bank is "loaned up," with no more excess reserves, its ability to create money ceases. And if it has deficient reserves, not enough to support its existing deposits, the bank must somehow get additional reserves. Otherwise, it has no choice but to call in loans or sell securities in order to bring its deposits back in line with its reserves. If a bank has checking account deposits of $10,000 but only $1,100 in reserves, it would be $100 short of meeting its required reserves. One way to set itself right with the Federal Reserve would be to call in $834 worth of loans. This would reduce its deposits to $9,166, at which level its $1,100 of reserves satisfies the legal 12 percent requirement.

It is through the fulcrum of these reserves that the Federal Reserve influences bank lending and investing and thereby the money supply. The Federal Reserve manipulates the reserves of the banking system and the amount of checking accounts that they can support through open market operations, reserve requirements, and the discount rate. These will be explored in detail in Chapter 15. For now, let's just take it for granted that the Federal Reserve controls bank reserves, hence the money supply, and move on to the next question.

HOW LARGE SHOULD THE MONEY SUPPLY BE?

In theory, the answer is simple enough. Presumably the supply of money affects the rate of spending, and therefore we should have enough money so that we buy, at current prices, all the goods and services the economy is able to produce. If we spend less, we will have idle capacity and idle people; if we spend more, we will wind up with higher prices but no more real goods or services. In other words, we need a money supply large enough to generate a level of spending on new goods and services—the economy's gross national product (GNP)—that produces high employment at stable prices. More money than that would mean too much spending and inflation, and less money would mean too little spending and recession or depression.

In practice, unfortunately, the answer is not nearly that simple. In the first place, decisions about the appropriate amount of money are often linked with the notion of countercyclical monetary policy, that is, a monetary policy that deliberately varies the amount of money in the economy—increasing it (or, more realistically, increasing the rate at which it is growing) during a recession, to stimulate spending, and decreasing it (or increasing it at a less than normal rate) during a boom, to inhibit spending. As we will see in subsequent chapters, there is considerable debate over the desirability of such attempts at economic stabilization.

The more fundamental issue for us is to understand how changes in the money supply can influence people's *spending* in a consistent way. What a change in the money supply can do is to alter people's *liquidity*. Money, after all, is the most liquid of all assets. A liquid asset, as mentioned in Chapter 1, is something that can be turned into cash—that is, sold or "liquidated"—quickly, with no loss in dollar value. Money already *is* cash. You can't get more liquid than that!

Since monetary policy alters the liquidity of the public's portfolio of total assets—including, in that balance sheet, holdings of real as well as financial assets—it should thereby lead to portfolio readjustments that involve spending decisions. An increase in the money supply implies that the public is more liquid than formerly; a decrease in the money supply implies that the public is less liquid than before. If the public had formerly been satisfied with its holdings of money relative to the rest of its assets, a change in that money supply will presumably lead to readjustments throughout the rest of its portfolio.[1]

In other words, these changes in liquidity should lead to more (or less) spending on either real assets (cars and television sets) or financial assets (stocks and bonds). If spending on real assets expands, demand for goods and services increases, production goes up, and GNP is directly affected. If spending on financial assets goes up, the increased demand for stocks and bonds drives up securities prices. Higher securities prices mean lower interest rates. The fall in interest rates may induce more spending on housing and on plant and equipment (investment spending), thereby influencing GNP through that route.[2]

---

[1]Of course, if monetary policy could increase the money supply while all other assets of the public remained unchanged, people would not only be more liquid but also wealthier. As we will see in Chapter 15, however, monetary policy can alter only the composition of the public's assets; it cannot change total wealth *directly*.

[2]Since this point will come up again and again, it is worth devoting a moment to the *inverse* relationship between the *price* of an income-earning asset and its effective *rate of interest* (or yield). For example, a long-term bond that carries a fixed interest payment of $10 a year and costs $100 yields an annual interest rate of 10 percent. However, if the price of the bond were to rise to $200, the current yield would drop to $\frac{10}{200}$, or 5 percent. And if the price of the security were to fall to $50, the current yield would rise to $\frac{10}{50}$, or 20 percent. Conclusion: a rise (or fall) in the price of a bond is reflected, in terms of sheer arithmetic, in an automatic change in the opposite direction in the effective rate of interest. To say the price of bonds rose or the rate

Underlying the effectiveness of monetary policy, therefore, is its impact on the liquidity of the public. But whether a change in the supply of liquidity actually does influence spending depends on what is happening to the demand for liquidity. If the supply of money is increased but the demand expands even more, the additional money will be held and not spent. "Easy" or "tight" money is not really a matter of increases or decreases in the money supply in an absolute sense, but rather increases or decreases relative to the demand for money. In the past half century we have had hardly any periods in which the money supply actually decreased for any sustained length of time, yet we have had many episodes of tight money because the *rate* of growth was so small that the demand for money rose faster than the supply.

If people always respond in a consistent manner to an increase in their liquidity (the proportion of money in their portfolio), the Federal Reserve will be able to gauge the impact on GNP of a change in the money supply. But if people's spending reactions vary unpredictably when there is a change in the money supply, the central bank will never know whether it should alter the money supply a little or a lot (or even at all!) to bring about a specified change in spending.

The relationship between changes in the money supply and induced changes in spending brings us to the speed with which money is spent, its *velocity* or rate of turnover. When the Federal Reserve increases the money supply by $1 billion, how much of an effect will this have on people's spending, and thereby on GNP? Say we are in a recession, with GNP $100 billion below prosperity levels. Can the Fed induce a $100 billion expansion in spending by increasing the money supply by $10 billion? Or will it take a $20 billion—or a $50 billion—increase in the money supply to do the job?

VELOCITY: THE MISSING LINK

Clearly, this is the key puzzle that monetary policy must solve if it is to operate effectively. After all, the central bank is not in business to change the money supply just for the sake of changing the money supply. Money is only a means to an end, and the end is the total volume of spending, which should be sufficient to give us high employment but not so great as to produce excessively rising prices.

of interest fell is saying the same thing in two different ways. We will return to these matters in Chapter 5.

When the Federal Reserve increases the money supply, the recipients of this additional liquidity *probably* spend some of it on goods and services, increasing GNP. The funds thereby move from the original recipients to the sellers of the goods and services. Now *they* have more money than before, and if they behave the same way as the others, they too are *likely* to spend some of it. GNP thus rises further, and at the same time the money moves on to yet another set of owners, who in turn *may* also spend part of it, thereby increasing GNP again. Over a period of time, say a year, a multiple increase in spending and GNP could thus flow from an initial increase in the stock of money.

This relationship between the increase in GNP over a period of time and the initial change in the money supply is important enough to have a name: the velocity of money. Technically speaking, velocity is found, after the process has ended, by dividing the cumulative increase in GNP by the initial increase in the money supply.

Similarly, we can compute the velocity of the *total* amount of money in the country by dividing total GNP (not just the increase in it) by the *total* money supply. This gives us the average number of times each dollar turns over to buy goods and services during the year. In 1987, for example, with a GNP of $4,500 billion and an average money supply of $740 billion during the year, the velocity of money was 4,500 divided by 740, or 6.08 per annum. Each dollar, on the average, was spent about six times in purchasing goods and services during 1987.

With this missing link—velocity—now in place, we can reformulate the problem of monetary policy more succinctly. The Federal Reserve controls the supply of money. Its main job is to regulate the flow of spending. The flow of spending, however, depends not only on the supply of money but also on that supply's rate of turnover, or velocity, and this the Federal Reserve does *not* have under its thumb. Since any given supply of money might be spent faster or more slowly—that is, velocity might rise or fall—a rather wide range of potential spending could conceivably flow from any given stock of money.

If it weren't for the complications introduced by velocity, decisions about the appropriate money supply would be fairly simple, and there would be little disagreement among rational people. However, complications there are, and a central problem of monetary theory is the exploration of exactly what determines the velocity of money—or, looked at another way, what determines the volume of spending that flows from a change in the supply of money. As we shall see, disagreements over the determinants and behavior of velocity underlie part of the debate over economic stabilization policy.

But there's more. The Federal Reserve has to worry not only about the relationship between money and spending but also about whether prices or production responds to increased spending. More GNP is good if it corresponds to more production but not so good if it means higher prices. Either outcome is possible. And that brings us to inflation. The next few pages provide an overview, with the nitty gritty reserved for Chapters 23 and 24 on monetary theory.

MONEY AND INFLATION

Consumer prices are now about *nine* times higher than in the late 1930s and more than triple what they were in 1970. Since 1970 prices have risen at an annual average rate of 6 percent a year; at that rate, prices *double* every twelve years.[3]

Who is responsible for inflation? Is money the culprit? Can we bring an inflationary spiral to a halt if we clamp down on the money supply? The classic explanation of inflation is that "too much money is chasing too few goods." The diagnosis implies the remedy: stop creating so much money and inflation will disappear.

Such a diagnosis has been painfully accurate during those hard-to-believe episodes in history when runaway hyperinflation sky-rocketed prices out of sight and plunged the value of money to practically zero. Example: Prices quadrupled in revolutionary America between 1775 and 1780, when the Continental Congress opened the printing presses and flooded the country with currency. The phrase "not worth a continental" remains to this day. The situation in Germany after World War I was even more extreme; prices in 1923 were 34 billion times what they had been in 1921. In Hungary after World War II, it took 1.4 nonillion pengö in 1946 to buy what one pengö could purchase a few years earlier (one nonillion equals 1,000,000,000,000,000,000,000,000,000,000).

Severe breakdowns of this sort are impossible unless they are fueled by continuous injections of new money in ever-increasing volume. In

---

[3]As a special bonus, we give you "the rule of 72" for growth rates. If something (anything) is growing at a compound annual rate of *x* percent, to find out how many years it will take to *double,* divide 72 (the magic number) by *x.* For example, if prices are rising at 6 percent a year, they will double in 72 ÷ 6 = 12 years. It isn't precise to the dot, but it's a useful rule of thumb.

While we're on such things, here's another rule of thumb: if you listen carefully to a cricket, the number of times it chirps in 15 seconds plus 37 equals the temperature in degrees Fahrenheit.

such cases money is undoubtedly the inflation culprit, and the only way to stop inflation from running away is to slam a quick brake on the money creation machine.

However, hyperinflation is not what we have been experiencing in this country in recent years. During World War II consumer prices rose by about 30 percent. In the immediate postwar years (1945–1949), after wage and price controls were removed, they climbed another 30 percent. None of this was unexpected or particularly unusual. Prices typically rise in wartime and immediately thereafter.

The unusual thing about prices and World War II is not that they rose so much during and immediately after it, but that they have never declined since. Quite the contrary—prices have continued onward and upward to this day, virtually without interruption, producing the longest period of continuous inflation in American history. In all prior times of war, prices had gone up during and immediately after hostilities but then had fallen back somewhat. Not this time. In all prior peacetimes, price increases had been interrupted from time to time by occasional corrective periods of stable or declining prices. No longer.

From 1950 through 1988, the cost of living increased in every year but one (1955). The annual rate of inflation over the entire thirty-nine year period averages out at more than 4 percent per year. Moreover, even during periods of recession, such as 1974 and 1981, inflation was still very much with us, with prices rising twelve and nine percent respectively in those years.

This type of creeping inflation is something new. Is money the culprit here, too?

Unlike its role in hyperinflation, money is not so obviously the only culprit when it comes to the everyday variety of inflation we have experienced over the years. Let's take a look at some evidence before jumping to conclusions. The five-decades-plus from 1930 to 1987 are instructive:

1. During the 1930s, the money supply (M1) increased by 35 percent, but consumer prices *fell* 20 percent.

2. In the 1940s, the money supply increased by 200 percent, but prices rose by "only" 70 percent.

3. The 1950s provide the best fit: the money supply and prices both rose by about 25 percent.

4. In the 1960s the relationship deteriorated slightly: the money supply increased by 45 percent, and consumer prices rose by slightly less than 30 percent.

5. During the 1970s, the money supply rose by 90 percent, and prices rose by 105 percent.

6. From the beginning of 1980 through 1987, the money supply rose by 90 percent, and prices rose by 50 percent.

You can be your own judge, but the data seem to imply that money has a lot to do with all types of inflation. People cannot continue buying the same amount of goods and services at higher and higher prices unless the money supply increases. If the money supply today were no larger than it was in 1950 ($115 billion), prices would have stopped rising long ago—and so would real economic activity.

A qualification is in order: an increase in the money supply is a *necessary* condition for the continuation of inflation, but it is probably not a *sufficient* condition. Increases in the money supply will not raise prices if velocity falls (as in the 1930s). Even if velocity remains constant, an increase in the money supply will not raise prices if production expands. When we are in a depression, for example, the spending stimulated by an increase in the money supply is likely to raise output and employment rather than prices. Furthermore, in the short run at least—and sometimes the short run is a matter of several years—increased spending and inflation can be brought about by increases in velocity without any increase in the money supply.

Let us end this section with a summary statement of the role of money in the inflation process. Does more money *always* lead to inflation? No, but it can under certain circumstances, and if the increase is large enough it probably will. Case 1: If the central bank expands the money supply while we are in a recession, the increased spending it induces is likely to lead to more employment and a larger output of goods and services rather than to higher prices. Case 2: As we approach full employment and capacity output, increases in the money supply become more and more likely to generate rising prices. However, if this increase is only large enough to provide funds for the enlarged volume of transactions accompanying real economic growth, inflation still need not result. Case 3: Only when the money supply increases under conditions of high employment *and* exceeds the requirements of economic growth can it be held primarily responsible for kindling an inflationary spiral.

The time factor and the extent of inflation are also relevant. In the short run, an increase in monetary velocity alone (generated by increasing government or private spending), with a constant or even declining money supply, can finance a modest rate of inflation. The longer the time span, however, and the higher the rise in prices, the

---

Can It Happen Here? In 1985, Inflation in Bolivia Was 11,700 Percent.

Many Americans were frantic when consumer prices in the United States rose at a double-digit rate (13 percent) back in 1979 and 1980. What would life be like if inflation hit not double but *quintuple* digits, as it actually did—at 11,700 percent—in Bolivia in 1985?

Life in the world of hyperinflation was both tragic and absurd. People had to carry around suitcases full of money in order to buy ordinary goods and services, since all payments had to be made in paper money. Paper money was necessary because the rapid rate of inflation made the use of checks and credit cards impractical; the time they took to clear made the figures on them obsolete. A startling example: the number of pesos a new luxury Toyota automobile cost in 1982 would buy just three boxes of aspirin in 1985.

According to the *Wall Street Journal*, the 1,000-peso bill, the most commonly used, cost more to print than it purchased. It bought one tea bag. To buy an average-size television set with 1,000 peso bills, customers had to haul money weighing more than 68 pounds to the store. A new 100,000-peso note was printed to ease the burden. At the official exchange rate, however, it was worth only $2 (U.S.). On the black market, where it was more realistically valued, it was worth no more than 80 U.S. cents.

As a result, the financial system practically ceased to exist, the economy could not function on a day-to-day basis, and barter replaced monetary exchange in many parts of the country.

---

less likely that velocity can do the job by itself. Over the longer run, the money supply must expand for inflation to persist.

Conclusions: More money does not always lead to inflation (Cases 1 and 2), but sometimes it does (Case 3). In the short run, inflation can make some headway without any change in the money supply, but rising prices cannot proceed too far too long unless inflation is fueled by an expanding money supply.

SUMMARY

1. Control over the money supply rests with the Federal Reserve, which tries to regulate the supply of money so that we have enough spending to generate high employment without inflation.

2. Checking accounts, which make up the bulk of the money supply, come into being when banks make loans and buy securities. They vanish when bank loans are repaid or banks sell securities.

3. The Federal Reserve regulates bank lending and the money supply through its control over bank reserves.

4. By changing bank reserves and thereby the money supply, the Fed alters people's liquidity and, it is hoped, their spending on goods and services, which in turn helps determine GNP, the level of unemployment, and the rate of inflation.

5. The relationship between money and spending depends on how rapidly people turn over their cash balances. This rate of turnover of money is called the velocity of money. Since any given supply of money might be spent faster or more slowly—that is, velocity might rise or fall—a rather wide range of potential spending could conceivably flow from any given stock of money.

6. Inflation has been one of our most troublesome economic problems for fifty years.

7. In cases of hyperinflation, the money supply is clearly the main culprit.

8. Increases in the money supply are a necessary but not a sufficient condition for the creeping type of inflation we have been experiencing.

9. More money does not always lead to inflation, because velocity can fall and output can expand. In the long run, however, inflation cannot continue unless it is fueled by an expanding money supply.

Suggestions for Further Reading

Three good books devoted entirely to inflation are R. J. Ball, *Inflation and the Theory of Money* (Chicago: Aldine, 1965); James A. Trevithick and Charles Mulvey, *The Economics of Inflation* (New York: Wiley, 1975); and Thomas M. Humphrey, *Essays on Inflation* (Federal Reserve Bank of Richmond).

CHAPTER 3

Financial Instruments and Markets

Financial markets are basically the same as other kinds of markets. People buy and sell, bargain and hassle, win and lose, just as in the flea markets of Casablanca and Amsterdam or the gold markets of London and Zurich. In financial markets they buy and sell securities, like stocks and bonds, which are less tangible than hot bracelets or cold gold bars but are no less valuable. Stocks and bonds can be very valuable indeed, even though they are nothing but pieces of paper.

Since we will be discussing bonds, stocks, and mortgages throughout this book, we devote a number of sections in this chapter to explaining the similarities and differences among such financial instruments. In addition we provide a bird's-eye view of the money and capital markets, where billions of dollars worth of these and other instruments are bought and sold every day. But first we set the stage by offering an overview of what financial markets do within the context of the economy as a whole.

THE NATURE OF FINANCIAL MARKETS

Financial markets are the transmission mechanism between saver-lenders and borrower-spenders. Through a wide variety of techniques, instruments, and institutions, financial markets mobilize the savings of millions and channel them into the hands of borrower-spenders who need more funds than they have on hand. Financial markets are conduits through which those who do not spend all their income can make their excess funds available to those who want to spend more than their income.

Saver-lenders stand to benefit because they earn interest or dividends on their funds. Borrower-investors stand to gain because they get access to money to carry out investment plans they otherwise could not finance (and that presumably yield more than the interest they pay). Without financial markets, savers would have no choice but to hoard their excess money, and borrowers would be unable to realize any investment plans except those they could finance by themselves.

Financial markets give savers additional options besides that of simply holding their savings in the form of cash. They can, if they wish, *buy securities* with the money. Similarly, through financial markets borrowers can finance their investment plans even though they may not have previously accumulated funds to draw upon. They can *sell securities* to obtain the funds they need.

Schematically, Figure 1 illustrates in simplified form the flow of funds from ultimate saver-lenders, through financial markets, to ultimate borrower-spenders. Ultimate lenders are on the left, ultimate borrowers on the right. Funds flow from left to right, either directly (from ultimate lenders to ultimate borrowers via financial markets) or indirectly (through financial institutions, such as banks and insurance companies, which we discuss in detail in the next chapter). The liabilities issued by ultimate borrowers, known as *primary securities*, flow in the opposite direction, from right to left, as they are purchased by

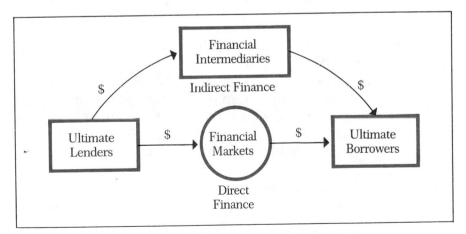

FIGURE 1 Flows of Funds From Lenders to Borrowers

either ultimate lenders (direct finance) or financial institutions (indirect finance).

Ultimate lenders are typically households, although from time to time business firms and governmental bodies—federal, state, and local—also lend substantial amounts. *Ultimate borrowers* are mostly business firms and governments, although households are also important as consumer credit and mortgage borrowers. The financial market in which the transaction takes place generally takes its name from the borrowers' side of the market, more specifically from the particular kind of primary security involved—the government bond market, the municipal bond market, the mortgage market, the corporate bond market, the stock market, and so on. Sometimes, however, it is the lender who gives the market its name, as, for example, the market for bank loans.

The existence of highly developed, widely accessible, and smoothly functioning financial markets is of crucial importance in transmitting savings into the hands of those desiring to make investment expenditures. Those who can visualize and exploit potentially profitable investment opportunities are frequently not the same people who generate current saving. If the financial transmission mechanism is underdeveloped, inaccessible, or imperfect, the flow of funds from household saving to business investment will be impeded, and the level of economic activity will fall below its potential.

Assume, for example, that a significant portion of otherwise feasible investment plans is not undertaken because of lack of financing, due to the failure of financial markets to channel funds effectively from savers able to lend to business firms anxious to borrow. The end result of reduced investment spending is likely to be a level of economic activity far below what could have been reached had financial markets operated more effectively.

A concrete example of the failure of financial markets to channel funds effectively arises when there is a lack of adequate information about borrowers seeking funds and/or lenders wanting to lend them. This highlights the main function of any market—to bring buyers and sellers together. In financial markets, it is buyers and sellers of credit. If some potential borrowers, for example, are unaware of financial markets—or if knowledge about sources of funds is not widely disseminated—then some investments that could have been undertaken won't be, even though there are savers who would have willingly lent the funds at rates of interest equal to, or less than, what investors would have been willing to pay.

A similar situation could arise as far as savers are concerned. Some may not be aware of lending opportunities. Instead of being put to work, funds are put under the mattress and less investment takes place (which in turn lowers saving as income declines). But well-developed financial markets do not permit such waste and inefficiency.

Several kinds of institutions have emerged to help channel funds between savers and investors. Perhaps the most prominent are investment banks, such as Salomon Brothers, Goldman Sachs, and Morgan Stanley. These firms gather information on the ultimate buyers of securities and, for a fee, help issuers market their securities at the most favorable price. In essence, investment bankers are information and marketing specialists for newly issued securities.

Once securities are issued, another related set of institutions help to provide a "secondary market" where existing securities can be bought and sold by different investors. Perhaps the most prominent secondary market is the New York Stock Exchange, but there are also so-called over-the-counter markets in many securities as well.

We will return to these topics in Chapter 29, where we discuss the structure and performance of securities markets. At this point let's turn to the instruments themselves, so that we can better appreciate why stocks, bonds, and mortgages are so valuable, even if they are only pieces of paper.

BONDS REPRESENT BORROWING

Bonds exist in a wide variety of forms. For example, there are corporate bonds, U.S. government bonds, and state and local government (often called municipal) bonds. But in each and every case they represent the same thing, namely, the borrowing of money by the corporation or governmental body that originally sold the bond.

When IBM, let's say, or Uncle Sam, or the state of Wyoming wants to raise a few million dollars, what it frequently does is print up fancy pieces of paper—called *bonds*—and try to sell them. Many individuals and financial institutions are interested in buying these fancy pieces of paper, because the paper states that the issuer (that is, the borrower, IBM) promises to pay whoever owns the bond (the lender) certain interest payments at specified dates in the future.

The paper also states when the bond will mature—that is, the date when the loan will be paid off to whoever owns the bond at that time. Some bonds have an original maturity of only a few years, while others may not come due for twenty or thirty years. At times in the past some governments have even sold perpetual bonds, called *consols;* these keep paying interest forever, because they have no maturity date at all. In all cases, however, bonds always denote *borrowing* by whoever issued them.

Most bonds, like those just mentioned, promise to pay a certain number of dollars of interest each year for a stated number of years and then to repay the principal amount at maturity. Traditionally, bonds have been issued with coupons attached that bondholders can clip and send in every six months or every year to collect the interest that is due. (For that reason, bonds are often referred to as *coupon securities.*)

More recently, however, some bonds have been issued *without* coupons. Naturally enough, they are referred to as *zero-coupon* bonds. These securities are sold at a price well below their stated face value, with the difference representing the interest that will be earned by the bondholder over the life of the instrument. Treasury bills—obligations of the U.S. government with one year or less to maturity—are the oldest securities of this sort. In Chapter 5 we will go into the details of how interest is calculated on coupon-bearing and zero-coupon securities.

There are many other differences among bonds. One of the most important has to do with the way their interest is taxed. State and local bonds, or municipals, are often called *tax-exempts,* because their interest is exempt by law from federal income taxation. (Their interest is also usually exempt from state income taxes in the state where they are issued.) Interest on corporate bonds and on federal government securities *is* subject to federal income taxes.

On the other hand, interest on federal government bonds is not subject to state and local income taxation. In the past, state and local income taxes have been relatively low compared with federal taxes, so exemption from state and local taxes was not so important. In recent years, however, state and local income taxes have grown to become a much larger percentage of the taxpayer's total taxes. If this trend continues, perhaps in the future U.S. government bonds, rather than municipal bonds, will be the ones that are called "tax-exempts."

STOCKS REPRESENT OWNERSHIP

While bonds denote borrowing, stocks represent ownership. Holding a stock certificate means that the holder owns part of the corporation. Thus there are only *corporate* stocks, no U.S. government or state and local government stocks, since individuals cannot "own" governments (at least not legally). Corporations raise money in several ways: by borrowing from banks, for instance, or by selling bonds, or by selling shares in ownership—that is, selling stocks. While bondholders receive interest, the income that stockholders receive is called dividends.

The two main types of stocks—often they are called equities or shares—are *preferred* stock and *common* stock. Preferred stockholders get a *fixed* dividend, and they are entitled to it before the common stockholders get anything. Common stockholders get what is left over after preferred stockholders have received their fixed payments; in other words, common stockholders get a *residual* or *variable* dividend that fluctuates with the company's profits. That's nice if the company has been doing well, but not so pleasant otherwise. There is also *convertible* preferred stock, which can be converted into common stock at a predetermined price.

Once stocks are issued, they are traded on a number of markets in this country and abroad, with common stock prices fluctuating with the fortunes of particular companies and with economic conditions in general. Actually, many buyers of common stocks seem to be more interested in capital gains (the difference between the purchase price and the selling price) than in dividends, possibly because they think they can get rich more quickly with capital gains than with dividends.

There are several measures of trends in overall common stock prices, that is, in common stock prices in general rather than in the price of any one particular stock. Two of the better-known measures are Standard & Poor's 500 Stock Index, which is based on the prices of 500 stocks, and the New York Stock Exchange Composite Index, which is based on all the stocks (more than 1,500) listed on the New York Stock Exchange. However, the most popular and widely followed measure of all, even though it is the least representative, is the Dow Jones Industrial Average, which is based on the prices of only 30 stocks.

A market in which stock prices are rising, by the way, is called a *bull market,* while one in which stock prices are falling is a *bear market.* Similarly, *bulls* are traders who expect stock prices to rise, while *bears* expect them to fall. (It is often said on Wall Street that bulls make money and bears make money but pigs never do; so don't be a hog!)

With bonds and preferred stocks having fixed income payments, and common stocks variable income payments, we have come upon one of the main similarities as well as one of the main differences among securities. *All securities share a common characteristic in that they represent a claim to a stream of payments, often called cash flows, in the future.* In particular, the purchaser or owner of a security has a claim against the issuer or original seller of the security. It is the precise nature of that claim that distinguishes different types of securities.

Bonds and preferred stocks generate fixed dollar payments in the future, while common stocks produce variable dollar payments. The key message, however, is that *all* securities represent claims to cash flows, and the nature of those cash flows is what helps to determine the value (price) of the securities.[1]

MORTGAGES INVOLVE REAL ESTATE

Mortgages are debts incurred by someone who is borrowing in order to buy land or buildings, with the land or buildings serving as security, or collateral, for the lender. Like bonds, mortgages are debt instruments that promise to pay interest for a stated number of years and then repay the face value or principal at maturity. They are frequently amortized, which means that the principal is gradually repaid, along with the interest, during the life of the mortgage.

Mortgages are classified into three types: one- to four-family home mortgages, multifamily residential mortgages (apartment houses), and commercial (including farm) mortgages. They often run twenty-five to thirty years until maturity, although some are considerably shorter. Mortgages are also classified by whether or not they are insured by a government agency, either the Federal Housing Authority (FHA) or the Veteran's Administration (VA). These so-called FHA-VA mortgages are contrasted with conventional mortgages, which do not carry any government insurance.

Mortgages have undergone considerable change in the 1980s. Traditionally they were normal *fixed-rate* securities, with the interest rate fixed over the life of the loan. But in the early eighties they led the movement to *variable-rate* (or *floating-rate*) debt, with the interest rate adjusted periodically—say, every six months—to reflect changes in the financial environment.

An unusual characteristic of mortgages is the uncertainty that exists for the lender with respect to inflows of cash. Even if the interest rate is fixed, homeowners will often prepay their mortgages if they move

---

[1]In Chapter 5 we present a formula that can be used to value fixed cash flows on a bond.

to a new location or if interest rates fall and they can refinance their indebtedness (borrow again) on better terms. This prepayment uncertainty makes mortgages less desirable than other forms of debt from the lender's viewpoint.

Some of the uncertainty is reduced when individual mortgages are packaged together in a "pool" and sold as a unit. Mortgage pools have become a popular form of financial investment, with buyers (lenders) relying on the large number of mortgages in the pool to help smooth out cash flows. The most popular type of mortgage pool is insured by the Government National Mortgage Association (Ginnie Mae), a division of the Department of Housing and Urban Development.

Mortgage pools are also referred to as *pass-through securities* (such as Ginnie Mae Pass-Throughs), because the interest and principal on the underlying mortgages are passed through to the investors in the pool by the originators of the mortgages. For example, after a savings and loan association (which we meet in the next chapter) makes a series of mortgage loans to individuals, it applies for insurance from Ginnie Mae and is then allowed to form a pool of mortgages that can be sold to the investing public. All interest payments and principal prepayments on the mortgages are passed through to the investors who have purchased the pool. Obviously there's a lot of bookkeeping involved, so the originator of the pool (the savings and loan association) receives a servicing fee for its time and trouble.

OPTIONS AND FUTURES CONTRACTS

Options and futures contracts are not used by corporations or individuals to raise funds. Nevertheless, they have become such important financial instruments in managing risk exposure that it is helpful to have at least a nodding acquaintance with them. Options and futures are often lumped together, because they both represent contractual agreements between two parties concerning some third asset. For example, there are options contracts on gold and on Treasury bonds and there are also futures contracts on gold and Treasury bonds. Thus, both options and futures are often called derivative financial instruments, because they derive their value from a so-called underlying asset. Options and futures are also similar in that they are both traded on organized securities exchanges. For example, the Chicago Board Options Exchange conducts trading in options on common stock and the Chicago Board of Trade sponsors trading in Treasury bond futures.

But the differences between these two instruments far outweigh their similarities. First let's look at *futures contracts*, because they are less complicated. A futures contract deals in both rights and obligations regarding the underlying commodity. In particular, the buyer of a futures contract, also called the long, has the right and obligation to receive the underlying commodity, say Treasury bonds, at some future date. The seller of the contract, also called the short, has the right and obligation to deliver the Treasury bonds on a specific date in the future. The price at which the Treasury bonds will be transferred is negotiated when the contract is sold by the short to the long on the floor of a futures exchange.

Thus, both parties know exactly how much Treasury bonds (or gold) will cost them in six months or a year. If prices go up in the meantime, the long (who is entitled to pay the lower agreed-upon price) makes money and the short (who has agreed to deliver at the lower price) loses money. One reason people buy and sell futures contracts, therefore, is that they disagree on the future course of prices for an underlying asset and hope to profit as prices move in their anticipated direction. Another reason is that selling or buying the asset at a known price at a specific date in the future eliminates the risk of price fluctuations for someone who must buy or sell the asset in the future.

Options contracts also deal in rights and obligations with respect to an underlying asset, but these rights and obligations are separated. In particular, a *call option* gives the owner the right to buy the underlying asset, such as IBM stock or gold or Treasury bonds, at a fixed price (called the *strike price*) for a specific time interval, such as six months. A *put option* gives the owner the right to sell the underlying asset at a fixed price. The sellers of these options, called option writers, have the obligation to sell or buy the underlying assets as the case may be, and in return receive a payment, called the option premium.

Obviously, options are a complicated business, one that we cannot get into in detail right now. But it should be clear that options are potentially important instruments for dealing with the risks of price movements in the underlying assets. We will return to these topics in Chapter 33.

Before leaving, let's take another look at how the financial markets as a whole are organized. Generally, a distinction is drawn between the market for long-term securities—more than a year in original maturity—called the "capital market," and the market for shorter-term issues, the "money market."

THE CAPITAL MARKET

By far the largest part of the capital market, in terms of dollar volume of securities outstanding, is the stock market, as Table 1 indicates. About 70 percent of all the outstanding stocks are owned by individuals; the rest are held by such institutional investors as pension funds, mutual funds, and insurance companies (in that order), all of which we will meet in greater detail in the next chapter.

Most one- to four-family home mortgages—some of which are insured by the Federal Housing Authority or by the Veterans' Administration—are acquired by savings and loan associations and savings banks, but commercial banks are also important lenders in this area. Multifamily mortgages are purchased mostly by thrift institutions (savings and loan associations and savings banks), commercial mortgages mainly by life insurance companies and commercial banks.

In the corporate bond market, life insurance companies are the main lenders (they own a third of the corporate bonds), followed by pension and retirement funds. State and local government bonds are bought primarily for their tax-exempt feature, since their interest is exempt from federal income taxes. Commercial banks and high-income households own most of the total outstanding.

U.S. government securities are generally bought by a wide variety of purchasers, including the Federal Reserve, commercial banks, in-

TABLE 1
The Capital Market: Securities Outstanding
(End of 1986)

Type of Instrument	Amount Outstanding*
Corporate stocks (at market value)	$2,950
Residential mortgages	1,910
U.S. government securities (marketable, long-term)	1,200
Corporate bonds	1,010
U.S. government agency securities	800
Consumer loans	720
Commercial and farm mortgages	650
State and local government bonds	500

*In billions of dollars.

SOURCES: Federal Reserve Flow of Funds Accounts and *Federal Reserve Bulletin.*

dividuals, and foreigners. The same is true of the securities of various government agencies, such as the Federal Home Loan Banks, the Federal National Mortgage Association, and the Federal Land Banks; most of these are guaranteed, formally or informally, by the full faith and credit of the federal government.

In many of these sectors of the capital market, active trading takes place daily for outstanding issues—especially for stocks and for U.S. government securities, to a lesser extent for corporate and for municipal (state and local) bonds. Trading is facilitated by a variety of institutions, including securities dealers and brokers, with expensive communications facilities, under the watchful eye of government regulators such as the Securities and Exchange Commission. We will explore the functioning of all these markets in greater depth in Part 5.

In other sectors, such as consumer credit, there is virtually no secondary market at all—that is, no trading in outstanding securities—so that these securities have little marketability and liquidity. In the residential mortgage market, the movement to mortgage pools spearheaded by such government-sponsored programs as the Ginnie Mae pass-throughs has facilitated a secondary market in mortgages (see Chapter 31) and thereby given home mortgages a degree of liquidity they formerly lacked.

Trading is most active, as noted, in the stock and bond markets, but even there it does not compare with the dollar volume of turnover that daily characterizes the money market, especially in Treasury bills.

THE MONEY MARKET

In contrast to the capital market, with its long-term securities, the money market specializes in short-term instruments that almost by definition are highly liquid—that is, readily marketable, with little possibility of loss. If you need to raise cash quickly and are forced to dispose of long-term securities, you can take a beating; but if you have short-term securities, chances are you can sell them without taking much of a loss. The short-term securities will mature pretty soon anyway, so if you can hold off a little while you can redeem them at face value when they mature. In addition, it is simply a fact of life, embedded in the mathematics of bond yields and prices, that for long-term securities a small change in interest rates involves a large change in price, whereas for short-term securities even a large change in yield involves only a small change in price.

For example, a rise in yield from 10 to 12 percent on a $10,000 face

TABLE 2
The Money Market: Securities Outstanding
(End of 1986)

Type of Instrument	Amount Outstanding*
Negotiable bank CDs (large denomination)	$450
U.S. Treasury bills	430
Commercial paper	320
Bankers' acceptances	60

*In billions of dollars.

SOURCES: Federal Reserve Flow of Funds Accounts and *Federal Reserve Bulletin.*

value thirty-year bond bearing a 10 percent coupon involves a fall in price from $10,000 to $8,348. A similar rise in yield on a three-month security of similar coupon involves a fall in price from $10,000 to only $9,700.[2]

For this reason, business firms and others with temporary surplus funds buy money market instruments rather than long-term securities. They purchase short-term money market securites and thus earn interest without much risk exposure. Commercial banks are particularly important participants in the money market, both as lenders and borrowers, as they adjust their legal reserve positions, invest temporarily idle balances, or sell some of their securities to raise funds in anticipation of forthcoming business demands for loans.

U.S. Treasury bills are the most liquid money market instrument, with about $430 billion outstanding. Treasury bills are short-term debts of the U.S. government. Typically, they are issued for three months or six months or a year. They are highly marketable and actively traded by both financial institutions and nonfinancial corporations. Treasury bills have been around since 1929.

In 1961 Treasury bills were joined by bank CDs, when the First National City Bank of New York (now Citibank) introduced the large-denomination ($100,000 and over) negotiable certificate of deposit. As Table 2 indicates, there are now more CDs outstanding than Treasury bills. Negotiable CDs are deposits and thus liabilities of the issuing banks. But they are interest-earning assets to the corporations that hold them; they are attractive to corporate treasurers, since they are readily marketable through securities dealers, such as Salomon Broth-

[2]For a more general proof, see Chapter 5.

ers and Morgan Stanley, who specialize in buying and selling them. Thus a corporate treasurer who needs cash quickly can sell off CDs before they mature. The negotiable CD offers corporate treasurers an alternative to Treasury bills or other money market instruments. By raising the rate they pay on CDs, banks can entice corporate surplus funds that might otherwise go into Treasury bills.

Commercial paper is also largely held by corporate treasurers. It represents short-term liabilities of *prime* business firms and finance companies. *Bankers' acceptances,* the least important of the main money market instruments, arise mostly in the course of international trade transactions.

In addition to the above, the daily purchase and sale of "federal funds" (unsecured liabilities of commercial banks that are settled by a transfer of funds on the same day the transaction is made) are also of major importance in the money market, particularly with respect to the role of commercial banks. In a typical federal funds transaction, a bank with excess reserves will sell funds to a bank with deficient reserves (often on a overnight basis) at an agreed-upon interest rate. We will encounter federal funds in a number of chapters; just remember, federal funds as the term is used here has no necessary connection with the U.S. Treasury.

SUMMARY

1. Financial markets are the transmission mechanism between saver-lenders and borrower-spenders. Ultimate lenders supply funds to ultimate borrowers either directly, by buying primary securities, or indirectly, by buying the liabilities of specialized financial institutions, which in turn buy the primary securities.

2. Well-functioning financial markets facilitate the growth of GNP by giving both lenders and borrowers options they would not otherwise have, thereby increasing both saving and investment.

3. Government, corporate, and municipal bonds all indicate the same thing—that the issuer has borrowed funds at a specified interest rate for a stated period of time.

4. Traditionally, bonds have been coupon-bearing securities. Recently, however, zero-coupon bonds have become popular. With zeros, lenders obtain their interest by the difference between the purchase price and the redemption value.

5. Stocks represent ownership rather than indebtedness. Preferred stocks receive fixed dividends, similar to bond interest, but common stocks get variable dividends that depend on the company's profitability.

6. Mortgages are debts incurred by borrowers who are buying land or buildings. The property serves as collateral for the lender in case of borrower bankruptcy. Mortgage pools are groups of mortgages put together and purchased by an investor as a unit.

7. Options and futures contracts are contractual agreements between two parties concerning a third underlying asset. Although they are not used for borrowing by corporations or individuals, they are important tools in managing risk.

8. In the final analysis, all securities are similar in that they entitle the owner to a series of future cash payments. However, the terms and precise pattern of cash flow varies among specific instruments.

9. The capital market refers to the market for long-term securities, such as corporate stocks and bonds. The money market refers to the market for short-term securities (one year or less in original maturity), such as Treasury bills and negotiable bank CDs. Money market instruments are more liquid than capital market securities.

Suggestions for Further Reading

A classic on the bond market, although it is somewhat dated now, is David M. Darst, *The Complete Bond Book* (New York: McGraw-Hill, 1975). For the stock market, see Burton G. Malkiel, *A Random Walk Down Wall Street*, 4th ed. (New York: Norton, 1985).

The operations of the money markets are examined in depth in Timothy Q. Cook and Timothy D. Rowe, eds., *Instruments of the Money Market*, 6th ed. (Federal Reserve Bank of Richmond, 1986); Wesley Lindow, *Inside the Money Market* (New York: Random House, 1972); Yale L. Meltzer, *Putting Money To Work: An Investment Primer* (Englewood Cliffs, N.J.: Prentice-Hall, 1984); and Marcia Stigum, *The Money Market*, rev. ed. (Homewood, Ill.: Dow Jones–Irwin, 1983).

CHAPTER 4

Financial Institutions: Purposes and Profile

Financial institutions—such as banks, insurance companies, and pension funds—are called by a special name: financial intermediaries. They dominate the financial scene at home and abroad. It is virtually impossible to spend or save or lend or invest money nowadays without getting involved with some kind of financial intermediary in one way or another. In this chapter we formally introduce the various kinds of financial intermediaries that are prominent in this country and show how they go about their business. In order to set the stage, let's first get a perspective on what these institutions do within the framework of the overall economy. In particular, let's try to understand why the transmission of funds between savers and investors, as described in the beginning of the last chapter, frequently is accomplished through the good offices of financial intermediaries.

THE ROLE OF FINANCIAL INTERMEDIARIES

Financial intermediaries are nothing more than financial institutions—commercial banks, savings banks, savings and loan associations, credit unions, pension funds, insurance companies, and so on—that act as agents, transferring funds from ultimate lenders to ultimate borrowers. They borrow from Peter in order to lend to Paula. What all financial intermediaries have in common is that they acquire funds by issuing their own liabilities to the public (savings deposits, savings and loan shares) and then turn around and use this money to buy primary securities (stocks, bonds, mortgages) for themselves.

Because these institutions exist, savers who do not want to hoard their cash under a mattress but who feel hesitant about going directly into the financial market to purchase corporate bonds or stocks or mortgages (primary securities) because they feel that these assets are perhaps too risky—or because they don't know about the availability of such items—have a third choice. They can "purchase" savings deposits or savings and loan shares. In that way they can hold a relatively safe and quite liquid financial asset, yet still earn *some* interest income. At the same time, corporations and potential home-owners can sell their bonds, stocks, and mortgages to the financial intermediaries rather than to the original savers themselves. Financial intermediaries, in brief, "intermediate" between ultimate saver-lenders and ultimate borrowers.

Financial intermediation, or indirect finance, is precisely this process: savers deposit funds with financial institutions rather than directly buying bonds or mortgages, and the financial institutions, in turn, lend to the ultimate borrowers. *Disintermediation* is the reverse: savers take funds out of deposit accounts, or reduce the amounts they normally put in, and invest directly in primary securities such as stocks and bonds.

Financial institutions are in a better position than individuals to bear and spread the risks of primary security ownership. Because of their large size, intermediaries can diversify their portfolios and minimize the risk involved in holding any one security. They are experts in evaluating borrower credit characteristics. They employ skilled port-folio managers and can take advantage of administrative economies in large-scale buying and selling.

Competition among financial intermediaries forces interest rates to the lowest level compatible with the intermediaries' evaluation of the risks of security ownership. These yields are lower than if the primary securities were held by individual investors, who are unable to mini-mize their risks as efficiently.

It is worth noting that since financial intermediation tends to lower interest rates, or at least to moderate any increase, it has been highly beneficial to our rate of economic growth. A high rate of economic growth requires a large volume of real investment. The lower the rate of interest that ultimate borrowers must pay, the greater their expenditure on real investment.[1]

The beneficial effect of intermediation on economic growth can also be seen from the viewpoint of risk bearing. Intermediaries are better able than individuals to bear the risks of lending out capital. As was previousy stressed, ability to diversify, economies of scale, and expertise in lending account for this comparative advantage of institutions over individuals. As financial intermediaries own a larger and larger portion of the marketable securities outstanding, the subjective risk borne by the economy is lowered, interest rates are reduced, and more real investment takes place. Funds are channeled from ultimate lenders, through intermediaries, to ultimate borrowers more efficiently than if the intermediaries did not exist.

FINANCIAL INSTITUTIONS IN PROFILE

Let's now turn to individual financial institutions. We are most interested in exactly how these institutions *intermediate* between saver-lenders and borrower-spenders. So we will pay special attention to the *composition* of their liabilities and assets, because they acquire funds from saver-lenders by "selling" their own liabilities and then turn around and obtain earning assets when they disperse the funds to borrower-spenders. By paying a lower interest rate when they acquire funds than they charge when dispersing them, financial institutions hope to make a profit on the differential.

In fact, from this perspective, financial intermediaries are just like any other firm—they are motivated by profits. In the process of turning a profit they just happen to accomplish an important economic objective, channeling funds from savers to investors.

Although all financial institutions have a lot in common, there are also substantial differences among them. Ranked in terms of asset size, for example, as in Table 1, commercial banks are easily the largest. In addition to sheer size, the composition of liabilities and assets also differs significantly from one type of financial institution to another.

1. *Commercial banks* are the most prominent of all financial institutions. There are about 15,000 of them, ranging from Citibank,

---

[1]In recent years financial intermediation has grown but interest rates have frequently risen, because "all other things" have not remained constant. (In Parts 4 and 5 we discuss these "other things.") Without financial intermediation, interest rates would have risen even higher.

TABLE 1
Financial Institutions, Ranked by Asset Size
(End of 1986)

Institution	Asset Size*
Commercial banks	$2,170
Savings and loan associations	1,160
Life insurance companies	900
Private noninsured pension funds	640
State and local government retirement funds	470
Mutual funds	410
Sales and consumer finance companies	400
Property and casualty insurance companies	350
Money market mutual funds	290
Mutual savings banks	240
Credit unions	170

*Total financial assets, in billions of dollars.

SOURCE: Federal Reserve Flow of Funds Accounts.

with over $150 *billion* in assets, to thousands of small banks scattered throughout the country, many of which have less than $50 *million*.

Commercial banks are also the most widely diversified in terms of both liabilities and assets. Their major source of funds used to be demand deposits (checking accounts), but in the past two decades savings and time deposits—including certificates of deposit—have become even more important than demand deposits. As we saw in Chapter 1, the main difference between savings and time deposits is that time deposits have a scheduled maturity date.

With these funds commercial banks buy a wide variety of assets, ranging from short-term government securities to long-term business loans and home mortgages. Because of their importance we will devote all of Chapters 8 and 10 to commercial banks.

2. *Savings and loan associations* (S&Ls) have traditionally acquired almost all their funds through savings deposits—usually called shares instead of deposits—and used them to make home mortgage loans. This was their original purpose—to encourage family thrift and home ownership. For the most part, S&Ls are still oriented in these directions, but changes are taking place

rapidly. The Banking Act of 1980—formally known as the Depository Institutions Deregulation and Monetary Control Act of 1980—granted them the power to issue checking accounts (usually called NOW—for negotiable order of withdrawal—accounts) and also to make consumer loans.

Subsequently, the Garn–St. Germain Depository Institutions Act of 1982 gave savings and loans additional authority with respect to consumer loans and also gave them power to make business loans.[2]

There are about 3,000 savings and loan associations in the United States, located from coast to coast. They encountered serious problems in the late 1970s and early 1980s because such a large proportion of their liabilities was in the form of savings deposits—which in effect are payable on demand—while so many of their assets consisted of fixed-rate long-term mortgages, a lot of them acquired when interest rates were much lower.

Typically S&Ls pay an interest rate of, say, 6 percent for their savings deposits and then turn around and make home mortgage loans at a higher rate, say 10 percent. The 4 percent differential is supposed to cover their operating costs and yield a profit. However, imagine the problems they face when short-term interest rates rise to, say, 12 percent: they are caught in a profit squeeze, because they have to pay 12 percent to get new money and also to prevent an outflow of their existing deposits, while their assets are still earning 10 percent (or even less) because most of them were acquired long ago.

We will examine the savings and loan industry and its difficulties in more detail in Chapter 7.

3. *Mutual savings banks* are practically identical with savings and loans except that there are only about 800 of them, concentrated mostly on the East Coast. Both are often called "thrift institutions." As their name implies, mutual savings banks are legally structured as "mutuals" or "cooperatives," with the depositors or shareholders "owning" the institution. As a result of the Garn–St. Germain Act of 1982, however, they can now easily switch from mutual to stock form of ownership, and many of them have done just that.

[2]This important piece of legislation also permitted deposit-type financial institutions to establish money market deposit accounts. The Garn–St. Germain Act was named after its Congressional sponsors, Senator Jake Garn of Utah and Representative Fernand St. Germain of Rhode Island.

Like S&Ls, savings banks have traditionally obtained most of their funds in the form of savings deposits and used the money mainly to make home mortgages. However, the Banking Act of 1980 also gave them the power to issue demand deposits (NOW accounts) and to make consumer and some business loans.

Since savings banks are so similar to S&Ls, they face identical problems when interest rates rise. They have to pay more to get new money and to retain a lot of what they have, but the return they get on most of their assets fails to rise correspondingly, since these are long-term mortgages acquired years ago.

4. *Life insurance companies* rank third in asset size, right after commercial banks and S&Ls. They insure people against the financial consequences of death, receiving their funds in the form of periodic payments (called premiums) that are based on mortality statistics. They can predict with a high degree of actuarial accuracy how much money they will have to pay out in benefits this year, next year, even ten or twenty years from now. They invest accordingly, aiming for the highest yield consistent with safety over the long run. Thus a high percentage of their assets is in the form of long-term corporate bonds and long-term mortgages, although the mortgages are typically on commercial rather than residential properties.

   We will look more closely at life insurance companies and other nondeposit financial institutions in Chapter 9.

5. *Pension and retirement funds* are similar to life insurance companies in that they are mainly concerned with the long run rather than the short run. Their inflow of money comes from working people building a nest egg for their retirement years. Like life insurance companies, pension and retirement funds are able to predict with a high degree of accuracy how much they will have to pay out in pensions (called annuities) for many years into the future. Since they face few short-term uncertainties, they invest mainly in long-term corporate bonds and high-grade stocks.

6. *Property and casualty insurance companies*, on the other hand, are more likely to encounter short-run liquidity needs. They insure homeowners against burglary and fire, car owners against theft and collision, doctors against malpractice suits, and business firms against negligence lawsuits, among other things. With the premiums they receive—big ones from car owners under twenty-five years old—they buy high-grade municipal

and corporate bonds, high-grade stocks, and short-term money market instruments such as Treasury bills (for liquidity).

7. *Sales and consumer finance companies* specialize in lending money for people to buy cars and take vacations and for business firms to finance their inventories. Many of them, like the General Motors Acceptance Corporation, are owned by a manufacturing firm and lend money mainly to help retailers and customers buy that firm's products. Others, like Household Finance and Beneficial Finance, mainly make small consumer loans. They get their funds by selling their own short-term promissory notes (called commercial paper) to business firms with funds to invest for a short while, as well as by selling their own long-term bonds.

8. *Credit unions* are generally included, along with S&Ls and mutual savings banks, in the category of "thrift institutions." There are about 15,000 of them, some in every state in the Union, most quite small but a few with assets exceeding $1 billion. They are organized as cooperatives for people with some sort of common interest, such as employees of a particular company or members of a particular labor union or fraternal order or church. Credit union members buy shares, which are the same as deposits, and thereby become eligible to borrow from the credit union.

   Until recently credit unions offered only savings deposits and made only consumer loans. Like S&Ls and mutual savings banks, however, they have had their powers broadened considerably. They can now offer checking accounts (called credit union share drafts) and can also make long-term mortgage loans.

9. *Mutual funds* are frequently but not exclusively stock market–related institutions. Pooling the funds of many people of moderate means, the fund's management invests the money in a wide variety of stocks, thereby obtaining diversification that individuals acting alone probably could not achieve. Shareholders can always redeem or sell back their shares if they wish, but the price they'll receive from the fund depends on what has happened to the stocks it holds. Buying shares in a mutual fund is thus much more risky than buying a savings deposit or a money market instrument, like a Treasury bill, but it is less risky than buying stocks on your own. In addition to mutual funds that buy stocks, there are many others that specialize in corporate or municipal bonds or other kinds of securities.

10. *Money market mutual funds* are something else again. They were the growth phenomenon of the 1970s and early 1980s. From only $2 billion in 1974 they exploded to $45 billion by 1978 and then to a startling $200 billion by 1982. They are like the old-fashioned kind of mutual fund just described in that people buy shares in a fund. However, the fund's management does not invest the money in the stock market or in corporate or municipal bonds. Instead, it purchases highly liquid short-term money market instruments, such as large-size bank negotiable CDs, Treasury bills, and high-grade commercial paper.

FINANCIAL INSTITUTIONS ARE BECOMING MORE ALIKE

So far in this chapter we have emphasized the differences among financial institutions, traditional distinctions that have deep historical and institutional roots. But in recent years these differences have been eroding, making depository institutions increasingly alike. By the turn of the century it will be difficult to tell them apart.

For instance:

1. Traditionally, demand deposits have been the exclusive province of commercial banks, with other deposit-type institutions legally barred from offering checking account facilities. In the 1970s, however, thrift institutions began offering NOW accounts, which are just checking accounts under another name. The Banking Act of 1980 confirmed their right to do so, with the result that now S&Ls, mutual savings banks, and credit unions all offer some type of checking account. Even money market mutual funds have gotten into the act, though they are not mentioned in the Banking Act of 1980.

2. Traditionally, only commercial banks made business loans, while savings and loans and savings banks specialized in mortgage lending and credit unions in consumer loans. However, the Banking Act of 1980 and the Garn–St. Germain Act of 1982 enlarged the lending powers of all the thrifts, so that now S&Ls and savings banks can make consumer and business loans and credit unions can make mortgage loans.

The net result of these changes is that the traditional specialization of financial institutions is breaking down. Deposit-type institutions are becoming more general and more alike. In a sense, they are all in the process of becoming commercial banks, dealing in checking accounts as well as time deposits and becoming more diversified in their assets. In addition, distinctions between deposit and non-deposit types of financial institutions are also eroding, as we shall see in our discussion of the Glass-Steagall Act in Chapter 9.

SUMMARY

1. Financial intermediation involves financial institutions acquiring funds from the public by issuing their own liabilities and then using the funds to buy primary securities. Disintermediation is the reverse: savers take their funds out of financial institutions and buy the primary securities themselves.

2. Financial intermediation leads to lower interest rates, because financial institutions can bear the risks of primary security ownership better than individuals can. They also have economies of scale and more skilled portfolio management than is available to most individuals acting on their own.

3. Commercial banks are the largest of all financial institutions in terms of asset size, followed by savings and loan associations, life insurance companies, and pension and retirement funds.

4. Commercial banks are not only the largest but also the most widely diversified in both their liabilities and their assets. However, the Banking Act of 1980 (the Depository Institutions Deregulation and Monetary Control Act) and the Garn–St. Germain Depository Institutions Act of 1982 broadened the asset and liability powers of thrift institutions, so they are rapidly becoming more and more like commercial banks.

Suggestions for Further Reading

The discussion of the role of financial intermediaries in the economy is derived primarily from John G. Gurley, "Financial Institutions in the Saving-Investment Process," *Proceedings of the 1959 Conference on Saving and Residential Financing* (United States Savings and Loan League, 1959). A very popular introduction to this general area is Dorothy M. Nichols, *Two Faces of Debt* (Federal Reserve Bank of Chicago).

For more on financial institutions and what they do, see Robert P. Black and Doris E. Harless, *Nonbank Financial Institutions* (Federal Reserve Bank of Richmond). Two classics on financial intermediaries are a book by John G. Gurley and Edwin S. Shaw, *Money in a Theory of Finance* (Washington,

D.C.: Brookings Institution, 1960) and an article by James Tobin, "Commercial Banks as Creators of Money," in *Banking and Monetary Studies,* ed. Deane Carson (Homewood, Ill.: Irwin, 1963).

For careful historical surveys of legislative developments regarding financial institutions, see Jean M. Lovati, "The Growing Similarity Among Financial Institutions," Federal Reserve Bank of St. Louis *Review* (October 1977), and *Leveling the Playing Field: A Review of the DIDMCA of 1980 and the Garn-St. Germain Depository Institutions Act of 1982* (Federal Reserve Bank of Chicago, 1983).

CHAPTER 5

Calculating Interest Rates

Interest rates are the most pervasive element in the financial world. They affect everything that financial institutions do, and their implications extend into just about every nook and cranny of financial markets. Bank managers wouldn't dream of making investment decisions without first considering the outlook for interest rates. Consumers decide where to put their savings depending in large part on where they can get the best interest rate on their funds. Business managers take interest rates into account in deciding when to borrow, how much, from whom, and for how long. Most importantly, interest rates serve as a yardstick for comparing different types of securities. Given the importance of interest rates, it is worthwhile exploring how they are calculated and their relationship to the prices of securities.

SIMPLE INTEREST

Suppose you lend someone $100 for a year at 8 percent annual interest. How much would you get back at the end of the year? There is a formula for calculating the dollar amount of interest that you probably remember from high school:

$$\text{Principal} \times \text{Rate} \times \text{Time (in years)} = \text{Interest}$$
$$\$100 \quad \times \quad .08 \quad \times \quad 1 \quad = \quad \$8$$

The amount you'd get back at the end of the year would be the principal ($100) plus the interest ($8) or a total future amount of $108:

$$\begin{aligned}
\text{Total Future Amount} &= \text{Principal} + \text{Interest} \\
&= \text{Principal} + (\text{Principal} \times \text{Rate}) \\
&= \text{Principal} \, (1 + \text{Rate}) \\
&= \$100 \, (1 + .08) \\
&= \$108
\end{aligned}$$

This example illustrates that if you are offered a choice between a dollar today and a dollar a year from now, you should take the dollar today, because you could lend it out and turn it into more than a dollar a year from now. Time, in other words, is worth money. A dollar in hand is worth *more* than a dollar due a year from now. Another way of expressing the same thought is to say that a dollar due a year from now is worth *less* than a dollar today (because interest can make today's dollar grow over the course of a year).

With *simple* interest at an 8 percent annual rate, $100 loaned out today will yield $8 interest at the end of a year, another $8 interest at the end of a second year, $8 interest at the end of a third year, and so on.

$$\text{Principal} \times \text{Rate} \times \text{Time (in years)} = \text{Interest}$$
$$\$100 \quad \times \ .08 \ \times \qquad 3 \qquad = \quad \$24$$

The total amount you'd have at the end of three years would be the principal ($100) plus the interest ($24) or $124. It's hard enough to get rich to begin with, but even harder if you lend your money out at simple interest. At least insist on *compound* interest, which is just as easily available—usually more so—and over time generates much more rapid growth.

COMPOUND INTEREST

Compound interest produces more rapid growth because it involves interest on interest. With annual compounding, the interest that accumulates during a year is added to the principal at year's end, so that the following year your money earns interest on interest.

Banks, for example, usually pay compound interest to depositors who put their money into bank savings accounts. The interest depositors earn is periodically added to their principal, so that it in turn starts to earn interest. Some banks convert the interest to principal annually, while others do so semi-annually, quarterly, monthly, or even daily. They advertise that interest is compounded annually, semiannually, or whatever it may be. We'll stick to annual compounding to illustrate how compound interest works.

With annual compounding at an 8 percent interest rate, $100 loaned out today will yield $8 interest at the end of a year, an additional $8.64 interest at the end of a second year, a further $9.33 at the end of a third year, and so on. Compare this $25.97 of total interest after three years to the $24 that accumulates with simple interest. The difference appears small, but over long periods of time it becomes stupendous. For instance, $100 lent at 8 percent *simple* interest would grow to $900 in a hundred years; at 8 percent *compound* interest over the same time period, $100 would grow to $219,976!

Let's examine compound interest a bit more closely. If you deposit $100 in a bank at 8 percent annual interest, what is your deposit worth after a year? The answer, of course, is $108. More formally: $100 (1 + .08) = $108. What is it worth after two years? Because of compounding (receiving interest on interest), it becomes $108 (1 + .08) = $116.64. What the second year really amounts to is $100 (1 + .08) (1 + .08), or $100 (1 + .08)^2 = $116.64. On the same basis, after three years the deposit would be worth $100 (1 + .08)^3, after four years $100 (1 + .08)^4, and so on.

If $100 today at 8 percent interest is worth $108 a year from now, and $116.64 two years from now, we can work *backward* and say that $108 a year from now must be worth only $100 today, and that $116.64 two years from now must also be worth only $100 today. In the previous paragraph, we applied an interest rate to increase a present sum into the future; now, when we work backward, we are *discounting* to reduce a future sum back to its *present value* (time is money). Putting it a bit more formally, we have simply transposed the previous paragraph's

$$100 (1 + .08) = \$108 \qquad \text{into} \quad \frac{\$108}{(1 + .08)} = \$100$$

$$\text{and} \quad \$100 (1 + .08)^2 = \$116.64 \quad \text{into} \quad \frac{\$116.64}{(1 + .08)^2} = \$100$$

We will return to the concept of present value shortly. First, though, let's become better acquainted with some interest rates on marketable coupon-bearing securities, like corporate, municipal, and government bonds. The interest rate that is most frequently referred to in bond markets is called *yield to maturity,* but a couple of other bond interest rates are often mentioned by securities buyers and sellers and are quoted in the financial sections of many newspapers—namely, the *coupon rate* and the *current yield.* Let's look first at the coupon rate and the current yield and then return to yield to maturity.

COUPON RATE ON BONDS

Suppose you pay $900 for a $1,000-face-value 8 percent–coupon bond that will mature in ten years and that you expect to hold until maturity. *What annual interest rate will you be getting on that security? In particular, what return will you be earning if you invest in the security?*

You have to be careful to keep clear exactly which interest rate you are talking about. In this instance the *coupon rate* is 8 percent, which merely means that printed on the face of the bond is a statement that each year the holder of the bond will get an interest payment, from the bond's issuer, amounting to 8 percent of the $1,000 face value, or $80. (Most bonds pay interest semiannually, which in this case would mean payments of $40 twice a year, but for simplicity we'll assume only one payment a year of $80.)

If you had paid the full $1,000 face value for the bond, you would indeed be getting 8 percent interest. But bond prices may rise and fall for many reasons, as we'll see in the next chapter. In this case, you are paying only $900, so although the coupon rate printed on the bond specifies 8 percent, you will actually be earning more than 8 percent because you paid less than $1,000. But *how much more* than 8 percent?

CURRENT YIELD

We take a step in the right direction by examining the current yield. The current yield is calculated as the annual dollar interest payment divided by the price you paid for the bond, or $80/$900 = 8.89 percent. At first glance this looks like a reasonable way to figure the interest rate, until you realize that it neglects receipts accruing beyond a one-year time horizon. In our case this understates the true yield, because when the bond matures in ten years you'll have a $100 capital gain (because you paid only $900, but when the bond matures it will be redeemed at its $1,000 face value).

YIELD TO MATURITY

Yield to maturity is the most accurate and widely used measure of interest rates in financial markets. It takes into account the factors that current yield neglects. Back in the section on compound interest we noted that, at 8 percent annual interest, $100 today will be worth $108 a year from now, $116.64 two years from now, $125.97 three years from now, and so on. Putting this formally: $100(1 + .08) = $108; $100(1 + .08)^2 = $116.64; and $100(1 + .08)^3 = $125.97.

We also noted that we could work backward and *discount a future sum back to its present value:* at 8 percent interest, $108 due a year from now would be worth $100 today (its present value), $116.64 due two years from now would be worth $100 today, and $125.97 due three years from now would also be worth $100 today. That is:

$$\frac{\$108}{(1 + .08)} = \$100; \quad \frac{\$116.64}{(1 + .08)^2} = \$100; \quad \frac{\$125.97}{(1 + .08)^3} = \$100$$

This concept of present value enables us to compare securities with different time dimensions. The illustration above, for example, shows that, when the annual interest rate is 8 percent, three pieces of paper—one promising $108 in a year, one promising $116.64 in two years, and one promising $125.97 in three years—are all equally valuable. Each of them is worth exactly the same ($100).

With this background in mind, let's now turn to the concept of yield to maturity. *The yield to maturity of a security is that particular interest rate (or rate of discount, as it is commonly called) that will make the sum of the present values of all the expected future payments of the security equal to its purchase price.*

The easiest way to understand that italicized sentence is with a concrete example. We have been discussing paying $900 for a $1,000-face-value 8 percent–coupon bond that will mature in ten years. What annual interest rate will it provide? Unless we can answer that question, we have no way of comparing it to other bonds that are available in the market, so we won't be able to tell if it's a good buy or a poor one.

Assuming that the interest is paid annually rather than semiannually, this piece of paper promises eleven future payments—ten interest payments of $80 each and one face value payment of $1,000. The price of the bond is $900, which means that anyone who wants to receive those future payments has to give up $900 today. The yield to maturity of this bond is *that particular rate of discount* (let's call it *r*) *that will make the sum of the present values of all eleven expected future* *payments equal $900.* (In corporation finance textbooks, by the way, this r is called the internal rate of return rather than yield to maturity.)

If we can find r in the following equation, we will have calculated the annual yield to maturity of this security:

$$\$900 = \frac{\$80}{(1 + r)} + \frac{\$80}{(1 + r)^2} + \frac{\$80}{(1 + r)^3} + \cdots + \frac{\$80}{(1 + r)^{10}}$$
$$+ \frac{\$1000}{(1 + r)^{10}}$$

We could figure out r by trial and error, trying one rate of discount (say 9 percent) and then another (10 percent) until we zero in on one that makes all the terms on the right-hand side of the equation add up to $900. But that would be a time-consuming process. It would be a lot quicker and easier just to look it up in a book of bond yield tables, where it's all worked out for us. Such tables show the yield to maturity in this particular case to be 9.58 percent per annum. (Notice that this is well above the current yield of 8.89 percent.)

What if you don't have a book of bond yield tables handy? Well, most business-type hand calculators are programmed to provide such information. If you have a business-oriented hand calculator, enter the yearly coupon payments ($80), the face value that will be paid on maturity ($1,000), the number of years to maturity (10), and the purchase price of the bond ($900). Press the right keys, and in a moment the calculator will give you the annual yield to maturity: 9.60 percent.

The hand calculator's 9.60 percent yield to maturity differs slightly from the bond table's 9.58 percent. The reason is that we assumed only one interest payment a year when entering data into the calculator, whereas bond tables are constructed on the assumption of semiannual interest payments. Since we've been simplifying all along in this example by assuming interest is paid annually, we might as well stick with that assumption and, to be consistent, use 9.60 percent as the appropriate yield to maturity.

In terms of yield to maturity, therefore, if you invested $900 in this particular security you'd get an annual interest rate of 9.60 percent on your money from now until the bond matures ten years from now. The yield to maturity is an accurate measure of the return on your investment in the security, because it compares all future dollar payments (including any capital gain) with the amount of money needed to get those future payments (namely, the price of the security).

So far we've been discussing yield to maturity in very specific terms, using the example of a particular security. The concept is too important, however, to leave at that. We should generalize the concept so it can be applied to a variety of cases. Here is the general formula for the yield to maturity (r) of a fixed-income security that pays a dollar coupon (C) in each of n years, has a face value (F) that will be paid off at maturity n years from now, and has a current price (P):

$$P = \frac{C_1}{(1 + r)} + \frac{C_2}{(1 + r)^2} + \frac{C_3}{(1 + r)^3} + \ldots + \frac{C_n}{(1 + r)^n}$$
$$+ \frac{F_n}{(1 + r)^n}$$

What the general formula tells us is that if we know the price of a security, its coupon payments, its face value, and its maturity, we can find its annual yield to maturity (r). The yield to maturity is whatever rate of discount will make the sum of the present values of all future payments equal the purchase price.

Obviously, we could also use the same general formula to determine a security's *price*, provided we know the rate of interest to begin with. In other words, if we know r, the coupon payments (C), the face value (F), and the years to maturity (n), we can solve for the present value of the bond or the price (P) we should be willing to pay for it. We'll come back to this way of looking at the equation later in the chapter.[1]

HOLDING PERIOD YIELD

Having emphasized how great yield to maturity is as an interest rate measure, we're now going to take it all back. Well, not all of it, but some of it, anyway. Yield to maturity is indeed the best (that is, the most accurate) interest rate measure for people who, as the term implies, plan on holding a security to maturity. However, many people and financial institutions buy bonds—even long-term ones—expecting to sell them well *before* the bonds are scheduled to mature.

[1]Actually the "present value" formula in the text can be used quite generally to value anything with future cash flows, not just securities. An investor might project future cash flows for an investment in a firm or building as C_1 through C_n. If the purchase price of the firm or building were given, then the formula would generate the internal rate of return on the investment. In Chapter 20 we note that an investor compares this internal rate of return on an investment with the interest rate to determine whether the investment is worth undertaking. Thus, the present value formula has diverse applications in money and finance.

For instance, let's return to our $1,000-face-value 8 percent–coupon bond, scheduled to mature in ten years, that we just bought for $900. Bond prices go up and down for a variety of reasons, many of which we'll explore in the next chapter. Let's say that we expect bond prices to go up for three years and then down. So we anticipate holding the bond not ten years but only three, after which we'll sell it. Clearly, yield to maturity isn't very relevant in this case, since we don't plan to hold the security that long.

Because this is such a common situation, the concept of "holding period yield" has been developed to cover it. Holding period yield is a modification of yield to maturity, with changes to make it appropriate for those who do not expect to hold a bond until it matures. Specifically, holding period yield includes the coupon interest for as long as it is received plus whatever sale receipts are received when the bond is disposed of before maturity.

Assume we've bought our bond for $900 and after three years the price has risen to $1,100. Following an appropriate celebration, we proceed to sell it, as planned. What has been our holding period yield?

We received a coupon payment of $80 at the end of one year, another $80 at the end of the second year, a third $80 at the end of three years, plus $1,100 at the end of the third year. The holding period yield is that annual rate of discount (r) that will make the sum of the present values of the coupon payments and of the sale receipts equal to the purchase price:

$$\$900 = \frac{\$80}{(1 + r)} + \frac{\$80}{(1 + r)^2} + \frac{\$80}{(1 + r)^3} + \frac{\$1,100}{(1 + r)^3}$$

Our holding period yield (r) turns out to be 15.27 percent per annum. It is found on a calculator by modifying the computation of yield to maturity. Just plug in the yearly coupon payments ($80), the amount realized from the sale ($1,100) in place of face value, the number of years held (3) in place of years to maturity, and the purchase price of the bond ($900).

ZERO-COUPON BONDS

Most bonds are like the $1,000-face-value 8 percent–coupon bond that we have been using for illustrative purposes; most corporate, government, and municipal bonds do indeed have coupons attached to them that entitle the holder to specific interest payments periodically. In the case of our bond, the coupon rate of 8 percent means that each

The Million Dollar Lottery: A Case of Misleading Advertising?

One illustration of the time value of money arises in connection with state lotteries in which the lucky winner gets paid over a period of time rather than getting the entire sum all at once. "Buy a ticket and win a million dollars!" reads the advertisement. But often it turns out that what the winner really gets is $50,000 now followed by $50,000 a year for the next nineteen years.

However, $50,000 now followed by $50,000 a year for nineteen years is worth considerably less than a million dollars.

Following the present value formula in the text and assuming an 8 percent interest rate:

$$\text{Present Value} = \$50,000 + \frac{\$50,000}{(1+.08)}$$

$$+ \frac{\$50,000}{(1+.08)^2} + \cdots + \frac{\$50,000}{(1+.08)^{19}}$$

Converting each of the payments to present value and adding produces a sum total of $530,180. Not bad, but it's a long way from a million!

year the holder of the bond will get an interest payment, from the bond's issuer, amounting to 8 percent of the bond's $1,000 face value, or $80.

However, the last decade has witnessed the growing popularity of a new kind of bond—zero-coupon bonds, which do not entitle the holder to get any coupon interest payments whatsoever. The only thing the owner of such a bond gets is the face value, when the bond eventually matures.

Why would anyone ever think of buying a bond that doesn't make any interest payments? As with many things, whether or not it is worth buying depends on how much it costs. We've already seen that if you pay $900 for an 8 percent-coupon bond with a $1,000 face value, you'll get an annual yield to maturity of 9.60 percent on your money over the next ten years. What if someone offers you the same bond but without any coupons—that is, a piece of paper promising $1,000 in ten years and nothing else? In fact, if you can get that piece of paper at a price of only $400, you will *also* get 9.60 percent on your money over the next ten years!

Yields to maturity on zero-coupon bonds follow the same principles as on coupon securities, but they are easier to calculate because there is only one payment—the face value, which is due on maturity. Thus the yield to maturity formula simplifies to:

$$Price = \frac{Face\ Value}{(1 + r)^n}$$

In the case of zero-coupon bonds, yield to maturity is that rate of discount (r) which makes the present value of a single payment (the face value), due in n years, equal to the current price. If we already know what r we want, we can use the same formula to solve for the present value or price of the bond.

In our example, with a face value of $1,000 due in ten years, if we know the annual interest rate we want—say we want r to be 9.60 percent—then we can solve for the price. With a hand calculator, the price turns out to be $399.85.

TREASURY BILLS

The most common zero-coupon securities aren't bonds at all but rather Treasury bills—short-term obligations of the federal government, with maturities of a year or less at the time they are issued. The formula for calculating the yield on a zero-coupon Treasury bill with one year to maturity is:

$$Price = \frac{Face\ Value}{(1 + r)}$$

The exponent n disappears in the denominator, because it is equal to unity when the maturity of the security is one year. We will examine yields and other aspects of Treasury bills in greater detail in Chapter 30.

THE INVERSE RELATIONSHIP BETWEEN YIELDS AND BOND PRICES

As early as Chapter 2 (see footnote 2), we mentioned that higher interest rates mean lower bond prices and lower interest rates mean higher bond prices. We can use the general present value formula (the last formula in the "Yield to Maturity" section) to demonstrate why this is so: if a bond's coupon payment (C) and face value (F) are fixed, a higher yield to maturity (r) must imply a lower bond price (P). Similarly, a lower yield must imply a higher bond price. If either r or P changes, the other will automatically change in the opposite direction.

For instance, what if you paid not $900 but $925 for our illustrative ten-year 8 percent–coupon bond with a face value of $1,000? What annual yield to maturity would you be getting then? Plug in $925 instead of $900; the yield to maturity, according to our trusty hand calculator, would fall from 9.60 to 9.18 percent. What if you paid only $875? Then yield to maturity would rise to 10.04 percent.

We have been assuming that we know P and want to find the resulting interest rate. We could do it the other way around: we could try to get a certain target yield to maturity and then search for the price that would provide it. For instance, enter 12 percent as a target r and then find the price that would produce that annual yield to maturity (assuming, of course, that C and F are fixed). The answer must be a price *below* $875, since $875 gives us only a 10.04 percent yield. We find that a price of $774 would produce a 12 percent yield to maturity.

The special case of a consol—or perpetual bond—best illustrates the inverse relationship between yields and bond prices. A consol is a bond with no maturity date at all. It promises that the holder will receive a fixed annual dollar payment forever, with no redemption date. In that case, with n approaching infinity, the general present value formula collapses (you'll have to take our word for it) into simply:

$$Price = \frac{C}{r}$$

Here it becomes obvious that, with C given, the rate of interest (r) and the price have to move inversely. If r rises, the price must fall, and if r falls, the price must rise.

WHY LONG-TERM BONDS ARE RISKIER THAN SHORTS

We can also use the general formula for the present value or price of a bond to explain why a change in interest rates affects long-term bond prices so much more than it affects prices of short-term securities. For long-term securities, a small change in interest rates involves a large change in price, whereas for short-term securities even a big change in yield involves only a small change in price.

Here's an illustration. Take two bonds, each of which has a face value of $1,000 and an 8 percent coupon; one has twenty years until maturity and the other has only two years. Both are currently priced at par (that is, at $1,000), so that yield to maturity in each case is 8 percent, the same as the coupon rate.

Assume that suddenly, for reasons no one fully understands, all interest rates rise by two percentage points. Yield to maturity in each case goes up to 10 percent. This rise in yield involves a fall in price from $1,000 to $830 for the twenty-year bond, but a fall in price from $1,000 to only $965 for the two-year security.

In brief, the longer a bond's maturity, the more its price will be affected by a change in the general level of interest rates. This has enormous implications for capital gains and losses. When all interest rates fall, long- and short-term, long-term securities rise dramatically in price, but not short-term ones. Similarly, when all interest rates rise across the board, long-term bonds—but not the shorter ones—drop drastically in price.[2]

The general present value formula explains why this is so. The formula shows that the price or present value of a bond consists of the sum of the discounted present values of all its future payments. The longer the maturity of a security, the greater will be the effect of a change in r on the price, because there are more future payments and they will be discounted over a longer period of time. The longer period of time is crucial: remember that discounting a payment due in twenty years isn't just dividing by $(1 + r)$ but by $(1 + r)^{20}$.

In other words, you can get rich quickly with long bonds, but you can also go down the drain. Long-term bonds are riskier than short-term bonds because the threat of potential loss is greater. Then why do people buy them? Because they often yield more than shorts, and also because hope springs eternal: maybe interest rates will fall and long-term bond prices will skyrocket!

It should also be pointed out that long-term bondholders do not necessarily suffer *out-of-pocket* losses whenever interest rates rise and bond prices fall. An out-of-pocket loss is suffered only if the bonds are sold. Owners who can hold on until their bonds mature will have

---

[2]Length of time to maturity is the most important factor affecting bond prices when interest rates change, but it is not the only one. Coupon size is also relevant: the smaller the coupon, the more a bond's price will be affected by a change in interest rates. An 8 percent–coupon bond will be more volatile in price than one with a 10 percent coupon. (Most volatile of all would be a long-term zero-coupon bond.) Portfolio managers often mathematically combine maturity and coupon size in order to estimate a bond's riskiness more precisely than is possible with maturity alone. The combination of the two is called a bond's "duration." For more on the subject, see the Appendix to Chapter 28.

paper losses but eventually receive the full face value of the bonds when they redeem them.

NOMINAL VERSUS REAL INTEREST RATES

So far we have discussed only nominal interest rates. "Nominal" in this sense means measured in money as distinct from actual purchasing power. Nominal interest rates—that is, market interest rates as quoted in the newspapers—provide an accurate measure with respect to purchasing power when consumer prices are stable, because then the purchasing power of money remains constant over time. But when consumer prices are rising, as during periods of inflation, nominal interest rates become misleading with respect to purchasing power.

Inflation means that lenders will get back dollars that have less purchasing power than the dollars they originally loaned out. Assume a 10 percent nominal interest rate and a 6 percent annual rate of inflation. If you lend someone $100 for a year, at 10 percent interest, you'll receive back $110 a year later. But with prices 6 percent higher, it will take you all of $106 to buy what you could have gotten for $100 last year. In terms of purchasing power, the $110 you now have buys only $4 more of goods and services than the $100 you loaned out a year ago. Although the nominal interest rate is 10 percent, 6 percent inflation has shrunk the inflation-adjusted or real interest rate to only $4/$100, or 4 percent.

The *nominal* interest rate measures the increment in dollars as a percent of dollars loaned out ($10/$100). The *real* interest rate measures the increment in purchasing power as a percent of purchasing power loaned out ($4/$100). *In a nutshell, the real interest rate is the nominal interest rate minus the inflation rate.*[3]

Actually, there are two concepts of the real interest rate: the ex ante or expected real rate and the ex post or realized real rate. The ex ante or expected real interest rate is the nominal interest rate minus the *expected* rate of inflation. The ex post real rate is the nominal interest

[3]The 4 percent real interest rate in this example is an approximation. It takes $106 to buy what $100 could have bought a year ago, leaving an apparent $4 increment in purchasing power. But that $4 can no longer buy what $4 could have bought a year ago. Because of the 6 percent inflation, $4 now can only buy what $3.77 could have bought last year ($4/1.06 = $3.77). Thus the precise real rate of interest in this example is not 4 percent but only 3.77 percent. Nevertheless, it has become customary to ignore this refinement, so that the real rate of interest is generally calculated simply as the market interest rate minus the inflation rate.

rate minus the actual or *realized* rate of inflation. More on this in the next chapter.

SUMMARY

1. Even simple interest demonstrates that time is money, that a dollar today is worth more than a dollar due a year from now (because today's dollar can grow to more than a dollar by earning interest during the year).

2. Compound interest produces more rapid money growth than simple interest because compounding involves the payment of interest on interest.

3. The yield to maturity of a security is that rate of discount that will make the sum of the present values of all future payments flowing from the security equal to its purchase price. Conversely, the present value or price of a security consists of the sum of the discounted present values of all its expected future payments. The yield to maturity is a useful yardstick for comparing returns on different securities.

4. Because many buyers do not hold securities to maturity, the yield to maturity formula is often modified to provide a security's holding period yield.

5. Zero-coupon bonds are securities with a payment at maturity but no coupons. A consol, on the other hand, has coupon payments but no maturity.

6. The present value formula shows why there is an inverse relationship between yields and bond prices. It also shows why a change in interest rates affects the prices of long-term securities more than the prices of short-term ones, making long-term securities riskier than short-term securities.

7. It is important to distinguish between "real" and "nominal" interest rates. The real interest rate is the nominal rate minus the rate of inflation.

Suggestions for Further Reading

A useful small paperback on the matters discussed in this chapter is Gary E. Clayton and Christopher B. Spivey, *The Time Value of Money* (Philadelphia: W. B. Saunders, 1978). Advanced topics are covered in Sidney Homer and Martin L. Liebowitz, *Inside the Yield Book* (Englewood Cliffs, N.J.: Prentice-Hall, 1972). For more on zero-coupon bonds, see Lawrence R. Rosen, *Investing in Zero Coupon Bonds* (New York: Wiley, 1986). Finally, an interesting essay on the significance of compounding is Stanley Diller's "The Power of Compound Interest," in the *American Banker* (March 20, 1980).

CHAPTER 6

The Level of Interest Rates

Now that we are experts in how to calculate interest rates, let's see what determines whether they are high or low and how they have behaved historically. There are many different interest rates—rates on car loans, on home mortgages, on government securities, on corporate bonds, and so on. However, most interest rates move up and down together, so that we can simplify matters by discussing "the" interest rate, with "the" rate conveniently standing for all rates taken as a group. Later, in Chapter 28, we will look at individual interest rates separately and explore differences among them.

SUPPLY AND DEMAND DETERMINE THE INTEREST RATE

The interest rate is a price, like the price of apples or Bruce Springsteen tapes or copies of Ritter and Silber. With the interest rate, however, the price we are talking about is the price of credit or borrowing money—the price that lenders receive and borrowers have to pay. Because the interest rate is a price, like all prices it must be determined by supply and demand. Supply of and demand for what? Of *credit* or *loanable funds*—funds that lenders are willing to make available for borrowers to borrow.

In any competitive market, whether for apples or textbooks, interaction between supply and demand determines price and quantity exchanged. Financial markets are no exception. In fact, we can best illustrate the story by drawing familiar supply and demand curves. In Figure 1 the interest rate is shown on the vertical axis and the quantity of credit or loanable funds on the horizontal axis. The upward-sloping supply-of-funds curve represents the commonsense notion that lenders will be willing to extend more credit the higher the interest rate they receive (holding everything else constant, including things like borrower credit-worthiness). The downward-sloping demand-for-funds curve represents borrower behavior: the lower the interest rate, the more funds borrowers are willing to borrow (once again holding everything else constant, like the prospects for business activity).

It should not be terribly surprising to you that the equilibrium interest rate is at the intersection point of the supply and demand curves—producing a yield of 5 percent in Figure 1. Equilibrium, you may recall from basic economics (or high school physics, if that's a better memory), means no tendency for change. Thus, in Figure 1 the interest rate will stay at 5 percent because that's where the quantity of funds lenders want to lend just equals the quantity of funds borrowers want to borrow. At any other interest rate, there is an excess of either borrowers or lenders, and competitive pressure will force the rate toward its equilibrium level. For example, at 6 percent lenders want to lend more than borrowers want to borrow; competition among

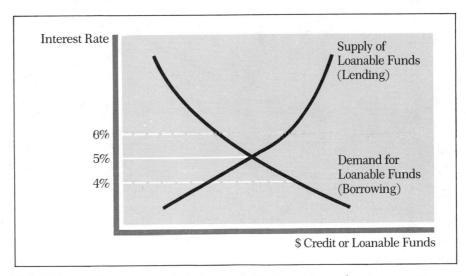

FIGURE 1 Supply and Demand Determine the Interest Rate

lenders forces the interest rate down. Similarly, at 4 percent borrowers want to borrow more than lenders want to lend; competition among borrowers forces the interest rate up. Once the interest rate gets to 5 percent, there is no tendency for it to change as long as the supply and demand curves stay where they are.[1]

Analyzing interest rates by supply and demand assumes that financial markets are competitive, so that supply and demand pressures will be reflected in price (interest rate) changes. It rules out the conspiracy theory of interest rates—the view that rates are rigged by a few insiders with substantial market power.

It is hard to believe that any one person, institution, or group of

[1] Instead of talking about how the supply of and demand for credit or loanable funds determine the rate of interest, we could talk about the same thing in terms of how the demand for securities and the supply of securities determine the price of securities (see the diagram below). To supply credit (lend) is equivalent to *demanding* financial assets (securities)—financial institutions lend, for example, by purchasing financial assets. To demand credit (borrow) is the same as *supplying* securities—business

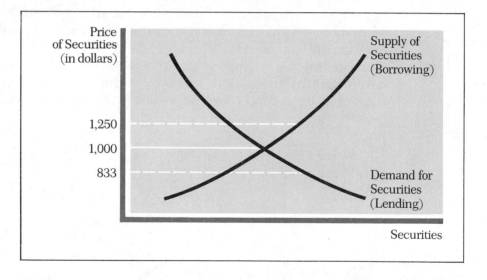

firms borrow by selling their bonds or other IOUs. Look at the diagram and compare it with Figure 1 in the text. At a price of $833 (which corresponds, let us say, to the 6 percent *yield* in Figure 1, assuming a 5 percent *coupon* on a $1,000 bond), relative eagerness to buy securities—or lend—would drive up the price of securities, just as Figure 1 shows that it would drive *down* the rate of interest. And at a price of $1,250, corresponding to a 4 percent yield, relative eagerness to sell securities—to borrow—would drive down the price of securities, just as Figure 1 shows that such circumstances would drive *up* the rate of interest.

institutions has anywhere near enough power to rig interest rates in this country. There are simply too many lenders engaged in the business of lending, and therefore too many alternatives open to most would-be borrowers, to permit any tightly-knit clique of lenders to control the price of credit. Lenders charging more than prevailing rates would price themselves out of the market and lose business to their competitors. Similarly, borrowers trying to borrow at cheaper than prevailing rates would find themselves outbid for funds by others who are willing to pay the market price.

WHY DOES THE INTEREST RATE FLUCTUATE?

Once the interest rate reaches equilibrium—like 5 percent in Figure 1—why doesn't it just stay there? Why does it change so often?

The interest rate fluctuates, like other competitive prices, because of shifts in the demand and/or supply curves. Before going into the details, let's focus on the mechanics. Perhaps you remember from your introductory economics course that we should distinguish between movements *along* a demand or supply curve and a *shift* in the curve. When the amount demanded or supplied changes in response to a change in the interest rate, then we have a movement *along* a demand or supply curve. On the other hand, a *shift* in a curve occurs when the amount demanded or supplied changes, at each interest rate, in response to something else—such as, for example, a change in expectations regarding inflation.

Figure 2 illustrates (a) a movement along a demand curve and (b) a shift in the curve. Moving down demand curve (a) from x to y to z is a movement along the demand curve. As the interest rate falls, the amount demanded increases. A shift in demand takes place when the amount demanded increases at each interest rate, as from demand curve (a) to demand curve (b). Of course, the amount demanded could also *decrease* at each interest rate, in which case the curve would shift to the left.

When talking about a movement along a single demand or supply curve, we'll always refer to a change in "amount demanded" or "amount supplied." On the other hand, when we say demand or supply has increased (or decreased), we'll mean the whole curve has shifted to the right (or the left).

Making this distinction helps to avoid confusion. When mortgage

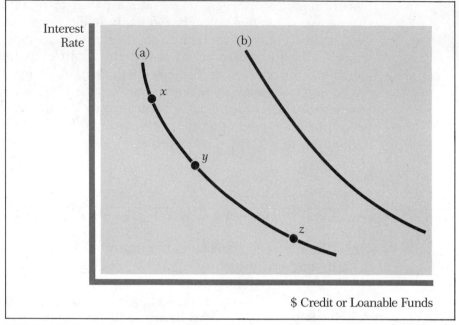

FIGURE 2 Movement Along a Demand Curve vs. a Shift in Demand

interest rates fall, for example, many potential home buyers decide to borrow funds and buy a home because now they can afford the monthly mortgage interest payments. That's an increase in the amount of loanable funds demanded in response to a change in the interest rate—a movement down *along* a single demand curve. In this case, a fall in the interest rate causes an increase in the amount demanded. On the other hand, say many tenants suddenly find themselves with more money and decide they can afford to buy their own homes, even at higher mortgage rates. This is a rightward *shift* in the demand curve.

It should be fairly obvious that anything that causes the demand or supply curves to shift position will cause the equilibrium interest to change. For example, in Figure 3, starting out with supply curve *S* and demand curve *D* produces a 5 percent equilibrium interest rate. If the demand curve shifts from D to D' and the supply curve stays put, the equilibrium interest rate will rise to 6 percent. If, on the other hand, the supply curve shifts from S to S' and the demand curve stays where it was (at D), then the new equilibrium interest rate will be 4 percent.

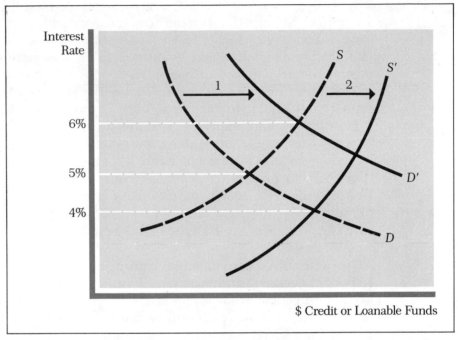

FIGURE 3 Shifts in Demand (1) or Supply (2) Curves Can Change the Equilibrium Interest Rate

BEHIND SUPPLY AND DEMAND

Now that we know that shifting supply and demand curves for loanable funds underlie gyrations in interest rates, let's see if we can go one step further. The level of interest rates will go up when the demand for loanable funds increases or when the supply of loanable funds decreases. What might lie behind such shifts in the demand and supply curves? First, let's look at demand.

Most borrowing comes from.

1. Business firms, borrowing to acquire inventories or buy capital equipment;
2. Households, borrowing to buy cars, consumer goods, or homes;
3. State and local governments, borrowing to build sewer systems, roads, schools, and so on; and
4. The federal government, borrowing to finance federal budget deficits.

Anything that increases the eagerness to borrow of any of these sectors would shift the demand for loanable funds to the right and drive interest rates higher. Some such factors might be anticipated improved profits on the part of business firms; expectations of higher incomes on the part of consumers; large population increases resulting in the need for more state and local services; or a big buildup in military outlays producing larger federal budget deficits.

Now let's turn to supply. Why might the supply of loanable funds—lending—decrease? Most lending comes from financial institutions or directly from individuals. Banks and other financial institutions sometimes have to curtail their lending because governmental authorities, like the Federal Reserve, make it difficult for them to lend. The ability of individuals to lend depends in part on how much they save; if they save less, they will generally lend less, exerting upward pressure on interest rates.

We will not go behind supply and demand in similar detail with respect to declines in interest rates. We trust your own ingenuity. In general, of course, what makes interest rates fall are decreases in the demand for loanable funds and/or increases in the supply. You can take it from there.

THE IMPORTANCE OF EXPECTATIONS

One element underlying *both* supply and demand deserves special mention because it is so important. That element is expectations.

In the previous chapter, in our discussion of nominal versus real interest rates, we showed how to calculate the real rate of interest given a particular nominal interest rate and a specific rate of inflation. Now we have a somewhat different concern: will a change in *expectations* of inflation alter the equilibrium nominal interest rate itself?

Changes in inflationary expectations clearly affect equilibrium interest rates by shifting the curves for both the demand for and supply of loanable funds. Borrowers expecting inflation to accelerate will *increase their demand* for loanable funds, shifting the demand curve to the right, because they look forward to repaying their borrowings in depreciated dollars. On the other hand, lenders expecting a speed-up in inflation will *decrease their supply* of loanable funds, shifting the supply curve to the left, because they anticipate getting repaid with money of diminished purchasing power. On both counts, the end result of increased inflation *expectations* will be higher nominal interest rates. Similarly, expectations of a slowdown in inflation will decrease demand, increase supply, and produce lower rates.

Usually, however, matters are not so neat and tidy. Our example assumed that everyone agrees in their expectations about inflation. In the real world, such unanimity about the future, or about anything else for that matter, hardly ever exists. Under such circumstances, the consequences for interest rates are more complicated.

Expectations about inflation aren't the only expectations that affect interest rates. Indeed, probably the most important expectations are those with respect to interest rates themselves. Borrowers who expect interest rates to rise will try to borrow more now, before they go up. And lenders who expect rates to rise will be reluctant to lend now, preferring to wait until they are higher. Expectations about future interest rates are sometimes *self-fulfilling prophesies:* increased demand for loanable funds and decreased supply combine to produce the higher rates that were anticipated.

CYCLICAL AND LONG-TERM TRENDS IN INTEREST RATES

Now let's see if our supply-demand framework can shed some light on how interest rates have behaved over the past four decades. Chart 1 plots the yields on long-term government and corporate bonds since 1950 to represent the overall movement in rates. The shaded areas on the chart indicate periods of business cycle recession—that is, periods when the economy is growing relatively slowly and unemployment is increasing. Each shaded area begins at the peak of a business cycle expansion and ends at the bottom (or trough) of the ensuing recession.

A number of generalizations can be drawn from Chart 1:

1. *The level of interest rates tends to rise during periods of business cycle expansion and fall during periods of cyclical recession.* Yields go up when business conditions are good, because that's when business firms and households generally increase their demand for loanable funds. Businesses borrow more to accumulate inventories in anticipation of increased sales, and households buy more goods and services on credit because the future looks bright for them, too. The opposite takes place in recessions, when both businesses and consumers rein in their use of credit so that the demand for loanable funds shifts to the left and interest rates fall.

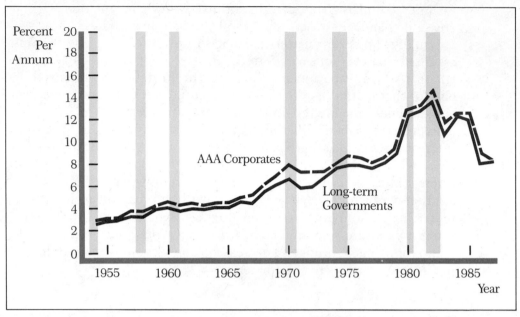

CHART 1 Trends in Interest Rates Since 1950

Supply curve shifts reinforce these effects on interest rates. The Federal Reserve usually tightens credit in business cycle expansions, shifting the supply of loanable funds to the left, raising interest rates. And the Fed typically eases credit during recessions, which increases the supply of credit, lowering interest rates.

2. *The level of interest rates has been on an upward long-term trend since 1950.* There are some exceptions, but for the most part each cyclical trough in interest rates has been higher than the previous trough, and each cyclical peak has similarly been higher than the one before. This upward trend is probably due to a number of factors, the two most important of which are large federal budget deficits, which force the U.S. Treasury to borrow huge amounts every year, and investor nervousness about future inflation. Inflationary expectations, as we have seen, can generate forces that raise interest rates. Inflation accelerated between the 1950s and the 1980s, so it is not surprising that nominal interest rates followed a similar trend.

    Needless to say, there is much more to the story of how interest rates are determined. In fact, much of our discussion in Chapters 19 through 25 on monetary theory focuses on how interest rates are influenced by economic activity, the central bank, and, of course, inflation. Although this chapter's discussion of supply and demand for loanable funds has broken some ground, there are plenty of complications to keep you busy later on.

SUMMARY

1. The interest rate is the price of credit and as such is determined by the supply of and demand for credit or loanable funds. It fluctuates because of shifts in demand and/or supply.

2. A movement along a supply or demand curve can be distinguished from a shift in the curve.

3. Interest rates rise when the demand curve for loanable funds shifts to the right and/or when the supply curve shifts to the left. Rates fall when the demand curve shifts to the left and/or the supply curve shifts to the right. Behind demand and supply are the borrowing requirements of businesses, households, and governments, and the monetary policies of the Federal Reserve.

4. Expectations also underlie the demand for and supply of loanable funds, especially expectations regarding inflation and expectations with respect to interest rates themselves. Expectations about interest rates often turn into self-fulfilling prophesies.

5. Interest rates tend to rise during periods of business cycle expansion and fall during recessions. This reflects increased demand for loanable funds during expansions and decreased demand during recessions.

6. The long-term trend of all interest rates has been upward since 1950. Much of this uptrend is a reflection of the increase in inflation between the 1950s and 1980s.

Suggestions for Further Reading

For historical perspective, an outstanding source is Sidney Homer, *A History of Interest Rates*, rev. ed. (New Brunswick, N.J.: Rutgers University Press, 1975). See also Roger G. Ibbotson and Rex A. Sinquefield, *Stocks, Bonds, Bills, and Inflation: The Past and the Future* (Charlottesville, Va.: Financial Analysts Research Foundation, 1982). A provocative analysis of interest rates is contained in Wall Street guru Henry Kaufman's *Interest Rates, the Markets, and the New Financial World* (New York: Times Books, 1986).

PART II

INTERMEDIARIES AND BANKS

The Regulation and Structure of Depository Institutions

One of the major influences on financial institutions is the regulatory environment within which they operate. In this chapter we look at the structure and regulation of depository institutions—commercial banks, thrift institutions (S&Ls, savings banks, and credit unions), and money market mutual funds. Actually, money market funds are not really deposit institutions, at least not in the full sense the others are, but they do offer checking account facilities and are included on that basis.

Since commercial banks are so much bigger than the others and occupy such a pervasive role in the functioning of the economy, most of the chapter is devoted to them. A number of questions spring to mind. Is there enough competition and flexibility in banking to make it a dynamic and innovative industry, responsive to private needs and public goals? Are banks safe places for your money? Who supervises them, in what ways and for what purposes?

After we have looked at the banking system, we will turn to the structure and regulation of thrift institutions and money market mutual funds. At the end we will spend some time with Regulation Q, a federal regulation that has helped shape the financial system as we know it.

THE DUAL BANKING SYSTEM

The American commercial banking system is known as a *dual* banking system because its main feature is side-by-side federal and state chartering (and supervision) of commercial banks. It has no counterpart in any other country. Indeed, it arose quite by accident in the United States, the unexpected result of legislation in the 1860s that was intended to shift the authority to charter banks from the various state governments to the federal government.

The National Currency Act of 1863, the National Bank Act of 1864, and related post–Civil War legislation established a brand new federally chartered banking system, under the supervision of the Comptroller of the Currency (within the U.S. Treasury). The idea was to drive the existing state-chartered banks out of business by imposing a prohibitive tax on their issuance of state banknotes (currency issued by state-chartered banks), which in those days was the principal form of circulating money. However, state-chartered banks survived and eventually flourished, because public acceptance of demand deposits in lieu of currency enabled state banks to remain in business despite their inability to issue banknotes.

Thus today we have a dual banking system: federally chartered banks, under the aegis of the Comptroller of the Currency, and state-chartered banks, under the supervision of each of the various states. Federally chartered banks are for the most part larger institutions, but state-chartered banks are more numerous. In mid-1986, as Table 1 indicates, two-thirds of the commercial banks had state charters, but

TABLE 1
Status of Insured Commercial Banks, 1986
(Dollars in billions)

All Commercial Banks	Number of Banks 14,186		Total Deposits $1,806	
	No.	Percent	Amount	Percent
National banks	4,866	34	$1,048	58
State banks	9,320	66	758	42
F.R. member banks	5,954	42	1,298	72
Nonmember banks	8,232	58	508	28

SOURCE: Federal Reserve, data for June 30, 1986.

the one-third with national charters held over half the deposits in the banking system.

In 1913, with the passage of the Federal Reserve Act, another supervisory layer was added as national banks were required to become member banks of the Federal Reserve System, while state banks were permitted the option of joining or not. At present, as can be inferred from Table 1, most state banks are not members of the Federal Reserve System. Nevertheless, member banks, both state and national, hold 72 percent of the total deposits in the banking system.

An additional supervisory structure was laid atop the edifice with the establishment of federal deposit insurance in the 1930s. All Federal Reserve member banks, and thus all national banks, are required to be insured by the Federal Deposit Insurance Corporation (FDIC). State nonmembers retain the option of having federal deposit insurance or not, but virtually all commercial banks have chosen to have federal deposit insurance coverage, because it would be difficult to attract deposits without it. (We will return to the FDIC later in this chapter.)

As matters now stand, a national bank is subject to the supervisory authority of the Comptroller of the Currency, the Federal Reserve, and the FDIC. A state member bank is subject to the regulatory authority of the state in which it is located (usually exercised through a state banking commission), the Federal Reserve, and the FDIC. A state bank that is not a member of the Federal Reserve is subject to its state's regulations plus the FDIC. A unique feature of the system is that the regulated can choose their regulator: state banks can shift to national charters and vice versa, state member banks can shift to nonmember status and vice versa. An economic historian might be able to detect the application of Gresham's law to bank supervision: bad regulators drive out good regulators.[1]

[1]Since every money and banking textbook should tell you what Gresham's law is— and since this is as good a chance as any—here it is. Sir Thomas Gresham (1519– 1579), financial adviser to Queen Elizabeth I, is said to have coined the phrase "bad money drives good money out of circulation," meaning that if two types of money of the same denomination serve as media of exchange, one containing less valuable (or debased) metal and the other containing more valuable metal, the coins containing the less valuable metal will remain in circulation while the more valuable coins will be hoarded. The bad money (the money with less valuable intrinsic content) will drive the good money (the money with more valuable intrinsic content) out of circulation, because everyone will try to hold on to the more valuable and pass on the less valuable.

Concrete examples of Gresham's law occur daily. Dimes and quarters minted in 1965 and since have been 75 percent copper and 25 percent nickel bonded to a pure

The justification for the dual banking system—side-by-side federal and state bank regulation—is that it is supposed to foster change and innovation by providing alternative routes through which banks can seek charters and do business. It is claimed that a dual banking system is more responsive to the evolving banking needs of the economy than a single system would be. The validity of these arguments is difficult to assess, but whatever their merits no one has been marching in the streets demanding change in the status quo. The dual banking system seems to be working tolerably well, regardless of its logic.

MULTIPLE FEDERAL AUTHORITIES

The dual banking system has aroused considerably less controversy than the existence of multiple and sometimes conflicting supervisory authorities at the federal level. Dispute among the federal banking agencies was especially marked during the regime of James J. Saxon as Comptroller of the Currency, from late 1961 to late 1966. The Comptroller repeatedly sought to depart from established precedent, only to be met by resistance from the more conservative Federal Reserve and FDIC.

The Federal Reserve and the Comptroller clashed frequently over the interpretation of certain laws. Relations between the FDIC and the Comptroller were also strained, even though the Comptroller is one of the three members of the FDIC's Board of Directors. Amity was not furthered by Comptroller Saxon's refusal, after a while, to attend FDIC Board meetings.

Different interpretations of the same statutes and intermittent dissension that has punctuated relations among the federal supervisory agencies have led many to recommend that all federal chartering, examination, and supervisory responsibilities be combined in a single agency. The proposal has always foundered, however, on lack of consensus as to which agency—the Federal Reserve, the FDIC, or the Comptroller of the Currency—is most appropriate. Notice that consolidation at the federal level would not affect the dual banking system, since state chartering and supervision would continue to exist.

---

copper core; previously they had been 90 percent silver and 10 percent copper. In light of the relatively high price of silver, the intrinsic value of a coin minted in 1965 or later is much less than one minted before 1965. The result, à la Gresham, is that post-1964 dimes and quarters (bad money) remain in circulation while an estimated $2.5 billion of the more valuable earlier coins (good money) have disappeared into private hoards.

Despite the fact that one study group after another has seen fit to recommend unification at the federal level—disagreeing only in how that unification might best be achieved—the existing tripartite arrangement remains. In 1978 Congress attempted to achieve some coordination by establishing a five-member Federal Financial Institutions Examination Council. The Council consists of a member of the Federal Reserve Board, the Comptroller of the Currency, and the heads of the FDIC, the Federal Home Loan Bank Board, and the National Credit Union Administration. Its purpose is to try to develop uniform reporting, examination, and regulatory standards for all financial institutions supervised by federal agencies.

The present system is defended by some on the grounds that divided federal authority, like the dual banking system, provides an element of flexibility, fostering innovation and change, that would be lacking if all federal banking powers were concentrated in one agency. On the other hand, if there is to be federal supervision of banking at all, it would appear axiomatic that it should be consistent in application and operated at minimum cost—which implies that one supervisory body is preferable to three, especially when the three tend to disagree fairly often among themselves.

It has to be admitted, however, as an argument in favor of the status quo, that federal regulatory agencies, in general, have not compiled a particularly outstanding record for imaginative leadership, for stimulating innovation, or even for protecting (not to mention furthering) the public interest. While a forward-looking, able, and conscientious single federal banking authority would undoubtedly be an improvement over present arrangements, lack of these qualities in a consolidated agency might only make matters worse.[2]

DEPOSIT INSURANCE AND THE FDIC

During the 1920s bank failures averaged about 600 a year, and during the years 1930–1933 over 2,000 a year! Read that sentence over again, so you really appreciate how huge those numbers are and get some idea of how many people lost their life savings as bank after bank disap-

[2]In the early 1980s a high-level governmental task force recommended a reorganization of federal regulatory responsibilities, but the recommendations fell on deaf ears. See *Blueprint for Reform: Report of the Vice President's Task Group on Regulation of Financial Services* (Washington, D.C.: Government Printing Office, 1984). The Federal Reserve's views on regulatory restructuring can be found in the July 1984 issue of the *Federal Reserve Bulletin.*

peared. At the end of 1933 there were fewer than 15,000 commercial banks remaining out of 30,000 that had been in existence in 1920. It is not surprising, therefore, that Congress established the Federal Deposit Insurance Corporation (FDIC) in response to this historic debacle. The ramifications of its establishment are with us to this very day.

The FDIC was created by the Banking Act of 1933 to insure deposits at commercial and mutual savings banks.[3] Companion legislation created the Federal Savings and Loan Insurance Corporation to do the same for savings and loan associations, and in 1970 the National Credit Union Administration initiated deposit insurance for federally chartered credit unions. FDIC deposit insurance became effective on January 1, 1934, with coverage limited to $2,500 per depositor per bank. This was raised to $5,000 in mid-1934, $10,000 in 1950, $15,000 in 1966, $20,000 in 1969, $40,000 in 1974, and $100,000 in 1980.

According to FDIC survey data, the present coverage provides full insurance for about 99 percent of the *depositors* in insured banks. With respect to the dollar volume of deposits, however, the 1 percent of depositors not fully covered hold *uninsured* balances that constitute a fourth of the dollar value of total deposits. In other words, although almost all depositors are fully insured (that is, they have less than $100,000 in their accounts in any single bank), a fourth of the deposits in terms of dollar volume are not insured. A $150,000 negotiable certificate of deposit (CD), for example, would be insured for $100,000 and uninsured for the $50,000 balance.

Although nominal insurance coverage is $100,000 per depositor per bank, in fact actual coverage may be greater (never less), depending on the procedure used by the FDIC in taking over a failed bank. The FDIC may allow the bank to go into receivership, the so-called *payoff* method. In such cases the FDIC sends its agents to the bank, verifies the deposit records, and then pays out funds directly to each depositor up to a limit of $100,000. Thereafter the FDIC shares, on a pro rata basis with the claims of depositors in excess of their insurance and with the other creditors, in the residual proceeds realized from liquidation of the failed bank's assets. The FDIC reports that, after liquida-

---

[3]The typical point of view of the banking community in 1933, with respect to the feasibility of federal deposit insurance, was summarized in the gloomy conclusion that "the plan is inherently fallacious . . . one of those plausible, but deceptive, human plans that in actual application only serve to render worse the very evils they seek to cure." (*The Guaranty of Bank Deposits*, Economic Policy Commission, American Bankers Association, 1933, p. 43.) On this basis, organized banking groups generally opposed legislation establishing the FDIC.

tion, those with deposits in excess of the insurance limit have usually received back over ninety cents on the dollar, but often only after a wait of several years.

Alternatively, the FDIC may succeed in merging the failed bank with a healthy one, the so-called *assumption* method. The deposits of the failed bank are assumed by another bank into which the distressed one is merged and are made available in full to the depositors. The FDIC may assist in this procedure, either by making loans to the bank taking over or by relieving it of some of the weaker assets of the failed bank. The assumption method has been the one most often used in recent years; in such cases the FDIC has in effect completely insured all depositors to the *full* amount of their deposits, regardless of the technical insurance coverage limit.

In addition, in a few cases the FDIC has extended loans to a bank in difficulty and allowed it to continue in business. Two examples are Detroit's Bank of the Commonwealth, which received loans totaling $35 million from the FDIC in 1972, and Philadelphia's First Pennsylvania Bank, which received $300 million of FDIC credit in 1980. Both continued operating thereafter. The treatment of the Continental Illinois National Bank of Chicago in 1984, the largest bank "failure" in U.S. history, was somewhat different, as we shall see in the following.

The original capital of the FDIC was provided by a levy on the Treasury and the Federal Reserve Banks, amounting to $289 million, which was fully repaid in 1948. In addition, insured banks are assessed annually one-twelfth of 1 percent of their *total* deposits (not just their insured deposits). Frequently, the effective rate of these assessments has been reduced by rebates that the FDIC has returned to the banks.

Were the banking system to collapse, an insurance fund of $18 billion, which is what it amounts to now, is obviously insufficient to pay off several hundred billion dollars of currently insured deposits. The FDIC has additional legislative authority to borrow up to $3 billion from the U.S. Treasury in case of emergency, but such numbers are really meaningless. The reasoning underlying the FDIC does not involve calculations of actuarial probability, but rather the basic premise that the very existence of federal deposit insurance eliminates the possibility of large-scale bank failure. By insuring deposits under the auspices of the federal government, backed by the implied support of the United States Treasury to whatever extent necessary, the FDIC has successfully eliminated the old-fashioned "run on the bank" by frightened depositors that formerly heralded another bank failure. If people hear their bank is "in trouble" now, they hardly pay attention.

They're insured, so who cares? Thanks to this simple but effective device, savings have been made safe and the banking system has prospered in the last fifty years as never before.

However, a word of caution: Although apprehensive depositors no longer form long lines waiting to withdraw their funds from a bank that is rumored to be in trouble, a less obvious but very large deposit drain can still occur through the failure of corporate treasurers to renew outstanding large-size negotiable certificates of deposit—they simply let their CDs "run off." Corporate treasurers are exceedingly careful about which banks they put their funds in, since large-size CDs ($100,000 and over) are insured only up to the $100,000 insurance limit. Similarly, large corporate checking accounts will be transferred quickly from a bank in trouble to one that is considered safe.

Bank failures have increased sharply in the last few years. They averaged only 6 a year from 1960 through 1974 and 11 a year from 1975 through 1981, but then they jumped to 42 in 1982, 48 in 1983, 79 in 1984, 120 in 1985, 138 in 1986, and 184 in 1987. This increase is a by-product of financial deregulation, which has created a riskier environment and therefore more likelihood that banks will fail.

One banking collapse that isn't included as a failure in the 1984 figures because technically it wasn't allowed to fail is Chicago's Continental Illinois National Bank. With over $40 billion in assets, Continental Illinois was the seventh largest bank in the United States at the end of 1983. Continental made a number of risky loans, many of which turned bad, and in May of 1984 rumors circulated that the bank was in trouble. As a result, many institutional depositors—corporations, money market mutual funds, and other banks, foreign as well as domestic—that had been holding Continental's large-size CDs and other obligations decided not to renew. This silent and invisible "run" on the bank removed about $8 billion of the bank's deposits in a matter of days and about $20 billion in a couple of months.

The bank was kept afloat by FDIC intervention of a most unusual sort: the FDIC took over $3.5 billion of Continental's bad loans and also injected $1 billion of capital by acquiring, for that sum, 80 percent of the bank's common stock. In effect, the FDIC "nationalized" the bank—the first such nationalization of a bank in this country—by taking 80 percent of ownership and appointing new top management. As part of the arrangement, the Federal Reserve lent the FDIC $3.5 billion.

The rescue of Continental Illinois has raised a number of disturbing issues. When many small or medium-sized banks fail, the FDIC uses the payoff method and depositors are reimbursed only up to the

$100,000 deposit insurance limit. When a giant bank like Continental Illinois threatens to go under, however, all depositors are in effect insured for the full amount of their deposit, whether or not it is over the $100,000 limit. Is it fair to treat depositors of small and large banks differently?

Also, is it appropriate, in a capitalistic free enterprise system, to have the government take over a troubled bank? Is this a precedent that might lead to further nationalization of banking in the future, or is it a rare case that deserves special treatment?

A related question has arisen about the wisdom of the FDIC's *fixed-rate* deposit insurance premiums. That is, all insured banks are assessed identical annual premiums, namely, one-twelfth of 1 percent of deposits (less any rebate, which is also identical for all). All other kinds of insurance—life insurance, auto insurance, health insurance— vary premium payments with risk: the greater the risk, the higher the premium. Under the circumstances, some banks may be tempted to reach out for riskier higher-yielding loans, knowing that they will not be penalized by higher insurance premiums and that in any event their depositors will be bailed out.

An alternative that the FDIC has been considering is to price deposit insurance, like other insurance, on a risk-adjusted basis. Banks with riskier portfolios would pay higher premiums. Problems arise because it is difficult to measure a bank's overall portfolio risk with any degree of precision. Nevertheless, the idea deserves further exploration.

BANK SIZE DISTRIBUTION AND THE McFADDEN ACT

The objectives of bank supervision, regulation, and insurance are to protect the safety of depositors' funds and promote a viable and smoothly functioning banking system—one that will encourage saving, channel funds from savers to borrowers, enable borrowers to get funds on reasonable terms, and foster economic stability and growth. All of this means that the objectives of bank supervision, regulation, and insurance are to make sure that banks are both safe and competitive. The FDIC and bank examinations are designed to ensure safety, while other aspects of supervision are intended to promote competition.

In down-to-earth terms, competitive conditions mean that customers can shop around, that they have alternatives. For example, are the opportunities open to depositors sufficiently varied to give them an array of choices with respect to deposit terms and yields, so they can pick those that best suit their particular needs? Similarly, do borrowers who are refused a loan at one bank have alternatives open to them—other banks to which they can turn? Do banks actively seek customers, either depositors or borrowers, by offering more service or better terms than rival banks are offering?

With more than 14,000 commercial banks in the United States, there would appear to be, on the face of it, a high degree of robust competition in banking. However, as Table 2 indicates, a large percentage of banks are very small institutions, with less than $50 million of assets per bank. Indeed, almost 9,000 of the banks in the country—62 percent of them—are that small (see lines 1 and 2 in the table). These 9,000 banks have only 8 percent of the aggregate assets in the banking system. Most of them are in small, one-bank towns.

At the other end of the scale, about 500 large banks (the last two lines of Table 2), only 3 percent of the total, have 70 percent of all bank assets.

If the large number of very small banks were the product of natural evolution, it would indicate that the optimum (low-cost) size bank is probably a very small institution. Their large numbers would attest to their competitive viability.

In fact, the reason for so many very small banks in this country does not have much to do with their successful adaptation to changing economic needs or their innovative capabilities. It is that most of them are *sheltered* from competition by state anti-branching stat-

TABLE 2

Size Distribution of Insured Commercial Banks (End of 1985)

Asset Size	No. of Banks	% of Total Banks	% of Total Assets
Less than $25 million	5,251	36	3
$25–50 million	3,742	26	5
$50–100 million	2,808	20	7
$100–500 million	2,091	15	15
$500 million–1 billion	209	1	5
Over $1 billion	315	2	65
TOTALS	14,416	100	100

SOURCE: FDIC.

utes, to which the federal banking authorities defer. Many very small banks would be unable to remain in business if a large bank opened up a branch next door. The fact that in many states the large bank is legally prohibited from doing so is what permits many small banks to survive.

The McFadden Act of 1927 prohibits banks from branching across state lines and permits national banks to branch within a state only to the same extent as state-chartered banks. At present, about a dozen states, mostly in the Midwest, permit only unit banking; that is, no branches at all are allowed. Another dozen states allow only some limited form of branching. The remaining states permit unlimited statewide branching. In summary, *the McFadden Act prohibits interstate branching everywhere and requires that a federally chartered bank abide by the branching laws of the state in which it is headquartered.* [4]

The result is that the McFadden Act and state anti-branching statutes, not economic circumstances, are the principal determinants of the number of banks in the United States. If there were fewer banks, and more of them were close to optimum size, the general public would be better served. The proof is that almost half the banks in the country are in the dozen no-branching states, where the average bank size is much smaller than in unlimited branching states.

However, there are many signs in the wind that the McFadden Act's prohibition against interstate branching is on its last legs. Here are some of the signs pointing in that direction:

1. In 1981, two savings and loan associations in financial trouble— the West Side Federal Savings and Loan of New York City and the Washington Savings and Loan of Miami Beach, Florida—were merged into the Citizens Federal Savings and Loan Association of San Francisco (then owned, by the way, by National Steel Corporation). The result was the first nationwide savings and loan association, and it was renamed exactly that: First Nationwide Savings and Loan Association, with 150 branches in California,

---

[4] Actually, federal branching laws are contained not only in the McFadden Act of 1927 but also in the National Bank Act of 1864, the Banking Act of 1933, and the Douglas Amendment to the Bank Holding Company Act of 1956. The Douglas Amendment prohibits bank holding companies from acquiring banks across state lines, unless expressly permitted by state law. However, in financial circles the McFadden Act is commonly understood as meaning the whole network of restrictive federal branching laws.

Florida, and New York. As such, it serves as a model for banks to emulate as soon as they can.

2. In 1982 and 1983 Citicorp, parent holding company of New York's giant Citibank, was given permission to acquire (a) the Fidelity Savings and Loan Association of California (with more than eighty branches in that state), (b) the First Federal Savings and Loan of Chicago, and (c) the Biscayne Federal Savings and Loan of Miami, Florida. All three thrift institutions were on the verge of failure, and to prevent their going down the drain Citicorp was permitted to buy them. Net result: Citicorp has the nucleus of a nationwide branch banking system already in place.

3. In May of 1983 BankAmerica Corporation, parent holding company of San Francisco's giant Bank of America, was given permission by the regulatory authorities to buy Seafirst Corporation, the biggest bank holding company in the Northwest ($9.6 billion in assets) and owner of the Seattle First National Bank. The Seattle bank needed a rescue operation to save it from failure. Result: BankAmerica has established an interstate branch foothold. If it is acceptable here, why not elsewhere?

4. In December of 1986 Chemical Bank of New York announced the acquisition of Texas Commerce Bank, making Chemical the country's fourth largest bank. (Chemical was ranked seventh in size at the time, Texas Commerce twenty-seventh.)

5. The McFadden Act and related legislation prohibit bank holding companies from acquiring banks across state lines, *unless expressly permitted by state law.* In recent years, a host of states have enacted legislation specifically permitting reciprocal interstate banking: banks from State X can locate here if our banks can locate in State X. These include Alaska, Connecticut, Georgia, Florida, Illinois, Indiana, Kentucky, Maine, Massachusetts, Michigan, New York, Rhode Island, South Carolina, and Utah. In other words, the states may successfully outflank federal statutes prohibiting interstate branching by enacting their own permissive legislation. Indeed, in 1985 the U.S. Supreme Court expressly upheld such state laws permitting reciprocal interstate branching.

6. The geographic limitations that the McFadden Act places on branches do not apply to nonbank subsidiaries. Both national and state banks can establish bank-related subsidiaries and affiliates anywhere in the country. New York banks now have mortgage

company subsidiaries in Florida, California banks have finance company affiliates in Texas, and Chicago banks have loan production offices in New York.

Everything considered, the first steps toward nationwide branch banking appear to have been taken. Most observers believe that it will be commonplace by the turn of the century.

DO THE GIANT BANKS POSE A MONOPOLY THREAT?

So far we have emphasized that there are probably too many very small banks in the United States, too small for efficient operation. What about the other end of the scale—where each of a few Giant Banks has over $20 *billion* in assets? This handful of banks, one-tenth of 1 percent of all the banks in the country, holds a third of all the banking system's assets. Do these sixteen Giants, listed in Table 3, pose a clear and present monopoly danger?

Opinions differ on this, of course, but at this stage in history the Giant Banks appear to be more benign than malignant. This is not

TABLE 3
The Sixteen Giants

Bank	Assets*
Citibank (New York)	153
Bank of America (San Francisco)	91
Chase Manhattan (New York)	82
Morgan Guaranty (New York)	69
Manufacturers Hanover (New York)	62
Chemical (New York)	58
Bankers Trust (New York)	55
Security Pacific (Los Angeles)	48
Wells Fargo (San Francisco)	39
First National (Chicago)	34
Continental Illinois (Chicago)	32
First National (Boston)	25
Mellon (Pittsburgh)	24
First Interstate (Los Angeles)	22
Marine Midland (Buffalo)	22
Irving Trust (New York)	21

*In billions of dollars, end of 1986.

SOURCE: *The American Banker.*

because they are particularly generous, home-loving, or patriotic—at least no more so than any of us—but simply because, large as they are, they still face sufficient competition to keep them in line. Close on their heels are another seventy banks with assets between $5 and $20 billion, and close behind *them* come another hundred with assets between $2 and $5 billion.

The monopoly threat is further ameliorated in this country by legislation that forbids banking and industrial operations by the same firm. In some other countries—Japan is the outstanding example—giant banks are affiliated with giant manufacturing firms under common ownership, representing a vast concentration of economic power. If Chase Manhattan Bank, Xerox, and IBM could merge into a huge combine, as is permissible in Japan—where they are called *zaibatsus*—then we would really have something to worry about.

One development of the past twenty years that contributed to the fear of bigness in banking is the growth of one-bank holding companies. In the late 1960s and early 1970s all the nation's large banks converted their corporate structure to holding company form, with the holding company owning the bank as well as other subsidiaries. The primary motivation for the growth of one-bank holding companies was not an attempt to form vast financial-industrial combines, like Japan's *zaibatsus.* The underlying reasons were much more mundane: an effort on the part of American banks to evolve into new functional areas—such as data processing activities, insurance services, mutual fund sales, investment advisory services, and so on—in which, *as banks,* they could not fully participate. Faced with legal and regulatory constraints on their ability, as banks, to move into diversified financial activities, they turned to the holding company format as a way out. The holding company becomes an umbrella, sheltering under a single corporate structure the bank and various affiliated subsidiaries that can legally offer an array of financial services.

The apparition of potential *zaibatsus* was put to rest once and for all by congressional legislation in 1970 regulating one-bank holding companies. The legislation specified that they must confine their activities to fields "so closely related to banking as to be a proper incident thereto." The supervisory body is the Board of Governors of the Federal Reserve System. Thus one-bank holding companies cannot engage in manufacturing, communications, or any other industry not "closely related" to banking.

The future activities of one-bank holding companies are still unclear. The Federal Reserve, pursuant to the 1970 legislation, has ruled that they may engage in certain specified activities, such as some forms of insurance underwriting, acting as an investment or financial adviser and providing bookkeeping or data processing services. But litigation continues in the courts; for example, in 1971 the Supreme Court ruled that one-bank holding companies could not operate their own mutual funds, and in 1976 the Federal Reserve decided that they should not be permitted to operate travel agencies, because that activity is not "closely related" to banking. The outcome of other suits, still pending, will be a crucial factor in deciding the shape of banking in the future.

SAVINGS AND LOAN ASSOCIATIONS AND SAVINGS BANKS

Savings and loan associations may be federally or state chartered. Of the roughly 3,000 S&Ls in existence, slightly more than half are chartered by the states in which they operate and the rest by the federal government. Virtually all of them, however, are members of the Federal Home Loan Bank System (FHLBS), which is to S&Ls what the Federal Reserve System is to commercial banks. The Federal Home Loan Bank System, like the Federal Reserve System, consists of twelve regional Banks plus a supervisory board in Washington.

The Federal Home Loan Bank Board regulates S&Ls by chartering them, conducting examinations, and reviewing applications for branches and mergers. Branching for S&Ls fundamentally depends on state laws, but it tends to be much more liberal than for commercial banks, and branching across state lines is not uncommon.

The Federal Home Loan Bank System also supports S&Ls by making loans to them when they are otherwise short of funds; the FHLBS raises the money by selling its own securities and then uses the funds to make loans to savings and loan associations. While Federal Reserve lending to financial institutions is usually expected to be repaid fairly rapidly, FHLB loans to S&Ls are often for extended periods of time.

Savings banks were the first thrift institutions in the country. The Provident Institution for Savings in Boston and the Savings Fund Society in Philadelphia were founded in 1816, whereas the first S&L, the Oxford Provident Building Association in Philadelphia, was not organized until fifteen years later. Nowadays, though, for all practical purposes savings banks and savings and loans are hard to tell apart except by their names.

The 800 savings banks, concentrated on the eastern seaboard, are almost all state chartered; federal chartering of savings banks was not begun until 1978. Because most are state chartered, they are state regulated and state supervised.

Under the Depository Institutions Deregulation and Monetary Control Act of 1980, otherwise known as the Banking Act of 1980, both S&Ls and savings banks must hold reserves against their checking account and business time deposit liabilities, as specified by the Federal Reserve; as a *quid pro quo,* they have full access to temporary borrowing from the Federal Reserve when needed.

Most savings banks are insured by the FDIC, up to the standard $100,000 per depositor, just like commercial banks. S&Ls, on the other hand, are typically insured by the Federal Savings and Loan Insurance Corporation (FSLIC), also up to $100,000 per depositor. While the FDIC is an independent agency, the FSLIC is a subsidiary of the Federal Home Loan Bank System, and its policies are determined by the Federal Home Loan Bank Board. At the end of 1986, the FDIC insurance fund amounted to $18 billion, but because of numerous savings and loan failures the FSLIC fund had run out of money.

As we saw in Chapter 4, both S&Ls and savings banks had serious difficulties in the late 1970s and early 1980s, because of the rise in the general level of interest rates. Their liabilities were mostly short-term, while their assets were chiefly sunk in relatively low-yielding fixed-rate long-term mortgages. As a result many S&Ls went down the drain.

The Garn–St. Germain Depository Institutions Act of 1982, which we mentioned previously in Chapter 4, was intended primarily as a rescue operation for savings and loan associations and savings banks. It authorized them to offer money market deposit accounts, enabling thrifts to compete on an equal footing with money market mutual funds, and it also gave them enhanced power to make business and consumer loans. In addition, S&Ls and savings banks were given wide flexibility to alter their charters if they wished to do so: now they can easily convert from a state to a federal charter and can also switch between being a savings bank and being a savings and loan, or between mutual and stock-type ownership. The Act also enlarged the powers of federal insurance agencies to aid troubled institutions, including making loans to them and arranging mergers across state lines.

However, the Garn–St. Germain Act of 1982 failed to stem the tide of thrift institution failures. S&Ls in depressed farm and energy states were especially hard hit, so much so that by early 1987 the Federal Savings and Loan Insurance Corporation had run out of money and was declared technically insolvent. In 1987 Congress passed legislation intended to help the FSLIC get back on its feet. The insurance fund was allowed to raise $11 billion through new government-guaranteed bond issues. Given the rate of S&L failures, however, it is doubtful whether this will be enough.

As an aside, it is useful to note that there are a number of government-sponsored efforts to support the activities of mortgage-related financial institutions. Perhaps the most popular is the Federal National Mortgage Association, also known as Fannie Mae, established by Congress in 1938. It later became part of the Department of Housing and Urban Development (HUD) and in 1968 became a privately owned corporation with certain ties to the government. Fannie Mae buys mortgages from S&Ls and other institutions that no longer wish to hold them as investments and finances these so-called secondary market operations primarily by issuing bonds to the public.

Fannie Mae's performance in the mortgage market is complemented by the work of Ginnie Mae, more properly called the Government National Mortgage Association. A relative newcomer to the mortgage market scene, Ginnie Mae was established by Congress in 1968 as part of HUD. Since 1970, Ginnie Mac has made a name in connection with the "pass-through program." Instead of buying mortgages and financing these acquisitions by issuing her own securities, Ginnie Mae guarantees the timely payment of interest and principal on packages or pools of mortgages that are insured by the Federal Housing Administration (FHA) or the Veterans Administration (VA). These pools of mortgages are put together by private mortgage originators such as savings and loan associations or mortgage bankers. GNMA pass-through securities are attractive to such investors as pension funds and insurance companies because of their government guarantee and liquidity. The pass-through program has made mortgages look very much like bonds to some investors, thereby broadening the source of mortgage funds.

In 1970, Congress established the Federal Home Loan Mortgage Corporation (FHLMC) as a subsidiary of the Federal Home Loan Bank System. Dubbed Freddie Mac by the investment community, this latest creation does just about what Ginnie Mae does, except that instead of FHA-VA mortgage-backed securities, Freddie Mac creates participation certificates in conventional mortgages and sells them to ultimate investors. As with Ginnie Mae, the objective is to attract heretofore nontraditional funds into the mortgage market by packaging individual mortgage loans into a bondlike instrument.

All these government and government-sponsored agencies are very active, especially during periods of tight money, in helping to finance mortgage activity. They have, in fact, led to concern in the capital markets over the "federalization of the mortgage market."

CREDIT UNIONS

The first credit union in this country was established in Manchester, New Hampshire, in 1909. Credit unions now number about 15,000, making them the most numerous of the thrift institutions. They have not been subject to the same problems as S&Ls and mutual savings banks, because the bulk of their lending has always taken the form of relatively short-term consumer loans.

Credit unions may be federally or state chartered, but the majority have federal charters. State-chartered institutions are regulated and supervised by the states in which they operate and the federally chartered ones by the National Credit Union Administration in Washington. The National Credit Union Share Insurance Fund, run by the National Credit Union Administration, provides deposit insurance (up to $100,000 per depositor) for both state and federally chartered credit unions.

Like savings and loans and savings banks, credit unions are required by the Banking Act of 1980 to hold reserves against their checking accounts as specified by the Federal Reserve. In return, they have access to the temporary borrowing facilities of the Fed.

MONEY MARKET MUTUAL FUNDS

There are now about fifty money market mutual funds that have assets of over $1 billion each, as compared with none only about fifteen years ago. You will not find a money market mutual fund with a drive-in window at your local shopping center, because all transactions are by mail, phone, or some related form of telecommunication. They are not regulated or supervised by any banking-type agency, either state or federal, and since they have no brick-and-mortar branches there are no regulations about where they can locate. However, as mutual funds they do come under the overall regulation of the Securities and Exchange Commission in Washington, which provides protection to shareholders against fraudulent practices and other potential abuses.

The Current Regulatory Structure in Brief

Federal Reserve (FR).   Established as an independent agency in 1913. Supervises and examines state-chartered banks that are members of the FR System and regulates all bank holding companies, regardless of charter.

Comptroller of the Currency.   Established in 1863 as an office within the U.S. Treasury Department. Charters, regulates, examines, and supervises nationally chartered banks.

State Banking Departments.   Charter, regulate, examine, and supervise state-chartered banks and thrifts. In practice, share authority over state-chartered institutions with federal insurer.

Federal Deposit Insurance Corporation (FDIC).   Established as an independent agency by the Banking Act of 1933. Insures deposits at virtually all commercial banks and most savings banks. Examines and supervises state-chartered banks that are not members of the Federal Reserve System. Acts as receiver for most banks, both state and national, placed in receivership.

Federal Home Loan Bank System (FHLB).   Created in 1932 as an independent agency to provide a central credit system for savings and loan associations. Governed by a board in Washington and twelve regional Federal Home Loan Banks. Responsible for chartering, regulating, examining, and supervising federally chartered S&Ls, and extends loans to

them to meet liquidity requirements. The FHLB also administers the FSLIC.

Federal Savings and Loan Insurance Corporation (FSLIC).   Created in 1934 under management of FHLB. Insures deposits at savings and loan associations. Also acts as receiver in cases of liquidation.

National Credit Union Administration (NCUA).   Established in 1970 as an independent agency to charter, regulate, examine, and supervise federal credit unions.

National Credit Union Share Insurance Fund (NCUSIF).   Created in 1970 under management of NCUA. Insures deposits at federal credit unions and insured state-chartered credit unions.

U.S. Department of Justice.   May review proposed mergers, acquisitions, and related changes in the structure of financial industry and sue to block those believed to be anti-competitive.

Securities and Exchange Commission (SEC).   Established under 1933 and 1934 legislation to regulate securities brokers and dealers and securities markets. Mutual funds, including money market funds, are now also under its jurisdiction. Specifies and enforces public disclosure requirements and regulates "insider" trading. Involved with banks particularly with respect to bank holding companies and public disclosure regarding such matters as problem loans.

Shares in money market mutual funds are not insured by any governmental agency.[5]

Because money market funds generally offer checking account privileges—in most cases only for checks of $500 or more—their "deposits" or shares are included as part of the money supply (M2). However, they are not subject to the reserve requirements that the Federal Reserve enforces on all other institutions offering demand deposits. So far the Fed has not strongly protested this anomaly.

Why did money market mutual funds grow so fantastically in the late 1970s and early 1980s? Obviously the extraordinarily high short-term money market interest rates available back then must have had something to do with it. But that alone is only a partial explanation. For the full answer, we have to bring into the picture something called Regulation Q—the interest rate ceilings that used to be imposed on savings and time deposits by federal law. Let's examine Regulation Q for a moment and see how it helped shape the structure of all deposit-type institutions, and why it gave birth to money market mutual funds, among other things.

REGULATION Q: REQUIESCAT IN PACE

Through Regulation Q, the Federal Reserve used to set the maximum interest rates that commercial banks were allowed to pay on their time and savings deposit liabilities. The maximum interest rates that savings banks and savings and loan associations could offer depositors were also regulated. (In addition, banks were prohibited from paying any interest at all on checking deposits. In effect, the checking deposit interest rate ceiling was set at zero.)

Regulation Q was enacted in the Banking Act of 1933, on the ground that excessive interest rate competition for deposits during the 1920s had undermined the soundness of the banking system. It was believed that competition among commercial banks for funds had driven deposit rates up too high. To cover their costs, banks acquired high-yielding but excessively risky low-quality assets. This deterioration in

[5]The main difference between money market mutual funds and other depository institutions is that the money funds (like all mutual funds) do not have any capital (or surplus) on their balance sheets. In other words, money funds distribute all of their earnings on assets to their shareholders (less a management fee). Other financial intermediaries retain some portion of their earnings to build up capital. One consequence of this difference is that the return earned on money funds can never be fixed; it must always fluctuate with earnings on assets.

the quality of bank portfolios, it was said, contributed to the collapse of the banking system in the early 1930s. Abolition of interest rate competition for deposits, by setting legal rate ceilings, was seen as rooting out the basic element weakening the banking system. Similar arguments were responsible for the imposition of comparable ceilings over S&Ls and savings banks starting in 1966, although, in an effort to reward S&Ls and savings banks for their home mortgage concentration, the ceiling on their deposit rates was set $\frac{1}{4}$ percent higher than at commercial banks.

In retrospect, it is not at all clear that the historical experience which led to Regulation Q was correctly interpreted at the time. Interest rates on bank time and savings deposits actually declined during the 1920s, and thorough investigation since has failed to substantiate any appreciable deterioration in the quality of bank assets during that period.

Regulation Q effectively prevented aggressive, well-managed banks from offering depositors more attractive interest rates than the bank next door. Banks that wanted to compete for funds by bidding more for deposits were legally prohibited from doing so; as a result, of course, depositors were deprived of the higher yields that more vigorous price competition among banks would have produced.[6]

More specifically, Regulation Q caused intermittent financial *dis*-intermediation during the tight-money episodes of the 1960s and 1970s, and again in 1981. During those periods, money market interest rates rose but deposit interest rates were held down by Regulation Q. With deposit interest rates substantially below market rates, savers stopped moving funds *into* financial institutions; instead, they moved them *out.* People took money out of savings accounts and put it directly into money market instruments and other primary securities, thereby bypassing the intermediaries. As we saw in Chapter 4, this behavior is known as financial disintermediation. Financial intermediation describes savers depositing funds with financial institutions, which then turn around and buy primary securities (such as bonds, stocks, and mortgages). Financial disintermediation is the reverse: savers take funds *out* of their deposit accounts, or reduce the amounts they normally put in, and directly buy the primary securities themselves.

---

[6]In addition, Regulation Q discriminated against the small saver. Higher interest rates were permitted on large deposits (over $100,000) than on small ones. See Edward J. Kane, "Short-Changing the Small Saver," *Journal of Money, Credit and Banking* (November 1970).

Disintermediation put the intermediaries under severe pressure. With substantial withdrawals and minimal inflows of new funds, their profit position was threatened, their solvency was endangered, and their ability to lend evaporated.

The disintermediation effects of Regulation Q were softened over the years by regulatory changes. In 1970 the Federal Reserve eliminated the rate ceilings on large-size ($100,000 and over) negotiable CDs that mature in less than three months, in order to ease money market pressures stemming from the collapse of the Penn Central Railroad. And in 1973 the Fed eliminated the ceilings on longer-maturity large-size CDs as well.

Equally important, especially in forestalling disintermediation during the tight-money episode of 1978–1979, was a new six-month money market time certificate that commercial banks and thrift institutions were allowed to issue starting in mid-1978. The interest rate on these was tied to the Treasury bill rate, so that depositors could receive high money market yields without withdrawing their funds from depository institutions. They could merely shift their funds for six months from a passbook savings account to a money market time certificate in the same bank or S&L. However, these were not permitted in denominations below $10,000, leaving smaller depositors out in the cold.

Money market mutual funds were the private sector's answer to this under-$10,000 gap. A new kind of financial institution, they were created in response to the restrictions of Regulation Q. With large depositors able to get the benefits of high money market rates—since large CDs of $100,000 and over were freed from deposit rate ceilings in 1970 and 1973—and with both Treasury bills and money market time certificates available in denominations no lower than $10,000, there was room for ingenuity and innovation on behalf of small depositors.

This ingenuity produced money market mutual funds, which gathered together the funds of many small savers, in batches as small as $1,000 and $2,000, and then proceeded to buy high-yielding large-size CDs and other money market instruments, such as commercial paper, in denominations of $25,000, $50,000, and $100,000. Since they were not subject to Regulation Q, the money market funds could pass these high yields on to their shareholders. By pooling their funds, small savers were thus able to gain access to money market yields that had been barred to them by Regulation Q.

By the end of 1982, money market mutual funds had achieved tremendous popularity. They had total assets of over $200 billion, a lot of which had formerly been held by banks. This loss of business prompted banks to lobby for similar powers—that is, for the ability to compete with money market mutual funds by offering something comparable. Partly in response to such pressure, Congress passed the Garn–St. Germain Depository Institutions Act of 1982, one section of which stipulated that depository institutions could introduce a money market deposit account that had limited checking privileges *and* carried market interest rates.

Money market deposit accounts at commercial banks and thrift institutions have proved enormously successful. As a result of this innovation, banks have regained much of the business they had lost to money market mutual funds, especially since money market accounts at banks and thrifts are federally insured up to $100,000 while accounts at money market mutual funds are not. The new accounts have eliminated incentives for further disintermediation.

The Banking Act of 1980 put an end to Regulation Q. The Act established a Depository Institutions Deregulation Committee, which gradually phased out interest rate ceilings on time and savings deposits and eliminated them entirely on April 1, 1986.[7] The Act also put an end to the ban against paying interest on personal (but not business) checking accounts by permitting all depository institutions to offer NOW (Negotiable Order of Withdrawal) accounts, which are in effect interest-bearing checking accounts.

SUMMARY

1. The United States has a dual banking system, involving side-by-side federal and state chartering and supervision of commercial banks. State-chartered banks are more numerous, while federally chartered banks are larger. It is claimed that a dual banking system is more responsive to the evolving banking needs of the economy than a single system would be.

2. The multiplicity of federal supervisory authorities—the Federal Reserve, the Comptroller of the Currency, and the FDIC—frequently creates confusion and conflict. There is general agreement that one federal supervisory authority would be preferable to three, but there is no consensus as to which one of the three would be best.

[7]This demise of Regulation Q is properly noted in the title of this section, "Requiescat In Pace," more commonly known by the initials R.I.P. which becomes "Rest In Peace" for those of us who have forgotten our elementary Latin.

3. FDIC insurance of bank depositors has eliminated the old-fashioned "run" on a bank in trouble, but deposits can still evaporate as holders of a bank's large-size CDs let them run off. A number of questions have arisen recently about deposit insurance, including the wisdom of fixed-rate premiums. An alternative would be to price deposit insurance, like other insurance, on a risk-adjusted basis.

4. The McFadden Act of 1927 prohibits interstate branching and requires that a federally chartered bank abide by state branching laws. One result is that the United States has more than 14,000 commercial banks, most of them very small institutions. However, there are many signs in the wind that the McFadden Act's prohibition against interstate branching is on its last legs.

5. The Giant Banks appear to pose no near-term monopoly threat, especially since one-bank holding companies must confine their activities to fields "closely related" to banking.

6. Savings and loan associations are supervised by the Federal Home Loan Bank Board and insured by the FSLIC. Savings banks are mostly state supervised and insured by the FDIC. Credit unions are supervised by the National Credit Union Administration and insured by the National Credit Union Share Insurance Fund. The Garn–St. Germain Depository Institutions Act of 1982 was intended mainly as a rescue operation for thrifts.

7. Money market mutual funds come under the overall supervision of the Securities and Exchange Commission. So far they have escaped the reserve requirements of the Federal Reserve even though their shares are included as part of the money supply (M2). The growth of money market mutual funds has slowed down considerably since depository institutions began offering money market deposit accounts in 1982.

8. Regulation Q, which set maximum legal interest rates on time and savings deposits, was responsible for reducing competition among depository institutions and for stimulating the growth of money market mutual funds. When market interest rates rose above Regulation Q's ceilings, depositors withdrew their funds from depository institutions, or put in less than usual, and moved their money into primary securities either on their own or via money market mutual funds (financial disintermediation).

9. The Garn–St. Germain Act permitted depository institutions to offer money market deposit accounts comparable to money market mutual fund shares. The money market deposit accounts offer market interest rates and limited check-writing facilities. They have eliminated incentives for further disintermediation.

Suggestions for Further Reading

The literature on bank structure is extensive. The classic in the field is David Alhadeff's *Monopoly and Competition in Banking* (Berkeley: University of California Press, 1954). Also see his "Barriers to Bank Entry," *Southern Economic Journal* (April 1974). Recent changes in bank structure are discussed in Donald T. Savage, "Developments in Banking Structure," *Federal Reserve Bulletin* (February 1982).

The McFadden Act is analyzed in *Geographic Restrictions on Commercial Banking in the United States: The Report of the President* (Washington, D.C.: Government Printing Office, 1981). The entire Summer 1980 issue of the *Journal of Bank Research* is also devoted to it. See also the article on "Interstate Banking: The Drive to Consolidate," by Constance Dunham and Richard F. Syron, in the Federal Reserve Bank of Boston's *New England Economic Review* (May–June 1984).

On problems of bank regulation, Marriner Eccles' analysis of many years ago is still sound and up to date: it is in his autobiography, *Beckoning Frontiers* (New York: Knopf, 1951), pp. 266–286. See also Kenneth Spong, *Banking Regulation: Its Purposes, Implementation, and Effects,* 2d ed. (Federal Reserve Bank of Kansas City, 1985). Another very useful book on regulation and its historical development is Carter H. Golembe and David S. Holland, *Federal Regulation of Banking* (Washington, D.C.: Golembe Associates, 1986). Also highly recommended: Elbert V. Bowden and Judith L. Holbert, *Revolution in Banking,* 2d ed. (Reston, Va.: Reston Publishing Company, 1984).

With respect to the FDIC, see Edward J. Kane, *The Gathering Crisis in Federal Deposit Insurance* (Cambridge, Mass.: MIT Press, 1985), and Irvine H. Sprague, *Bailout: An Insider's Account of Bank Failures and Rescues* (New York: Basic Books, 1986).

Closely related to structure and regulation is the role of bank examination. On this see George J. Benston's monograph, *Bank Examination* (New York University, Institute of Finance, 1973). And if you get a chance, be sure to see W. C. Fields (as Egbert Sousé) in the movie *The Bank Dick.* Franklin Pangborn plays the part of the bank examiner, J. Pinkerton Snoopington.

CHAPTER 8

Commercial Bank Asset and Liability Management

Banks are business firms. Banks may not look like Frisbee factories, but then King Kong doesn't look much like Rudolph the Red-nosed Reindeer either. They are both animals, nevertheless.

Like Frisbee manufacturers, bankers buy inputs, massage them a bit, burn a little incense, say the magic words, and out pops some output from the oven. If their luck holds, they can sell the finished product for more than it cost to buy the raw materials in the first place.

For bankers, the raw material is money. They buy it at a long counter they set up in the store, then rush around to the other side of the counter, sit down behind a huge desk (a little out of breath), and sell it as soon as they can to someone else. If they're really good at their business, sometimes they can even sell it back to the same person they bought it from (a trick bankers picked up from Los Angeles used-car dealers).

About the only way you can tell whether bankers are buying money or selling it is to observe whether they're standing up or sitting down. For some unknown reason, probably an inherited trait, bankers always stand up when they buy money (take your deposit), but invariably sit down when they sell it (make loans or buy securities). In this chapter we'll look first at what happens when they're sitting down and then at what they do when they stand up.

USES OF BANK FUNDS

Tables 1 and 2 show the major trends in the past quarter-century in uses of bank funds. Table 1 contains the dollar amounts and Table 2 the percentage distribution. What trends do they show?

TABLE 1
Assets of Insured Commercial Banks, 1960–1986
(In billions of dollars)

	1960	1970	1986
Cash assets	52	93	374
U.S. govt. and agency securities	61	75	283
State and local govt. securities	17	69	139
Other securities	3	3	55
Business loans	43	112	599
Mortgage loans	29	73	510
Consumer loans	26	66	324
Other loans	19	63	266
Miscellaneous assets	6	22	355
TOTAL	256	576	2,905

SOURCE: FDIC *Annual Reports* and *Federal Reserve Bulletin.* All figures are as of year end.

TABLE 2
Assets of Insured Commercial Banks, 1960–1986
(Percentage distribution)

	1960	1970	1986
Cash assets	20	16	13
U.S. govt. and agency securities	24	13	10
State and local govt. securities	7	12	5
Other securities	1	1	2
Business loans	17	19	21
Mortgage loans	11	13	17
Consumer loans	10	11	11
Other loans	8	11	9
Miscellaneous assets	2	4	12
TOTAL	100	100	100

SOURCE: See Table 1.

Banks have obviously cut way back on the proportion of their funds in cash assets and their holdings of government securities—from 44 percent of total assets in 1960 to only 23 percent in 1986. These have been replaced chiefly by loans of all sorts, which are up from 46 percent of total assets in 1960 to 58 percent in 1986.

Bank holdings of government securities are highly marketable and can be liquidated on short notice. Aside from the long-run decline in holdings of government securities, there are also cyclical fluctuations that are not captured by Tables 1 or 2. Traditionally, banks buy government securities during recessions, when private loan demand is slack, and then sell them off during business recoveries, when private loan demand is vigorous. Thus bank holdings of government securities are a residual use of funds. They show a countercyclical pattern, rising when business conditions decline and falling when the business cycle is on the upswing. Loans in general, and business loans in particular, move in the opposite direction, that is, in harmony with the business cycle.

The category "other loans" includes billions of dollars of loans to foreign governments in 1986 that were not present in 1960 or 1970, when almost all loans were domestic. Many of the foreign loans now on the books have turned sour as third-world borrowers have not paid either the interest or the principal on schedule. We will discuss this problem and its implications in Chapter 10.

Why is it that no *stocks* are included among bank assets? The reason is that commercial banks have traditionally been barred by law from owning stocks, on the ground that stocks are too risky. This prohibition dates from the National Currency Act of 1863 and the National Bank Act of 1864 and has been reaffirmed repeatedly in subsequent legislation. Banks *do* buy billions of dollars worth of stocks, but not for themselves; they buy them for the trusts, estates, and pension funds that they manage for others. Such trust department holdings are not included among a bank's own assets.

SOURCES OF BANK FUNDS

Tables 3 and 4 show the major trends over the past quarter-century in sources of bank funds. Table 3 contains the dollar amounts and Table 4 the percentage distribution.

Notice first how demand deposits, which used to be *the* major source of bank funds—61 percent in 1960—have shrunk in importance, declining to 18 percent by 1986. This decline is traceable to the

TABLE 3
Liabilities and Capital of Insured Commercial Banks, 1960–1986 (In billions of dollars)

	1960	1970	1986
Demand deposits	156	247	507
Passbook savings deposits	55	99	155
Time deposits*	18	110	1,014
Large-size negotiable CDs	0	26	267
Miscellaneous liabilities	6	54	782
Equity capital	21	40	180
TOTAL	256	576	2,905

*Excluding large-size ($100,000 and over) negotiable certificates of deposit. Includes money market deposit accounts.

SOURCE: FDIC *Annual Report* and *Federal Reserve Bulletin.* All figures are as of year end.

TABLE 4
Liabilities and Capital of Insured Commercial Banks, 1960–1986 (Percentage distribution)

	1960	1970	1986
Demand deposits	61	43	18
Passbook savings deposits	22	17	5
Time deposits	7	19	35
Large-size negotiable CDs	0	5	9
Miscellaneous liabilities	2	9	27
Equity capital	8	7	6
TOTAL	100	100	100

SOURCE: See Table 3.

legal prohibition against banks paying interest on demand deposits, combined with the general increase in interest rates on other types of assets that has taken place over this period of time. Individuals and business firms are reluctant to hold any more demand deposits than they really need for their day-to-day payments. They have learned that it pays to economize on their checking accounts, since to hold more than is absolutely necessary means sacrificing interest income.

Savings and time deposits, on the other hand, have expanded from only 29 percent of bank funds in 1960 to 49 percent in 1986. Savings and time deposits are frequently lumped together, but in the tables we have disaggregated them into three components: passbook savings deposits, time deposits (not counting large-size negotiable certificates of deposit), and large-size ($100,000 and over) negotiable CDs. One reason for the separation is that their relative growth rates have differed considerably over the period.

Passbook savings deposits are the traditional form of savings account, held mostly by individuals and nonprofit organizations. A little blue (sometimes green) passbook has been the standard symbol of a savings account for generations, and until the late 1960s such passbook accounts represented the bulk of total commercial bank savings and time deposits. Time deposits consist of certificates of deposit with a scheduled maturity date and are held by business firms as well as by individuals. They have swept well ahead of passbook savings deposits in recent years.

With passbook savings accounts, funds can be withdrawn from the savings account at any time. Technically, thirty days' notice is required prior to a withdrawal, but this requirement is universally waived. On the other hand, if depositors want to withdraw funds from a time deposit before the scheduled maturity date, they are subject to substantial penalties, such as the forfeiture of interest.

The growth of time deposits was given particular impetus by the "invention" of the *negotiable* certificate of deposit in 1961. Usually issued in denominations of $100,000 and over, the negotiable CD can be sold if one has to raise cash before it matures. Thus it serves as an alternative to Treasury bills for corporate treasurers with excess funds to invest for a short time.

Tables 3 and 4 also show a huge increase in "miscellaneous" liabilities over the past twenty years. These include a wide variety of *nondeposit* sources of funds, such as:

1. Borrowings from the Federal Reserve.

2. Borrowings in the federal funds market: federal funds are an unsecured loan between banks (often on an overnight basis) that is settled by a transfer of funds the same day the loan is made.

3. Borrowings by banks from their foreign branches, from their parent holding companies, and from their subsidiaries and affiliates.

4. Repurchase agreements: banks often sell securities and agree to buy them back at a later date (often the next day). When a bank sells securities to a corporation or to another bank under an

agreement to repurchase—called RPs or "repos"—the bank commits itself to buying the securities back on a specified future date at a predetermined price. In effect, since the bank has the use of the funds until the securities are repurchased, the bank is borrowing funds with the securities as collateral; the interest rate is determined by the difference between today's selling price and tomorrow's higher repurchase price. With overnight RPs, the bank gains access to short-term funds, which it hopes to use profitably, and the corporation earns interest while sacrificing virtually no liquidity. When such a transaction is made between a bank and one of its own corporate depositors, the bank's balance sheet shows a rise in borrowings and a corresponding drop in demand deposit liabilities.[1] More on RPs in Chapter 30.

A final source of bank funds, and one that has become increasingly important although it does not show up on the tables, arises from the sale of assets through a technique called *securitization.* Banks pool and package some of their loans into securities and sell these loan-backed securities, which are collateralized by the underlying assets, to investors, thereby raising new funds. Such securities can be backed by mortgage loans, automobile loans, credit card loans, or any other bank assets that can be pooled and packaged for resale. The idea originated in 1970 with Ginnie Mae mortgage-backed pass-throughs (see Chapter 3) and has recently spread to other components of bank loan portfolios.

BANK CAPITAL

The final source of funds on Tables 3 and 4 is equity capital, which means the difference between total assets and total liabilities on a bank's balance sheet.[2] The function of equity capital is to serve as a buffer, so that if a bank experiences hard times depositors will not be immediately affected. As in any business, equity capital serves as a

[1]The widespread growth of overnight RPs in recent years has increased skepticism regarding the value of the M1 money supply figures as a reliable measure of liquidity in the economy. See William L. Silber, *Commercial Bank Liability Management* (Chicago: Association of Reserve City Bankers, 1978), pp. 42–45, and Gillian Garcia and Simon Pak, "Some Clues in the Case of the Missing Money," *American Economic Review* (May 1979).

[2]This measure of equity capital has no necessary connection with the value of a bank as measured by the value of its stock in the stock market. Accountants and finance majors worry about such discrepancies, but we don't have to.

TABLE 5
Equity Capital to Risk Assets, 1960–1986*

	1960	1970	1986
(1) Equity capital	21	40	180
(2) Risk assets	143	408	2,248
(1) ÷ (2)	15%	10%	8%

*Equity capital and risk assets in billions of dollars.

SOURCE: FDIC *Annual Reports* and *Federal Reserve Bulletin.*

cushion against adversity. (In return, of course, stockholders also get dividends, the fruits of prosperity.)

As Table 4 shows, equity capital has held stable at around 7 percent of total sources of funds for many years. But meanwhile the overall riskiness of bank assets has increased. Bank examiners measure the riskiness of bank portfolios by subtracting cash assets and U.S. government securities from total assets. Thus, as Table 2 shows, 56 percent of bank assets were risk assets in 1960, 71 percent in 1970, and 77 percent in 1986. The ratio of the dollar amount of equity capital to risk assets (from Tables 3 and 1) is shown in Table 5.

It is clear from Table 5 that the ratio of equity capital to risk assets has declined. This has led many bank regulators to question the adequacy of bank capital today and to suggest that banks go about rebuilding their capital positions (by retained earnings and new stock flotations) to regain the levels of capital relative to risk assets that were typical fifteen or twenty years ago.

Bankers, on the other hand, typically prefer to operate with less rather than more equity. Because equity is usually more expensive than deposits or other short-term borrowed funds, a bank's profitability is enhanced the less it relies on equity and the more it relies on deposits and other debt. As a result, there is constant conflict between bankers and the supervisory authorities as to how much bank capital is appropriate.

LIQUIDITY AND PROFITABILITY

Bank management is a never ending tug-of-war between liquidity and safety, on the one hand, and earnings and profitability on the other. The more liquid an asset, the less it usually yields. But banks are

business firms, with stockholders; presumably they want to earn profits. Why not forget about liquidity, then, and buy only high-yielding
(less liquid) assets? The reason is that because of the unique structure
of their liabilities, banks *need* liquidity; that is, they need assets that
are quickly convertible into cash, with little or no loss in value. So
bank management faces an endless conflict (a conflict of interest?).

The nature of their liabilities confirms banks' need for liquidity on
the asset side. Demand deposits, for example, are all payable, as their
name implies, on *demand.* And so are passbook savings deposits, for
all practical purposes. Thus, a far larger proportion of commercial bank
liabilities is payable on demand than is the case with any other type
of business. But, of course, if a bank holds only highly liquid assets
to meet any conceivable volume of withdrawals, it will probably not
cover its costs and will have to go out of business.

Tables 6 and 7 show the income and expenses of all insured commercial banks since 1960. Notice how interest *expenses* have grown—to

TABLE 6
**Operating Income, Expenses, and Net Income of Insured
Commercial Banks, 1960–1986 (In billions of dollars)**

	1960	1970	1986
Operating Income			
Interest on loans	6.8	24.0	189
Interest on securities	2.3	6.5	42
Service charges and fees	.8	2.0	8
Other operating income	.8	2.2	30
TOTAL	10.7	34.7	269
Operating Expenses			
Salaries and wages	2.9	7.7	42
Interest on deposits	1.8	10.5	116
Interest on other borrowed funds	—	2.0	24
Other operating expenses	2.2	7.4	68
TOTAL	6.9	27.6	250
Net Operating Income	3.8	7.1	19
Securities gains (losses)	(.4)	(.1)	4
Taxes	1.4	1.9	5
Net After-Tax Income	2.0	5.1	18

SOURCE: FDIC *Annual Reports* and *Federal Reserve Bulletin.*

TABLE 7

Operating Income and Expenses of Insured Commercial Banks, 1960–1986 (Percentage distribution)

	1960	1970	1986
Operating Income			
Interest on loans	63	69	70
Interest on securities	21	19	16
Service charges and fees	8	6	3
Other operating income	3	3	11
TOTAL	100	100	100
Operating Expenses			
Salaries and wages	42	28	17
Interest on deposits	26	38	46
Interest on other borrowed funds	—	7	10
Other operating expenses	32	27	27
TOTAL	100	100	100

SOURCE: FDIC *Annual Reports* and *Federal Reserve Bulletin.*

56 percent of total costs in 1986, more than three times larger than salaries and wages.

Having to *pay out* so much in interest puts added pressure on bank portfolio decision-makers to acquire assets that *return* enough in interest to make the bank a profitable enterprise. This illustrates concretely the dilemma constantly facing bankers: they must maintain liquidity (because of the nature of their liabilities), and yet they are always tempted to reduce liquidity (to generate profits).

By almost any measure, bank liquidity has declined substantially over the years 1960–1986. One traditional rule-of-thumb measure that is widely used to gauge bank liquidity is the ratio of total loans to total deposits. It is an inverse measure: a lower loan/deposit ratio indicates a rise in bank liquidity, a higher loan/deposit ratio a decline in bank liquidity. If you compare the data in Tables 1 and 3, you will find that the loan/deposit ratio rose from 51 percent in 1960 to 65 percent in 1970 and to 87 percent in 1986.[3]

For the banking *system*—all the banks taken together—ultimate

[3]For 1960, 117/229 = 51%; for 1970, 314/482 = 65%; and for 1986, 1,699/1,943 = 87%. These figures are for all insured commercial banks. Larger banks typically have higher loan/deposit ratios than smaller ones.

liquidity is provided by the Federal Reserve. But what about an *individual* commercial bank? How can a single commercial bank best provide for its liquidity needs without excessively impairing its profitability?

LIABILITY MANAGEMENT

The past twenty-five years have witnessed a dramatic change in bank liquidity practices. Provision for liquidity used to be sought almost entirely on the asset side of the balance sheet. Banks stocked up with liquid assets, especially short-term government securities, and then sold them off when they needed funds.

Starting in the early 1960s, however, banks began increasingly to draw their liquidity from the *liabilities* side of the balance sheet. Instead of taking their liability structure as given and tailoring their assets to fit, they began to take a target asset growth as given and adjust their liabilities to hit the target. Liability management was facilitated by the growth of the negotiable CD market, which started in early 1961. More and more banks—especially the larger ones—came to rely on their ability to buy (borrow) money when they needed liquidity. Why store up liquidity in short-term, low-yielding assets, when it could always be bought in the market when needed? Why turn away creditworthy potential borrowers with talk of being "loaned up"— only to see them get loans from competitors—when the necessary funds could always be bought by selling new CDs?

The expansion of the federal funds market during the 1960s also played a significant role in the development of bank liability management. In an old-fashioned federal funds transaction, a bank with excess reserves would sell some of its excess to a bank with deficient reserves, on an overnight basis and at an agreed-upon interest rate. Nowadays, when a bank needs funds, it can borrow by creating an unsecured liability called a federal funds liability. Only another bank or deposit institution (such as an S&L) can lend funds in the federal funds market. In all cases, federal funds are transferred on the same day a transaction is concluded.

For a bank seeking to make up a reserve deficiency, the federal funds market is an alternative to borrowing from the Federal Reserve. Since buying federal funds and borrowing from the Federal Reserve at the discount rate are alternatives, the interest rate on federal funds never rose above the discount rate until the mid-1960s. If the federal funds rate went above the discount rate, a bank needing reserves would merely use the discount window instead of buying federal funds from another commercial bank.

Since the mid-1960s, however, the daily federal funds rate has rarely been *below* the discount rate. This is because in recent years the market has changed its nature. It used to involve only banks making temporary last-minute adjustments in their reserves. Now a number of large banks use the federal funds market to make virtually continuous net purchases, even when they are not faced with a reserve shortage; they are using the federal funds market to acquire funds on a more or less permanent basis. Thus federal funds are just another bank liability (included under Miscellaneous liabilities in Tables 3 and 4) used to expand lending ability.

The paradoxical result is that the shortest of all money market transactions—the overnight purchase of federal funds—has become in many respects more like a capital market than a money market instrument. In fact, in recent years some federal funds transactions are extended for maturities of one or two months. This serves as a good lesson in why you cannot draw a hard and fast line between the money and capital markets. Virtually all financial markets are interconnected and interrelated, in one way or another. We will return to these interactions in Chapter 28 when we examine the structure of interest rates.

INTEREST RATE RISK AND FLOATING RATE LOANS

Closely related to the liquidity-profitability tug-of-war in bank management are considerations regarding relative maturities of liabilities versus assets. *Traditionally, banks have borrowed short and loaned long.* That is, their sources of funds have been mostly short-term (overnight federal funds borrowing is an extreme example), which they use to buy longer-term assets (thirty-year mortgages are an example at the other extreme). Banks pay less on their short-term borrowings than they get on their longer-term loans, thereby covering their administrative costs and perhaps making a profit. This is generally the case, because short-term interest rates are usually lower than long-term rates.

Borrowing short and lending long, however, exposes banks to *interest rate risk:* if interest rates should rise, banks may find themselves paying more for their short-term sources of funds—which they have to refinance continually—than they will be getting on their long-term assets. For example, assume banks are paying 10 percent for short-term funds and getting 13 percent on five-year business loans; for one reason or another, all interest rates go up five percentage points; now banks are in a bad way, because they are paying 15 percent for short-term money, which they have to renew often, but they are still getting the same old 13 percent on their existing five-year business loans. This is exactly the sort of problem that drove so many savings banks and savings and loan associations out of business.

Banks have responded to the fluctuating rates of recent years by shifting the interest rate risk to their customers, charging *floating* (or variable) rates instead of fixed interest rates when they make business, consumer, or mortgage loans. Floating rates move up and down with the general level of interest rates, so that banks are sure to continue earning more than they pay out even when rates rise. With floating rates, it is the borrowers who assume the interest rate risk, because if the general level of rates rises they have to pay more. It is still possible for borrowers to obtain fixed rate loans, but banks nowadays prefer to make their loans at floating rates. As a result, borrowers frequently have to pay a premium (a higher rate) to get the peace of mind of a fixed-rate loan.

DISCRETIONARY FUNDS MANAGEMENT

The central focus of bank management today is a modified form of liability management, best described as discretionary funds management. It revolves around the strategic employment of interest-sensitive funds—whether liabilities *or* assets—that can be increased or decreased at the bank's initiative.

In relatively large institutions, the management meets at least monthly, often weekly, to project expected movements in *non* discretionary funds—anticipated inflows and outflows that are beyond the bank's immediate control. These would include expected extensions or repayments of business loans, projected inflows and outflows of time and savings deposits, and so on. The result of all these nondiscretionary flows is either a projected *net outflow* of funds or a projected *net inflow*, which the bank must accommodate in the short run. An expected net outflow means that funds must be raised to fill the gap; an expected net inflow means that there are surplus funds to dispose of.

It is the *discretionary* liabilities and assets that will be used to raise funds or dispose of them, as the case might be. If a bank needs to raise funds because it has a projected net outflow, it might buy federal funds, sell Treasury bills, sell securities under repurchase agreements, or borrow through CDs or from the Federal Reserve. If it has funds to dispose of because it has a projected net inflow, it might sell federal funds, buy Treasury bills, lower its CD rate and let CDs run off, and so on. Whether a discretionary item is an asset or a liability is relatively unimportant in the bank's financing decision. The most basic consideration is to raise funds at minimum cost or to allocate a surplus to maximize profits.

These alternative sources of funds all stand on a common footing in that each of them can—at a price—supply a dollar of liquidity which is just as good as a dollar of liquidity acquired from any other source. In brief, at any one time a choice exists among an array of alternatives as to how liquidity might be acquired. It is more rational to make this choice in terms of relative costs and risks than to worry about whether it is assets or liabilities that are involved.

Finally, it should be emphasized that fundamental to the state of bank liquidity are three basic factors that are often overlooked: (1) federal monetary-fiscal policies, to maintain a prosperous economy in which the anticipated income of borrowers will actually be realized so that they are able to repay their loans on time; (2) federal deposit insurance protection, which has more or less eliminated the old-fashioned "run on the bank" that used to spark liquidity crises; and (3) the Federal Reserve itself, in times of unforeseen widespread financial emergency standing by as a "lender of last resort."

SUMMARY

1. Over the past few decades, commercial banks have sharply reduced their holdings of government securities in favor of loans of all sorts. However, their government securities still show countercyclical fluctuations.

2. On the liabilities side, demand deposits and passbook savings deposits, which were 83 percent of bank liabilities in 1960, shrank to 23 percent in 1986. Their place was taken by time deposits, large-size negotiable CDs, and miscellaneous liabilities, such as Federal funds purchases and the sale of securities under repurchase agreements.

3. The ratio of equity capital to risk assets has been falling, and so has bank liquidity as measured by the loan/deposit ratio.

4. Bank management is a continuous tug-of-war between liquidity and profitability. Banks need liquidity because such a large proportion of their liabilities is payable on demand, but typically the more liquid an asset the less it yields.

5. Traditionally, banks have borrowed short and loaned long, which exposes them to the consequences of interest rate risk if rates should rise. They have responded by shifting the risk to their customers, by charging floating instead of fixed rates when they make loans.

6. Liability management replaced asset management in the 1960s as the main method of providing for bank liquidity. In turn, exclusive reliance on liability management has been superseded by discretionary funds management, incorporating both assets and liabilities and choosing among alternatives on the basis of relative costs and risks.

Suggestions for Further Reading

The problems of bank liquidity are discussed in surprisingly modern terms in Walter Bagehot's classic *Lombard Street* (New York: Scribner's, 1873; reprinted, Homewood, Ill.: Irwin, 1962), and in Lloyd W. Mints, *A History of Banking Theory* (Chicago: University of Chicago Press, 1945).

For a more up-to-date treatment of bank asset and liability management, see William L. Silber, *Commercial Bank Liability Management* (Chicago: Association of Reserve City Bankers, 1978). A thorough analysis of the implications of securitization is in Christine Pavel, "Securitization," Federal Reserve Bank of Chicago *Economic Perspectives* (July–August 1986).

A good discussion of bank capital is in James G. Ehlen, Jr., "A Review of Bank Capital and Its Adequacy," Federal Reserve Bank of Atlanta *Economic Review* (November 1983). See also Anthony M. Santomero, *Current Views on the Bank Capital Issue* (Association of Reserve City Bankers, 1983).

Managing a Bank's
Money Position

I

The legal obligation to hold reserves leads to the problem of managing a bank's reserve position, usually called managing its "money position." This Appendix explains how a bank's required reserves are computed and how a bank's "money desk" manager goes about the job of meeting those requirements.

First, the simple rules of the game:

1. All depository financial institutions have to hold required reserves against both their demand deposit and their business or non-personal time deposit liabilities.

2. Although we will add further details later (in Chapter 15), for the present assume that reserve requirements are *12 percent* against demand deposits and *3 percent* against business-owned time deposits.

3. Only two assets can be used to fulfill these requirements, namely cash in vault and deposits in the regional Federal Reserve Bank. Neither of these earn any interest, so while a bank must hold enough reserves to meet its requirements it has an incentive not to hold any more than that.

116

II

From here on, however, matters get more complex. The first complication of these simple rules is that reserve requirements are not imposed against a bank's total demand deposits but against its *net* demand deposits. Net demand deposits are a bank's total demand deposit liabilities minus both (a) cash items in process of collection and (b) demand balances due *from* domestic banks. Both of these deductions are *asset* items on a bank's balance sheet. Deducting them from a bank's total demand deposit liabilities avoids requiring reserves twice against what is really the same deposit. In other words, by allowing these two deductions the Fed avoids double counting the demand deposit liabilities of the banking system to the public.

For example, take the asset item "cash items in process of collection." Say you have an account in the King Kong National Bank and you write a check and give it to a storekeeper who deposits it in the Godzilla State Bank on the other side of town. This is a new demand deposit liability for Godzilla, but until the check clears, King Kong still has your demand deposit on its books too. In fact, for the moment King Kong doesn't even know you have written that check, so it is still figuring you have the same demand deposit and is still holding a required reserve against it.

If both banks had to hold reserves against these deposits, they would both be holding reserves against what really amounts to one and the same deposit. What Godzilla, the storekeeper's bank, does until the check clears is list an offsetting item on the asset side of its balance sheet, namely "cash item in process of collection." This is subtracted from its total demand deposits when it computes its net demand deposits, so for now only King Kong has to hold reserves against this deposit.

Then when the check clears in a day or so, several things happen: the King Kong National Bank receives your check back, cancels it, and removes your demand deposit from its books; and the Godzilla State Bank removes the entry "cash items in process of collection" from its assets (because the check is no longer "in process" of collection—it has actually been collected). Now King Kong no longer has the deposit and no longer has to keep reserves against it. The deposit is now officially at Godzilla, and that is the bank that has to hold reserves against it.

Similar logic—avoiding double counting of the banking system's demand deposit liabilities to the public—is also behind the other deduction, "demand balances due *from* domestic banks." These are simply interbank deposits as carried on the books (as assets) of the *depositing* bank. Say you deposit a $100 check in your account at King Kong National. Also let's say that King Kong is a correspondent of a large city bank, the Bank of America (also known as the Mighty Joe Young Bank and Trust Company). A correspondent bank holds deposits with another bank, usually to facilitate check clearing and for other services. King Kong therefore may very well make a $100 deposit of its own in the Bank of America. When King Kong does this, it enters an asset on its books "demand balance due from the Bank of America." King Kong deducts this from its total demand deposits when calculating its net demand deposits, because in effect it has shifted the deposit to the Bank of America. It is the Bank of America that must now hold reserves against this $100 deposit.

Once a bank's net demand and business time deposits are determined, the level of required reserves can be calculated based on the applicable required reserves ratio. The money desk manager's job is to hit that target level of reserves right on the nose. A *lower* than target volume of reserves will penalize the bank, because banks that are deficient in their reserves have to pay a penalty on the deficiency to the Federal Reserve. A *higher* than target volume of reserves will also penalize the bank in the form of lost income, since surplus reserves earn no interest. We now turn to the next complication, calculating the specifics of a bank's required reserves.

III

A bank's required reserves are computed on a daily-average basis over a two-week period, starting on a Tuesday and ending on Monday two weeks later. However, required reserves against time deposits and those against demand deposits are computed over different two-week periods.

Figure 1 illustrates how this works. It shows, first, business time (as opposed to personal time) deposits for a bank as of the close of business each day during a period that starts on Tuesday of Week 1 and goes through Monday of Week 3. They are as follows:

Time Deposits Reserve Computation Period

	Day	Time Deposits	Day	Time Deposits
Week 1:	Tues	$180 million	Tues	$208 million
	Wed	200	Wed	202

Time Deposits Reserve Computation Period (*Continued*)

	Day	Time Deposits		Day	Time Deposits
	Thur	205		Thur	200
	Fri	190		Fri	195
	Sat	190		Sat	195
Week 2:	Sun	190	Week 3:	Sun	195
	Mon	215		Mon	235

Time deposits = $2,800 million ÷ 14 = $200 million daily average

Notice that Friday's closing figure counts three times, since it counts for Saturday and Sunday as well. On the basis of these deposit figures, how much required reserves does this bank have to hold against business time deposits? Given reserve requirements of 3 percent, it needs required reserves of $6 million against its $200 million daily average business time deposits. (There are no reserves required against personal time deposits.)

IV

What about required reserves against net demand deposits? The computation period for figuring reserves against demand deposits starts two weeks after the computation period for time deposits ends. As Figure 1 shows, it starts on Tuesday of Week 5 and runs through Monday of Week 7. These are the numbers in Figure 1:

Demand Deposits Reserve Computation Period

	Day	Demand Deposits		Day	Demand Deposits
Week 5:	Tues	$137 million		Tues	$136 million
	Wed	139		Wed	105
	Thur	115		Thur	120
	Fri	125		Fri	130
	Sat	125		Sat	130
Week 6:	Sun	125	Week 7:	Sun	130
	Mon	133		Mon	100

Demand deposits = $1,750 million ÷ 14 = $125 million daily average

	Sun	Mon	Tue	Wed	Thur	Fri	Sat
Week 1			td=180 vc=10	td=200 vc=9	td=205 vc=7	td=190 vc=8	td=190 vc=8
Week 2	td=190 vc=8	td=215 vc=6	td=208 vc=6	td=202 vc=11	td=200 vc=9	td=195 vc=7	td=195 vc=7
Week 3	td=195 vc=7	td=235 vc=9					
Week 4							
Week 5			dd=137	dd=139	dd=115 FR=13	dd=125 FR=14	dd=125 FR=14
Week 6	dd=125 FR=14	dd=133 FR=11	dd=136 FR=10	dd=105 FR=16	dd=120 FR=8	dd=130 FR=10	dd=130 FR=10
Week 7	dd=130 FR=10	dd=100 FR=14	(Need 38 more in FR)				

td = time deposits computation period
dd = demand deposits computation period
vc = vault cash reserve holding period
FR = deposit in Federal Reserve reserve holding period

FIGURE 1 Illustrative Reserve Computation and Holding Periods

These are the daily closing figures for net demand deposits at this bank. Notice again that Friday's figures count for Saturday and Sunday as well. Reserve requirements are 12 percent of $125 million so required reserves against demand deposits are $15 million.

Combined with $6 million of required reserves against time deposits, total required reserves for this bank amount to $21 million.

V

This $21 million of required reserves must be held in the form of vault cash and/or deposits in the Fed. However, a distinction is made between the two: the vault cash that is used to satisfy the requirements is the cash on hand during the *same* two weeks as the bank's time deposit liabilities are computed, that is, from Tuesday of Week 1 through Monday of Week 3. But the deposits in the Federal Reserve are those that are held a few weeks later.

Here is our bank's cash in vault at closing time daily from Tuesday of Week 1 through Monday of Week 3 (see Figure 1):

Vault Cash Reserve Holding Period

	Day	Vault Cash		Day	Vault Cash
Week 1:	Tues	$10 million		Tues	$ 6 million
	Wed	9		Wed	11
	Thur	7		Thur	9
	Fri	8		Fri	7
	Sat	8		Sat	7
Week 2:	Sun	8	Week 3:	Sun	7
	Mon	6		Mon	9

Vault cash = $112 million ÷ 14 = $8 million daily average

VI

Now the money desk manager knows exactly what has to be done during the final reserve holding period, which is Thursday of Week 5 through Wednesday of Week 7 (see Figure 1). The money desk manager has to hit a reserve target, in the form of average daily deposits in the Fed, of $13 million—$21 million required reserves minus $8 million already satisfied by vault cash.

As Figure 1 indicates, the bank is somewhat on the short side as the last two days of the reserve holding period approach; the daily average reserve balance at the Fed is only $12 million, when it should be $13 million to put the bank on target:

Deposit in Fed Reserve Holding Period

	Day	Dep in Fed		Day	Dep in Fed
Week 5:	Thur	$13 million		Thur	$ 8 million
	Fri	14		Fri	10
	Sat	14		Sat	10
Week 6:	Sun	14	Week 7:	Sun	10
	Mon	11		Mon	14
	Tues	10		Tues	?
	Wed	16		Wed	?

Deposit in Federal Reserve = $144 million ÷ 12 = $12 million daily average

To get up to the target of $13 million daily average will require a balance of $19 million at the Fed on Tuesday and the same on Wednesday, the final day of the reserve holding period, or some combination of the two that adds up to 38. Then $182 million ÷ 14 will equal a $13 million daily average.

Actually, the rules do not require such pinpoint accuracy. The Fed permits a bank to run an excess or a deficiency of as much as 2 percent of required reserves and to carry that excess or shortage over into the next reserve holding period. So if the money desk manager can get within $420,000 of the target (2 percent of $21 million = $420,000), the excess can be applied or the deficiency made up in the next reserve holding period.

A money desk manager who wants to *increase* a bank's reserves will start selling assets, like Treasury bills, or borrowing money—in the federal funds market, via CDs, or maybe from the Federal Reserve. Naturally, the least-cost alternative will be the most attractive: it would be cheaper to sell Treasury bills that are yielding 10 percent than to borrow in the federal funds market at 12 percent.

To *reduce* reserves a money desk manager would do the opposite: buy Treasury bills, sell federal funds, or perhaps pay off any outstanding indebtedness to the Federal Reserve. Relative interest rates would greatly influence the choice among these alternatives.

Why is the money desk manager's job so difficult? Because so many things that affect a bank's reserve balance are not within the bank's control. Every check that is written by a depositor of the bank—or received by a depositor—alters the bank's reserves. If a large corporate depositor writes a big check, the bank's reserves fall; if many large corporate depositors do so, the bank's reserves fall a lot. The opposite happens if depositors receive checks and send them in to the bank to be credited to their accounts; then the bank's reserves at the Fed rise. A large bank will have thousands of such transactions each day, often with unpredictable net effects on its reserves. You can always tell who the money position managers are in large banks: they have glazed eyes and they twitch a lot. But there are compensations: they get paid well and have long vacations.

VII

The system of reserve requirements we have just described is known as "contemporaneous reserves" and has been in effect only since 1984. It replaced a system of "lagged reserves" that was much simpler in conception but that many felt failed to provide the Federal Reserve with sufficient control over the money supply. Ironically, the present system is only "contemporaneous" in connection with demand deposits; with respect to time deposits it is lagged even more than the old system.

With the old lagged reserve requirement system that was in effect prior to 1984, banks knew what their reserve requirements were two full weeks before they had to hold the reserves. The time gap between the creation of deposits, which gave rise to required reserves, and the time when the reserves actually had to be held was believed by many to weaken the Federal Reserve's control over deposit creation.

With the present system of contemporaneous reserves, there is only a two-day gap between the creation of required reserves for demand deposits and the holding of these reserves by depository institutions. Whether or not it has been successful in strengthening the Fed's control over the money supply (M1) is still a matter of some contro versy, especially since the lag is now even longer than it used to be for time deposits (which are part of M2).

CHAPTER 9

Nondeposit
Financial Institutions

Once upon a time, so the story goes, there were deposit financial institutions and nondeposit financial institutions and never the twain did meet. Those days are fast disappearing. The sharp differences between deposit and nondeposit institutions are fading, as various financial institutions aggressively invade each other's territories. In this chapter we will look at each of the major nondeposit financial institutions as well as at the overlaps and conflicts that are now erupting.

LIFE INSURANCE COMPANIES

The first life insurance company in the United States (the Presbyterian Ministers' Fund) was established shortly before the Revolutionary War and is still in existence. There are now more than 2,000 life insurance companies in the country, with assets of about $900 billion at the end of 1986. Some, like Prudential Insurance Company and Metropolitan Life, are among the largest and best-known corporations in the world.

Life insurance companies are structured as either stock companies or mutual associations. In stock companies the business is owned and controlled by regular stockholders; in mutuals ownership and control technically rest with the policyholders. Over 90 percent of the life insurance companies now in existence are stock companies, but the mutuals are much larger and control more than half the assets. Both Prudential and Metropolitan Life, for example, are organized as mutuals.

Life insurance companies are supervised and regulated almost entirely by the states in which they operate. Regulation covers virtually every aspect of the business, including sales practices, premium rates, and allowable investments. A company must be licensed and file reports in all states in which it sells life insurance. Regulation is usually by a state insurance commissioner, who is sometimes also the state banking commissioner.

Firms marketing life insurance used to specialize almost exclusively in selling "whole life" policies to individuals. Such policies have a constant premium which the policyholder pays through the entire life of the policy. In the early years of the policy, this constant premium is higher than actuarial probabilities warrant, but later on it becomes lower than required by actuarial probabilities. (Actuaries are statisticians who specialize in mortality probabilities.) Since the earlier premiums are higher than necessary in terms of actuarial statistics, whole life policies build up reserves. These reserves provide savings that yield a cash value the policyholder can borrow against or take outright at any time by canceling the policy.

Whole life policies contrast with "term" life insurance, in which premiums are relatively low at first but then rise as policyholders grow older and have a higher statistical probability of dying. Term life insurance policies are pure insurance and involve no reserves or savings element.

For a number of years, the savings feature of whole life insurance has produced a rate of return to policyholders that has been well below yields obtainable on alternative investments, such as Treasury bills or money market mutual funds. As a result there has been a pronounced shift by the public away from whole life policies in favor of term insurance. Term insurance gives the same amount of protection at a generally lower premium; with the money they save in premiums, people can buy assets that yield a higher rate of return than provided by the savings component of a whole life policy.

In response, the life insurance industry has begun to change its ways drastically, to recapture the funds that it used to receive but that are now flowing elsewhere. It has redesigned its product, selling more group insurance (through employers, for example) than policies to individuals and inventing new kinds of insurance policies that offer higher yields than were formerly available. For example, some new types of policies combine term life insurance with investment in a money market fund or something similar, like a stock market mutual fund. To facilitate these adaptations to a changing environment, a number of life insurance companies have acquired firms with expertise in money market funds, the stock market, and related areas.

In line with these developments, life insurance companies have also altered their investment policies. Traditionally, they used the policy premiums they received (in excess of what they paid in benefits) mainly to buy long-term corporate bonds and commercial mortgages. Lately, however, they have branched out into riskier ventures, such as common stocks and real estate. Metropolitan Life, for instance, paid $400 million in 1981 to buy the Pan Am Building in New York City.

PENSION FUNDS

A lot of people are financially better off dead than alive, because when they die their life insurance policies pay out a hefty amount. The problems arise when they stay alive too long after they've finished their working careers and find out that social security doesn't come anywhere close to meeting their day-to-day retirement needs, not to mention buying an occasional luxury item. Pension plans are intended to fill this gap, enabling retirees to maintain a decent standard of living.

A private pension plan is run by a trustee—possibly a bank, an insurance company, or a pension fund manager—whose job is to administer the pension arrangements agreed to by the employer or group of employers and their employees. All pension plans involve the twin problems of *vesting* and *funding* of future benefits.

An employee's pension benefits are said to be vested when the employee can leave the job and still retain pension benefits already earned. Many firms require that a person be on the payroll for a given number of years before future benefits are vested; if he or she quits or is fired before then, all pension rights are forfeited. Other plans provide for something like 25 percent vesting after so many years, with a gradual increase to 100 percent after a number of additional years. The specific provisions about vesting are obviously among the most important clauses in any pension plan contract. Employers generally prefer to delay vesting as long as possible so that an employee will think twice (or three times) before quitting to go elsewhere.

Equally important are the stipulations about funding. A pension liability is fully funded when enough money has been set aside so that, after earning an assumed rate of return, there will be sufficient funds to pay the promised pension when it comes due. Because of the power of compound interest over time, the entire final amount does not have to be set aside today. If the money is expected to earn 10 percent interest, then only $1,000 has to be set aside today to fully fund a pension of $1,100 due a year from now . . . or a pension of $17,450 due thirty years from now (because $1,000 $(1 + .10)^{30}$ = $17,450).[1]

Given those figures—$1,100 a year from now or $17,450 thirty years from now, and an assumed 10 percent yield—if *less* than $1,000 is set aside today, then the pension is said to be only partly funded. Many companies have a low level of funding, planning to meet their pension commitments mainly out of current earnings when the pensions come due. This works, of course, only if earnings remain sufficient to meet such liabilities. Clearly, the higher the level of funding the safer the pension. The social security system, for instance, is largely unfunded. It pays current pensions mainly out of current social security tax receipts, which is one reason it is in trouble.

Because of abuses and mismanagement in many private pension plans, in 1974 Congress enacted the Employee Retirement Income Security Act (ERISA), which established minimum reporting, disclosure, vesting, funding, and investment standards to safeguard employee pension rights. The same legislation also created the Pension Benefit Guaranty Corporation—known, believe it or not, as Penny Benny—which is a sort of pension FDIC. It guarantees some pension benefits in case a company goes bankrupt or is otherwise unable to meet its accrued pension liabilities.

In addition to employer-sponsored pension plans, some individuals are also given tax incentives to set up their own pension plans—Keogh Plans for self-employed people and Individual Retirement Accounts (IRAs) for working people who are not covered by company-sponsored pension plans.[2] These are usually established in the form of a deposit account in a bank or thrift institution or in the form of shares in a mutual fund of some sort, with the interest or dividends tax-deferred until retirement.

One aspect of pensions worthy of special mention is the matter of gender. Women, on average, live seven years longer than men. Because of this, many pensions used to pay a smaller monthly retirement income to women than to men (because on average women live to collect more monthly checks). In 1983, however, the U.S. Supreme

---

[1]See Chapter 5 for additional details.
[2]Keogh Plans are named after Representative Eugene F. Keogh of New York, who sponsored the legislation that created pension plans for self-employed individuals.

Court, by a 5–4 vote, ruled that unequal monthly benefits for men and women are illegal on the grounds that it is a form of discrimination based on sex. The Court held that an *individual* woman may not be paid lower monthly benefits than a man simply because women *as a group* live longer than men. It ruled that monthly benefits have to be equal, even though this means that on average women will collect more than men over their lifetimes.

Similar gender issues also exist in the field of insurance, by the way, where premiums based on relative risk are standard practice. Life insurance policies typically cost women less than men in monthly premiums because, since women live longer than men on average, their premiums will earn interest for the insurance company longer before they have to be used to pay death benefits. In other words, because they live longer women are better life insurance risks than men. In auto insurance, women also generally pay smaller premiums than men of the same age because accident records show that women are better risks—that is, they are involved in fewer accidents. On the other hand, health insurance policies are often *more* expensive for women than for men. There is considerable controversy about these sex differentials in insurance; unlike the controversy over pensions, however, thus far they have not been resolved by either legislation or court decision.

PROPERTY AND CASUALTY INSURANCE COMPANIES

Property and casualty insurance companies cannot plan ahead as easily as life insurance companies, because they have no simple equivalent of actuarial mortality tables to tell them how much they will probably have to pay out every year into the indefinite future. About 3,500 companies nationwide offer insurance against casualties such as automobile accidents, fire, theft, personal negligence, malpractice, and almost anything else you can dream up. Lloyd's of London, it is said, will insure against *any* contingency—at a price.

In dollar terms, automobile liability insurance is the most important of all forms of property and casualty insurance. The most unusual insurance policy of all time is probably the retroactive fire insurance the MGM Grand Hotel in Las Vegas purchased *after* its disastrous 1980 fire, in which 84 people died and 700 were injured. Since there was uncertainty about how much the fire might cost the hotel as the result of negligence lawsuits, the hotel insured itself against payments above a certain amount. The second most unusual is probably the $50

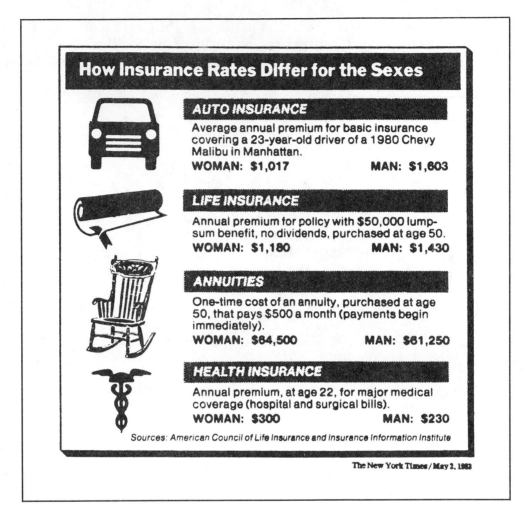

How Insurance Rates Differ for the Sexes

AUTO INSURANCE

Average annual premium for basic insurance covering a 23-year-old driver of a 1980 Chevy Malibu in Manhattan.

WOMAN: $1,017   MAN: $1,603

LIFE INSURANCE

Annual premium for policy with $50,000 lump-sum benefit, no dividends, purchased at age 50.

WOMAN: $1,180   MAN: $1,430

ANNUITIES

One-time cost of an annuity, purchased at age 50, that pays $500 a month (payments begin immediately).

WOMAN: $64,500   MAN: $61,250

HEALTH INSURANCE

Annual premium, at age 22, for major medical coverage (hospital and surgical bills).

WOMAN: $300   MAN: $230

Sources: American Council of Life Insurance and Insurance Information Institute

The New York Times / May 2, 1983

million of strike insurance the major league baseball owners wisely bought before the start of the 1981 season—it put them in a comfortable bargaining position when the players went on strike for seven weeks that year.

Property and casualty insurance companies, like life insurance companies, are regulated and supervised almost exclusively by the states in which they operate. There is little federal involvement. State insurance commissions set ranges for rates, enforce operating standards, and exercise overall supervision over company policies. Their investment policies reflect the fact that they are fully taxed and that casualty losses can be unexpected and highly variable. Thus they are heavy buyers of tax-free municipal bonds and liquid short-term securities.

MUTUAL FUNDS

Money market mutual funds have been prominent on the American financial scene since the 1970s, as we saw in Chapters 4 and 7, but way back in the 1950s stock market mutual funds—generally called just "mutual funds" or "investment companies"—were all the rage. A mutual fund pools the funds of many people; the managers of the fund invest the money in a diversified portfolio of securities and try to achieve some stated objective, like long-term growth of capital or high current income or perhaps only modest current income but minimum risk.

Open-end mutual funds, which are the typical kind, offer redeemable shares in the fund for sale to the general public. Such shares represent a proportionate ownership in a portfolio of securities held by the mutual fund. With an open-end fund, a shareholder can at any time go directly to the fund and buy additional shares or cash in (redeem) shares at their net asset value (NAV). The NAV per share is calculated daily on the basis of the market value of securities owned by the fund and is published each day in the financial section of major newspapers.

Say a mutual fund owns securities with an aggregate market value of a million dollars at the close of today's stock market, has no liabilities, and has ten thousand shares outstanding. The NAV of one share in this particular fund would be a million dollars divided by ten thousand shares, or $100 a share. If the stocks that make up the fund's portfolio fall in value, its NAV per share will drop correspondingly.

Many funds sell their shares directly to the public at the current NAV. These are called "no-load" funds. Others, however, known as "load funds," charge a sales commission, often as much as $8\frac{1}{2}$ percent of NAV.

Closed-end investment companies, which are in the minority, are completely unlike those just described. Closed-end funds issue only a limited number of shares and do not redeem their own shares on demand, like open-end funds. Instead, the shares of closed-end funds are traded in the stock market, and if you want to buy or sell them you have to deal with a third party, just as you would in buying or selling shares in IBM or Xerox.

Mutual funds are regulated by the Securities and Exchange Commission under the provisions of the Securities and Exchange Acts of 1933 and 1934 and the Investment Company Act of 1940. The primary objective of regulation is the enforcement of reporting and disclosure requirements and protection of investors against fraudulent practices by fund managers.

Mutual funds grew very rapidly in the fifties and most of the sixties, but they came on hard times in the seventies and early eighties (aside from money market mutual funds, which grew for very special reasons, as we saw in Chapter 7). However, the resurgence of the stock market in the eighties carried mutual funds to new heights of popularity. Many investors have been especially attracted in recent years to "families" of mutual funds, where a number of mutual funds operate under one management umbrella and where investors can easily transfer money among funds within the family. Typically a family of mutual funds will include bond and money market funds along with a variety of stock mutual funds.

SECURITIES BROKERS AND DEALERS AND INVESTMENT BANKERS

Neither securities brokers and dealers nor investment bankers are listed as major financial institutions in Table 1 of Chapter 4, because they have relatively small amounts of assets of their own. However, they are crucially important as intermediaries in the distribution and trading of huge amounts of securities, including corporate stocks, bonds, state and local government securities, and U.S. government securities.

The difference between investment bankers on the one hand and brokers and dealers on the other involves the distinction between *primary* and *secondary* securities markets. Primary markets refer to the sale and distribution of securities when they are *originally issued* by the money-raising corporation or governmental unit. Secondary markets involve the *subsequent trading* of those securities once they are already outstanding. The New York Stock Exchange is an example of a secondary market.

Investment bankers operate in primary markets, selling and distributing new stocks and bonds directly from the issuing corporations to their original purchasers. Brokers and dealers are involved in secondary markets, trading "used" or already outstanding securities.

The difference between brokers and dealers is that brokers do not buy or sell for their own account. They match buyers and sellers of a particular security and earn a commission fee for bringing the two together. Dealers, on the other hand, "take positions" in securities: they buy them for their own account hoping to resell at a higher price. If they are wrong, and the price falls before they can unload, their hoped-for profit becomes a loss instead.

Many of the nationwide stock exchange firms, like Merrill Lynch and Shearson Lehman act in all these capacities. They are called stockbrokers, or brokerage houses, because they act as agents in executing orders to buy or sell securities on the various stock exchanges. At times they also act as dealers and at other times as investment bankers. We will return to all these matters in Chapter 29, when we explore the functioning of securities markets in detail.

Our main interest at the moment, however, is in the ways in which a number of large stock exchange firms have branched out in the last few years to provide new kinds of financial services that used to be considered beyond their province. Merrill Lynch was the innovator, starting the ball rolling in 1977 with its Cash Management Account (CMA). The CMA consists of a financial package that includes a credit card, instant loans, check-writing privileges, investment in a money market mutual fund, and complete record keeping—including monthly statements.

Such services bring brokerage houses close to being in the banking business. In fact, as Table 1 indicates, Prudential-Bache, Dreyfus (a leading mutual fund manager), and Merrill Lynch, the nation's largest stockbroker, have all recently gone out and acquired banks of their own! Can banks respond to the challenge by turning around and going into the securities or mutual fund business themselves? So far the answer is technically no, and the reason they can't is called Glass-Steagall.

THE GLASS-STEAGALL ACT

The Banking Act of 1933, known as the Glass-Steagall Act, separated commercial banking and investment banking, where the latter refers specifically to issuing, underwriting, selling, or distributing stock or bond offerings of corporations. Commercial banks had become deeply involved in the sale and distribution of new stock and bond offerings in the 1920s, not always with happy results. There were suspicions that banks on occasion dumped new offerings into trust funds that they managed because they couldn't sell them to anyone else. To avoid such conflicts of interest, the Banking Act of 1933 divorced commercial from investment banking. Banks involved in both areas were forced to choose one or the other.[3]

Commercial banks are still permitted to distribute new offerings of federal government securities and "full faith and credit" general obligations of state and local governments. But Glass-Steagall forbids them to get involved in new offerings of corporate stocks or bonds or municipal revenue bonds. Revenue bonds differ from general municipal obligations in that they are not backed by the full taxing power of the state or local government; bondholders have a claim only on the revenues of a specific project being financed, such as a toll road or a state university dormitory (maybe even yours). The Act has also been interpreted as meaning that commercial banks cannot offer mutual funds, including money market mutual funds.

Commercial banks believe they are being discriminated against by the provisions of the Glass-Steagall Act. After all, securities firms and investment bankers—not to mention life insurance companies—have penetrated the banks' deposit and checking account business via money market mutual funds and CMAs, but commercial banks can't penetrate the securities business with their own mutual funds or by distributing new municipal revenue bonds or new corporate securities of any sort.

In fact, as we have mentioned and as Table 1 shows, several securities firms (Dreyfus, Prudential-Bache, Merrill Lynch) have acquired their own commercial banks, even though Glass-Steagall would appear to prohibit such mixing of commercial and investment banking under one corporate roof. How is it possible?

It has been done through a loophole in the law. Technically, a commercial bank is defined in the statutes as an institution that both accepts deposits *and* makes business loans. What Dreyfus and the others have done is to stop their newly acquired banks from performing one of these two functions—either one, it doesn't matter which—so that now the bank is technically no longer a commercial bank! The bank purchased by Dreyfus, for instance, no longer makes business loans and sold off its existing loan portfolio to another bank. Thus, technically speaking, it is not a commercial bank any more. As a matter of fact, it is often referred to as a *nonbank bank*—a strange name that

[3]The Banking Act of 1933 is called the Glass-Steagall Act after its two principal sponsors, Senator Carter Glass of Virginia and Representative Henry B. Steagall of Alabama. While we're at it, Representative Louis T. McFadden was from Pennsylvania. Quick now: What is the McFadden Act? (Check Chapter 7.)

TABLE 1

You Can't Tell the Players Without a Scorecard: Financial Merger and Acquisition Milestones in the Eighties

April 1981	PRUDENTIAL INSURANCE, the world's largest insurance company, acquires BACHE HALSEY STUART SHIELDS, one of the nation's largest stock brokerage houses with assets of $3 billion and 200 offices.
June 1981	AMERICAN EXPRESS, a major financial service company, acquires SHEARSON LOEB RHOADES, one of the nation's largest brokerage firms, with assets of $2.9 billion and 270 offices.
August 1981	PHIBRO CORPORATION, reputed to be the world's largest publicly held commodities trader, acquires SALOMON BROTHERS, one of the world's largest private investment bankers and bond traders.
October 1981	SEARS, ROEBUCK, & COMPANY, the nation's largest retailer, with 850 retail department stores (and already owner of SEARS SAVINGS BANK in California and ALLSTATE INSURANCE) acquires COLDWELL, BANKER, one of the country's largest real estate brokers, with 430 offices, and also DEAN WITTER REYNOLDS, one of the nation's largest stockbrokers, with assets of $2.3 billion and 300 offices.
July 1982	SHEARSON/AMERICAN EXPRESS acquires BALCOR, a large real estate investment concern.
December 1982	DREYFUS CORPORATION, a leading mutual fund, acquires a small commercial bank in New Jersey.
January 1983	BANKAMERICA of San Francisco, one of the country's largest bank holding companies, acquires CHARLES SCHWAB, the nation's largest discount stock brokerage firm. The acquisition was approved by the U.S. Supreme Court in June of 1984.
March 1983	PRUDENTIAL-BACHE acquires a small commercial bank in Georgia.

TABLE 1   (*continued*)

March 1983	CITICORP of New York, one of the country's largest bank holding companies, announces plans to buy a small bank in South Dakota, where the state legislature has enacted a law that permits state-chartered banks to own insurance companies.
August 1983	SECURITY PACIFIC NATIONAL BANK of Los Angeles buys a seat on the New York Stock Exchange.
September 1983	SHEARSON/AMERICAN EXPRESS acquires INVESTORS DIVERSIFIED SERVICES.
January 1984	The New Jersey Banking Commissioner announces plans for MERRILL LYNCH, the nation's largest stockbroker, to start a commercial bank in New Jersey.
April 1984	SHEARSON/AMERICAN EXPRESS acquires LEHMAN BROTHERS KUHN LOEB, one of the country's largest investment banking houses.
November 1984	EQUITABLE LIFE ASSURANCE SOCIETY, the nation's third largest life insurance company, announces the acquisition of DONALDSON, LUFKIN & JENRETTE, a leading securities broker.
December 1985	FORD MOTOR COMPANY acquires FIRST NATIONWIDE SAVINGS, the country's eighth largest thrift institution, with operations in many states.
January 1986	The U.S. Supreme Court, by a vote of 8 to 0, rules that the Federal Reserve does not have authority to regulate or restrict so-called nonbank banks (i.e., limited-service banks).
January 1987	The U.S. Supreme Court, by a vote of 8 to 0, rules that commercial banks may establish or acquire discount brokerage facilities anywhere in the country, regardless of existing restrictions on bank branching.
December 1987	SHEARSON LEHMAN BROTHERS announces the acquisition of E.F. HUTTON & COMPANY, one of the country's largest retail brokerage firms.

has arisen in financial circles to describe such limited-service institutions.

Of course, banks have not reacted passively to this invasion of their turf. As Table 1 indicates, BankAmerica (parent holding company of the Bank of America) has acquired Charles Schwab & Company, a discount stockbroker, and Citicorp (parent holding company of Citibank) is moving into the insurance business. Security Pacific National Bank of Los Angeles has bought a seat on the New York Stock Exchange. These are straws in the wind.

Where will it all end? In light of the breakdowns in barriers separating financial institutions over the past decade, it is likely that new legislation in the 1990s will carry that trend even further. Many observers expect that banks will soon be able to compete by being empowered to offer their own mutual funds and to sell and distribute new municipal revenue bonds. At the same time, investment banking and brokerage firms will make further intrusions into the banking business. Before long, it will be difficult to tell one kind of financial institution from another.

SUMMARY

1. Life insurance companies used to specialize in selling whole life policies to individuals. Whole life policies involve a savings element, while term life insurance does not. Since that savings feature has produced a relatively low rate of return, there has been a pronounced shift on the part of the public in favor of term insurance.

2. In response, the life insurance industry has begun to emphasize group rather than individual insurance and to invent new kinds of policies that offer higher yields. Some combine term insurance with investment in a money market or stock market mutual fund. This helps explain why Prudential bought Bache and American Express acquired Shearson Loeb Rhoades and Lehman Brothers. It also explains why life insurance companies have been moving into somewhat riskier investments.

3. Two crucial aspects of private pension plans are the provisions regarding vesting and funding. Because of abuses in these areas, in 1974 Congress enacted the Employee Retirement Income Security Act (ERISA) in an attempt to safeguard employee pension rights.

4. Securities brokers and dealers and investment bankers have recently branched out into new kinds of financial services, such as Merrill Lynch's

Cash Management Account (CMA), which includes checking account privileges as well as a variety of other financial services.

5. The Banking Act of 1933, usually called the Glass-Steagall Act, divorced investment and commercial banking. As a result, commercial banks are unable to offer their own mutual funds or to sell and distribute newly issued corporate securities or municipal revenue bonds.

6. Glass-Steagall is under attack from all sides and is not likely to survive much longer. Securities firms have been buying banks and turning them into nonbank banks. And banks have been buying brokerage houses and seats on the stock exchange. Before long, it will be difficult to tell one kind of financial institution from another.

Suggestions for Further Reading

On insurance, a good reference is *The Consumers Union Report on Life Insurance,* 4th ed. (New York: Holt, Rinehart & Winston, 1980). A highly readable and to some extent controversial book is Andrew Tobias, *The Invisible Bankers,* subtitled "Everything the Insurance Industry Never Wanted You to Know" (New York: Simon & Schuster, 1982). Also good reading: Ronald Kessler, *The Life Insurance Game* (New York: Holt, Rinehart & Winston, 1985).

With respect to pension funds, see Peter F. Drucker, *The Unseen Revolution: How Pension Fund Socialism Came to America* (New York: Harper & Row, 1976); William C. Greenough and Francis P. King, *Pension Plans and Public Policy* (New York: Columbia University Press, 1976); Jeremy Rifkin and Randy Barber, *The North Will Rise Again: Pensions, Politics and Power in the 1980s* (Boston: Beacon Press, 1978); and Dan M. McGill, *Fundamentals of Private Pensions,* 5th ed. (Homewood, Ill.: Irwin, 1984).

On the Banking Act of 1933 (Glass-Steagall), see Larry R. Mote, "Banks and the Securities Markets," Federal Reserve Bank of Chicago *Economic Perspectives* (March–April 1979); Christine Pavel and Harvey Rosenblum, "Banks and Nonbanks: The Horse Race Continues," Federal Reserve Bank of Chicago *Economic Perspectives* (May/June 1985); and Anthony Saunders, "Securities Activities of Commercial Banks," Federal Reserve Bank of Philadelphia *Business Review* (July–August 1985).

An up-to-date survey of the investment banking industry is Ernest Bloch's *Inside Investment Banking* (Homewood, Ill.: Dow Jones–Irwin, 1986). For the *real* lowdown, focusing on the 1984 takeover of Lehman Brothers Kuhn Loeb by Shearson/American Express, see Ken Auletta, *Greed and Glory on Wall Street: The Fall of the House of Lehman* (New York: Random House, 1986).

CHAPTER 10

International Banking

Only thirty years ago, United States banks, with few exceptions, stayed within their own national borders. The field of international banking was dominated by British banks. But things have changed dramatically. Now many large U.S. banks do a significant part of their business overseas, lending to foreigners. Correspondingly, foreign banks do a lot of business in this country, lending to Americans.

AMERICAN BANKS ABROAD

In 1960, only eight United States banks had branches abroad, and the assets of those branches totaled less than $4 billion. By 1980, only twenty years later, almost 200 American banks had established foreign branches, and the assets of those branches exceeded $400 billion. What accounts for this remarkable expansion of U.S. banks into foreign countries?

One reason is the rapid growth of foreign trade and of U.S. multinational corporations that took place during the sixties and seventies. American firms engaged in importing or exporting, and American multinationals with subsidiaries and affiliates abroad, often need banking services overseas. Foreign banks can do the job if necessary, but a branch of an American bank abroad can be even more convenient:

there are no language problems; the firm and the branch share common business customs and practices; and in the case of multinationals the parent firm and parent bank may already have longstanding ties with each other.

In addition to branches abroad, U.S. banks also participate in international financing through Edge Act corporations, which are domestic subsidiaries engaged strictly in international banking operations. In 1919 Congress passed the Edge Act (named after Senator Walter Edge of New Jersey) to allow U.S. banks to establish special subsidiaries to facilitate their involvement in international finance. Edge Act corporations are located in the United States, but they are exempt from the McFadden Act's prohibition against interstate branching, so that a bank can have Edge Act subsidiaries in several different states—one in Florida, for example, specializing in financing trade with Latin America, one in New York, one on the West Coast, and so on.

FOREIGN BANKS IN THE UNITED STATES

Just as U.S. banks have a major presence abroad, so foreign banks play a significant role in this country. For example, in a typical year about 20 percent of the dollar volume of all commercial bank business loans in the United States is made by branches or subsidiaries of foreign-owned banks.

Many large and well-known banks are foreign-owned: Marine Midland of Buffalo is owned by the Hong Kong and Shanghai Banking Corporation; Union Bank of Los Angeles is British-owned; California First Bank of San Francisco is Japanese-owned; Harris Trust of Chicago is owned by the Bank of Montreal; and the European American Bank (New York), successor to the failed Franklin National Bank, is owned by a consortium of six foreign banks whose home bases are Austria, Belgium, England, France, Germany, and the Netherlands. All in all, more than 900 offices of foreign banks are currently operating in the United States.

Foreign banks do business here through four main organizational forms: they may open a *branch* of the parent bank, open or buy a *subsidiary* bank, establish an *agency*, or open a *representative office*. A branch is an integral part of the foreign bank and usually carries that bank's name. A subsidiary is legally separate from the foreign bank that owns its stock; the subsidiary usually has its own charter and may or may not carry the name of its foreign owner. Both branches and subsidiaries are full-service banking institutions. Agencies have more limited powers than either branches or subsidiaries; they can make loans but cannot accept deposits. Representative offices cannot accept deposits *or* make loans; they mostly make contacts with potential customers of the parent organization (by holding dinner parties) and perform public relations functions (by sponsoring rock or philharmonic concerts). Foreign banks can also complicate matters further by having Edge Act corporations in the United States.

Until 1978, foreign banks operating in the United States were largely unregulated. They did not have to hold reserves with the Fed, they were able to branch across state lines, and they had numerous other rights and privileges denied to domestic banks. This was changed by the International Banking Act of 1978, which brought foreign banks under essentially the same federal regulations that apply to domestic banks.

EURODOLLARS

The spread of international trade and the growth of American multinationals encouraged branching by American banks overseas, but these were not the only factors stimulating the establishment of foreign branches. The maximum deposit rates permitted under Regulation Q played a part as well.

In the 1960s, when Regulation Q still imposed interest-rate ceilings on large-size CDs in the United States, European banks were able to offer more attractive yields to potential depositors than U.S. banks were allowed to pay. Not only were there no interest-rate ceilings in most countries abroad, but in addition reserve requirements and other regulations were typically less onerous than in the United States. As a result, foreign banks could outbid American banks for time deposits.

These deposits in foreign banks—mainly in London—not only paid higher yields than American banks could offer but, as an added inducement for the convenience and safety of Americans, were recorded as payable *in dollars* rather than in pounds or francs or whatever the money of the host country happened to be. Naturally enough, such deposits came to be known as *Eurodollars.* The term has since been broadened to mean deposits in banks abroad—still mostly in London but now in other places in Europe and in Asia and the Caribbean as well—that are on the banks' books as payable in U.S. dollars rather than in the money of the country where the bank is located.

Eurodollars are created when an American transfers a dollar deposit from an American bank to a foreign bank and keeps it there *in dollars*

Don't Throw Away Those Old Czarist Bonds!

Government bonds of leading nations are usually considered to be of very high quality. Sometimes, however, completely unexpected developments interfere with the orderly payment of interest and principal, and then even government bonds can end up in default.

One of those "unexpected developments" is a successful armed revolution that overthrows the government in power—the one that originally issued the bonds—and establishes a new government in its place. The new government invariably repudiates all outstanding debts of its predecessor, so that creditors at home and abroad are left with long faces and fancy-looking bonds that aren't worth the paper they're printed on; under the circumstances, they might as well be used as wallpaper or thrown out with the rest of the trash.

But wait! All is not necessarily lost! Maybe the wisest thing to do is to pack the bonds with the rest of the family memorabilia and store them in the attic for your great-great-grandchildren.

Case in point: the bonds of the Imperial Russian Government, the government of the Czars that was overthrown in 1917.

We're not sure whether Ingrid Bergman was or wasn't Anastasia—youngest daughter of Czar Nicholas II, the last Russian czar—but we do know that Czarist bonds weren't worth a wooden ruble for half a century after the Communists took over in 1917.

However, in 1986, almost seventy years after the revolution, the Soviet Union and Great Britain formally agreed on settlement terms for the $200 million of British-held Czarist bonds in default. British bondholders will not get full value, but they will get something.

There has been no comparable settlement yet with the United States, but there may be sometime soon. And perhaps the People's Republic of China, which has refused to make any payments on government bonds issued before the Communists came to power in 1949, will come to a similar accord with foreign bondholders.

In any event, if you know anyone who still has some pre-Communist Russian or Chinese government bonds, tell them to hang on a while longer. Prospects are looking better all the time.

(rather than switching to pounds, say, if the bank to which the money is transferred is in London). Eurodollars are also created when a foreign holder of a deposit in a U.S. bank does the same thing, as when a French exporter gets paid with a check drawn on an American bank and deposits the check in a Paris bank with instructions to retain it as a dollar deposit instead of exchanging it into an equivalent amount of francs. Why would anyone want to do this? Because dollars are still considered safer than most other kinds of money and are still more generally acceptable in international transactions than any other kind of money.

In response, many American banks decided to open their *own* branches abroad in order to escape domestic regulations and to bid for funds on a more equal basis with their foreign competition. During periods of tight money, when their ordinary domestic sources of funds dried up because of Federal Reserve restraint, Regulation Q, and financial disintermediation, American banks turned around and borrowed these Eurodollars back from their foreign branches as one aspect of their growing reliance on liability management. Eurodollars are now an integral and accepted part of overall global bank asset and liability management.

At the end of 1986, the foreign branches of U.S. banks held total assets of $450 billion. Of this total, $140 billion was in London branches and a similar amount in branches in the Bahamas and the Cayman Islands in the Caribbean. Branches in London are easy to understand: London has been an international financial center for centuries and remains the heart of the Eurodollar market. But how did the Bahamas and the Caymans ever get into the act?

The Bahamas and the Caymans are tax havens, with almost zero taxation and practically no regulation. Virtually all the assets in branches there are held not by full-service branches but by "shell" branches—primarily bookkeeping operations, with fund-raising and lending decisions emanating from the banks' head offices in the United States. A rise in British taxes in the early 1970s led to a substantial shift in loan operations from London to the Bahamas. The Cayman Islands subsequently came into the picture when the Bahamas achieved their independence, giving rise to anxiety (since proven unfounded) that this might lead to increased Bahamian regulation and taxation.

DOMESTICALLY BASED INTERNATIONAL BANKING FACILITIES

In late 1981, in an effort to bring some of this offshore Eurodollar business back home, the Federal Reserve approved the establishment of International Banking Facilities (IBFs) on American soil. Caribbean branches flourished because they operate in an environment almost entirely free from regulation and taxation. The purpose of IBFs is to offer banks comparable conditions here and thus lure offshore banking back to the United States. Thus both American and foreign banks can now have IBFs that are within the geographic confines of the United States but are regulated as though they were located abroad. In effect, an IBF is a domestic branch that is treated by the Federal Reserve as if it were a foreign branch. Their transactions are considered offshore transactions, free from such domestic regulations as reserve requirements and deposit insurance assessments.

It is not necessary for a parent bank to open up a separate office to establish an IBF. Essentially, IBFs are bookkeeping operations, just like shell branches. A bank wanting to start an IBF simply notifies the Federal Reserve and then segregates its IBF assets, liabilities, and related transactions from all others. This creates a new set of books that are exempt from the usual rules and regulations that apply to domestic transactions. Moreover, many states have enacted legislation exempting the income of IBFs from state and local taxes, thereby providing an environment that closely resembles tax havens abroad.

So much for the good news; the bad news is that the services of IBFs are not available to domestic residents. IBFs can transact only business that is international in nature with respect to both sources and uses of funds. They are permitted to accept deposits from and lend funds to foreign-based customers only. Foreign subsidiaries of American multinationals are included among the eligible depositors and borrowers, provided the funds do not come from domestic sources and are not used for domestic purposes.

Thus far IBFs have been a resounding success. Although they have been allowed only since December 1981, by the end of 1987 they already had assets of about $250 billion.

AMERICAN BANKS AND THE INTERNATIONAL DEBT PROBLEM

At the beginning of this chapter, we noted that nowadays many large U.S. banks do a significant part of their business abroad, lending to foreigners. Indeed, a number of them have lent so much overseas that in some years they earn more of their income from international operations than from domestic operations. This has brought problems as well as rewards. The problems stem from the fact that many foreign borrowers—especially third-world countries—have not been able to pay their debts on time, threatening the financial viability of the banks that made the loans.

By way of background, many non-oil-exporting countries began to encounter serious financial problems when the Organization of Petroleum Exporting Countries (OPEC) jacked up international petroleum prices in 1973–74 and again in 1979–80. Non-oil-producing countries found themselves short of funds because so much of their money was needed to buy petroleum at inflated prices. Many third-world countries were especially hard hit.

At the same time, OPEC nations were rolling in money, with billions of surplus dollars, as funds poured in for their oil. They spent a lot on armaments, on consumer goods, at Las Vegas baccarat tables, and they still had plenty left over. Much of the surplus was invested in large-denomination bank certificates of deposit, especially the CDs of major American banks.

The banks, behaving as intermediaries, turned around and lent much of this money to needy deficit third-world nations. The process came to be known as the *recycling of petrodollars.* The banks acquired OPEC money by selling CDs to Middle Eastern sheiks and then used the funds to extend loans to Brazil, Mexico, Argentina, and many other deficit countries. Total third-world international indebtedness was estimated at almost a trillion dollars at the end of 1984.

At the time, during the 1970s, recycling petrodollars in this way appeared to be an ideal way to avoid the potential disaster that seemed to face third-world countries squeezed by oil prices. The Arabs found a safe interest-bearing haven for their surplus money, the banks found what appeared to be creditworthy borrowers on whom they could turn a profit, and desperate third-world countries found a number of Santas handing out money when it wasn't even Christmastime.

Hiding in the background, however, was the fact that banks had put their credit on the line. The chickens came home to roost when worldwide recession in the early eighties reduced the export markets of many third-world countries, making it almost impossible for them to earn the dollars required to pay their debts to American banks. And higher interest rates in the United States also made matters more difficult. Since most of the loans were floating-rate loans, the interest rates on third-world debts fluctuated with American rates; higher U.S. interest rates meant higher rates on outstanding foreign loans as well as on any new ones that might be negotiated. As a result of these and related economic developments, since 1981 one country after another has announced that it cannot meet its interest payments when they are due, not to mention repaying the principal, and has requested that its debt be restructured and rescheduled.

TABLE 1

Selected Banks: Loans Outstanding to Four Latin American Countries (End of 1984; in millions of dollars)

	Argentina	Brazil	Mexico	Venezuela	Total	As % of Bank Capital
Citicorp	$1,200	$4,900	$2,900	$1,300	$10,300	160%
Bank America	425	2,721	2,766	1,508	7,420	145
Manufacturers Hanover	1,293	2,424	1,969	1,083	6,709	206
Chase Manhattan	845	2,830	1,750	1,280	6,705	169
J.P. Morgan	754	1,981	1,228	464	4,427	119
Chemical	373	1,447	1,435	767	4,022	158
Bankers Trust	250	891	1,297	380	2,818	134

SOURCE: Keefe, Bruyette and Woods, Inc.

Table 1 shows the potential impact on several major U.S. bank holding companies of such nonpayment of foreign debt. Given their risk exposure to just four Latin American countries, each of the bank holding companies listed could lose an amount that exceeds its total capital. In other words, widespread default could quickly wipe out each bank's capital and leave it technically insolvent (that is, with liabilities greater than its assets).

A number of banks responded to the evolving problem in 1987 by establishing added reserves to shore up their capital. Nevertheless, there are widespread fears that defaults could undermine confidence in the entire banking system, and not only in this country. Thus the International Monetary Fund (the IMF)—an international organization—has played a major role in trying to see that the international debt problem does not get out of hand. How it will all eventually work itself out is still a matter of much conjecture.

SUMMARY

1. Close to 200 American banks have branches or subsidiaries abroad, with assets of $450 billion in foreign branches at the end of 1986. In addition to

branches abroad, American banks also participate in international financing through Edge Act corporations, which are subsidiaries located in the United States that specialize in the financing of foreign trade.

2. Just as American banks have a major presence abroad, so foreign-owned banks play a significant role in this country. About 20 percent of the dollar volume of all commercial bank business loans is made by foreign-owned institutions. The International Banking Act of 1978 brought foreign banks in the United States under essentially the same federal regulations that apply to domestic banks.

3. American regulation helped create the Eurodollar market. Eurodollars are deposits in banks abroad (no longer just in Europe) that are carried on the banks' books in dollars, rather than in the money of the countries where the banks are located. As one aspect of their liability management, American banks use their foreign branches to bid for Eurodollars; then the parent bank borrows these funds when other sources of funds dry up or become relatively more expensive.

4. Since late 1981 American banks have been allowed to establish International Banking Facilities (IBFs) in the United States. IBFs are shell branches located here but treated for regulatory and tax purposes as though they were abroad. They have been permitted in order to recapture some of the offshore Eurodollar business that has flourished in tax havens such as the Bahamas and the Cayman Islands.

5. During the 1970s, petrodollars were recycled through American banks to third-world countries. Subsequently, however, many third-world borrowers have been unable to repay their debts on schedule. If defaults are widespread, many major U.S. banks could become technically insolvent. Indeed, the stability of banking worldwide could even be threatened.

Suggestions for Further Reading

International banking is analyzed in Norman S. Fieleke, "International Lending on Trial," in the Boston Fed's *New England Economic Review* (May–June 1983). Other discussions of international lending are contained in Anthony Sampson, *The Money Lenders* (New York: Viking, 1982); Darrell Delamaide, *Debt Shock: The Full Story of the World Debt Crisis* (New York: Double-day, 1984); Benjamin J. Cohen, *In Whose Interest? International Banking and American Foreign Policy* (New Haven, Conn.: Yale University Press,

1986); and S. C. Gwynne, *Selling Money* (New York: Weidenfeld and Nicolson, 1986).

If you want to learn more about Eurodollars, see Milton Friedman, "The Eurodollar Market: Some First Principles," Morgan Guaranty *Survey* (October 1969); Jane Sneddon Little, *Eurodollars: The Money Market Gypsies* (New York: Harper & Row, 1975); and Anatol B. Balbach and David H. Resler, "Eurodollars and the U.S. Money Supply," Federal Reserve Bank of St. Louis *Review* (June–July 1980).

C H A P T E R   1 1

Financial Innovation

Fed or reserve for thereby
Broaders

Not too many years ago, financial transactions were relatively simple matters. To earn interest, you went to a savings bank with cash and opened a passbook savings account. To earn capital gains in the stock market, you bought some shares of IBM or General Motors. And to pay for everyday expenses, you either dug into your wallet for cash or else wrote a check on your commercial bank checking account (hoping your last deposit would cover it).

Now things are very different. A savings account is no longer the only choice open to savers: money market deposit accounts, NOW accounts, and money market mutual funds offer competitive opportunities. In the stock market, you no longer have to like IBM or General Motors in order to make a killing; financial futures and options markets allow you to buy or sell the entire market, all at once, without playing favorites. And if you are afraid you don't have enough in your bank account to cover that last check you wrote, you can always rush down to the bank's automatic teller machine—even at 2 A.M.—and add a few dollars so your check doesn't bounce.

As we've seen in the last few chapters, the financial system has changed a great deal in recent years. Financial innovation has spawned new *institutions* (such as money market mutual funds), new *products* (such as NOW accounts), and new *markets* (such as exchange-traded options and financial futures), thereby transforming a conservative, old-fashioned group of industries like banking and insurance into the new and highly sophisticated *financial services industry.* In this chapter let's step back for a moment and see how it all came about. In other words, what have been the causes of financial innovation? Why did all these changes take place at this particular time in history?

CIRCUMVENTING REGULATION

One of the most popular explanations of financial innovation is that it is a response to excessively constricting government regulation. In particular, innovation is viewed as a means of *avoiding* regulation!

Take money market mutual funds as an example: they are institutions that probably never would have come into existence if it hadn't been for Regulation Q. Bank depositors were frustrated in the 1970s because they could not get market interest rates on their money because of the interest rate ceilings imposed by Regulation Q. Even banks that *wanted* to pay market interest rates in order to keep their old depositors, or to attract new ones, weren't allowed to do so. Depositors with a few thousand dollars turned to buying Treasury bills in order to get a market return, but then the U.S. Treasury stepped in and raised the minimum denomination of its bills from $1,000 to $10,000, thereby making it impossible for many people to buy them.

Within that environment, money market mutual funds were established by entrepreneurs who saw an unfilled need in the financial system and figured out a way to satisfy it. Since money market mutual funds were brand new and politicians had not yet decided to shackle them with regulations, they were free to offer competitive market interest rates. Their usefulness was demonstrated by the fact that within a few years their assets grew to over $200 billion.

Other innovations are also traceable to the ramifications of Regulation Q. For instance, as interest rates on securities rose during the sixties and seventies, Regulation Q's ceiling on rates severely limited the ability of banks to obtain additional funds. After all, who would want to deposit money in a bank at only 4 percent when one could buy Treasury bills or put dollars into a money market mutual fund and get twice as much?

As banks found themselves with profitable loan opportunities but not enough funds to satisfy them, they had no alternative but to devise new ways to raise money. In fact, just about all the instruments of liability management discussed in Chapter 8 came into being in response to this need for additional funds. Negotiable CDs were "invented" in 1961, and Eurodollars, as we saw in Chapter 10, became a source of bank funds shortly thereafter. American banks established branches abroad partly because foreign countries did not have deposit rate ceilings like Regulation Q. Banks lured funds into their foreign branches by offering attractive interest rates to depositors abroad and then transferred these funds to the United States to make domestic loans.

Obviously, circumventing regulatory restraint was an important element in stimulating recent financial innovation, but it was not the sole motivating factor. Other forces, such as the double-digit inflation that characterized the late 1970s, progressive legislation, the burst in technological advances, and the philosophy of deregulation, were important as well. Each of these will be discussed in turn.

DOUBLE-DIGIT INFLATION

The double-digit inflation of the late seventies and early eighties had profound social and economic consequences, including the stimulation of financial innovation. We had 13.3 percent inflation in 1979 and 12.4 percent in1980. From the start of 1978 to the end of 1981, inflation averaged about 11 percent per annum! Double-digit interest rates invariably accompany or follow close on the heels of double-digit inflation, as we saw in Chapter 6. As a result, a number of financial institutions—especially mutual savings banks and savings and loan associations—found themselves on the verge of bankruptcy because they were paying more to retain deposits than they were earning on most of their assets.

The reason was that most of the assets of these institutions consisted of *long-term* mortgages they had acquired in the fifties and sixties, when inflation was in single digits and interest rates were relatively low. In the late seventies and early eighties, however, the double-digit interest rates that accompanied double-digit inflation turned many previously profitable savings banks and savings and loan associations into losers. They were still earning the *old* interest rates on their long-term assets, mostly 25- and 30-year mortgages, but they had to pay the newer and much higher interest rates on a substantial portion of their liabilities. Their innovative response was the abandonment of *fixed-rate* loans in favor of *floating-rate* (also called *variable-rate*) uses for their funds. With floating-rate loans, the interest rate is tied to some prominent rate, such as the Treasury bill rate. The rate therefore rises and falls with the general level of market interest rates.

Floating-rate mortgages and floating-rate business and consumer loans shift the risk involved in higher rates from lenders to borrowers, as we have already discussed in earlier chapters. When the general level of interest rates rises, the higher rates are applied to "old" loans as well as to new ones. Financial institutions are no longer caught in a "rate squeeze" in which they are taking in less interest than they are paying out. The interest they take in on their assets is linked in some fashion to the interest they pay out on their liabilities, so whenever the interest rate on their liabilities goes up, the interest rate on their assets rises, too.

Financial innovation has been stimulated not only by high interest rates but also by the wide *fluctuations* in interest rates in recent years. During the fifties and sixties, interest rates did not fluctuate nearly so much as they do nowadays. Widely fluctuating interest rates imply greater risk, because they mean widely fluctuating securities prices; when rates rise, securities prices fall, and when rates fall, securities prices rise (as we saw in Chapter 5).

Among many innovative responses in the market designed to reduce this additional risk are (1) zero-coupon bonds, and (2) the development of widespread trading in financial futures. Zero-coupon bonds enable investors to lock in a specific yield for a stated period of time, often as long as twenty or thirty years, regardless of what happens to market interest rates during that interval. With ordinary coupon bonds, the purchaser has the problem of reinvesting the interest payments (coupons) to achieve a target yield. This problem does not arise with zero-coupon bonds, because there are no coupons to begin with. Similarly, futures markets enable market participants to agree today on a future transaction price, thereby removing uncertainty as to what that price will be.[1]

LEGISLATIVE ENCOURAGEMENT

The first section of this chapter focused on regulatory factors that for *negative* reasons provided a stimulus to financial innovation. We saw that attempts to *circumvent* governmental regulations have led to the introduction of new financial institutions, products, and markets. Government is not always such a negative force, however; indeed, in

---

[1] In stock market futures, the contracts are written on market indices such as Standard and Poor's 500. That's why we said above that you can buy or sell the market as a whole with financial futures. For a complete discussion see Chapter 33.

U.S. Is Altering Rules to Accommodate Growing Market in 'Zero-Coupon' Bonds

By Alan Murray

Staff Reporter of The Wall Street Journal

WASHINGTON—The Treasury Department, as expected, is moving to accommodate the growing market in "zero-coupon" bonds.

The Treasury said yesterday that it will allow banks and securities dealers to sell separately the interest payments and principal of the 10-year notes and 30-year bonds it will auction next month.

The Treasury also said it is eliminating the "call" provision on the 30-year bonds, which currently enables the Treasury to buy back the bonds at their face value after 25 years.

The plan for separate interest-payment sales was first disclosed last August. Zero-coupon securities pay no interest but are sold at deep discount from their face value.

Institutions buying Treasury securities will be able to request that each semiannual interest payment and the principal be registered separately by Federal Reserve banks. Each payment may then be sold as a zero-coupon bond.

The program will be known as Separate Trading of Registered Interest and Principal of Securities, or "Strips"—an acronym that reflects the market jargon for the practice of selling separate bond interest payments, known as stripping.

Currently, some dealers buy Treasury securities, put them in special trusts and then sell claims on individual interest payments or on the principal, using trade names like "CATS" and "Tigrs" for the claims. The Treasury plan will eliminate the need for such elaborate trust arrangements.

Cutting Financing Costs

By facilitating trade in Treasury zero coupons, department officials hope to cut

News Item *Financial Innovation in Action*

several respects it has also made *positive* contributions to financial innovation in recent years.

Example One: Ginnie Mae pass-through securities emerged primarily through government initiative. The Government National Mortgage Association (hence "Ginnie Mae") pass-through program was inaugurated by the Department of Housing and Urban Development. The pass-through program successfully increased the liquidity of mortgages and thereby increased the flow of credit to the mortgage market (more on this in Chapters 28 and 31).

Example Two: Individual Retirement Accounts (IRAs) and Keogh Accounts are both products of Congressional legislation. IRAs are retirement funds that employed people can set up for themselves. Keogh Accounts are designed for *self*-employed people, like doctors and free-lance illustrators or writers. Both IRAs and Keoghs have become extremely popular, no doubt because of the tax benefits they the interest costs of financing the federal debt and make zero-coupon securities less expensive and more readily available.

"This is the most significant innovation in debt financing during the first Reagan term," said Thomas Healey, department assistant secretary. "It may cause the market to look at Treasury debt in a radically different way."

Following the sale of 10-year notes and 30-year bonds next month, the Treasury will also make Strips available for the 10-year and 30-year securities sold last November. The 20-year bond sold in November will also become eligible for the program after May 15.

"Over time, we plan to make all the securities for which there is an interest eligible" for Strips, Mr. Healey said.

Purchase Minimum

The minimum amount of a security that a bank or broker must buy to qualify for Strips will vary with the interest rate. The minimum, which will be announced by the Treasury along with the results of each auction, will be set to produce a semiannual interest payment of $1,000 or a multiple of $1,000. The securities themselves are generally sold in multiples of $1,000.

Thus, if a security carries a coupon rate of 10%, an institution wishing to sell separate interest payments must buy at least $20,000 of the security, resulting in semiannual interest payments of $1,000. If a security carries an interest payment of, say, 11.25%, the Treasury will set a minimum of $160,000, producing semiannual interest payments of $9,000. Banks and brokers will then be allowed to sell zero-coupon bonds in $1,000 denominations.

Zero-coupon bonds have become increasingly popular in recent years, especially with such investment institutions as pension funds, which project their capital needs far into the future. A zero-coupon bond is appealing to such investors because it lets them assure future payment by investing a fraction of that amount now.

Since mid-1982, about $45 billion of Treasury securities have been turned into zero-coupon bonds.

Wall Street Journal, January 16, 1985

offer. Contributions to the funds can be used under specific conditions as deductions from income subject to federal tax; both the principal and the interest and/or dividends that the funds earn is deferred from taxation until the owner actually withdraws them, usually after retirement. Such deferment of taxes allows money to grow at a much faster rate than it would if interest and/or dividends were subject to income taxes each year.

Cynics might say that the main reason Congress enacted the legislation giving rise to IRAs and Keoghs is that the principal federally sponsored retirement fund—social security—has been coming apart at the seams. Many people who formerly counted on social security to support them in their old age have become disillusioned as social security has periodically come close to running out of money. In order to encourage *private* provision for pensions, in place of the not-too-healthy public pension system, Congress offered the inducement of tax breaks to those who would establish their own pension plans and fund them themselves. In any event, whatever the motivation, it was governmental legislation that initiated and promoted these innovative private pension plans.

Example Three: In 1976 Congress passed legislation that for the first time allowed mutual funds to pass the tax-exemption feature of state and local government securities along to their shareholders. That is, mutual funds could buy tax-exempt municipal securities, and shareholders in such mutual funds wouldn't have to pay federal income taxes on the interest earned.

As a result, many mutual funds have been established that specialize in acquiring state and local bonds. The market for municipal securities was thereby greatly broadened, because mutual funds can buy a more diversified basket of municipal securities than individual investors can buy, since they have so much more money at their disposal.

An individual investor with a given amount of money can therefore acquire lower-risk municipal securities with no sacrifice of yield by putting the money into a mutual fund instead of buying one or two municipal securities directly. The opportunity to acquire a diversified assortment of state and local government securities appeals to many high-income investors, and state and local governments have been able to sell more securities at lower interest rates than had previously been possible.

Mutual funds also gave the municipal bond market additional liquidity, because shares in a mutual fund are generally easier to sell than individual state or local government securities. Again, therefore, governmental legislative initiative helped bring about an innovative improvement in financial markets.

THE PHILOSOPHY OF DEREGULATION

In analyzing why so much innovation has been taking place at this particular time in history, let us not forget the widespread acceptance of what has come to be known as the philosophy of deregulation. Between 1975 and 1985 a wave of deregulation swept through the U.S. economy. It began in the Carter administration and has been endorsed and furthered by the Reagan administration. Probably the most prominent industry to have been deregulated has been the airline industry, but many others have also been freed from the encumbrances of government regulatory restraint.

In the field of finance there has always been a special conflict between *safety* and *flexibility*. That is, it has traditionally been felt that a considerable amount of government regulation is required to make sure that banks and other financial institutions handling other people's money are run prudently and safely. Thus banks are not allowed to invest in the stock market (too risky), and they are examined periodically by the banking authorities to make sure they follow the rules with respect to the loans they make and the securities they buy.

On the other hand, too much regulation can excessively limit management discretion and flexibility. Management decision-making needs some leeway if it is to be imaginative and forward-looking in coping with the short- and long-run problems faced by every dynamic firm and industry. If no imagination or independent judgment can be exercised in running a firm or a bank, then good management people will get bored and go elsewhere, to other industries, and the firm or bank will stagnate. Too much legislated built-in safety can have negative as well as positive effects.

Historically, the United States has erred on the side of safety in banking and finance, often sacrificing managerial flexibility in order to gain more safety. In recent years, however, the balance has shifted somewhat. We still want a lot of built-in safety, but we are not willing to give up quite as much flexibility in order to get it. The philosophy of deregulation has had an impact on the financial services industry as well as on other segments of the economy.

The basic philosophy underlying deregulation is that free markets and private initiative are better able to cope with changes in the economic environment than a network of rigid and inflexible governmental rules and regulations. Private management is also more motivated to figure out less costly and more productive ways of doing things, because it stands to gain (with higher profits) if new methods of production or new products successfully reduce costs or expand sales.

As the philosophy of deregulation has become more widespread, many financial institutions have been encouraged to experiment and test the limits of governmental rules and regulations. Thus many banks have edged their way into insurance and stock brokerage, just as many stock market firms have acquired small banks and then converted them into "nonbank banks." The result of all this breaching of the regulations has been increased motivation for change and the encouragement of innovation throughout the financial services industry. Were there no spirit of deregulation in the air, such innovations would probably be introduced much more hesitantly, if at all.

TECHNOLOGICAL CHANGE

Technology is the traditional stimulus to change, and it is as powerful in financial markets as anywhere else. The technological revolution typified by computers has had an obvious impact in the field of finance. For example, it would be impossible to have automated teller machines without computerization of the deposit/withdrawal function. Computerization has also been crucial in the development of credit cards to the advanced level they have reached. Modern computer-generated methods of information storage, retrieval, and transmission underlie many of the changes that have taken place in the financial services industry.

Modern technology has revolutionized the speed and cost of processing information, and the financial consequences are probably still in their infancy. In the next decade, the financial implications of such technological developments are likely to go well beyond what we can imagine today.

Technological change, of course, is generally considered a major source of improvement in economic welfare. Technological innovations expand the proverbial economic pie, allowing everyone to have more without forcing anyone to have less, thereby making it possible for everyone's standard of living to rise.

Financial innovations have similar effects. In the case of financial innovation, however, the main areas of welfare gain are improvements in the ability to bear risk (futures markets), lowered transactions costs (automated teller machines), and avoidance of the consequences of outmoded governmental regulation (money market mutual funds as an end run around Regulation Q).

NECESSITY IS THE MOTHER OF INVENTION

We should not leave our discussion of financial innovation without tying it in with the broad principles regarding invention and innovation more generally. The best known principle is summarized in the popular aphorism "necessity is the mother of invention." It should be clear that new financial institutions, products, and markets come into use and remain there because of a demand for them, a need that keeps them in existence more than temporarily. This point can be illustrated by examples of successful innovations that extend beyond the experience of the 1970s and 1980s.

Credit cards, introduced during the 1950s and 1960s, could not have become so widespread without the technological computer base that enables them to function so effectively. Nevertheless, no matter how advanced the technology, credit cards would not have become so popular if they hadn't fulfilled an underlying consumer need. People simply enjoy the ability to spend without paying up immediately. And credit cards facilitate that process.

Similarly, commercial banks introduced consumer loans and term loans (business loans with more than one year to maturity) in the 1930s, because they perceived a demand for such loans waiting to be satisfied. Banks had tried to make short-term business loans, but business borrowers turned elsewhere in search of longer-term funds. In order to keep their customers, banks changed their policies and extended their loans to four or five years in place of the one-year loans they had been trying to make previously.

Returning to the 1970s, money market mutual funds would have faded rapidly from the scene if they did not satisfy a need. In this case, more clearly perhaps than any other, necessity was the mother of invention. Depositors, prevented from getting market interest rates by Regulation Q, turned enthusiastically to money market mutual funds as soon as the alternative became open to them.

On the basis of such evidence, we can conclude that if someone perceives a need that is currently not being fulfilled and can invent a way to satisfy that need, chances are such an innovation will prove successful. Innovations that do not meet that criterion will probably fall by the wayside. In other words, if you build a better mousetrap, the world will beat a path to your door—provided people need to catch mice!

SUMMARY

1. One of the most popular explanations of financial innovation is that it is a response to outmoded and excessively restrictive governmental regulation.

2. That partially explains the reasons for financial innovation, but it is not a complete explanation. Double-digit inflation, high interest rates, wide fluctuations in interest rates, progressive government legislation, the philosophy of deregulation, and technological change are also important factors that have helped to stimulate financial innovation.

3. Above all, however, necessity is the mother of invention. Unfilled needs give rise to ways to satisfy them; conversely, unless an innovation fills a need it will not become a permanent part of the financial services industry.

Suggestions for Further Reading

One of the earliest systematic studies of financial innovation is by Stuart Greenbaum and Charles Haywood, "Secular Change in the Financial Services Industry," *Journal of Money, Credit and Banking* (May 1974). For historical perspectives, see Richard Sylla, "Monetary Innovations and Crises in American Economic History" in *Crises in the Economic and Financial Structure*, ed. Paul Wachtel (Lexington, Mass.: D.C. Heath, 1982); and *Financial Innovation*, ed. William L. Silber (Lexington, Mass.: D.C. Heath, 1975). A more recent overview appears in William L. Silber, "The Process of Financial Innovation," *American Economic Review* (May 1983). An emphasis on the regulatory role in innovation is found in Edward Kane's "Accelerating Inflation, Technological Innovation and the Decreasing Effectiveness of Banking Regulation," *Journal of Finance* (May 1981).

Finally, see Alfred Broaddus, "Financial Innovation in the United States—Background, Current Status, and Prospects," Federal Reserve Bank of Richmond *Economic Review* (January–February 1985).

CHAPTER 12

The Payments System

The payments system has become a rather glamorous topic, with focus on the technological revolution that promises to replace checks with electronic messages and turn bankers into robots. It was only about a hundred years ago that checks displaced currency as the dominant means of payment in the economy, sparking a revolution of its own. To provide a perspective on current and future developments, therefore, it is useful to review briefly the evolution of the payments system during the past century. We can then turn to a science fiction view of the payments system of the future—ever mindful that all too often today's science fiction turns out to be tomorrow's reality.

THE CURRENT PAYMENTS SYSTEM

Back in Chapter 1 we showed how monetary exchange is superior to a barter-based system. In particular, using a medium of exchange to consummate transactions cuts down the time needed for exchange. It also facilitates trade among strangers, because the medium of exchange is readily identifiable and acceptable in the settlement of obligations. But the contribution of monetary exchange depends, in part, on exactly what serves as money in such a system. For example, in the good old days gold and other metals served as money because only they were readily acceptable in trade. Paper currency came into the picture because coins and bullion were cumbersome media of exchange. As long as the banks that issued the currency could redeem it in "real money"—the underlying metal—paper currency was acceptable in trade and served as a more convenient means of payment.

But even currency has its drawbacks as a medium of exchange. It is still fairly bulky—$10,000,000 even in $100 bills fills quite a few attaché cases—and it can be easily stolen. Settling obligations by shipping currency can be inconvenient as well as expensive. Coin and currency are a substantial improvement over barter, but consummating a transaction in cash is still costly, especially when payments must be made over some distance.

Checks came into use precisely to overcome such costs. A check is simply an order to a bank to transfer funds from one person's account to someone else's. Instead of paying out $20,000 in $100 bills to buy a new deluxe sports car, you write a check instructing your bank to shift $20,000 from your checking account to the car dealer's account. The transaction can be completed without the need to move any currency out of the bank's safekeeping. And that's the way most transactions are completed nowadays. Payments are made via debits and credits on a bank's books rather than through an exchange of cash.

The actual check-based payments system is complicated by the fact that buyers and sellers do not usually have checking accounts at the same bank. Thus when a check is drawn on one bank ordering payment to an account at another bank, the two banks must settle accounts with each other. Many of the institutional complications in the current payment system arose in connection with interbank settlement of claims.

The local clearinghouse is the oldest kind of institution used to settle interbank claims. Representatives from local banks gather once (or twice) a day at an agreed-upon time and place to settle via a single exchange of cash the net inflow or outflow required against all other local banks. The advantage is that only *net* cash balances are exchanged. Thus if Banc One (Columbus, Ohio) is presented with $10 million in checks drawn by its depositors and holds $9 million in checks drawn on other local banks, it will have to ante up only $1 million, the net debit to other members of the local clearinghouse.

Processing checks drawn against out-of-town (nonclearinghouse) banks is more complicated. To accomplish this efficiently, banks maintain checking accounts with each other, called correspondent balances. For example, when a Chicago bank receives a check drawn against a bank in Toledo, Ohio, it will forward the check for collection to a Chicago institution that is the Toledo bank's correspondent—or to the correspondent of a correspondent. In this way a check is eventually debited to the proper bank, although it may take a rather circuitous trip in the process. Nevertheless, many of our checks are currently collected through the network of correspondent balances.

By far the most influential force in the collection of checks, however, is the Federal Reserve System. When the Fed was established in 1913, one of its main functions was to facilitate the check collection process, especially for out-of-town checks. In fact, the Federal Reserve operates a nationwide clearinghouse for settling interbank transfers of funds. Checks are collected by debiting and crediting bank reserves on the books of the regional Federal Reserve Banks, as will become clear in Chapter 14. The Fed operates regional check processing centers to sift and tabulate the mass of paper generated by the checking system.

An important innovation speeding check clearance was taken in the 1950s with the adoption of a nationwide standardized system of Magnetic Ink Character Recognition (MICR) imprinted on checks. The odd-looking numerals on the bottom of checks identify a particular bank, the Federal Reserve District in which it is located, the account number of the depositor, and other information. The MICR imprint enables checks to be sorted by machines for more rapid processing.

Actually, MICR is already old-fashioned, because the use of *electronic* communications to transfer funds, in place of written orders on pieces of paper, is already well advanced. Three main electronic systems are now operating:

Fed Wire is a sophisticated telecommunications system operated by the Federal Reserve. It consists of a nationwide network of interconnected computers through which instructions can be transmitted to transfer funds from one bank to another. Actual payment, or settlement, is accomplished by debits and credits to the reserve balances of the banks at the Federal Reserve. In other words, if a bank in New York wants to transfer some reserve balances to a bank in Los Angeles, as part of a Fed funds transaction, it can be done almost instantaneously by sending the proper instructions over the Fed Wire. Millions of dollars can thus be transferred on the books of the participating banks in nanoseconds.[1]

CHIPS, an acronym for Clearing House Interbank Payment System, is operated by the banks associated with the New York Clearing House.

---

[1] A nanosecond is one-billionth of a second.

The CHIPS network specializes in *international* transfers of funds, with computer terminals at large banks in the United States and Europe tied in to a central computer located in New York.

SWIFT, which stands for the Society for Worldwide Interbank Financial Telecommunications, is another internationally oriented funds transfer system. Headquartered in Belgium, it is similar to CHIPS in that it handles mostly international transfers.

Fed Wire, CHIPS, and SWIFT transfer millions of dollars at one time. But small consumers have also been affected by the computer revolution. Automated teller machines (ATMs) are now available in most parts of the country, enabling bank customers to make deposits or withdrawals twenty-four hours a day. And in some areas purchases and sales of goods or services can be processed by point of sale (POS) terminals connected on line with a bank's computer. With a POS terminal, payment is made at the checkout counter by the cashier pushing a series of keys which electronically debit the buyer's bank account and credit the seller's. The Fed also operates a number of automated clearinghouses (ACHs) which process computer tape orders to pay rather than checks. Thus far the ACHs are most often used for preauthorized regular payments, such as monthly mortgage or utility bills, or to receive direct credits of salary or social security payments.

There is little doubt that electronics will make further inroads on paper as the primary mechanism for settling transactions. The cost of processing the sheer volume of paper will continue to spur innovative practices. To provide a flavor of what it might be like in a full-fledged electronic funds transfer system (EFTS), let's take a somewhat fanciful view of how it might work out. Be careful, though, because it may be closer than you think.

THE PAYMENTS SYSTEM OF THE FUTURE

A few decades from now, coins will probably still be with us for inserting into vending machines that we can then shake and bang to release our aggressions. But checks may well have vanished. Check payment, as we have just seen, is really nothing more than a bookkeeping operation to begin with. As a method of dispersing information about how the books should be kept, checks are—in light of present and foreseeable technology—notoriously cumbersome, slow, unreliable, and inefficient.

More in keeping with the twenty-first century will be a vast nationwide balance sheet and clearing system in which debits and credits can be rung up virtually instantaneously by electronic impulse. Every individual and every transacting organization of whatever sort will be tagged at birth with a number and a slot on the "books" of a computerized nationwide accounting and payments system, a National Ledger, as it were.

Credits and debits to each individual account will be made by the insertion of a twenty-first-century version of a credit card into a twenty-first-century version of a telephone or teletype. Instead of a written piece of paper instructing a bank to credit this account and debit that one—that is, a check, with its necessary physical routing from place to place—the insertion of a plastic card into the appropriate receptacle will automatically credit and debit both accounts instantaneously. With high-speed computers, magnetic tape storage, remote feed-ins, and satellite transmission, it should not be too difficult to devise a system whereby the proper code will serve as a means of verifying the validity of the electronic instructions to the Great Master Bookkeeper in the Sky.

Eliminating checks would be only one of the many advantages that would emerge from such a system. All financial assets are nothing more than a representation of someone else's liability or evidence of equity. Current practice, which consists of inscribing same on embossed parchment, has been absurd for at least two generations. There is no need for stocks and bonds to look like Pronouncements of State by King Henry VIII. As everyone is fully aware, a simple computer print-out would do just as well. However, soon after the turn of the millenium, even that will not be necessary, since it will all be recorded automatically on the magnetic tape of the National Ledger as soon as a stock or bond is sold or a transaction made.

A National Ledger payments system will be possible in a surprisingly few years. Already its introduction depends more on costs and financial evaluations regarding its profitability than on purely technological considerations. It remains to be seen whether the necessary services will be provided by one firm, an association of private financial and nonfinancial firms, or the government, alone or in partnership with private enterprise.

With methods of communication and the dissemination of information perfected to the ultimate degree by the year 2000, in all likelihood, financial markets will finally take on the characteristics of the purely competitive markets that economists have been talking about in classrooms since the days of Adam Smith. Instead of simple buy and sell orders, or bid and offered quotations, potential buyers and sellers

Judge Refuses Man's Request To Let Him Become a Number

MINNEAPOLIS, Feb. 13—A district court judge today denied the request of a Minneapolis man who wanted his name changed to a number, saying that it would be "an offense to basic human dignity."

Michael Herbert Dengler filed a petition in October seeking to assume legally the name 1069, which he said he had used for more than four years. Mr. Dengler cited philosophical reasons for his request, saying that each of the numerals had symbolic significance to him. Taken together, he said, the numerals "describe what is inherent in me."

He was out of town and could not be reached for comments on the ruling.

Mr. Dengler, a 32-year-old former resident of North Dakota, had twice been denied such permission by courts in that state. The North Dakota Supreme Court conceded that "One Zero Six Nine" might qualify as a name, but balked at his use of numerals instead of words.

Opened Checking Account

However, after Mr. Dengler moved to Minnesota he opened a checking account as 1069, and he displays a Social Security card also identifying him by number. He said he had little trouble passing checks bearing the unusual name.

"I just write the check and say, 'Would I write a bad check with a name like this?'" he said.

But Mr. Dengler said that he had been discriminated against by potential employers and utility companies that refused to accept his number as a name. In an interview for a job at a large corporation, a personnel officer reportedly told him: "You come in here with a name. We'll give you a number."

Mr. Dengler's attorney, Timothy Geck, said at a court hearing in Minneapolis that several utilities had refused to give his client services as 1069 without a court order making it official. The Northwestern Bell Telephone Company, for example, would give Mr. Dengler only an unlisted telephone number as 1069, Mr. Geck said.

Judge Donald Barbeau of Hennepin County District Court said he believed Mr. Dengler was sincere in his philosophical motives for requesting the change, but said that he could not "in good conscience add to today's inhumanity by giving it the stamp of judicial approval."

"Dehumanization is widespread and affects our culture like a disease in epidemic proportions," Judge Barbeau wrote in his opinion. "To allow the use of a number instead of a name would only provide additional nourishment upon which the illness of the dehumanization is able to feed and grow to the point where it is totally incurable."

Mr. Geck said, after learning of the decision, that "there is a very good likelihood" that Mr. Dengler would appeal the ruling to the Minnesota Supreme Court.

New York Times, February 14, 1978

News Item *The Twenty-First Century?*

Update: Mr. Dengler did indeed appeal to the Minnesota Supreme Court, which ruled in 1980 that he could not use the name 1069 but that One Zero Six Nine was permissible. The court noted that this would be much like Juan Nyen.

of financial assets will be able to transmit complete demand and supply schedules electronically to a central clearing computer, specifying the amounts of various securities they wish to buy or sell at various prices.

Of course, this in itself would not be quite sufficient to meet classroom standards for a purely competitive market, since one of the prerequisites for such a market is that the participants possess perfect foresight regarding the future as well as perfect knowledge of the present. But even that might be incorporated by feeding probability forecasts into the Giant Maw of the computer. Is it too farfetched to suggest that such forecasts might even involve some of the parapsychological techniques—like clairvoyance and precognition—currently under study at some of our most prestigious universities and on several all-night radio programs?

Economic policy-making will also mean something quite different in the twenty-first century from what it means today. Monetary and fiscal policy are far too uncertain in their impact for use in the Century of Efficiency that will follow the present Century of Progress.

By that time, all assets and liabilities as recorded on the National Ledger will be subject to increase or decrease by any given percentage by Executive Order, thereby instantaneously altering the wealth of every individual and every business firm in the country. If aggregate spending does not respond promptly in the direction and amount desired, further asset-valuation adjustments can be fine-tuned until the reaction of the private sector conforms to what is deemed necessary to assure the Good Life for all.

Given human nature, this may possibly give rise to the problem of "valuation evasion"—that is, an illegal market in which assets are valued and transactions effected at prices other than those recorded on the National Ledger. The result would be the accumulation of unrecorded wealth for those involved in such dealings. If this gains currency, so to speak, an entire underground financial system—complete with (unreported) deposits, handwritten checks, and a subterranean check-routing network—is likely to spring up in opposition to the more efficient computerized and satellite-supervised official payments system.

The most effective remedy to prevent such undermining of the common welfare would be to bar all participants in Financial Subversion from access to the National Ledger. Practitioners of too-private enterprise would thus be consigned to deserved financial ostracism as Subverters of the National Happiness.

Such a solution would have the self-evident virtue of safeguarding the Sinews of our Efficiency, while at the same time being consistent with the preservation of our Cherished Freedoms.

P.S. If you understand all of this, let us know what it means.

SUMMARY

1. An efficient payments system reduces the cost of completing transactions by devising low-cost media of exchange to replace higher-cost means of payment. Checks are a less costly payments mechanism than either currency or metal, hence checks have dominated both during much of the twentieth century.

2. Check clearing among banks is facilitated by a number of institutional arrangements, including clearinghouses, correspondent balances, and the Federal Reserve System.

3. A number of electronic transfer mechanisms currently supplement the system of check collection, including Fed Wire, CHIPS, and SWIFT. More recently, computer transfers through automated clearinghouses have become routine for preauthorized regular payments.

4. The payments system of the future is limited only by the confines of current imagination. One thing will surely be with us, however: a subterranean economy to circumvent excessive control and documentation. "The more things change, the more they remain the same" is as true of the payments system as of everything else.

Suggestions for Further Reading

A number of articles in various issues of the *Federal Reserve Bulletin* have described the payments mechanism, including Earl Hamilton, "An Update on the Automated Clearinghouse" (July 1979); James Brundy, David Humphrey, and Myron Kwast, "Check Processing at the Federal Reserve Offices" (February 1979); and George Mitchell and Raymond Hodgdon, "Federal Reserve and the Payments System" (February 1981). For an interesting historical study see Kenneth Garbade and William Silber, "The Payment System and Domestic Exchange Rates: Technological Versus Institutional Change," *Journal of Monetary Economics* (January 1979).

For a discussion of the payments system of tomorrow see Lawrence Ritter and Thomas Atkinson, "Monetary Theory and Policy in the Payments System of the Future," *Journal of Money, Credit, and Banking* (November 1970); Mark J. Flannery and Dwight M. Jaffee, *The Economic Implications of an Electronic Monetary Transfer System* (Lexington, Mass.: Lexington Books, 1973); and *The Future of the U.S. Payments System,* Proceedings of Conference (Federal Reserve Bank of Atlanta, 1981).

But for the real truth first read Aldous Huxley's *Brave New World* (New York: Harper & Row, 1932) and George Orwell's *1984* (New York: Harcourt, Brace, 1949). Then go see Stanley Kubrick's *2001: A Space Odyssey* and Charlton Heston in *Planet of the Apes.*

PART III

THE ART
OF CENTRAL
BANKING

CHAPTER 13

Who's In Charge Here?

Monetary policy is the responsibility of the Federal Reserve, but to whom is the Federal Reserve responsible? We saw in the beginning chapters of the book that the money supply should be set to give us high employment without inflation. The Federal Reserve checks the money supply, but who checks the Fed?

The answer to that question is so complex that if we unravel it successfully (which is not too likely a prospect), we will either have unveiled one of the great socioeconomic creations in the annals of civilization, comparable to the invention of indoor plumbing, or unmasked one of the most devious schemes ever contrived by the human mind to camouflage the true locus of clandestine power.

According to some, the Federal Reserve is responsible to the Congress. But it is the President, not Congress, who appoints the seven members of the Board of Governors of the Federal Reserve System, who occupy the stately building at Twentieth Street and Constitution Avenue, Washington, D.C. The President also selects from among those seven the Chairman of the Board of Governors, the principal policy-maker of the central bank.

On that basis, one might surmise that the Federal Reserve is responsible to the executive branch of government, in the person of the President. However, since each member of the Board has a fourteen-year term, the current President can appoint only two of the seven members of the Board of Governors, unless there are deaths or resignations. Even the Chairman may be the appointee of the previous administration. Furthermore, it is Congress that created the Federal Reserve in 1913, and it is Congress, not the President, that has the authority to alter its working mandate at any time. In 1935, for example, Congress chose to throw two administration representatives off the Board of Governors—the Secretary of the Treasury and the Comptroller of the Currency, both of whom had been ex officio members— simply because they were representatives of the executive branch.

Others, more cynical, have suggested that the Federal Reserve is mostly responsible to the private banking community, primarily the 6,000 commercial banks that are member banks of the Federal Reserve System. The member banks do in fact choose six of the nine directors of each regional Federal Reserve Bank, who in turn appoint the presidents of the regional Federal Reserve Banks, including the president of the most aristocratic of all, the Federal Reserve Bank of New York. It may or may not be significant that the annual salary of the President of the Federal Reserve Bank of New York is about double the salary of the Chairman of the Board of Governors in Washington.

Who's in charge here, anyway?

FORMAL STRUCTURE OF THE FEDERAL RESERVE SYSTEM

The statutory organization of the Federal Reserve System is a case study in those currently popular concepts, decentralization and the blending of public and private authority. A deliberate attempt was made in the enabling congressional legislation, the 1913 Federal Reserve Act, to diffuse power over a broad base—geographically, between the private and public sectors, and even within the government—so that no one person, group, or sector, either inside or outside the government, could exert enough leverage to dominate the direction of monetary policy.

As Figure 1 shows, the Board of Governors of the Federal Reserve System consists of seven members, appointed by the President with the advice and consent of the Senate. To prevent presidential board-packing, each member is appointed for a term of fourteen years, with one board member's term expiring at the end of January in each even-

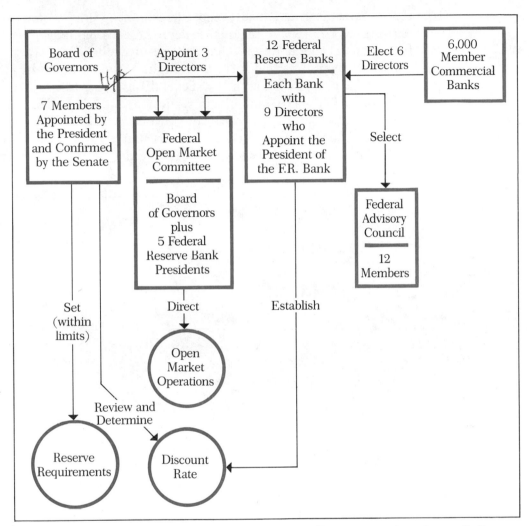

FIGURE 1 The Formal Structure and Policy Organization of the Federal Reserve System

numbered year. Furthermore, no two board members may come from the same Federal Reserve District. The Chairman of the Board of Governors, chosen from among the seven by the President, serves a four-year term. However, the Chairman's term does not coincide with the presidential term, so an incoming President is usually saddled with an already appointed Chairman at the beginning of the new administration. The Board is independent of the congressional appropriations process and partly exempt from audit by the government's watchdog, the General Accounting Office, because its operating funds come from the earnings of the twelve regional Federal Reserve Banks.

The regional Federal Reserve Banks, one in each Federal Reserve District, are geographically dispersed throughout the nation—the Federal Reserve Bank of New York, the Federal Reserve Bank of Kansas City, the Federal Reserve Bank of San Francisco, and so on (see Figure 2). Each Federal Reserve Bank is privately owned by the member banks in its district, the very commercial banks it is charged with supervising and regulating. Each member bank is required to buy stock in its

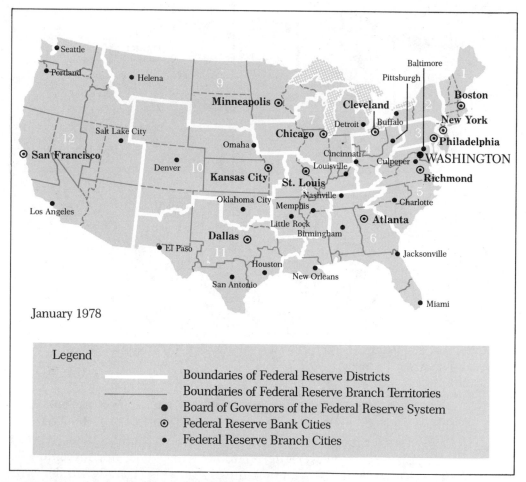

January 1978

Legend

——————————— Boundaries of Federal Reserve Districts
—————————— Boundaries of Federal Reserve Branch Territories
● Board of Governors of the Federal Reserve System
⊙ Federal Reserve Bank Cities
• Federal Reserve Branch Cities

FIGURE 2 The Federal Reserve System

SOURCE: *Federal Reserve Bulletin.* R. W. Galvin, Cartographer.
NOTE: Hawaii and Alaska are in the Twelfth Federal Reserve District.

district Federal Reserve Bank equal to 6 percent of its own capital and surplus. Of this 6 percent, 3 percent must be paid in and 3 percent is subject to call by the Board of Governors. However, the profits accruing to ownership are limited by law to a 6 percent annual dividend on paid-in capital stock. The member bank stockholders elect six of the nine directors of their district Federal Reserve Bank, and the remaining three are appointed from Washington by the Board of Governors. These nine directors, in turn, choose the president of their Federal Reserve Bank, subject to the approval of the Board of Governors.

The directors of each Federal Reserve Bank also select a person, always a commercial banker, to serve on the Federal Advisory Council, a statutory body consisting of a member from each of the twelve Federal Reserve Districts. The Federal Advisory Council consults quarterly with the Board of Governors in Washington and makes recommendations regarding the conduct of monetary policy.

Legal authority is similarly diffused with respect to the *execution* of monetary policy, as Figure 1 indicates. The Board of Governors has the power to set reserve requirements on bank time and demand deposits, for example, but it cannot set them outside the bounds of the specific limits imposed by Congress.

Open market operations (see Chapter 15) are directed by a body known as the Federal Open Market Committee (FOMC), composed of the seven-member Board of Governors plus five of the Reserve Bank presidents. Since the members of the Board of Governors are appointed by the White House, and the Reserve Bank presidents are appointed by the directors of each Federal Reserve Bank, who are (six of nine) elected by the member commercial banks, the diffusion of authority over open market operations spans the distance from the White House to the member bank on Main Street. In addition, although open market operations are directed by the FOMC, they are executed at the trading desk of the Federal Reserve Bank of New York by a person who appears to be simultaneously an employee of the FOMC and the Federal Reserve Bank of New York.

Legal authority over discount rates (again, see Chapter 15) is even more confusing. Discount rates are "established" every two weeks by the directors of each regional Federal Reserve Bank, but they are subject to "review and determination" by the Board of Governors. The distinction between "establishing" discount rates and "determining" them is a fine line indeed, and it is not surprising that confusion occasionally arises as to precisely where the final authority and responsibility lie.

THE REALITIES OF POWER

So much for the Land of Oz. Actually, the facts of life are rather different, as the more realistic Figure 3 illustrates.

By all odds, the dominant figure in the formation and execution of monetary policy is the Chairman of the Board of Governors of the Federal Reserve System. The Chairman is the most prominent member of the Board itself and the most influential member of the FOMC and is generally recognized by both Congress and the public at large as *the* voice of the Federal Reserve System. Although the Federal Reserve Act appears to put all seven members of the Board of Governors on more or less equal footing, over the past fifty years the strong personalities, outstanding abilities, and determined devotion to purpose of the chair-

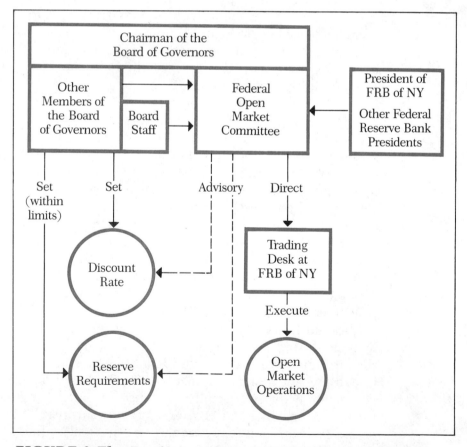

FIGURE 3 The Realities of Power Within the Federal Reserve System

men have made them rather more equal than the others. As adviser to the President, negotiator with Congress, and final authority on appointments throughout the system, with influence over all aspects of monetary policy as Chairman of both the Board of Governors and the FOMC, the Chairman for all practical purposes is the embodiment of the central bank in this country.

The other six members of the Board of Governors also exercise a substantial amount of authority, more so than is indicated in the formal paper structure of the system, because with the passage of time primary responsibility for monetary policy has become more centralized and concentrated in Washington. When the Federal Reserve Act was passed in 1913, it was thought that the Federal Reserve System would be mainly a passive service agency, supplying currency when needed, clearing checks, and providing a discount facility for the convenience of the private commercial member banks. At that time there was no conception of monetary policy as an active countercyclical force. Since then, of course, the central bank has shifted from passive accommodation to active regulation, from the performance of regional service functions to the implementation of national economic policy. This shift has been accompanied, naturally enough, by a rise in the power of the centralized Board of Governors in Washington and a corresponding decline in the role of the regional Federal Reserve Banks and their "owners," the commercial banks.

It would not be unrealistic to describe the central bank today as headquartered in Washington, with twelve field offices throughout the nation. These field offices may be known by the rather imposing name of Federal Reserve Banks, and they do indeed retain a certain degree of autonomy in expressing their views on the wisdom of various policies. But even so they essentially amount to little more than branches of the Washington headquarters.

Closely related to the Board of Governors in the informal power structure, and deriving influence through that association, is the Board's professional staff of economic experts and advisers. The long tenure in the Federal Reserve System of many senior staff economists, their familiarity with Federal Reserve history, and their expertise in monetary analysis give them a power base that is to a large extent founded on the respect with which they, as individuals, are held throughout the System. Through daily consultation with the individual Governors and written and oral presentations before each meeting of the FOMC, staff personnel exert an indefinable but significant influence on the ultimate decision-making process. In fact, three members of the Board's staff have been elevated to the Board itself, via presidential nomination (Robert Holland in 1973, Charles Partee in 1976, and Lyle Gramley in 1980).[1]

Aside from the Board of Governors, its Chairman, and its staff, the only other body playing a major role in Federal Reserve policymaking is the FOMC, which meets about every five or six weeks in Washington. Of the twelve members on the FOMC, a majority of seven are the Board of Governors themselves. The other five are Reserve Bank presidents. The President of the Federal Reserve Bank of New York is a permanent member of the FOMC, and the other eleven Federal Reserve Bank presidents rotate the remaining four seats among themselves.

The statutory authority of the FOMC is confined to the direction of open market operations, but in recent years it has become the practice to bring all policy matters under review at FOMC meetings. Although only five of the Reserve Bank presidents are entitled to vote at any one time, typically all twelve attend every meeting and participate in the discussion. Thus potential reserve-requirement and discount-rate changes are, in effect, decided upon within the FOMC, with the twelve Reserve Bank presidents participating in an advisory capacity. The Board of Governors, however, always has the final say on reserve requirements and discount rates if matters should come to a showdown, particularly since legal opinion appears to be that, in case of disagreement, the Board's power to "review and determine" discount rates overrides the authority of the individual Reserve Banks to "establish" them.

The status of the President of the Federal Reserve Bank of New York in the nation's financial center lends the role a unique position in the hierarchy. A president of the New York Reserve Bank who is inclined to use this leverage, as Allan Sproul did a generation ago and Benjamin Strong did before him, can mount a substantial challenge even to the Chairman of the Board of Governors. Since such a challenge would have little legal foundation, it would have to be based on the prestige of the presidency of the Federal Reserve Bank of New York and the forcefulness of the person who holds the position.

But where, in the corridors of power, does this leave the member banks, the directors of each Federal Reserve Bank, and the Federal Advisory Council? Pretty much shut out, if the truth be known.

The member banks do indeed "own" their district Federal Reserve

---

[1] In 1978, Nancy Teeters became the first woman member of the Board of Governors. The first black member of the Board was Andrew Brimmer, who was appointed in 1966.

Bank, but such stockholding is mostly symbolic and carries none of the usual attributes of ownership. The member banks also have a major voice in electing the directors of their Reserve Bank, but the directors in turn have responsibilities that are largely ceremonial. True, they appoint the members of the Federal Advisory Council, but the Federal Advisory Council serves mostly a public relations purpose and has little to do with actual policy-making. The directors of each Federal Reserve Bank also choose the president of their Reserve Bank, subject to the approval of the Board of Governors. But the "subject to approval" clause has meant, in practice, that the most the directors can really do is submit a list of nominees for the position of president. On several occasions the choice of the directors of a Federal Reserve Bank has not met with approval from Washington; such cases have made very clear exactly where ultimate authority is lodged.

THE PROBLEM OF FEDERAL RESERVE INDEPENDENCE

The fact that ultimate authority over monetary policy resides in Washington brings to the fore the relationship between the central bank and the other branches of government also responsible for overall national economic policy—the Congress and the administration, the latter personified by the President.

The Federal Reserve is a creature of the Congress. The Constitution gives Congress the power "to coin money and regulate the value thereof." On this basis, in 1913 Congress created the Federal Reserve as the institution delegated to administer that responsibility on its behalf. Congress requires periodic accountability by the Federal Reserve and has the authority to amend the enabling legislation, the Federal Reserve Act, any time it sees fit.

Essentially, Congress has given the Federal Reserve a broad mandate to regulate the monetary system in the public interest and then has more or less stood aside and let the monetary authorities pursue this objective on their own and to the best of their abilities. Congress has also attempted to minimize interference from the administration by giving each member of the Board of Governors a fourteen-year term, thereby sharply limiting any single President's influence over the Board.

This semi-independent status of the central bank is a source of continuous friction. Some members of Congress believe that the Federal Reserve has carried its "independence" much too far. There has been some concern over its freedom from congressional appropriations and its partial exemption from standard government audit. Also, the Federal Reserve's responsibility on occasion for tight money and high interest rates has stimulated some intensive questioning at congressional hearings, including frequent scoldings of Federal Reserve officials by populist-minded members of Congress who get uptight about tight money.

Others, in Congress and out, have complained that the Federal Reserve simply has not done a very good job, that we would all be better off if Congress laid down some guidelines or rules to limit the discretion available to the monetary authorities in conducting their business. We will discuss such proposals in Chapter 23.

The relationship between the central bank and the President has also aroused considerable controversy. Many feel that the Federal Reserve should be a part of the executive branch of government, responsible to the President, on the grounds that monetary policy is an integral part of national economic policy and should therefore be coordinated at the highest level (that is, by the President), along with fiscal policy, as a component part of the administration's total program for economic growth and stability.

To do otherwise, it is charged, is both undemocratic and divisive— undemocratic because monetary policy is too important to be run by an elite group of experts insulated from the political process, and divisive because monetary and fiscal policy should not work at cross-purposes. Since fiscal policy proposals are clearly within the President's domain, monetary policy should be as well. A Federal Reserve independent of presidential authority conflicts with the administration's responsibility to promulgate and coordinate an overall economic program.

The case for central bank independence from the President, on the other hand, rests on the pragmatic basis that subordination of the central bank to the executive branch of government invites excessive money creation and consequent inflation. The charge that an independent Federal Reserve is undemocratic is countered by the reminder that the central bank is still very much responsible to Congress, which can amend the Federal Reserve Act any time it wishes. In addition, the President holds frequent meetings with the Chairman of the Board of Governors, the Secretary of the Treasury, and the Chairman of the Council of Economic Advisors.

It is feared by many, and not without historical justification, that if the monetary authority is made the junior partner to the President or the Treasury (the fiscal authority), monetary stability will be sacrificed to the government's revenue needs—the government will be tempted to seek the easy way out in raising funds, by printing money or borrowing excessively at artificially low interest rates, in preference to the politically more difficult route of raising taxes or cutting back on government spending. The sole purpose of an independent monetary authority, in brief, is to forestall the natural propensity of governments to resort to inflation.

*   *   *   *   *

The rest of Part 3 takes an intensive look at Federal Reserve methods of control. We will explore how the Fed regulates the money supply and the difficulties the Fed has in trying to hit its monetary targets. We will also examine the effects that federal budget deficits have on the money supply and on Federal Reserve decision-making. To work our way around these important policy issues requires a fair amount of attention to the nitty gritty; but that's what it's all about.

SUMMARY

1. The dominant figure in the formation and execution of monetary policy is the Chairman of the Board of Governors of the Federal Reserve System. The Federal Open Market Committee is the major policy-making body within the System. It is composed of the seven members of the Board of Governors and five Reserve Bank presidents.

2. The Federal Reserve is accountable to the Congress but is legally independent of the executive branch of government. This semi-independent status of the Federal Reserve has been a source of frequent conflict. It is defended on the ground that the central bank must have considerable independence to counteract the natural propensity of governments to resort to inflationary methods of financing themselves.

Suggestions for Further Reading

For a formal description of the Federal Reserve's structure, read *The Federal Reserve System: Purposes and Functions*, 7th ed. (Washington, D.C.: Board of Governors of the Federal Reserve System, 1984). On the internal workings of the Fed, see C. R. Whittlesey, "Power and Influence in the Federal Reserve System," *Economica* (February 1963); David P. Eastburn, "The Federal Reserve as a Living Institution," in *Men, Money, and Policy: Essays in Honor* of Karl R. Bopp (Federal Reserve Bank of Philadelphia, 1970); and Jane W. D'Arista, *Federal Reserve Structure and the Development of Monetary Policy* (Staff Report, House Committee on Banking and Currency, U.S. Congress, 1971). A particularly interesting study on the internal operations of the Federal Reserve is by Thomas Havrilesky, William P. Yohe, and David Schirm, "The Economic Affiliations of Directors of Federal Reserve District Banks," *Social Science Quarterly* (December 1973).

A recent widely-discussed book on the Fed is William Greider's *Secrets of the Temple: How the Federal Reserve Runs the Country* (New York: Simon & Schuster, 1987).

For the real flavor and excitement of central banking, two books are *must* reading: Marriner Eccles's autobiography, *Beckoning Frontiers* (New York: Knopf, 1951); and the *Selected Papers of Allan Sproul,* published by the Federal Reserve Bank of New York in 1980 (you can get a copy of the Sproul book for free if you write to the Federal Reserve Bank of New York and ask for it). Mariner Eccles was a member of the Board of Governors from 1934 to 1951 and its Chairman from 1934 to 1948. Allan Sproul was president of the Federal Reserve Bank of New York from 1941 to 1956.

Finally, for an insightful look at the Fed in recent years, emphasizing the human element in policy-making, see Cary Reich, "Inside the Fed," *Institutional Investor* (May 1984).

CHAPTER 14

Bank Reserves and the Money Supply

Now that we know who is responsible for our nation's monetary policy, let's see exactly how the Federal Reserve goes about doing its job. It will take all of four chapters to really understand exactly what is going on. We know from our overview in Chapter 2 that the money supply plays an important role in helping to determine overall economic activity. We also suggested that there is a connection between the Federal Reserve, bank reserves, and the money supply. Although it is possible to explore the details in any number of ways, we take the following approach. In this chapter we examine the relationship between bank reserves and the money supply. In Chapter 15 we survey the tools available to the Federal Reserve to carry out its objectives. In Chapter 16 we focus precisely on the connection between the Fed's tools and bank reserves. And finally, in Chapter 17 we tie things together by examining how the Federal Reserve establishes its targets and carries out its game plan.

As we saw in Chapter 1, most of our country's money supply does not consist of coins and dollar bills. Rather, the money supply is composed mainly of demand deposits (checking accounts) in commercial banks and in other kinds of financial institutions. In Chapter 2, we briefly explored how bank reserves play a crucial role in creating those demand deposits. Now it's time to examine the process in much greater detail; it is by regulating the reserves of banks and other finan-

183

cial institutions that the Federal Reserve gets sufficient leverage to control the aggregate amount of demand deposits in the country and thereby the nation's money supply.

CHECK CLEARING AND COLLECTION

We already know a lot about how financial institutions work from Chapter 4 in Part 1 and from all the chapters in Part 2, but a quick review won't hurt. This time we're going to change our perspective and focus on demand deposits in particular and especially on the relationship between reserves and demand deposits. To really understand what's going on, let's go into the banking business.

Assume that we sell stock and raise $5 million to start a bank, that we buy a building for $1 million and open our doors for business. Our bank's balance sheet on opening day would look like this:

ASSETS		LIABILITIES AND NET WORTH	
Cash	$4,000,000	Net Worth	$5,000,000
Building, etc.	1,000,000		

The balance sheet could stand some improvement. Too much cash. Doesn't earn any interest. So we immediately take three-quarters of the cash and buy government bonds with it. The T-account, showing the *changes* that occur in our balance sheet, looks like this:

A		L & NW
Cash	− $3,000,000	
Government bonds	+ 3,000,000	

Next, for purposes that will become clear shortly, we take another $900,000 and ship it to our regional Federal Reserve Bank, to open up a deposit in our bank's name:

A		L & NW
Cash	−$900,000	
Deposit in Fed	+ 900,000	

During the course of the first few days, we gleefully welcome long lines of new depositors who open up accounts with us by depositing $2 million worth of checks drawn on *other* banks—where they are closing out their accounts, because they like our ambience better. Our T-account for these deposits is as follows:

A	L & NW
Cash items in process of collection +$2,000,000	Demand deposits +$2,000,000

A demand deposit in a bank is an asset for the depositor. It is part of the depositor's wealth. For the bank, however, it is a *liability*, a debt, because the bank is obligated to pay it—indeed, to pay it *on demand*. A demand deposit must be paid any time the depositor wishes, either by handing out currency across the counter or by transferring the funds to someone else upon the depositor's order. That is precisely what a check is: a depositor's order to a bank to transfer funds to whoever is named on the check, or to whoever has endorsed it on the back.

We now have $2 million of checks drawn on other banks that our new customers have deposited with us. We have to "collect" these checks; so far they are just "cash items in process of collection." If we had the time, we could take each check to the bank on which it is drawn, ask for currency over the counter, and then haul it back to our own bank. Since this would get tedious if we had to do it every day, what we do instead is what other banks do: rely on the Federal Reserve to help us in the check collection process. Federal Reserve Banks play a pivotal role in collecting checks, so vital that we must digress a moment to see how they do it.

As we saw in the last chapter, there are twelve Federal Reserve Banks around the country—in New York, Atlanta, Dallas, Minneapolis, San Francisco, and so on. Every deposit-type financial institution is affiliated with one of them. The Federal Reserve Banks themselves have little direct contact with the public; mostly they deal with the government and with financial institutions. Through facilities they provide, however, checks are efficiently collected and funds transferred around the country. The primary collection vehicle is the deposit that each financial institution maintains with its regional Federal Reserve Bank, which is one reason we deposited $900,000 in our Federal Reserve Bank two T-accounts back.

Let's see how the collection process works. We take the $2 million worth of checks our new customers have deposited, checks drawn on other banks, and ship the whole batch of them to the Federal Reserve Bank. The Fed credits us with these checks by increasing our "deposit in the Fed" by that amount. At the same time, it *deducts* $2 million from the "deposits in the Fed" of the banks on which the checks were drawn. It sends these checks to the appropriate banks, with a slip notifying them of the deduction, and the banks in turn deduct the proper amounts from their depositors' accounts. The T-accounts of the whole check collection process look like this, with the arrows showing the direction in which the checks move:

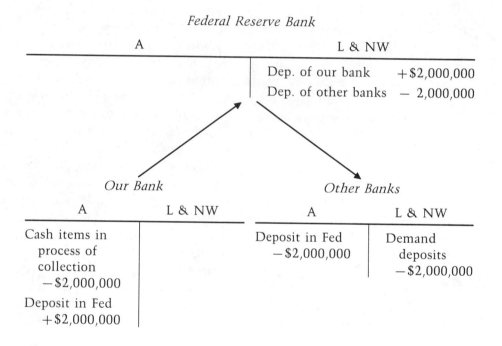

We can summarize this collection process in a few words. When a bank receives a check drawn on another bank, it gains deposits in the Fed equal to the amount of the check. Conversely, the bank on which the check was drawn loses deposits in the Fed of the same amount.[1] We will see soon that deposits in the Fed are part of a bank's reserves.

[1]Notice that the deposits of banks in the Federal Reserve Bank are *liabilities* of the Federal Reserve Bank (although assets of the commercial banks), just as deposits of the public in a commercial bank are liabilities of the bank (although assets of the depositors).

We can rephrase the above into an important banking principle: *When a bank receives a check drawn on another bank, it gains reserves equal to the amount of the check. Conversely, the bank on which the check was drawn loses reserves of the same amount.*

Two minor complications. One: What if some of the institutions involved are not members of the Federal Reserve System? No problem. All financial institutions that accept checkable deposits, whether they are member banks or not, must hold reserves in the form of either vault cash or deposits with the Fed (or with another bank that in turn holds them with the Fed). So they will either clear checks directly through the Fed or clear them indirectly through arrangements with a so-called correspondent bank that holds such reserves. Two: What if the two financial institutions involved are in different Federal Reserve Districts, so they have deposits in two *different* Federal Reserve Banks? Again no problem. The Federal Reserve has its own Inter-District Settlement Fund, where the twelve Federal Reserve Banks all hold accounts, and they settle up in such cases by transferring balances among themselves on the books of the Inter-District Settlement Fund.

So where do we stand now? Let's take a look at our bank's balance sheet, after all the above transactions have been incorporated into it:

A		L & NW	
Cash	$ 100,000	Demand deposits	$2,000,000
Deposit in Fed	2,900,000	Net worth	5,000,000
Government bonds	3,000,000		
Building, etc.	1,000,000		

Looking at this balance sheet reminds us that according to law commercial banks and other deposit-type financial institutions have to hold part of their assets in the form of reserves. As mentioned above, all banks are required to hold reserves—*in the form of either cash or deposits in the Fed*—as specified by the Board of Governors of the Federal Reserve. How does our bank stand with respect to reserves? To simplify matters, let's assume that all banks, ours included, have to hold reserves equal to a flat 10 percent of demand deposits.

We *have* reserves—cash and/or deposits in the Fed—of $3 million. With demand deposits of $2 million, we *need* reserves equal to 10 percent of that figure, or $200,000, to satisfy our legal obligation. Thus we have *excess* reserves of $2.8 million. That simple calculation, computing the amount of a bank's excess reserves, is crucially important in the banking business.

What should we do now? Unfortunately, with this balance sheet we are not too profitable. We have a lot of excess reserves that are earning no interest, and not enough income-producing assets. All we have in the way of interest-bearing assets is the $3 million of government bonds we bought. Banks make profits mostly by making loans, earning the difference between the interest charged on the loan and the cost of deposits. Surely we can hustle up some good loans—preferably to people who don't need the money, because they are obviously the ones who deserve it most (and are most likely to pay us back).

Let's assume we can find enough creditworthy borrowers who want to take out loans. Then a big question faces us: *how much can we safely lend without endangering our legal reserve position?*

DEPOSIT EXPANSION: THE SINGLE BANK

To answer the question of how much we can safely lend, we need to know two things: (1) how much excess reserves we have, and (2) what happens when we make a loan. We already know how much excess reserves we have—$2.8 million. So let's take a moment to examine what happens when we make a loan.

When a bank lends, the borrower does not ordinarily take the proceeds in hundred-dollar bills; more likely, the borrower takes a brand-new checking account instead. On the bank's balance sheet, loans (an asset) and demand deposits (a liability) both rise. A bank *creates* a demand deposit when it lends. In effect, since demand deposits are money, banks create money.

How much, then, can we lend? Since the only limit on our creation of demand deposits appears to be the requirement that we hold a 10 percent reserve, a superficial answer would be that we can lend—and create demand deposits—up to a limit of ten times our excess reserves. We have excess reserves of $2.8 million, so why not lend ten times that, or $28 million? If we did, here is what would happen:[2]

A		L & NW	
Loans	+$28,000,000	Demand deposits	+$28,000,000

[2]Actually, a bank would typically "discount" the loan—that is, deduct the interest in advance, giving the borrowers somewhat less than $28 million. For the sake of convenience, let's ignore this detail.

And our new balance sheet would look like this:

A		L & NW	
Reserves { Cash	$ 100,000	Demand deposits	$30,000,000
Deposit in Fed	2,900,000	Net worth	5,000,000
Government bonds	3,000,000		
Loans	28,000,000		
Building, etc.	1,000,000		

We now have some good news and some bad news. First the good news: we have a fairly large amount of demand deposit liabilities—$30 million—and our reserves, at $3 million, are legally sufficient to support them. It appears we have found a veritable gold mine. In business hardly a month, only a $5 million investment, and here we are collecting the interest on $3 million of government bonds *and* $28 million of loans.

But wait a minute, because here comes the bad news: we haven't really looked into what happens *after* a borrower takes out a loan. Most borrowers don't take out loans and pay interest on them just to leave the funds sitting there. They want to *spend* the money. And when they do, they'll write checks on those brand-new demand deposits. The checks will probably be deposited in *other* banks by their recipients, and when they clear through the Federal Reserve we'll *lose reserves*. (Remember that a bank on which a check is drawn loses reserves equal to the amount of the check.) Thus, for our bank:

A		L&NW	
Deposit in Fed	−$28,000,000	Demand deposits	−$28,000,000

If our deposits in the Fed are only $2.9 million to begin with, we can hardly stand by calmly while they fall by $28 *million*. We'll wind up in jail instead of on the Riviera. Something has clearly gone very wrong. What has gone wrong, obviously, is that we miscalculated our lending limit, the amount we could safely lend—"safely" meaning without endangering our legal reserve position.

What, then, is our safe lending limit? It is the amount of reserves we can afford to lose, and we already know what that is: our *excess reserves. A bank can lend up to the amount of its excess reserves, and no more.* If it tries to lend more, it will find itself with inadequate reserves as soon as the borrowers spend the proceeds of the loans and the checks are collected through the Federal Reserve's check-collection facilities.

So let's start over again. Our excess reserves are $2.8 million. If we lend that amount, our balance sheet entry is:

	A		L & NW	
Loans	+$2,800,000		Demand deposits	+$2,800,000

When the borrowers spend the funds, assuming the checks are deposited in other banks, we have:

	A		L & NW	
Deposit in Fed	−$2,800,000		Demand deposits	−$2,800,000

Which leaves our balance sheet as follows:

	A		L & NW	
Reserves	Cash	$ 100,000	Demand deposits	$2,000,000
	Deposit in Fed	100,000	Net worth	5,000,000
	Government bonds	3,000,000		
	Loans	2,800,000		
	Building, etc.	1,000,000		

Now, after all checks have cleared, we end up with deposits of $2 million and reserves of $200,000, which is right on the dot; our reserves equal one-tenth of our deposits. But notice that we got there by shrinking our reserves, *not* by expanding our deposits (as in the previous disastrous example). We shrank our reserves by lending an amount equal to the excess, which resulted in an equivalent reduction in our reserves in the ordinary course of events.[3]

---

[3]*An important note:* Calculation of excess reserves to estimate lending ability should always be made *prior* to extending new loans, without including the reserves needed to support the new loan-created deposits. For example, after we made the $2.8 million of loans noted above, demand deposits went up by the same amount, so that required reserves rose by $280,000. But that $280,000 increase in required reserves does not

Notice also that the purchase of securities would have the same effect on reserves as lending, except that the drop in reserves would probably occur even more rapidly. If we bought securities for the bank, we would generally not open a deposit account for the seller but simply pay with a check drawn on the bank (payable via our account at the Fed). As soon as the check cleared, our reserves would fall by that amount.

The conclusion of this section is worth emphasizing: a single bank cannot safely lend (or buy securities) in an amount greater than its excess reserves, as calculated *before* it makes the loan. But it *can* lend or buy securities up to the amount of its excess reserves without endangering its legal reserve position.

An individual bank can therefore create money (demand deposits), but only if it has excess reserves to begin with. As soon as it has created this money—in our case, $2.8 million—it *loses* it to another bank when the money is spent. This is the key to the difference between the ability of a single bank to create money as compared with the banking system as a whole.

DEPOSIT EXPANSION: THE BANKING SYSTEM

When we lent our $2.8 million and created demand deposits of that amount for the borrowers, they soon spent the funds, and we lost both the newly created deposits and reserves of a like amount. That ended *our* ability to lend. But in the check-clearing process, some other banks *gained* $2.8 million of deposits and reserves, and those other banks can expand *their* lending, for now *they* have excess reserves.

Let's simplify our calculations at this point and assume that instead of having excess reserves of $2.8 million and lending that amount, we had excess reserves of only $1,000 and had lent that. This will make the numbers easier to work with. When the checks cleared, some other banks would have gained $1,000 of deposits and reserves, and those other banks could now continue the process, for they now have excess

---

affect our lending ability, because so long as those $2.8 million of deposits are there, our reserves are more than ample. It is not until those loan-created deposits disappear—when the borrowers write checks on their new deposits—that our reserves will drop, as the checks are collected in favor of other banks through the Federal Reserve. By that time, however, we won't need reserves against those deposits, since they will no longer be on our books.

reserves. If the entire $1,000 were deposited in one bank (Bank B), that bank's T-account would look like this:

Bank B

A		L & NW	
Deposit in Fed	+$1,000	Demand deposits	+$1,000

Bank B can now make loans and create additional demand deposits. Assuming it was all loaned up (that it had zero excess reserves) before it received this deposit, how much could Bank B lend? Less than we did, because its excess reserves are not $1,000 but only $900—it has new reserves of $1,000, but it needs $100 of that as reserves against the $1,000 deposit.

If Bank B does indeed make a $900 loan, we should start to sense what is going to happen. Its loans and deposits will both rise by $900, and when the borrowers spend the funds its *reserves* and deposits will both fall by the same amount. Net result: Its demand deposits will drop back to $1,000, its reserves to $100, and its lending (and money-creating) ability will be exhausted.

However, when Bank B's borrowers spend their $900, giving checks to people who deposit them in other banks (such as Bank C), the very check-clearing process that takes reserves and deposits away from Bank B transfers them *to* Bank C:

Bank C

A		L & NW	
Deposit in Fed	+$900	Demand deposits	+$900

Now Bank C can carry the torch. It can lend and create new demand deposits up to the amount of *its* excess reserves, which are $810. As the process is repeated, Bank D can lend $729 (creating that much additional demand deposits), Bank E can lend $656.10, Bank F $590.49, and so on. Because the reserve requirement is 10 percent, each bank in the sequence gets excess reserves, lends, and creates new demand deposits equal to 90 percent of the preceding one. If we add $1,000 + $900 + $810 + $729 + $656.10 + . . . the summation of the series approaches $10,000.

When expansion has approached its $10,000 limit, the banking *system* will have demand deposits that are a multiple of its reserves—demand deposits will be $10,000 on the liabilities side and reserves $1,000 on the asset side for all banks taken together. (At the same time, of course, banks will also have $9,000 in other assets—loans, in our example.) For the banking system, this final stage is reached not by shrinking reserves, as in the case of a single bank, but by expanding deposits. The key: While each individual bank loses reserves after it lends—in the check-clearing process—some bank always gains the reserves another bank loses, so reserves for the entire banking system do not change. They just get transferred from bank to bank. However, as banks lend more and more, demand deposit liabilities grow, thereby reducing *excess* reserves even though the total reserves of the system do not change. This continuous decline in excess reserves eventually sets a limit on further expansion.

In more general terms, how much can the banking system expand demand deposits? While a single bank can lend (and create demand deposits) only up to the amount of its excess reserves, the banking *system* can create demand deposits up to a *multiple* of an original injection of excess reserves.

The particular expansion multiple for the banking system depends on the prevailing required reserve ratio. In our example, with a reserve requirement of $\frac{1}{10}$, the multiple is ten (an original increase of $1,000 in excess reserves can lead to an eventual $10,000 increase in demand deposits). If the reserve requirement were $\frac{1}{5}$, the multiple would be five (an original increase of $1,000 in excess reserves could lead to a potential $5,000 increase in demand deposits). In general, *the demand deposit expansion multiplier is always the reciprocal of the reserve requirement ratio.* In brief, for the entire banking system:

$$\text{original excess reserves} \times \frac{1}{\text{reserve ratio}} = \frac{\text{potential change in}}{\text{demand deposits}}$$

We can derive this formula more formally. We have been assuming that each bank lends out all of its excess reserves. The process of deposit expansion can continue until all excess reserves become required reserves because of deposit growth; then no more deposit expansion can take place. At that point, total reserves (R) will equal the required reserve ratio on demand deposits (r_{dd}) times total demand deposits (DD). That is:

$$R = r_{dd} \times DD$$

Dividing both sides of the equation by r_{dd} (which is a legal operation even in the banking business) produces:

$$\frac{R}{r_{dd}} = \frac{r_{dd} \times DD}{r_{dd}}$$

$$R \times \frac{1}{r_{dd}} = DD$$

Using the familiar delta (Δ) sign to denote "change in," we have:

$$\Delta R \times \frac{1}{r_{dd}} = \Delta D$$

where the change in reserves initially produces excess reserves in that amount until demand deposits are created in sufficient magnitude by the banks to put all the reserves in the required category.[4]

DEPOSIT CONTRACTION

A change in demand deposits can, of course, be down as well as up, negative as well as positive. If we start with a *deficiency* in reserves in the formula, a negative excess, the potential change in demand deposits is negative rather than positive. Instead of money being *created* by banks when they lend or buy securities, money is *destroyed* as bank loans are repaid or securities sold.

When someone repays a bank loan, the bank has fewer loans outstanding and at the same time deducts the amount repaid from the

---

[4]An even more formal derivation of the relationship between changes in reserves and changes in deposits uses the formula for the sum of the (geometric) series discussed above in the text. In particular, the change in demand deposits due to an increase in reserves can be expressed as follows:

$$\Delta DD = \Delta R \left[1 + (1 - r_{dd}) + (1 - r_{dd})^2 + \ldots + (1 - r_{dd})^n \right]$$

There is a formula (white and bubbly) which gives the sum of the geometric progression within the brackets. As n gets infinitely large, the formula becomes:

$$\frac{1}{1 - (1 - r_{dd})} = \frac{1}{r_{dd}}$$

or, believe it or not:

$$\Delta DD = \Delta R \times \frac{1}{r_{dd}}$$

borrower's demand deposit balance. There are fewer demand deposits in existence; money has disappeared. Similarly, if a bank sells a bond to one of its own depositors, it takes payment by reducing the depositor's checking account balance. If it sells a bond to a depositor in another bank, the other bank winds up with fewer demand deposit liabilities.

The potential multiple contraction in demand deposits follows the same principles discussed above for the potential expansion of demand deposits, with one exception: the entire downward multiple change in demand deposits could conceivably take place in one single bank.

Say that a bank has a $1,000 reserve deficiency. It is then faced with two stark alternatives: it must either (a) increase its reserves by $1,000 or (b) decrease its demand deposits by ten times $1,000, or $10,000 (assuming a reserve requirement of 10 percent).

Let's take the second alternative first. The bank could decrease its demand deposits by the entire $10,000 by demanding repayment of that many loans or by selling that many securities *to its own depositors.* Loans (or bonds) would drop by $10,000 on the asset side, demand deposits would drop by the same amount on the liabilities side, and the reserve deficiency would be eliminated. In this case, the single bank alone bears the entire multiple decrease in the money supply.

It is more likely that the bank will choose the first option, increasing its reserves by $1,000. One way it could go about this is by borrowing $1,000 in reserves from the Federal Reserve, an alternative we will discuss more fully in the following chapter. Another way is by selling $1,000 of bonds on the open market, making the reasonable assumption that they will be bought by depositors in other banks (our bank being just a little fish in a veritable sea of banks). After the checks are cleared, the bank's deposits in the Fed will be $1,000 higher, and its reserves will be adequate once again.

But the reserves gained by Bank A will be another bank's loss. Some other bank—the bank where the purchaser of the bond kept the account—has lost $1,000 of deposits and $1,000 of reserves. Assuming that this second bank, Bank B, had precisely adequate reserves before this transaction, it now has a $900 reserve deficiency. It has lost $1,000 of reserves, but its requirements are $100 lower because it has also lost $1,000 of demand deposits, so its deficiency is only $900.

Bank B will now have no choice but to (a) get $900 in additional reserves, or (b) reduce its demand deposits by ten times $900, or $9,000. If it sells $900 of bonds to depositors in other banks, it gets its reserves, but in doing so it puts the other banks $810 in the hole.

Thus the multiple contraction process continues very much like the multiple expansion process ($1,000 + $900 + $810 + $729 + $656.10 + . . .), and the summation of the series again approaches $10,000. At each stage, the bank that sells securities gains reserves, but at the expense of other banks, since the buyers of the bonds pay by checks that are cleared via the transfer of reserves on the books of the Federal Reserve Bank. Reserve deficiencies are shuffled from bank to bank, just as in the expansion process reserve excesses are shuffled from one bank to another.

There is a difference, however. When banks get *excess* reserves, they *may* lend more and increase the money supply; when they have *deficient* reserves, they *must* reduce their demand deposits. We usually assume that banks will want to lend out all their excess reserves and expand demand deposits to the maximum, because they earn interest on the loans generated in the process, and the interest earned on the loans exceeds the interest cost of the source of funds, demand deposits. But there can be exceptions, as we will see in the Appendix to this chapter.

Control over bank reserves thus gives the Federal Reserve considerable power over demand deposits, which you may recall from Chapter 1 are the major component of the M1 measure of the money supply. Thus, if the Fed can inject excess reserves into the banking system, it can *permit* commercial banks to expand the money supply by a multiple of the injection. If it can impose a deficit reserve position on the banking system, it can *force* a multiple reduction in the money supply.

In the following chapter we will see exactly how the Fed goes about changing the level of reserves available to the banking system. First, however, the Appendix adds a few complicating elements to deposit creation that we have so far ignored in the interest of simplicity.

SUMMARY

1. All deposit-type financial institutions are legally required to hold reserves, in the form of either vault cash or deposits in their local Federal Reserve Bank.

2. When a bank receives a check drawn on another bank, it gains reserves (through the clearing process) equal to the amount of the check. Conversely, the bank on which the check is drawn loses reserves of the same amount.

3. A single bank can safely lend, and create demand deposits, up to the amount of its excess reserves. If it tries to lend more, it will find itself short

of reserves as soon as the borrowers spend the proceeds of the loans and the checks clear through the Fed's check-collection facilities.

4. However, the banking system as a whole can lend, and create demand deposits, up to a multiple of an original injection of excess reserves. The demand deposit expansion multiplier is the reciprocal of the reserve requirement ratio.

5. A bank with deficient reserves must either (a) increase its reserves by the amount of the deficiency or (b) reduce its demand deposits by a multiple of the deficiency. Again, the multiple is the reciprocal of the reserve requirement.

6. Banks with excess reserves *may* lend more and increase the money supply. Banks with deficient reserves *must* either increase their reserves or reduce their demand deposits.

Suggestions for Further Reading

In case you feel you don't have a firm grasp of the basic principles underlying deposit expansion and contraction, try reading Dorothy M. Nichols's excellent pamphlet, *Modern Money Mechanics: A Workbook on Deposits, Currency, and Bank Reserves*, which is available free from the Federal Reserve Bank of Chicago (P.O. Box 834, Chicago, Illinois 60690).

Three Complications

The previous discussion suggested that it would be fairly easy for the Fed to generate just about any money supply it wanted. In this Appendix we show that such a view is rather naïve.

In terms of our formula from the chapter, a change in bank reserves (ΔR) times the reciprocal of the demand deposit reserve ratio (r_{dd}) gives us the maximum potential change in demand deposits (ΔDD). Say the reserve requirement against demand deposits (all checking accounts) is 15 percent and the Fed increases bank reserves by \$1,000:

$$\Delta R \times \frac{1}{r_{dd}} = \Delta DD$$

$$\Delta R \times \frac{1}{.15} = \Delta DD$$

$$\Delta R \times 6\frac{2}{3} = \Delta DD$$

$$\$1,000 \times 6\frac{2}{3} = \$6,667$$

The actual change in demand deposits will reach the maximum of $6,667 as long as banks lend out all their excess reserves. If we were to draw up a consolidated T-account for the entire banking system following this $1,000 injection of reserves, showing the changes that take place in the balance sheets of all banks taken together, our formula tells us it would look like this:

Final Position, All Banks Taken Together
($1,000 change in reserves; r_{dd} = 15 percent)

A		L & NW	
Reserves		Demand deposits	+$6,667
(cash + deposit in Fed)	+$1000		
Loans and securities	+ 5,667		

But this is just the first approximation. Looking a bit deeper, we find that fundamental difficulties face the Fed in its efforts to control the money supply, even with such precision like formulas. These problems can be categorized into three main complications.

1. The simple case abstracts from the fact that, *as demand deposits expand, the public is likely to want to hold part of its increased money supply in the form of currency.* When people need more currency, they simply go to their bank and cash a check. On the bank's balance sheet, both cash (an asset) and demand deposits (a liability) fall. The bank's excess reserves also fall by 85 percent of the withdrawal, assuming a 15 percent reserve ratio.

Notice that a $100 currency withdrawal does not directly change the public's money holdings; it simply switches $100 from demand deposits to dollar bills, leaving the total money supply unaltered. But it *does* deplete bank excess reserves by $85, because a $100 demand deposit uses up only $15 in reserves, whereas a $100 cash withdrawal subtracts a full $100 of reserves (remember that cash in bank vaults counts as reserves). Draining of currency into the hands of the public thus depletes bank reserves dollar for dollar and thereby cuts back the expansion potential of the banking system.

Let's assume that for every $1 in demand deposits, the public wants currency holdings of about 30 cents. That is, the ratio of currency to demand deposits (c/dd) is about 30 percent. This, of course, alters our demand deposit expansion formula. It is fairly easy to see the changes that are necessary: what we have to do is incorporate the currency/demand deposit ratio into the formula.

We continue to assume that banks lend out all their excess reserves. We saw in our chapter that demand deposits could expand until all excess reserves become required reserves (because of deposit growth)—that is, until the demand deposit reserve requirement (r_{dd}) times the growth in demand deposits (ΔDD) equals the change in reserves (ΔR).

But now, when reserves rise initially by ΔR, not only will they be absorbed by demand deposit growth, but in addition some of these reserves will *leave* the banking system as the public holds more currency (equal to c/dd times the growth in demand deposits). Although banks will still expand their demand deposits until all reserves are in the required category, *they will be unable to retain all the initial change in reserves.* Since the initial injection of reserves eventually winds up as either required reserves or as currency held by the public, we have:

$$\Delta R = (r_{dd} \times \Delta DD) + (c/dd \times \Delta DD)$$

Factoring out the ΔDDs gives us:

$$\Delta R = (r_{dd} + c/dd) \times \Delta DD$$

and finally:

$$\Delta R \times \frac{1}{r_{dd} + c/dd} = \Delta DD$$

where the *initial change* in reserves (ΔR) is no longer fully retained within the banking system, because part leaks out into currency holdings outside the system. This total—reserves plus currency outside the banks—is the *monetary base* (B). When the Federal Reserve injects reserves, it is really adding to the monetary base, since some of these reserves will shift over into the form of currency holdings outside the banking system.

Let us now return, with our new formula, to our illustrative example. Assume a currency/demand deposit ratio of 30 percent, along with our 15 percent demand deposit reserve requirement, and our familiar injection of $1,000 of reserves by the Fed. Because of the currency drain, the $1,000 of additional reserves are not all kept by the banks, so that in our new formula we should properly refer to a $1,000 increase in the monetary base (B) rather than in reserves. What we get, after all is said and done, is a multiple expansion potential for demand deposits that is considerably smaller than before—now it is not 6.67, but only 2.22:[1]

$$\Delta B \times \frac{1}{r_{dd} + c/dd} = \Delta DD$$

$$\Delta B \times \frac{1}{.15 + .30} = \Delta DD$$

$$\Delta B \times \frac{1}{.45} = \Delta DD$$

$$\Delta B \times 2.22 = \Delta DD$$

$$\$1,000 \times 2.22 = \$2,222$$

Now an initial $1,000 injection of reserves produces an eventual maximum increase in demand deposits of only $2,222. If we again draw up a consolidated T-account for all banks, following a $1,000 initial boost to reserves, the final results will look like this:

Final Position, All Banks Taken Together
($1,000 initial change in reserves; r_{dd} = 15 percent;
and now adding cash drain: c/dd = 30 percent)

A		L & NW
Reserves		Demand deposits + $2,222
(cash + deposit in Fed)	+ $333	
Loans and securities	+ 1,889	

Memorandum: currency drain (i.e., currency outside the banks, held by the public): + $667

Notice that, because of the currency drain, the banking system *retains* as reserves only $333 of the original $1,000. With a 15 percent reserve requirement, this amount can support demand deposits of only $2,222. The other $667 has moved *out* of the banking system into the hands of the general public, on the premise that the public wants to

[1]This multiplier is strictly correct only if ΔB is initially all reserves.

hold 30 cents more currency when it gets \$1 more demand deposits (667 = 30% of 2,222).

The total change in the M1 measure of the *money supply* due to the *initial* change in reserves (= change in the monetary base) is the sum of the change in demand deposits and the change in currency. We have just seen that currency goes up by 30 percent of 2,222, or more generally:

$$\Delta \text{currency} = c/dd \times \Delta DD = c/dd \times \frac{1}{r_{dd} + c/dd} \times \Delta B$$

Hence, the total change in the money supply (ΔM) due to the initial change in reserves is:

$$\Delta M = \Delta DD + \Delta \text{currency}$$

$$= \frac{1}{r_{dd} + c/dd} \times \Delta B + \frac{c/dd}{r_{dd} + c/dd} \times \Delta B$$

which simplifies to:

$$\Delta M = \frac{1 + c/dd}{r_{dd} + c/dd} \times \Delta B$$

Using our numbers, the money supply multiplier is 2.889:

$$\Delta M = 2.889 \times \$1,000 = \$2,889$$

which is \$2,222 in demand deposits and \$667 in currency. This formula relating the change in money supply to an initial change in reserves is a lot more complicated than the simple inverse of the required reserve ratio that we derived in our chapter.

2. In the second place, we have to recognize that *banks have time deposits as well as demand deposits among their liabilities, and that these also require reserves.* To see how this affects the deposit multiplier, let's assume a reserve requirement on such deposits of 3 percent. While this is not as large as the reserve requirement against demand deposits, it does serve to absorb bank reserves and thereby further reduces the demand deposit expansion potential of the system. Assume further that the public wants to hold a ratio of commercial bank time deposits to demand deposits (td/dd) of about two to one. Since the reserve requirement against such deposits (r_{td}) averages 3 percent, this has to affect our demand deposit expansion formula. Using the

same logic as before, the new demand deposit multiplier turns out to be 1.961:[2]

$$\Delta B \times \frac{1}{r_{dd} + c/dd + td/dd\ (r_{td})} = \Delta DD$$

$$\Delta B \times \frac{1}{.15 + .30 + 2(.03)} = \Delta DD$$

$$\Delta B \times \frac{1}{.15 + .30 + .06} = \Delta DD$$

$$\Delta B \times \frac{1}{.51} = \Delta DD$$

$$\Delta B \times 1.961 = \Delta DD$$

$$\$1,000 \times 1.961 = \$1,961$$

We can extend this expression to the M1 measure of the money supply as a whole (not just demand deposits) by adding the increase in currency in circulation to the increase in demand deposits:

$$\Delta M1 = \Delta DD + \Delta \text{currency} = \frac{1}{r_{dd} + c/dd + (td/dd)\ (r_{td})} \times \Delta B$$

$$+ \frac{c/dd}{r_{dd} + c/dd + (td/dd)\ (r_{td})} \times \Delta B$$

[2]The derivation is as follows: The initial injection of reserves (ΔB) now gets absorbed by required reserves against demand deposits ($r_{dd} \times \Delta DD$); by currency ($c/dd \times \Delta DD$); and by required reserves against time deposits. The increase in time deposits (ΔTD) equals $td/dd \times \Delta DD$, and reserves against time deposits equal $r_{td} \times td/dd \times \Delta DD$. Therefore, we have:

$$\Delta B = (r_{dd} \times \Delta DD) + (c/dd \times \Delta DD) + (td/dd \times r_{td} \times \Delta DD)$$

Factoring out the ΔDDs gives us:

$$\Delta B = [r_{dd} + c/dd + (td/dd \times r_{td})] \times \Delta DD$$

and finally:

$$\Delta B \times \frac{1}{r_{dd} + c/dd + (td/dd)(r_{td})} = \Delta DD$$

which simplifies to:

$$\Delta M1 = \frac{1 + c/dd}{r_{dd} + c/dd + (td/dd)\,(r_{td})} \times \Delta B$$

If you work it out, you'll find that this yields an M1 money supply multiplier of 2.549.

The consolidated bank T-account for an initial $1,000 reserve increase under these circumstances is interesting:

Final Position, All Banks Taken Together
($1,000 initial change in reserves; r_{dd} = 15 percent;
currency drain c/dd = 30 percent; and now adding
time deposit growth: td/dd = 2 and
r_{td} = 3 percent)

A		L & NW	
Reserves (cash + deposit in Fed) + $412		Demand deposits + $1,961	
For demand deposits: + $294			
For time deposits: +118			
Loans and securities + 5,471		Time deposits + 3,922	

Memorandum: currency drain (i.e., currency outside the banks, held by the public): + $588 (= 30% of $1,961)

These results—fewer demand deposits but more total deposits and more bank lending compared with the previous T-account—reflect two things. The currency drain is now less, so the banking system retains more reserves. (The currency drain is less even though the c/dd ratio is the same, because currency outflows depend, by assumption, on the growth of demand deposits only.) And time deposits, while they use up reserves and thereby inhibit potential demand deposit expansion, do not remove reserves from the banking system the way currency drains do; with time deposits, banks can continue lending, and indeed they can lend even *more* than with an equivalent amount of demand deposits, because the reserve requirement against time deposits is lower.

This suggests that the reserve multiplier consequences for broader money supply definitions are still more complicated than for M1. In our last example, associated with a demand deposit multiplier of 1.961 and an M1 multiplier of 2.549, we have an M2 multiplier that is quite a bit larger: namely, 6.471. How do we know? Because we can see that an original reserve injection of $1,000 results in a $588 expansion of currency in circulation, a $1,961 increase in demand deposits, *and* a $3,922 increase in time deposits. These add up to a $6,471 increase in M2.

3. Finally, a last complication: *Banks may not always be willing to expand their loans (or securities purchases) up to the full amount of their excess reserves.* If some banks don't lend all their excess reserves (perhaps because they cannot find enough creditworthy borrowers) and don't buy additional securities (perhaps because they expect bond prices to fall), the whole sequence of lending and demand deposit creation cannot reach its theoretical maximum.

Banks that do not fully expand their loans won't lose all their excess reserves to other banks, so the other banks will be unable to lend as much. In addition, banks that do lend are likely to lose some reserves to the nonlenders, thereby rendering such reserves immobile. Thus the potential multiple can be realized only if *all* banks are willing to lend and/or buy securities up to the *full* amount of their excess reserves.

In the 1930s idle excess reserves were plentiful. In the past few decades most banks have stayed rather fully loaned up, so this has not been so much of a problem. Unused excess reserves have been small in amount and concentrated in small rural banks. But under some circumstances this situation might change. For example, it is quite possible that bank holdings of excess reserves could be a function of interest rates, high rates inducing banks to make more loans and hold less excess reserves, and low rates making it less costly for banks to hold excess reserves (they are not giving up much interest income by not lending). This raises the possibility that the money supply is a function of interest rate levels.

What do all these complications mean for the Federal Reserve, these successive modifications of our original simple demand deposit expansion multiplier? (Remember when it was just the reciprocal of the demand deposit reserve requirement?) They mean, most important, that the Fed's ability to control the money supply, even in its narrow definition, is not nearly as precise as we had originally thought. As it attempts to control the money supply, the central bank has to deal with currency drains, time deposit growth, and bank holdings of idle excess reserves. We can get away with using hypothetical numbers for the multipliers, but for the Fed that is simply not good enough. It has to predict with accuracy the various ratios for the coming weeks and months if it is to succeed in making the money supply what it wants it to be.

Suggestions for Further Reading

For a painstaking derivation of the demand deposit multipliers discussed in this Appendix, and a few others as well, see John T. Boorman and Thomas M. Havrilesky, *Money Supply, Money Demand, and Macroeconomic Models* (Boston: AHM, 1982), pp. 10–41. For an advanced treatment with some historical perspective, see Phillip Cagan, *Determinants and Effects of Changes in the Stock of Money, 1875–1960* (New York: Columbia University Press, 1965).

CHAPTER 15

The Instruments of Central Banking

In the last chapter we saw that bank lending and the money supply were related by some multiple to the level of bank reserves. The Federal Reserve exercises control over bank lending and the money supply by altering the reserves of commercial banks and of other deposit-type institutions and by influencing the deposit creation multiplier. The Fed accomplishes these objectives by changing reserve *requirements* relative to deposits and by changing the actual *amount* of reserves that financial institutions hold. First we'll look at reserve requirements and then we'll see how the Fed varies the actual amount of reserves through the discount rate and open market operations.

RESERVE REQUIREMENTS

Within limits established by Congress, the Federal Reserve can specify the reserve requirements that banks and other deposit-type institutions must hold against deposits. Congressional limits for banks were first established in the Federal Reserve Act of 1913 and reset a number of times since, most recently in the Banking Act of 1980 and the Garn–St. Germain Depository Institutions Act of 1982. This most recent legislation provided that *all* depository institutions—savings banks, savings and loans, and credit unions, as well as *all* commercial banks, whether members of the Federal Reserve System or not—are subject to the Fed's reserve requirements. As of the beginning of 1988 each depository institution had to hold reserves (in the form of vault cash or deposits in a regional Federal Reserve Bank) as follows:

1. Against *demand deposits* and similar checking-type accounts, reserves equal to:
   a. 3 percent of its *first $40 million* of demand deposits.[1]
   b. 12 percent of its demand deposits *in excess of that amount.* The Fed can vary this latter percentage within a range of 8 to 14 percent, and under emergency circumstances it can go as high as 18 percent.

2. Against *business-owned time and savings deposits:* reserves equal to 3 percent of such deposits. The Fed can vary this percentage within a range of zero to 9 percent. The Fed has ruled that the 3 percent requirement should be applied only to such deposits with an original maturity of less than one and a half years; longer maturities have no reserve requirement.

3. Reserve requirements against *personal* time and savings deposits, which used to exist, have been eliminated.

4. Against *borrowing from foreign banks or branches abroad:* reserves equal to 3 percent of the amount borrowed.

5. Finally, regardless of the above requirements, the first $3.2 million of reservable liabilities is *exempt* from reserve requirements. The Fed adjusts this $3.2 million figure upward annually by 80 percent of the annual percentage increase in total reservable liabilities in the country (similar to the annual adjustment mentioned in footnote 1).

Lowering the required reserve ratio for demand deposits—for example, from 12 to 10 percent—does two things. First, it instantly and automatically increases banks' excess reserves, since fewer reserves are now required against any given volume of demand deposits. A bank with demand deposits of $1,000 and reserves of $120 is all loaned up

---

[1]The $40 million figure (actually, $40.5 million) is adjusted upward annually by 80 percent of the annual percentage increase in total transactions accounts in the country. Example: If total transactions accounts in the country rise by 5 percent, the $40 million figure will be increased by 80 percent of 5 percent, which equals 4 percent. Four percent of $40 million equals $1.6 million. Accordingly, at the beginning of 1989 the amount would be increased from $40 million to $41.6 million.

when the reserve requirement is 12 percent; lowering it to 10 percent suddenly provides $20 of excess reserves. More excess reserves, of course, enable banks to make more loans, buy more securities, and expand demand deposits.

In addition, lowering the required reserve ratio also increases the demand deposit expansion *multiplier* for the entire banking system. As we saw in the previous chapter, the multiplier—at least in its simple form—is the reciprocal of the required reserve ratio. The smaller the ratio, the larger its reciprocal. Thus a decrease in the required reserve ratio from 12 percent (or about $\frac{1}{8}$) to 10 percent ($\frac{1}{10}$) would raise the deposit expansion multiplier from about eight to ten.

Raising the required reserve ratio—for example, from 10 to 12 percent—would have the opposite effects. It would create reserve deficiencies, or at least reduce excesses, *and* lower the potential for multiple expansion. Putting banks into a deficit reserve position would *force* them to call in loans and sell securities, bringing about a reduction in demand deposits, while smaller excesses would at least restrain lending and deposit creation.

Since the same reserve requirements apply to nonmember as well as to member commercial banks, membership in the Federal Reserve System has become essentially irrelevant. The problem of dropouts from the Federal Reserve System that occurred during the 1960s and 1970s has been resolved. Banks can no longer escape the requirement to hold zero-interest-bearing reserves by leaving the System. Also, since the same requirements apply to thrift institutions as to commercial banks, the distinction between them—as pointed out in earlier chapters—has become less important.

How crucial are reserve requirements for monetary policy? What would happen if the Federal Reserve eliminated reserve requirements entirely in order to increase bank profits?[2]

[2]Recall that reserve requirements are satisfied by holding vault cash or deposits in a bank's regional Federal Reserve Bank, neither of which earn any interest. Higher reserve requirements thus lower bank profitability by increasing the proportion of assets that yield no income.

The differential impact of reserve requirements on bank profitability was one of the main reasons behind passage of the Banking Act of 1980. Until it was enacted in March of 1980, the Fed's reserve requirements applied only to commercial banks and, further, only to those commercial banks that were members of the Federal Reserve System.

The adverse effect of the Fed's reserve requirements on their earnings led many member banks to reconsider their membership in the Federal Reserve System. Of the roughly 14,000 commercial banks in the United States, about one-third are chartered

Actually, even without formal reserve requirements the Fed would still be in business. Financial institutions would still need both cash to meet customer withdrawals and balances in the Fed to clear checks. As long as they have a demand for claims against the central bank, and as long as the central bank controls the supply of such claims, monetary policy can still work. While the Fed would lose one tool of monetary policy if it could no longer change reserve requirements, it could still influence the behavior of financial institutions.

There is one qualification: the size of the multiplier relationship between reserves and money supply might fluctuate considerably. This would make the job of controlling the money supply more difficult. Not impossible, but more difficult. And as we saw in the Appendix to the previous chapter, things are tough enough already.

DISCOUNTING AND THE DISCOUNT RATE

The Federal Reserve can also alter the excess reserves of banks and other depository institutions by changing the actual amount of reserves that financial institutions hold. One way this is accomplished is through the discount mechanism, by which the Fed lends reserves, temporarily, to the banks. The Fed charges an interest rate, called the discount rate, on such loans. In other words, banks faced with reserve deficits can temporarily borrow reserves from their regional Federal Reserve Bank at a price (the discount rate).

Say that a bank in Cucamonga, California, has a reserve deficiency of $1,000 (it needs $1,000 more reserves than it has). Rather than take the drastic step of calling in loans, and preferring not to sell securities, it can borrow the reserves it needs from the Federal Reserve Bank of San Francisco at the prevailing discount rate. If it did so, the T-accounts would look like this:

---

by the federal government (national banks) and two-thirds are chartered by the state in which they operate (state banks). National banks are *required* to be members of the Federal Reserve System, but state banks are free to join the System or not, as they wish.

During the 1960s and 1970s many state banks withdrew from the Federal Reserve System, giving up their membership to escape the Fed's reserve requirements, and some national banks even turned in their national charters and took out state charters for the same reason. State-administered reserve requirements were typically much lower than the Fed's requirements.

Federal Reserve Bank

A		L & NW	
Loan to Cucamonga Bank	+$1,000	Deposit of Cucamonga Bank	+$1,000

Cucamonga Commercial Bank

A		L & NW	
Deposit in Fed	+$1,000	Due to Fed	+$1,000

When a manufacturer borrows from a bank, the manufacturer receives a brand-new deposit at the bank. A bank is in the same position relative to the Federal Reserve: when it borrows from its friendly neighborhood Federal Reserve Bank, it receives a brand-new deposit at the Fed which increases its legal reserves.[3] The ability to borrow these reserves—to discount from the Fed—means that when it is faced with a reserve deficiency the Cucamonga bank does not have to call in loans or sell securities, and thus the money supply can remain unchanged.

The Federal Reserve tries to influence the willingness of banks to borrow reserves by changing the interest rate it charges on such loans (the discount rate). A lower discount rate will make the borrowing of reserves more attractive to banks, and a higher discount rate will make it less attractive.

The effectiveness of the discount mechanism as a means of injecting or withdrawing reserves is limited by the fact that the initiative for borrowing from the Fed rests not with the Fed but with the banks. Banks will want to borrow reserves only when they need them. If they already have ample reserves, there is no reason for them to borrow more, no matter how low the discount rate. During the 1930s and 1940s, for example, when banks generally had substantial excess reserves, the discount mechanism rusted from disuse, and changes in the discount rate became irrelevant. In recent decades, however, excess reserves have declined and discounting has once again become common, so that changes in the discount rate are more important as a tool of Federal Reserve policy. Nevertheless, since the initiative still rests

[3]Notice that the Cucamonga bank's deposit in the Fed is an asset of the Cucamonga bank, but a liability of the Fed (just as your deposit in a local bank is your asset but the bank's liability).

with the banks rather than with the Fed, the discount process is not a very efficient instrument for the Federal Reserve to use in injecting or withdrawing reserves when *it* wishes to do so.

The Banking Act of 1980 enlarged access to borrowing from the Federal Reserve to *all* depository institutions that have to hold reserves—which means nonmember as well as member commercial banks and also thrift institutions. Previously, only member banks had access to discounting, although in emergencies others could sometimes use it, too. Now, however, nonmember banks and thrift institutions have the same access to borrowing from the Federal Reserve that member banks have, and on exactly the same terms.

Stepping back a moment, we should note that discounting and the discount rate have a long and distinguished history in the evolution of central banking. Indeed, discounting was considered the *main* instrument of central banking throughout the nineteenth century and the first three decades of the twentieth. It reached its apogee in terms of prestige in 1931 (the same year that "The Star-Spangled Banner" was declared the national anthem by act of Congress). At that time, England's Macmillan Committee, somewhat carried away by the splendor of it all, reported that the discount rate "is an absolute necessity for the sound management of a monetary system, and is a most delicate and beautiful instrument for the purpose."[4] This was just at the time when the monetary system of virtually every country was collapsing into ruins, whether it had a delicate and beautiful discount rate or not.

It has been recognized for a long time that discount policy has two dimensions: the first is *price*, the discount rate, the rate of interest the Federal Reserve charges financial institutions when they borrow from the Fed. The second dimension has to do with the *quantity* of Federal Reserve lending, including Federal Reserve surveillance over the amount that each institution borrows and the reasons why it borrows. Let us examine quantity first and price second; each, in its turn, has been credited with the mystique of power that surrounds discounting.

Historically, the primary function of a central bank has been to stand ready to supply funds—promptly and in abundance—whenever the economy is in danger of coming apart at the seams because of a shortage of cash. While that is no longer its sole function, it is still one of its most important. The central bank is the ultimate source of

[4]*Report of the Committee on Finance and Industry* (London: His Majesty's Stationery Office, 1931), p. 97.

liquidity in the economy, because with its power over bank reserves it can increase (or decrease) the ability of the banking system to create money. Since no one else can do the job, it is the central bank that must be responsible for supplying funds promptly on those rare but crucial occasions when liquidity shortages threaten economic stability: "financial panics," the history books call them. Because of this responsibility, the central bank has traditionally been called the "lender of last resort."[5]

When the Federal Reserve Act was passed in 1913, its principal feature was the establishment of a discounting mechanism—facilities through which member banks could temporarily borrow funds from the Fed. Until that time there had been no such mechanism available (indeed, until then there was no central bank in this country, except for brief experiments in 1791 and 1816 with the First Bank and Second Bank of the United States).

The discount facilities instituted by the passage of the Federal Reserve Act in 1913 were supposed to provide a vehicle through which the Federal Reserve could quickly inject funds precisely where needed in order to stop a panic from spreading. Banks threatened with cash drains could borrow what they needed from the Fed—the lender of last resort. Thus they could get more reserves without any other bank losing them and thereby prevent an infection from becoming a plague.

In the ordinary course of events, however, bank use of the discount facility is rather routine, not at all panic-oriented, with banks borrowing here and there to make short-run adjustments in their reserves with no fuss or bother. A bank may find itself with an unexpected reserve deficit, for example, and need to borrow a few million to tide itself over the weekend.

The Fed has always stressed that ordinary run-of-the-mill borrowing of this sort (as contrasted with crisis situations) should not be used *too* often to get banks out of reserve difficulties. Banks should run their affairs so they do not have to rely on the Fed to bail them out every few weeks. Or, as the Federal Reserve usually puts it, discounting is considered a privilege, not a right, and privileges should not be

---

[5]The principle of the central bank as "lender of last resort" was eloquently articulated as long ago as 1873 by Walter Bagehot in *Lombard Street,* the first full-blown exposition of what central banking is all about. Many of his ideas stemmed from Henry Thornton's *An Enquiry into the Nature and Effects of the Paper Credit of Great Britain,* which was published in 1802.

"There's a run on the bank!"

Drawing by Robt. Day; © 1969 The New Yorker Magazine, Inc.

abused. Federal Reserve surveillance enforces the "privilege, not a right" concept by checking up on banks that borrow too much or too frequently.[6] A bank is supposed to borrow only because of *need*, and not go out and make a *profit* on the deal.

In particular, the Fed is sensitive to the possibility that banks may borrow from it and then turn around and use the money to purchase higher-yielding securities. The Fed does not want a bank borrowing from it at a 10 percent discount rate and then using the funds to buy a short-term security yielding 12 percent. Nor does the Fed like it when a bank borrows from it too often, in effect using the discount facility as a more or less permanent source of funds.

One Fed method of preventing "abuse" of the discount facility is tighter surveillance procedures: it checks up on why banks are borrowing and what they are doing with the money. Another way is simply to raise the price of borrowing—which brings us to the discount rate itself.

[6]In 1973, however, the Fed introduced a special "seasonal borrowing privilege" that encourages small banks to borrow to cover most of their recurring reserve needs arising from seasonal swings in loans or deposits (as happens to banks in agricultural and resort areas).

THE DISCOUNT RATE AND MARKET INTEREST RATES

The objective of changing the discount rate is just what the Federal Reserve says it is: a higher discount rate discourages borrowing from the Fed, and a lower discount rate encourages it. These results flow from the least-cost alternatives facing banks with reserve deficiencies. A higher discount rate makes it relatively more advantageous to sell securities to get additional reserves, and a lower discount rate makes it relatively more advantageous to borrow from the Fed. Actually, "higher" and "lower" in absolute terms are not as important as the relationship between the discount rate and market interest rates. Discounting is discouraged (by cost considerations) when the discount rate is *above* other short-term interest rates, and encouraged when it is *below* market interest rates.[7]

In some countries the discount rate is often kept above short-term market interest rates, so that it is a *"penalty rate,"* a means of restraining excessive commercial bank use of the central bank's borrowing facilities. In the United States, on the other hand, the discount rate is usually, although not always, held below the Treasury bill rate, so that the Fed has to rely more on surveillance than cost to prevent "abuse of the discount privilege."

How does a change in the discount rate affect market interest rates? The two are not *directly* connected. A higher or lower discount rate alters bank borrowing from the Fed, thereby changing bank reserves, bank lending, the money supply, and finally market interest rates. This is a rather weak linkage, however, since a change in the discount rate affects reserves and the money supply far less than other tools available to the Federal Reserve.

Careful examination, however, reveals that *changes* in the federal funds rate and in Treasury bill yields typically *precede* changes in the discount rate. The federal funds rate and Treasury bill yields rise, probably because of Federal Reserve open market operations (which we discuss in the next section), and then—after they have risen quite a while and often quite a bit—the discount rate moves up. Or bill rates fall and then the discount rate is lowered. In other words, a change in the discount rate is likely to come *after* a basic change in market interest rates has already occurred. This is not always true, of course, but it is generally the case.

[7]See R. Alton Gilbert, "Benefits of Borrowing from the Federal Reserve when the Discount Rate is Below Market Interest Rates," Federal Reserve Bank of St. Louis *Review* (March 1979).

One possible way that changes in the discount rate might directly affect market interest rates is through the "announcement effect" produced when a discount rate change comes unexpectedly. An unanticipated rise in the discount rate is likely to lead bondholders to expect tight money and higher interest rates (lower bond prices). They sell bonds to avoid capital losses, thus hastening the drop in bond prices and the rise in interest rates.

The key is that the rise in the discount rate under such circumstances generates expectations regarding future interest rates. But if, prior to the change in the discount rate, the public had already observed tightening in the credit markets due to other Federal Reserve operations, the actual announcement itself would produce very little reaction. In fact, the bond markets might be relieved of uncertainty, and interest rates might fall back a bit. The change in the discount rate thus usually confirms what is going on but does not initiate it.

OPEN MARKET OPERATIONS

The most important way the Federal Reserve alters the actual amount of reserves the banks hold is not by discounting, but by buying and selling government securities—technically known as open market operations. Undertaken at the Fed's own initiative, open market operations are the mainstay of Federal Reserve policy.

About $1,700 billion worth of marketable government securities are outstanding. They are held as investments by the public—by individuals, corporations, financial institutions, and so on. Over $200 billion are held by the Federal Reserve System. These government securities came into being when the United States Treasury had to borrow to finance budget deficits. Some are long-term bonds, running twenty or thirty years until maturity, and others are shorter term, all the way down to Treasury bills, which are issued for only a few months. The existence of this pool of widely held marketable securities, with many potential buyers and sellers, offers an ideal vehicle through which the Federal Reserve can affect bank reserves. Federal Reserve purchases of government securities increase bank reserves, and Federal Reserve sales decrease them. Here's how it works:

When the Federal Reserve *buys* $1,000 of government securities, much as you might buy a stock or a bond on one of the stock exchanges, it pays with a check drawn on itself. If the Fed buys the securities directly from a commercial bank—say, from a bank in Succasunna, New Jersey—the Succasunna bank sends the Fed's check to its regional Federal Reserve Bank (the Federal Reserve Bank of Philadelphia) and has its deposit at the Fed—its reserves—increased by $1,000. The Succasunna bank's excess reserves rise by the full amount of the transaction, and with more excess reserves it can make more loans and increase its demand deposits.

The T-accounts for a Federal Reserve purchase of government securities directly from a commercial bank are:

Federal Reserve

A		L & NW	
Govt. securities	+$1,000	Deposit of Succasunna Bank	+$1,000

Succasunna Commercial Bank

A		L & NW	
Deposit in Fed	+$1,000		
Govt. securities	−1,000		

But what the central bank giveth, the central bank can taketh away. When the Federal Reserve *sells* government securities out of its portfolio, it *gets paid* for them, and everything is reversed. Say the Fed sells $1,000 of government securities directly to our friendly Succasunna bank; the Succasunna bank now has gained $1,000 worth of securities, which is good, but it has to pay for them, which is bad. The Fed takes payment by deducting that sum from the Succasunna bank's deposit at the Federal Reserve, thus diminishing its reserves. If you were to draw up the T-accounts for the transaction, everything would be exactly the same as the T-accounts above, except that every plus sign would become a minus and every minus sign a plus. The Succasunna bank's excess reserves fall by the full amount of the transaction; if it had no excess reserves, now it has a $1,000 reserve deficiency.

Note that the Federal Reserve could achieve the same ends—that is, change bank reserves—by buying or selling any asset, such as record albums or any type of bond or stock. The reason for limiting its open market operations to the purchase and sale of government securities is quite obvious: who would determine whether the Federal Reserve should buy Cyndi Lauper or Bruce Springsteen? General Motors stock or IBM? The Federal Reserve is smart enough, at least in this respect, not to get involved in the really important decisions.

Of course, when the Federal Reserve buys (or sells) government securities, it has no assurance that a bank will be the other party to the transaction. But it doesn't matter whether the securities the Fed buys are being sold by a bank or by someone else, nor is it important whether the securities the Fed sells are ultimately bought by a bank or by someone else. In either case, when the Fed buys, bank reserves go up, and when the Fed sells, bank reserves go down.

For example, suppose that when the Fed bought $1,000 of government securities, the seller of the securities wasn't the Succasunna bank but an insurance company in Mishawaka, Indiana. It wouldn't matter if the insurance company were in Cut Off, Louisiana; Zap, North Dakota; Searchlight, Nevada; or even Eureka, California. However, *this* insurance company happens to be in Mishawaka, Indiana.[8]

In any case, when the Fed buys, it still pays for the securities with a check drawn on itself. When the insurance company deposits the check in its local commercial bank, the Mishawaka bank now has the Federal Reserve's check (an asset), and it gives the insurance company a demand deposit. In turn, the Mishawaka bank sends the check to its regional Federal Reserve Bank (the Federal Reserve Bank of Chicago) and receives in exchange a $1,000 addition to its reserves.

The T-account for the insurance company shows that it now has $1,000 less in government securities and $1,000 more in its demand deposit account at its local commercial bank. For the Federal Reserve and the Mishawaka bank, the T-accounts for such a Federal Reserve purchase look like this:

Federal Reserve

A		L & NW	
Govt. securities	+$1,000	Deposit of Mishawaka Bank	+$1,000

Mishawaka Commercial Bank

A		L & NW	
Deposit in Fed	+$1,000	Demand deposit of Ins. Co.	+$1,000

[8]Speaking of place names reminds us of Zzyzx Road (believe it or not), which you will encounter on Interstate 15 about fifty miles out of Barstow on the way to Las Vegas.

Notice that in this case the commercial bank's excess reserves go up, but not by the full amount of the transaction. The bank has $1,000 more of reserves, but it needs $100 more (assuming a 10 percent reserve requirement) because its deposits have gone up by $1,000; thus its *excess* reserves have risen by $900. However, the money supply has *already* risen by $1,000, so the ultimate potential effect on the money supply is the same regardless of where the Fed buys its securities. To summarize:

1. If the Fed buys $1,000 of government securities directly from commercial banks, bank excess reserves rise by the full $1,000 and the banking system can then create $10,000 of new money (assuming a 10 percent reserve requirement);

2. If the Fed buys from nonbanks, bank excess reserves rise by only $900 and the banking system can create $9,000 of new money. But the money supply has already gone up by $1,000, and $9,000 + $1,000 also equal $10,000. So, in the end, the ultimate effect on the money supply of either type of open market purchase turns out to be the same.[9]

Commercial banks are unable to do anything to offset these measures. if the Fed wants to reduce bank reserves by open market sales, there is nothing the banks can do about it. By lowering its selling price, the Fed can always unearth a buyer. Since it is not in business to make a profit, the Fed is free to alter its selling price as it wishes. And while any single commercial bank can replenish its own reserves by selling securities to other banks—or to individuals who keep their accounts in other banks—the reserves of the other banks will then decline. Reserves replenished by one bank are lost by others. Total bank reserves must fall by the value of the securities sold by the Federal Reserve.

As suggested in Chapter 2 (see footnote 1 in that chapter), it should now be clear why a contraction or expansion in the money supply via pure monetary policy does not change the total size of the public's portfolio (its wealth) directly. The public gives up an asset, or incurs

[9]Similarly, were the Fed to *sell* securities to an insurance company, everything would be exactly the same as the T-accounts immediately above, except the signs would be reversed. Our Mishawaka bank would find its excess reserves diminished by $900 (not by $1,000, because although its reserves would be $1,000 lower, its deposit liabilities would also be that much lower). When the Fed sells securities directly to commercial banks, on the other hand, bank excess reserves fall by the full amount of the sale. However, in both cases the potential effect on the money supply is the same.

a liability, as part of the very process through which currency or demand deposits rise; the reverse occurs when demand deposits decline. For example, if the money supply is increased by Federal Reserve's open market purchases of securities, the increased demand deposit acquired by the public is offset by the reduction in its holdings of government securities (they were purchased by the Federal Reserve). In any subsequent expansion of demand deposits by bank lending or security purchases, the public acquires an asset (demand deposits) but either creates a liability against itself in the form of a bank loan or sells to the bank an asset of equal value, such as a government bond.

CONDUCTING OPEN MARKET OPERATIONS

Now that we understand the mechanics of open market operations, let's see how the Federal Reserve implements its policies. Although monetary policy is made in Washington, open market operations are actually conducted in New York—in a well-guarded trading room on the eighth floor of the Federal Reserve Bank of New York, which is only a few blocks from Wall Street. The Federal Open Market Committee (FOMC) in Washington decides on the general aims and objectives of monetary policy, but then it is up to the New York Federal Reserve Bank's Peter Sternlight, Manager of the System Open Market Account, to do the actual buying and selling to carry out the FOMC's intentions.

Sternlight's location in the heart of the New York financial district puts him in close contact with the dealers with whom the Fed does business when it buys or sells government securities. Every morning of the work week, the Account Manager meets with some of the securities dealers to get the "feel of the market," and even the opening handshakes (firm or limp? dry or sweaty palms?) probably give him a hint of whether the market is likely to be strong or weak, bullish or bearish. (It is said that on occasion Sternlight has been known to shock the dealers by the judicious use of one of those little hand buzzers that they sell in novelty shops.)

Feedback from the securities dealers is only one component of the vast array of data and information marshaled by the Account Manager in mapping his plans for open market operations on any given day. His starting point, of course, is the stance of monetary policy as expressed by the FOMC with respect to bank reserves, the money supply, and interest rates. Given these targets, Sternlight has to figure out how to achieve them by open market operations—should he buy or sell, how much, from or to whom, and when?

Each morning, a little after 9:30, the Account Manager receives a report on the reserve position of the banking system as of the night before. A key indicator of whether the quantity of reserves is high or low relative to demand is provided by the federal funds rate, the rate charged on funds lent by one bank to another. If many banks have excess reserves and only a few have deficiencies, the federal funds rate is likely to fall, because there will be many eager lenders and few borrowers. On the other hand, if many banks have reserve deficiencies and only a few are in surplus, the rate will rise, because there will be many eager borrowers and few lenders. The federal funds rate thus provides the Fed with a sensitive barometer of reserve supply relative to demand.

A little later in the morning, the Account Manager is provided with a detailed projection by his research staff. It covers expected movements in various items that can affect the reserve position of the banking system—including currency holdings of the public (which show considerable seasonal variation), deposits in foreign accounts at the Federal Reserve banks, and other technical factors. As we will see in the next chapter, a change in any of these can cause reserves to go up or down and thereby affect bank lending capabilities, interest rates, and growth in the money supply. For example, as the public cashes checks in order to get more currency, commercial banks must pay out vault cash and thereby suffer a loss in reserves.

A call is also made to the U.S. Treasury to determine what is likely to happen to Treasury balances in tax and loan accounts at commercial banks—deposits of the U.S. government generated by tax payments of the public and receipts from bond sales—and to find out what is likely to happen to Treasury balances at the Federal Reserve banks, from which most government expenditures are made. As funds are shifted from Treasury tax and loan accounts in commercial banks to Treasury balances at the Federal Reserve, the commercial banking system loses reserves.[10]

By 11:00 A.M., Peter Sternlight has a good idea of money market conditions, including what is happening to interest rates, and of anticipated changes in the reserve position of the banking system. He also knows what the FOMC wants. If the FOMC had asked for moder-

[10]The discussion of the last two paragraphs on the impact of various items on bank reserves will be explained in detail in the next chapter.

ate growth in reserves to sustain moderate growth in the money supply, and if all the other technical factors just discussed are expected to pour a large volume of reserves into the banking system, he may decide that open market *sales* are necessary to prevent an excessive expansion in reserves. If, on the other hand, he expects to find reserves going up too little or even declining as a result of these other forces, he may engage in large-scale open market purchases. It is clear, therefore, why knowledge of the amount of government securities that the Federal Reserve bought or sold on a given day, or during a given week, in itself tells us almost nothing about the overall posture or intent of monetary policy. Many purchases and sales are used to offset technical influences on reserves.

At 11:15 it is time for a daily long-distance conference call with a member of the Board of Governors in Washington and one of the Federal Reserve Bank presidents. Sternlight outlines his plan of action for the day and explains the reasons for his particular strategy. Once his decision is approved, the purchase or sale of securities (usually Treasury bills) takes place. The Account Manager instructs the traders in the trading room of the Federal Reserve Bank of New York to call the forty or so primary government securities dealers and ask them for firm bids for stated amounts of specific maturities of government securities (in the case of an open market sale) or for their selling price quotations for stated amounts of specific maturities (in the case of an open market purchase). While the Federal Reserve does not engage in open market operations to make a profit, it still insists on getting the most for its money, and it is assured of that by vigorous competition among the various dealers in government securities. (More on government securities dealers in Chapter 30.)

The Account Manager may instruct his traders to buy or sell securities outright—that is, involving no additional commitments. Or he may decide that he prefers to inject or withdraw reserves only *temporarily*, say for several days. One type of open market operation is particularly well suited to the temporary injection of reserves, namely, buying government securities under *repurchase agreements*. With a "repo" the Fed buys the security with an agreement that the seller will repurchase it on a specific date in the future, usually within a week or so. When the Fed buys, reserves go up, but when the security is sold back to the dealer a week or so later, reserves drop back down again.[11]

A "reverse repo" is designed to do the opposite. It *withdraws* re-

[11]The term *repo* takes its name from the dealer's point of view. That is, the dealer sells to the Fed under an agreement to repurchase the securities. Repos are discussed in greater detail in Chapter 30.

serves from the banking system temporarily. With a reverse repo, also called a matched sale-purchase agreement, the Fed sells securities but simultaneously agrees to buy them back at a specific date in the future. When the Fed sells, reserves fall; but later when the Fed buys the securities back, reserves are restored.

In recent years, the Fed has relied to an increasing extent on repos and reverse repos. In terms of the dollar volume of open market operations, they now greatly exceed outright purchases and sales.

It takes only about half an hour for the traders to complete their "go-around" of the market and execute the open market operation. By 12:30 the Account Manager and his staff are back to monitoring bank reserve positions via the federal funds rate and to keeping track of trends in financial markets in general. If necessary to implement the original objective, the manager is prepared to engage in further open market operations during the afternoon.

SUMMARY

1. The Federal Reserve regulates bank lending and the money supply through its control over bank reserves and the deposit creation multiplier.

2. All depository institutions are equally subject to the Fed's reserve requirements, regardless of whether they are commercial banks, savings and loans, savings banks, or credit unions, and regardless of Federal Reserve membership. Until the Banking Act of 1980, the Fed's reserve requirements applied only to commercial banks that were members of the Federal Reserve System.

3. By changing the required reserve ratio, the Fed alters bank excess reserves and simultaneously changes the deposit expansion multiplier for the banking system. Lower required reserve ratios mean easier money, while higher ratios imply tighter money.

4. Discounting and the discount rate have a long and distinguished history, dating back to the nineteenth-century concept of the central bank as a "lender of last resort."

5. By changing the discount rate, the Fed affects the willingness of banks to borrow reserves from the Federal Reserve. Reducing the discount rate usually confirms an easier monetary policy, while increasing the discount rate usually confirms tighter money.

6. Most important, by buying or selling government securities (called open market operations), the Fed supplies banks with additional reserves or takes away some of their reserves. Fed buying increases bank reserves (easier money), while Fed selling decreases reserves (tighter money).

7. Open market operations are not conducted in Washington but at the Federal Reserve Bank of New York. Repos and reverse repos have become much more important than outright purchases and sales in recent years.

8. By changing bank reserves and thereby the money supply, the Fed alters people's liquidity and, it is hoped, their spending on goods and services, which in turn helps determine GNP, the level of unemployment, and the rate of inflation.

Suggestions for Further Reading

Two informative articles on reserve requirements are William Poole and Charles Lieberman, "Improving Monetary Control," *Brookings Papers on Economic Activity* (No. 2, 1972); and George Garvy, "Reserve Requirements Abroad," Federal Reserve Bank of New York *Monthly Review* (October 1973).

The standard works regarding discounting and the discount rate are W. W. Riefler, *Money Rates and Money Markets in the United States* (New York: Harper, 1930); R.C. Turner, *Member Bank Borrowing* (Columbus: Ohio State University Press, 1938); and Warren L. Smith, "The Discount Rate as a Credit Control Weapon," *Journal of Political Economy* (April 1958). An article that explores in some detail the seminal ideas of Henry Thornton and Walter Bagehot is Thomas M. Humphrey, "The Classical Concept of the Lender of Last Resort," Federal Reserve Bank of Richmond *Economic Review* (January–February 1975). See also Daniel L. Thornton, "The Discount Rate and Market Interest Rates: Theory and Evidence," Federal Reserve Bank of St. Louis *Review* (August–September 1986).

Detailed explanations of the formulation and execution of open market operations can be found in Howard L. Roth, "Federal Reserve Open Market Techniques," Federal Reserve Bank of Kansas City *Economic Review* (March 1986), and in two publications by Paul Meek: *U.S. Monetary Policy and Financial Markets* (Federal Reserve Bank of New York, 1982) and *Open Market Operations* (Federal Reserve Bank of New York, 1985). Also very useful: William C. Melton, *Inside the Fed: Making Monetary Policy* (Homewood, Ill.: Dow Jones–Irwin, 1985).

CHAPTER 16

Understanding Movements in Bank Reserves

Adding and subtracting bank reserves are simple matters when all that's needed are pluses and minuses on textbook T-accounts. But in the real world simple T-accounts are replaced by complicated balance sheets that frequently seem to hide the truth. To understand the specific factors influencing bank reserves, we must look at the balance sheet of the Federal Reserve.

In the previous chapter we noted that both open market operations and lending at the discount window can change the volume of bank reserves and, therefore, the potential level of the money supply. Not surprisingly, we will see that both open market operations and discounting show up in specific items on the Fed's balance sheet. But there are other entries on the Fed's balance sheet that can offset or exacerbate these movements in reserves. Some are not even under the discretionary control of the Federal Reserve. Thus we have to examine the Fed's balance sheet to help explain why the central bank sometimes has difficulty controlling total bank reserves.

As if this weren't sufficiently complicated, it is also true that activities of the U.S. Treasury can add or absorb bank reserves. It is therefore necessary to expand the determinants of bank reserves beyond the Fed's balance sheet to get the entire picture. This expanded view goes by the rather imposing name of the *bank* (or *depository institutions*) *reserve equation*. In fact, it is nothing more than a tally sheet of the

TABLE 1

**The Federal Reserve's Balance Sheet
(End of 1987; in billions of dollars)**

Assets		Liabilities & Capital Accounts	
Gold certificates (including special drawing rights)	$ 16.1	Federal Reserve notes outstanding	$ 212.9
Coin	0.4	Bank deposits (reserves)	41.8
Loans	3.8	U.S. Treasury deposits	5.3
U.S. govt. and agency securities			
Owned outright	226.5	Foreign and other deposits	1.3
Held under repurchase agreements	4.9		
Items in process of collection	8.0	Deferred credit items	7.2
		Miscellaneous liabilities	
Miscellaneous assets	15.8	and capital accounts	7.0
	$ 275.5		$ 275.5

SOURCE: *Federal Reserve Bulletin.*

sources and uses of reserves. Nevertheless, it is so useful for monitoring trends in reserves that it is often billed as the fundamental framework of monetary control.

In the first two sections of this chapter we present the Fed's balance sheet and the monetary accounts of the U.S. Treasury. We use T-accounts to show how the specific items influence reserves. In the last two sections we combine these balance sheets into the reserve equation and show how it can be used to monitor Federal Reserve policies.

THE FED'S BALANCE SHEET

Table 1 is the somewhat simplified balance sheet of the Federal Reserve System at the end of 1987.[1] Each of the items on both the assets and liabilities sides deserves some explanation, since each of them reflects something that has an effect on reserves.

[1] If you look in the back of the *Federal Reserve Bulletin,* you will find the Fed's balance sheet in a table labeled "Federal Reserve Banks: Condition and Federal Reserve Note Statements."

The general proof of that last statement—that every item on the Fed's balance sheet has an effect on reserves—is so obvious it's easy to overlook. So here it is:

1. By definition, on *any* balance sheet, total assets = total liabilities (including net worth or "capital accounts").
2. With respect to the Fed, its total liabilities include reserves—they are "bank deposits" in the Fed—plus that part of "Federal Reserve notes outstanding" which is in bank vaults.
3. Therefore, bank reserves must equal total Federal Reserve assets minus all other Federal Reserve liabilities (and capital accounts) besides bank reserves.

All of which can be put more formally:

Definition 1: Fed assets = Fed liabilities + Fed capital accounts

Definition 2: Fed liabilities = bank reserves + other Fed liabilities

Thus (by substitution): Fed assets = bank reserves + other Fed liabilities + capital accounts

Therefore (rearranging terms):

Bank Reserves = Fed assets − (other Fed liabilities + capital accounts)

At this point, it is clear that anything affecting a Fed asset or a Fed liability has to alter reserves *unless it is offset somewhere else in the balance sheet.* If total Fed assets rise, for example, and there are no changes in "other liabilities," then reserves have to rise. Or if Fed liabilities other than reserves rise, and no asset changes, then reserves have to fall. It all follows from the fundamental accounting identity: total assets = total liabilities plus capital accounts.

To understand the mechanics underlying the process, it will be useful to examine more closely each of the major items on the Fed's balance sheet. We will see exactly how increases in each of the Fed's assets expand bank reserves and how increases in "other liabilities" decrease bank reserves. We can then isolate the uncontrollable items that complicate the Fed's influence over reserves.

1. *Gold certificates (including special drawing rights),* equal to $16.1 billion in Table 1, are Federal Reserve assets that arise in connection with U.S. Treasury gold purchases, regardless of whether the

gold is purchased from abroad or from domestic mines. Say the U.S. Treasury buys $100 million of newly mined gold from the Get Rich Quick Mining Company in Dodge City, Kansas. The Treasury pays for the gold with a check drawn on its deposit in the Federal Reserve; the Get Rich Quick Mining Company deposits the check in its local commercial bank, which sends it to the Fed for collection, and as a result bank reserves rise by $100 million, as we see in the following T-accounts:

T-Accounts for a Purchase of Gold

U.S. Treasury		Federal Reserve		Commercial Bank	
A	L	A	L	A	L
Gold +$100			Dep. of commercial bank +$100	Dep. in FRB +$100	Dep. of mining co. + $100
Dep. in FRB −$100			Dep. of Treas. −$100		

So far, this illustrates that if a Fed liability other than bank reserves falls, and there are no offsetting entries, then bank reserves must rise. But when gold is involved, that is not the end of the story. The Treasury has used up part of its checking account balance at the Fed. To replenish it, the Treasury issues to the Fed a "gold certificate" (a claim on the gold) equal in value to the dollar amount of gold purchased, and the Fed in exchange credits the Treasury's deposit account by a similar amount, as follows:

T-Accounts for Issuance of Gold Certificates

U.S. Treasury		Federal Reserve	
A	L	A	L
Dep. in FRB + $100	Gold certif. outstanding + $100	Gold certif. + $100	Dep. of Treas. + $100

In this latter transaction, Federal Reserve assets (namely, gold certificates) have risen but reserves are not affected, because a liability other than reserves (namely, Treasury deposits) has risen simultaneously.[2] However, the net result of both of these transactions is still an increase in bank reserves. (A gold *sale* by the Treasury would *reduce* bank reserves, with all the above entries being the same except opposite in sign.)[3]

2. *Coin* on the asset side of the Federal Reserve balance sheet consists of coins and bills issued by the U.S. Treasury (a liability of the Treasury) that the Fed happens to have in its vaults (equal to $0.4 billion in Table 1). Mostly it consists of coins. If some bank sends a truckload of pennies to the Fed, cash goes up on the asset side of the Federal Reserve's balance sheet and that bank's reserves go up on the liability side.

3. *Loans* (or bank borrowings), totaling $3.8 billion in Table 1, have been examined in detail via T-accounts in the last chapter. When banks borrow from the Fed the banks' reserves rise, and when they repay such debts their reserves decline.

4. *U.S. government and agency*[4] *securities* are acquired by the Fed when it engages in open market operations, as we saw in the T-accounts of the last chapter. When the Fed buys securities, bank reserves expand; when the Fed sells securities, bank reserves contract. Table 1 shows that at the end of 1987, $226.5 billion of securities were held outright and an additional $4.9 billion were held as part of repurchase agreements (more on this toward the end of the chapter).

5. *Items in process of collection* on the asset side of the Fed's balance sheet is an entry that arises in the course of clearing checks. The entry "deferred credit items" on the liabilities side is generated

[2]As you can see, this step is nothing more than a sterile bookkeeping operation since this "monetization of gold" comes *after* the gold stock has already affected bank reserves. In fact, some gold purchases are not "monetized" by the Treasury (no gold certificates are issued for them), and yet they affect bank reserves just the same.

[3]We will discuss "special drawing rights" (SDRs) in Chapter 36. They constitute only $5.0 billion of the $16.1 billion in Table 1. SDRs result from international monetary arrangements made in recent years. They are a supplement to gold in international finance, and an increase in U.S. holdings of SDRs affects bank reserves exactly the same as an inflow of gold.

[4]Agency issues are securities of government-sponsored institutions, such as the Federal Home Loan Banks and the Federal National Mortgage Association (see Chapter 7). Agency obligations account for only about $9 billion of the $231 billion in Table 1.

by the same process. Although each of these entries is rather obscure, the difference between them—"float"—is well known and has often caused serious short-term disruptions in bank reserves. A somewhat detailed treatment, therefore, is worthwhile.

Let's take a specific example. Say you have an account in the Safe & Sound National Bank and you see in the local newspaper that for only $100 you can get an antique spittoon and bedpan (matching set, last one left, accept no substitutes!). So you rush downtown and are lucky enough to get them, paying the $100 by check. The antique dealer has his checking account at the Last Laugh National Bank, in a neighboring town. He deposits your check in Last Laugh, which sends it in to the Fed for collection.

So far so good, and indeed we saw all this before in Chapter 14. But in reality things are just a bit more complicated. Back in Chapter 14 we said that the Fed would simply add $100 to the Last Laugh Bank's deposit in the Fed, deduct that amount from your Safe & Sound Bank's reserve account, and that would be that. Although the end results are accurate enough, the mechanics are not quite that simple, as the T-account below indicates:

T-Accounts for Federal Reserve Float

Federal Reserve Bank

A		L	
(a) Items in process of collection:		Deferred credit items:	
Safe & Sound Bank +$100		Last Laugh Bank	+$100
		Deferred credit items:	
		Last Laugh Bank	−$100
(b)		Bank deposits:	
		Last Laugh Bank	+$100
(c) Items in process of collection:		Bank deposits:	
Safe & Sound Bank −$100		Safe & Sound Bank	−$100

When the Fed receives your check from Last Laugh, it doesn't *immediately* credit Last Laugh's reserve account and reduce Safe & Sound's reserve account. What it does is give Last Laugh "deferred credit," meaning that Last Laugh's reserve account will be credited in due course, according to a prearranged time schedule. At the same time it considers the check "in process of collection" from Safe & Sound. Thus the first pair of entries, labeled (a), in the Fed's T-account.

Next step: After a day or two, depending on the time schedule, Last Laugh will formally receive an addition to its reserve account—the pair of entries labeled (b) above. Notice that, for the moment, *after* step (b) but *before* step (c), "items in process of collection" on the Federal Reserve's balance sheet exeeds "deferred credit items" by $100. This $100 difference is known as Federal Reserve *float,* and it adds to total bank reserves because it means that *one bank's reserves have been increased, but so far no other bank's reserves have been reduced.*

Finally, when the check is actually collected from Safe & Sound, then Safe & Sound's reserve account will be reduced, which is step (c). At that time, "items in process of collection" will also decline, and both float and total reserves will fall by $100, returning to their original amounts.

Float—the difference on the Fed's balance sheet between the asset "items in process of collection" and the liability "deferred credit items"—arises because many checks are not collected within the time period established for crediting the reserves of banks depositing checks with the Fed. According to the time schedule now in use, all checks must be credited to a depositing bank's reserve account no later than two days after they are received by the Fed.

With respect to its effect on bank reserves, adding $0.8 billion at the end of 1987 according to Table 1, the importance of float is not so much that it exists but that it fluctuates considerably. Float usually rises when bad weather grounds planes and causes delays in the mails, since this interferes with the delivery of checks en route for collection. A rise in Federal Reserve float increases total bank reserves, but such gains are temporary since subsequent declines in float reduce reserves.[5]

Note: On the Fed's balance sheet, the sum of bank borrowing, U.S. government and agency security holdings, and Federal Reserve float is frequently referred to as "Federal Reserve credit."

6. *Federal Reserve notes outstanding* are most of our $1, $2, $5, $10, and $20 bills (and so on up the ladder), an asset to those of us

---

[5]As electronic debiting and crediting replaces checks as the means of transferring funds, the volatility of float will be a diminishing problem (see Chapter 12). For more details on float, see Arline Hoel, "A Primer on Federal Reserve Float," Federal Reserve Bank of New York *Monthly Review* (October 1975).

who are fortunate enough to have any. But to the Fed they are just another liability, totaling $212.9 billion in Table 1. When your local bank finds itself running short of currency, it cashes a check at its regional Federal Reserve Bank and the Fed sends an armored car to deliver some more tens and twenties. This is recorded as shown in the following:[6]

T-Accounts for Shipment of Currency From Fed to Banks

Federal Reserve Bank		Commercial Bank	
A	L	A	L
	F.R. notes outstanding +$100	Cash in vault +$100	
	Dep. of bank −$100	Dep. in FRB −$100	

When commercial banks or thrift institutions ship currency back to the Fed, of course, the entries are the same but opposite in sign. Which means that when the Fed receives an inflow of Federal Reserve notes, its assets do not rise; instead, its Federal Reserve note liabilities decline, because there are fewer Federal Reserve notes *outstanding*. (Federal Reserve notes in the possession of the Federal Reserve are just so much paper—if they are frayed or worn, they are burned; if they are still serviceable, they are stored awaiting the day when banks will want them again.)

[6]What if the Fed includes in its shipment some Treasury-issued coin or some Treasury-issued $5 or $10 bills? To the extent that this occurs, then instead of the Fed liability "Federal Reserve notes outstanding" rising, what happens is that the Fed asset "coin" falls. In *either* case, bank deposits at the Fed fall.

So when the item "Federal Reserve notes outstanding" rises, bank deposits at the Fed fall, and vice versa. But these transactions—shipments of currency back and forth between depository institutions and the Federal Reserve Banks—do not in themselves alter bank reserves. They just exchange one kind of reserve (a deposit at the Fed) for another (cash in vault). However, if the *public* decides to hold more currency—perhaps because Christmas is approaching and people need more coins and bills to spend—then bank reserves fall dollar for dollar with the currency drain:

T-Accounts for Public Holding More Currency

Commercial Bank		Public	
A	L	A	L
Cash in vault − $100	Demand deposits − $100	Demand deposits − $100	
		Currency + $100	

When currency is returned to the banking system, as in the weeks after the Christmas season ends, then bank reserves rise dollar for dollar with the currency reflow. The T-accounts are the same as above, except opposite in sign. If the currency is then shipped back to the Fed, banks are merely exchanging reserves in the form of currency for reserves in the form of deposits at the Fed.

7. *U.S. Treasury deposits,* amounting to $5.3 billion in Table 1, are just what the name implies: deposits of the Treasury held in the Federal Reserve Banks. The Treasury keeps most of its working balances in "tax and loan accounts" at many commercial banks throughout the country. This is where tax payments and the receipts from bond sales are initially deposited. But when the Treasury wants to spend the money, it first shifts its funds to a Federal Reserve Bank and then writes a check on its balance at the Fed. The Treasury can shift its balances from commercial banks to the Fed prior to making payments by writing a check on its balance at commercial banks and giving the check to the Fed.[7] As a result, Treasury deposits at the Fed rise and bank reserves fall:

[7]The Treasury's balances are actually shifted by electronic instructions wired to banks, not by writing paper checks.

T-Accounts For Shift in Treasury Balances from Banks to Fed

U.S. Treasury		Federal Reserve Bank		Commercial Banks	
A	L	A	L	A	L
Dep. in comm. bank −$100			Comm. bank dep. −$100	Dep. in FRB −$100	Dep. of Treasury −$100
Dep. in FRB +$100			Treasury dep. +$100		

However, when the Treasury actually spends the funds, then its deposits at the Fed fall and reserves rise again. Say the Treasury spends $100 on paper clips. It pays a supplier of paper clips with a check drawn on its balance at the Fed, the supplier deposits the check in his or her local commercial bank, the bank sends it in to the Fed, and— *voilà!*—as Treasury deposits at the Fed decline, bank reserves are increased:

T-Accounts For Treasury Spending

U.S. Treasury		Federal Reserve Bank		Commercial Banks	
A	L	A	L	A	L
Dep. in FRB −$100			Comm. bank dep. +$100	Dep. in FRB +$100	Demand dep. +$100
Paper clips +$100			Treasury dep. −$100		

This completes our analysis of bank reserves and the balance sheet of the Federal Reserve. In addition, however, many transactions of the U.S. Treasury also affect bank reserves. Some of these transactions we have already discussed, but they bear repeating from the independent viewpoint of the Treasury; others—like the issuance of Treasury currency—have not yet been taken into account. Let's turn to the Treasury's influence on bank reserves.

THE U.S. TREASURY'S MONETARY ACCOUNTS

First of all, strictly speaking, it is the Treasury, not the Fed, that officially buys and sells gold on behalf of the government. As we have seen, after it buys some gold, the Treasury usually issues an equal amount of gold certificates (a Treasury liability) and hands them to the Fed (for whom they are an asset), so that the Treasury can replenish its deposit account at the Fed. However, as the T-accounts at the beginning of this chapter show, it is really the gold purchase that increases bank reserves, not the subsequent issue of gold certificates. Since gold, per se, does not appear on the balance sheet of the Fed, we had to talk about the gold certificates while we were confining ourselves to the Fed's balance sheet. But now that we are bringing the Treasury explicitly into the picture, we can go right to the heart of the matter: when the Treasury buys gold, bank reserves rise, and when the Treasury sells gold, bank reserves fall.[8]

A second aspect of Treasury operations that affects bank reserves is changes in the Treasury's deposits at the Federal Reserve banks. Since we have just seen the T-accounts illustrating this process, there is no need to repeat them.

Finally, we have to take account of the fact that the Treasury also issues a small amount of our currency, including all of our coins. Actually, the Bureau of Engraving and Printing operates the printing presses for bills (this is not the same thing as the Government Printing Office, although for all practical purposes maybe there isn't much difference), and the Bureau of the Mint manufactures the coins in three coin factories that are located in Denver, Philadelphia, and San Francisco. Both of these bureaus are departments of the U.S. Treasury.

The impacts on bank reserves of changes in Treasury currency outstanding are the same as the effects of Federal Reserve notes. Thus the T-accounts presented above apply here as well. The reason is straightforward: there is no difference between currency that is in the form of Federal Reserve notes and currency (such as United States notes or silver certificates) that is issued by the U.S. Treasury. Regardless of who issued it, all coin and bills in bank vaults count as reserves. Thus when the public decides it wants to hold more currency—because a trip to the supermarket calls for a fifty-dollar bill rather than a twenty—then bank reserves fall dollar for dollar with the drain of currency out of bank vaults into the purses of the public. It doesn't matter whether the currency leaving the banks is in the form of Federal Reserve notes or Treasury-issued money. And conversely, when the

---

[8]You can confirm the ultimate significance of gold rather than gold certificates by noting that if you were to consolidate the balance sheets of the Treasury and the Fed, gold certificates would cancel each other—since they are a liability of the Treasury and an asset of the Fed—leaving only the gold itself.

public redeposits its change—nickels, quarters, and a few dollar bills—back in the banking system, bank reserves rise dollar for dollar with the currency reflow regardless of the type of currency being redeposited.

THE BANK RESERVE EQUATION

We have now become acquainted with all the factors that affect bank reserves, and we can put them together in a full and complete "bank reserve equation." The reserve equation is nothing more than a record of the sources and uses of bank reserves. It is actually rather simple to visualize conceptually, as long as you remember the accounting at the beginning of this chapter plus the fact that Treasury currency in bank vaults also counts as reserves.

Thus, bank reserves = total Fed assets *minus* all Fed liabilities and capital accounts *other than* those Fed liabilities that constitute bank reserves *plus* Treasury currency in bank vaults. This is usually put more formally, as in Table 2, but it amounts to the same thing.[9]

Table 2, the bank reserve equation, looks a bit different from Table 1, the Fed's balance sheet, but the differences are really minor. "Factors supplying reserves" in Table 2 correspond roughly to Federal Reserve assets, and "factors absorbing reserves" correspond roughly to Federal Reserve liabilities; in addition Treasury-issued currency is also incorporated into Table 2.

In brief, Table 2, the bank reserve equation, is simply the consolidation of the Fed's balance sheet with the Treasury's monetary accounts. Some of the altered items are as follows. Federal Reserve float in Table 2 is the excess of the Fed asset from Table 1 called "items in process of collection" over the Fed liability "deferred credit items." Gold stock in Table 2 replaces gold certificates in Table 1 because, as we have seen, it is the purchase or sale of the gold itself that affects bank reserves, not the issuance of gold certificates. "Treasury currency outstanding" in Table 2, the only really new item as compared with Table 1, includes all Treasury-issued currency regardless of who holds it; that is, it is counted here whether it is held by the public, commercial banks, the Federal Reserve, or even the Treasury itself. Thus under the "factors absorbing reserves" in Table 2 we include both Federal Reserve

[9]You can find the reserve equation in the *Federal Reserve Bulletin* in a table titled "Reserves of Depository Institutions and Reserve Bank Credit."

TABLE 2
The Bank Reserve Equation
(End of 1987; in billions of dollars)

Factors supplying reserves:	
Federal Reserve credit:	
U.S. govt. and agency securities	$ 231.4
Loans	3.8
Float	0.8
Miscel. Federal Reserve assets	15.8
Gold stock (including SDRs)	16.1
Treasury currency outstanding	18.2
	286.1
Less factors absorbing reserves:	
Currency in circulation (i.e., outside the Federal Reserve, the Treasury, *and bank vaults*)	203.2
Treasury cash holdings	0.5
Treasury, foreign, and other deposits with Federal Reserve banks	8.2
Miscel. Federal Reserve liabilities and capital	7.1
	219.0
Equals bank reserves:	
Bank deposits with Federal Reserve banks	41.8
Currency in bank vaults	25.3
	$ 67.1

SOURCE: *Federal Reserve Bulletin.*

Notes and Treasury-issued currency as part of "Currency in circulation." This item absorbs reserves because it refers to currency held by the nonbank public—that is, currency that is *outside* the Federal Reserve, the Treasury, and the banks. Currency of any sort that may be held by the Treasury is included in the figure for "Treasury cash holdings."[10]

[10]For more detail on the consolidation of the Fed's balance sheet with the Treasury's monetary accounts, see Arthur W. Samansky, *Statfacts: Understanding Federal Reserve Statistical Reports* (Federal Reserve Bank of New York, 1981). However, to *really* understand the accounting nitty-gritty you'll have to dig into the *Supplement to Banking and Monetary Statistics,* Section 10 (Board of Governors of the Federal Reserve System, 1962), pp. 1–13.

We should mention that in the bank reserve equation as actually published by the Federal Reserve, the term "currency in circulation" is defined as Federal Reserve Notes

Thus, the bank reserve equation presented in Table 2 is really just a formal summary of the sources and uses of bank reserves. As we mentioned in the beginning of the chapter, it is obvious that other factors besides Federal Reserve decisions can influence bank reserves. These could cause problems for the Fed in controlling reserves and hence the money supply. The Federal Reserve, in fact, uses the reserve equation to keep track of these forces. Let's see how it is done.

PUTTING IT ALL TO USE

In chapter 14, when we related demand deposits to reserves via the deposit expansion multiplier (the simplest multiplier is demand deposits = total reserves times the reciprocal of the demand deposit reserve ratio), we assumed that the Fed could control the volume of reserves by judicious use of open market operations. But from the reserve equation, we see that this is no simple matter. Movements in float, gold, Treasury deposits, currency in circulation, and the other items listed in Table 2 have to be forecast and monitored. Only then can Fed open market operations hope to come close to the mark in terms of bank reserves. Open market operations, therefore, cannot be fully understood, or properly executed, without the bank reserve equation.

For example, if reserves are rising because of a temporary decline in the Treasury's balance at the Fed, open market sales may be used to *offset* such influences. Open market operations of this type are called *defensive* because they are aimed at defending a target level of reserves

and Treasury-issued currency held outside the Fed and the Treasury. In other words, "currency in circulation" as published by the Fed includes currency held by the banks as well as that held by the nonbank public. From the point of view of bank reserves this is illogical, as the Fed itself admits. It is illogical because "currency in circulation" is treated as an entry that reduces reserves in the reserve equation, but in fact currency held by banks is part of their reserves. The Fed's published version winds up with reserves held in the form of deposits at the Fed, to which vault cash is added back in to get total reserves. Our version corrects the structure of the reserve equation, redefining "currency in circulation" as only that currency held by the nonbank public. The Fed's reasons for its form of presentation are mainly historical, as explained on page 7 of the *Supplement to Banking and Monetary Statistics* mentioned above.

Another way of looking at vault cash, suggested by Professor Robert S. Holbrook, is that because of lagged reserve accounting (see Chapter 8) vault cash *does* reduce total reserves this week, so that at any moment vault cash *can* be viewed as a competing use of reserves and not as a source.

from "outside" influences. Another example would be increased Fed purchases of government securities in December to offset seasonal increases in currency holdings by the public. December may mean mirth and cheer to most of us, but to practitioners of the dismal science in the Fed's trading room it means "pump up reserves to offset currency drains."

As we saw in the previous chapter, there is a special type of open market operation that particularly lends itself to defensive uses, namely, buying government securities under repurchase agreements. Under a repo the Fed buys the security with an agreement that the seller will repurchase it on a specific date in the future (usually within seven days). As Table 1 indicates, $4.9 billion of government securities were held under repurchase agreements at the end of 1987. A reverse repo is designed to sop up reserves over a short interval; that is, the Fed sells government securities and agrees to repurchase them at some date in the near future (this is also called a matched sale-purchase agreement).

By their very nature, repos and reverse repos are *temporary* injections or deletions of reserves and might be interpreted as always being in the defensive category. But that would be falling into the well-known pitfall of identifying a specific Federal Reserve action with a particular objective. Never, never, never, do that. Once you do, the Fed denies it and then makes sure you're wrong by going out and doing just the opposite—using repos and reverse repos continuously to change reserves over a long period of time. In fact, in terms of volume of transactions, repos and reverses far outweigh outright purchases and sales.[11]

Which brings us to the *dynamic* variety of open market operations. Dynamic open market operations are aimed at either increasing or decreasing the overall level of bank lending capacity by changing the level of bank reserves. Even here, the volume of purchases or sales must be undertaken in light of movements in all the other factors in Table 2 that affect bank reserves. For example, if an increase in reserves is desired and the reserve equation shows that all other sources of reserves will be expanding, open market purchases may be completely unnecessary. For these reasons, it is not really possible for an outsider

---

[11]Table 1 shows that the volume of securities *held* under repurchase agreements at any given time is relatively small, but the number and volume of repo transactions are enormous. The reason they don't appear on the Fed's balance sheet is that repos expire and the securities are returned to their original owner.

Prices Rise on Fed Purchases

Treasury Issues Benefit

By Michael Quint

Prices of Treasury securities rose slightly yesterday, with all of the gains coming in the second half of the day after the Federal Reserve bought an undisclosed amount of notes and bonds for its own account.

The Fed's purchases were welcomed by securities dealers, as it was an opportunity to them to reduce their holdings from the auction last week of $16 billion of 3-, 10- and 30-year Treasury issues. After declining byabout 1/3 point prior to the Fed's 1:30 P.M. purchases, all three of the new issues closed with price gains of 1/3 to 1/4 point.

Economists and Fed watchers said the purchases were not a sign of any change in monetary policy, although the effect of the Fed's purchases will be to increase the supply of reserves in the banking system during the week beginning tomorrow, and put downward pressure on short-term interest rates.

"The Fed's purchases are viewed as a purely technical operation, and did not signal any change in monetary policy," said Albert Gross, senior vice president and economist at Refco Inc., a securities firm.

The Fed typically buys Treasury securities at this time of year, analysts explained, because it needs to provide the banking system with enough reserves to offset the funds drained from the banking system as the public increases its holdings of cash during the holiday shopping season. "They did the same thing this time last year," Mr. Gross said.

By the time trading stopped in the Treasury market, prices were at their highest levels of the day, with new 11 percent notes due in 1986 offered at 100⅜, up 5/32 point, to yield 10.84 percent, while the 11¾ percent notes due in 1993 were offered at 100⅝, up ¼ point, to yield 11.65 percent. In the long bond market, the 12 percent Treasury issue due in 2013 was offered at 102¼, up 6/32, to yield 11.71 percent.

In the Treasury bill market, rates were generally unchanged, with three- and six-month issues bid at 8.79 percent and 8.95 percent respectively. Although Congress has not yet approved an increase in the Treasury debt ceiling, Treasury officials announced yesterday their intention to proceed with a $12.4 billion bill auction on Monday that will retire an equal amount of maturing bills. The next Treasury financing that would normally be used to raise funds as well as retire maturing debt is the two-year note auction tentatively scheduled for Nov. 22.

New York Times

News Item *The Holiday Shopping Season Causes Defensive Open Market Operations*

to distinguish defensive from dynamic open market operations, because the Fed is usually buying and/or selling on a continuous basis—sometimes offsetting "outside" influences on reserves, sometimes changing the total level of reserves, and sometimes even offsetting the offsetting changes. It is generally agreed, however, that the bulk of the Fed's open market operations—as much as 80 or 90 percent of total purchases and sales—are in the defensive category.

FOCUSING ON THE MONETARY BASE

There has been considerable controversy over what specific variable the Fed should try to control in order to regulate the money supply. The control variable is often called an operating target, because it is the *immediate* objective of open market operations. We can show how to change Table 2 to focus on one popular alternative to bank reserves—the monetary base.

The definition of the monetary base is total reserves plus currency held by the nonbank public. The reserve equation can be altered quite easily to focus on the monetary base; just shift "currency in circulation" down to the bottom of Table 2, to join bank reserves. Then, in terms of Table 2, what we would have is (Federal Reserve credit + gold stock + Treasury currency outstanding) *less* (Treasury cash holdings + Treasury, foreign, and other deposits with the Federal Reserve Banks + miscellaneous Federal Reserve liabilities and capital) = the monetary base (i.e., bank reserves + currency in circulation).

It is important to recognize that an open market operation, which changes the Fed's holdings of government securities in Table 2, produces a dollar-for-dollar change in bank reserves or the monetary base only if all the other items listed in Table 2 remain the same. Thus, simply controlling the Fed's portfolio of government securities does not necessarily guarantee hitting a bank reserve or monetary base target. The advantages of alternative targets in helping the Fed achieve some goal of monetary growth will be explored in detail in the next chapter.

SUMMARY

1. The main message of this chapter is that hitting a particular target for bank reserves takes a fair amount of work, planning, and coordination. The Fed cannot simply assume that changes in its holdings of government securities will translate into reserve movements. The Fed must look at all the sources and uses of bank reserves.

2. We showed via T-accounts that all the items on the Federal Reserve's balance sheet, as well as some U.S. Treasury operations, have a potential effect on bank reserves. A convenient summary of the influences on bank reserves is provided by the bank reserve equation.

3. The most important item supplying reserves is U.S. government and agency securities held by the Federal Reserve. The largest alternative use of

reserves is currency in circulation. Thus open market operations and the public's use of currency are key factors in the reserve equation. This does not mean, however, that the other entries can be ignored. Whenever these other factors fluctuate without warning, as float often does, there can be significant complications for the Federal Reserve.

4. The Fed maintains a particular target level of reserves by conducting *defensive* open market operations to offset movement in other items in the bank reserve equation. *Dynamic* open market operations are used to alter the overall level of reserves.

Suggestions for Further Reading

The best sources for details on the Federal Reserve's balance sheet and the factors affecting member bank reserves are Dorothy M. Nichols, *Modern Money Mechanics* (Federal Reserve Bank of Chicago), and Arthur W. Samansky, *Statfacts: Understanding Federal Reserve Statistical Reports* (Federal Reserve Bank of New York, 1981). Both are available for the asking. See also *The Federal Reserve System: Purposes and Functions* (Board of Governors of the Federal Reserve System, 1984). Current and historical data can be found in the monthly *Federal Reserve Bulletin.* The distinction between defensive and dynamic open market operations was first made by Robert V. Roosa in *Federal Reserve Operations in the Money and Government Securities Markets* (Federal Reserve Bank of New York, 1956). This is still a useful booklet, but unless your library has it you are out of luck, because it is out of print.

C H A P T E R   1 7

Hitting the Monetary Targets

In chapter 15 we spoke of the important daily conference call between the manager of the System Open Market Account, located in the Federal Reserve Bank of New York, a member of the Board of Governors in Washington, D.C., and a president of one of the other Federal Reserve banks currently serving on the Federal Open Market Committee (FOMC). We have never listened in to what is said during one of these calls, but we can make a pretty good guess at the conversation, much as sports commentators are able to surmise what is said at those all-important conferences between the quarterback and his coach in the closing minutes of a game, or the even more important huddle between a pitcher and catcher with people on second and third and none out. It probably goes something like this:

OPERATOR: Kansas City and Washington are standing by, New York. Will you deposit $3.35, please?

NEW YORK: You mean it's our turn to pay? Hold on a minute, operator, we don't seem to have enough change here.

WASHINGTON: This is Chairman Greenspan on the line.

NEW YORK: Sorry, there's no one here by that name.

WASHINGTON: No, you don't seem to understand, I'm Chairman Alan Greenspan and I want . . .

NEW YORK: Hello, Alan. Sorry for the mix-up, but we've just hired a few Ph.D.s to answer the phones, and they haven't gotten the hang of it quite yet.

WASHINGTON: I know just what you mean. Say, we've got a problem here. Our staff says the 6½ to 9 percent range for M1 should replace as the main target the 4 to 6½ percent range on M2. Or is it the other way around?

NEW YORK: Frankly, our people have urged me to look at the M3 numbers, trying to hit the fourth-quarter-to-fourth-quarter growth figures, rather than the two-month targets. They say the M1 ball game is over.

KANSAS CITY: Hello? Hello? When do we start?

As we said, we've never listened in, but the implication that the Federal Reserve has been concerned with money supply targets is certainly authentic, and so is the uncertainty over precisely which monetary objective to shoot for. Ultimately, of course, the Fed is concerned with the performance of the economy—inflation, economic growth, and so on. But it has used money supply targets as a guideline in measuring the initial impact of its actions.

In the preceding chapters we described who runs the Federal Reserve, the tools at the Fed's disposal, and the way Federal Reserve actions influence bank reserves and the money supply. It is now time to put it all together to see how well the Federal Reserve meets its obligations. First, we take a more detailed look at the formulation of policy through what is known as the Federal Open Market Committee's directive. Second, we review the reasons for the particular game plan that is followed. We then analyze the linkages between Fed operating targets and the money supply objectives. At the end we should have a pretty good idea of why the Fed sometimes has trouble hitting its targets.

THE FOMC DIRECTIVE

The FOMC meets in Washington about once every five or six weeks. At the beginning of each meeting the staff of the FOMC, comprising economists from the Board of Governors and the district Federal Reserve Banks, presents a review of recent economic and financial developments—what is happening to prices, unemployment, the balance of payments, interest rates, money supply, bank credit, and so on. Projections are also made for the months ahead. The meeting then proceeds to a discussion among the committee members; each expresses his or her views on the current economic and financial scene and proposes appropriate monetary policies.

The FOMC directive, embodying the committee's decision on the direction of monetary policy until the next meeting, is voted on toward the end of each meeting, with dissents recorded for posterity. If economic conditions are proceeding as expected the month before and the current stance of monetary policy is still appropriate, the previous directive may remain unaltered. If conditions have changed, the directive is modified accordingly.

In recent years, the FOMC directive has usually contained six or seven paragraphs. The first few review economic and financial developments, including the behavior of real output, inflation, monetary aggregates, and interest rates. The third or fourth paragraph then turns to a general qualitative statement of current policy goals. For example, at the meeting on March 31, 1987, the goals of the FOMC were set forth as follows:

> The Federal Open Market Committee seeks to foster monetary and financial conditions that will foster reasonable price stability over time, promote growth in output on a sustainable basis, and contribute to an improved pattern of international transactions.

While the statement of goals does not contain everything—we know that the FOMC is not trying to eliminate highway fatalities (at least not yet)—it does include virtually every objective of stabilization policy. This general statement of goals is rarely changed significantly. Toward the end of 1975, for example, when the country was in a deep recession, the phrase "encourage economic expansion" replaced "foster reasonable price stability" as the first goal mentioned.

Immediately following this general statement, the directive presents long-run target ranges for the monetary aggregates that are thought to be consistent with the broadly stated goals. At the meeting of March 31, 1987, the annual targets were stated as follows:

> In furtherance of these objectives the Committee . . . established growth ranges of 5½ to 8½ percent for both M2 and M3 from the fourth quarter of 1986 to the fourth quarter of 1987. . . . The associated range for total domestic nonfinancial debt was set at 8 to 11 percent for 1987.

There are four important points to recognize in this statement. First, the goals for the monetary aggregates are stated for M2 and M3, rather than for a single measure of money supply. Second, the target growth ranges for each monetary aggregate are rather broad. Third, just for good measure, the Committee throws in a target for total debt growth during the year. Finally, because of particular uncertainties, the Committee chose not to set a specific target for M1 during 1987. These sources of flexibility reflect the Fed's uncertainty over the precise linkages between the aggregates and the ultimate goals of policy.

The last order of business in the FOMC directive is to specify the immediate prescription for implementing these longer-run objectives. In that March 1987 meeting, the immediate targets were described:

> In the implementation of policy for the immediate future, the Committee seeks to maintain the existing degree of pressure on reserve positions. . . . This approach is expected to be consistent with growth in M2 and M3 over the period from March through June at annual rates of around 6 percent or less. Growth for M1 is expected to remain below its pace in 1986. The Chairman may call for Committee consultation if it appears . . . that reserve conditions . . . are likely to be associated with a federal funds rate persistently outside a range of 4 to 8 percent.

Two points are worth emphasizing here. First, we now have money supply targets that are specified over a shorter time horizon. These targets usually set three-month growth rates that are designed to take into account "special events" that might call for deviations from the annual objectives. For example, previous shortfalls or overshooting in the annual growth paths are counteracted over these shorter intervals.

The second point to note is that while the Fed's short-run objectives are still couched in terms of money supply growth, the directive also mentions reserve targets to implement the desired growth in the aggregates. Thus in outlining its so-called operating targets, the Committee states (somewhat mysteriously) that behavior of reserve aggregates should be consistent with targeted money supply growth. The numerical reserve targets are not disclosed publicly with any greater precision; yet they are the focal point of the Fed's operating targets.

As we will see below, a number of specific reserve targets are available, including total reserves, nonborrowed reserves, and even the broader monetary base. But the Fed never lets on exactly how much growth it would like to see in any particular measure. It keeps its options open because it is not quite certain about precisely how much reserve growth will produce the desired path in money supply.

The emphasis in this 1987 FOMC directive is on the monetary and reserve aggregates. It wasn't always that way. Until the late 1970s the Fed paid most of its attention to interest rates (especially the federal funds rate) and credit market conditions. The main surviving reference from that era is the specification of an expected range for the prevailing federal funds rate in the last line of the directive. Apparently the federal funds rate has been eclipsed by reserve targets, but clearly it has not disappeared totally. At times, in fact, it again takes over center stage from the reserve targets. And this is not too surprising, since the Fed's impact on reserves is simultaneously transmitted to the federal funds market, as we shall see in a moment.

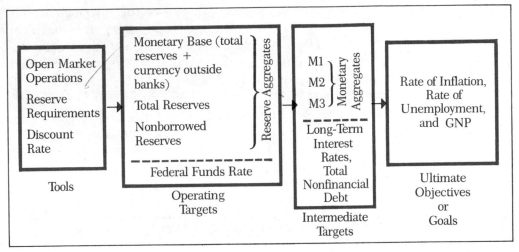

FIGURE 1 The Fed's Game Plan

THE FED'S STRATEGY

Figure 1 summarizes the FOMC game plan as described in the directive. Notice that the ultimate goals are separated from the Fed's tools by two sets of intervening targets. These operating and intermediate targets are more immediately responsive to Federal Reserve actions than the ultimate goals regarding inflation and unemployment. Fed officials believe that by formulating these intermediate steps they can more easily and quickly judge whether they are on the right track than if they waited for a signal from overall economic activity. As long as the linkages work reasonably well, it makes sense to use the intervening objectives.[1]

The Fed's plan is established in the following way (more or less): First, it decides upon the rate of growth in GNP that is most consistent with the rates of inflation and unemployment that are the objectives for the year. Then the Fed sets the range for monetary growth that is expected to generate the target rate of GNP growth. Given that desired range for monetary growth—say 5 to 8 percent for M2—the Fed then sets a target range for the growth in reserves—say 3 to 5 percent— which will produce the desired rate of growth in money.

The key to the usefulness of both operating and intermediate targets rests with the connecting linkages on each side: from the tools to

[1]For a contrary view on the value of such signals, see Benjamin M. Friedman, "The Inefficiency of Short-Run Monetary Targets for Monetary Policy," *Brookings Papers on Economic Activity* (No. 2, 1977).

operating targets, from the operating targets to the intermediate targets, and finally to the ultimate goals. Each of these steps has been fraught with controversy in the past. In fact, in each of the target boxes in Figure 1 there is a list of alternative objectives that can be pursued. The operating targets include several possible reserve measures, while the intermediate targets list the conventional measures of money supply. In addition, below the dashed line in each of the boxes, the interest rate and credit alternatives to the reserve and monetary aggregates are included as well. The advantages and disadvantages of these alternatives will be discussed in the next two sections.

OPERATING TARGETS: RESERVES AND THE FEDERAL FUNDS RATE

The Federal Reserve has had trouble deciding which operating target it prefers:

1. Before October, 1979, the Fed favored the federal funds rate as its main operating target.

2. However, the seventies were marked by double-digit inflation. In an effort to gain better control over the money supply and thereby tame inflation, in October of 1979 the Fed switched its operating target from the federal funds rate to the reserve aggregates. Reserve aggregates were the dominant operating target from October 1979 until mid-1982.

3. By mid-1982, double-digit inflation had been replaced by double-digit unemployment as the major economic problem in the country. The Fed reacted by trying to lower interest rates in an effort to stimulate more borrowing and spending. It thus started to pay attention again to the federal funds rate as an operating target. The Fed still pays lip-service to the reserve aggregates, as the March 1987 directive indicates, but since mid-1982 it has devoted at least as much attention to the federal funds rate—sometimes emphasizing one operating target and sometimes the other.

This schizophrenia gives rise to a problem, however, inasmuch as there is often an irreconcilable conflict between federal funds rate targets and reserve targets. To understand why this is so, let's spend a few paragraphs explaining how the federal funds market works.

Federal funds are immediately available funds that are lent, usually on an overnight basis, between banks. Thus, in the simplest case, if

Banc One (Columbus, Ohio) needs funds and First Third (Cincinnati) has an excess, then First Third can "sell" funds to Banc One for immediate delivery. The exchange of funds is accomplished by a transfer of reserves on the books of the Federal Reserve System today and will be returned tomorrow, unless another transaction is made. The interest rate charged on such overnight transactions is called the federal funds rate.[2] While federal funds are now used by banks for many purposes besides simple reserve adjustments (see the section on liability management in Chapter 8), our focus here is the way the federal funds rate reflects Fed pressure on bank reserves.

A simple example follows. Suppose the Fed sells securities because it wants to reduce bank reserves. If a customer of Banc One buys the securities, the bank will lose reserves. Its first response usually will be to replenish the funds by an overnight purchase in the federal funds market. Since the Fed has made reserves less available, Banc One's efforts will force up the federal funds rate; the demand for funds in the federal funds market will exceed the supply, and the price (the interest rate) is pushed up.

In this case the Fed's objective of reducing reserves is harmonious with an increased federal funds rate. The problem with using the federal funds rate as a target stems from the fact that it can sometimes induce inappropriate Federal Reserve actions. For example, suppose First Third is confronted with an increased demand for loans associated with an inflationary surge in economic activity. When the loan is made and checking deposits are created, First Third needs reserves. It turns to the federal funds market, where its efforts to borrow push up the rate. In this case, if the Federal Reserve had established a federal funds rate guideline, it would be induced to expand reserves to meet the demand. While this action would keep the federal funds rate on target, it would produce an inflationary surge in bank reserves.

In general, it is not possible to establish independent targets for reserves and federal funds. That lesson is brought home loud and clear from basic micro economics. A monopolist who wants to fix the price of something at a target level must accomodate to shifts in demand, supplying more when buyers predominate to prevent the price from

---

[2]Alternatively, an overnight transfer of reserves can occur with a sale of government securities and an agreement to repurchase them (at a higher price, to reflect the interest rate) on the following day. The so-called "repo" market is closely linked with the federal funds market, since they are both sources of overnight funds. In the rest of this discussion, we use the federal funds rate to represent all sources of overnight funds. See Chapter 30 for details on Repurchase Agreements.

rising and withdrawing supply when buyers disappear to prevent the price from falling. Similarly, if the Fed wants to control the federal funds rate it must add to or subtract from reserves in order to accommodate to shifts in the demand for reserves. To establish independent targets for reserves and the federal funds rate is an exercise in futility.

Even if the Fed were to choose reserves (and not the funds rate) as its sole operating target, there would still be the task of implementing the next linkage—between reserves and the various measures of money supply as intermediate targets. There are two major problems in this area. First, the Federal Reserve is not able to control total reserves precisely. As we saw in Chapter 15, for example, banks can borrow reserves from their regional Federal Reserve banks. Discounting adds to reserves just as open market operations do, but discounting is at the individual bank's initiative rather than the Fed's. Thus either First Third, Banc One, or even Chase, Citibank, or First Chicago can generate an increase in total reserves to support deposits. The Fed discourages such borrowing either by raising the discount rate or, after some demonstrated abuse, by refusing to lend to the offending bank. In the meantime, however, the level of reserves goes off track.

The second problem in the linkage between a reserve operating target and the intermediate money supply objective has to do with instability in the multiplier relationship between reserves and deposits. The discussion in the Appendix to Chapter 14 showed that only in the simplest case were demand deposits equal to total reserves multiplied by the inverse of the required reserves ratio. There were numerous complications in the relationship. For example, if banks don't make loans based on all of their reserves, but instead hold some reserves in excess of what is required, the multiple expansion in deposits is cut short. Moreover, to the extent that the public withdraws currency from the banking system, the process of deposit creation with a given level of initial reserves is short-circuited; banks lose reserves dollar for dollar when currency leaks out of the system (see the T-accounts in Chapter 16). Finally, if M1 is the intermediate target, the reserve multiplier may be relatively simple, while if M2 or M3 is the preferred monetary aggregate (for reasons given in the next section), the reserve multiplier linkage will be much more complicated, and will depend, in part, on the mix of deposits with different reserve requirements.

To summarize: A given level of total reserves can support more or less deposits depending upon (1) the mix of deposits with different reserve requirements; (2) the propensity of banks to hold excess reserves; and (3) the leakage of reserves into currency. In fact, the currency drain has led some critics to propose that the Fed focus its attention on the sum of reserves plus currency—the monetary base.

Note that in the operating target box of Figure 1, there are three alternative measures of reserve aggregates—the monetary base, total reserves, and nonborrowed reserves. Even if a reserve aggregate approach is chosen by the Fed, there remains the added complication of which reserve aggregate to focus on. The truth is that the difference between total reserves and the monetary base as the operating target is less important than either of these versus nonborrowed reserves (that is, total reserves less bank borrowings from the Fed). The reason is that bank borrowings from the Fed expand precisely when the Fed tries to contract reserves; similarly, borrowings contract precisely when the Fed tries to expand reserves. As we saw in Chapter 15, bank borrowings at the discount window respond to the spread between the federal funds rate and the discount rate. Federal Reserve open market sales to reduce reserves push up the federal funds rate, sending banks scurrying to the discount window to pick up cheap funds. Thus closer control over total reserves requires some tinkering with the discount mechanism. Until that happens, we'll just have to live with some slippage between Fed actions to control reserves and the induced impact on the monetary aggregates.[3]

INTERMEDIATE TARGETS: WHICH MONEY SUPPLY?

It seems, from our discussion thus far, that the Fed has more than its share of trouble trying to control its reserve target. Unfortunately, this is only part of the story. The Fed must use its reserve target to hit a money supply objective. In Table 1 of Chapter 1 we described three series the Fed uses to monitor the money supply: M1, M2, and M3. These measures appear as potential intermediate targets in the figure we just looked at describing the Fed's game plan. In the Appendix to Chapter 14 we derived the money multipliers that link reserves to the different money supply measures. Stability of these multipliers gives the Fed the control it needs to conduct monetary policy. And controllability is the first requirement of a good intermediate target.

The second requirement of an intermediate target is that it be

---

[3]There have been proposals to make the discount rate a true penalty rate; for example, it could be set at one percent above the federal funds rate. Thus far the Federal Reserve has resisted this logical solution, primarily out of historical sentiment (although the Fed always seems to give a fancier reason).

closely linked with the ultimate goals concerning inflation and unemployment—or, more practically, the rate of growth in GNP. On this score, the potential for controversy lies in the linkages between the financial sector and real spending decisions. Both the theory and the empirical evidence for these linkages are discussed at length in Part 4. At this point we need only to recall the discussion in Chapter 2 about the velocity of money—the rate at which money balances are spent on real goods and services. The greater the stability and predictability of the velocity of a particular measure of the money supply, the better that monetary aggregate is as an intermediate target.

In the good old days, this used to be a relatively straightforward proposition. M1, consisting of currency and checking accounts, was widely acknowledged as the best measure of immediately spendable funds. Hence the linkage between M1 and GNP was accepted as the most reliable relationship between a financial aggregate and spending, and M1 was considered the best monetary target. But the growth of savings deposits and time deposits as close substitutes for checking accounts forced many economists to reconsider their devotion to the M1 definition. As far back as the mid-1950s, John Gurley and Edward Shaw, Keynesian economists at Stanford, popularized the notion that the deposit liabilities of savings and loan associations, savings banks, and other financial intermediaries (see Chapter 4) must be monitored in order to get an accurate fix on whether monetary policy was expansionary or contractionary.[4] In recent years, with still newer financial instruments on the scene, the Gurley-Shaw argument would favor either the M2 or M3 definition of money. For somewhat different reasons, Milton Friedman has long advocated that both commercial bank demand deposits and savings deposits paint a better monetary picture than M1 alone. On the other hand, Monetarists Karl Brunner and Allan Meltzer have favored the narrower definition of money.[5]

Now let's turn to the credit side of the picture. The intermediate targets listed below the dashed line in Figure 1 include both long-term interest rates and a credit aggregate. In fact, this second item under the dashed line in the intermediate target box is something of a hybrid:

[4]A theoretical treatment of their arguments is found in *Money in a Theory of Finance* (Washington, D.C.: Brookings Institution, 1960).
[5]For Friedman's views see Milton Friedman and Anna Schwartz, *A Monetary History of the United States, 1867–1960* (Princeton, N.J.: Princeton University Press, 1963). Brunner's arguments appear in "The Role of Money and Monetary Policy," Federal Reserve Bank of St. Louis *Monthly Review* (July 1968), and Meltzer's view is in "The Demand for Money: The Evidence from the Time Series," *Journal of Political Economy* (June 1963).

it is an aggregate—*total* nonfinancial debt—but it is a *credit*, rather than monetary, aggregate. While its precise orientation is, therefore, somewhat in doubt, its lineage is unambiguous: Ben Friedman, a prominent Keynesian from Harvard (and no relationship to Milton except that they are both first-rate economists) has long advocated the use of credit aggregates to supplement the purely monetary side of the picture.[6] In 1983 the Federal Reserve recognized the wisdom of just one more compromise and added total nonfinancial domestic debt to the aggregates it now monitors.

Interest rates have made a comeback since mid-1982, so let's review the advantages and disadvantages of interest rates versus the aggregates as intermediate targets. The main virtue of using a monetary aggregate target is that it helps to insulate automatically the overall level of economic activity from unanticipated shifts in business or consumer spending. Thus if the Fed's ultimate goal is some level of economic activity that reflects its desired inflation/unemployment combination, pursuit of a monetary aggregate target will help to sustain that level of economic activity from uncontrolled shifts in spending. Let's look at an example of how the monetary aggregate target automatically provides stability compared with the interest rate target.

Suppose there is a burst of unanticipated investment spending because business firms expect higher prices next year. As long as reserves and the money supply are kept on target, the jump in business demand for credit to carry out the spending plans will cause interest rates to rise. This will force others to rethink their spending plans, thereby mitigating the inflationary burst in the economy. But if the Fed had targeted on interest rates, then the unanticipated jump in interest rates would require the Fed to push them back down again. Thus the Fed would be led to supply more bank reserves to support a higher level of money supply, thereby sanctioning an inflationary jump in economic activity. Interest rate targets, then, are poor protection against unanticipated changes in real spending decisions.

An interest rate target would, however, insulate the economy from unanticipated shifts in the demand for money. For example, if people reduced their cash balances and started to spend more, the declining demand for money would push down interest rates. The Fed would cut back on reserves and money supply if it were following an interest rate

[6] The formal statistical case for such aggregates is presented in Benjamin M. Friedman, "Using a Credit Aggregate Target to Implement Monetary Policy in the Financial Environment of the Future," in *Monetary Policy Issues in the 1980s* (Federal Reserve Bank of Kansas City, 1982). See also his *Monetary Policy in the United States: Design and Implementation* (Washington, D.C.: Association of Reserve City Bankers, 1981).

target, which is precisely what it should do to keep spending from accelerating. In this case, the interest rate target insulates the economy from unanticipated shifts in money demand.

Whether the Federal Reserve should focus on money supply or on interest rates depends, therefore, on whether money demand is more or less predictable than business investment plans. Congress is sufficiently impressed by the need to focus on the monetary aggregates to require the Federal Reserve to testify regarding its target growth rates for various measures of the money supply. Twice a year Fed representatives appear before the House and Senate Banking Committees to explain planned monetary objectives and to review recent results. Let's see how the Fed has performed in recent years.

THE FED'S TRACK RECORD

Judging whether the Federal Reserve has hit its monetary target would seem, at first glance, to be a fairly straightforward proposition. First you see what the Fed said it would do; you then compare that with what happened; and *voilà*—pass or fail, depending upon whether the Fed hit the bull's-eye. To see why things are not that simple requires some attention to the details.

As we saw in the FOMC directive, the Fed sets target *ranges* for monetary growth. And in the past, these ranges have been rather wide, reflecting, no doubt, the well-known proverb: Big Target Means Sharp Shooter. Should the Fed be judged on whether it gets inside the rather broad ranges established for monetary growth, or should deviations from the midpoint be the relevant criterion? Second, the Fed sets both annual and three-month growth targets for M1, M2, and so on. Should performance be based on the shorter- or longer-run objectives? Third, growth rates are notoriously sensitive to the starting point, the so-called base period. Should the growth in money during the year be measured from the average level of the previous year to the average level of the current year, or should it be measured from the fourth quarter of the previous year to the fourth quarter of the current year (which reflects the growth that took place *during* the current year)?

The proper answers to these questions should reflect the sensitivity of the ultimate goals of Fed policy to the errors implied by each measure. Because there is no consensus on this matter, we present the results according to the Fed's own preferred procedures.

Chart 1 shows the record for M1, M2 and M3 from the second half of 1985 through the third quarter of 1986. The actual growth rate in

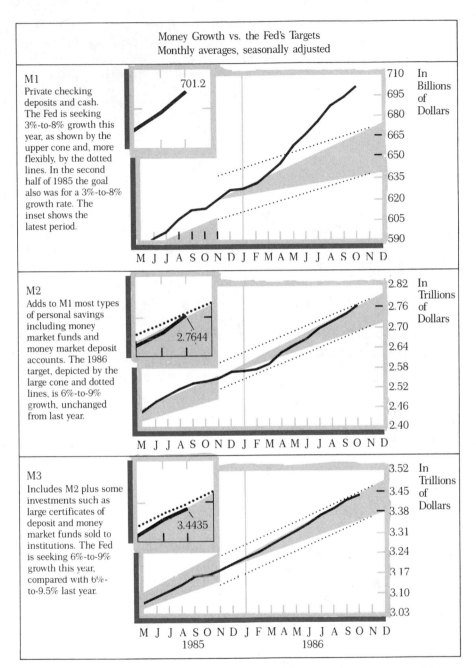

Money Growth vs. the Fed's Targets
Monthly averages, seasonally adjusted

M1
Private checking deposits and cash. The Fed is seeking 3%-to-8% growth this year, as shown by the upper cone and, more flexibly, by the dotted lines. In the second half of 1985 the goal also was for a 3%-to-8% growth rate. The inset shows the latest period.

701.2

In Billions of Dollars

M J J A S O N D J F M A M J J A S O N D

M2
Adds to M1 most types of personal savings including money market funds and money market deposit accounts. The 1986 target, depicted by the large cone and dotted lines, is 6%-to-9% growth, unchanged from last year.

2.7644

In Trillions of Dollars

M J J A S O N D J F M A M J J A S O N D

M3
Includes M2 plus some investments such as large certificates of deposit and money market funds sold to institutions. The Fed is seeking 6%-to-9% growth this year, compared with 6%-to-9.5% last year.

3.4435

In Trillions of Dollars

M J J A S O N D J F M A M J J A S O N D
1985   1986

CHART 1 Money Growth vs. the Fed's Targets (Monthly averages, seasonally adjusted)

SOURCE: *The Wall Street Journal*, November, 1986.

each aggregate is represented by the heavy solid line in each of the three panels of the chart. The target ranges for 1986 are represented two ways: by the dotted *parallel lines* and by the solid lines that outline a *cone* emanating from the fourth quarter of 1985. Each of these alternative methods for calculating the target ranges delivers the identical message: growth rates in M2 and M3 during 1986 were well within the Fed's boundaries, while M1 growth was well above the prescribed path.

The Fed does not like to see such dissension among the aggregates. There was a straightforward solution, as we saw in the FOMC directive earlier in the chapter: suspend the M1 targets so that they will no longer mar the Fed's record.

The moral of the story seems to be that if you make the rules you hardly ever lose the ballgame. Actually, Congress makes the rules for the Fed and has so far not been terribly upset by the Fed's performance. It does seem that the weight of the evidence suggests that the Fed is doing a reasonable job of hitting its targets. An alternative explanation is that if monetary events turn out to be a disaster, Congress will need a convenient scapegoat. And the Federal Reserve might fill that role quite well.

SUMMARY

1. The Federal Reserve's strategy for implementing monetary policy is summarized in a directive issued about once every five weeks by the Federal Open Market Committee. Operating targets for reserves are set so that the Fed can best hit its intermediate money supply targets. The money supply objectives are supposed to implement the Fed's ultimate goals in terms of inflation and unemployment.

2. The ideal operating target should be immediately responsive to such Fed tools as open market operations and should link rather closely with the money supply.

3. The federal funds rate reflects the initial thrust of changes in bank reserves. While the interest rate on federal funds used to be the main operating target, it often gave off unreliable signals. It was replaced in October 1979 by a reserve-based operating target, but the federal funds rate subsequently made a comeback.

4. The connection between reserves and the money supply is complicated by currency drains and shifts among deposit categories, and by the ability of banks to borrow at the discount window.

5. Focus on the monetary aggregates as intermediate targets stems from the stability and predictability of their linkage with overall economic activity. The choice between M1, M2, and M3 as the best intermediate target is still open to debate, although M1 clearly seems to be losing the battle.

6. The Fed has not been terribly precise in hitting its money supply objectives. There are some signs that their execution has improved with practice.

Suggestions for Further Reading

A detailed study of everything you ever wanted to know about the monetary control procedures of the Fed is contained in a two-volume analysis entitled *New Monetary Control Procedures* (Board of Governors of the Federal Reserve System, February 1981). For those of you who don't want to read all of that, a nice review of the magnum opus (plural: opera) is the "Review Essay" by Stephen M. Goldfeld in the *Journal of Money, Credit and Banking* (February 1982). In addition, that particular issue of the *Journal of Money, Credit and Banking* contains an interesting debate on Fed policy: "Is the Federal Reserve's Monetary Control Policy Misdirected? A Debate," by Allan Meltzer, Robert Rasche, Stephen Axilrod, and Peter Sternlight. Finally, a broad summary of the Fed's strategy appears in Paul Meek, *U.S. Monetary Policy and Financial Markets* (Federal Reserve Bank of New York, 1982).

A great deal of useful background material on targets and indicators is contained in *Improving the Monetary Aggregates: Report of the Advisory Committee on Monetary Statistics* (Board of Governors of the Federal Reserve System, June 1976); and "A Proposal for Redefining the Monetary Aggregates," *Federal Reserve Bulletin* (January 1979). The final definition of the aggregates (so far) is "The Redefined Monetary Aggregates," *Federal Reserve Bulletin* (February 1980).

The seminal article comparing the advantages and disadvantages of money supply targets versus interest rates is William Poole, "Optimal Choice of Monetary Policy Instruments in a Simple Stochastic Macro Model," *Quarterly Journal of Economics* (May 1970). For an English translation of the mathematics, see Poole's "Rules of Thumb for Guiding Monetary Policy" in *Open Market Policies and Operating Procedures*, Board of Governors of the Federal Reserve System (July 1971).

Two recent books that are worth reading are David M. Jones, *Fed Watching* (New York: New York Institute of Finance, 1986); and William C. Melton, *Inside the Fed* (Homewood, Ill.: Dow Jones–Irwin, 1985).

Budget Deficits and the Money Supply

When the Government spends more than it receives in tax receipts, it runs a deficit. The easiest way to finance the deficit is to print up the money and pay the bills. But that option is not open to the U.S. Treasury. Congress in its infinite wisdom conferred on the Federal Reserve System, not the U.S. Treasury, the responsibility of printing money and regulating its supply. What the Treasury *can* do is to sell bonds and use the proceeds to meet its obligations. In the process of carrying out its debt finance and spending functions the Treasury complicates the Fed's job of controlling the money supply.

In the first section of this chapter we examine alternative procedures for financing government spending in general, and a deficit in particular, and explore their effects on bank reserves and the money supply. In the next section we confront the controversial issue of whether deficits are responsible for excessive growth in the money supply and hence are inherently inflationary. Although the connection between deficits, the money supply, and inflation is part of the conventional wisdom, we will see that the linkages are far more subtle than most people realize.

FINANCING GOVERNMENT SPENDING

It is useful to identify five ways available to the U.S. Treasury to finance government spending: (1) collecting taxes; (2) borrowing from the nonbank public; (3) borrowing from the banking system; (4) borrowing from the Federal Reserve; and (5) printing money. Each method has somewhat different implications for bank reserves and the money supply.

1. *Taxation.* Assume the government decides to spend an additional $100 million on water pollution control equipment and chooses to raise the money by levying taxes on everyone who takes more than one shower a week. As the taxes are collected, they are initially deposited in the Treasury's accounts at commercial banks throughout the country, called the Treasury's "tax and loan accounts." Thus demand deposits (DD) at commercial banks are transferred from private ownership to Treasury ownership. The relevant T-accounts look as follows:

T-Accounts for Taxation

U.S. Treasury		Fed. Res. Banks		Commercial Banks		Nonbank Public	
A	L	A	L	A	L	A	L
DD in comm. bank + $100					DD of Public − $100	DD in comm. bank − $100	Taxes due − $100
Taxes due − $100					DD of Treasury + $100		

As a result of this step alone, the money supply falls by $100 million, since government deposits are not counted in the money supply.[1] Bank reserves, however, are not yet affected.

Before the Treasury spends the money, it usually shifts the funds from the commercial banks to a Federal Reserve Bank so that it can make its disbursements from a central account. *This* step depletes total bank reserves by $100 million, as the following T-accounts show:

[1]The money supply is defined as currency and demand deposits owned by the nonbank public, because it is designed to measure the *private* sector's liquidity.

T-Accounts for Shifting Funds to the Federal Reserve

U.S. Treasury		Fed. Res. Banks		Commercial Banks		Nonbank Public	
A	L	A	L	A	L	A	L
DD in comm. bank − $100			Comm. bank dep. − $100	Dep. in FRB − $100	DD of Treasury − $100		
DD in FRB + $100			Treasury deposit + $100				

Having raised $100 million and shifted it from commercial banks to its account at the Federal Reserve, the government now spends it. When expenditures are made, the Treasury writes checks on its demand deposit account at the Fed to pay its suppliers. The suppliers deposit the checks in commercial banks, and the banks send the checks to the Fed for collection. The result is that the money supply *and* bank reserves go back up by $100 million:

T-Accounts for Government Spending

U.S. Treasury		Fed. Res. Banks		Commercial Banks		Nonbank Public	
A	L	A	L	A	L	A	L
DD in FRB − $100			Comm. bank deposit + $100	Dep. in FRB + $100	DD of public + $100	DD in comm. bank + $100	
Goods & services + $100			Treasury deposit − $100			Goods & services − $100	

By combining all the effects of acquiring funds via taxation and spending the money, we see that after all is said and done neither the money supply nor bank reserves are altered. The money supply falls when taxes are collected, but it rises by the same amount when the government spends the proceeds. Similarly, bank reserves at first decline when the Treasury shifts the funds to its account at the Fed, but then reserves are replenished when the Treasury spends the money.[2]

2. *Borrowing from the nonbank public.* Alternatively, suppose that people who take more than one shower a week amount to a substantial voting bloc (not very likely), and Congress decides it would be the better part of valor not to tax them. Instead, the Treasury finances its spending—now *deficit* spending—by borrowing, specifically by selling bonds to the nonbank public. The T-accounts are the same as for taxation, except that this time people get a government security for their money instead of a receipt saying they paid their taxes:

T-Accounts for Borrowing from Nonbank Public

U.S. Treasury		Fed. Res. Banks		Commercial Banks		Nonbank Public	
A	L	A	L	A	L	A	L
DD in comm. bank + $100	Debt outst. + $100				DD of Public − $100	DD in comm. bank − $100	
					DD of Treasury + $100	Govt. bond + $100	

Again, as with taxation, this action reduces the money supply, transferring it from the pockets of the public to the accounts of the Treasury. When the Treasury shifts the funds to the Fed, bank reserves are also reduced, but as soon as the government spends the funds the money supply and bank reserves bounce back to where they had been originally (we have already seen the T-accounts for both of these transactions). The net result of the government's financing its deficit by borrowing from the nonbank public: just as in the case of taxation, after all is said and done neither the money supply nor bank reserves are altered (although this time the public does wind up with more government bonds than before).

[2]While the end result of the government's taxation and spending is to leave the money supply and bank reserves unchanged, the *timing* of the shifting of funds from tax and loan accounts at commercial banks to the Fed, and of subsequent expenditures, creates reserve management problems for the Federal Reserve, as we saw in Chapter 16.

3. *Borrowing from the commercial banking system.* The Treasury need not sell its securities to the nonbank public. Instead of the public, the commercial banks might buy them. The ultimate net effects would depend on whether the commercial banks (a) are fully loaned up to begin with (zero excess reserves) or (b) have excess reserves. To see why this is so, let's examine each possibility.

(a) If the banking system is fully loaned up to begin with, it will not be able to buy the government securities unless it first disposes of other assets. This is because the purchase of the government securities would result in an increase in Treasury demand deposits at commercial banks, against which required reserves must be held. To release sufficient reserves, private deposits have to be reduced by a corresponding amount. By selling $100 million of other investments to the public, the banks can now buy $100 million of government bonds from the Treasury. The relevant T-accounts are as follows, with the banks' liquidation of other investments above the dashed line and their subsequent acquisition of government securities below it:

*T-Accounts for Borrowing from the Commercial Banking System
(Zero excess reserves)*

U.S. Treasury		Fed. Res. Banks		Commercial Banks		Nonbank Public	
A	L	A	L	A	L	A	L
				"Other" securities − $100	DD of Public − $100	DD in comm. bank − $100	
						"Other" securities + $100	
DD in comm. banks + $100	Debt outst. + $100			Govt. bonds + $100	DD of Treasury + $100		

In effect, the banks have sold some of their other securities and replaced them with new government bonds. These transactions, by themselves, decrease the money supply, because the public has fewer deposits. (Although the Treasury has gained deposits, Treasury deposits are not counted as part of the money supply, as we pointed out earlier.) But, as in our previous cases, the Treasury shifts its funds to its account at the Fed and then spends them. When the funds are spent, the public's money holdings are restored to their former level. Once again, there is no change in either total bank reserves or the money supply.

(b) On the other hand, if banks have excess reserves to begin with, then they will not have to dispose of other securities or call in loans in order to make room for their new purchases of Treasury securities. Thus that part of the T-accounts above the dashed line will not be necessary. The banks buy the Treasury bonds and open up a new deposit for the Treasury; the Treasury shifts its balance to the Fed and then spends the money. When the Treasury spends, individuals receive brand-new demand deposits (for which they give up goods and services). Under these circumstances, financing a deficit by borrowing from the banks *increases the money supply* by as much as the deficit (although it does not alter total bank reserves).[3]

4. *Borrowing from the Federal Reserve.* The Treasury could borrow the money directly from the Federal Reserve:

T-Accounts for Borrowing from the Federal Reserve

U.S. Treasury		Fed. Res. Banks		Commercial Banks		Nonbank Public	
A	L	A	L	A	L	A	L
DD in FRB + $100	Debt outst. + $100	Govt. bonds +$100	Treasury deposit + $100				

In this case the Treasury does not have to shift the funds to the Federal Reserve before spending them; they are already there. Also, this method of borrowing reduces neither the money supply nor bank reserves. The government merely sells some bonds to the Fed, gets a checking account for them, and is in business.[4] Painlessly. Thus, when

---

[3]Note that since banks had excess reserves to begin with, the money supply could have increased without any Treasury financing. The only role played by the deficit in this case is to induce banks to lend out all excess reserves.

[4]In ordinary circumstances, the Treasury does not sell securities *directly* to the Federal Reserve. Rather, newly issued bonds are brought to market through auctions held by the Federal Reserve banks. The Fed acts as the Treasury's fiscal agent, distributing issues to ultimate buyers (see Chapter 30 for a more complete discussion). Securities

the Treasury *spends* the funds, the public winds up with more demand deposits and the banks with more reserves, as our T-accounts for government spending (which we saw earlier) show. Indeed, this way of financing a deficit has the same effects as printing greenbacks. It increases both the money supply *and* bank reserves.

5. *Printing money.* Instead of borrowing from the Federal Reserve, the Treasury could (if Congress permitted it) do the same thing by printing currency, depositing it with the Fed and then spending from its account at the Fed. The T-accounts for printing money are almost the same as those for borrowing from the Fed; the only difference is that the Treasury would give the Fed non-interest-bearing currency instead of interest-bearing bonds. But that is a meaningless difference, since at the end of the year the Federal Reserve turns over most of its interest earnings to the Treasury anyway:

T-Accounts for Printing Money

U.S. Treasury		Fed. Res. Banks		Commercial Banks		Nonbank Public	
A	L	A	L	A	L	A	L
DD in FRB + $100	Currency outst. + $100	Treasury currency + $100	Treasury deposit + $100				

In the end, therefore, it is the Federal Reserve and not the Treasury that decides whether or not deficit financing will be tantamount to printing money. If the Fed buys the securities, new money is created; if the Fed refuses and the public buys the securities, no additional cash is created.

CAN A DEFICIT SUBVERT MONETARY POLICY?

Obviously the deficit has to be financed in some way. We have just seen, however, that it is the Federal Reserve's prerogative to decide how much will come in the form of new money and how much must come through the ultimate sale of bonds to the public. The Fed can

---

dealers buy newly issued Treasury obligations for their inventory, to distribute to their customers. Our example in the text would be implemented if the Federal Reserve bought back some of these newly issued securities from dealers.

make the Treasury's financing job easier by "monetizing the debt," that is, by buying some of the newly issued securities. But turning new debt into new money may not be in the public interest. After all, in the long run, just about everyone agrees that excess money creation is inflationary (see Chapter 2). In fact, the reason Congress created the Federal Reserve was to keep the printing press away from the Treasury: to make deficit spending costly by forcing the Treasury to pay interest on its debt. In that way the inflationary consequences of a deficit would be mitigated.

When the Federal Reserve monetizes the debt by buying Treasury securities, it lets the Treasury get to the printing presses through the back door. And that's precisely what Congress doesn't want (or at least says it doesn't).[5]

There are some who contend that the Federal Reserve is often *forced* to accommodate excessive Treasury borrowing through new money creation. Despite the institutional separation between bond sales by the Treasury and money creation by the Federal Reserve, sometimes there is political pressure on the Fed to monetize the deficit. That pressure stems from the fact that Treasury bond sales by themselves will raise interest rates. After all, the Treasury is a borrower just like everyone else. And when the Treasury comes to market it must induce individuals to part with their hard-earned dollars. The only way to do that is to raise the interest rate that is offered.

If the Federal Reserve is committed to a policy of holding down interest rates, then it has no choice but to buy Treasury securities whenever interest rates start to rise. But the only time the Federal Reserve made such a commitment to keep rates from rising was during and immediately after World War II. At that time the Federal Reserve agreed to peg the price of government securities to reduce the interest cost of financing the war. In effect, the Fed bought whatever bonds the public didn't want to hold; it monetized the debt to whatever extent was necessary to keep interest rates from rising.[6]

The Federal Reserve extricated itself from the burden of blindly supporting the price of government securities through a compromise between the Treasury and the Federal Reserve that became known as

[5]It makes no difference whether the Fed buys some old securities when the Treasury sells new ones or whether the new securities are purchased. In either case, the Fed is monetizing some of the debt.

[6]Note that pegging the price of bonds meant that the Fed lost control over its own holdings of bonds, hence it lost control over the supply of reserves. Whenever anyone wants to control the *price* of anything, control over the *quantity* exchanged is lost in the process.

the Treasury–Federal Reserve Accord. On March 4, 1951, the Federal Reserve and the Treasury issued a joint statement:

> The Treasury and the Federal Reserve System have reached full accord with respect to debt management and monetary policies to be pursued in furthering their common purpose to assure the successful financing of the Government's requirements and, at the same time, to minimize monetization of the public debt.

The key phrase for the Federal Reserve was the last one: "to minimize monetization of the public debt."

Chart 1 shows the annual growth rate in the federal debt (the solid line) as well as the annual growth rate in the money supply (the broken line) between 1970 and 1987. It is obvious from the chart that there isn't very much relationship between the growth rates in the money supply and federal debt. Although there is little doubt that other measures of the importance of federal deficits could be developed, the implication of this simple overview is that large increases in federal deficits have had no persistent impact on money supply growth.

Although Chart 1 suggests no overall relationship between government debt and money growth, that does not negate the fact that at

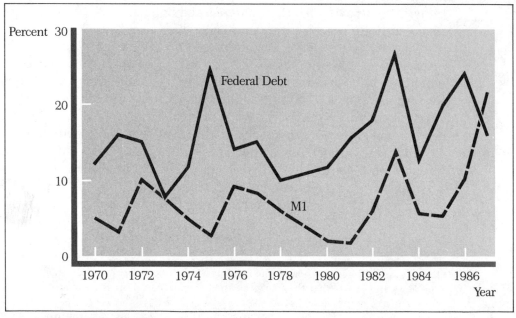

CHART 1 Growth Rates in Money and Federal Debt

SOURCE: *Federal Reserve Bulletin.*

times the deficit does cause trouble.[7] The picture is simply too broad to identify such effects. The fact that past deficits do not seem to have been excessively monetized by the Federal Reserve stems, in part, from the nature of the historical increase in government debt. Much of the deficit emerged during cyclical downturns in the economy, when reduced incomes generated smaller tax receipts. These deficits will not usually drive up interest rates because private credit demands are relatively low during recessionary periods. Thus there is little pressure on the Fed to monetize the automatic deficits that emerge in a recessionary economy. The real problem for the Federal Reserve occurs when the deficit expands during periods of economic expansion. Such deficits can be generated by an excessive increase in government spending, and that could very well lead to pressure on the Fed to monetize the debt.

To sum up: Deficits can at times be responsible for inducing faster growth in the money supply, but there is little evidence of such a systematic bias in recent years.

SUMMARY

1. When the U.S. Treasury sells bonds to finance a deficit, the impacts on bank reserves and the money supply are different depending upon who buys the bonds: (a) if either the nonbank public or banks with zero excess reserves buy the bonds, then the money supply and reserves remain unchanged; (b) if banks with excess reserves buy the bonds, an increase in the money supply results but reserves are not affected; (c) if the Federal Reserve buys the bonds, both the money supply *and* bank reserves increase.

2. The purchase of newly issued bonds by the Federal Reserve is the modern-day equivalent of printing money to finance a deficit. The only new wrinkle is that it is the Federal Reserve, rather than the Treasury, that makes the ultimate decision whether or not to create more money. Thus it is the Fed, not the Treasury, that fundamentally decides whether or not a deficit will be financed in an inflationary way.

3. A large deficit may induce the Federal Reserve to buy new Treasury securities if the deficit drives up interest rates when the Fed is trying to keep

[7]For empirical evidence see Michael J. Hamburger and Burton Zwick, "Deficits, Money, and Inflation," *Journal of Monetary Economics* (January 1981).

them down. This extreme case of "monetizing the debt" occurred during, and immediately after, World War II.

4. There is little formal evidence that deficits during the 1970s and 1980s have been responsible for inducing an increased rate of growth in M1. It is possible, however, that over short intervals of time deficits could elicit faster growth in the money supply.

Suggestions for Further Reading

Most of the literature on the monetary effects of a deficit discusses the relationship between deficits and inflation. For the argument that deficits are benign in this respect, see Scott E. Hein, "Deficits and Inflation," Federal Reserve Bank of St. Louis *Review* (March 1981). Evidence to the contrary is in Michael J. Hamburger and Burton Zwick, "Deficits, Money, and Infla-tion," *Journal of Monetary Economics* (January 1981). See also Aris Protopapadakis and Jeremy J. Siegel, "Are Government Deficits Monetized?" Federal Reserve Bank of Philadelphia *Business Review* (November–Decem-ber 1986).

Finally, for an interesting psychological perspective with some history and economic statistics, see Thomas J. Sargent, "The Ends of Four Big Inflations," in Robert E. Hall, ed., *Inflation: Causes and Effects* (Chicago: University of Chicago Press, 1982).

PART IV

MONETARY THEORY

CHAPTER 19

The Foundations of Monetarism

The first question we asked in this book was: what is the "right" amount of money? The answer depends on how money influences the economy, which in turn depends on what determines the overall level of spending. Monetarist and Keynesian economists have somewhat different views of the world in general and money in particular. This chapter and the others in Part 4 explore the analytical foundations and empirical evidence that underlie their outlooks.

The origins of Monetarism lie in the Classical economics of Adam Smith (1723–1790) and his friends. The two cornerstones of the Classical system are Say's Law, which deals with interest rates, employment, and production, and the quantity theory, which explains the role of money. Both concepts are essential to the proper functioning of the Classical world; both were attacked by John Maynard Keynes when the Classical wisdom was supposedly laid to rest in 1936; and both were resurrected by modern monetarism and refined during the 1970s and 1980s.

To understand the role of money according to Classical thinking, we must first see what determines GNP (the total value of goods and services produced). We start, therefore, with Say's law of markets and work our way toward the somewhat more famous quantity theory of money. Along the way we'll stop to consider some specifics: Classical interest theory as well as the demand for money.

SAY'S LAW

Jean Baptiste Say (1767–1832) summarized the Classical school's income and employment theory with the now familiar maxim, "Supply creates its own demand." Dubbed Say's law, it meant quite simply that the economy could never suffer from underemployment or succumb to Thomas Malthus' fear of under-consumption. Total spending (demand) would always be sufficient to justify production at full employment (supply). Let's spend some time making clear why this is the case.

Given current technology, potential output of the economy is determined by the size of the labor force available to work with the existing stock of capital goods (plant and equipment). This production function, in technical terms, defines the total supply of goods and services that can be produced. Say argued that production would be at the full employment level, since spending would always be great enough to buy all the goods and services that could be produced. Why? Because of the interplay of market forces, guided by what Adam Smith referred to as an "invisible hand."

If people who wanted to work couldn't find a job, they would offer their services for less money and would be snapped up by eager entrepreneurs. Entrepreneurs who found it difficult to sell slow-moving items would promptly lower their prices and watch their inventories disappear. Flexible wages and prices would assure that all markets would be cleared, all goods sold, all people employed—except economists, who would have nothing to do, since everything worked just fine without them. The interplay of market forces under the guiding principle of laissez faire (noninterference) would bring about the best of all possible worlds.

To represent Classical economics as having an entirely uniform outlook, however, would be unjust to some prominent precursors of modern Keynesian ideas. The Reverend Thomas Malthus (1766–1834) could hardly believe that *he,* a man of the cloth, was unable to see the invisible hand, so he proceeded to launch a sustained and vigorous attack on it. Spurning the microeconomic details, Malthus argued as follows: while the production of goods and services generates *income* in the same amount as total output, there does not seem to be anything to force *spending* to equal total production. Supply might create its own purchasing power (income), but not its own demand (spending). In particular, if people try to save too large a fraction of their income—more than firms want to invest—part of the goods produced will be left unsold, entrepreneurs will cut back their production, and unemployed labor and capital will result. This argument was later refined and formalized by Keynes, as we shall see in the next chapter.[1]

However, the Classical economists cannot be disposed of so simply. People save part of their income, but such funds do not disappear. They are borrowed by entrepreneurs to use for capital investment projects. Savers receive interest on their funds, and borrowers are willing to pay, as long as they expect to earn a return on their investment in excess of the rate of interest.

But what made the Classical economists so sure that all saving would actually be invested by entrepreneurs? If saving went up, would investment go up by the same amount? In Classical economics, *the rate of interest* is the key; according to Classical theory, the interest rate would fluctuate to make entrepreneurs *want to invest* what households *wanted to save.* As is emphasized in the Appendix to this chapter, this equality between desired saving and desired investment is sufficient to maintain production at the assumed level, in this case, full employment. The next section explains in greater detail this Classical theory of interest rate determination. It is really an elaboration of one of the market mechanisms underlying Say's Law.

CLASSICAL INTEREST THEORY

Back in Chapter 6 we described how the level of interest rates was determined by the supply of and demand for loanable funds. Classical economists obviously recognize the importance of supply and demand but focus their attention on saving and investment—the two main factors that, in the long run, underlie the supply of and demand for loanable funds. With saving creating a supply of funds and investment generating the demand for funds, classical economists had a firm handle on the forces underlying the level of interest rates. Let's see how classical economists presented this more fundamental approach to interest rate determination in the long run.

Saving, according to Classical economics, is a function of the rate of

---

[1]There is a distinction between the accounting identity that income or output equals actual expenditure and the possibility that income may not equal *desired* expenditure. The Appendix to this chapter discusses these relationships, which are relevant both for Classical and Keynesian economics. Because of the accounting identity between income and output we use these terms interchangeably throughout the text.

interest. The higher the rate of interest, the more will be saved (see Figure 1), since at higher interest rates people will be more willing to forgo present consumption. The rate of interest is an inducement to save, a reward for not giving in to baser instincts for instant gratification by consuming all your income. It does not pay, by the way, to make too much of this Classical assumption, because Classical interest theory worked just as well if saving did not depend on the interest rate—that is, if saving were a vertical line in Figure 1.

As long as investment is a function of the rate of interest, increasing as the rate of interest declines (as illustrated by the negatively sloped investment line in Figure 1), Classical interest theory and Say's law remain alive and well. Since it is crucial to our story, let's examine why the amount of investment should increase with a fall in the rate of interest.

Investment in physical capital is undertaken because capital goods— buildings, machines, or anything that is not used up immediately— produce services in the future. A new plant or machine is used by an entrepreneur to produce goods and services for sale. A business firm

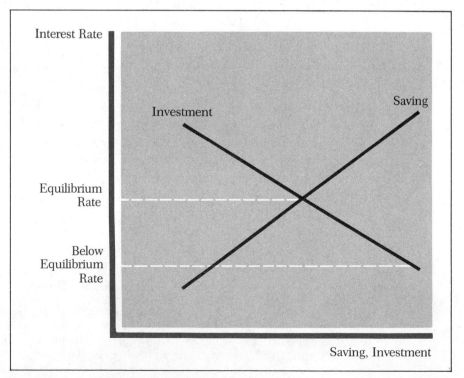

FIGURE 1 Classical Interest Theory

will invest in more capital if the expected return exceeds the rate of interest paid on the funds borrowed to make the investment. A lower rate of interest induces entrepreneurs to undertake more investment. They will accept projects of lower expected profitability, because the cost of borrowing funds is less.[2]

Figure 1 includes a supply of funds curve (people's saving) and a demand for funds curve (entrepreneurs' demand for investment). The rate of interest is in equilibrium (no tendency to change) at the point of intersection between saving and investment, where total saving is equal to total investment: everyone who wants to borrow funds is able to, and everyone who wants to lend can do so. If the rate of interest were below equilibrium, as shown in Figure 1, entrepreneurs would want more funds than savers were ready to provide, and competition would force the interest rate upward. If the rate of interest were above equilibrium, savers would want to lend more funds than entrepreneurs wanted to invest, and competition would force the cost of funds downward.[3]

But things don't usually stay in equilibrium for very long. If people really listened to some of Thomas Malthus's dire predictions of the consequences of unrestrained population growth, they might decide to save more at every rate of interest. The entire saving function would then shift to the right (Figure 2). At the old equilibrium interest rate, desired saving now exceeds the amount of investment that entrepreneurs are ready to make. That is precisely what Thomas Malthus said was wrong with the Classical system—people would spend too little in the form of consumption, they would save too much (more than entrepreneurs cared to invest), and unemployment would follow.

But not really. The excess of saving over investment puts downward pressure on the rate of interest, as savers try to lend out their funds. As the rate of interest declines, some people will give in to their baser instincts and spend a greater part of their income (saving less and enjoying it more). At the same time, the decline in the rate of interest

---

[2]The entrepreneur need not borrow for the interest rate to be important in the calculation. If funds are already available, the alternative to increasing capital equipment is to lend the funds at the going rate of interest. At a lower rate of interest, lending becomes a less attractive use of the entrepreneur's funds and real investment becomes more attractive. The rate of interest *must* fall to elicit more investment spending because of our old friend from microeconomics, the law of diminishing returns. More investment means a larger capital stock, and, given the labor force and current technology, there is reduced marginal productivity (profitability).

[3]Return to Chapter 6 for additional details on how the supply of and demand for funds determine the level of interest rates.

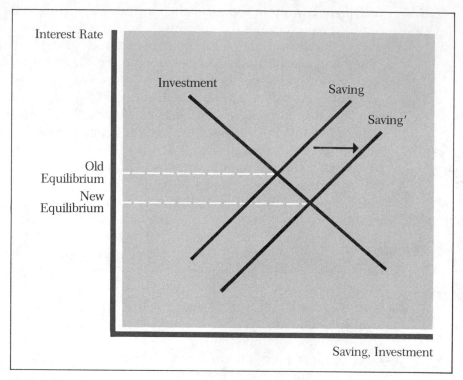

FIGURE 2 Increased Saving Calls Forth Increased Investment

will encourage business firms to expand their investments. As Figure 2 shows, the rate of interest will settle at a lower equilibrium, at which point all that is saved out of current income is still invested by entrepreneurs.

Where in all this does money fit in? The interest rate is influenced in the long run only by the saving of the public (determined by their habits of thriftiness) and by capital investment of entrepreneurs (determined by the productivity of capital). Money plays no role in this area of the Classical system. It influences neither employment, the rate of interest, nor production. Real things are determined by real forces. Total goods and services produced and total employment are determined by the supply of capital, the labor force, and existing technology; the interest rate is determined by the thriftiness of the public and the productivity of capital. Money plays no role in the real sector of the economy. Instead it is treated separately—via the second pillar of the classical edifice, the Quantity Theory—where it determines the price level.

THE QUANTITY THEORY OF MONEY

Money, according to the Classicists, is a veil that must be pierced to examine the determinants of real economic activity. Money affects the price level, but nothing else. An increase in the supply of money leads to an increase in the prices of all goods and services, but everything else—most notably the level of real economic activity, the rate of interest, and people's real income—remains unchanged. This conclusion expresses the quantity theory of money. It implies that money is *neutral* with respect to the real sector of the economy. The logic behind this is as follows.

We start with the *equation of exchange*, which is not the quantity theory but simply an identity, a truism:

$$(1) \qquad\qquad MV = PY$$

where M is the supply of money, V is velocity or its rate of turnover, P is the price level, and Y is the level of *real* income.

On the right-hand side of equation 1, total output of goods and services is represented by Y; that is what is produced by labor and capital given the technology currently available. Y is usually referred to as *real* GNP. The price level, P, is an index of the current prices of all goods. When Y is multiplied by P we have the *nominal* level of GNP, or GNP measured in current prices.[4] On the left-hand side of the equation, the stock of money (in dollars) is represented by M. When multiplied by its velocity, the number of times such dollars are used in the purchase of goods and services, the product MV also equals total spending. The equation of exchange says that total spending (MV) equals the value of what is bought (PY).[5]

The equation of exchange was originally put forth in a slightly different form. The level of real income on the right-hand side was replaced by T, the total level of transactions. The total level of transactions exceeds the level of GNP, because there are many transactions

[4]Throughout this book when we use the term GNP by itself we mean the real value of goods and services produced. The phrase *nominal* GNP is used to distinguish real output from the nominal value. As long as prices remain unchanged, movements in nominal GNP and real GNP are one and the same. When the price level changes, movements in *real* GNP and *nominal* GNP differ, as we will see with concrete examples in the rest of this chapter. For a discussion of how price indices are constructed, see any basic text on economics, such as William J. Baumol and Alan S. Blinder, *Economics*, 3rd ed. (New York: Harcourt Brace Jovanovich, 1985).

[5]As we saw in Chapter 1, velocity is *defined* as nominal GNP $\div M$, or, in these terms, $PY \div M$. Substituting $PY \div M$ for V on the left-hand side of (1) yields $PY = PY$, which is accepted as a truism even by those from Missouri.

that are excluded from GNP. Purchases and sales of *financial* assets and of *existing* assets—such as stocks and bonds, old homes, and works by the Great Masters, are not part of current production and hence are not included in GNP.[6] When the equation of exchange is written as:

$$(2) \qquad\qquad\qquad MV = PT$$

the velocity figure on the left-hand side is called transactions velocity.

Equation (1) is the most frequently used version of the equation of exchange. It is really the most meaningful approach, since our main concern is with GNP and not with total transactions. Thus all our subsequent discussion will be in terms of equation (1) and the "income" velocity of money. Irving Fisher, the brilliant Yale economist who is unfortunately known for his advice to buy just before the stock market crashed in 1929, was the most eloquent expositor of the equation of exchange as we have just presented it.[7]

There is still another version of the equation of exchange, however, associated with economists at Cambridge University, in England. So before discussing how we progress from the simple identity expressed by equation (1) or (2) to the quantity theory as used by Fisher and other Classical economists, let us give equal time to our friends across the Atlantic.

The Cambridge economists viewed the equation of exchange in a slightly different light. Instead of concentrating on the rate of turnover of a given stock of money during the year (its velocity), they concentrated on the fraction of total expenditure that people hold in the form of money. Simple algebraic manipulation of equation (1) produces the Cambridge "cash-balance approach" to the equation of exchange:

$$(3) \qquad\qquad\qquad M = kPY$$

where k is the fraction of spending that people have command over in the form of money balances. Obviously $k = 1/V$, so equations (1) and (3) are equivalent from an algebraic standpoint (for some unknown reason, when the Cambridge economists divided both sides of equation (1) by V they changed $1/V$ to the letter k). And (3), like its predecessors, is still a truism—an identity that must be true by definition. This latest version does represent a different orientation, however. In fact, equation (3) readily lends itself to interpretation as a *demand for money equation.*

[6]See Baumol and Blinder, *Economics*, Chapter 17, for a summary of GNP accounting.
[7]See Irving Fisher, *The Purchasing Power of Money* (New York: Macmillan, 1911).

But we are running a bit ahead of ourselves. It is time to convert the equation of exchange, whatever its form, from an algebraic identity—which it has been so far—into an analytical tool. Let's move, in other words, from the *equation of exchange* (an identity) to the *quantity theory of money* (a cause-and-effect hypothesis).

We started this section by saying that the quantity theory implied that increases in the supply of money cause increases in the price level. We can now be even more precise: according to the quantity theory of money, a change in the money supply produces a *proportionate* change in the price level—for example, if the money supply doubles, so does the price level. This cause-and-effect conclusion follows from two basic propositions (a nice word for assumptions) of the Classical school. First, on the right-hand side of equation (1), $MV = PY$, Y is assumed fixed at full employment (now you know why we started out with Jean Baptiste Say). Second, velocity is assumed to be fixed by the payment habits of the community. If $MV = PY$, and V and Y are assumed to be fixed, then if M doubles it follows that P *must* double. For example, if V and Y are fixed at 4 and 100 respectively, then a supply of money equal to 25 is consistent with a P equal to 1. If M doubles to 50, P must double to 2.

To understand the process involved, we need only recall the discussion in Chapter 2 of how people react to changes in the money supply brought about by central bank operations. Start out in equilibrium, with all people satisfied with the liquidity of their portfolio. Assume the Federal Reserve doubles the money supply. Liquidity rises. If people were formerly satisfied with their liquidity position, now they will try to get rid of their excess money balances by spending more. This increase in the demand for goods and services drives up prices, because total real output cannot expand—it is fixed at the full employment level by virtue of Say's law. If people were in equilibrium before a doubling of M, they will stop trying to spend the increased money balances only after their total expenditures have also doubled. Since real output is fixed, a doubling of total spending must cause prices to double. End result: Money stock held by the public has doubled, nominal GNP has doubled, the price level has doubled, V is the same as before, and so is *real* GNP.

Note carefully that Classical economists (as well as their Monetarist descendants) insist on clearly distinguishing the real versus nominal consequences of anything in general, and money in particular. A change in the money supply leaves the real amount of goods and services produced (real GNP) unchanged, but increases the dollar value of GNP (nominal GNP).

MONEY DEMAND AND THE QUANTITY THEORY

The two versions of the quantity theory, $MV = PY$ and $M = kPY$, are algebraically equivalent and also produce the same cause-and-effect implications for the relationship between money and prices. For explaining the transmission mechanism as we just have, and for what is to come later, the cash-balance version ($M = kPY$) is superior (in keeping with the best British tradition). The cash-balance equation can be interpreted as a demand for money function, as we mentioned above. Assume that $k = \frac{1}{4}$. Then if PY or nominal GNP equals $400, this means that people want to hold one fourth of nominal GNP, or $100, in cash balances; if GNP climbs to $600, the amount of money demanded rises to $150; and if GNP doubles to $800, money demand doubles to $200.

The fraction of nominal GNP that people want to hold in the form of money, k, is determined by many forces. It is essentially a *transactions demand* for money. Thus, since money is used as a medium of exchange, the value of k is influenced by the frequency of receipts and expenditures; if you are paid weekly, you can manage with a smaller daily average cash balance than if you are paid monthly. Second, the ease with which you can buy on credit (the use of credit cards) also influences k by permitting people to reduce the average balance in their checking accounts. Money is also used as a temporary abode of purchasing power—waiting in the wings until you summon it and exercise control over real goods and services. Thus an individual may hold more or less, depending upon whether he or she expects to be out of a job for four months or two months of the year. For the community as a whole, so the argument goes, all these factors average out and are fairly stable, hence the public winds up wanting to hold a stable and/or predictable level of money balances.

Looking at the cash-balance version of the quantity theory ($M = kPY$) as a demand for money equation, it is easy to see that the doubling of prices (and hence nominal GNP) produced by a doubling of the money supply follows directly from the equilibrium condition that the amount of money demanded must equal the supply. When M doubles, people have twice as much money as they want to hold (money supply exceeds the amount demanded), given that nothing else has changed. So they start to spend it. They stop spending when they want to hold the increased money supply (when the amount of money demanded grows into equality with the supply). That occurs when nominal GNP has doubled.

It is also possible to look at this new equilibrium position in a slightly different way. Namely, the *real* amount of money that people hold is the same in both the initial and final positions. The real amount of money is given by the actual money supply deflated by the price level, or M/P, where that tells you the amount of real goods and services that is "controlled" by the cash balances people hold. For example, if you hold a $1,000 checking account you control $1,000 worth of goods and services; if you have a $2,000 checking account but the price level has doubled, you still control the same real volume of goods and services.

The cash-balance version of the quantity theory, in fact, emphasizes that people try to fix their real money balances, not the dollar value of their cash holdings. Thus when the supply of money doubles, the public has twice as many *real* balances as it wants, given the old price level and real GNP. People try to get rid of those excess real balances by spending. But since the real output of goods and services is fixed at full employment, only prices respond to the increased demand for goods. Prices will continue to rise until people stop trying to spend those extra real balances. And that happens when they have none left, that is, after prices have doubled so that real balances are back to their original level ($M/P = 2M/2P$ is a famous theorem in Boolean algebra).

AGGREGATE DEMAND AND SUPPLY: A SUMMARY

In keeping with the best tradition of Classical economics, it is useful to summarize the discussion thus far within a supply/demand framework. This will serve us well later in bridging the Monetarist and Keynesian outlooks and will also form the foundation for analyzing inflation.

Figure 3 may not look exactly like the supply/demand graph you learned to love in basic economics, but it really is. Price is measured on the vertical axis and quantity is on the horizontal axis. In the macroeconomic framework, price refers to the price level of all goods, P, and quantity refers to the aggregate real output of all goods and services, Y. Since output (or production) and income are one and the same (two ways of measuring GNP—as shown in the Appendix to this chapter), we label the horizontal axis income. However, in our discussion we will use the terms income and output interchangeably.

The supply schedule in Figure 3 is a vertical line to represent the Classical assumption that the volume of goods and services that can be produced is fixed at full employment (Y_{FE}). In particular, changes

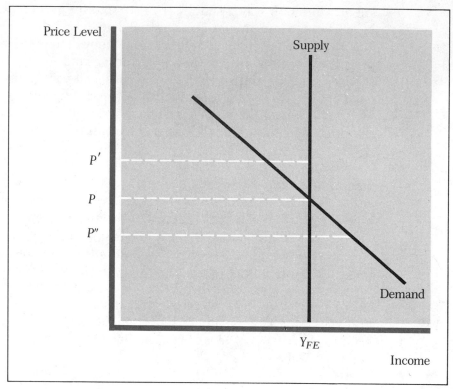

FIGURE 3 The Equilibrium Price Level

in the price level do not influence the supply of goods and services. (We encounter similar vertical supply schedules at the microeconomic level for many commodities in the very short run as well as for things like land in the long run.)

The demand schedule in Figure 3 is negatively sloped. While this is the normal shape, the reason is somewhat different in the macroeconomic context. The aggregate demand schedule is drawn for a given level of the money supply (M). And as we have just seen, a given stock of money buys more goods and services with a lower price level. Hence a lower price level means that the amount of goods and services demanded is greater.[8]

[8]Note that the normal microeconomic reasons for demand rising when prices fall are not relevant in the macroeconomic context. First, lower prices usually generate a larger amount demanded because a particular commodity is cheaper and consumers substitute it for other goods. But in the macro framework we are dealing with all goods together, and all prices are falling, hence the "substitution effect" is not relevant. Second, lower prices usually increase the amount demanded because people's incomes

The intersection of supply and demand in Figure 3 indicates the equilibrium price level. Since the supply of goods is fixed by Say's law, the demand schedule tells us only what price level will clear the market. If the price level were higher than P (as at P' in Figure 3), the aggregate demand for goods and services would be too low, and businesses would have to lower prices to sell all their output. If the price level were lower than P (as at P''), the aggregate demand for goods and services would exceed what is available, and businesses would raise prices to ration the existing supply (and to make a handsome profit). Thus P is the equilibrium price level.

Note that price flexibility is the key to the Classical school's argument that the level of real output would be at full employment. If the price level in Figure 3 were for some reason stuck at P', then aggregate demand for real goods would be below full-employment output (Y_{FE}). That's why we said earlier, in our discussion of Say's law, that flexible wages and prices would insure that all goods would be sold and all labor employed. Now we see clearly that if this weren't the case, aggregate demand for real goods would be too low. Downward rigidity in prices is one of the elements Keynes focused on in analyzing the behavior of economic activity at less than full employment, as we'll see in the next chapter.

Figure 4 allows us to identify the demand schedule more precisely. In particular, when there is a shift in the entire demand curve, we see that the price level rises from P to P'. Our discussion in the previous sections showed that increases in the money supply raise the price level. From Figure 4 we see that this occurs because higher levels of M increase the aggregate demand for goods and services. In particular, in Figure 4 at the old price level, P, the public had just the right amount of real cash balances (given the old money supply). When the supply of money is increased, the demand for goods and services at every price level goes up, because real cash balances are higher. This is represented in the figure by a rightward shift of the demand curve. The net result of this increased demand, however, is simply to raise the price level to P' because the aggregate supply of goods and services is fixed at full employment.

Our algebraic discussion in the previous sections was more specific

_____

can now buy more. But in the macro framework all prices, including the price of labor (wages), are falling. Thus the "income effect" of price decreases is irrelevant. That's why we appealed to our real money supply discussion. In particular, even though prices are falling, the stock of money is fixed by the central bank. Thus, as the value of real balances increases, because prices are falling, the amount demanded for all goods taken together rises.

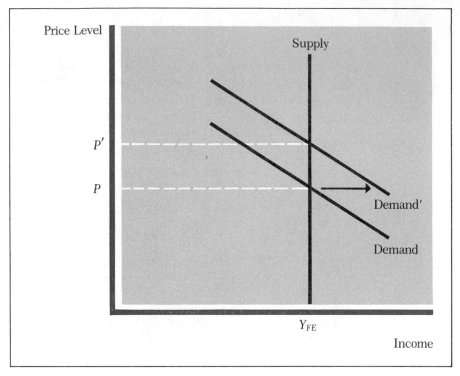

FIGURE 4 An Increase in Aggregate Demand Raises Prices

than the graphics, because we could show that changes in the money supply lead to proportional changes in prices under the quantity theory. But the pictures emphasize an important dimension as well: the quantity theory is really a specific statement of the aggregate demand for goods and services. In particular, this theory emphasizes that changes in the money supply raise prices by changing aggregate demand.

We have also just identified the source of the popular notion that inflation stems from "too much money chasing too few goods." In the context of Classical thinking, continued expansion in the money supply raises the aggregate demand for goods; with a fixed supply of goods, the result is rising prices, which is exactly what we mean by inflation. The Classical message, therefore, is that inflation is a monetary phenomenon: unless the money supply increases, the price level is stable. As we will see in Chapter 23, this is not the same conclusion reached by the Keynesian story on inflation.

REAL VERSUS NOMINAL RATES OF INTEREST

Once inflation enters the picture, we must return to amend our discussion of interest rate determination. Until now there was no need to consider the distinction between the real rate of interest and the nominal rate. The reason is that real and nominal yields are the same when the inflation rate is zero. Thus our discussion above, showing how saving and investment determine the rate of interest, is unambiguous: a given nominal rate of interest (in terms of dollars earned) is the same as the real yield (in terms of real goods and services earned) when the price level remains unchanged.

We pointed out in Chapter 5, however, that if inflation occurs, the real yield on a bond is calculated as the nominal rate less the rate of inflation. In particular, a $1,000 one-year bond that promises $50 in interest has a 5 percent nominal yield. But if the rate of increase in the price level is 2 percent, then it takes $1,020 next year just to buy what $1,000 would have purchased a year earlier. Thus only $30 of the $50 interest payment represents additional real goods and services that can be bought. In this case, therefore, the *real* yield is $30 per $1,000, or 3 percent. A convenient rule of thumb is as follows: the real yield is equal to the nominal rate minus the rate of inflation.

All of this is more arithmetic than economics. But Irving Fisher, of quantity theory fame, was the first to put the common-sense arithmetic together with some economic analysis. In particular, Fisher argued that if savers and investors expected inflation, they would force up the nominal rate of interest to include an inflation premium. The real rate would remain unchanged at the level determined by saving and investment, just as the nineteenth-century Classical economists said. But the nominal rate would increase by the expected rate of inflation.

The argument is as follows. Savers who were previously satisfied with, say, a 5 percent yield on bonds when inflation was zero will save less and lend less when the expected rate of inflation jumps to two percent—after all, their savings will buy fewer real goods next year. Investors, meanwhile, will want to borrow even more funds when they expect 2 percent inflation—after all, they'll be investing in goods and services that can be sold at even higher prices next year. Thus at the old interest rate of 5 percent there is a greater demand for funds and a smaller supply. The level of interest rates is forced up to bring saving and investment back into equality. When the nominal yield rises to 7 percent, and the real rate of interest is back at 5 percent, lenders and borrowers will once again have consistent saving and investment plans.

More specifically, unless the nominal rate of interest rises by the expected rate of inflation, the real rate of interest (the nominal rate minus the expected rate of inflation) will be too low. As we saw in Figure 1, when the real rate is below equilibrium, desired investment exceeds saving and the real rate of interest is pushed up. So Fisher's addendum to the purely Classical interest theory was that, in equilibrium, the nominal rate of interest would increase by the expected rate of inflation and the real rate would remain unchanged (determined by saving and investment at full employment).

MODERN MONETARIST MODIFICATIONS

Monetarists adhere to virtually all the tenets of Classical economics. However, they have made some modifications. For example, they have been known to use the quantity theory as a framework for describing the relationship between M and PY rather than just M and P. This approach recognizes the fact that real output may deviate temporarily from full employment and represents an attempt at describing what influences overall economic activity rather than just the price level. No doubt part of the Monetarist thrust in this direction stems from Keynesian preoccupation with real GNP and the Monetarist desire to show that the quantity theory can do the job just as well.

A Monetarist reading of the quantity theory experiments discussed earlier would go something like this. Start with $MV = PY$ and assume that velocity is 4 and the money supply is $50. Thus the total value of GNP is $200. If the money supply increases to $100, nominal GNP must rise to $400. If this increased money supply occurs during a period of unemployment, then real output (Y) will increase. On the other hand, if the economy is already at full productive capacity, then prices alone will respond as in the Classical tradition.

It must be emphasized, however, that this broader view of the quantity theory can never wander very far from the first pillar of Classical economics: Say's Law. Modern Monetarists still view the invisible hand as pushing the economy toward the full employment level of production (Y_{FE}). Any increases or decreases in Y stemming from expansions or contractions in M are viewed as temporary. As we will see in Chapter 23, much of this discussion hinges on a more precise

The Money Supply and the Great Depression

Most people believe that the Great Depression of the 1930s was started by the stock market crash of 1929. In fact, although the stock market crash might have initiated the depression, according to many economists the depth and duration of the depression must be largely attributed to the major contraction in the money supply that followed in the wake of the stock market's collapse.

First the dimensions of the depression: Gross national product in the United States was $104 billion in 1929. In 1930 it declined 13 percent to $90 billion, and in the three subsequent years GNP continued to shrink to a low point of only $56 billion in 1933. Unemployment soared: from 3 percent of the civilian labor force in 1929 to an intolerable 25 percent in 1933!

In 1939, a decade after the stock market crash, GNP was still below its 1929 level and unemployment was still 17 percent of the civilian labor force.

To a large extent, the depth and duration of the depression were due to what happened to the money supply and the associated impact on spending. M1 (currency plus checking accounts) was $26 billion in 1929. By 1933, though, M1 had declined by 23 percent, to only $19 billion. In other words, almost a fourth of the money supply simply disappeared.

This money supply contraction resulted from the collapse of the banking system. In the four years 1930 through 1933, more than 9,000 commercial banks failed, wiping out billions of dollars of deposits (there was no federal deposit insurance yet, since the FDIC didn't begin operations until 1934).

It was 1936 before the money supply recovered to its 1929 level. No wonder the depression was so deep and lasted so long.

specification of the aggregate supply and demand schedules that were just introduced.

A second modification of Classical thought occurred with Milton Friedman's revival of the quantity theory during the 1950s.[9] Friedman replaced the idea of the stability of velocity with the less militant notion that it is predictable. Or, looked at another way, money demand may not be a fixed fraction of total spending, but it is related to *PY* in a close and predictable way. Obviously this provides a looser linkage between changes in money and prices, one that must be de-

[9]See Milton Friedman, ''The Quantity Theory of Money—A Restatement'' in his *Studies in the Quantity Theory of Money* (Chicago: University of Chicago Press, 1956).

scribed in statistical terms rather than with a simple arithmetical example.[10] Nevertheless, if people respond in a predictable way to changes in the money supply, much of the Classical heritage is sustained.

Perhaps the most important Classical tradition that is upheld by modern Monetarists is the inherent stability of the economy at full employment. This explains the Monetarist rejection of governmental attempts to fine-tune economic activity. A higher level of economic activity requires more capital and labor or technological improvements; more money only leads to inflation. The answer to cyclical downturns is to wait for the natural upturn. Government intervention is unnecessary and potentially damaging.

Monetarists have added still another wrinkle to the futility of government efforts at fine tuning—rational expectations. This perspective, as we will see in greater detail in Chapter 24, emphasizes that people formulate expectations based on all available information, including their knowledge of how the economy behaves. Recognizing that the economy tends toward full employment implies that any attempt at increasing the money supply to reduce unemployment will not be successful. People will immediately equate increases in money supply with an offsetting rise in prices. Thus there will not be any expansionary impact on real economic activity, because increases in money supply simultaneously generate expectations of higher prices.

To some extent, these are the implications of Classical economics that sparked the Keynesian revolution. While modern Monetarists have popularized the notion of a self-correcting economy, enticing even some Keynesian disciples, there are still significant areas of disagreement between the two schools of macroeconomics. In the next chapter we outline the Keynesian viewpoint and then return to the Monetarist-Keynesian dialogue in Chapters 23 and 24.

SUMMARY

1. Modern Monetarism traces its roots to Classical economics. The two main concepts of Classical thinking on money and aggregate economic activity are Say's Law and the quantity theory.

[10]The collection of essays cited in footnote 9 was Friedman's first attempt at statistical confirmation of the quantity theory. We will survey some of the more recent evidence in Chapter 25.

"Mr. Semple, who wants to stimulate the economy, help the cities, and clean up the environment, I'd like you to meet Mr. Hobart, who wants to let the economy, the cities, and the environment take care of themselves. I'm sure you two will have a lot to talk about."

Drawing by Stan Hunt; © 1976 by The New Yorker Magazine, Inc.

2. Say's Law emphasizes that the economy is inherently stable at full employment. Any deviations from that level of economic activity are only temporary. A key mechanism promoting stability is the flexibility of interest rates. Saving and investment are brought into equality through variations in the interest rate.

3. The quantity theory of money states that the impact of money in Classical economics is limited to the price level. Increases in the money supply raise prices, and decreases in money reduce the price level. Money is neutral with respect to the real sector of the economy. There is a clear distinction between real and nominal magnitudes.

4. At the heart of the quantity theory is a stable demand for money. More particularly, the demand for real cash balances is a predictable fraction of real GNP. This stability allows the quantity theory to predict that changes in money supply will be reflected in spending, and hence in prices.

5. The quantity theory can also be viewed as a statement about what determines the aggregate demand for goods and services. In particular, it says that increases in the money supply raise aggregate demand. With aggregate

supply fixed at full employment, the impact of an increase in the money supply is to raise prices.

6. The real rate of interest is determined by saving and investment. When expectations of inflation emerge, the nominal rate of interest is forced up to include an inflation premium, leaving the real rate unchanged.

7. Modern Monetarists treat the quantity theory more flexibly than their Classical ancestors did. Money influences spending in a predictable way rather than in a rigid numerical fashion. Moreover, if the economy is at less than full employment, even real output might respond to changes in the money supply. But the natural tendency toward full employment eliminates any systematic impact on real output of changes in money supply.

Suggestions for Further Reading

Two books by Irving Fisher, *The Theory of Interest* (New York: Macmillan, 1930) and *The Purchasing Power of Money* (New York: Macmillan, 1911) are the most comprehensive treatments of Classical interest theory and the quantity theory, respectively. More recently, Milton Friedman has "modernized" the quantity theory; see "The Quantity Theory of Money—A Restatement" in his *Studies in the Quantity Theory of Money* (Chicago: University of Chicago Press, 1956).

GNP Definitions and Relationships

This is a review of basic aggregate economic relationships that are relevant for both Monetarist and Keynesian analyses. We discuss the circular flow of income and output, the separation between saving and investment, and other paradigms of praxeology and catallactic concepts. Of course, if you have forgotten the meaning of some of the simple terms in the last sentence, you should read on to refresh your memory.

THE CIRCULAR FLOW OF SPENDING, INCOME, AND OUTPUT

Let's start by taking a simplified view of the economy, dividing its participants into two groups: business firms and households. Firms produce goods and services for sale; households buy these goods and services and consume them. Households are able to buy the goods and services produced by firms because they also supply firms with all the land, labor, capital and entrepreneurship required for production; hence they receive as income the total proceeds of production. The total value of the goods and services produced is called gross national product (GNP), or more simply national income (Y), and it can be measured by either the total output sold by firms *or* the total income received by households (in the form of wages, rent, interest, and profits).

These relationships are summarized in Figure 1, the inner circle recording flows of *real* things (factors of production to firms and goods and services to households), the outer circle recording the associated *money* flows (income payments to households and money expenditures to firms). The money flow relationship can be written symbolically as $C = Y$, where C stands for household spending on consumer goods and Y stands for national income or GNP.

As long as firms sell all their output, they will continue to produce at that level. As long as we assume that all the income received by

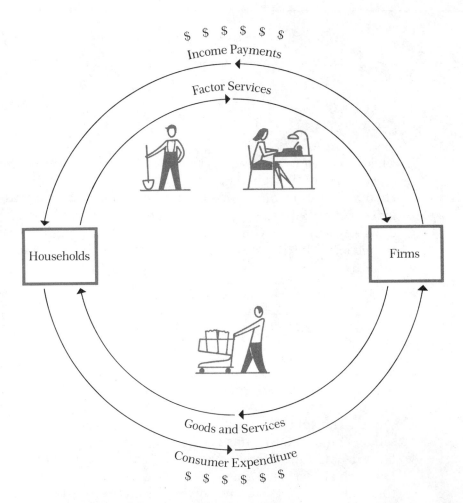

FIGURE 1 The Circular Flow of Spending, Income, and Output

households is spent on the goods and services produced, production equals sales, output equals demand, and we are in equilibrium (there is no tendency for anything to change). But if we keep this up much longer, you will have fallen asleep in the very position you are now in, maybe still holding this book (also equilibrium). So we modify things a bit to make our hypothetical economy more like the real one.

SAVING AND INVESTMENT

Households don't spend all their income; they usually save some fraction. Saving represents a leakage in the circular flow. Total income of households (which is equal to the total value of goods and services produced by firms) does not all return to firms in the form of consumption expenditures. Saving (S) is defined simply as total income (Y) minus consumption spending (C)—that is, $S = Y - C$. It may not have anything specifically to do with putting the money in a bank, under the mattress, or in the stock market. Households may do any of these things with their savings—that is, with the excess of their income over their spending on consumer goods. For now we are not concerned with their financial transactions, just with the fact that failure to spend all income implies that total expenditure is less than total income (and total production). If things remained that way, output would exceed sales and firms would want to cut back production.

But all is not lost. Consumer goods are not the only thing that firms produce. Firms themselves add to their stock of production facilities or to inventories—they buy goods and services for their own use, which we call investment spending (I). If firms *want to invest* (I) exactly what households *want to save* (S), then all that is produced will once again be sold, but this time to both households (for consumption) and business firms (for investment). And, of course, the level of output will be one of equilibrium (hooray). This happy state of affairs is summarized in Figure 2 and can be represented as $C + I = Y$. Note that we can also describe the situation as one in which the leakage from the household spending stream (saving) is equal to business spending on investment, or, in symbols, $S = I$.

In Figure 2 we have labeled the connecting link between saving and investment the financial markets. Decisions to save are often made by people very different from those who invest—saving is done by the little people in the economy who scrimp to hold their spending down

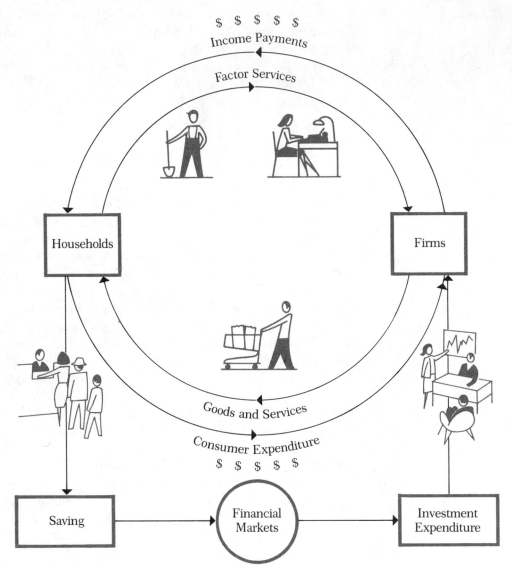

FIGURE 2 The Circular Flow Including Saving and Investment

in order to prepare for a rainy day, while investment is done by corporate executives sitting at huge oval desks with thirteen phones and four secretaries. These seemingly diverse groups are brought together by financial markets, with the savings of ordinary people borrowed by the corporate executives and then spent on investment goods, so that both groups may continue along their merry way.

The word "investment" is frequently confusing, because it is used to mean different things. Here it means the purchase of "real" productive facilities, like factories and machine tools, whereas in common usage "investment" often refers to purely financial transactions, like buying stocks and bonds. Buying stocks and bonds can have implications for "real" investment (the purchase of factories and machine tools), but they are clearly different things. We will usually reserve the term "investment" for buying productive facilities, as we are using it here. In later chapters, however, we will occasionally fall into common parlance and use it for buying financial assets, like stocks and bonds; in that case, the purely financial meaning will be clear from the context.

It is important to emphasize that for equilibrium output to occur when saving equals investment it is necessary that households *want to save* the same amount as business firms *want to invest.* As we noted earlier in this chapter, Classical economics assumed that the interest rate would bring desired saving and investment together.

We have to distinguish this condition (where desired S = desired I) from one in which S and I are equal simply by definition. That is, saving is defined as $Y - C$. But $C + I = Y$, so that I also equals $Y - C$. Thus, by definition, S must always equal I, since both equal $Y - C$. But *this* equality is an ex post accounting identity, always true by definition. It is not an ex ante behavioral equality arising from what people *want* to do. Only when people *want* to save what firms *want* to invest will income be in equilibrium (remain unchanged). A concrete example is given in the next chapter.

So far we have ignored the government (wishful thinking?). It too introduces a leakage between income payments and household consumption expenditures—namely, taxes (T). When the government collects taxes, households have less to spend on consumer goods (and less to save). If some other form of spending did not increase when taxes were levied, production once again would exceed the sum of all types of expenditures, and economic activity would decline. But the government could lend these funds to business firms so they could increase investment spending, or the government itself could buy goods and services from business firms.

If *desired* spending in the form of consumption (C), investment (I), and government expenditure (G) equals total output, or $C + I + G = Y$, then that level of production will be maintained. Note that we can also describe the situation as one in which total leakages from the spending stream, saving plus taxes, equals total spending injections in the form of investment and government expenditure, or $S + T = I + G$. For simplicity, we may sometimes refer to the left-hand side as total saving and the right-hand side as total investment.

Although we have now relaxed many of the hypothetical assumptions that populated our simple economy, we have still not introduced foreigners—exports and imports. Such a radical step is usually reserved for an entirely separate section in most textbooks. Ours is no exception.

ANOTHER CATALLACTIC CONCEPT[1]

We can look at the same subject, total spending in the economy, from a slightly different angle. So far we have viewed total spending as consisting of three categories, $C + I + G$. This breakdown is in terms of who does the spending—consumers, business firms, or government. But total spending could also be viewed as consisting of the quantity of money in existence (M) multiplied by the average number of times each dollar is spent on goods and services during a given period of time, which, as we noted in this chapter, is called velocity (V) or the rate of turnover of money.

This way of looking at total spending ($M \times V$) is in terms of *what* is spent rather than *who* does the spending. An analogy: If two people are alternating driving a car, and one drives 50 miles and the other 30 miles, the total number of miles driven equals 80. A different way of finding the total miles driven is to calculate how many hours were spent driving and the average speed per hour—say, two hours at an average speed of 40 miles per hour. Total: 80 miles. This second way makes who is doing the driving irrelevant, just as with $M \times V$ it is irrelevant who is doing the spending. Since both $M \times V$ and $C + I + G$ are formulas for total spending, we can also equate $M \times V$ with *GNP* (as can be seen in Table 1). At times one way of looking at the process may be more fruitful, and at times the other may be more illuminating.[2]

We have seen in this chapter that Classical economists and their Monetarist descendants prefer the money-velocity link with total

[1]Literally: exchange concept. Paradigm of praxeology = model of human action.
[2]The equality between MV and $C + I + G$ properly refers to nominal GNP, since $MV = PY$. As we will see in Chapter 23, this is one of the focal points of the Monetarist-Keynesian dialogue.

TABLE 1

**Components of Spending = Income, 1970–1987
(Dollars in billions)**

Year	C	+	I	+	G	=	GNP	=	M	×	V
1970	620		150		220		990		220		4.50
1980	1670		420		540		2630		420		6.26
1987	2,850		720		930		4,500		740		6.08

SOURCE: *Annual Reports*, Council of Economic Advisors.

spending. We will see in the next chapter that Keynesian economists prefer to emphasize the impact on GNP of consumption, investment, and government spending. Part of the difference stems from the fact that Monetarists discuss both real and nominal GNP, while Keynesians focus almost exclusively on real GNP, as we shall see later.

CHAPTER 20

The Keynesian Framework

John Maynard Keynes, first baron of Tilton (1883–1946), did many things differently. We are not concerned here with his ability to make a fortune speculating in the market while simultaneously teaching at King's College, Cambridge; nor with his infatuation with the finer things in life—ballet, drama—and his editorial supervision for many years of the technical *Economic Journal;* nor with his unique abilities in the fields of mathematics, philosophy, and literature. Rather, we are concerned with his contribution to economics in his book, *The General Theory of Employment, Interest and Money,* published in 1936: how it revolutionized the thinking of all economists since, how it replaced Classical economics as the conventional wisdom, and how it led to a different outlook on employment, interest, and money.

Before going into the details of Keynes's contributions to macroeconomics and monetary theory and the refinement of his ideas at the hands of other economists (collectively labeled Keynesians), it will be helpful to set the stage by noting an essential difference in Keynes's outlook compared with that of his Classical teachers. Keynes was concerned with the short run, while Classical economists were preoccupied with the long run. Keynes's attitude toward the concern of his Classical mentors is best illustrated by his now-famous dictum: "In the long run, we are all dead."

Classical economics explained why fluctuating prices and interest

rates would continuously push economic activity toward full employment. But Keynes argued that these free market forces could take
considerable time to work themselves out. And in the short run there
could be lengthy periods of underemployment. While it is difficult to
delineate the borderline between the short run and long run, the six
years of worldwide depression preceding the publication of Keynes's
magnum opus seemed too long to wait for Classical market forces to
restore full employment.

Keynes was preoccupied with what determined the level of real
economic activity during those lengthy recession or depression intervals between the full employment points of the Classical school. Real
output could increase without any increase in the price level if we
started out in a sufficiently depressed state. All of Keynes's basic analysis assumes that the price level is fixed.[1] Therefore, throughout this
chapter, all changes in GNP represent real changes. Moreover,
throughout this book, whenever GNP appears without a modifier, it
refers to *real* GNP. As in the last chapter, real GNP is represented by
the letter Y.

Keynes obviously had to focus on the aggregate demand for goods
and services, since full employment supply was irrelevant for his particular problem. Theoretically, he could have chosen the quantity
theory to describe aggregate demand, just as he had done in his Classical life before 1936. But in his new incarnation he had other plans for
money, quite different from the quantity theory. Moreover, he believed he had to introduce a new set of analytical tools to deal with
unemployment, since Classical economics had almost nothing to say
about such matters. Keynes wanted to design a model of GNP determination that would explain how economic activity could be in equilibrium at *less* than full employment. Who or what was to blame for a
depressed level of economic activity? To what extent is money the
culprit?

A model is like a map. It does not include every detail of the actual
terrain; rather, it incorporates only those characteristics that are essential in explaining how to go from one point to another. Don't be turned
off, therefore, if Keynes's model appears to be highly aggregative, ignoring many specifics and making many heroic assumptions. That is precisely what models are supposed to do: strip away the superfluous detail
and get down to basics. The ultimate test, of course, is whether that
simplified view of the world cuts through to explain actual behavior.

---

[1]Toward the end of this chapter we will describe how this looks in terms of the
aggregate supply and demand framework introduced in Figure 3 of the last chapter.

WHEN SAVING DOESN'T EQUAL INVESTMENT

The Appendix to the previous chapter showed that for GNP to be at an equilibrium level—that is, no tendency for change—all that is produced must be sold to consumers or willingly added to the capital stock as investment by business firms. We also said that this equilibrium condition could be stated in another way: total saving *desired* by households must equal total investment *desired* by firms. In that way the leakage out of the spending stream in the form of saving would be made up by desired investment spending by firms, and everyone would be happy.

We also mentioned in the Appendix that ex post (after all is said and done) saving is always equal to investment. Only in the ex ante (desired) sense is equality of saving and investment an equilibrium condition. Let's take a very specific example of these relationships to set the stage for our discussion in the rest of the chapter.

Assume entrepreneurs produce $1,000 billion of output (Y) at full employment and expect to sell $800 billion to consumers (C) and want to use the remaining $200 billion for investment (including inventory accumulation). They will continue producing at that rate only if their sales are realized. If consumers plan to buy $800 billion in consumer goods and services and therefore *desire* to save $200 billion, all is well. But what if consumers decide they want to spend only $700 billion on consumer goods, which means they want to save $300 billion? What will give?

Assuming that consumers succeed in implementing their spending plans, entrepreneurs will wind up selling only $700 billion, although they have produced $800 billion in consumer goods and services. Clearly their selling plans have been disappointed, and they wind up with an *extra* $100 billion in (unwanted) inventories. In fact, they *wind up* investing $300 billion (the same as saving): their planned capital accumulation of $200 billion plus $100 billion of *unintended* inventory accumulation. Saving (S) equals investment (I) ex post, but *desired* savings exceeds *desired* investment by $100 billion.

The key Classical-Keynesian confrontation involves precisely such circumstances: what happens when *desired* saving exceeds desired investment? The Classics had a series of simple answers based on a single principle—*prices adjust* when there is an excess supply of or demand for any good (or all goods together). Therefore, when there is an excess supply that isn't being sold, entrepreneurs reduce their prices to get rid of unsold inventories, workers lower their wage demands to stave off unemployment, and the rate of interest (the *price* of borrowing) decreases when saving exceeds investment. The fall in the interest rate lowers desired saving (increasing desired consumer spending directly) and raises desired investment, until desired saving and investment are again equal and entrepreneurs are content with their previous (full employment equilibrium) level of production. All of this was stated more formally in the preceding chapter.

But Keynes was not sympathetic. Prices are sticky and probably wouldn't decline as inventories piled up. Wages are notoriously resistant to decreases and, even more important, fluctuations in the rate of interest do not equilibrate desired saving and desired investment. The rate of interest is determined in the money market; it equilibrates the supply and demand for money, not saving and investment. (And that is why Keynes dropped the quantity theory, as we will see in greater detail later.)

Assuming that the rate of interest doesn't bring saving into equality with investment, what happens as a result of the undesired inventory accumulation? Keynes thought that the level of real output, rather than prices, would respond most quickly. Entrepreneurs with unwanted accumulating inventories would probably cut back production. Output would fall as long as desired saving exceeded desired investment. Since the price level was unchanged, both real output and income would decline. How far? Until desired S equaled desired I, when a new equilibrium GNP, lower than before, would be reached. To help us see how far GNP would fall when desired saving exceeds desired investment, Keynes invented the consumption function (or, looked at another way, the saving function).

CONSUMPTION AND SIMPLE GNP DETERMINATION

We start by determining equilibrium production, or GNP, where GNP is measured by both income received and output sold (as described in the Appendix to the previous chapter). Figure 1 is the familiar Keynesian cross diagram. On the horizontal axis we measure real income and real output (both represented by Y) and on the vertical axis we measure different types of expenditure. For simplicity we label the horizontal axis income and the vertical axis expenditure. The line drawn from the origin at an angle of 45° marks off equal magnitudes on each axis (remember isosceles triangles from basic geometry?), hence it traces the equilibrium condition $E = Y$, or expenditure equals income.

Expenditure takes two forms: consumption and investment (we'll ignore the government for a while). Keynes argued that consumption

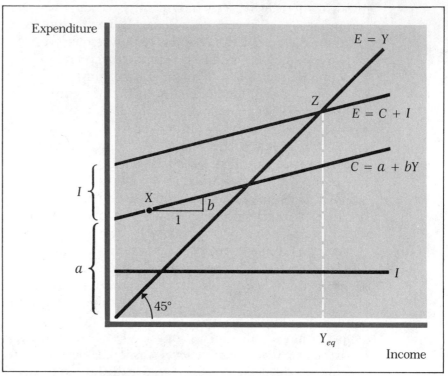

FIGURE 1 Spending Determines Income

spending (C) depends mainly on the level of income (Y)—more income, more consumption. In Figure 1, therefore, desired consumption is a simple linear function of Y:

$$C = a + bY$$

The letter b is the slope of the line, or $\Delta C/\Delta Y$, the change in consumption per unit change in income (see point X in Figure 1). It is called the marginal propensity to consume and is assumed to be less than 1. For example, if b is .8, that means an increase in Y of $100 raises C by $80. (It also means that saving goes up by $20.)

   The a in the consumption function is the constant term. It records the level of C if Y were zero (presumably people eat even if they have no income—many of us have relatives like that), and it also sums up all other influences on consumption besides income. For example, if you had bought Xerox when it was $1 a share (only as far back as 1958), you would now be consuming a lot more than if you bought silver when it was $50 an ounce (January 1980). Thus the consumption function might shift up or down, recorded by larger or smaller values for a, if people are wealthier or poorer, although our equation still says they would consume $8 out of every $10 *increment* in earned income.

As far as investment (I) is concerned, Keynes agreed with the Classics that it is a function of the rate of interest on bonds. Entrepreneurs compare the expected rate of return on a prospective investment with the rate of interest.[2] They invest as long as the rate of return exceeds the rate of interest and continue up to the point at which the expected return on the last investment just equals the rate of interest. If the rate of interest declines, then investment projects with lower expected

---

[2]Note that since prices are fixed and inflationary expectations are zero, all nominal rates are the same as real rates.

The rate of return on an investment is determined by the expected future dollar revenues on the project and the current cost of the investment. In particular, if an investment is expected to generate $105 next year and requires a cash outlay of $100, we can calculate the rate of return quite simply. It is that rate of discount which equates the expected future revenues with the current cost, or $100 = \dfrac{105}{1 + q}$, where q is the rate of discount or, in our terminology, the rate of return. In our case it is clearly equal to .05, or 5 percent. We call q the rate of discount because it reduces (discounts) the $105 that is due next year to its current value (time is money). See Chapter 5 for a similar discussion.

Looked at another way, $100 put out at 5 percent for 1 year (100×1.05) produces $105 one year hence. This perspective also gives a clue as to how one ought to treat revenues two years hence. Namely, $100 left at 5 percent for two years produces 100×1.05 after one year, or $105, which is then reinvested and generates $110.25 after the next year ($105 \times 1.05 = \$110.25$). In general, therefore, if R_1 is the expected revenue two years from now, it must be discounted twice or

$$C = \frac{R_2}{(1 + q)(1 + q)} = \frac{R_2}{(1 + q)^2}$$

The general formula for the rate of return is as follows. If revenues of R_1, R_2 ... R_n are expected over the next n years, then the rate of discount q which equates C, the current cost, to the expected stream of revenues, as in

$$C = \frac{R_1}{(1 + q)} + \frac{R_2}{(1 + q)^2} + \ldots + \frac{R_n}{(1 + q)^n}$$

is called the rate of return on the investment project. Relax—you have at least 13 seconds to perform the necessary computations.

Those of you who still remember Chapter 5 may recall that this equation is very similar to the one used to calculate the yield (rate of return) on a bond. Just substitute P (the price of the bond) for C, put the coupons (C_1 through C_n) where the R's are, and replace q with the rate of interest (r). In fact, once you do that, the formulas are the same, which is just fine since in both cases we're measuring rates of return. Of course, that doesn't make it any easier to calculate these things.

returns become profitable and investment will increase. For now we take the rate of interest as given. We also take expectations as given, which is an even more questionable proposition. Under such conditions, investment is some constant amount (say \$200 billion), as indicated by the horizontal line labeled I in Figure 1.

Equilibrium output is represented by the line $E = Y$, where total desired expenditure (E) equals total income, Y. Total desired expenditure is the sum of desired C and desired I, or, in Figure 1, line $E = C + I$, which is the vertical addition of C ($= a + bY$) and I. The point at which the total desired expenditure line ($E = C + I$) crosses the expenditure-equals-production line ($E = Y$) is equilibrium income (Y_{eq}). Point Z in Figure 1 is an example. At the level of production Y_{eq}, desired expenditure equals income.

It is also true that *desired* saving equals desired investment at that same income level. Desired saving is given by the difference between income and desired consumption (that is, $S = Y - C$). It can be measured by the vertical difference between the 45° line and the consumption function. In Figure 1 the only point at which saving (the vertical difference between the 45° line and the consumption function) equals investment (the difference between the $E = C + I$ line and the consumption function) is at income Y_{eq}.

In Figure 2 we have plotted the saving function explicitly, where Y is measured along the horizontal axis and dollars saved or invested are on the vertical axis. Saving is defined as $Y - C$, so that desired saving, S, equals $Y - (a + bY)$. Rearranging terms (and factoring the Y term) gives:

$$S = -a + (1 - b)Y$$

which is called the saving function. The marginal propensity to save equals 1 minus the marginal propensity to consume (out of each dollar increment in Y, a person spends b cents and saves $1 - b$ cents). From Figure 2 it is also clear that only at income Y_{eq} is desired saving equal to investment. At higher levels of income, desired saving exceeds desired investment; at lower levels of income, desired saving is less than desired investment.

CHANGES IN GNP

Will production and income stay at level Y_{eq} in Figure 1 forever? It will if the consumption function (and hence the saving function) remains where it is, and if desired investment is also unchanged. Is that

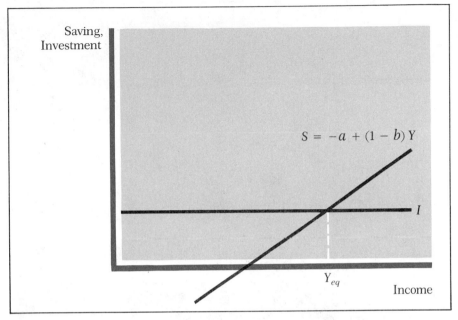

$$S = -a + (1 - b)Y$$

I

Y_{eq}

Saving, Investment

Income

FIGURE 2 Saving and Investment Determine Income

good? Yes, *if* Y_{eq} is the full employment level of economic activity. But not only wouldn't Keynes guarantee that it would be full employment, he was convinced that it would be only a fortuitous accident if it were. He reasoned that the level of economic activity is subject to wide swings because the level of investment is highly unstable. The consumption function is quite stable—you can always count on dumb households to consume a predictable percentage of income. But if entrepreneurs became uncertain about future sales prospects—especially about what other business firms were planning to do—then desired investment spending would decline and GNP would fall.

There are two ways to see *how far* GNP declines when desired investment spending falls. Let us first look at what happens in terms of total spending (investment and consumption) when desired investment falls—the wide-angle approach of Figure 1. We can then look at it from the standpoint of the investment-saving relationship—the isolated camera on S and I of Figure 2.

In Figure 3 we have replotted Figure 1's equilibrium point Z and the equilibrium income associated with the old total spending function $E = C + I_{old}$. If desired investment now falls to I_{new}, then the total desired spending function declines to $E = C + I_{new}$, the new equilibrium point is at N, and income declines to $Y_{new\ eq}$. The decline in

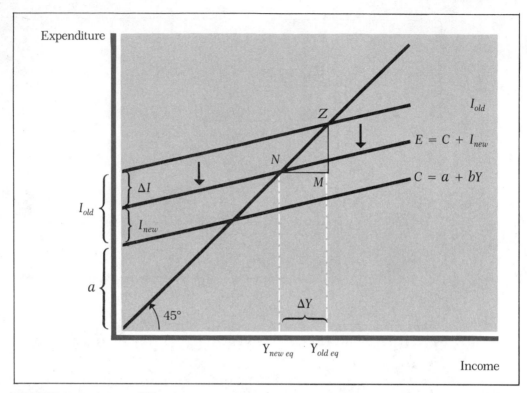

FIGURE 3 A Decline in Investment Spending Reduces _Y_ by a Multiple of the Change in Investment

income is written as ΔY (the change in Y) and is measured by the change in income along the horizontal axis or by the distance MN (constructed parallel to the horizontal axis). As can be seen in Figure 3, the decline in income _exceeds_ the decline in investment: the decline in income is ZM, which is equal to MN by construction, while the drop in investment is only part of ZM.

Why does income change by some _multiple_ of the change in investment spending? Quite simply, because when investment changes and income begins to decrease (or increase), there is a further _induced_ change in consumer spending. Consumption is a function of income, and whenever there is a change in Y, consumption spending is affected by the amount $b\Delta Y$, where b is the marginal propensity to consume.

How large is the ΔY associated with a particular ΔI? GNP will change by the sum of the changes in both components of expenditure, namely $\Delta I + \Delta C$. Algebraically:

$$\Delta Y = \Delta I + \Delta C$$

But we know that, after all is said and done, $\Delta C = b\Delta Y$ (from our consumption function). Substituting $b\Delta Y$ for ΔC we have:

$$\Delta Y = \Delta I + b\Delta Y$$

We can now solve for the unknown value of ΔY by isolating the ΔY terms on the left side. We do this by subtracting $b\Delta Y$ from each side, which yields:

$$\Delta Y - b\Delta Y = \Delta I$$

Factoring the ΔY terms on the left side gives us:

$$\Delta Y(1 - b) = \Delta I$$

Dividing both sides by $(1 - b)$ produces:

$$\Delta Y = \Delta I \frac{1}{1 - b}$$

where $1/(1 - b)$ is known as the *multiplier.* If b, the marginal propensity to consume, equals .8, then the change in income will be 5 times the initial change in investment. If $b = .5$, the change in income will be 2 times the initial ΔI.[3]

The second way of looking at this process is to impose our desired S equals desired I condition for equilibrium. In Figure 4 we see that at income $Y_{old\,eq}$ investment I_{old} equals desired saving. When invest-

---

[3]The multiplier is sometimes derived by more explicit use of the successive rounds of consumption flowing from the initial ΔI. This is called period analysis, and it goes something like this. Initially ΔI produces a direct change in income, ΔY, equal to the ΔI. But then consumption changes by $b\Delta Y$ (which is equal to $b\Delta I$). This leads to a further change in consumption, $b(b\Delta I)$. This goes on, with the successive additions to GNP getting smaller and smaller because b is less than unity, hence b^2 is smaller than b, b^3 is smaller than b^2, and so on. The total ΔY is equal to the initial change in investment plus all of the subsequent changes in consumption (which stem from the initial $\Delta I = \Delta Y$). Or $\Delta Y = \Delta I + b\Delta I + b^2\Delta I + b^3\Delta I + \ldots + b^n\,\Delta I$. The right-hand side is a geometric progression whose sum is given by

$$\Delta I \times \frac{(1 - b^n)}{(1 - b)}$$

Since b is less than unity, b^n approaches zero as n gets large; hence we have

$$\Delta Y = \Delta I \times \frac{1}{(1 - b)}$$

which (surprisingly enough) is the same expression we derived in the text! These successive rounds of consumption were lumped together in the text into one $b\Delta Y$, by saying "after all is said and done," while here we build it up from each round of ΔY.

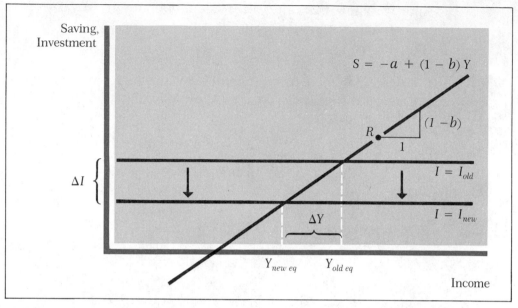

FIGURE 4 A Decline in Investment Spending Reduces Y by a Multiple of the Change in Investment

ment falls to I_{new} and income is still at $Y_{old\,eq}$, desired saving exceeds desired investment and income must fall. Income falls enough to reduce desired saving until it is equal to investment. But we know from our saving function (see point R in Figure 4) exactly how much saving changes per unit ΔY:

$$\Delta S = (1 - b)\Delta Y$$

Since desired ΔS must equal desired ΔI in equilibrium, we can impose the following condition:

$$\Delta I = \Delta S$$

and then directly relate ΔI to ΔY by substituting $(1 - b)\,\Delta Y$ for ΔS. Hence:

$$\Delta I = (1 - b)\Delta Y$$

Dividing both sides by $(1 - b)$ produces:

$$\Delta Y = \Delta I \frac{1}{1 - b}$$

which, to our great chagrin, is the same multiplier formula as before.

AUTONOMOUS VERSUS INDUCED CHANGES IN GNP

Figures 3 and 4 suggest that anything that shifts the *position* of the total desired spending function will alter GNP. Such shifts in the position of the spending function are produced by *autonomous* spending changes (autonomous = independent; in our case, independent of GNP). The larger the size of the autonomous change in spending, the greater will be the change in economic activity.

But the multiplier story was based on the fact that autonomous spending changes also *induce* further changes in spending—in our case, via the consumption function. The larger the propensity to spend out of increments in income, or the larger the *slope* of the spending function (the larger *b* is), the greater will be the induced change in spending, and thus the greater will be ΔY.

Now you can see why Keynes divided spending into the two categories of consumption and investment. What he was really interested in was induced versus autonomous spending decisions. He argued that consumption spending is largely induced, while investment spending is largely autonomous (independent of income, but a function of the expected rate of return on capital and the rate of interest). Of course, investment prospects might be influenced by sales (current and future), which are certainly related to GNP. Similarly, desired consumption may change independently of current income; the constant term in the consumption function, *a*, shifts when Xerox goes from $10 per share to $100 per share. Nevertheless, Keynes still felt consumer spending was largely induced (by *Y*), while investment spending was largely independent (of *Y*).

It is worth noting that the multiplier expression derived above can be modified quite simply to take account of other sources of ΔY. In particular, ΔY is related to *any* autonomous change in spending (ΔA) by the same $1/(1 - b)$ factor. Or:

$$\Delta Y = \Delta A \frac{1}{1 - b}$$

For example, if the consumption function shifts upward, then ΔA equals the difference between the old and new levels of autonomous consumption spending. Just like ΔI, this produces a direct change in *Y* that then causes further changes in *Y* via the conventional reaction of consumption to income.

The great problem of macroeconomics, according to Keynes, was that changes in autonomous spending would spark fluctuations in economic activity—rather wide fluctuations, via the multiplier, if the induced component of expenditure were large. These wide fluctuations in GNP would be associated with unemployment when GNP fell below its full employment level as a result of a decline in autonomous spending. What to do? The Classical response to such a situation was to do nothing—laissez faire. Keep hands off and let the long run work things out. But that was not the Keynesian response.

GOVERNMENT TO THE RESCUE

Keynes was the original Big Spender. If the private sector doesn't spend enough to keep everyone employed, let George do it (King George, of course). Government spending and taxation could be manipulated to offset the autonomous forces buffeting GNP and thereby restore full employment.

It is not very difficult to add government expenditure and taxes to our simple model. GNP is equal to the total of all expenditures in the economy—consumption, investment, and government:

$$C + I + G = Y$$

Assuming that government spending is some fixed level G, we can simply add another line to Figure 1 for autonomous government

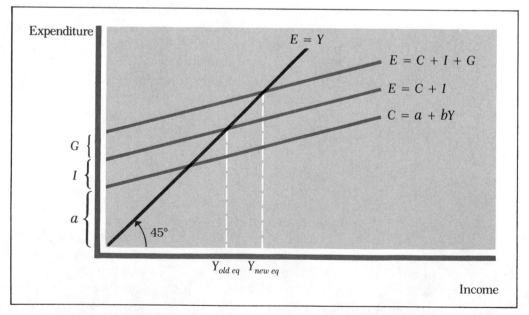

FIGURE 5 Adding Government Spending Raises Income

"There are plenty of jobs around. People just don't want to work."

Drawing by Drucker; © 1972 The New Yorker Magazine, Inc.

spending. This is done in Figure 5, where $Y_{new\ eq}$ is the new equilibrium level of income when government spending is added.

The government usually finances its expenditures by taxation. Taxes do not lower spending directly, in the same sense that government expenditure directly changes spending. Rather, taxes reduce the amount of income that households have available for consumption expenditure. Consumption is not so much a function of GNP but of *disposable* income, where that is defined as equal to income minus taxes $(Y - T)$. We therefore have a new consumption function, written as:

$$C = a + b (Y - T)$$

Or, after carrying out the multiplication we can write the consumption function as:

$$C = a + bY - bT$$

It is easy to see from either way of writing the consumption function that when taxes go up by $10, consumption declines by b times that amount (or if $b = .8$, by $8). The reason is quite simple: people treat a dollar of income taken away by the government the same way they treat any other decline of a dollar's worth of income—they reduce consumption expenditure by the marginal propensity to consume times the change.

Taxes, in fact, introduce the same type of leakage between income and spending that saving does. From the standpoint of our model it

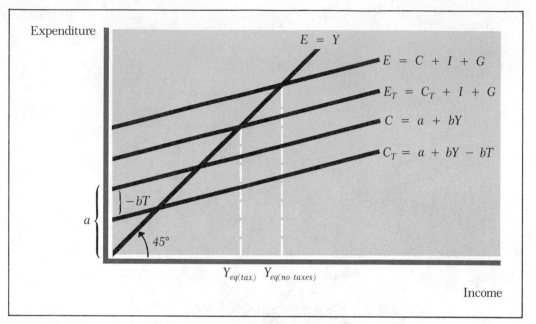

FIGURE 6 Introducing Taxes Lowers Income

makes no difference whether people reduce their consumption because they just happen to feel like it or because the government says it would be nice if they did (curiously, if you don't feel like it in the second case, you wind up getting a striped uniform and free room and board for between one and five years). In either case, the consumption function shifts downward. Figure 6 shows the equilibrium levels of GNP with and without taxes. Figures 5 and 6 also suggest that changes in both government spending and taxes produce multiplier effects on GNP. In this respect they are just like any other kind of autonomous expenditure. But there is one big difference: both taxes and government spending can be changed by government policy.[4]

The moral of the model of GNP including government expenditure and taxation is that the economy need not be buffeted about by autonomous changes in investment spending. Entrepreneurs may cut their desired investment spending if they get nervous, but nothing need happen to GNP as long as the government keeps its collective head and either increases *its* spending or lowers taxes so that consumers can increase theirs. In either case, the autonomous decline in investment

---

[4]We will ignore the fact that taxes vary with the level of income. It does change the nature of the model slightly, but for our purposes we are better off without that complication.

spending could be offset by government *fiscal policy* (fiscal means pertaining to the public treasury or revenue, from the Latin *fiscus*). Whether or not the timing and magnitude of changes in G and T would be appropriate, given the institutional setup, is another matter (and will be discussed in later chapters). But the possibility of improving on the workings of the free market is certainly evident.

This returns us to an important issue mentioned earlier: is fiscal policy even necessary? Why doesn't income remain at full employment, with desired saving and investment brought into equality via fluctuations in the rate of interest, as the Classical economists said would happen? Why did Keynes, a truly Classical economist before he became a Keynesian, reject the Classical theory of interest rate determination? And what did he put in its place?

MONEY AND THE RATE OF INTEREST

Our exposition of the Keynesian model so far is very much like its Classical counterpart in at least one respect: money doesn't matter. While the Classics said economic activity was set at the full employment level, and Keynes said it would settle at the point where total desired expenditure equaled production—which might be less than full employment—up to this point *neither* model has the money supply affecting real economic activity. The Classics, as we saw in the previous chapter, deflected its impact to the price level. Keynes, the financial wizard of Cambridge, took a bolder position: the rate of interest is a monetary phenomenon. It is not determined by saving and investment, the way the Classics said, but by the supply of and demand for money.[5] Keynes also said that money might affect the level of real economic activity, but only to the extent that it first influenced the rate of interest. Changes in the rate of interest would then alter desired investment spending and thereby change the level of GNP.

The first order of business in investigating the rate of interest is to establish the framework by noting how Keynes divided the decision-making in his model of macroeconomic activity. So far, the analysis of income and expenditure revolves around two decisions: (1) household choice between spending income and saving it, with the latter

[5]Obviously, since prices are fixed and inflation is not part of the picture, Keynes is referring to the real rate of interest when claiming it is a monetary phenomenon. The Classical picture of the real rate is Figure 1 of the last chapter, which shows saving and investment as determining the real rate of interest.

defined simply as nonconsumption; and (2) business firm decisions regarding the level of investment spending. These parts of the Keynesian system deal only with *flows*: consumption, saving, investment, and income over a given time period. It is, in the accountant's terminology, the "income statement" of the economy, with an implicit time dimension. We have also noted that none of these decisions involve any financial transactions; they deal only in *real* goods and services.

Money introduces an entirely new dimension to the macro model. Money is a *financial asset*, which is held in an individual's portfolio just as one holds a savings account at a bank, a corporate equity, or a Treasury bond. In other words, money is part of an individual's wealth—part of a person's balance sheet, in accountant's terms. The interest rate is determined by the third decision in the Keynesian scheme of things: (3) decisions of the public regarding the composition of its financial asset holdings.

Let's divide the public's portfolio into two types of assets: money and everything else. As we've seen before, money can be defined in many specific ways. For our purposes, the main distinction is that money has a fixed rate of interest, without any risk. Sometimes the rate is fixed at zero, as with currency, but that's not necessarily so, as with some checking accounts. The key is that no capital losses or gains are incurred on the asset called money. Money is also used as the medium of exchange (to conduct transactions). Thus money is the most liquid of all assets, where liquidity is defined as the ability to turn an asset into the medium of exchange quickly with little or no loss in value. For lack of a better name, we'll call all other assets "bonds." The price of a bond can vary in terms of the medium of exchange, so the owner can suffer capital losses or reap capital gains. The realized rate of interest on a bond can be above or below what was expected at the time it was purchased, depending on whether interest rates rise or fall subsequently (as we saw in Chapter 5).

Money is a riskless asset, and bonds are risky assets. If people are risk averters—that is, if they dislike risk—then they will demand a higher expected return (yield to maturity) on risky assets compared with riskless assets (more on this in Chapter 26). Thus a choice is necessary: how much of one's portfolio should go into money and how much into bonds?

It is important to note that the more bonds and less money held in a portfolio, the greater the uncertainty over total portfolio yield. For example, if I have $100, all in cash, my return is certain. If I put it all into bonds yielding 10 percent, I expect my return to be just that: 10 percent. But if interest rates rise substantially after my purchase, my

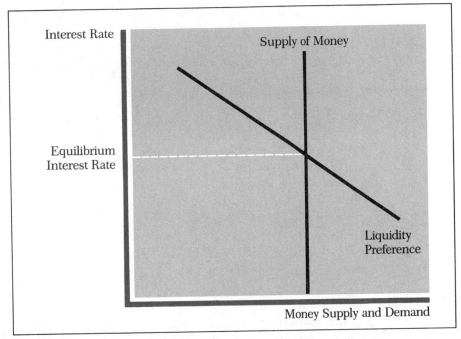

FIGURE 7 Keynesian Interest Theory

$100 bond might be worth (could be sold for) only $75. In this case my expected 10 percent yield would be reduced by the capital loss of $25. If I had held $50 in cash and invested only $50 in bonds, I would have lost only half as much. More bonds in a portfolio mean more risk.

Our composite bond in this analysis includes all risky assets—equities, corporate bonds, municipals, even long-term government bonds. We'll assume that an efficient combination of risky assets has been derived. In Chapter 28 we'll return to the structure of yields on risky securities. For now we are concerned only with the choice between money and the composite bond of Keynes. It is this decision that determines the overall expected return, the "average" interest rate, on bonds.

The demand for money, called *liquidity preference* by Keynes, is a function of the rate of interest. In Figure 7 the horizontal axis measures the quantity of money, while the rate of interest is on the vertical axis.[6] The demand-for-money function is negatively sloped—the lower the rate of interest, the larger the amount of money demanded.

---

[6]As the previous footnote mentioned, since the rate of inflation is zero the rate of interest on the vertical axis is the real rate, which is also equal to the nominal rate.

There are a number of reasons for this negative relationship between quantity of money demanded and rate of interest. Keynes argued that people had an idea of some "normal" rate of interest, as though the rate of interest were attached to its "normal" level by a rubber band. When the rate of interest *declines,* more and more people become convinced that it will snap back to its "normal" level, that is, that interest rates *will rise in the future.* If they hold bonds when rates are rising, they will suffer capital losses. In other words, the public, trying to avoid capital losses, would want to hold fewer bonds (but more money) as interest rates decline. This relationship has been called the speculative demand for liquidity because people are speculating on future bond prices.

A less restrictive approach to the negative relationship between demand for speculative money balances and the interest rate stresses interest rates as compensation for risk bearing.[7] A high rate of interest means that the cost of being liquid and safe (holding money) is great, in terms of the interest forgone. A high interest rate is an inducement to hold a large portion of one's assets in bonds (bond demand is high) and only a little in cash. At lower interest rates, the opportunity cost of (what one gives up by) holding money is much less. Since it feels good to be liquid, the amount of money demanded is greater at lower rates of interest. In more formal terms, people are risk averse—they don't like risk. There must be an inducement to hold a riskier port-folio, one with a larger amount of bonds. The inducement is a higher rate of interest.

Either approach to the demand for money explains its negative relationship to interest rates (as interest rates fall the amount of money demanded rises). Coupled with a fixed supply of money, determined by the central bank (a rather bold assumption), the rate of interest is in equilibrium when the amount of money demanded equals the supply. We know that the interest rate is in equilibrium then (as in Figure 7), because below the equilibrium rate the demand for money exceeds the fixed supply. If the rate of interest momentarily fell *below* the equilibrium rate, people would want more money than they have and would try to sell bonds to get it. The attempt to sell bonds drives bond prices down and interest rates up, until—at the equilibrium rate—people are satisfied with their portfolios of money and bonds.

[7]This approach was first formally presented in James Tobin's article, "Liquidity Prefer-ence as a Behaviour Toward Risk," *Review of Economic Studies* (1958). It is less restrictive than Keynes's original discussion, because it does not require people to expect a "normal" level of interest rates. It also puts the money versus bonds decision within a general model of portfolio choice (see Chapter 26).

At a rate of interest *above* the equilibrium rate, people would have more money than they want. They would try to get rid of their excess money balances by purchasing bonds. Bond prices would be driven up and interest rates down, until people were again happy with their holdings of money and bonds. This is at the equilibrium interest rate, of course.[8]

Our introductory discussion in Chapter 6 described the interest rate as determined by the supply of and demand for loanable funds, or looked at another way (see footnote 1 of Chapter 6) by the supply of and demand for bonds. It should not be too difficult to see why Keynesian analysis can look at the supply of and demand for money, rather than looking at the bond market directly, and say that the rate of interest is determined by equilibrium in the money market. As long as the total size of the public's portfolio, its wealth, is fixed—and in the short run this is a reasonable assumption—then a change in the demand for money relative to supply would be reflected in a one-to-one relationship by an opposite change in the demand for bonds relative to supply. In other words, if the demand for money goes up, it necessarily implies that people want to hold fewer bonds, and vice versa. Looking only at the supply and demand for money is perfectly consistent with our earlier discussion, because a change in one market is automatically reflected in the other.

MONETARY POLICY

What causes the rate of interest to change? Clearly, if either the demand for money or the supply of money shifts position, the equilibrium interest rate would change. For now, assume that the money-demand function is given, and let us examine the impact of changes in the money supply on interest rates and economic activity.

In Figure 8, let's start out with the money supply at $60 billion and the equilibrium interest rate as indicated. Assume the central bank increases the money supply (the magic word, as Captain Marvel said, is Shazam) from $60 to $70 billion. At the old rate of interest, the amount of money that people are now holding is greater than what they want. People try to dispose of their excess money balances (re-

[8]A sensitive assumption embedded in this analysis is that money and bonds are substitutes only for each other: an excess demand for one means there is an excess supply of the other. Neither is considered a direct substitute for real goods and services. This turns out to be a distinction between modern Monetarists and Keynesians, as we shall see in Chapter 23.

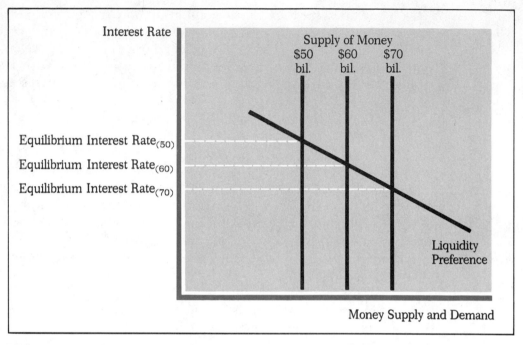

FIGURE 8 Effect of Changing the Money Supply on the Interest Rate

duce their liquidity) by buying bonds, driving the price of bonds up and the interest rate down until the interest rate has fallen sufficiently to make people content to hold the new level of cash (and stop trying to buy bonds). This happy state of affairs occurs at the lower equilibrium interest rate(70), when the amount of money demanded now equals the new supply.[9]

[9]Since some forms of money balances pay interest—such as some checking accounts—it is at least conceivable that the larger supply of money could be absorbed by a higher interest payment on money balances rather than a lower interest rate on bonds. The excess supply of money requires only a decrease in the differential between the rate on bonds and the rate on money (so that people are induced to hold relatively more of the latter). One reason all bond rates fall, rather than the rate on money rising, has to do with the zero interest rate on currency and the fact that currency and demand deposits exchange on a one-to-one basis. Thus the rate of interest paid by banks on demand deposit balances cannot wander very far from the zero rate paid on currency. As a result, the major burden of adjustment to changes in the supply of money falls on all other rates of interest, rather than the own-rate on money. For a similar discussion, see James Tobin "A General Equilibrium Approach to Monetary Theory," *Journal of Money, Credit, and Banking* (February 1969).

The implications of the increased money supply for economic activity are clear—a lower interest rate on bonds means higher investment spending, *ceteris paribus* (a key phrase meaning everything else held constant, often used by economists to produce unexpected results). In terms of our GNP-determining diagrams earlier in the chapter, the investment line shifts up and GNP goes up by the increase in *I* (induced by the decline in the interest rate) times the multiplier.

A decrease in the money supply produces just the opposite results. We start once again with a money supply of $60 billion in Figure 8, and this time let the central bank *decrease* the money supply to $50 billion (the magic word is obviously Mazahs). At the old equilibrium rate of interest, the amount of money that people are now holding is less than the amount they want to hold. People try to sell bonds to get more cash, bond prices decline, and interest rates rise until people are satisfied with their new money balances. They stop trying to

---

Money and Credit Are Not the Same Thing

When you lend a friend $50, the amount of *credit* in the economy is increased by $50. However, the amount of *money* is not altered one iota; your friend has $50 more money than before, but you have $50 less, so in the aggregate there's no net change at all in the amount of money. Credit and money may look alike but they are two very different things.

Credit is a *flow* concept, involving transactions that take place over a period of time. For instance, say you borrowed $3,000 during 1989. That kind of transaction, or series of transactions, belongs on an income statement, in this case one covering the year 1989.

Money, on the other hand, is a *stock* concept, referring not to a transaction but to something in existence at an instant in time. Say you had $500 cash on hand on December 31, 1989. That sort of thing goes on a balance sheet, say one drawn up for midnight on December 31, 1989.

Credit could be converted to balance sheet form, but then it wouldn't be the amount borrowed or loaned during a year. Instead, it would have to be the net result of what happened not only during the year but during all previous years as well: it would have to be an entry like "outstanding debts payable" or "outstanding loans receivable" on December 31, 1989.

In any event, don't let all this accounting terminology obscure the main point: credit and money may have some similarities but they are *not* the same thing.

sell bonds when a new equilibrium is established at the higher interest rate$_{(50)}$.[10]

The implications for aggregate economic activity are the reverse of the case in which the money supply was increased. This time we have a higher interest rate on bonds, and investment will decline; GNP goes down by the drop in I (induced by the rise in the interest rate) times the conventional multiplier.

The negative relationship between the demand for money and the rate of interest is an important component of the Keynesian model of GNP determination. It provides a link between changes in the supply of money and the level of economic activity.

But what Keynes giveth, Keynes can take away. If an increase in the money supply does *not* lower the interest rate, investment spending will not be affected. Keynes proceeded to question the efficacy of monetary policy under certain conditions. He argued, for example, that at very low interest rates the money-demand function becomes completely flat. In Figure 9 it is easy to see that a very flat demand-for-money function means that increases in the money supply could no longer reduce the rate of interest. In particular, an increase in the money supply from $50 billion to $60 billion lowers the interest rate, but a further increase to $70 billion fails to produce any additional decline.

What causes the money-demand function to enjoy the horizontal position? Keynes argued that at very low interest rates everyone would expect interest rates to rise to more "normal" levels in the future. In other words, everyone would expect bond prices to fall, therefore no one would want to hold bonds and the demand for liquidity (money)

---

[10]An interesting sidelight: When the interest rate is above the equilibrium level, the public has more money than it wants and it tries to get rid of its excess cash (by buying bonds). When the interest rate is below the equilibrium level, the public wants more money than it has and it tries to get its hands on more cash (by selling bonds). *But it never succeeds, because the supply of money*—which is the amount the public has—*is determined not by the public but by the Federal Reserve.* When people buy or sell bonds to one another, all they do is shuffle the money supply around among themselves, moving it from one pocket to another. What the public *does* succeed in doing is changing the price of bonds—or the interest rate—until it reaches the (equilibrium) level where people are *content* to hold the same amount of money they held all along.

It is also interesting to note that when the money supply changes, the Keynesian result is that the interest rate adjusts to induce people to hold the new level of cash balances. In the Classical world, when the money supply changes, the prices of all goods and services adjust until people restore their *real* cash balances to their original level. More on this in Chapter 23.

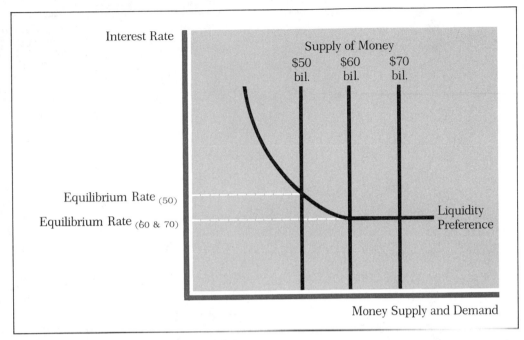

FIGURE 9 Keynesian Liquidity Trap

would be infinite. Any increase in money supply would simply be held by the public (hoarded), and none of the increased liquidity would spill over to the bond market. No one, in fact, would willingly hold bonds. In this "liquidity trap," as Keynes called the flat portion of the money-demand function, monetary policy does not alter interest rates and therefore is completely ineffective. More generally, the flatter the liquidity-preference function, the less effective monetary policy is in changing interest rates, hence in influencing GNP.

It should be obvious that monetary policy will also be less effective in changing GNP if investment spending is not very responsive to changes in the rate of interest. An interest-insensitive investment function means that even a large change in the rate of interest will not alter investment spending very much. Thus a given change in the money supply will raise GNP by less if investment spending does not respond to interest rates.

Modern Keynesians have pointed out, however, that investment spending is not the only linkage between money supply and GNP. Consumers may also change their spending in response to variations in the interest rate. In particular, we noted above that consumer wealth—the value of stocks and bonds—influences consumption expenditure. A lower rate of interest means that the prices of bonds rise. Thus consumers will spend more when interest rates fall because they feel wealthier. In terms of our earlier diagrams, this wealth effect of a decrease in the interest rate causes the consumption function to shift upward.

We can conclude by noting that a change in the money supply will have a larger impact on GNP when the interest rate changes by a lot and when investment and consumption expenditures are sensitive to interest rates. The interest rate influences expenditure through changes in the cost of borrowed funds as well as via a somewhat more modern wealth effect.

TRANSACTIONS DEMAND AND MONETARY POLICY

The concept of a speculative demand for money, related to the rate of interest, was a Keynesian innovation. Before Keynes came along, classical economists had emphasized that the only reason people would want to hold money was for transactions purposes—to buy goods and services—as we saw in the previous chapter. An increase in GNP leads to an increase in the amount of money demanded (at every rate of interest), because people need more cash to carry out the higher level of transactions. Keynes also acknowledged this transactions demand, although he did not himself appear to realize all its implications.[11]

Figure 10 shows how a change in the demand for money (at every rate of interest) affects the interest rate. We start out with a given money supply and a given money-demand (liquidity-preference) function. Together they determine the equilibrium interest rate. Now suppose that people become more nervous than normal, perhaps because they expect a decrease in money supply. They seek ultimate relief by building up the proportion of cash in their portfolios. In other words, at every rate of interest people want more money (and fewer bonds) than before. Say the demand for money increases (ΔLP) by the amount ab. This happens at each rate of interest, so that we now have a new money-demand function to the right of the old. At the old

[11]Keynes also discussed a precautionary demand for money: people hold cash to provide for unforeseen contingencies. This demand was considered constant or was lumped together with transactions balances. In the next chapter we expand on the implications of transactions demand. In particular, since changes in income alter transactions demand and interest rates, we determine the level of income and interest rates simultaneously.

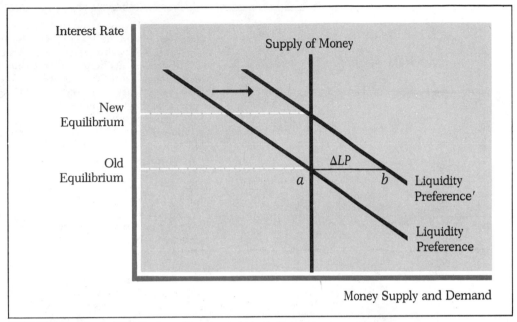

Interest Rate

Supply of Money

New
Equilibrium

Old
Equilibrium

ΔLP

a b

Liquidity
Preference'

Liquidity
Preference

Money Supply and Demand

**FIGURE 10 A Shift in the Demand for Money Changes the
Interest Rate**

equilibrium rate of interest, the amount of money demanded is larger than the fixed supply. To get more cash, people try to sell bonds, driving bond prices lower and interest rates higher until a higher equilibrium interest rate is established. The case of a decrease in the demand for money can be treated symmetrically. The money-demand function shifts to the left and the interest rate declines.

Something similar happens when the level of income changes. Let's say that income rises. People now demand more money balances at every rate of interest to carry out the higher level of transactions, the demand-for-money function shifts to the right, and the rate of interest rises. In an economy that is growing, perhaps because investment spending is rising, the rate of interest would rise because of the increase in transactions demand for money—unless, of course, the central bank expands the supply of money to provide for those transactions balances.

Now you know why we said back in Chapter 2 that "easy" or "tight" money is not really a matter of increases or decreases in the money supply in an absolute sense, but rather of increases or decreases relative to demand. In a growing economy, the money supply must

How Rockwell Makes Killing On High Rates

By Thomas Petzinger Jr.
Staff Reporter of The Wall Street Journal

PITTSBURGH—While record interest rates are burdening and even bankrupting some businesses, others are making a killing in the short-term money markets.

With a lot of cash, it's easy. Rockwell International Corp., the diversified manufacturer, is a prime example. The short-term cash held by Rockwell earned $78.8 million in the fiscal year ended Sept. 30, compared with $507.5 million of pretax income from Rockwell's automotive, electronics, aerospace and general manufacturing operations. "The way things are going, we should run well over $100 million in interest income this year," says Robert A. DePalma, Rockwell's chief financial officer.

Rockwell has about 18 domestic cash investments totaling $570 million, mainly in bank certificates of deposit and time deposits held abroad, earning interest at rates as high as 20.375% a year. Even counting another $200 million in cash invested by Rockwell operations in Canada and Europe, that's "really a small part of the corporation's total assets" of $4.43 billion, says William L. Neely, treasurer. But he says it's "a hell of a big number in terms of the total earnings of the company."

Prime Rate "Madness"

For manufacturers, high interest rates raise the cost of financing their own operations and make it harder for their customers to buy. Bank lending rates, ranging from 20% to 21½% on short-term credit to the biggest and most creditworthy companies, are driving some manufacturers into court and are delaying others' expansion plans. Rockwell itself is encountering a downturn in its automotive business, which supplies parts for the depressed automobile and truck industry. "This 20% prime is madness, absolute madness," Mr. DePalma says.

Although its windfall interest income is helping Rockwell through hard times, some analysts worry over the temptation to sacrifice long-term investment for short-term gain. At Rockwell, managers "are all well aware of the fact that we're making 20%"—on cash—"and they're maybe going to make 10%" on other assets, Mr. Neely says. "When they see their margins shrinking, they reduce their operating assets, mainly inventories and receivables, in order to maintain their overall return, and they turn the cash over to me." Nonetheless, he insists that Rockwell will continue to plough money into expansion and improvement. "You can't stop the lifeblood of the company, which is capital," he says. "The liquidation of this company isn't in the cards."

At most large companies, cash management has grown sophisticated ever since the cost of money began climbing in the mid-1960s, from a long-term rate of less than 5%. Now most big companies collect and disburse cash through computers linked with their banks. Credits and debits get posted electronically, permitting companies to earn interest almost instantaneously.

Getting the Last Buck

The companies release the cash at the last possible minute. Like others, Rockwell doesn't stick cash in its checking account before writing a check, but waits until the check will be presented for payment. Meanwhile the float, the cash that will go to settle the check, earns interest. "We've always been intense about wringing the last buck out of excess cash," Mr. Neely says.

At rates above 20%, the intensity turns

News Item *Business Firms Always Try to Economize on Cash, Especially When Interest Rates Are High*

Rockwell International Corp.'s Cash Moves This Month

Date	Amount Invested in Eurodollars	Maturity	Rate
12/2	$20 million	2 days	17⅛%
12/5	$15 million	3 days	20
12/8	$25 million	30 days	20⅛
	$35 million	30 days	20⅜
12/16	$35 million	182 days	19⅛
12/17	$15 million	overnight	20⅜
12/22	$35 million	28 days	20¾

to obsession. When Rockwell collects cash at a remote office outside its computer network, for example, "We're sure as hell going to double our effort to pick it up and get it deposited on Friday instead of Monday, even if it means flying there to get it," says L. Richard Cribbs, Rockwell's cash management director. On Friday, Dec. 5, Rockwell collected $15 million from a customer and, although no airplane heroics were needed, got it deposited in a time account that day at a New York bank at an annual rate of 20%. By Monday, the deposit had earned about $25,000 in interest.

Wall Street Journal, December 31, 1980

increase because the demand for money will rise along with the growth in GNP. Unless the central bank increases the money supply, interest rates will rise.

The transactions demand for money is probably affected by the interest rate as well as by income. It is very likely that higher interest rates reduce the demand for transactions balances. For example, assume you are paid $4,000 monthly (probably dropped out of school and became an apprentice plumber). You deposit the entire amount in the bank, spend it evenly over the month, and wind up at zero. Your *average* daily cash balance is $2,000. This is your transactions demand. But if interest rates on bonds were sufficiently high, you'd be willing to go to the cost and trouble to take half your salary at the beginning of the month ($2,000) and buy a bond, put the other $2,000 in your bank to be spent during the first fifteen days, and then when that runs out sell the bond and spend the second $2,000 over the last half of the month. What this means is that your average daily cash balance is only $1,000 (you go from $2,000 to zero evenly over fifteen days). What you gain from this is the higher interest on the funds invested in the bond market. And as long as the gain exceeds the costs, it's worth doing.

Your initial reaction might be: it would take an awfully high rate of interest to make me go through such shenanigans. That could be. But if you were a large corporation with a few million dollars in idle cash, the investment of that money could be very profitable. Most economists agree that the transactions demand for money, like the speculative demand, is a function of the rate of interest.[12] For some purposes it can be ignored or played down—but not if you are a corporate treasurer.

An interesting sidelight on the transactions demand discussion is the role played by credit cards. The easiest way to look at this is that credit cards permit a transaction to take place without a cash balance. In other words, people could theoretically invest all their cash at the beginning of the month in bonds, pay for everything via those little plastic cards, and then at the end of the month sell the bonds, put the proceeds into the bank, and write one check to the credit card company (which could be the bank itself). Although this is an extreme example, it indicates how credit cards get into the model and how their growth affects the economy. Greater use of credit cards reduces the demand for money (at every interest rate), thereby lowering interest rates, permitting investment and GNP to increase.

EXPECTATIONS AND MONETARY POLICY

Most simple economic models assume that expectations are exogenous, that is, they are determined outside the system.[13] This one is no exception. An important implicit assumption is that changes in the money supply are imposed by our central bank, the Federal Reserve, and that such policy changes are *unanticipated*. Under such circumstances, monetary policy alters the interest rate by more or less, depending on the conditions described above.

But whether an increase or decrease in the stock of money causes a *simultaneous* movement in interest rates in the predicted direction depends crucially on whether or not the change in policy was anticipated. In particular, if everyone expects the Federal Reserve to cut

[12]The interest sensitivity of transactions demand was first pointed out by William J. Baumol, "The Transactions Demand for Cash: An Inventory Theoretic Approach," *Quarterly Journal of Economics* (November 1952). For an application of modern cash management techniques stemming from Baumol, see Rita M. Maldonado and Lawrence S. Ritter, "Optimal Municipal Cash Management," *Review of Economics and Statistics* (November 1971). A somewhat more general treatment of household behavior is Robert J. Barro and Anthony M. Santomero, "Household Money Holdings and the Demand Deposit Rate," *Journal of Money, Credit, and Banking* (May 1972).
[13]More sophisticated economic models require that expectations for variables in the model (such as interest rates) conform with the predictions of the model. This is called "rational expectations" and will be discussed in Chapter 24.

back on the money supply next week or next month, a change in interest rates is likely to occur beforehand, with little or no effect at the time the money supply is actually altered. The reasoning is straightforward: if everyone expects the Fed to reduce the money supply in the future—and therefore expects interest rates to rise—then profit-maximizing bondholders will try to sell bonds *now* to avoid expected capital losses. Bond sales will drive down bond prices, driving up interest rates until they just about equal the expected rate next period. Thus when the money supply is, in fact, cut back next week or next month, rates don't move at all.

Incorporating expectations about policy movements into our model is possible but cumbersome. It is simulated by a shift in the demand-for-money function at every interest rate. In our particular example, when we say that bondholders want to sell to avoid capital losses, we are saying, in effect, that the demand for bonds decreases—or, in terms of our picture, that the demand for money increases at every rate of interest. That means the money-demand function shifts to the right, as in Figure 10, increasing the rate of interest with the same supply of money.[14]

Thus an anticipated monetary policy will change interest rates before it is implemented. This is not especially surprising once it is put into the framework of our model, but it can be troublesome for policy-makers when portfolio managers get into the habit of forecasting stabilization behavior. More on this in Chapter 24.

AGGREGATE DEMAND AND SUPPLY

So far we have described all the factors that can influence the aggregate demand for goods and services according to Keynes. As we mentioned at the very beginning of this chapter, since Keynesian analysis assumes prices are fixed because of a depressed state of the economy, all the impacts on aggregate demand discussed up to now correspond to changes in real income and output as well. It will be useful, nevertheless, to put the Keynesian model into a formal supply/demand framework, just as we did for Classical economics in Chapter 19. This will

[14]In the example of the previous paragraph, when the *anticipated* decrease in the money supply actually takes place, there is no increase in the level of rates at that time precisely because the demand for money simultaneously decreases by the same amount at that time. The reason is that people no longer expect the Fed to reduce the money supply. Thus, the demand for money returns to its original position.

highlight the similarities and differences between Keynes and the Classics, permit a brief insight into Keynesian causes of inflation, and also let us see what is meant by supply-side economics.

In Figure 11 we put the price level on the vertical axis and GNP on the horizontal axis, just as we did in Figure 3 of the previous chapter. Don't get nervous simply because until now aggregate spending ($C + I + G$) has been plotted in the figures against income (Y). Now we are interested in how aggregate demand varies when the price level changes, so Figure 11 plots income (output) as a function of price. We have different pictures tailored to answer different questions.

The aggregate supply schedule in Figure 11 is in two parts: a horizontal segment, which reflects the fact that prices do not increase at less than full employment, and a vertical part, which is the Classical school's supply schedule, showing that only prices (not real income) increase after full employment (assumed equal to Y_{FE}) is reached.

The aggregate demand schedule (D) is negatively sloped for the

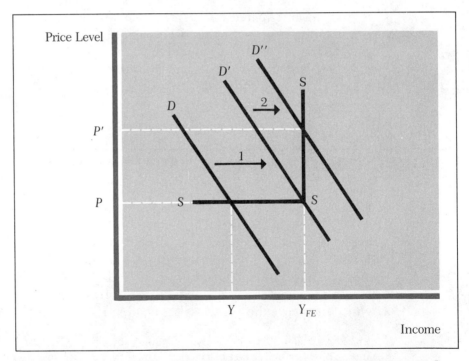

FIGURE 11 Increases in Aggregate Demand Raise Real Income or Prices, Depending on the Shape of Aggregate Supply

same reason as in the Classical world: a lower price level raises the real supply of money balances, which in turn increases the aggregate demand for goods and services. But in the Keynesian world, this rise in the real supply of money has a very specific channel of influence on GNP. It occurs through the impact of rising real balances on the interest rate (as in Figure 8) and the impact of a lower interest rate on investment spending and hence GNP.

Equilibrium GNP is given by the intersection of aggregate demand and supply in Figure 11. If we start with D, the level of real income is Y and the price level is P. Thus far, Figure 11 adds nothing to our analysis, since we had assumed all along that prices were fixed. The only plus is that we now know that prices are fixed at some level P (big deal).

If aggregate demand increases from D to D' in Figure 11, when aggregate supply is horizontal, the level of real output rises from Y to Y_{FE} and the price level remains at P. The rightward shift in the aggregate demand schedule can result from an increase in any of the autonomous expenditure categories discussed earlier. Thus D could shift to D' because of an increase in investment (I) or government expenditure (G), or because of a decrease in taxes which increases consumer spending (C). Note also that an increase in the money supply (M) will also shift D to D'.[15] What Figure 11 emphasizes for us is that the multiplier effects of autonomous expenditures correspond to increases in real income (without any change in the price level) as long as the aggregate supply schedule is horizontal.

But if aggregate demand increases further, from D' to D'', after aggregate supply has become vertical, then shifts in aggregate demand will result in price increases (from P to P') rather than increased real income. Thus, when the aggregate supply function is vertical, the multiplier effects of autonomous spending translate into changes in *nominal* GNP rather than real GNP.

What emerges from this is that when the economy is at or near full employment, Keynesian aggregate demand analysis can be used together with the aggregate supply curve to explain upward pressure on prices, or inflation. Anything that shifts the aggregate demand schedule to the right—whether it is increased government spending, increased consumer spending, or increased money supply that increases investment spending—will force up the price level. Notice that this explanation of what influences the price level is somewhat different

[15]Recall that an increase in M shifts D because at *every* price level there are more real cash balances, which lowers interest rates and raises investment spending.

from that of Classical economics. In Chapter 19 we showed that, according to Classical thinking, shifts in the aggregate demand schedule reflect changes in the money supply; in fact, the aggregate demand schedule embodies the quantity theory. This is a fundamental distinction between the Classical/Monetarist view of inflation and the Keynesian theory and will be discussed again in Chapter 23.

At this point it is appropriate to mention the role of so-called supply-side policies in macroeconomics. Keynes himself had little reason to focus on aggregate supply, since in the depressed economy of the simple Keynesian model there are more than enough goods and services to go around. But in a full employment setting, the only way to increase real output is to expand productive capacity. That would be represented in Figure 11 by a rightward shift in the vertical segment of aggregate supply (Y_{FE} would shift to the right). Supply-side economics focuses primarily on the impact of government policies on the aggregate supply schedule. Although this is very different from the Keynesian focus, the two are by no means contradictory.[16]

As we mentioned early in Chapter 19, the productive capacity of the economy is determined by the supply of labor, capital, and available technology. Policies that increase any of these production factors will increase potential real output. The government does not directly control any of these, but its tax policies influence the willingness of households and business firms to supply labor and invest in capital. In particular, higher tax rates may very well discourage work and investment, because labor and entrepreneurs are denied some fraction of the income they earn.

According to supply-siders, the main consequence of reducing tax rates is increased production incentives. This view contrasts with the Keynesian emphasis that a reduction in taxes raises aggregate demand. Up to now we have considered the effect of a tax reduction only on the aggregate demand schedule in Figure 11; supply-siders contend that the tax impact on the aggregate supply schedule can be even more important. Thus they *could* argue that reducing taxes when the economy is at full employment need not cause prices to rise. In particular, if the vertical portion of the aggregate supply schedule shifted to the right by more than the movement in aggregate demand, prices could even fall. Whether this is in fact the case can be clarified only by empirical evidence.

The role of Keynesian, Monetarist, and supply-side mechanisms in

---

[16]Note that the quantity theory is in the same boat as Keynesian analysis, because it focuses almost exclusively on aggregate demand.

the inflationary process will be discussed in greater detail in Chapter 23. Meanwhile, in the next chapter we treat you to the pleasure of a more complicated Keynesian aggregate demand model.

SUMMARY

1. Keynesian analysis maintains that the level of production is determined by the aggregate demand for goods and services. This differs from Classical economics, which argued that production occurs at full employment. The main difference between Keynes and the Classics is that Keynes did not think that fluctuating prices and interest rates would push the level of economic activity toward full employment, especially in the short run.

2. The Keynesian model focuses on the determinants of aggregate demand in order to pinpoint the level of production. Demand is divided into consumption, investment, and government expenditure. To Keynesians the consumption function is a key behavioral relationship, because it allows them to explain how consumer spending varies with income. Thus when there is a change in autonomous spending (such as an increase in investment), income changes by some multiple (because of induced consumption spending).

3. Government expenditure and taxation play an important role in influencing the level of aggregate demand. Changes in taxes and government expenditures have multiplier effects on income and can be used to offset the effects on GNP of autonomous changes in investment.

4. According to Keynesians, the demand for and supply of money determine the level of interest rates. This view differs from the Classical quantity theory, in which the supply of and demand for money determine the price level. The Keynesian result stems from the behavioral assumption that the demand for money is interest-sensitive plus the fact that the price level does not vary.

5. Changes in the money supply alter the level of interest rates in the Keynesian world. The impact on economic activity is then determined by the response of investment spending and the subsequent multiplier effects on GNP. The greater the impact of money supply changes on interest rates, and the larger the sensitivity of spending to interest rate changes, the larger the effect of monetary policy on GNP.

6. All Keynesian analysis focuses on the aggregate demand for goods and services. It assumes that aggregate supply is sufficient to accommodate increased demand without raising prices. Any increases in aggregate demand at

full employment will raise prices and cause inflation. Supply-side policies emphasize the need to generate increased real output at or near full employment.

Suggestions for Further Reading

Keynesian ideas all stem, of course, from John Maynard Keynes, *The General Theory of Employment, Interest and Money* (New York: Harcourt, Brace, 1936). Having become a true classic (defined as a book that is no longer read, just referenced), it has been interpreted on many levels. One of the best interpretations is Alvin Hansen, *A Guide to Keynes* (New York: McGraw-Hill, 1953). A more advanced treatise is Axel Leijonhufvud (pronounced Leijonhufvud), *On Keynesian Economics and the Economics of Keynes* (Oxford University Press, 1968).

CHAPTER 21

The ISLM World

Why confuse things with a more complicated model of GNP determination? Is it worth the effort? Haven't we said that a good model is like a good map—it tells you how to get from one place to another without detailing every curve in the road, every bump in the terrain? True enough. But sometimes a few complications make life more interesting. Versatility is the password. Being adaptable to more than one use is a desirable characteristic for a model.

The more complex model of GNP determination is known as *ISLM* analysis. Among its many attractions, it shows how monetary and fiscal policy interact with each other; it shows what determines the relative multiplier effects of each; it provides a partial integration of the Classical and Keynesian systems into one conceptual framework; and it demonstrates some of the fundamental features distinguishing the Classical and Keynesian outlooks. As in the previous chapter, most of the analysis assumes a fixed price level, so that we still are concerned with the level of real GNP. In the next-to-last section we will analyze the implications of flexible wages and prices, and at the end we will show how the *ISLM* model collapses into an aggregate demand schedule.

MONEY, INTEREST, AND INCOME

In Chapter 19 we noted that the Classical economists stressed the transactions demand for money. Keynes, as we saw in Chapter 20, also discussed this transactions demand, although he did not himself seem to perceive all its ramifications. In particular, because transactions demand increases with income, the rate of interest rises as income rises. Thus not only does the interest rate help determine income; in addition, income helps determine the interest rate.[1] Causation runs both ways—from the interest rate to income and from income to the interest rate. Fortunately, this is not an insurmountable problem. The economy winds up with a determinate level of each, but our model must be reformulated to take this into account.

We begin, in Figure 1, with three alternative money-demand functions, each associated with a different level of economic activity.[2] The liquidity-preference function associated with Y_1 is for a level of GNP that is less than Y_2, which in turn is less than Y_3. Each level of GNP has its own liquidity-preference function, because at higher income levels more money is demanded for transactions purposes (at every rate of interest). The horizontal distance between any two demand-for-money functions is equal to the difference in the demand for money at the two levels of GNP. If we use the Classical formulation coming out of Cambridge (as discussed in Chapter 19), we can write:

$$\text{demand for money} = kY$$

or

$$\Delta \text{ demand for money} = k\Delta Y$$

The latter implies that the demand for money will change by k times the change in the level of GNP (where k equals, for example, .25). In terms of Figure 1, this means that the horizontal distance between any two liquidity preference curves equals $k\Delta Y$.

The demand for money is really a function of two variables—income and the interest rate. The equilibrium condition (amount of money demanded = money supply) no longer provides an interest rate; rather, it provides combinations of income (Y) and the interest rate

---

[1]The one exception is the liquidity trap, introduced in the last chapter, where the rate of interest is given and is independent of everything except public psychology.

[2]The discussion in the remainder of this chapter will be based on geometric analysis. For those who prefer algebra, the Appendix to the chapter presents the entire model, and its implications, in equation form.

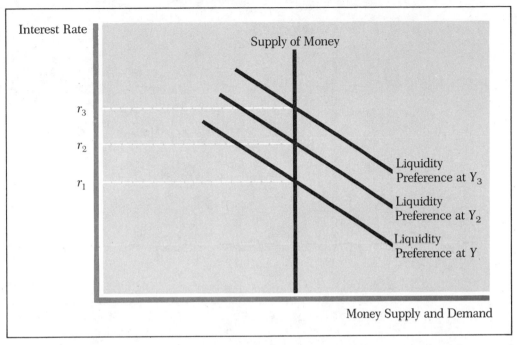

FIGURE 1 How to Derive the *LM* Curve: At Higher Levels of Income, the Demand for Money Rises and So Do Interest Rates

(r) which satisfy the condition that money demand equals money supply *when the money supply is fixed.* In fact, according to Figure 1, a positive relationship between Y and r is needed to keep the amount of money demanded equal to the fixed money supply. A higher level of GNP (compare Y_2 with Y_1) is associated with a higher interest rate (r_2 versus r_1). This relationship between Y and r that satisfies the equilibrium condition in the money market is plotted in Figure 2, where the interest rate is still on the vertical axis but now we have income on the horizontal axis. The line is labeled *LM* because it is the locus of combinations of Y and r that satisfy the *l*iquidity-preference-equals-*m*oney-supply equilibrium condition.

How should you "read" the *LM* curve? In either of two ways. For a series of alternative interest rates, it tells you what the resulting income would have to be to make the demand for money equal to the (fixed) supply of money. *At higher interest rates,* there is less money demanded, *so income must be higher* to increase the demand for transactions balances if the total demand for money is to remain equal to the (fixed) supply. *Or,* for a series of alternative income levels, Figure 2 tells you what the resulting interest rate would have to be to

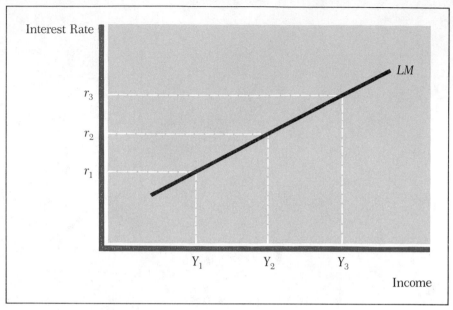

FIGURE 2 The *LM* Curve

make the demand for money equal to the fixed supply. *At higher income levels,* more transactions money is desired, *so the interest rate must be higher* to shrink the demand for money balances if total demand is to remain equal to the fixed supply.

Before you write to the folks back home and tell them that the pundits from Wall Street said that an increase in the interest rate raises GNP, or that an increase in GNP raises the interest rate, rest assured that nothing of the sort has been said—so far. In fact, we can't even determine Y and r as yet, much less say anything about how each of these variables changes. All we have is one relationship (equation or equilibrium condition) and two variables, Y and r, and you remember enough high school algebra to know that you need at least two equations to determine the equilibrium values of two variables.

We *will* produce another relationship between Y and r, based on the equilibrium condition in the market for goods and services (the $C + I + G = Y$ or the $I = S$ equilibrium condition). This great unification and solution, which will knock your socks off, is scheduled to take place in about ten pages. But before that cataclysmic experience, it will be helpful for subsequent policy discussions to elaborate on the factors determining the slope of the *LM* curve and shifts in its position. Both of these help determine the relative size of monetary and fiscal policy multipliers.

ALL ABOUT *LM*

The determinants of the slope of the *LM* curve are best illustrated by going over the reasons for its positive slope. Take point *A* in Figure 3. Assume that the amount of money demanded equals the fixed money supply at that point, hence combination Y_1 and r_1 lies on the *LM* curve. To see whether a second (Y, r) combination that also satisfies the equilibrium condition (money demand = money supply) lies above and to the right of *A* (like point *B*), or below and to the right (like point *D*), let us first pick a point *C* which differs from *A* only in the level of income.

At point *C*, the rate of interest is still r_1 but income is Y_2 (above Y_1). Since income is higher at point *C* than at point *A*, the transactions demand for money is greater at *C*. Nothing else is changed, so point *C* must have a larger demand for money than the (fixed) supply. To set matters right, the interest rate must *rise* to reduce the demand for money and thereby restore the equality between demand and supply.

The slope of line *AB* (the *LM* curve) in Figure 3 is determined by two factors. *The first is the size of the gap between money demand and supply at point C.* If the increment in the amount of money

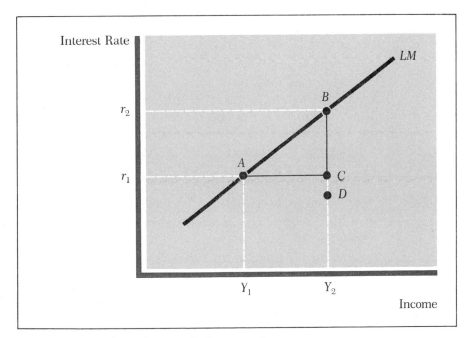

FIGURE 3 The Slope of the *LM* Curve

demanded per unit ΔY is large, then the amount demanded will be a lot higher at C than at A, and the increase in r needed to restore equilibrium (to lower the amount demanded) will be large. In other words, if transactions demand is great, then the level of r needed to maintain demand-supply equality at Y_2 will be great, point B will be higher than otherwise, and the slope of the LM curve will be steeper.

The second factor influencing the slope of the LM curve is the interest-sensitivity of money demand. For a given excess of money demand over supply at point C in Figure 3, the greater the interest-sensitivity of liquidity preference, the *smaller* the necessary increase in the rate of interest to restore equilibrium. This is so because when liquidity preference is highly interest-sensitive, then even a small increase in r reduces the amount of money demanded by a lot. In other words, at Y_2 the rise in r needed to insure demand-supply equality will be smaller the greater is the sensitivity of demand to r; point B will be lower than otherwise, and the slope of the LM curve will be flatter.

To summarize: The slope of the LM curve will be steeper the greater is the income-sensitivity of demand for money, and the less is the interest-sensitivity of demand for money; the LM curve will be flatter the less is the income-sensitivity of the demand for money, and the greater is the interest-sensitivity.

MONETARY POLICY AND THE *LM* CURVE

What causes the LM curve to shift *position* (in contrast to a change in its slope)? It does get boring having it in the same position, so the monetary authorities rush to the rescue. An increase in the supply of money moves the LM curve to the right, and a decrease in the money supply moves the LM curve to the left. *By shifting the position of the LM curve, the Federal Reserve can increase or decrease the potential equilibrium level of GNP associated with a given interest rate.* Let's see why a change in the money supply shifts the LM curve.

In Figure 4 we start with the LM curve associated with money supply M_1. All points on that curve satisfy the condition that the amount of money demanded $= M_1$. Take point a, with interest rate r_1 and income Y_1. Now increase the money supply to M_2. At point a the new larger money supply now exceeds the demand for money. What can restore equilibrium between the demand for money and

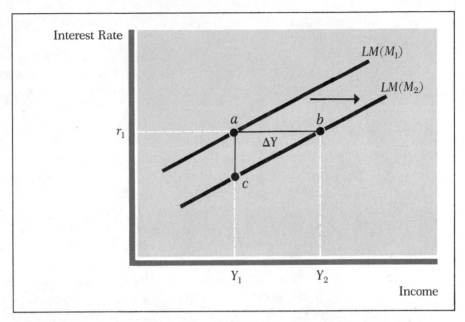

FIGURE 4 An Increase in the Money Supply Shifts the LM Curve to the Right

money supply? Clearly, if *income* rises, the transactions demand for money will go up, hence some point to the right of *a*, say point *b*, will now represent equilibrium between demand and supply. Therefore, the new *LM* curve, $LM(M_2)$, the one with combinations of Y and r that satisfy demand equal to the new larger money supply, must be to the right of the old *LM* curve. (A similar argument shows that the *LM* curve must shift to the left if there is a decline in money supply.)

We can say exactly how far to the right (or to the left) the new *LM* curve must be. If the supply of money increases by ΔM, the amount of money demanded must change by the same amount in order to restore equilibrium. But we know that the transactions demand for money changes by k times the change in income ($k\Delta Y$). So income must change until $k\Delta Y$ equals ΔM (assuming nothing else changes, which is what we are doing by looking at the horizontal differences between two *LM* curves, with the interest rate held constant). The demand for money will increase to match the enlarged supply when $k\Delta Y = \Delta M$, or when $\Delta Y = \Delta M/k$, which we can also write as $\Delta Y = 1/k \times \Delta M$. In other words, the horizontal distance between two

LM curves is equal to $1/k \times \Delta M$ (or the difference in Figure 4 between Y_1 and Y_2 is $1/k \times \Delta M$).[3]

But a change in income is not the only way for a change in the money supply to be absorbed into the economy. The interest rate can fall, and this would also raise the amount of money demanded. This is represented in Figure 4 by point c, which lies directly below point a; that is, we are still at income Y_1, but this time it is the interest rate that has fallen to restore equilibrium between the amount of money demanded and the new (larger) supply of money.

Unfortunately, we cannot as yet say exactly where the new increased money supply leads us. *Will it all be absorbed by increases in GNP, or will it all be absorbed by declines in the interest rate?* That question is a biggie! Our introductory discussion in Chapter 2 suggested that expansion in M will lead to *both* a higher GNP and a lower interest rate. Hence, if we start out at point a in Figure 4, the new equilibrium of the economy lies somewhere *between* points b and c. The Classical economists, however, said an increase in M will all be absorbed by transactions demand. We cannot yet answer the question because we don't really know where we started from. In order to find out where the devil we are, we must introduce the goods sector of the economy—saving and investment.

THE GOODS MARKET

Economic activity and interest rates are affected by behavior in the market for goods and services as well as in the money market. The counterpart to the money-demand-equals-money-supply equilibrium condition is the equilibrium between desired saving and investment (or total desired expenditure equals production). The equilibrium levels of GNP and interest rate must satisfy two equilibrium conditions: the condition that $I = S$ as well as money demand = money supply—which is a good thing, because with two variables, Y and r, we need two equations if both variables are to be determined simultaneously.

To describe the combinations of Y and r needed for equilibrium in

[3]Recall from Chapter 19 that when there is no interest-sensitivity of the demand for money, then $1/k$ equals velocity. Under those conditions, the horizontal distance (which holds the rate of interest constant) between the two LM curves equals ΔM times velocity. This will be important in the next chapter, unless you decide not to read it because things are complicated enough as is.

the goods market, we must recall the investment function from Chapters 19 and 20. Desired investment spending is negatively related to the rate of interest; a fall in the rate of interest raises the level of investment spending. A higher level of investment spending, in turn, implies a higher level of GNP. These relationships are best depicted graphically. We will then discuss them in more general terms.

In Figure 5(a) the saving function is drawn together with three alternative levels of investment, each one associated with a different rate of interest. "Investment (r_1)" assumes rate of interest r_1, "investment (r_2)" assumes rate of interest r_2 (a higher rate than r_1), and so on. Figure 5(b) depicts the same situation, but from the total expenditure point of view. The three total expenditure lines are associated with the three different levels of investment.

The alternative levels of investment are derived from the investment function in Figure 6, where the rate of interest is measured on the vertical axis and the level of investment is on the horizontal axis. Interest rate r_3 is the highest rate and is associated with the lowest level of investment $I(r_3)$; interest rate r_1 is the lowest rate and is associated with the highest level of investment $I(r_1)$. The change in the amount of investment per unit change in the rate of interest $(\Delta I / \Delta r)$ measures the sensitivity of investment spending to changes in the rate of interest.

It should be obvious from Figures 5(a) and 5(b) that there is a negative relationship between Y and r as far as the goods market is concerned. Lower interest rates are associated with higher income levels as long as the equilibrium condition—saving equals investment—is satisfied. This relationship between Y and r is summarized in Figure 7, with r measured on the vertical axis and Y on the horizontal axis. (At this point, *we* are having difficulty distinguishing the horizontal from the vertical and who's on what—so keep your eyes open.) The locus of points satisfying the investment-equals-saving equilibrium condition is called the *IS* curve.

How should you "read" the *IS* curve? As with the *LM* curve, in either of two ways. For a series of alternative interest rates, it tells you what income must be to make saving equal to investment. *At higher interest rates,* there is less investment, *so income must be lower* to shrink saving (which is a function of income) to the point where it equals the smaller volume of investment. *Or,* for a series of alternative income levels, it tells you what the interest rate must be to make saving equal to investment. *At higher income levels,* saving is larger, *so the interest rate must be lower* to expand investment to the point where it equals the larger volume of saving.

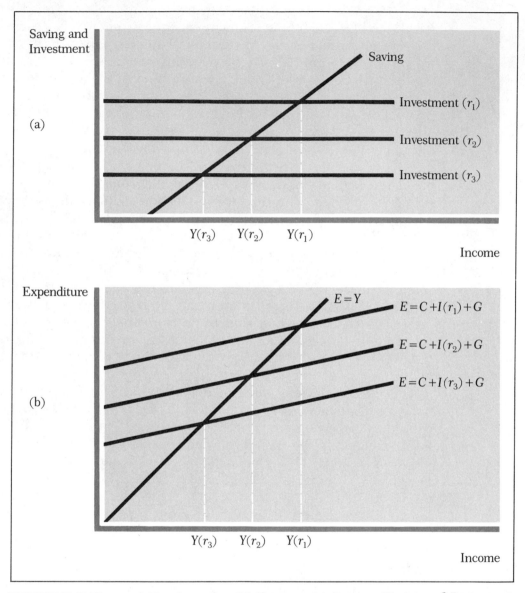

FIGURE 5 How to Derive the *IS* Curve: At Lower Rates of Interest the Level of Investment Is Higher, and So Is the Level of Income

Perhaps now you can appreciate our advice earlier in the chapter, with respect to the *LM* curve, suggesting that you not pass on that particular information about the relationship between Y and r. Now there are two relationships between Y and r. While more of a good

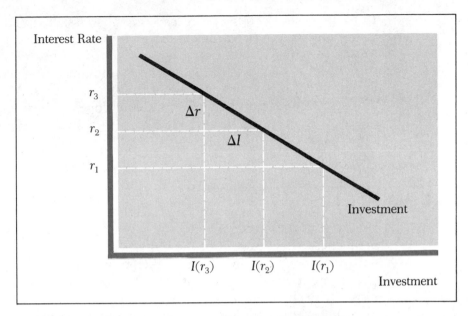

FIGURE 6 The Investment-Demand Function

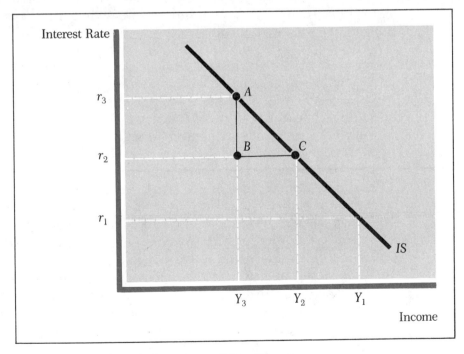

FIGURE 7 The *IS* Curve and Its Slope

thing is usually better, it can lead to embarrassing situations. In our case, however, it will rescue our model from indeterminacy. But before presenting the Missouri Compromise (named after those who refused to believe it was possible), let's take a quick look at the factors that determine the slope and position of the *IS* curve; these are the things, along with the factors that determine the slope and position of the *LM* curve, that influence the relative magnitudes of the monetary and fiscal policy multipliers on GNP.

ALL ABOUT *IS*

To see why the *IS* curve looks the way it does, what makes it flatter or steeper, what moves it to the right or to the left, let us examine its negative slope in greater detail. Take point A in Figure 7 and assume that combination (r_3, Y_3) satisfies the condition that saving equals investment: hence A lies on the *IS* curve. Now let us move to point B, which differs from A only in having a lower interest rate (r_2 compared with r_3). But a lower rate of interest implies a higher level of investment. Hence, if $I = S$ at point A, then I must *exceed* S at point B. In order to restore equilibrium, saving must be brought up to equality with investment. There's no better way to do it (in fact, no other way at all in our model) than for income to rise, say to Y_2, which raises saving (by the marginal propensity to save times ΔY). At point C saving is once again equal to investment, and it too is admitted to that select group of points on the *IS* curve.

The slope of the *IS* curve is determined by the size of the discrepancy between I and S at point B—that is, by the sensitivity of investment to a unit change in the interest rate—and by the responsiveness of saving to increases in income (the marginal propensity to save). For example, if investment is very sensitive to changes in r (in Figure 6, if the investment function were flatter, so that ΔI per unit Δr were larger), then investment would exceed saving by a lot at point B in Figure 7. In order to increase saving by a lot, income would have to rise a lot; point C would be further to the right than it is, and the *IS* curve would be flatter. If the marginal propensity to save were very large, however, the increase in Y need not be very large to restore equilibrium, point C would be more to the left, and the *IS* curve would be steeper.

All of this could be said in somewhat less formal terms. The fall in the rate of interest at point B compared with point A raises investment spending. This ΔI, in turn, raises the level of GNP by ΔI times the "simple" multiplier, $1/(1 - b)$, of the previous chapter. This increase in GNP is measured from point B to point C. (Note that this assumes quite explicitly that the rate of interest remains the same both before and after the increase in Y, and that is accomplished by drawing a *horizontal* line from B to C.) Hence, the more sensitive investment spending is to changes in the rate of interest, the flatter the slope of the IS curve will be and the larger the multiplier effect. This is perfectly consistent with the story just told in terms of the marginal propensity to save, because the larger the marginal propensity to save ($= 1 - b$), the smaller the multiplier of the simple Keynesian model.

To summarize: A *highly* interest-sensitive investment function and a *low* marginal propensity to save imply a flat IS curve; a low interest-sensitivity of investment and a high marginal propensity to save imply a steep IS curve.

The *position* of the IS curve (in contrast to its slope) is altered by any change in autonomous spending, such as government spending, private investment that is independent of the rate of interest, or private consumption spending that is independent of income (or, looked at from another standpoint, private saving that is independent of income, such as changes induced by government taxation). Such shifts in autonomous spending disturb the $I = S$ (or $E = Y$) equilibrium condition. The equilibrium combinations of Y and r will, therefore, be altered. This can be seen by looking either at saving-equals-investment equilibrium or income-equals-expenditure equilibrium. We will spare you the agony of doing it both ways (just this once) and concentrate on the expenditure-equals-income approach.

In Figure 8 let's start out with IS curve $IS(G_1)$. At every point, saving equals investment and desired total expenditure equals income. Now assume government spending goes up, from G_1 to G_2. From Figure 5(b) it is clear that under such conditions each of the total-expenditure functions would shift upward, producing a higher level of Y for each interest rate. In Figure 8, therefore, an increase in G implies a shift to the right of the IS curve, say to $IS(G_2)$—that is, a higher level of Y for each rate of interest.[4]

Similar shifts in the IS curve would be brought on by increases or decreases in investment spending that are independent of the rate of interest. How might that come about? If entrepreneurs suddenly expect higher future dollar returns on investment projects, the rate of

[4]An increase in taxes, on the other hand, implies a lower level of consumption in Figure 5(b), hence each of the total expenditure lines is lower than before and the level of Y associated with each rate of interest is less. Result: The IS curve shifts to the left.

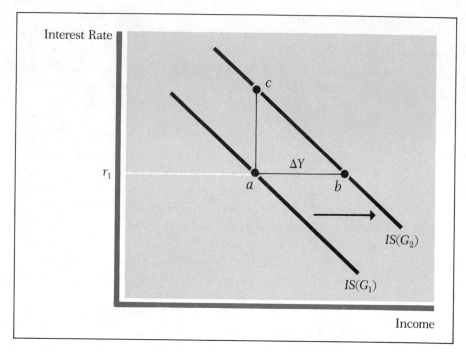

FIGURE 8 An Increase in Government Spending Shifts the *IS* Curve to the Right

return discussed in Chapter 20 will increase and some investment spending will be undertaken that otherwise would not have been. Keynes thought such shifts would, in fact, occur quite often and in substantial magnitude. Entrepreneurs are a fickle group, very sensitive to anything (war and peace) and anyone (presidents and reporters) that might influence the future profitability of their investments. Their actions tend to shift the investment demand function (Figure 6) to the right or left, thereby shifting the *IS* curve to the right or left as well.

We can also say exactly how much the *IS* curve shifts to the right or left because of a change in autonomous spending. A change in autonomous spending, ΔA, produces a change in GNP by the amount ΔA times the Chapter 20 multiplier, $1/(1-b)$, assuming no changes in other categories of spending (besides consumption via the change in income). In Figure 8, the horizontal distance between two *IS* curves—for example, point *a* to point *b*—measures the difference between two levels of income, assuming that some type of autonomous spending has increased but the rate of interest remains constant. That would equal ΔA times our old multiplier friend $1/(1-b)$. Therefore, an increase in autonomous spending—such as a change in government spending—shifts the *IS* curve to the right by ΔA times $1/(1 - b)$, while a decrease in autonomous spending shifts the *IS* curve to the left by ΔA times $1/(1 - b)$.

But there really is *another* possibility. The increase in autonomous spending need not raise GNP if some other category of spending simultaneously contracts. If, at the same time that government spending goes up, private investment spending is discouraged (because the rate of interest rises), it is conceivable that GNP could remain unchanged. This possibility is recognized explicitly in Figure 8 by point *c*, which is directly above *a*, implying no change at all in GNP. Instead, the rate of interest has risen sufficiently so that total spending remains the same: income equals desired expenditure at point *c* as well as point *b*, saving equals investment at both points, and so both are on the new *IS* curve.

Keynesians seem to agree that a change in government spending will raise GNP a lot, hence we will wind up near point *b* when *G* goes up. The Classical economists, on the other hand, felt that the level of output would be unaffected by changes in any particular category of expenditure. An increase in *G* would be accompanied by a decrease in some other kind of spending, leaving income unchanged (we would move to point *c*). We can't really tell what will happen until we bring the *IS* curve together with the *LM* curve, derive equilibrium *Y* and *r* simultaneously, and then examine the way these variables respond to monetary and fiscal policy within that *general* equilibrium framework.

THE SIMULTANEOUS DETERMINATION OF INCOME AND INTEREST: *IS* AND *LM* TOGETHER

The equilibrium levels of GNP and the interest rate must satisfy equilibrium in the money market (money demand = money supply or $LP = M$), *and* in the product market ($I = S$). In Figure 9 we have drawn an *LM* curve for a given money supply and an *IS* curve for a given level of government expenditure and taxation and a given investment function (relating *I* to *r*). The equilibrium *Y* and *r* must be at the intersection point of the *IS* and *LM* curves, point *E*, since only at that point does saving equal investment *and* liquidity preference (*LP*) equal the money supply. At any other point, one or both of these equilibrium conditions are violated, and dynamic forces will move income and the interest rate toward point *E*.

Let's see what happens if the economy is not at point E in Figure 9. Take point A on the IS curve. Saving equals investment, but money demand is less than money supply. (The latter is so because point A is directly above point B, which is on the LM curve. At point B we know $LP = M$. Since point A has a higher rate of interest, the amount of money demanded is less, so with a given money supply we have LP less than M.) People want to hold less money than they have at point A. To get rid of the money they start to buy bonds, driving bond prices higher and the interest rate lower. As the interest rate falls, investment rises and so does income—and, believe it or not, we are sliding down the IS curve toward E.

At point B, money supply equals money demand because we are on the LM curve, but investment exceeds saving (point B is directly below A; at A we know $S = I$; at B the interest rate is lower, hence I exceeds S). The excess of I over S leads to an increase in production as entrepreneurs try to replenish falling inventories. As income rises, the rate of interest is driven up because the money supply is fixed and people start to sell bonds in order to get additional transactions balances. We are now climbing up the LM curve toward E.

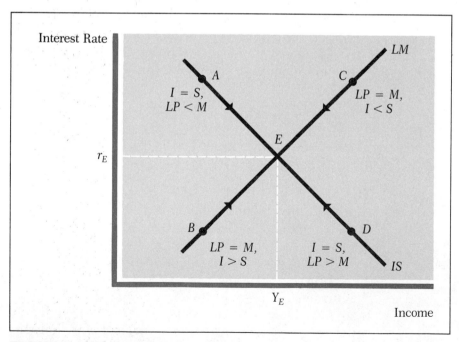

FIGURE 9 The Simultaneous Determination of Income and Interest (Fantastic!)

At points to the right of E, dynamic forces would lead to a fall in the level of income. At C we have $LP = M$, but desired investment is less than desired saving (see if you know why—hint: compare with D). Entrepreneurs cut back their production in order to reduce inventory accumulation. As GNP falls there is a reduction in the need for transactions balances, people start buying bonds with the extra cash, bond prices rise, and interest rates decline—we return to E by sliding down the LM curve. Finally, at point D investment equals saving, but LP exceeds M. People try to sell bonds to get more cash, bond prices fall, interest rates rise; investment spending starts to fall and income falls along with it—we climb the IS curve until we get to E.

Equilibrium point E has the nice property that if the economy is not there, dynamic forces will restore that particular combination of Y and r. It is a *stable* equilibrium. As long as the IS and LM curves remain in the same position, any deviation of income from Y_E will set forces in motion to restore that level of output; the same is true of interest rate r_E.

But there is nothing sacred about income Y_E. It may or may not be a full employment level of output. We have noted no tendency for the economy to ensure that Y_E is full employment, although we will suggest a few things later on. If Y_E happens to be full employment, all is well. But if it isn't, and the army of unemployed becomes restless, the government may step in to produce full employment. As we noted in the previous chapter, it could use monetary policy or fiscal policy. We have all the tools to do a complete analysis of the impact of such policies on GNP.

MONETARY AND FISCAL POLICY

Monetary Policy: We have now reached the point where we can put all of our slopes and shifts to good use. Figures 10, 11, and 12 summarize the way monetary policy influences economic activity, and the factors affecting the size of the multiplier effects on GNP within the *ISLM* framework.

In Figure 10, if we start with LM and IS, the equilibrium level of income is Y and the interest rate is r. An increase in the money supply, for example, shifts the LM function to LM', reducing the interest rate to r' and increasing GNP to Y'.[5]

[5]All the examples are in terms of increases in the money supply. A decrease would simply shift the LM curve to the left and all the changes would be just the reverse.

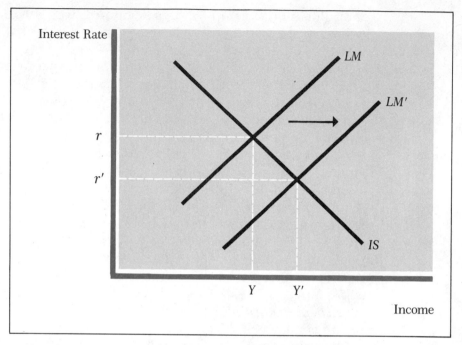

FIGURE 10 An Expansionary Monetary Policy

Figure 11 shows that an increase in money supply (*LM* shifts to *LM'*) raises GNP by more, the *flatter is the IS curve.* With the relatively steep *IS* curve, the increase in income is only to Y_s, while with the flatter *IS* curve the increase is to Y_f. The flatter *IS* curve can be due to a highly interest-sensitive investment function.[6] Hence, the fall in *r* due to an increase in *M* raises the level of investment by a lot. The impact of monetary policy on GNP is more powerful under such conditions.

Figure 12 is somewhat more complicated. It illustrates that an increase in the money supply is more powerful *the less the sensitivity of money demand* to changes in the interest rate. If the demand for money is rather insensitive to changes in the rate of interest, the *LM* curve is steeper. An increase in money supply would shift LM_{steep} to

---

[6]The wealth effect of interest rates on consumption also makes the *IS* curve flatter, thereby increasing the impact of a change in the money supply on GNP. The reasoning is as follows: a decline in the rate of interest not only increases investment spending directly but also increases wealth (by raising bond prices) and thereby induces consumers to spend more. For a given decline in the rate of interest, therefore, both investment and consumption go up, causing income to rise by a larger amount.

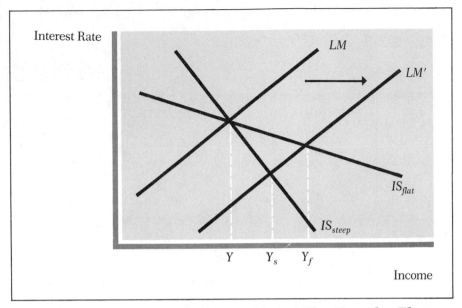

FIGURE 11 Monetary Policy Is More Effective the Flatter the *IS* Curve

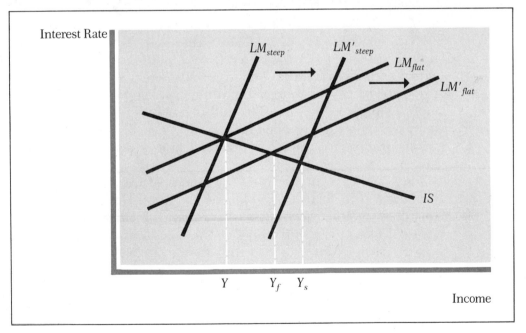

FIGURE 12 Monetary Policy Is More Effective the Steeper the *LM* Curve

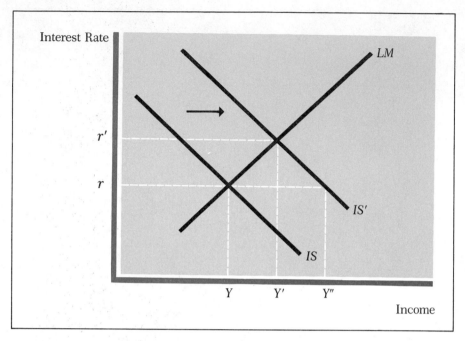

FIGURE 13 An Expansionary Fiscal Policy

LM'_{steep} or LM_{flat} to LM'_{flat}.[7] The former implies an increase in GNP from Y to Y_s, while the latter implies a shift from Y to Y_f. The explanation is as follows: The *less* the interest-sensitivity of the demand for money, the *larger* the decline in the rate of interest when money supply is increased (because the amount of money demanded increases only slightly when there is only a small fall in r); therefore, with a big drop in r (needed to increase money demand), the induced increases in investment spending and GNP are large.

Fiscal Policy: The nature of the impact of fiscal policy on GNP is summarized in Figures 13, 14, and 15. An increase in government spending (or a decrease in taxes) shifts the *IS* curve to the right.[8] In Figure 13 there is a shift from *IS* to *IS'*. Equilibrium GNP goes from Y to Y' at the same time that the interest rate is driven *up* from r to r'. The interest rate goes up because there is increased transactions

[7]Notice that the *horizontal* distances between the curves in the two sets are identical because the income sensitivity of the demand for money is the same in both cases; hence the *potential* increase in GNP due to the increased money supply is the same (at the old equilibrium interest rate).

[8]A decrease in government spending or an increase in taxes shifts the *IS* curve to the left, and all the impacts are the reverse of those in the text.

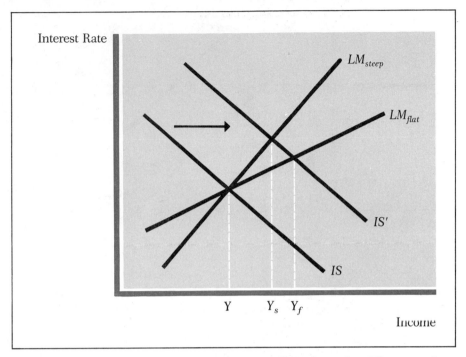

FIGURE 14 Fiscal Policy Is More Effective the Flatter the LM Curve

demand for money associated with the rise in GNP; therefore, with a fixed money supply, r must rise to keep $LP = M$.

Up to now this interest rate effect has been suppressed in evaluating the impact of ΔG (or any change in autonomous spending) on economic activity. It has significant consequences, however. It *reduces* the size of the autonomous expenditure multiplier, hence the power of fiscal policy, because the increase in the interest rate reduces investment spending at the same time that government expenditure is going up. If the rate of interest had remained unchanged, the increase in GNP would have been to Y''. The size of the horizontal shift in the *IS* curve is equal to ΔG times $1/(1 - b)$, and the increase from Y to Y'' is equal to that. But the actual increase in GNP is less (only to Y'), because the interest rate goes up and investment spending is reduced somewhat (now you know why we called $1/(1 - b)$ the "simple" multiplier). In fact, this decrease in investment when government spending rises has come to be known as the "crowding out" effect.

The size of the government expenditure multiplier (and thus the effectiveness of fiscal policy) is greater, the smaller is the offsetting

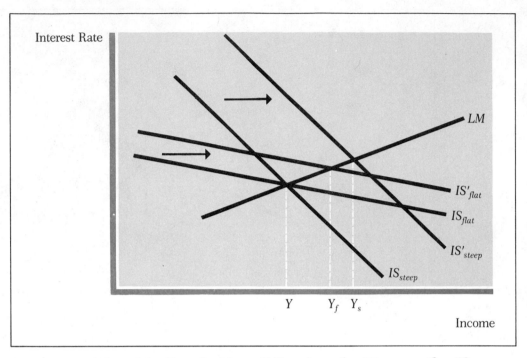

FIGURE 15 Fiscal Policy Is More Effective the Steeper the *IS* Curve

effect of rising interest rates on investment spending. In Figure 14 the rightward shift in the *IS* curve has a smaller impact on GNP with the steeper *LM* curve than with the flatter *LM* curve. When a steep *LM* curve is due to small interest-sensitivity of liquidity preference, for example, the increased transactions demand for money as GNP rises requires a large increase in the rate of interest to bring total money demand back into equality with money supply. The large rise in the rate of interest cuts off a large amount of private investment—there is a large "crowding out" effect—hence the net impact on GNP is relatively small.[9]

Figure 15 is another rather complicated diagram. It indicates that the less the interest-sensitivity of investment, the larger is the government expenditure multiplier, and thus the more effective is fiscal policy. If investment spending is insensitive to changes in the rate of interest,

[9]The steep *LM* curve can also be due to a large transactions demand for money. In this case, the increase in *Y* produces a large rise in the demand for money, forcing the rate of interest to rise by a lot in order to bring money demand back into equality with the fixed money supply.

TABLE 1
A Summary of Monetary and Fiscal Policy Effectiveness

Then	(1) If LP is very sensitive to r	(2) If I is very sensitive to r
(A) The LM curve is	flatter	—
(B) The IS curve is	—	flatter
(C) Monetary policy is	less effective	more effective
(D) Fiscal policy is	more effective	less effective

the IS curve is steeper. An increase in government spending either shifts IS_{steep} to IS'_{steep}, raising GNP to Y_s, or shifts IS_{flat} to IS'_{flat}, raising GNP to Y_f. The increase in the rate of interest cuts off more investment the greater the sensitivity of investment to the rate of interest; hence the rise in income is smaller under such circumstances.[10]

As a reward for reading this far and still remaining conscious (check your pulse), Table 1 summarizes the factors influencing the relative effectiveness of monetary policy and fiscal policy. Start at the top of columns (1) and (2), with the statement, for example, "If LP is very sensitive to r" and then proceed to the extreme left-hand column for "*Then* (A), (B), (C) and (D)." The implications of each statement for *ISLM* analysis and monetary and fiscal policy are recorded in the table.

KEYNES AND THE CLASSICS

Velocity, one of the cornerstones of the Classical system, seems to have disappeared from our Keynesian framework. Where has velocity gone? It has disappeared behind the LM curve. Since a particular LM function is drawn for a *given* money supply, as one moves up along an LM function, the income velocity of money is necessarily going up. Income is rising but the money supply is constant, so Y/M ($= V$) has to rise. In Figure 16, three different IS curves produce three different levels of GNP, as well as three different levels of velocity: V_1 (equal

[10]Notice that the horizontal distances between the IS curves in the two sets are identical. This is so because, if the rate of interest is held constant, the *potential* increase in GNP due to an increase in government spending is the same (because the marginal propensity to consume is assumed to be the same).

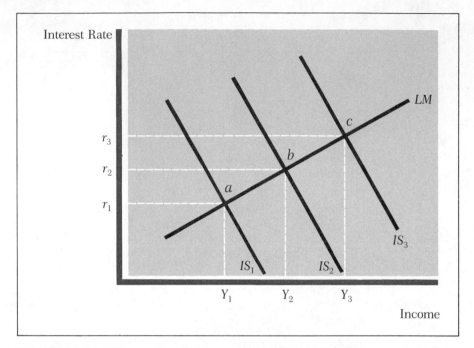

FIGURE 16 When the *IS* Curve Shifts, Both Income and Velocity Rise

to Y_1/M) at a; V_2 $(= Y_2/M)$ at b; and V_3 $(= Y_3/M)$ at c.[11] V_3 is greater than V_2, which is greater than V_1.

The rightward shifts in the *IS* curve in Figure 16, associated with (for example) increased levels of government spending, succeed in raising GNP by raising velocity. In fact, velocity goes up because the demand for money is sensitive to the rate of interest. The rise in the rate of interest induces the public to hold less speculative balances (or, more generally, to make more economical use of all money balances), permitting more cash to be used for carrying out transactions.

If the demand for money were totally *insensitive* to the interest rate, then velocity would be constant and GNP would not be affected by shifts in autonomous spending. An interest-insensitive demand for money means that money demand depends *only* on income. For a given supply of money, there is only one level of income at which the

[11]Velocity is properly defined as PY/M, but in our discussion prices are fixed so that movements in velocity are identified with Y.

equilibrium condition, $LP = M$, is satisfied. The LM curve is vertical at that level of GNP, as shown in Figure 17—implying that no matter how high government spending rises, the level of GNP cannot go up because then LP would exceed M.

It is the fixed money supply that prevents GNP from rising under such circumstances. If autonomous spending goes up, illustrated by the rightward shifts in the IS curve in Figure 17, the result is an increase in the rate of interest, cutting off investment spending. The rate of interest rises until the drop in interest-sensitive investment spending is equal to the autonomous increase in spending, resulting in no increase in GNP. The "crowding out" effect is complete. (We will return to the implications of a vertical LM curve in the next chapter.)

Another feature of $ISLM$ analysis is that it integrates the Classical and Keynesian theories of interest rate determination. In Chapter 20 the simplified Keynesian view was that the interest rate was a purely monetary phenomenon, determined by the supply of and demand for money. The Classical school, on the other hand, argued that the inter-

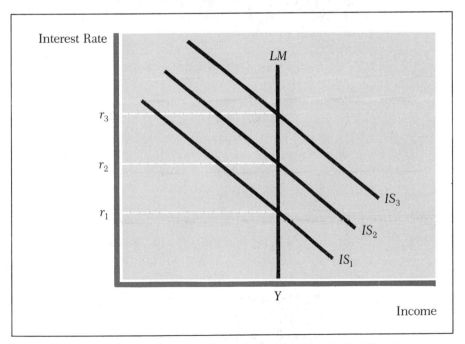

FIGURE 17 When the LM Curve is Vertical, Shifts in the IS Curve Raise Neither Income nor Velocity

est rate was a "real" phenomenon, determined exclusively by saving and investment.[12] In our current treatment both monetary factors, embodied in the *LM* curve, and real factors, embodied in the *IS* curve, affect the interest rate. An increase in the money supply, by shifting the *LM* curve to the right, lowers the rate of interest, as Keynes suggested. An increase in autonomous investment, by shifting the *IS* curve to the right, raises the rate of interest, as the Classics suggested.

This partial rehabilitation of Classical interest rate theory forces us back to the question we raised earlier: Why don't variations in the rate of interest automatically bring about full employment in the Keynesian system, as the Classical economists argued would happen? Having resurrected this much of Classical theory, can we bring Say's Law back to life as well?

WHEN WILL FULL EMPLOYMENT PREVAIL?

The Classical argument that the level of economic activity would tend toward full employment can be put into the Keynesian *ISLM* framework by allowing the price level to vary. Figure 18 shows an equilibrium level of income and interest rate associated with *IS* and *LM*. Let's assume that the level of GNP that would generate full employment is Y_{FE}. Quite clearly, equilibrium economic activity at Y is too low to justify employing all those who want to work at the going wage rate. Unemployment is the result.

The Keynesian apparatus makes it perfectly clear that the only way employment will increase is for aggregate economic activity to increase; only if desired spending increases will GNP increase beyond Y toward Y_{FE}. So far we have no reason to suspect that either the *IS* curve or the *LM* curve will shift to the right, hence no reason to suspect that output Y will not remain at that level unless there are increases in government spending or the money supply.

But the Classical economists said we needn't wait for government intervention. With less than full employment, workers would lower their wage demands and prices would be lowered as entrepreneurs tried to sell the output they produced with the increased labor that they hired (more workers would presumably be hired at lower wage

[12]Recall once again that this controversy refers to the real rate of interest. As long as inflationary expectations are zero, real rates equal nominal rates. Moreover, as long as inflationary expectations are unchanged, changes in nominal interest rates correspond to changes in real rates.

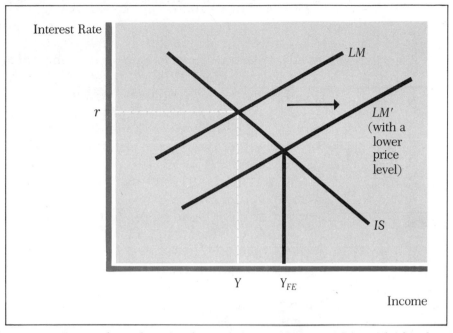

**FIGURE 18 The Classical Position: Lower Prices Shift the
LM Curve to the Right and Automatically Produce Full
Employment**

rates). However, if both prices *and wages* are falling, there is no reason
to expect consumers to spend more—goods cost less but individuals
receive less money for their work, so their *real* income hasn't increased. Investment spending is also not likely to be affected directly.
Entrepreneurs pay less for their inputs because of the decline in prices,
but they must also expect to receive a smaller dollar return on outputs;
the two are likely to cancel each other and expected profitability
should be more or less unchanged. Indeed, all our behavioral relationships are in *real* terms; people see through falling prices accompanied
by falling incomes, so consumption, investment, and money-holding
decisions are unaffected by equal movements in dollar incomes and
prices. Thus, it seems that both the *IS* and *LM* curves in Figure 18 will
remain unchanged, aggregate demand will remain at its old level (*Y*),
workers just hired will be fired, and the level of employment will be
back where it started.

Nevertheless, the Classical economists had an ace in the hole: *one
thing clearly affected by a fall in the price level is the real value of
the supply of money.* As we saw in previous chapters, if the money

supply is fixed at $1,000 and the price level is one, its real value (in purchasing power) is the same as if the money supply were $2,000 and the price level were doubled. But if we start out with a $2,000 money supply and the price level is cut in half—presto, the real money supply doubles (for example, from $2,000/2 to $2,000/1)! This increase in the real value of the money supply due to falling prices is the mechanism through which the economy would move itself from a position of less than full employment to full employment. Here's how.

In terms of Figure 18, falling prices shift the *LM* curve to the right for the same reason that an increase in money supply does: falling prices increase the real value of the money supply and thereby create an excess of (real) money supply over the (real) demand for money. Falling prices continue as long as people are unemployed, so that the increased real value of the money supply continues to shift the *LM* curve to the right, lowering the interest rate and increasing desired investment. This process would continue until the *LM* curve in Figure 18 is shifted from *LM* to *LM'* (the latter associated with a lower price level than at the original position), at which point economic activity is at full employment.

The Keynesian attack on this Classical mechanism was not confined to the argument that prices and wages are sticky and inflexible and not likely to fall very promptly. The Classical school, in fact, stressed that unemployment was the result of such downward inflexibility in wages and prices. Keynes said, however, that there were at least two other circumstances that would stall the move toward full employment. The first is the case of a *liquidity trap*, in which an increase in the money supply would not lower the interest rate, as we noted at the end of the last chapter. As long as the liquidity preference function is perfectly horizontal, an increase in the money supply, real or nominal, is associated with the same rate of interest. The *LM* curve is horizontal under such conditions,[13] and no matter how far the price level declines, the interest rate won't fall, investment spending will remain unaltered, and so will aggregate output and employment. This situation is depicted in Figure 19.

The second case in which falling prices fail to work is when investment is highly *insensitive* to the rate of interest. The *IS* curve is very steep. Under such conditions, declining prices and the induced reduction in the rate of interest will be unable to raise investment to a

---

[13]Recall that the *LM* curve is flatter the greater the interest-sensitivity of money demand. In the liquidity trap, money demand is infinitely interest-elastic, hence the *LM* curve becomes totally flat.

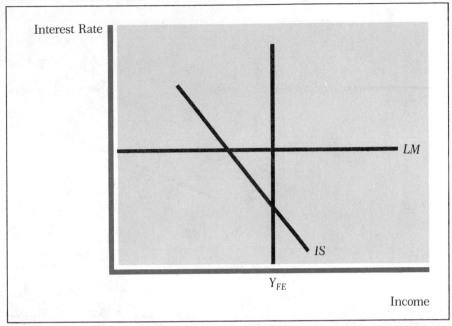

FIGURE 19 An Extreme Keynesian Position: A Liquidity Trap

sufficiently high level to generate full employment spending, as in Figure 20.

But Classical economics wasn't built on such a fragile link between the monetary sector and spending on goods and services. The Classical argument that we have just presented based the automatic tendency toward full employment on the rightward shift in the *LM* curve due to increases in the real value of the money supply. This is a thoroughly "Keynesian" mechanism, in the sense that money affects the economy only through the interest rate. But falling prices not only lower the interest rate, they also make people's real money balances worth more, and this might have a more direct impact on economic activity. People would be wealthier in addition to being more liquid. And if more liquidity wouldn't help (because of, say, the liquidity trap), more wealth (in the form of real balances) certainly would. A cash balance of $10 may not mean you're very rich if the price level is unity. But if the price level fell to $\frac{1}{10}$ of what it was, you'd have $100 in purchasing power; a drop to $\frac{1}{100}$ would make your $10 bill worth $1,000 (in purchasing power); and a decline in the price level to $\frac{1}{100,000}$ of what it was would make you a millionaire!

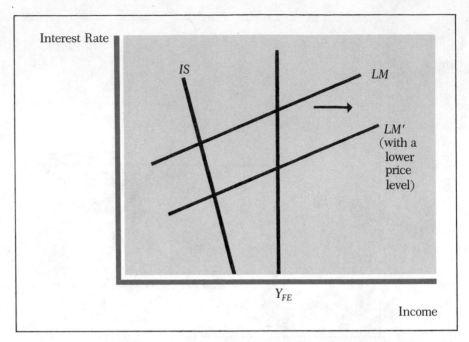

FIGURE 20 Another Extreme Keynesian Position: Investment Unresponsive to the Interest Rate

As we noted in our discussion of the consumption function in Chapter 20, an increase in wealth raises desired consumption at every level of income.[14] In terms of Figures 19 and 20, the *IS* curve would now shift to the right until it intersected the *LM* curve at the full employment level of GNP. Prices would then stop falling, and all those who wanted jobs would be employed (with so many millionaires, perhaps the unemployment problem would be eliminated by the army of the wealthy pulling out of the labor force).

Thus, in contrast to our initial impression, the complete Classical argument has *both* Keynesian curves, the *IS* and *LM*, moving to the right as a result of falling prices. Changes in the real value of money balances affect the rate of interest and indirectly influence investment spending (the rightward shift in *LM*), but they may also affect consumption spending directly (the rightward shift in *IS*).

[14]The wealth effect just discussed is called the real balance effect, to distinguish it from the influence of interest rates on wealth. As we mentioned in footnote 6, the interest-rate-induced wealth effect merely changes the slope of the *IS* curve (it depends on the interest rate, and the interest rate is on the vertical axis). The real balance effect *shifts* the *IS* curve because it alters spending at every rate of interest.

Keynes would say all this is fine, but by the time it comes about all those who wanted jobs will have passed through the Great Unemployment Window in the Sky. The Classical "do it yourself" path to full employment is lengthy and arduous. Unemployment can last a very long time if the economy is left to its own devices, with no help from its friends. So the Keynesian prescription is fiscal policy. Monetarists reflect their Classical ancestry by maintaining that flexible wages and prices will do the job. In Chapter 23 we use aggregate supply and demand analysis to describe these alternative viewpoints. It will be useful therefore to see how the *ISLM* model developed here meshes with that broader framework.

ISLM AND AGGREGATE DEMAND

Recall from the end of Chapter 19 that the aggregate demand curve relates the price level to the demand for real output. The *ISLM* model is concerned with a different relationship: the interest rate and the demand for real output. That's why price is on the vertical axis in the picture for the aggregate demand schedule (see Figure 11 in the last chapter), while the interest rate is on the vertical axis in the *ISLM* picture. The two models emphasize different relationships because they focus on movements in different variables. But both the *ISLM* model and the aggregate demand schedule focus on the *demand* for real output. Here are the specifics on how they are related.

It is relatively straightforward to generate a complete aggregate demand schedule from the *ISLM* model. Different price levels are associated with a family of *LM* curves, as in Figure 21(a). Given the curve *IS* in Figure 21(a), we have a number of equilibrium real income or output levels (Y_0, Y_1, and Y_2) associated with price levels P_0, P_1, and P_2. Figure 21(b) plots the demand for real output as an explicit function of those prices. The result is D, which is exactly what we call the aggregate demand curve.

It is also fairly easy to see the underlying factors causing the aggregate demand schedule to change position. Figure 21(a) shows that a rightward shift in the *IS* curve to *IS'* generates higher levels of GNP for any given price level. Thus the aggregate demand curve shifts from D to D' when any category of exogenous spending pushes the *IS* curve to the right. It follows that decreases in exogenous spending push the aggregate demand curve to the left.

Less obvious but also true, an increase in the stock of money shifts

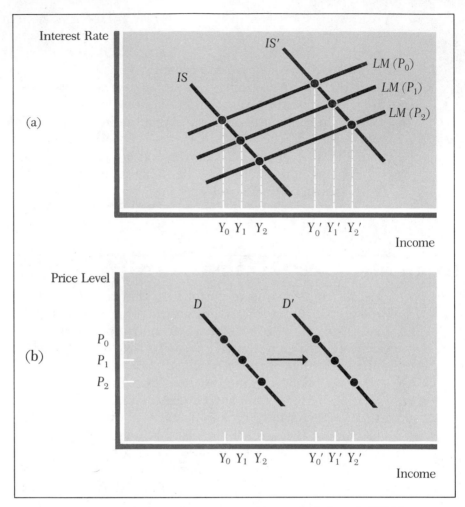

FIGURE 21 Deriving Aggregate Demand from *ISLM*

aggregate demand to the right. The reasoning is as follows: an exogenous increase in the money supply causes *each* of the *LM* curves in
Figure 21(a) to shift rightward (use your imagination); thus, a higher
level of demand for GNP is associated with any given price level, and
that's represented by a demand schedule like *D'* compared with *D* in
Figure 21(b). Similarly, decreases in the money supply will cause the
aggregate demand curve to shift to the left.

It is possible to describe in greater detail how the *IS* and *LM* curves
combine to determine the slope and the size of the shifts in the
aggregate demand schedule. For our purposes, you are no doubt happy
to know, it is more important simply to recognize the connection

between the *ISLM* world and the aggregate demand/supply framework. We will explore the implications in Chapter 23.

SUMMARY

1. The main advantage of *ISLM* analysis is that it shows the behavior of the money market and the product market in a single diagram. Keynes's earlier treatment ignored some crucial interactions. An important mechanism is that the interest rate both influences GNP (through investment) and is affected by it (through the demand for money).

2. The simple Keynesian fiscal policy multiplier ignores the fact that an expansion in aggregate demand raises interest rates. Thus in the *ISLM* model the impact of fiscal policy on GNP is tempered by rising interest rates that crowd out private investment.

3. Monetary policy raises GNP by lowering the interest rate and encouraging investment. The impact on GNP will be reduced, therefore, when either the interest rate can't be lowered much (because money demand is very interest-sensitive) or when investment spending is relatively insensitive to the interest rate.

4. Velocity, the cornerstone of Classical economics, is hidden behind the *LM* curve of the Keynesian model. Fiscal policy raises GNP by increasing the velocity of the existing money supply.

5. Flexible wages and prices will push aggregate demand toward full employment equilibrium even in the Keynesian world. That process is tempered by a very interest-sensitive money demand and by very interest-insensitive investment. Nevertheless, given enough time, wage-price flexibility will generate full employment even according to *ISLM* analysis.

Suggestions for Further Reading

The original presentation of the *ISLM* model was in John R. Hicks, "Mr. Keynes and the 'Classics': A Suggested Interpretation," *Econometrica* (April 1937). A good basic introduction to ISLM analysis is Robert J. Gordon, *Macroeconomics*, 3d ed. (Boston: Little Brown, 1984); or Stanley Fischer and Rudger Dornbusch, *Macroeconomics*, 3d. ed. (New York: McGraw-Hill, 1984).

APPENDIX

The Simple Algebra
of Income Determination

For the algebraically inclined, much of the discussion in Chapters 20 and 21 can be summarized succinctly in equation form. The economy is divided into two sectors: the goods or product market, comprising the demand for goods and services; and the monetary sector, comprising the demand for and supply of money.

THE MODEL

The product market can be described by four functional relationships (behavior equations) and one equilibrium condition (an identity). All the functional relationships are assumed to be linear, an assumption that simplifies exposition without doing excessive damage to real world applications. The functional relationships:

(1) $C = a + b(Y - T)$ Consumption (C) function
(2) $I = d - n(R)$ Investment (I) function
(3) $T = e + t(Y)$ Tax (T) function
(4) $G = \overline{G}$ Government spending (G)

and the equilibrium condition:

(5) $C + I + G = Y$ or $S + T = I + G$

where Y stands for GNP (income) and R for the interest rate. In each equation, the first lower-case letter represents the constant term of the function, and the second lower-case letter the coefficient of the independent variable (or the slope of the function); that is, b is the marginal propensity to consume ($\Delta C / \Delta (Y - T)$), and n is the interest-sensitivity of the investment function ($\Delta I / \Delta R$). Government spending is indicated by $\overline{G}$ and is exogenously fixed (imposed on the system from outside).

The *monetary sector* of the economy consists of two functional relationships and one equilibrium condition:

(6) $L = f - h(R) + k(Y)$ Liquidity preference (L) or demand-for-money function

(7) $M = \overline{M}$ Money supply (M)

(8) $L = M$ Equilibrium condition

THE *IS* AND *LM* FUNCTIONS

By solving equations (1) through (5), we find the *IS* function:

(9) $Y = \dfrac{a - be + \overline{G} + d}{1 - b + bt} - \dfrac{n}{1 - b + bt}R$

By solving equations (6) through (8), we find the *LM* function:

(10) $Y = \dfrac{\overline{M} - f}{k} + \dfrac{h}{k}R$ or $R = \dfrac{kY + f - \overline{M}}{h}$

EQUILIBRIUM INCOME AND INTEREST

By solving (9) and (10) simultaneously, we obtain equilibrium income (Y) and interest rate (R):

(11) $Y = \dfrac{1}{1 - b + bt + \dfrac{nk}{h}}(a - be + d + \overline{G} - \dfrac{nf}{h} + \dfrac{n\overline{M}}{h})$

(12) $R = \dfrac{1}{h(1 - b + bt) + nk}[ka - kbe + kd + k\overline{G}$
$+ f(1 - b + bt) - \overline{M}(1 - b + bt)]$

MULTIPLIER EFFECTS: ON INCOME

From (11) one can derive the multiplier effects on income, and from (12) one can derive the multiplier effects on the interest rate, that follow from a change in government spending (ΔG), an autonomous shift in the consumption or investment function (Δa or Δd), a shift in the tax function (Δe), a change in the money supply (ΔM), or an autonomous shift in the demand for money (Δf).

The multiplier effects on income, from (11), are:

$$(13) \qquad \frac{\Delta Y}{\Delta G \text{ or } \Delta a \text{ or } \Delta d} = \frac{1}{1 - b + bt + \dfrac{nk}{h}}$$

$$(14) \qquad \frac{\Delta Y}{\Delta e} = -\frac{b}{1 - b + bt + \dfrac{nk}{h}}$$

$$(15) \qquad \frac{\Delta Y}{\Delta M \text{ (or } -\Delta f)} = \frac{n}{h\,(1 - b + bt) + nk}$$

MULTIPLIER EFFECTS: ON THE INTEREST RATE

The multiplier effects on the interest rate, from (12), are:

$$(16) \qquad \frac{\Delta R}{\Delta G \text{ or } \Delta a \text{ or } \Delta d} = \frac{k}{h(1 - b + bt) + nk}$$

$$(17) \qquad \frac{\Delta R}{\Delta e} = -\frac{kb}{h(1 - b + bt) + nk}$$

$$(18) \qquad \frac{\Delta R}{\Delta M \text{ (or } -\Delta f)} = -\frac{(1 - b + bt)}{h(1 - b + bt) + nk}$$

POLICY IMPLICATIONS

A number of policy implications are contained in the above multiplier formulas. Among the more important are the following:

1. As (13) indicates, in the complete Keynesian system the multiplier effect on income of a change in government spending is *smaller* than the simple $\frac{1}{1-b}$ that is typically taught in beginning economics courses. It is smaller by the addition of $bt + \frac{nk}{h}$ to the denominator. Here's what it means: t represents tax rates (they cut back consumer spending); k is the transac-

tions demand for money (as income rises, the amount of transactions money desired increases, raising interest rates); n is the interest-sensitivity of investment spending (as interest rates rise, they cut back investment spending); h is the interest-sensitivity of the demand for money (if liquidity preference is very responsive to interest rates, it will take only a small rise in rates to induce people to reduce their cash holdings enough to provide the additional money needed for transactions purposes).

2. Compare (13) and (14): as long as b is less than unity, an increase in government spending will increase income by more than an equal increase in taxes will lower income. The multiplier for a change in government spending is larger than the multiplier for a tax change.

2a. It follows from the above that a simultaneous and equal increase in both government spending and taxes—that is, a balanced budget change in government spending (financed entirely by higher taxes)—will not leave income unchanged, but will increase it. Balanced budgets are not neutral with respect to income.

3. Equation (15) indicates that monetary policy will be *less* powerful in affecting income the larger is h (the responsiveness of liquidity preference to interest rates) and the smaller is n (the responsiveness of investment spending to interest rates).[1]

3a. As a special case of the above, if h is *infinite* (Keynesian liquidity trap) or n is *zero* (investment completely insensitive to interest rates), then the multiplier for $\Delta M = 0$ and monetary policy is useless.

3b. Under such circumstances ($h = \infty$ or $n = 0$), it follows that fiscal policy is the only alternative.

4. Conversely, (15) also indicates that monetary policy will be *more* powerful in affecting income the smaller is h and the larger is n.

[1] The effect of changes in h, n, or any of the other coefficients on the size of the multipliers can be verified by numerical examples (putting in actual numbers for each coefficient, calculating the multiplier, and then changing one of the coefficients and recalculating the multiplier), or by using calculus (take the derivative, for example, of $\Delta Y / \Delta M$ with respect to n, h, or k). Note also that the points made under 3a, 3b, 4a, and 4b are not discussed in this chapter. They correspond to points that will be made in the next chapter.

4a. As a special case of the above, if h is *zero* (liquidity preference completely insensitive to interest rates), then—from (13)—the multiplier for $\Delta G = 0$ and fiscal policy is useless.

4b. On the other hand, under such circumstances ($h = 0$), monetary policy is both necessary *and sufficient* to control income. If $h = 0$, equation (15) indicates that the multiplier for $\Delta M = \frac{1}{k}$; so long as k is constant in the liquidity-preference function, a change in the money supply will always change income by the constant $\frac{1}{k}$. That is, $\Delta M \times \frac{1}{k} = \Delta Y$, which is—surprise!—the same as the quantity theory of money ($M \times$ velocity $= Y$, with velocity constant and equal to $\frac{1}{k}$).

CHAPTER 22

Monetarists and Keynesians in the ISLM World*

Last chapter's ISLM model integrated the Classical and Keynesian outlooks on the determination of GNP and interest rates. We can now utilize this ISLM framework to articulate some of the controversies that have surrounded Monetarist and Keynesian thinking. Monetarists, as you may recall from Chapter 19, are modern-day Classical economists who often focus attention on the connection between money supply and economic activity. Keynesians, as we saw in Chapter 20, inherited a faith in the linkage between fiscal policy and economic activity from John Maynard Keynes. To complete this discussion, the first section of this chapter illustrates the polar positions of Monetarists and Keynesians as far as monetary and fiscal policy are concerned. The next section turns to the ISLM framework to explain why Monetarists contend that economic activity is inherently stable while Keynesians emphasize the need for an active attempt at economic stabilization. In the last two sections we turn to an explicit consideration of price flexibility in the ISLM world. From that vantage point we can see clearly why Monetarists contend that inflation is

*This chapter uses analytical techniques developed in Chapter 21. If you skipped Chapter 21, skip this one too. All this material is presented in Chapter 23 in a somewhat different framework.

always a monetary phenomenon and why Keynesians are less positive on the subject.

MONETARY POLICY, FISCAL POLICY, AND CROWDING OUT

Over strenuous objections from Monetarists, and recognizing that such an approach can risk doing an injustice to their cause, we can represent an oversimplified Monetarist position within the *ISLM* framework. In fact, near the end of the last chapter the Monetarist "special case" in the Keynesian model was set forth: a demand for money that is unresponsive to interest rates—depending on income only—and that produces a vertical *LM* function (see Figure 17 in Chapter 21 and the discussion related to it).

In that world, things are very simple. Velocity is constant. With a fixed money supply, GNP can't change and neither does velocity. The impact of a change in money supply on the level of income equals ΔM multiplied by velocity (V). This can be seen in Figure 1. Start with *LM* and *IS* and equilibrium income *Y*. An increase in the money

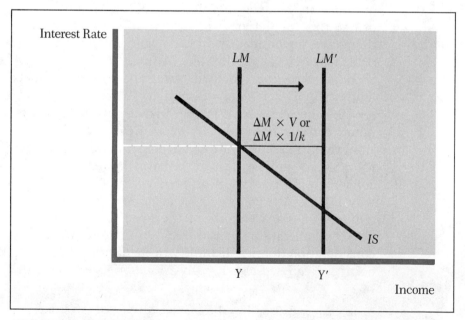

FIGURE 1 When the *LM* Curve Is Vertical, an Increase in the Money Supply Increases Income by ΔM Times Velocity

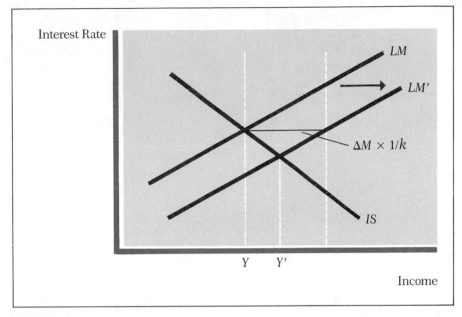

**FIGURE 2 When the *LM* Curve Is Not Vertical, an
Increase in the Money Supply is Less Powerful in
Increasing Income**

supply shifts the *LM* curve to the right by $\Delta M \times V$ (see footnote 3
of Chapter 21). The new equilibrium level of income is Y', and it is
obvious that the change in income from Y to Y' equals $\Delta M \times V$ *in
this case.* Income continues to rise until all the increased money
supply is absorbed into increased transactions demand.

On the other hand, as Figure 2 shows, when the *LM* curve is not
vertical but is positively sloped (as is the case when the demand for
money that underlies it is somewhat responsive to the rate of interest),
then the increase in income due to a change in the money supply will
be less than in Figure 1. In Figure 2 we have superimposed a set of
positively sloped *LM* curves (*LM* and *LM'*) on the Monetarist case of
Figure 1. While the horizontal distance between the two *LM* curves
is the same as before, the increase in income is clearly less than before.[1]
Why? Because the increase in the supply of money lowers the interest
rate, and at lower interest rates people will hold some of the increased
money supply in the form of "idle" balances rather than for transac-

[1]The horizontal distance between the two *LM* curves is the same as before, but now
it is simply called $\Delta M \times 1/k$, because $1/k = V$ only when the interest-sensitivity
of liquidity preference equals zero.

tions purposes. Thus the velocity or rate of turnover of the *total* money supply falls (some of it is now being held "idle"). But we are running a bit ahead of ourselves; let's wait until we come to the Keynesian analysis of money to complete this part of our story.

Let us reemphasize that the Monetarists are playing the game under protest—they don't like the rules of the Keynesian *ISLM* apparatus. It forces them into a situation where the change in money supply first lowers the interest rate, which increases investment, and thereby GNP. For Monetarists, the channels through which money influences spending are not restricted to interest rates, as will be emphasized in the next chapter. Thus while the vertical *LM* curve does convey some of the Monetarist flavor—that is, the stability of velocity—it still leaves a Keynesian taste. Moreover, as we stressed in Chapter 19, the assumption of stability in velocity is replaced by predictability in modern versions of Monetarism.

The Keynesian reservations about the potency of monetary policy can be summarized in a number of "special cases" in the *ISLM* model. First, an increase in money supply would not affect anything if the *LM* curve were horizontal at the relevant level of GNP, that is, if the liquidity trap were a reality.

Figure 3's money-supply-and-demand functions form the basis for

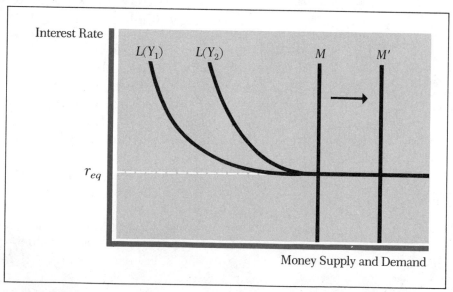

FIGURE 3 With a Liquidity Trap, an Increase in the Money Supply from *M to M′* Does Not Shift the *LM* Curve (see Figure 4)

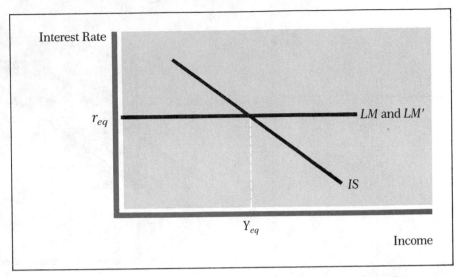

FIGURE 4 With a Liquidity Trap, an Increase in the Money Supply, Because It Does Not Shift the *LM* Curve, Does Not Change Income

constructing Figure 4's *LM* functions. If we increase the money supply from *M* to *M'* in Figure 3's liquidity trap, then we get no shift in the *LM* function in Figure 4. The *LM* curve with *M* (namely, *LM*) is the same as with M' (namely, *LM'*). As can be seen in Figure 4, when the *IS* curve intersects *LM* (or *LM'*), producing equilibrium income Y_{eq}, an increase in the money supply from *M* to *M'* does not lower the interest rate. All the increased money supply is held as idle balances. Equilibrium income is unchanged. More money and the same level of GNP imply a decrease in velocity—the hallmark of the Keynesian critique of monetary policy.

A second category of pitfalls for monetary policy concerns the *IS* curve. Even if the liquidity-preference function is well behaved, so that an increase in the money supply succeeds in lowering the rate of interest, there may still be no impact on GNP if investment is completely unresponsive to the rate of interest. From Chapter 21 we know that the *IS* curve is very steep if investment has little interest-sensitivity; with zero interest-sensitivity, the *IS* curve is vertical. Under such conditions, changes in the money supply do not affect income even though they may change the rate of interest. Figure 5 illustrates that situation. Start with *IS* and *LM* and equilibrium income *Y*. Then, an increase in the money supply causes a rightward shift in the *LM* curve to *LM'*, which merely lowers the interest rate

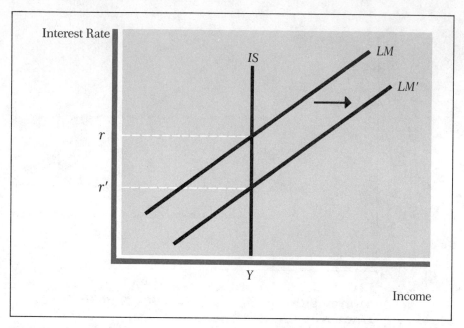

FIGURE 5 When the *IS* Curve Is Vertical, Monetary Policy Is Ineffective

with no impact on GNP. Once again, the money supply has gone up but GNP hasn't, with velocity falling as a result.

To summarize the monetary policy discussion: Monetary stimulus works in the Keynesian world when both the *IS* curve and the *LM* curve are "normal." Pathological cases of horizontal *LM*s and vertical *IS*s render monetary policy impotent. More generally, even when we are untroubled by horizontal *LM* curves and vertical *IS* curves, the impact of money on GNP is not the simple ΔM times a fixed velocity. For example, an increase in M may very well produce falling interest rates, more investment, and higher GNP. But GNP is not likely to rise in direct proportion to the change in M, because as interest rates decline, the speculative demand for money increases along with the transactions demand. In other words, velocity is likely to decline.

Turning to fiscal policy, the Monetarist and Keynesian polar cases in *ISLM* analysis produce symmetrical results. In particular, fiscal policy has a zero impact with a vertical *LM* curve, while it is completely effective (with no offsetting crowding out due to interest rate effects on private investment) with a horizontal *LM* curve.

Figure 6 illustrates these points. Let's start at point *a* with income *Y* and interest rate *r*. An increase in government spending (or a reduc-

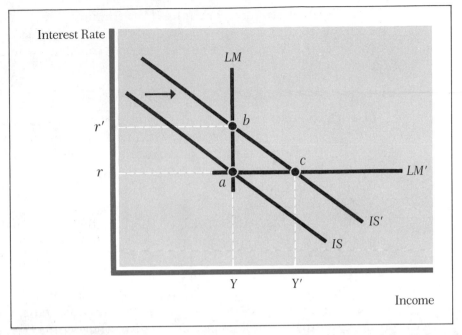

FIGURE 6 When the *LM* Curve Is Vertical, Fiscal Policy Is Completely Ineffective; When It Is Horizontal, It Is Totally Effective

tion in taxes) shifts the *IS* curve from *IS* to *IS'*. If the *LM* curve were *LM*, the new equilibrium would be at *b*, and the entire impact would be absorbed by a higher interest rate with no increase at all in GNP. In this case there is complete crowding out. But if the *LM* curve were *LM'*, the new equilibrium would be at *c* and the impact would be entirely on GNP, with no rise at all in the interest rate; in fact, since the rightward shift in the *IS* curve equals ΔG times $1/(1 - b)$, which also equals the change in GNP, the simple multiplier of Chapter 20 has returned in full bloom.

The general case of the positively sloped *LM* curve produces results that lie between the extremes, as we saw in the last chapter. An increase in government expenditure raises GNP, but by less than the "full multiplier" of the simple Keynesian system. This is because the interest rate goes up, cutting off some private investment (there is partial but not total crowding out). The rise in the rate of interest does not lower investment by as much as government spending increases, because the higher rate of interest also reduces the demand for money, permitting once-idle speculative balances to be used for carrying out the increased transactions associated with higher levels of GNP. It would seem, therefore, that unless the economy is characterized by the extreme case of zero interest-sensitivity of the demand for money (producing a vertical *LM* curve), even Monetarists would agree that fiscal policy could have some impact on GNP.

Not so fast, says Professor Friedman. The shape of the *LM* curve is only part of the story. Perhaps more important, the financing aspects of fiscal policy—especially in the long run—tend to dominate the direct impacts of a change in government spending or taxation. This is a more subtle dimension to crowding out, one that is unrelated to the slope of the LM curve. While the ISLM model is not designed for such purposes, we can use it to provide a flavor for the argument.[2]

When the government finances a deficit by selling bonds to the public, it increases the wealth of the private sector. That is because wealth is equal to the capital stock held by the private sector plus claims against the government (as long as we don't count the long-run tax liability needed to pay off the federal debt). Under the reasonable assumption that people want to hold increases in wealth in various assets (not just bonds), we expect that money *demand* should increase along with a bond-financed deficit. In other words, the increase in government bonds outstanding should raise the demand for money at every combination of income and interest rates. Note that the supply of money remains unchanged, because after the government receives cash from selling bonds it turns around and spends the money on goods and services (after all, the government sold bonds to *finance* spending).

An increase in money demand with a fixed money supply translates into a leftward shift in the LM curve. The new LM curve intersects the old IS curve at a lower level of GNP. Thus, a deficit financed by selling bonds crowds out private spending because it shifts the position of the LM curve, thereby raising interest rates, and not just because the slope of the LM curve implies that interest rates must go up when government spending rises. Note also that as long as the deficit persists, the LM curve continues shifting to the left.

The problem with this analysis is that it is incomplete. It introduces feedback from flows of spending (by the government) onto stocks of assets (bonds), but it has ignored other such relationships (such as the feedback from investment spending to the capital stock as well as the

[2]The following discussion is based on William L. Silber, "Fiscal Policy in IS-LM Analysis: A Correction," *Journal of Money, Credit, and Banking* (November 1970), and Alan S. Blinder and Robert M. Solow, "Analytical Foundations of Fiscal Policy," in *The Economics of Public Finance* (Washington, D.C.: Brookings Institution, 1974).

"In theory, yes, Mrs. Wilkins. But also in theory, no."

Drawing by Stan Hunt; © 1976 The New Yorker Magazine, Inc.

implications of financing the interest expenses on the bonds). More-over, stability of the system imposes limits to the leftward shift in the LM curve. Nevertheless, this added dimension to crowding out cannot be ignored.

To summarize: Crowding out occurs for two reasons: (1) the simple argument that more transactions associated with higher GNP raise money demand, thereby increasing interest rates and reducing invest-ment spending; (2) the more subtle argument that the dynamics of selling bonds to finance government deficits has a wealth effect on portfolios that raises interest rates as well.

IS THE PRIVATE SECTOR INHERENTLY STABLE?

The vertical and horizontal *LM* curves depict extreme Monetarist and Keynesian positions, respectively. Moderate wings in both camps assert only that the *LM* curve is "quite vertical" on the one hand or "somewhat flat" on the other. Such tendencies are sufficient to demonstrate the stability or instability of economic activity in the face of exogenous shifts in private investment.

Figure 7 shows two alternative *LM* curves: LM_{steep} and LM_{flat}.

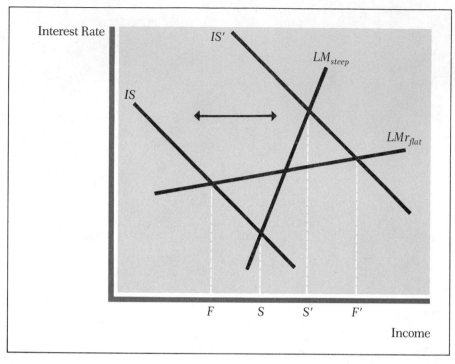

FIGURE 7 A Flatter *LM* Curve Means Wider Fluctuations in GNP Because of Exogenous Shifts in Investment

There are two *IS* curves representing shifts in autonomous investment. As can be seen in the picture, with LM_{steep} the induced fluctuation in GNP due to the shifting *IS* curve is *S* to *S'*. When the *LM* curve is LM_{flat}, however, the fluctuation in GNP is much wider, between *F* and *F'*. The key to the smaller fluctuation in GNP with LM_{steep} is that the level of interest rates fluctuates more than with LM_{flat}. Thus, when the *IS* curve shifts from *IS'* to *IS*, the interest rate falls a lot, inducing a large amount of endogenous investment to offset a large part of the decline in autonomous investment. With a flatter *LM* curve, the fall in the rate of interest is smaller and induced investment is less. Thus a steeper *LM* curve stabilizes the level of economic activity associated with a particular stock of money, because the interest rate fluctuates more. That's not quite how Monetarists would necessarily tell the story, but it's close enough.

When the economy operates near its full employment capacity, fluctuations in the price level help provide self-correcting stabilization. Figure 8 shows the intersection of *IS* and $LM(P_0)$ at Y_{FE}. We introduced Y_{FE} at the end of Chapter 21 to represent full employment

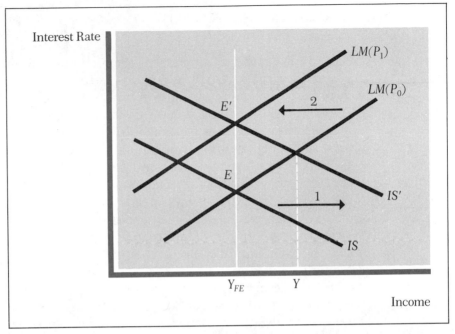

FIGURE 8 At Full Employment, Fluctuations in the Price Level Help Stabilize Economic Activity

GNP. The *LM* curve is labeled with a particular price index, P_0, since changes in the price level will affect the position of *LM.* Moreover, at full employment, we assume that prices rise in response to increases in aggregate demand. A shift in autonomous spending pushes *IS* to *IS'* and raises demand to *Y.* As a result, prices rise. With a fixed stock of money, this reduces the *real* supply of money, and the *LM* curve is pushed back toward the full employment line. This process stops once aggregate demand is back at full employment; in our picture this occurs at the intersection between *IS'* and $LM(P_1)$.

At the new equilibrium *E'* we have both a higher price level and a higher rate of interest. The higher price level (caused by an exogenous increase in spending) has reduced the real supply of money, raised interest rates, and pushed back aggregate demand to the full employment level. Thus the fixed supply of money, together with flexible prices and interest rates, insulates full employment economic activity from exogenous changes in investment. The process would be reversed (lower prices and lower interest rates) if there were a decrease in exogenous investment (shifting *IS* to the left). Notice that Figure 8 has the elements of an inflation story, as we will see shortly.

FLEXIBLE PRICES, THE NATURAL RATE OF INTEREST, AND REAL CROWDING OUT

Price flexibility has even more startling effects on the impacts of monetary and fiscal policy. In the first instance, when the economy is operating at or near full employment, and prices are flexible, the Keynesian interest rate mechanism gives way completely to Classical/Monetarist arguments. In particular, at full employment the rate of interest is independent of movements in the money stock. This can be seen in Figure 9, starting with *IS* and *LM* intersecting at Y_{FE} and r_{FE}. The latter is the real rate of interest because, as usual, we are assuming the absence of any inflationary expectations. As always, an increase in money supply shifts *LM* to *LM'*, apparently pushing down the interest rate from r_{FE} to r' and raising aggregate demand to Y'. But the excess of aggregate demand over Y_{FE} causes prices to rise. This reduces the real supply of money, pushing *LM'* back toward *LM*. After all is said and done, prices have risen until the *LM* curve is back where it started, since otherwise prices would keep on rising. And when *LM'* is back at *LM*, the real rate of interest is restored to its original level. Thus, at full employment, increases in money supply cannot reduce the interest rate below r_{FE}. Similar reasoning shows that *decreases* in the

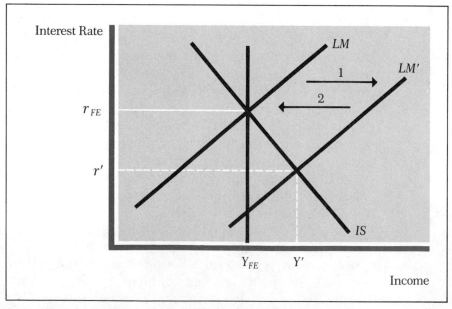

FIGURE 9 An Increase in Money Supply at Full Employment Doesn't Lower the Interest Rate

money stock will not raise interest rates above r_{FE} if prices fall when aggregate demand is below full employment.

The interest rate r_{FE} has a special name. It is called the natural rate of interest and is defined as that rate which equates saving and investment at full employment. It is determined by the intersection point between the IS curve and the Y_{FE} line. Shifts in the money stock can't change r_{FE}. Only shifts in the IS curve can, as we saw earlier in Figure 8. Thus at full employment only saving and investment (including government spending) determine the interest rate; money has nothing to do with it. At full employment, classical interest theory pops out of the Keynesian picture!

The implications for the effect of expansionary monetary policy on interest rates at full employment are twofold: (1) the real rate of interest is unchanged by increases in money supply; (2) nominal rates (not shown in the figures) will rise if inflationary expectations are generated by the increased money stock. The latter is quite likely, especially in the long run. Borrowers and lenders recognize that excessive expansion in money stock means rising prices. This will no doubt lead them to agree upon an inflation premium attached to the real rate of interest. With the real rate fixed at r_{FE}, the net result is an increase in nominal rates by the expected rate of inflation.[3]

The analysis of fiscal policy under flexible prices adds another dimension to the crowding out mechanism. In particular, we see that at full employment an increase in government expenditure is crowded out in *real* terms, even if the LM curve has a positive slope. Look again at Figure 8, which shows equilibrium at Y_{FE} with IS and $LM(P_0)$. The rightward shifts to IS' now represent an increase in government spending at full employment. Initially there is an increase in aggregate demand to Y', with investment demand declining (along the IS curve) to offset only part of the increase in government expenditure. A positively sloped LM curve permits such an expansion in aggregate demand. But that's not the end of the story. With aggregate demand, Y', exceeding full employment production, Y_{FE}, prices rise (from P_0 to P_1), pushing $LM(P_0)$ back toward $LM(P_1)$ and raising the interest rate still further. That process will continue until the new equilibrium, E', is reached. At that point the interest rate has increased by enough to cut off an amount of investment spending equal to the initial increase in government expenditure. How do we know? If that weren't the case,

---

[3]In the next chapter there is a more detailed discussion of the Monetarist and Keynesian views on real and nominal interest rate movements. Also, return to Chapter 6 for a simple discussion.

aggregate demand would still be above Y_{FE}, prices would still be rising, and so would the interest rate. (The logic is simply nauseating.)

Two points are worth noting in this example. First, the interest rate at full employment is obviously affected by shifts in the real sector of the economy, represented by the *IS* curve (even though it is unaffected by shifts in the monetary sector). Second, notice that nominal GNP is higher at *E'* compared with *E*. How do we know? Because real income is still at Y_{FE}, but prices are higher (P_1 versus P_0). Thus, while there is real crowding out at full employment even with a positively sloped *LM* curve, there isn't nominal crowding out as with the vertical *LM* curve.

The story at full employment is decidedly Monetarist-Classical, even when cloaked in a Keynesian framework. But that's not really as devastating to Keynesian protagonists as it initially seems. After all, at full employment Keynes was as Classical an economist as Milton Friedman and John Stuart Mill put together.

INFLATION

The *ISLM* model with price flexibility at full employment can tell either a Monetarist or a Keynesian story about inflation. In particular, we can identify when inflation is purely a monetary phenomenon, as Monetarists contend, and when it isn't.

We begin by noting again that aggregate demand is given by the intersection of the *IS* and *LM* curves. Start, in Figure 10, with *IS* and *LM* intersecting at the full employment income (Y_{FE}), so that the equilibrium income and the full employment income are one and the same. Now if *either* curve shifts to the right, aggregate demand for goods and services will exceed the economy's capacity to produce such output at the current price level; upward pressure on prices results. The process of rising prices is exactly what we mean by inflation.

For example, in Figure 10 assume the money supply is increased: the *LM* curve shifts to *LM'* and aggregate demand rises to *Y'*. Aggregate demand exceeds full employment output and prices are bid up, illustrating a classic case of inflation. The increased price level then reduces the *real* supply of money, and the *LM* curve begins to shift back toward its original position. The interest rate is pushed up and investment spending is reduced. Rising prices stop when aggregate demand is back at its old level—when the *LM* curve is back where it started. Note that in this case both the money supply and the price level are

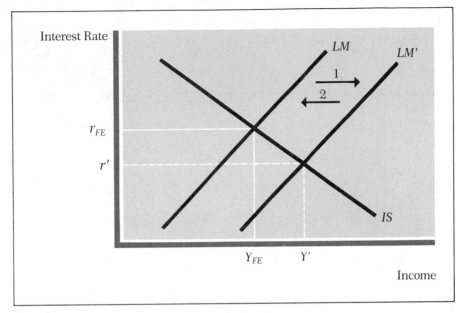

FIGURE 10 At Full Employment, an Increase in the Money Supply Shifts the *LM* Curve to the Right and Produces Inflation

higher than before, but the *real* money supply and *real* output are unchanged.

Note also that the interest rate remains unchanged as well. It is crucial to emphasize, however, that only the real rate of interest appears on the vertical axis. Under the inflation scenario, we cannot keep the nominal rate equal to the real rate (it is above the real rate, as we will see in the next chapter). Our picture always refers to real magnitudes.

An increase in the money supply raises prices, but the inflation provides its own cure—prices stop rising once the *real* supply of money falls back to its original level. Indeed, unless the money supply is increased again (producing another rightward shift in *LM*), inflation has stopped. Continuous injections of money, of course, will cause continuous rightward shifts in the *LM* curve and continuous inflation. Large and continued injections of money cause continuously large rightward shifts in the *LM* curve and produce hyperinflation.

As long as the *LM* curve is positively sloped—that is, as long as the demand for money is sensitive to changes in the interest rate—inflation can occur even if the money supply is constant. In Figure 11, again

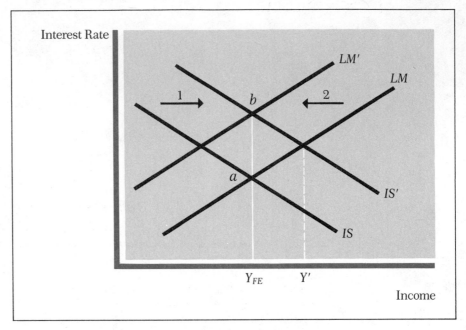

FIGURE 11 At Full Employment, a Shift in the *IS* Curve to the Right Produces Inflation Even Without an Increase in the Money Supply

start with *IS* and *LM* intersecting at the full employment income. This time the *IS* curve shifts to *IS'*—perhaps because of an increase in government spending. Aggregate demand, now *Y'*, exceeds Y_{FE} and prices start rising. But here too the inflation is brought to an eventual halt *if the money supply is held constant.* Rising prices—say from *P* to *P'*—reduce the real supply of money; because of that the *LM* curve shifts to the left (to *LM'* in Figure 11), and once again aggregate demand is at Y_{FE}, at which point the inflationary pressure ends.

In this case it is not increased money that causes inflation; the money supply, as we stressed, is held constant. Rather, it is the increased government (or consumer or investment) spending that raises aggregate demand above the full employment level. But the higher level of transactions associated with the increased price level (at the same level of *real* income, Y_{FE}) must be financed in some way. Nominal income has risen from $P \times Y_{FE}$ to $P' \times Y_{FE}$. This increased level of nominal income can be financed with the existing money supply because velocity has gone up ($P' \times Y_{FE}/M$ is greater than $P \times Y_{FE}/M$). Velocity increases because the demand for money is sensitive to the interest rate. As the interest rate rises, the amount of desired speculative money balances contracts, releasing funds for transactions purposes. (In Figure 11, velocity at point *b* is higher than at point *a*.)

While holding the money supply constant assures that the inflationary pressure of a once-and-for-all increase in the *IS* function will disappear, *continuous* rightward shifts in the *IS* curve—produced, let us say, by ever-increasing government expenditures—could *apparently* cause continuous inflation. But appearances are deceiving; inflation could not continue indefinitely, regardless of a rightward-shifting *IS* curve, if the money supply is really held constant. Here's why:

We just noted that rightward shifts in the *IS* curve can create inflation only when money demand is at least somewhat sensitive to interest rates; when the interest rate goes up, desired holdings of speculative money balances go down, permitting such funds to be used to carry out transactions. But it is generally agreed that speculative balances will eventually become depleted. In other words, the interest-sensitivity of money demand decreases with higher and higher interest rates, until it becomes zero when there are no more speculative balances left. At that point, the entire money supply is being used for transactions balances, and nominal GNP can rise no further.[4] Put somewhat differently, the velocity of money has reached its upper limit and can rise no further.

When this great moment arrives, the *LM* curve becomes vertical (zero interest-sensitivity), and further rightward shifts in the *IS* curve have no impact on aggregate demand. The only result is a higher interest rate. Here's the picture. Start out with *IS* and *LM* in Figure 12, intersecting again at the full employment income; shifting the *IS* curve to *IS'* produces aggregate demand *Y'*. Prices rise (say from *P* to *P'*), shifting *LM* to *LM'* and the new equilibrium to point *a*. The *LM* curve is now vertical, however, at level of real income Y_{FE} with the new price level (or at nominal income $P' \times Y_{FE}$).

Any further rightward shift in the *IS* curve, say to *IS"*, cannot raise aggregate demand because the existing money supply—remember, the money supply is being held constant—cannot support any higher level of transactions. Instead, the increased (say) government spending of so many billion dollars is fully offset by the rate of interest rising high

[4]In Chapter 20 we suggested that even the transactions demand for money is sensitive to the interest rate, because at higher interest rates it pays to economize on transactions balances. While this may very well be true, it is usually assumed that the transactions demand for money is less interest-elastic than speculative demand. Or, put somewhat differently, given the technology of the payments system at any specific time, there is a maximum rate of turnover—velocity—of a particular stock of money; therefore, the *LM* curve becomes vertical at high interest rates.

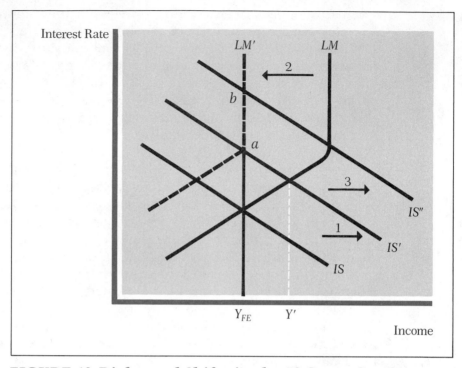

FIGURE 12 Rightward Shifts in the *IS* Curve Can No Longer Cause Inflation When the *LM* Curve Becomes Vertical

enough to *reduce* private investment by the same amount; total spending remains the same, with the increase in government spending crowding out an equal amount of private investment spending. The economy moves from point *a* directly to point *b* without suffering any inflation, just a higher rate of interest.

Our story is almost complete. The *ISLM* analysis has demonstrated the seemingly pretentious contentions of Monetarists that inflation can occur only for a short while in the absence of increases in the money supply. Sooner or later a constant money supply keeps inflation in check. But we also know that Monetarists recommend that long-run price stability requires a moderate but continuous constant rate of growth in the money supply. Thus we should show that increases in money supply do not always produce inflation. And that, too, can be illustrated in the *ISLM* world.

Increases in the money supply will not necessarily be inflationary if we recognize that full employment GNP grows over time, as the labor force and the stock of capital grow, and as technological progress

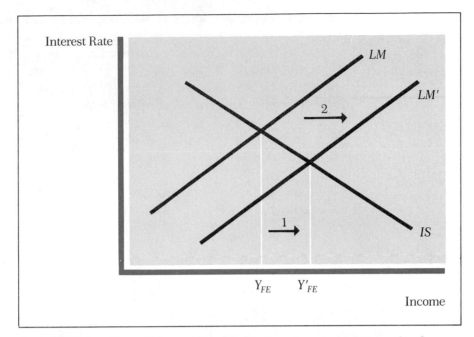

FIGURE 13 Over Time, the Full Employment Level of Income Moves to the Right, So That More Money Finances Real Growth Rather Than Inflation

increases productivity, enabling the economy to produce more real goods and services. In terms of our picture, the Y_{FE} line shifts to the right as the productive capacity of the economy increases. Aggregate demand *must* increase if we are merely to stay in the same place as far as the unemployment picture is concerned.

In Figure 13, if we start out with *IS* and *LM*, all is well when full employment GNP is represented by Y_{FE}. But by next year full employment output becomes Y'_{FE}, and unless aggregate demand increases via rightward shifts in the *LM* and/or *IS* curves, the current level of demand will be too small to generate full employment. In a growing economy, therefore, increases in the money supply (producing rightward shifts in the *LM* curve—say to *LM'*) are needed simply to maintain full employment.[5] Only if the rightward shift in the *LM* curve

[5]It is also usually recommended that as output grows, not only should the money supply increase, shifting *LM* to the right, but taxes should be reduced (or government spending increased) in order to shift the *IS* curve to the right as well. Which curve does most of the shifting to accommodate growth will affect the rate of interest and therefore the *composition* of aggregate demand, in terms of the proportion of consumption relative to investment spending.

intersects the *IS* curve *beyond Y'*$_{FE}$ will the increased money supply be inflationary. In other words, only if increases in the money supply exceed the transactions needs of a growing economy will inflationary pressures be generated.

Although the ISLM model has apparently successfully articulated the underpinnings of inflation according to Monetarists and Keynesians, the analysis has been unnecessarily constrained. It is far more appropriate to examine the inflation story within the framework of aggregate supply and demand introduced in Chapters 19 and 20. In the next chapter we turn to the aggregate supply and demand model for a more complete inflation discussion as well as for a general overview of the Monetarist and Keynesian outlooks.

SUMMARY

1. The "special" (or extreme) Monetarist and Keynesian slopes of the *ISLM* diagram help to highlight the polar positions on monetary and fiscal policy. In particular, a vertical *IS* curve and a horizontal *LM* make monetary policy impotent and fiscal policy supreme. A vertical *LM* curve, on the other hand, causes fiscal policy to lose its potency (complete crowding out) and raises monetary policy to its ultimate power (fixed velocity).

2. The demonstration that a steep *LM* curve insulates GNP from exogenous investment shocks highlights the stabilizing role of fluctuating interest rates on economic activity. Flexible prices add to that stabilizing mechanism.

3. Price flexibility at full employment restores the results of Classical interest rate theory: the level of the real rate of interest is determined only by saving and investment. A change in the money supply cannot alter this "natural rate of interest"; it can only influence nominal interest rates by changing inflationary expectations. Price flexibility at full employment also causes fiscal policy's impact on *real* GNP to be completely crowded out even with a positively sloped *LM* curve.

4. Inflation can result from either increases in money supply or autonomous increases in spending, as long as the *LM* curve is not vertical. At some point inflation becomes a purely monetary phenomenon, because the interest-sensitivity of money demand disappears (and *LM* becomes vertical).

5. Although the ISLM model has successfully illustrated a number of points in the Monetarist-Keynesian discussion, the model captures only part of the debate. In particular, it cannot depict in a simple way the controversy

over the financing side of fiscal policy, and it is incomplete in its analysis of inflation.

Suggestions for Further Reading

Two advanced articles on the complete Monetarist position, both by Milton Friedman, are: "A Theoretical Framework for Monetary Analysis," *Journal of Political Economy* (March–April 1970), and "A Monetary Theory of Nominal Income," *Journal of Political Economy* (March–April 1971). For an interesting discussion by leading Monetarists and Keynesians over the nature of the issues, see the comments by Karl Brunner, Allan Meltzer, James Tobin, Paul Davidson, Don Patinkin, and Milton Friedman in "A Symposium on Friedman's Theoretical Framework," *Journal of Political Economy* (September–October 1972). See Stanley Fischer, "Recent Developments in Monetary Theory," *American Economic Review* (May 1975) for a good historical survey.

Interest Rates Versus the Money Supply Under Uncertainty

In Chapter 17 we discussed the advantages and disadvantages of using the money supply versus the interest rate as a target of monetary policy. Monetarists generally prefer a money supply target, while Keynesians prefer an interest rate objective. At this point we can formalize the underlying analysis to demonstrate the pluses and minuses of each.[1]

The simplest point to demonstrate is that hitting a particular target in terms of the interest rate implies loss of control over the money supply, while hitting a money supply target implies loss of control over the interest rate. We don't even need *IS* and *LM* curves for that, just money demand and money supply curves. In Figure 1 let's assume that r^* is the target interest rate and that we start out with the original money supply and liquidity preference curves *M* and *LP*. If the demand for money shifts to *LP'*, then the Fed must accommodate the demand by shifting the supply curve to *M'* if the rate of interest is to remain at r^*. Therefore, to peg the interest rate the Federal Reserve must be willing to relinquish control over the money supply. Figure 2 shows why keeping control over the money supply implies greater

---

[1]The bulk of this discussion is based on an article by William Poole, "Rules of Thumb for Guiding Monetary Policy," in *Open Market Policies and Operating Procedures— Staff Studies* (Board of Governors of the Federal Reserve System, 1971).

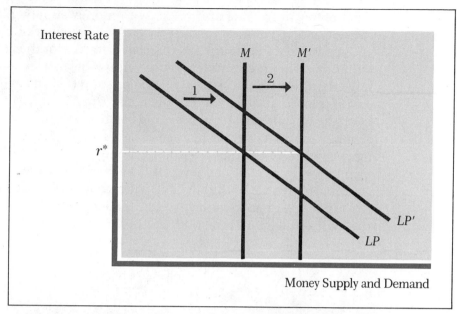

FIGURE 1 If the Federal Reserve Wants to Peg the Interest Rate, It Has to Abandon Control Over the Money Supply

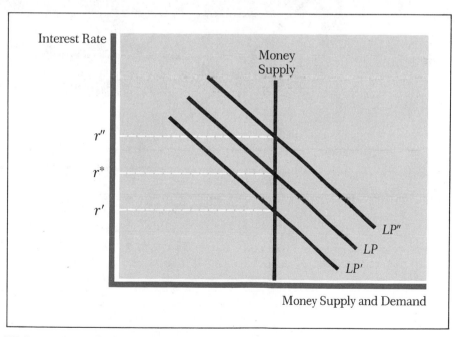

FIGURE 2 If the Federal Reserve Wants to Peg the Money Supply, It Has to Abandon Control Over the Interest Rate

fluctuations in the rate of interest: with money supply fixed, shifts in the demand for money produce interest rates between r' and r''.

Is it always better for the Fed to specify a target for the money supply rather than the interest rate, or vice versa? The answer is—it depends. Consider the situation where the major source of instability in GNP comes from unanticipated movements in the *IS* curve. In Figure 3 we have the *IS* curve shifting back and forth between *IS* and *IS'*. With a money supply target set by the Fed and a stable demand function for money, we have the upward sloping money market equilibrium curve pictured in Figure 3. The level of GNP varies between *A* and *B*.

Compare this variability in GNP with what occurs when the Fed sets the interest rate as its policy target. Under such conditions we have the horizontal money market equilibrium curve in Figure 3.[2] GNP

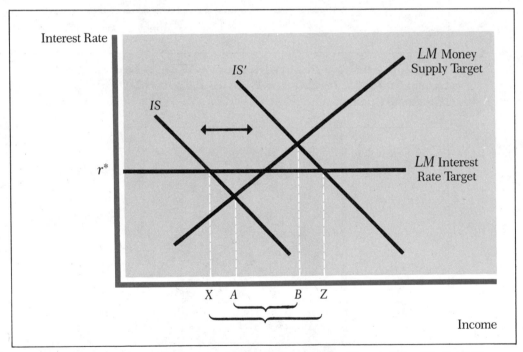

FIGURE 3 With an Interest Rate Target, an Unstable *IS* Curve Leads to Wider Variation in GNP Than If the Fed Had a Money Supply Target

[2]The *LM* curve is flat under such circumstances, because the Fed accompanies any increased demand for money with an increased supply, as we saw in Figure 1. Hence higher levels of *Y* (which increase the demand for money) are associated with the same level of interest, r^*. Notice that the definition of the *LM* curve is slightly

varies between *X* and *Z.* Clearly the money supply target is superior—it insures a smaller variability in GNP when the major source of instability is in the *IS* curve. A victory for the Monetarists.

When the game is played in the Keynesian ballpark, things turn out just the reverse. Here the demand for money is highly unstable. If the money supply is fixed by the Fed, and the demand for money shifts, then the *LM* curve moves between *LM* and *LM'* in Figure 4. With a fixed *IS* curve, GNP varies between *A* and *B.* But if the Fed uses an interest rate target, the relevant "*LM* curve" is again horizontal and there is no instability in GNP whatsoever. It stays put at *X.*

Monetarists insist that the most stable relationship in the economy (if not the world) is the demand for money. The Keynesian consump-

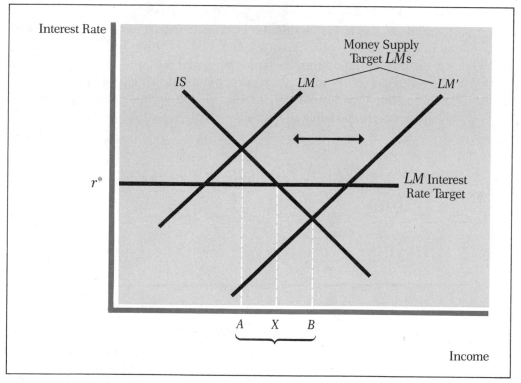

FIGURE 4 With a Money Supply Target, an Unstable *LM* Curve Leads to Wider Variation in GNP Than If the Fed Had an Interest Rate Target

different; it is the combination of *Y* and *r* with a *given* Federal Reserve policy and not a *given* money supply. That's why we've called the *LM* curve by its generic name: the money market equilibrium curve.

tion function is much less stable. The *IS* curve is therefore the major source of GNP instability. Figure 3 tells the truth—a money supply target is best. Keynesians argue that if anything is unstable it is Monetarists themselves. Not being psychiatrists, they'll settle for an unstable demand function for money. The *LM* curve is therefore the major source of GNP variability. Figure 4 tells the truth—an interest rate target is best.

As in most Monetarist-Keynesian disputes, the ultimate resolution lies in empirical evidence. No one believes that either the *IS* curve or the *LM* curve is perfectly stable. Unfortunately, there has been virtually no formal analysis of the *relative* stability of the underlying behavior in the real sector (*IS*) versus the monetary sector (*LM*). At least one observation does seem possible, however. Keynesians are the first to admit that investment is unstable. Hence, in order to assume a fixed or relatively stable *IS* curve, an accurately offsetting fiscal policy (such as *G* increasing whenever autonomous investment decreases) must be assumed. This makes the Keynesian case somewhat weaker than the Monetarist argument.[3] What this probably proves, in a somewhat broader context, is that if you want to win a debate you should never—but never—admit anything.

---

[3]Actually, the Monetarist case for a money supply target gets support from some Keynesians as well. The money supply acts as a built-in stabilizer, with interest rates fluctuating up and down to keep investment from rising too steeply or falling too far. There is an even more advanced argument in favor of the money supply target, based on rational expectations. See (at your own risk) Thomas Sargent and Neil Wallace, "Rational Expectations, the Optimal Monetary Instrument, and the Optimal Money Supply Rule," *Journal of Political Economy* (April 1975).

CHAPTER 23

Monetarists and Keynesians: An Aggregate Supply and Demand Perspective

At a conference of professional economists, Robert Solow, a prominent Keynesian from MIT, commented as follows on a paper presented by Milton Friedman: "Another difference between Milton and myself is that everything reminds Milton of the money supply; well, everything reminds me of sex, but I try to keep it out of my papers."

Monetarists do, in fact, make so much of the money supply that they are rather easy to caricature. It appears frequently in their professional papers circulated among economists; it figures prominently in their policy recommendations to the government; and some have even shown how it can make money in the stock market. But so far, at least, no evidence has been presented on its qualifications as an aphrodisiac. Don't, however, rule out the possibility.

The orientation of the President of the United States as a Keynesian or a Monetarist leads to very different approaches in economic policy-making. A Keynesian President would spend considerable time pressing Congress for countercyclical tax and expenditure legislation. A Monetarist President would spend more effort trying to convince everyone that things will get better by themselves, but to provide a proper noninflationary environment the Monetarist President would ask the Federal Reserve to keep money supply growth under control.

The basic Monetarist and Keynesian viewpoints were described in detail in Chapters 19 and 20. A more complicated exposition, the

ISLM model, was presented in Chapter 21, with the implications for Monetarists and Keynesians developed in Chapter 22. As it turns out, the most important elements of the Monetarist-Keynesian dialogue can be best articulated within the aggregate supply and demand framework discussed toward the ends of Chapters 19 and 20. In the rest of this chapter we put the details of the Monetarist and Keynesian models on the back burner and use the aggregate supply and demand pictures to explain the opposing positions on the stability of the economy, the relative effectiveness of monetary and fiscal policy, the causes of inflation, and the consequences for interest rates. Although these issues have been discussed in previous chapters, the unifying theme of aggregate supply and demand adds a unique and illuminating perspective. In the next chapter we will return to these issues from still another vantage point: rational expectations. By that time we should have a clear understanding of the Monetarist and Keynesian outlooks on just about everything.

IS THE PRIVATE SECTOR INHERENTLY STABLE?

Monetarists tend to believe that aggregate demand will be relatively unaffected by autonomous shifts in investment spending. Keynesians argue that unless there is an active attempt at stabilization, the level of economic activity and unemployment will fluctuate considerably when buffeted by entrepreneurial animal spirits.

Monetarists, reflecting their Classical ancestry, argue that any exogenous decrease in investment spending would be countered automatically by either increased consumption or interest-sensitive investment spending. The mechanism could be attributed, somewhat mysteriously, to the fixed money stock, resulting in a relatively fixed level of aggregate demand based on the quantity theory; or, in keeping with Classical interest theory, it could be attributed to a reduction in interest rates that would follow a downward shift in the investment function. The drop in interest rates would, in turn, stimulate investment spending, reduce saving (thereby increasing consumption), and make up for the initial drop in investment.

Keynesians are less impressed with the automatic offsets to gyrations in investment spending. First, the mysterious quantity theory linkage between money and aggregate demand is simply not part of the picture. Moreover, the interest rate does not necessarily respond to a drop in investment. And even if the interest rate did decline, there's no guarantee that it would induce very much additional spending.

Fluctuations in the price level are another source of stability, according to Monetarists. If, for example, consumption and investment didn't rise fast enough to offset the initial decline in investment spending, the resulting unemployment would drive down prices. A fixed money stock with lower prices means a larger real supply of money. This could stimulate spending directly via the quantity theory. Alternatively, the larger real supply of money would lower interest rates— in good Keynesian fashion—and investment spending would increase still further. The Keynesian response to such expected price effects is twofold: first, prices rarely decline; and second, the spending effects are too slow to rely on to restore full employment.

These arguments can be put somewhat more elegantly in terms of aggregate demand and supply. Recall from our earlier discussions that the aggregate demand schedule, labeled D in Figure 1, shows how the quantity of real income (or output) demanded varies with changes in the price level. In particular, decreases in prices increase the amount

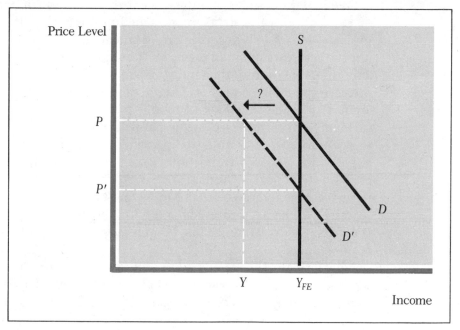

FIGURE 1 Monetarist Response to Declines in Exogenous Investment: Income Remains at the Full Employment Level

of goods and services demanded because real money balances increase when the price level falls.[1] The aggregate supply schedule, labeled S, shows how quantity produced varies with price. In Figure 1, the supply curve is vertical, reflecting the Classical assumption that quantity supplied is fixed at full employment.

First let's focus on aggregate demand. The quantity theory approach of Monetarists assumes a direct and powerful impact of increased real money balances on the demand for output. When people have more real cash balances, they want to spend more—period. For Keynesians, on the other hand, there are many things that can intervene between real money balances and demand. In particular, interest rates may not fall very much when money balances increase, because people may simply hold the additional cash balances. In addition, desired spending may not be very responsive to decreases in interest rates. All of this implies that the slope of the aggregate demand schedule, measuring how much of an increase in amount demanded occurs when prices fall, is flatter (and more stable) for Monetarists than for Keynesians. This slope is an important indication of how much of an offsetting (automatic) increase in aggregate demand occurs when prices fall.

Of equal if not greater importance is the stability (or predictability) of the entire aggregate demand schedule—whether it stays put or jumps around a lot. According to Monetarists, the major factor determining aggregate demand is the stock of money. Once that is fixed, the amount of real output demanded depends upon the price level—lower prices mean more goods and services demanded. Thus Monetarists argue that, once the stock of money is fixed, there will be relatively little impact on the aggregate demand schedule from exogenous shifts in spending. For example, if investment spending falls, Monetarists expect interest rates to decline, which reduces saving and increases consumption. For Keynesians, however, changes in investment do not necessarily generate offsetting movements in consumption expenditures. Thus the aggregate demand schedule will be pushed to the left if exogenous investment falls, because at every price level fewer goods are demanded.

Now let's put the economy through its paces. Our objective is to see whether GNP is stable at full employment. Obviously, this depends upon the behavior of the aggregate demand schedule, but it also de-

---

[1]Recall that a decrease in the price level does not increase people's real income directly, because a falling price level means both goods prices and factor prices (wages) are falling. Thus falling prices do not directly expand aggregate demand via a simple Keynesian consumption function argument.

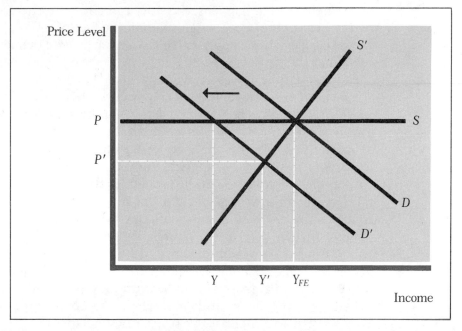

FIGURE 2 Keynesian Response to Declines in Exogenous Investment: Income Falls Below the Full Employment Level

pends upon the shape of aggregate supply. Thus, Figure 1 has the Monetarist vertical aggregate supply curve, while Figure 2 has the simple Keynesian horizontal supply curve (S) as well as a somewhat more realistic upward sloping supply curve (S').

Start with aggregate demand curve D in each figure, so that GNP is at the full employment level. Now ask what happens if businesses suddenly decide to invest less than they have been. From the Monetarist view of Figure 1, the demand schedule, D, may simply stay put, in which case aggregate economic activity remains at Y_{FE}. Some other form of spending will increase to take the place of the drop in investment. But if the aggregate demand curve does shift to D' in Figure 1, and the level of aggregate demand falls to Y at the old price level P, the resulting unemployed labor and unused capacity cause wages and prices to fall toward P'. As prices fall, the real quantity of money expands and aggregate demand increases along the new demand curve D'. Prices fall until demand is brought back into equality with aggregate supply at Y_{FE}.

In the Keynesian presentation of Figure 2, the leftward shift from D to D' most certainly takes place as a result of the fall in exogenous investment. If that happens, the story can end right there, when it has hardly begun. If prices are rigid even in the face of unemployment and excess capacity, the supply curve is S and aggregate demand and GNP remain at the depressed level Y. The Monetarist incentive to increase spending—falling prices—never appears.

The more realistic Keynesian case occurs when prices fall somewhat when production is below full capacity, and wages also decline *but at a slower pace.* This produces an aggregate supply curve that looks like S' in Figure 2.[2] With supply curve S', aggregate real output is above Y (where it would be if prices didn't fall) but is still below full employment income, Y_{FE}. The problem is that wages and prices do not fall far enough to stimulate sufficient new aggregate demand along D' to offset the decrease in exogenous investment.

Note that in both of the figures, if the demand curve were flatter, the fall in prices would not have to be that large to encourage more aggregate demand along the new demand curve D'. This would also reflect the Monetarist point of view: falling prices with a fixed stock of money will generate full employment because aggregate demand is very sensitive to increases in real money balances.

An important point to remember is that the upward-sloping Keynesian aggregate supply curve S' is only a short-run relationship. Even Keynesians recognize that with production below full employment there will be continued downward pressure on wages. As wages fall more, there will be an incentive for producers to move back to full employment production. Eventually, therefore, the vertical aggregate supply curve of Figure 1 comes into the picture, even for Keynesians. But the essential message is that the entire process takes time, and during that time the aggregate supply curve is not vertical. Thus, Keynesians argue, we should try to push up aggregate demand by monetary and fiscal policies.

To summarize: Monetarists tend to think that the aggregate demand curve is stable, given a particular money supply, and that the aggregate supply schedule is vertical. These conditions imply that exogenous shifts in investment leave GNP unchanged. Keynesians

[2]Here's one way of looking at why the supply curve is positively sloped. When wages (W) and prices (P) fall at the same rate, business firms' *real* wage expense (W/P) remains unchanged and they will hire the same number of workers as before. On the other hand, if wages fall less than prices, then firms will fire some workers and cut back their output of goods and services. That is precisely the implication of the positive slope in supply curve S': when prices fall, the supply of real output declines below the level that would fully employ all labor (and capital). We will return to this issue in our discussion of inflation later in this chapter.

argue that the aggregate demand curve is quite sensitive to exogenous changes in investment and that the aggregate supply schedule is not vertical. These circumstances imply that entrepreneurial animal spirits buffet the level of real income.

MONETARY POLICY, FISCAL POLICY, AND CROWDING OUT

Suppose the Keynesians have a point, and aggregate demand shifts to D' when business people are discouraged and cut back on their investment expenditures. Let's also put the economy into Figure 2 with the upward sloping supply schedule S'. Thus the reduction in aggregate demand reduces income to Y'. If we don't want to wait for further price adjustments to set matters right, then something must be done to push up aggregate demand. Monetary and fiscal policies are the two discretionary tools available to government policy-makers for precisely such circumstances.

According to the Monetarists, if the central bank increases the money supply, the aggregate demand schedule shifts to the right, reflecting increased demand for goods and services.[3] The transmission mechanism of an increase in money to spending is direct and certain. Extra cash balances do not first go into the bond market (as with Keynesians), where prices are forced up and interest rates pushed down. Rather, there is direct substitution between money and real goods.

For Keynesians, on the other hand, an increase in the money supply may very well shift the aggregate demand schedule rightward, but the impact is less certain than for Monetarists. The problem is that the transmission mechanism between money and spending is not quite so direct. According to Keynesians, falling interest rates can generate increased spending in a number of ways. The so-called cost-of-capital effect is the traditional impact of lower borrowing costs on the demand for investment goods. The wealth effect focuses on the impact of interest rates on securities prices: lower interest rates mean higher bond prices, and people respond to such capital gains by consuming more. Finally, the credit availability effect (to be discussed in Chapter

---

[3]Do not be confused on this point. Increases in real balances caused by falling prices are reflected in the *slope* of the aggregate demand curve, because prices are on the vertical axis; increases in real balances caused by an increase in the stock of money *shift* the aggregate demand curve, because at each price level (on the vertical axis) more goods and services will be demanded (measured on the horizontal axis).

25) asserts that lenders may simply increase the amount of funds offered to borrowers, thereby permitting them to expand their spending plans. When all these channels of money to spending are operative, then the impact of expanding the money supply on aggregate demand is quite potent. But in this very specific outlook, there's many a possible slip 'twixt the cup and the lip.

The Keynesian answer to the somewhat less certain effects of monetary policy is to focus on fiscal policy to stimulate aggregate demand. We started out with a reduction in autonomous investment expenditure that pushed the aggregate demand curve to the left. A simple solution is to offset that decrease by exogenously increasing government spending or raising consumer expenditure by a discretionary reduction in tax rates.

A Monetarist questions whether *any* exogenous shifts in expenditure, whether generated by business firms or by the government, influences aggregate demand. We saw earlier that, according to Monetarists, interest rates would fall to counteract the effects of decreased investment on aggregate demand. A symmetrical argument maintains that interest rates will rise when government spending goes up. Thus the government spends more but others, business firms and consumers, are induced to spend less because interest rates rise.

This process has often been called by a special name: crowding out. Because in the past it has received considerable attention as a central issue dividing Monetarists and Keynesians, it is worth some further elaboration.

We begin by noting that, initially, an increase in government spending raises aggregate demand directly, before anything else has happened. But the public's need for day-to-day transactions money is likely to rise along with aggregate demand. If the supply of money does not increase simultaneously, the public will find itself short of cash, will presumably sell off some financial assets to try to get additional money, and will thereby drive up interest rates. This crowding out effect may inhibit private investment spending, at least partly offsetting the expansionary impact of the government's spending. In brief, both the execution and the net impact of fiscal policy appear to be inextricably bound up with monetary implications. Moreover, it is especially important to consider how the government finances the increased expenditure (or the reduction in taxes).

The Keynesian position on these matters is that any fiscal action, no matter how it is financed, will have a significant effect on aggregate demand. Keynesians do not deny that interest rates are likely to rise unless new money is forthcoming to meet cash needs for day-to-day

The Crash of '87: A Policy Dilemma

The unprecedented drop of more than 20 percent in stock prices on October 19, 1987 sent shock waves through the financial world: securities firms were forced to close, stockbrokers lost their jobs, and investors lost their proverbial shirts. More than one trillion dollars in consumer wealth disappeared, quite literally, overnight. The savings of individuals who were "bullish on America" disappeared without a trace. For some, such as the elderly whose pension benefits evaporated, the damage was irreparable because they could not start afresh. For others, it meant that years of hard work went down the drain. Renewed vigilance over the suitability of stock market investments for many individuals is the only remedy for such personal trauma.

From a monetary and fiscal policy vantage point, the loss of one trillion dollars in consumer wealth aroused concern as to whether the wealth effect on consumer spending would be sufficiently powerful to cause a recession, or even worse, a depression. From a Keynesian outlook, the usual antidote of increased government spending was less than desirable because of the huge federal budget deficit; many viewed the ever increasing government debt as one of the uncertainties that precipitated the drop in stock prices to begin with. The only feasible remedy for an impending recession was an easier monetary policy. And that was the immediate response of the central bank to Black Monday: pump in liquidity to avoid a collapse in the system. Although the Fed clearly had to act as a lender of last resort to forestall a wave of bankruptcies, there was legitimate concern of an inflationary upsurge if the easier policy were maintained too long.

What to do? Only time will tell whether the emerging balance of monetary expansion and fiscal restraint was implemented successfully. If policy is devoted solely toward preventing a recession it may provoke inflation, while if it is geared primarily toward warding off inflation it may open the door to unemployment and depression. Do not bet on a quick resolution of this dilemma.

---

transactions. Thus they admit that a government deficit financed by money creation is more expansionary than one financed by bond sales to the public, and that both are more expansionary than increased government spending financed by taxation. But higher interest rates have dual effects. They may reduce private investment spending, but they may also lead people to economize on their cash balances, thereby supplying part of the need for new transactions money from formerly idle cash holdings.

As the Monetarists see it, a fiscal deficit financed by selling bonds to the public will not affect aggregate demand. True, the government will be spending more. But others will wind up spending less. Net result: No change in total spending. The rise in government spending will *initially* increase aggregate demand. However, this will increase the demand for cash for transactions purposes and drive up interest rates, and bond sales to finance the government's expenditures will drive up rates still further. The public will be buying government bonds and financing the government, instead of buying corporate bonds and financing business firms. Business firms will be crowded out of financial markets by the government. The rise in interest rates will reduce private investment spending by as much as government spending is increased, and that will be the end of the story. Government fiscal policy, unaccompanied by changes in the supply of money, merely changes the proportion of government spending relative to private spending.

It is useful to summarize the monetary and fiscal issues with a chronological flavor. The first leg of the debate focused on Keynesian skepticism over whether changes in the money supply influenced aggregate demand. The next step was the Monetarist counterattack on fiscal policy because of crowding out. And just as the respective positions on these items came under control, a third, as yet undiscussed, issue emerged as a focal point of concern: whether *countercyclical* policy has any impact on spending at all. The problem usually focuses on whether countercyclical movements in the money supply are anticipated and whether such anticipations lead to expected inflation and hence neutralize the money supply changes. To deal with this latest development properly, we first turn to issues of inflation and countercyclical policy. In the next chapter we extend the discussion to include rational expectations.

INFLATION, MONEY, AND THE PHILLIPS CURVE

The first issue dividing Monetarists and Keynesians is whether or not inflation is purely a monetary phenomenon. This issue turns on what influences the aggregate demand schedule. This is evident in Figure 3, which shows that if we start at full employment (where we always tend to be), with aggregate demand D and price level P, anything pushing demand to D' and D'' raises prices to P' and P''. The dynamics of P rising to P' and then P'' is precisely what we mean by inflation: rising prices. Thus Monetarists contend that since the aggregate demand schedule is likely to be stable at D unless the money supply

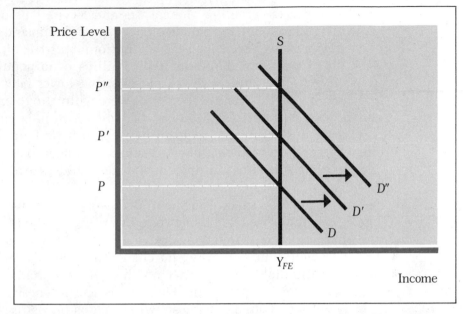

FIGURE 3 Anything Shifting Aggregate Demand to the Right Causes Inflation

changes, the main culprit behind shifts to D' and D'' is the Federal Reserve.

Keynesians, on the other hand, are not so quick to blame the Fed when inflation gets out of control. Any group of suddenly overexuberant spenders—government, business, or consumers—can push up aggregate demand and generate increases in prices. Obviously, the Keynesian position permits the blame for inflation to be attributed to expanding government deficits when the economy is at full employment. Monetarists, on the other hand, cannot rail against deficits per se as causing inflation. Only if the deficit induces the Federal Reserve to expand the money supply (see Chapter 18) will inflation follow.

Shifts in the aggregate supply schedule can also be charged with generating inflation. In fact, the so-called cost-push variety of inflation forces up prices precisely because it shifts the supply schedule in Figure 3 to the left. Higher costs (such as occurred with energy during the 1970s) restrict production, producing a period of rising prices. But Monetarists stress that such a once-and-for-all "supply shock" cannot account for persistent inflation; it is more of a one-shot deal. Except, of course, that if those shocks keep coming, then we have a multiple-shock deal.

A second issue dividing Monetarists and Keynesians on inflation concerns the possibility of a trade-off between inflation and unemployment. Keynesians have supported the notion of a trade-off, known as a Phillips Curve after Professor A.W. Phillips, who popularized the relationship. The Phillips Curve suggests that lower rates of unemployment could be obtained if only we were willing to tolerate a faster rate of increase in prices.[4] Monetarists, led by Milton Friedman, deny that there is a permanent trade-off between inflation and unemployment, arguing instead that once inflation was incorporated into people's expectations, the unemployment rate would return to its "natural" level.

Once again we can explain the underlying conflict in terms of our aggregate supply/demand framework, but this time the issue turns on the shape of supply function. Figure 3 is the Monetarist picture: a vertical supply curve showing no change in GNP (or employment) when inflation takes place, hence no Phillips Curve trade-off between inflation and unemployment. Figure 4 is the Keynesian picture: a positively sloped supply curve showing that as prices rise because of shifts in aggregate demand, real output expands *beyond* Y_{FE}. This higher level of income is produced by reducing the unemployment rate below what is normally considered full employment. Or, more generally, more inflation means less unemployment, as in the Phillips Curve.

This situation, unfortunately, requires some explaining in terms of worker behavior, wage-price lags, and inflationary expectations. Rest assured, however, that we will expose you to only the bare minimum

---

[4]The original article describing the relationship is "The Relation Between Unemployment and the Rate of Change in Money Wages in the United Kingdom, 1861–1957," *Economica* (1958). The graph of a Phillips curve looks like this:

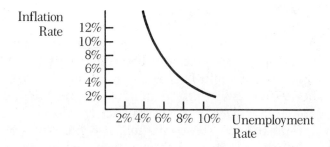

The negative sloped curve shows that lower rates of unemployment are associated with higher rates of inflation.

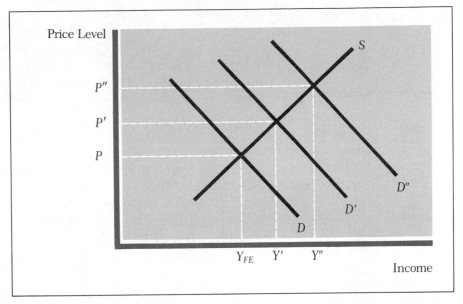

FIGURE 4 Inflation Causes Higher Income (and Lower Unemployment) with a Positively Sloped Supply Curve

(we really don't know very much more ourselves). The key to the debate focuses, once again, on whether the aggregate supply curve is vertical or positively sloped. A positive slope implies that real output varies positively with the price level. Our discussion back in footnote 2 showed that output varies positively with prices when wages change more slowly than prices. And that's reasonable, according to Keynesians, because many wage rates are set contractually, and contracts are not adjusted continuously. What this means is that when the price level falls, declining wages lag behind falling goods prices, and the real value of labor's compensation increases. That's why fewer workers are employed and less is produced when the price level declines. The other side of the coin is that when the price level rises, wages increase more slowly than prices, labor's real compensation falls, more workers are hired, and GNP goes up. And that's why the Keynesian picture shows a trade-off between inflation and unemployment.

Monetarists have emphasized, and economists of all persuasions now recognize, that a lower real wage cannot permanently induce workers to spend less time playing tennis and more time at the factory or behind the desk. Thus, after a while, labor will demand that wages be adjusted upward. Some workers may feel reluctant to do so right away because of a long-run contractual relationship with their employer, one that transcends what could be only a temporary erosion in the value of their paychecks. But as the inflation reality sinks in and workers come to *expect* a permanently higher rate of inflation, their wage demands become more vociferous. Wages will be pushed up by competitive pressure among employers. But once wages catch up to the higher rate of price increase, there is little incentive for business firms to produce more than they started with. Thus, production eventually returns to Y_{FE} and unemployment goes back to what is normally considered a full employment rate.

What we have just described is a slow but steady transition from the upward-sloping supply curve in Figure 4 to the vertical aggregate supply curve in Figure 3. Thus, after everything has adjusted, including inflationary expectations and labor-business contractual agreements, the aggregate supply curve must be vertical. In other words, the Phillips Curve eventually must show no trade-off between inflation and unemployment.

One of the main questions is, of course, how long can a temporary situation last? A more intriguing possibility is that if everyone knows that the trade-off is temporary, it may not even get started! In the next chapter we return to this discussion within the framework of rational expectations. For now let's turn our attention to the consequences of inflation and inflationary expectations for the level of interest rates.

INFLATION AND INTEREST RATES

Inflationary expectations are crucial to explaining how interest rates respond to changes in the money supply. In this area, however, we cannot appeal to the aggregate supply/demand framework for expositional help. English will have to suffice (sorry; we don't like it any more than you do).

Milton Friedman has argued that an *expansionary* monetary policy *raises* interest rates and a *contractionary* monetary policy *lowers* interest rates—just the reverse of standard Keynesian analysis. How does Milton do it? Here's the point: An increase in the money supply *may initially* lower interest rates, if the increased liquidity is spent on financial assets. But that is only the beginning. Once aggregate demand responds to the increased money supply (as it must in the Monetarist world), the transactions demand for money will increase, thereby driving interest rates upward. But this is hardly new. Mainstream Keynesians certainly wouldn't disagree. The Monetarists argue, however, that the "income effect" of the increased money supply will overwhelm the initial "liquidity effect," so that the interest rate will snap back past its original level.

If pressed on this last point, Keynesians might even acquiesce again. After a while interest rates *could* pass the original equilibrium, but it all depends on the speed and strength of the response in GNP to monetary expansion. Keynesians would focus their attention on the interim period—before GNP expands. And this interim period is sufficiently long to justify the statement: expansionary monetary policy *means* lower interest rates, and contractionary policy *means* higher rates.

But there's more to the Monetarist story, namely, inflationary expectations. In particular, if expectations of inflation are generated by an expansionary monetary policy, then this will cause a *further* increase in the level of *nominal* interest rates. The reason is as follows: suppose that when the expected rate of inflation is zero, the equilibrium interest rate is 5 percent. As we said in Chapter 19, if lenders expect prices to rise by 2 percent during the next twelve months and want to receive 5 percent in real terms, they will demand 7 percent from borrowers. As long as borrowers expect the same rate of inflation, they will go along with the higher nominal rate of interest. After all, if they were ready to pay 5 percent with no inflation, they should be equally eager to borrow money at 7 percent with 2 percent inflation—they will be paying off the loan in "cheaper" dollars.[5]

What might lead *both* borrowers and lenders to expect inflation and then arrive at a higher nominal rate of interest? You guessed it—an expansionary monetary policy. When such inflationary expectations are tacked onto the income effect, Monetarists contend that it is virtually certain that these two will dominate the initial liquidity impact and expansionary monetary policy will lead to higher nominal interest rates. An analogous argument can be made for contractionary monetary policy lowering interest rates.

Notice, by the way, that the Classical distinction between real and nominal rates is crucial in these arguments. Increases in money lead to inflation via the quantity theory. The interest rate (the *real* interest rate—the Classicists never spoke about fake rates) is determined by savers and investors. They "pierce the veil" of money and refuse to let inflation interfere with their agreed-upon *real* rate of interest. Thus

[5]Borrowers would like to pay only 5 percent. But as we saw in Chapter 19, competition for funds forces them to pay what lenders demand, unless they are willing to pass up some investment projects. But inflation will increase the expected *dollar* returns on investments, so that if a project was worth undertaking before it would be just as worthwhile with inflation and the higher nominal interest rate.

when the "inflation premium" described by Irving Fisher is added to the real rate, we see that increases in money supply raise the nominal rate of interest. Therefore, Milton Friedman, with an assist from Irving Fisher, concludes that an expansionary monetary policy raises interest rates.

The story just told, of nominal interest rates rising because of the inflationary expectations generated by expansionary monetary policy, can take on still another dimension. In particular, if policy-makers are *expected* to increase the money supply in an effort to lower interest rates, there will, in fact, not even be any temporary liquidity effect on real interest rates, since such anticipated money stock movements will have already been incorporated in portfolio decisions. For example, the liquidity effect of the anticipated increase in money stock will have already raised bond demand to take advantage of anticipated capital gains; thus no further bond price increases occur when the money stock actually increases. All that's left is the quantity theory effect, which says that increases in money stock raise prices. Thus the anticipated rate of inflation generated by expansionary monetary policy pushes up nominal interest rates. There simply aren't any intermediate steps.[6]

Although the expectations story sounds convincing, remember that Keynesians argue that the simple quantity theory operates only at or near full employment. At lower levels of economic activity, there is considerable slippage between money and prices. Even near what we designate as full employment there are wage and price rigidities because of contractual arrangements that interfere with any proportional relationship between money and prices.

Most observers contend, therefore, that it takes time for the inflation premium to be fully reflected in nominal interest rates. In the short run, lenders may have to settle for lower real interest rates. Instead of the nominal rate rising by 2 percent in our example above, it may rise by less, and therefore the real rate would fall somewhat when expected inflation jumped by 2 percent. Eventually, as lenders adjust their cash balances and borrowers alter their investment plans, the real rate returns to its long-run equilibrium level and the nominal rate rises above the real rate by the full expected rate of inflation.

How long is the long run? Ah, if we only knew the answer to that question, how simple life would be. We get closer to Irving Fisher's

[6]This discussion has applied the rational expectations argument to interest rates. More on this in the next chapter.

result even in the short run—say, within six months—as the delay in borrower and lender reactions gets shorter. Furthermore, when expectations of inflation respond quickly to economic forces, the Fisher result is likely to occur still more quickly. On the other hand, when delays are long and expectations of inflation respond slowly, then it takes longer for nominal rates to rise by the full amount of the expected inflation. As a general rule, it is a good bet that an increase in nominal rates of interest will closely follow a jump in inflationary expectations, but nominal interest rates are unlikely to respond immediately by the full amount Fisher suggested.

Can we really be this far into a book on money and not be sure which way interest rates respond to monetary ease or stringency? Yes and no—unequivocally.

We can summarize the discussion as follows. An increase in the money supply will immediately reduce both the nominal rate and the real rate of interest because of a liquidity effect. As inflationary expectations respond to the monetary expansion, nominal rates are driven up but by less than the inflationary surge. Thus the nominal rate could very well be above the original level of nominal (and real) rates while the real rate can be below it. After borrowers and lenders have completed all their adjustments, the real rate of interest will be back where we started and the nominal rate will have increased by the expected rate of inflation.[7] So now you can answer just about anything you want to the question of what happens to interest rates when the money supply expands, as long as you keep the real and nominal straightened out (don't worry, not many people can do that). To really confuse matters you might try to explain how decreases in the money supply produce an opposite set of results.

SHOULD A ROBOT REPLACE THE FEDERAL RESERVE?

We started this chapter with a discussion of whether the private sector is inherently stable. If the self-correcting mechanisms described above operate properly, there is little need for active monetary and fiscal policies to prevent economic fluctuations. In fact, these stabilizing mechanisms form the foundation for the Monetarist argument against

[7]The fact that expansionary monetary policy cannot reduce interest rates permanently explains why it is impossible for the central bank to make Congress happy by forcing down the cost of credit. It also explains why bondholders will not be forever wealthier because of increases in the money supply.

government attempts at "fine-tuning" the economy. It's simply not needed.

Keynesians claim that since the strength of these self-correcting forces is uncertain, we should use countercyclical monetary and fiscal policies to help insure full employment production. They implicitly assume that attempts at leaning against the economic trends—expansionary policy in recessions and contractionary policy during inflations—can only help. The problem is that attempts at countercyclical policy can actually wind up causing greater instability than would have otherwise been the case.

Milton Friedman was the first to point out the potentially destabilizing impacts of government countercyclical policy. To explain the argument we must recognize that the effects of changes in monetary policy or fiscal policy take time to work themselves out. In particular, there are lags in the impacts of monetary and fiscal policy on GNP. The empirical evidence on lags is presented later, in Chapter 25. For now it is sufficient to recognize that it takes time for changes in interest rates to alter business spending decisions and it takes time even for households to adjust their consumer expenditures to increased disposable income. Putting this little addendum on lags together with our aggregate demand story, we are able to show the potential damage of stabilization efforts. An alternative philosophy—rules rather than discretion—is proposed by Monetarists to mitigate the problem.

Assume that the Federal Reserve forecasts a recession six months from now. If the forecast is correct, and if a current expansion in the money supply would have an impact six months hence, well and good. But what if the Federal Reserve's crystal ball is not clear, and it is more than a year before the main impact of today's monetary policy is reflected in the economy? Then the effects of today's expansionary monetary policy are likely to be felt *after* the economy has passed the trough and is already on its way up.

As Figure 5 illustrates, the impact of today's easy money may exacerbate tomorrow's inflation. Tight money will have similarly delayed effects; it may be imposed with the best of intentions, to curtail a boom, but its real impact, being delayed, might accentuate a recession. Monetary policy is a destabilizer rather than a stabilizer!

On these grounds—the precarious nature of economic forecasting and the alleged length, variability, and unpredictability of the time lags involved—Friedman and some other Monetarists have given up on orthodox monetary policy. Friedman argues that the economy has been and is now inherently stable and that it would automatically tend to stay on a fairly straight course, as Figure 5 indicates, if only it were

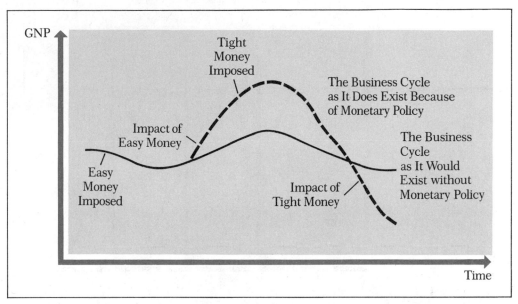

FIGURE 5 Friedman's Alleged Perverse Effects of Countercyclical Monetary Policy

not being almost continuously knocked off the track by erratic or unwise monetary policies. Conclusion: Quarantine the central bank. The best stabilization policy is no stabilization policy at all. Hasn't it all been said before:

They also serve who only stand and waite.

John Milton

What Professor Friedman proposes instead is that the Federal Reserve be instructed by Congress to follow a fixed long-run rule: increase the money supply at a steady and inflexible rate, month in and month out, year in and year out, regardless of current economic conditions. Set the money supply on automatic pilot and then leave it alone.

The specific growth rate—3, 4, or 6 percent—is less important than the principle. Once a figure is decided upon, no tinkering is permitted. In point of fact, the actual money supply growth rate is intended to keep prices stable and employment high by allowing aggregate demand to grow at the same rate as the economy's real productive capacity. This is illustrated in Figure 6 with our by now familiar aggregate supply and demand framework. But in this context, we allow the aggregate supply curve to shift rightward to reflect growth in capital and the labor force. Stable prices and full employment will be achieved

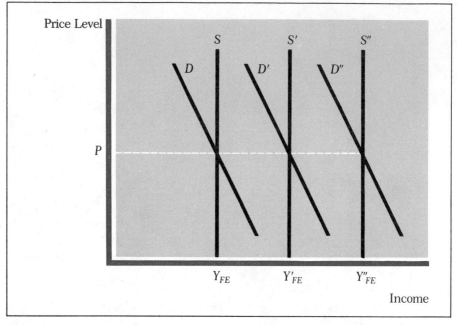

FIGURE 6 Aggregate Demand and Supply Shifting Together Over Time According to a Fixed Monetary Rule

when growth in the money supply pushes the aggregate demand schedule to the right along with aggregate supply (as in Figure 6).

The main advantage of a rule is that it would eliminate forecasting and lag problems and therefore remove what Friedman sees as the major cause of instability in the economy—the capricious and unpredictable impact of discretionary countercyclical monetary policy. As long as the money supply grows at a constant rate each year, be it 3, 4, or 6 percent, any decline into recession will be temporary. The liquidity provided by a constantly growing money supply will cause aggregate demand to expand. Similarly, if the supply of money does not rise at a more than average rate, any inflationary increase in spending will burn itself out for lack of fuel. Discretionary deviations by the central bank would interfere with the natural course of the economy and only make matters worse.

The United States Congress has been impressed enough to come part of the way toward a Friedman-type rule, in preference to allowing the Federal Reserve to rely entirely on its own judgment and discretion. In March 1975 both the House of Representatives and the Senate passed House Congressional Resolution 133, which instructed the Federal Reserve to "maintain long-run growth of the monetary and credit aggregates commensurate with the economy's long-run potential to increase production." It also required that the Fed report to Congress on its target monetary and credit growth rates. In November 1977 these provisions were incorporated into the Federal Reserve Act itself.

Whether one believes in a fixed rule or not, such reporting procedures have surely been beneficial. They have forced the Fed to assess its policies continuously in quantitative terms without shackling it with an inflexible formula. The objective is smoother monetary growth and the elimination of the extremely high (and extremely low) monetary growth rates that have often had harmful effects in the past.

Given the present state of knowledge, it is difficult to justify legislation at the present time that would circumscribe the Federal Reserve's actions more rigidly. Serious research on the subject is only in its early stages, and no consensus is apparent among economists who have worked in the area. It should be noted, however, that the variability of GNP before World War II (even excluding the Great Depression) was much larger than variability since World War II, and it is only in the latter period that stabilization policy has been active.[8]

Some proponents of activist stabilization policies argue that as long as there are some immediate impacts of policy on GNP, past errors of timing can be corrected. Thus expansionary monetary policy that acts too slowly to forestall a recession can be prevented from exacerbating the next round of inflation by a still more restrictive monetary policy. This possibility argues against a rule that would tie the hands of the stabilization authorities. Of course, the problem here is that ever larger doses of stimulus or restraint might be required to offset the detrimental lagged consequences of past policy. And that means that slight miscalculations might leave the system vulnerable to an explosion in either direction.

It is instructive that in the final analysis the extremists from both camps, Monetarist and Keynesian, have collectively ganged up on the Federal Reserve. The extreme Monetarists want to shackle it, because their concern with time lags leads them to believe it is both mischievous and harmful, and the extreme Keynesians want to subordinate it to fiscal policy. In the middle, squabbling but making more common cause than they had thought possible, are the moderates: moderate Monetarists, who believe that the forecasting-lag problem is not so great as to negate all the stabilizing effects of countercyclical monetary

[8]See Martin N. Baily, "Stabilization Policy and Private Economic Behavior," *Brookings Papers on Economic Activity* (No. 1, 1978).

policy; and moderate Keynesians, who believe that monetary policy has a powerful impact on spending and should be used along with fiscal policy with considerable caution.

It seems clear, after all is said and done, that central banking is still at least as much art as science. We simply do not know enough yet to legislate an eternal rule, or even a rule for the next six months, that the Federal Reserve must follow under any and all circumstances. Meanwhile, for better or worse, we appear to have no alternative but to rely on our best knowledge and judgment in the formulation of monetary policy. We can only try to make sure that the decision-makers are able and qualified men and women with open minds and the capacity to learn from experience.

SUMMARY

1. The Monetarist argument that the private sector is inherently stable stems from the automatic tendency for falling interest rates and prices to raise aggregate demand whenever exogenous spending falls. Keynesians claim that in the short run wages are less flexible than prices and that this will produce variations in GNP when there are exogenous shifts in aggregate demand.

2. Monetarists claim that the transmission mechanism between money and spending is direct. Additional cash balances are spent directly on real goods and services. According to Keynesians, however, the linkage between money and spending occurs through the interest rate, and in this case there is room for considerable slippage.

3. Keynesians contend that fiscal policy has a direct and powerful impact on spending. Monetarists claim that much of the expansionary impact of fiscal policy disappears because rising interest rates crowd out private investment.

4. Inflation is basically a monetary phenomenon, according to Monetarists, because aggregate demand depends primarily on the money supply. Keynesians claim that fiscal policy or other exogenous spending can cause inflation as well.

5. The existence of a Phillips Curve trade-off between inflation and unemployment depends upon the lags of wages and expectations behind changes in the price level. Even Keynesians would agree that in the long run there is no trade-off; but in the short run there is considerable disagreement.

6. Real interest rates initially fall after an increase in the money supply, but once inflationary expectations take hold, nominal rates rise. After a while

the real rate will return to its original level, but as long as inflationary expectations remain, the nominal level of rates will be higher.

7. The Monetarist case for a fixed rule to circumscribe stabilization policy stems from the possibility that the lagged effects of policy changes might cause greater instability in GNP. The key problem is accurately anticipating the timing of policy impacts on aggregate demand. Monetarists propose a fixed rule to prevent destabilizing effects. Keynesians believe the inflexibility imposed by a rule cannot be justified, given the present state of knowledge about the impact of policy on demand.

8. Many of these Monetarist-Keynesian arguments can be traced to differing views of the aggregate supply and demand curves. Monetarists tend to believe aggregate demand is stable once money supply is fixed; Keynesians see no reason to assume such stability. Monetarists say the aggregate supply curve is usually vertical; Keynesians claim it is horizontal some of the time and upward sloping much of the time.

Suggestions for Further Reading

An excellent discussion of the points of disagreement between Monetarists and Keynesians is Leonall C. Andersen, Lawrence R. Klein, and Karl Brunner in the September 1973 issue of the Federal Reserve Bank of St. Louis *Review.* In an attempt to settle matters once and for all, a conference was held at Brown University in 1974. The proceedings are available in Jerome L. Stein, ed., *Monetarism* (New York: North-Holland, 1976). Finally, the *Journal of Political Economy* has sponsored an aptly titled volume: *Milton Friedman's Monetary Framework: A Debate with His Critics* (Chicago: University of Chicago Press, 1974). They make it easy for you to order it by taking Master-Card or Visa (why not American Express?).

Professor Friedman's views on a rule for monetary policy are spelled out in his *A Program for Monetary Stability* (Bronx, N.Y.: Fordham University Press, 1959). The original statement on this subject was made by Henry Simons in "Rules Versus Authorities in Monetary Policy," *Journal of Political Economy* (February 1936). For an eloquent defense of countercyclical policy together with a concise treatment of the Monetarist-Keynesian debate, see Franco Modigliani, "The Monetarist Controversy, or Should We Forsake Stabilization Policies?" *American Economic Review* (March 1977).

An evaluation of Monetarist propositions in light of the 1979–82 so-called "monetarist experiment" in U.S. policy appears in articles by Benjamin Friedman, Bennet McCallum, James Pierce, and Milton Friedman in the *American Economic Review* (May 1984). As usual, no one agrees on what happened, but it's interesting to see why.

Rational Expectations: Theory and Policy Implications

Rational expectations, ice cream, and apple pie have at least one thing in common: it's hard to be against them. But the similarity ends there, because the implications of rational expectations are far more controversial than either of the other two—even if you're serious about counting calories.

Throughout our discussion of the Monetarist and Keynesian models, expectations have never been far from the surface. We saw in the last chapter that inflationary expectations are crucial determinants of the nominal interest rate. We also showed how inflationary expectations enter into wage agreements and thereby influence the shape of the aggregate supply curve and hence the Phillips curve trade-off between inflation and unemployment. Finally, back in Chapter 20 we indicated that expectations of monetary policy actions could affect the timing of interest rate responses to changes in the money supply.

In all these earlier discussions we never were very particular about how these expectations were formulated. Implicit in most discussions was the assumption that expectations of the future are based on the past: if price increases have been accelerating, for example, then inflation is *expected* to get worse. As it turns out, this seemingly innocuous formulation of expected inflation is not terribly rational, because it ignores other pieces of information that might be important to a proper estimate of future inflation.

The first order of business, therefore, is to describe precisely what is meant by rational expectations. We then turn to the implications for monetary and fiscal policy, the ability to control inflation and the consequences for interest rates.

WHEN ARE EXPECTATIONS RATIONAL?

If people use all available information to formulate expectations (of prices, interest rates, money supply, or anything else), then their expectations are considered rational. If people ignore information, then expectations are not rational. People are likely to be rational in formulating their expectations, because ignoring something is usually costly. For example, ignoring the news report of a freeze in Florida in formulating your expectation of orange juice prices next month is likely to cost you money. A rational forecast would suggest stocking up on orange juice before prices go up. Ignoring the information and relying on recent price trends to guide your spending plans will lead to inferior results. Thus, people have strong incentives to make rational forecasts and can be relied upon to act accordingly. If our models are to describe economic activity accurately, then the behavioral relationships must be based on rational expectations.

Let's examine in somewhat greater detail how inflationary expectations are formulated. Extrapolating recent price trends is often referred to as *adaptive* expectations. Thus, if inflation has been on the rise, adaptive expectations suggest that people expect inflation to continue to go up. But if at the same time that inflation is increasing the Federal Reserve restricts the money supply, and people are aware of this policy, then based on their knowledge of how the economy works, people would probably expect inflation to go down rather than up. Such expectations would be considered rational because they include information—what is happening to the money supply—that is relevant for properly forecasting inflation. Moreover, people will utilize that information, because spending, investing, and business decisions depend upon inflation forecasts. If inflation is expected to go down, certain job opportunities become more or less attractive, some investments become more or less attractive, and so on.

Notice that rational inflationary expectations include at least two items that were ignored by the less rigorous adaptive approach to forecasting: the behavior of the monetary authority and the structure of the economy. Since knowledge of what policy-makers will do and what economic models suggest are the consequences of such actions is potentially important for the future course of prices, it is crucial that rational expectations incorporate that information. The reason is not that we say so but that people will find it optimal (and profitable) to behave according to rational expectations.

A similar argument holds in forecasting securities prices—either bonds or equities—but even more so. Every scrap of information is likely to be exploited in formulating expected bond prices or stock prices, because there are direct, and often immediate, profit opportunities available in acting upon such information. This idea has an interesting implication for current securities prices: they will reflect all currently available information. For example, suppose a secret Federal Reserve document describing a surprise reduction in money supply growth were discovered in a Washington, D.C. trash can and were then published in the *Wall Street Journal.* Since the less expansionary monetary policy would lead to less inflation and lower nominal rates of interest, hence higher bond prices in the future, the demand for bonds would increase right now and bond prices would rise until there no longer was an opportunity to earn a profit. Thus, the information about the Federal Reserve's new policy would be incorporated in bond prices immediately upon its release.[1] In other words, securities prices fully reflect all available information.

This specific application of rational expectations to securities markets is often referred to as "efficient capital markets." We will return to this particular discussion in Chapter 29. In the remaining sections we examine the implications of rational expectations for stabilization policy.

ANTICIPATED VERSUS UNANTICIPATED MONETARY POLICY

Perhaps the most stunning implication of rational expectations is that when it is combined with the Classical world's assumption of completely flexible wages and prices, the result is that an *anticipated* monetary policy will have no impact on economic activity. The argument is complicated, so we will have to pay attention. It goes like this. Recall from the last chapter that the positively sloped aggregate supply

[1]Note that it isn't even necessary for this information to be available to everyone. Bond prices will jump even if only a few individuals know about Federal Reserve intentions. As long as they have funds to invest, we can rely on greed to push up prices until they reflect all available information.

curve implies that faster money supply growth leads to higher output and less unemployment as long as wages go up more slowly than prices. The argument is straightforward: if wages go up more slowly than prices it will pay business firms to hire more workers. The problem is that workers will permit their wages to rise more slowly than prices only as long as their inflationary expectations lag behind actual inflation. People will not work more if they expect a decline in their *real* wages (money wages adjusted for inflation to provide a measure of the goods and services the money wages can buy). But according to rational expectations, workers recognize the connection between inflation and money supply growth. Thus, if we start with an *anticipated* increase in the money supply, then the subsequent inflation will also be anticipated. And in that case, inflationary expectations keep pace with actual inflation and, because wages and prices are completely flexible, workers make sure that wages move up simultaneously with prices. Under those circumstances there won't be any increase in output or reduction in unemployment as a result of the anticipated increase in the money supply.

Note that if the money growth is not anticipated, the increased

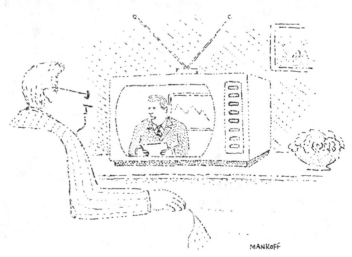

"On Wall Street today, news of lower interest rates sent the stock market up, but then the expectation that these rates would be inflationary sent the market down, until the realization that lower rates might stimulate the sluggish economy pushed the market up, before it ultimately went down on fears that an overheated economy would lead to a reimposition of higher interest rates."

Drawing by Mankoff; © 1981 The New Yorker Magazine Inc.

aggregate demand leads to higher prices that are not anticipated. Wages do, in fact, lag behind prices, and business firms hire more workers. The result: higher output and lower unemployment when money supply growth is not anticipated.

It is possible to illustrate the entire story within the aggregate supply and demand model as long as we remember to label each aggregate supply curve with the appropriate expected price level. In Figure 1 start with aggregate demand curve AD_1 and aggregate supply curve $AS(P^e_1)$, where P^e_1 indicates that the expected price level is P_1. The equilibrium price level given by the intersection point between AD_1 and $AS(P^e_1)$ is P_1 and equilibrium income is Y_E. An increase in the money supply shifts AD_1 to AD_2 and would raise output above Y_E if the aggregate supply curve remained $AS(P^e_1)$. But if the change in money supply is anticipated, the aggregate supply curve no longer is $AS(P^e_1)$ because the increased money supply is expected to increase

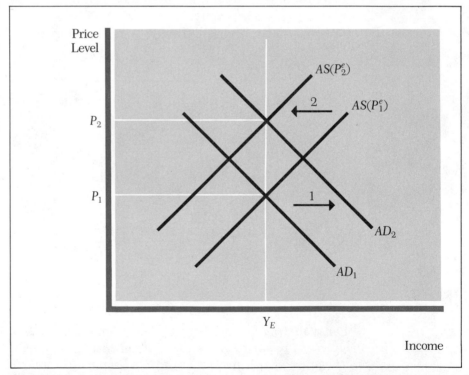

FIGURE 1 Anticipated Monetary Policy Shifts Aggregate Supply Along with Aggregate Demand, Leaving GNP Unchanged

the price level above P_1. The new aggregate supply curve under rational expectations is $AS(P^e_2)$, where the new equilibrium price level is equal to P_2. Thus, the end result of an anticipated change in the money supply is an unchanged level of economic activity and a higher price level.[2]

IMPLICATIONS FOR STABILIZATION POLICY

The distinction between anticipated and unanticipated monetary policy takes on still greater significance once we recognize that stabilization policy usually falls under the category of anticipated policy. If unemployment begins to rise and the Federal Reserve is known to pursue countercyclical monetary policy, then everyone expects the Federal Reserve to expand the money supply. As long as wages and prices are flexible, however, the expansion in money supply will lead to higher prices. Because people are aware of these relationships, expected inflation occurs simultaneously with the expansion in money supply, wages move up in tandem with prices, and the impact of the expansionary monetary policy on real economic activity is neutralized.

The cruel facts of rational expectations are that only random acts by the central bank—"erroneous" increases or decreases in the money supply—influence the level of economic activity. Systematic policies are useless. From this perspective, the discussions in the last chapter on rules versus discretion and whether the Federal Reserve should be a robot are irrelevant. No matter what systematic decision rule the Fed follows, it will not influence real economic activity—for better or worse.[3]

The outcome of the rational expectations world is decidedly Classical-Monetarist rather than Keynesian. Although rational expectations

[2]The proof that the new aggregate supply curve must be exactly $AS(P^e_2)$ is fairly complicated. It is based on the notion that the expected price level P^e_2 must be consistent with the actual new equilibrium price level P_2, and that neither has any tendency to change. This will occur where the level of output Y_E has no tendency to change as well, that is, Y_E is the full employment level of output.

[3]The irrelevance of policy in the rational expectations world was first presented in Thomas Sargent and Neil Wallace, "Rational Expectations, the Optimal Monetary Instrument, and the Optimal Money Supply Rule," *Journal of Political Economy* (April 1985).

does not necessarily support Milton Friedman's contention that the attempt at economic stabilization is destabilizing (since any systematic policy is neutralized), the close connection between money supply and inflation and the inherent stability of the economy at full employment are decidedly Monetarist-Classical propositions.[4] Rational expectations is sometimes referred to as the new classical economics.

But all is not lost for proponents of Keynesian thinking. Rational expectations combined with contractual rigidity in wages and prices modify the stark conclusions just described. In particular, even though inflationary expectations follow directly from expansionary monetary policy, and even though countercyclical policy will be anticipated, wages and prices are not determined by an auctioneer.[5] Unlike prices of stocks and bonds, wages are frequently set by contractual agreement. If that's the case, then wages may very well lag behind prices even if expectations of inflation are formed rationally. Somewhat more concretely, even when workers expect inflation to rise, they do not force up their wage demands instantaneously. Similarly, even if business firms expect a decrease in inflation, they do not reduce wages paid instantaneously. These sluggish adjustments are part of the implicit and explicit contractual arrangements in labor markets.

Without instantaneous adjustments in wages to reflect expected inflation, the positively sloped aggregate supply curve does not shift to the left in Figure 1. Thus, when AD_1 shifts to the right, the equilibrium level of output does, in fact, increase. From our new perspective these results occur not because expected inflation lags behind actual inflation—rational expectations do not permit that— but because wages simply do not adjust completely. Corporations hire more workers and output rises until the contractual arrangements run their course.

The battlefield between Monetarists and Keynesians over the effectiveness of stabilization policy has shifted once again. Instead of focusing on inflationary expectations the key ingredient now is labor contracts and rigid wages.[6] For some reason, that has a familiar ring to it.

---

[4]The rational expectations demonstration of the irrelevance of countercyclical policy *indirectly* supports the argument for a constant rate of monetary growth. In particular, large fluctuations in money supply associated with countercyclical stabilization policy increase the uncertainty of the economic environment and hence are undesirable.

[5]For a nice discussion of sluggish price adjustments see Stephen Cecchetti, "The Frequency of Price Adjustment," *Journal of Econometrics* (1986).

[6]See Stanley Fischer, "Long-term Contracts, Rational Expectations, and the Optimal Money Supply Rule," *Journal of Political Economy* (February 1977).

And for good reason, because wage rigidity is exactly where Keynes and his Classical mentors originally parted company.

INFLATION, THE PHILLIPS CURVE, AND CREDIBILITY

In the last chapter we described the Monetarist-Keynesian controversy over the Phillips curve: Keynesians argued that a trade-off existed between inflation and unemployment, while Monetarists claimed that there was no long-run trade-off. The key was the shape of the aggregate supply curve and whether inflationary expectations lag behind actual inflation. According to the Keynesians, the aggregate supply curve is positively sloped because expectations of inflation adjust more slowly than actual inflation to changes in underlying economic activity. Under such circumstances, policy-makers could increase the level of economic activity and reduce unemployment as long as they were ready to tolerate an increase in the rate of inflation. Monetarists, led by Milton Friedman, argued that in the short run this might be so, but after expectations have adjusted, the aggregate supply curve is vertical and no permanent trade-off is possible.

The rational expectations story pushes the Monetarist's long-run analysis into the short run by transforming a series of upward sloping aggregate supply curves into a vertical one. We begin, once again, with a change in the money supply that is fully anticipated. The increased money supply shifts the aggregate demand curve to the right. But as we saw in Figure 1, if wages and prices are flexible, whenever the Federal Reserve embarks on a countercyclical expansion in the money supply, the rightward shift in aggregate demand is met by a leftward shift in aggregate supply. In Figure 2, we illustrate these simultaneously shifting aggregate supply and demand curves that leave income and output at the "natural" full employment level Y_{FE}. The simultaneous shifts in aggregate supply and demand occur because the expansionary monetary policy that shifts AD_1 to AD_2 to AD_3 produces rational inflationary expectations that shift $AS(P^e_1)$ to $AS(P^e_2)$ to $AS(P^e_3)$. The equilibrium points in Figure 2 show an unchanged level of output at Y_{FE} combined with ever-increasing price levels. The result is that even though we have individual positively sloped aggregate supply curves, the outcome of a countercyclical monetary policy is a *de facto* vertical aggregate supply curve produced by simultaneous shifts in AS and AD. Thus, policy-makers are not confronted by a

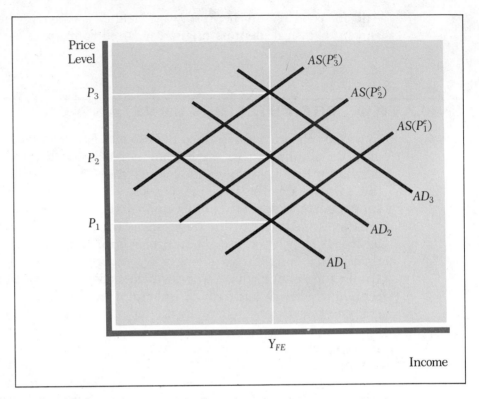

FIGURE 2 Anticipated Monetary Policy Can Affect Only the Price Level

Phillips curve trade-off between inflation and unemployment, because the positively sloped aggregate supply curve does not stay put.

Keynesians, of course, would respond that as long as wages and prices are set contractually, shifting aggregate supply curves would not eliminate the Phillips curve trade-off between inflation and unemployment. Even under rational expectations, the contractual rigidities remain and provide policy-makers with an avenue for influencing real economic activity.

For those of you with a soft spot for policy-making, do not think that a Phillips curve is necessary to provide a meaningful life. Although the absence of a trade-off between inflation and unemployment under rational expectations (with flexible wages and prices) deals a devastating blow to policy-makers trying to reduce unemployment, it creates a pleasant surprise for the inflation fighters. In particular, reducing inflation is accomplished painlessly. Let the central bank embark on a contractionary monetary policy and make certain that *everyone knows about it.* As long as the Federal Reserve's policy is credible, the leftward shift in the aggregate demand schedule produced by a reduction in the money supply is accompanied by a rightward shift in the aggregate supply curve. For example, if we start in Figure 2 with $AS(P^e_3)$ and AD_3 and price level P_3, the reduction in money supply shifts AD_3 to AD_2. Since everyone now expects the lower price level P_2, the aggregate supply curve also shifts to $AS(P^e_2)$. The economy moves from price level P_3 to price level P_2 painlessly—without any decrease in economic activity and without any increase in unemployment.

The key to this happy result is *credibility*. If the public suspects that the Federal Reserve will not stick to its guns, perhaps because the Fed is afraid that unemployment will increase, then the expected price level will not fall to P^e_2, and the aggregate supply curve will stay where it is. The result will be costly: a reduction in output and increased unemployment. Only if the Fed announces its policy and the public is convinced that it will pursue it at all costs will the costs turn out to be negligible.

How is this credibility accomplished? Rhetoric is usually not sufficient, especially in democratic societies where considerable political pressure can be brought to bear on policy-makers. Concrete policy changes are necessary to alter ingrained inflationary expectations. This is especially so in the case of hyperinflation, where exorbitant rates of inflation have taken hold of an economy. Under such circumstances, changing the monetary unit, introducing a truly independent central bank, and invoking severe fiscal restraint to balance the budget have had the desired effect. The hyperinflations suffered by Germany, Austria, Poland, and Hungary in the aftermath of World War I were reversed with hardly any reduction in real output as a result of an overhaul in the monetary-fiscal regimes in each of those countries.[7] Under more mundane circumstances, however, the search for a credible policy proceeds with much more caution. And that often dooms the experiment before it gets started.

At this point our discussion of the trade-off between inflation and unemployment sounds more like topics in advanced psychology than anything resembling economic policy. In part, that is the message of rational expectations. Economic policy-making is far more complicated than the Keynesian revolution had anticipated. And while wages and prices might not be sufficiently flexible to drive out countercyclical

[7] See Thomas Sargent, "The Ends of Four Big Inflations," in Robert E. Hall, ed., *Inflation: Causes and Consequences* (Chicago: University of Chicago Press, 1982).

policy completely, the effectiveness of the conventional Keynesian models must be modified by rational inflationary expectations.

INTEREST RATES AND ANTICIPATED MONETARY POLICY

The rational expectations message for interest rates is not much brighter than for countercyclical policy in general. Recall our discussion in the last chapter on how a change in the money supply affects the level of interest rates. We identified the Keynesian liquidity effect, which links an increase in money supply with a decline in both real and nominal interest rates. The Monetarists stress that this liquidity effect is only transitory, soon to be swamped by inflationary expectations that drive nominal rates above real rates. Keynesians have a short-run "liquidity" perspective when claiming that expansionary monetary policy lowers interest rates, while Monetarists have a longer-run perspective when emphasizing that interest rates go up because of inflationary expectations.

The rational expectations world is much simpler. An anticipated increase in the money supply leads to higher nominal interest rates immediately, while unanticipated increases in money supply produce lower nominal interest rates. The reasoning is straightforward. Anticipated increases in money supply produce inflationary expectations simultaneously with the expansion in money supply. Under such circumstances, lenders are reluctant to part with funds unless interest rates reflect the expected inflation and borrowers agree to pay higher rates because of the expected inflation. The liquidity effect never reduces interest rates, because inflationary expectations respond instantaneously. When the money supply jumps without warning, however, then the liquidity effect produces a drop in rates. In fact, if the expansion in money supply occurred without rhyme or reason, inflationary expectations might not get started until aggregate demand pushed up economic activity. And that might take sufficient time for the liquidity effect to remain for a while.

The lesson of the rational expectations story is harder to avoid in financial markets than in labor markets. When it comes to stocks and bonds, prices are not set by contractual agreement. Thus, the rational expectations distinction between the impacts of anticipated and unanticipated monetary policy on interest rates are important lessons. Nevertheless, the story cannot end here. Empirical evidence is the only way to resolve the policy disputes between Monetarists and

Keynesians, with or without rational expectations. And for answers we must turn to the next chapter.

SUMMARY

1. Expectations are rational when people take account of all available information in forecasting economic variables. In forecasting inflation, for example, rational expectations use information on what is happening to the money supply and what economic models predict the consequences will be for prices.

2. When expectations are rational and when wages and prices are completely flexible, anticipated monetary policies have no effect on economic activity. The result for stabilization policy, which is usually anticipated, is decidedly Monetarist-Classical: there is no impact of countercyclical policy on the level of economic activity.

3. The Keynesian viewpoint is that even if expectations are rational, wages and prices are not completely flexible because of contractual arrangements in labor markets. Under such circumstances, even an anticipated countercyclical monetary policy will have an impact on economic activity.

4. The rational expectations perspective eliminates even a temporary trade-off between inflation and unemployment. This means policy-makers cannot reduce unemployment below some natural level by increasing the rate of inflation. There is no short-run Phillips curve under rational expectations.

5. A contractionary monetary policy can reduce inflation without an increase in unemployment in the rational expectations world. As long as the anti-inflationary policy has credibility, the reduction in inflation will be painless.

6. Prices and yields in financial markets are sufficiently flexible to make the rational expectations world a reality. Under such circumstances, an anticipated monetary policy cannot influence real interest rates even in the short run. Anticipated monetary policy influences interest rates only through inflationary expectations.

Suggestions for Further Reading

The original demonstration of the ineffectiveness of monetary policy under rational expectations appears in Thomas Sargent and Neil Wallace, "Rational Expectations, the Optimal Monetary Instrument, and the Optimal Money Supply Rule"), *Journal of Political Economy* (April 1985). To really understand the argument as well as broader issues in rational expectations, see Thomas Sargent, "Rational Expectations and the Reconstruction of Macro-economics," Federal Reserve Bank of Minneapolis *Quarterly Review* (Summer 1980). The best defense of policy effectiveness even within the rational expectations world is John Taylor, "The Role of Expectations in the Choice of Monetary Policy," in *Monetary Policy Issues in the 1980s* (Federal Reserve Bank of Kansas City, 1982). Finally, Thomas Sargent, "The Ends of Four Big Inflations," in Robert E. Hall, ed., *Inflation: Causes and Consequences* (Chicago: University of Chicago Press, 1982) provides a delightful discussion of how credibility can help destroy inflation with hardly a whimper.

CHAPTER 25

Empirical Evidence on the Effectiveness of Monetary Policy

Theory, like punishment, is said to be good for the soul. But even the most philosophical among us realize that humans—and yes, even students—also require rewards that are somewhat more concrete. Having poked into every nook and cranny of the Monetarist-Keynesian dialogue over the effectiveness of monetary and fiscal policy, the time has come to reveal the Truth (with a capital T). Since many people believe that numbers are Truth, here they are aplenty.

What are the facts about the behavior of velocity? How powerful is the impact of monetary policy on economic activity? How are interest rates affected? What particular categories of spending are most influenced by money? After all, if monetary policy is to alter GNP, it cannot do it by mystic incantations; it has to do it by changing the consumer spending of households, the investment spending of business firms, or the expenditures of governments—federal, state, or local. In contrast to the theoretical discussion of previous chapters, we now turn to the *empirical* evidence.

LIVING WITH VELOCITY

We have seen that part of the Monetarist-Keynesian debate hinges on the behavior of velocity—Monetarists contending that it is relatively stable and that any changes are highly predictable, while Keynesians argue that either contention is an exaggeration. The facts are that velocity is neither perfectly stable nor fully predictable. The Federal Reserve, unfortunately, does not operate in a world designed for its own convenience. With a money supply of $500 billion, a miscalculation of only 0.1 in velocity means a $50 billion swing in GNP. And with a money supply of $1,000 billion, the GNP jump is twice as large. But all is not necessarily lost. While velocity is not fixed, neither do its movements appear to be random or perverse. If the Federal Reserve could discover the underlying determinants of fluctuations in velocity, it might still be able to coexist with such a moving target.

With that in mind, examining the last decade may provide a clue to developments in the next one. Chart 1 plots the historical course of three measures of velocity during the 1970s and 1980s, each one associated with a different money supply concept. The velocity figures for V1 are based on M1, V2 on M2, and V3 on M3. Two broad generalizations emerge from the picture. First, while none of the velocity measures has been completely stable, the meanderings of V2 and V3 have been quite tame. Of course, we just pointed out that even small miscalculations in velocity mean wide swings in GNP, especially for the more inclusive definitions of money. Nevertheless, the rather narrow range of movement in V2 and V3 is impressive. The second glaring message of Chart 1 is that V1 looks highly unpredictable. Those who prefer the narrow definition of money have some explaining to do.

First the facts. Velocity of M1 reached a peak of about 4 with the onset of the 1920s. It fell almost continuously during the Great Depression and World War II to an all-time low of about 2 in 1946. Since then, however, V1 has skyrocketed. It rose to 2.5 in 1950 and to 3.5 in 1960, passed its previous peak of 4 in 1965, pushed past 5 in the early seventies, and past 6 in recent years. Why has the velocity of M1 gone on its own trip, apparently giving Monetarism a bad name and making life difficult for the Federal Reserve? If we have a reasonable explanation, we may be able to claim that V1's behavior is predictable, and that's enough for most reasonable people.

The main reason for the post–World War II rise in velocity of M1 lies in the relatively narrow historical definition of M1—demand deposits plus currency—and the increasing attractiveness of other categories of financial assets—bonds as well as stocks, savings and loan shares as well as savings accounts in commercial banks—as prudent and desirable outlets in which to invest excess cash. These assets are highly liquid, almost as liquid as money, and yet they offer much

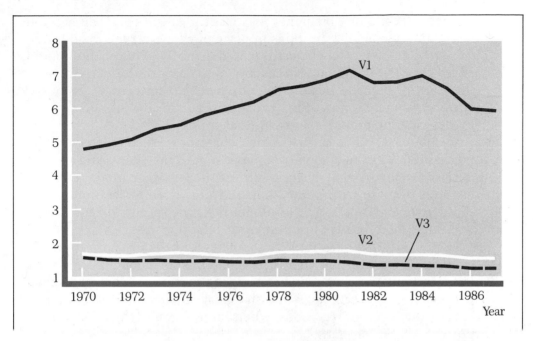

CHART 1 The Velocity of M1, M2, and M3.

SOURCE: *Wall Street Journal,* November, 1986.

higher interest rates than demand deposits. Attractive yields on financial assets other than money have led more and more people to wonder why they should ever hold any idle cash aside from what they need for day-to-day transactions purposes. Traditional concepts about how much cash on hand is really necessary for doing business have also come under reexamination. If money for day-to-day transactions purposes can be pared down, then some of it can be lent to earn higher interest. The money then moves to borrowers who can use it for current purchases. As a result, a larger volume of current spending flows from the same stock of money.

Corporate treasurers, in particular, have found that it pays dividends to scrutinize their cash holdings intensively. Could they manage to get along with somewhat less in the till than they had previously thought of as "normal" and invest a portion in high-yielding time deposits at commercial banks or in U.S. Treasury bills? Increasingly the answer has been "yes," and imaginative new techniques of cash management have been developed to facilitate the process (as well as some not-so-imaginative old techniques, such as becoming "slow payers" when bills come due).

This trend has not escaped the attention of consumers. They have learned to economize on money by substituting lines of credit at retail stores and financial institutions in place of cash reserves; in addition, the growing use of credit cards has drastically reduced household needs for day-to-day transactions money. What was formerly held in the form of demand deposits or currency, for emergency use or for current payments, now shifts to interest-bearing savings deposits or higher-yielding money market mutual funds.

In summary, it is clear that velocity has not been completely stable, nor has it fluctuated randomly or perversely.[1] There has been a pattern in the movements of M1 velocity during the postwar period—a persistent long-run rise with minor short-run dips during recessions. Even though we may not be able to pinpoint all the specific determinants, we can still see broad cause-and-effect relationships.

Higher interest rates lead to an increase in velocity by inducing business firms and households to economize on money. They hold less, lend out the excess, and others (the borrowers) can then spend it. Once learned, techniques of cash management are not easily forgotten, so that even in recessions, when interest rates fall, velocity does not drop back very far.

Furthermore, the long-run upward trend in M1 velocity over the past quarter-century suggests that fundamental structural relationships between the money supply and the spending habits of the community are apparently in the process of transition. New payment methods have been introduced (credit cards and automated funds transfers are prime examples), as financial innovation occurs side by side with technological innovation in industry. Such financial innovation, however, rarely takes root overnight. Established payment habits change only gradually.

Thus, although velocity is not fixed, neither is it likely to change drastically in the short run. And this is especially true for V2 and V3. The Federal Reserve may be able to live with such moving targets. By gaining further insight into what makes velocity move, the central bank might be able to establish a range of probabilities as to where velocity is likely to be tomorrow and the day after and to act on that basis. In other words, a morning line on velocity (not unlike the one your local bookie puts out on the races at Hialeah)—provided the odds were unemotionally calculated and continuously reassessed in the

---

[1]An early attempt at demonstrating the predictability of velocity is Karl Brunner and Allan H. Meltzer, "Predicting Velocity: Implications for Theory and Policy," *Journal of Finance* (May 1963).

light of emerging evidence—might still enable the Federal Reserve to come out a winner.

THE DEMAND FOR MONEY

We have just suggested that the historical movement in the velocity of M1 stems from many factors, including movements in interest rates, technology, and innovations in financial markets. To focus more precisely on the relative importance of each of these requires that we disentangle their separate influences. Only a formal application of statistical techniques to historical data on the money stock, interest rates, income, and other variables will permit us to identify the individual relationships. Indeed, economists have spent considerable effort estimating statistical counterparts to the money demand equations discussed in earlier chapters.[2] And the reasons for the effort are not difficult to understand—after all, the Monetarist and Keynesian heritages have a large stake in the outcome of such studies.

Just about every statistical study has shown that both the interest rate and the level of GNP influence money demand. In particular, higher interest rates significantly reduce the demand for cash balances. This result, by itself, contradicts extreme forms of Monetarism, which assume zero interest-sensitivity of money demand. On the other hand, none of the empirical investigations has ever isolated the Keynesian liquidity trap. More important, the estimated interest-elasticity of money demand has generally been quite low.[3] Thus the Monetarist outlook gains considerable support after all.

The question of the interest-sensitivity of money demand has historically been an important issue dividing Monetarists and Keynesians. But once the extreme positions—zero and infinite interest-elasticity—have been ruled out, the more sophisticated problem focuses on the *stability* of the money demand equation. After all, given the statistical results, the specific numbers are less important than their reliability

[2]See David Laidler, *The Demand for Money: Theories and Evidence* (New York: Dun-Donnelley Corp., 1977) for a review of the empirical evidence on money demand.

[3]In terms of the microeconomic division between elastic (greater than one) and inelastic (less than one) demand curves, the interest-sensitivity of money demand has been estimated as low as 0.15 and as high as 0.7 (see the Laidler book cited in footnote 2, especially pp. 122–130).

in forecasting future money demand. As long as the historical estimates are reliable predictors of money demand, then the Federal Reserve can gauge the proper amount of money to add to or subtract from the economy in order to hit a particular target of economic activity. On the other hand, if the particular estimates change a lot, or if the demand for money jumps around for no apparent reason, then changes in the money supply will be useless predictors of economic activity. Monetarists would obviously be unhappy at such results, and so would ecumenical Keynesians, who view both monetary and fiscal policies as potentially important stabilization weapons.

Most of the evidence suggests that the demand for money was quite stable until the mid-1970s; the predictive power of statistical money demand equations was quite good. Then, about the middle of 1974, the estimated demand equations for money went adrift. People were holding smaller money balances than the historical relationships suggested. This led to the celebrated mystery story—the case of the missing money.[4]

Mysteries are fun to read, but they pose problems for the authorities unless they can be solved. Explanations for the surprising shortfall in money holdings have ranged from technological developments, such as automated transfers of funds, to financial innovations, such as the use of money market mutual funds as substitutes for ordinary checking accounts. If the answer were primarily technological, then the shift in money demand in the mid-1970s would be a less troublesome once-and-for-all event. But a significant source of the shortfall in money demand since 1974 stems from financial innovation.[5] And many of these developments have been stimulated by rising interest rates (see Chapter 7).

Fortunately, it is somewhat premature to indict money demand as a hopeless case of manic-depression. First, the stability until the mid-1970s was quite impressive. Second, there was a confluence of forces during the 1970s, including bursts of inflation and unprecedented volatility in interest rates, that combined to generate unique pressures for change. Finally, and closely related to the last point, the regulatory environment was too antiquated to accommodate a smooth transition within established historical relationships. For example, much of the

[4]See Stephen M. Goldfield, "The Case of the Missing Money," *Brookings Papers on Economic Activity* (No. 3, 1976).
[5]See Gillian Garcia and Simon Pak, "Some Clues in the Case of the Missing Money," *American Economic Review* (May 1979).

innovative response to rising interest rates stemmed from the regulatory prohibitions against paying interest on demand deposits. Now that this restraint has loosened somewhat (again, see Chapter 7), there will be less incentive to circumvent regulations and destroy historical relationships in the process.

TIME LAGS IN MONETARY POLICY

The empirical evidence just presented on velocity and money demand provides some comfort to those promoting the relationship between money and economic activity. But the simple velocity and money demand approaches, even with carefully calculated probabilities, leave much to be desired as a guideline for Federal Reserve policy-making. In particular, they ignore time lags between changes in monetary policy and the impact on economic activity. They also ignore the more sophisticated statistical methodology used to construct entire models of the economy so that the impact of monetary policy can be simulated more elaborately. Both lags and econometric models add flesh to the skeleton of our theoretical models. First we look at lags, and then we introduce the power of econometric modeling.

By their own admission, Federal Reserve officials are not omniscient. If the economy starts to slip into a recession, it takes time before the experts realize what is happening so they can take steps to correct it. Similarly, if inflation begins to accelerate, it takes a while before the evidence verifies the fact.

Prompt recognition of what the economy is doing is not as easy as it sounds. For one thing, the available data are often inadequate and frequently mixed: new car orders will rise while retail department store sales are falling; farm prices may be dropping while employment in urban areas is rising. Furthermore, the economy rarely proceeds on a perfectly smooth course, either up or down. Every upsweep is interrupted from time to time by erratic dips; every decline into recession is punctuated irregularly by false signs of progress, which then evaporate. Is a change only a brief and temporary interruption of an already existing trend, or is it the start of a new trend in the opposite direction? No one is ever perfectly sure. This problem of getting an accurate "fix" on what is happening in the economy, or what is likely to happen in the near future, is called the *recognition lag* in monetary policy.

As soon as the recognition lag ends, the *impact lag* begins, spanning the time from when the central bank starts using one of its tools, such as open market operations, until an effect is evident on the ultimate objective—aggregate spending in the economy. It may take weeks before interest rates change significantly after a monetary action has begun. Changes in credit availability and money supply also take time. And a further delay is probable before actual spending decisions are affected. Once monetary policy does start to influence spending, however, it will most likely continue to have an impact on GNP for quite a while. All of this was swept under the rug in the theoretical models discussed in earlier chapters. But now it's time to add some flesh to that bare-bones description of the real world.

Regarding the *recognition* lag, rough evidence suggests that the Federal Reserve generally starts to tighten only a few months after a business cycle has reached its trough, while its move toward easing after a peak in the cycle is somewhat more delayed. This evidence is less than definitive, and it is likely that under some circumstances the monetary authorities will sense what is going on and take action more promptly than under other circumstances. Nevertheless, the inference that the central bank is typically more concerned with preventing inflation than with avoiding recession probably contains a grain of truth.

The *impact* lag is most conveniently discussed, along with the strength of monetary policy, in terms of the results that formal econometric models of the economy have produced. An econometric model is a mathematical-statistical representation that describes how the economy behaves. Such a model gives empirical content to theoretical propositions about how individuals and business firms, lenders and borrowers, savers and spenders react to economic stimuli. After such relationships are formalized in mathematical expressions, data on past experience in the real world are used to estimate the precise behavioral patterns of each sector. A model, therefore, is based on real-world observations jelled into a formal pattern by the grace of statistical techniques. Thrown into a computer, the model simulates the economy in action and grinds out predictions based on the formal interactions the model embodies.

Our knowledge of how best to construct such a model is far from complete. The same data can produce different results, depending on the theoretical propositions used to construct the model. As one cynic put it, "If one tortures the data long enough, it will confess."

A Keynesian model, for instance, would incorporate behavioral assumptions different from those of a Monetarist model and hence grind out a different set of predictions. Monetarist models frequently relate

Taking the Pulse of the Economy

Reading the financial news is somewhat complicated when the subject is overall economic activity. In fact, when measuring the performance of the aggregate economy there is no single number that does the job. Instead, a variety of statistics released by the government on a monthly or quarterly basis, and published in major newspapers, serve as important indicators. It is useful to divide these statistics into measures of aggregate output and unemployment on the one hand, and the price level and inflation on the other.

Aggregate Output and Unemployment

The most comprehensive measure of economic activity is real GNP. Estimates are released in April for the first quarter (January–March), in July for the second quarter (April–June) and so on. Although real GNP is released as a dollar figure, the most important feature is its rate of growth. Thus, if real GNP grows at an annual rate of $4\frac{1}{2}$ percent during a quarter, that is considered a fast pace of economic activity; if it grows by only 1 percent that would be slow.

The most important number released on a monthly basis is the unemployment rate. A 6 percent rate of unemployment is considered both politically acceptable as well as indicative of no inflationary pressures. Increases in the unemployment rate of one half of one percent during a one or two month period implies that economic activity is slowing down sufficiently to take its toll on the workforce.

The Price Level

The GNP deflator is the most comprehensive measure of the price level. It is a weighted average of prices of all goods and services produced in the economy. It is released quarterly along with data on GNP. A rate of increase in the deflator of 3 or 4 percent on an annual basis has been considered acceptable in recent years.

Two somewhat narrower measures of inflation are released monthly: the consumer price index and the producer price index. As suggested by their names, the former measures the rate of change in prices of goods purchased by the typical consumer (as defined by the Department of Commerce) while the latter measures price changes at the wholesale level. For obvious reasons, although the consumer price index is a less comprehensive measure of the price level than the GNP deflator, it receives the lion's share of attention because it measures how inflation influences each of us directly in our role as consumers. Once again, a 3 or 4 percent increase on an annual basis is considered acceptable; 6 or 8 percent is not.

total GNP to money supply directly, on the basis of a predictable velocity assumption. Keynesian models, on the other hand, involve considerable efforts to explain the determinants of consumption spending, investment spending, and liquidity preference. With regard to monetary policy in particular, the Keynesians' model tries to show explicitly the linkages between money supply, interest rates, and real spending decisions. And if something is left out, they have only themselves to blame.

Since both Monetarists and Keynesians are presumably interested in the truth, it is reasonable to assume that their models have been specified with that objective in mind. Let's review the evidence to see if some consensus emerges.

THE IMPACT OF MONETARY POLICY ON GNP

The Federal Reserve Board, working with economists at several universities, has developed an econometric model of the behavior of economic aggregates in the United States. Many other economists have done similar work at universities and financial institutions. But our discussion will be based primarily on the Federal Reserve model, which was prepared specifically to evaluate the impact of stabilization policies on economic activity. The results of Monetarist models, such as the one constructed at the Federal Reserve Bank of St. Louis, will be contrasted with the Fed model.

It is important to emphasize at the outset that these econometric models are evolutionary phenomena, constantly revised and altered to reflect new and different perspectives about economic reality. Moreover, the numerical estimates of how the economy responds to a change in monetary policy (and fiscal policy as well) vary with the specific conditions of economic activity. Thus the numbers reported later provide a general flavor of how the models simulate economic and financial responses to policy, but they should be viewed as impressionistic. In fact, we must append the Surgeon General's warning: these numbers are dangerous to your health. They cannot be distributed without prescription. Minors will not be admitted even with parental guidance.

The Federal Reserve's model articulates rather carefully the impact of monetary policy on various categories of spending. Indeed, the channels of transmission are clearly set out in mathematical splendor.

We will give some of the details later, but at this point it is best to concentrate on an overview of the model's findings for monetary policy.

The latest version of the Fed's model shows that a 1 percent increase in the money supply raises real GNP by about 1 percent after one year. During the next four quarters, prices rise so that nominal GNP goes up still further—by almost 2 percent after two years.[6] After about three years the impact on real GNP has just about disappeared, and the entire impact of the 1 percent increase in money supply is felt on prices.

Earlier versions of the Fed model took longer for monetary policy to work its way through the economy. Back then Monetarists were unhappy with such results and suspected that the architects of the Federal Reserve's model unwittingly left something out of their complicated system of equations. As a result Monetarist economists at the Federal Reserve Bank of St. Louis developed a simple model that related GNP directly to the money supply, without any intervening steps. And after all was said and done, this model also showed that a 1 percent change in money supply increased GNP by about 1 percent after a year. The so-called St. Louis model was silent, however, on the division of GNP between real and nominal magnitudes, as well as on what happened after the first twelve months.

The surprising outcome is an apparent consensus that monetary policy has a significant impact on economic activity within a year. The problem is that after this initial period the impact of the monetary expansion is passed on to higher prices. And this result could occur more quickly if conditions were ripe. More specifically, since the Fed's equations do not model rational expectations (and the St. Louis approach is silent on the issue), the potential for an immediate impact on prices cannot be ruled out.

Regarding the question of time lags, it should be noted that it takes time for an open market operation by the Federal Reserve to have an impact on the money supply. Reserves provided through open market purchases, for example, must work their way through the banking system as banks make loans and buy securities. If we measure the lag in monetary policy from the time when the Federal Reserve injects reserves through open market operations, then we must add on a few months to the delayed response in GNP to monetary policy.

[6]See "Structure and Uses of the MPS Quarterly Econometric Model of the United States," *Federal Reserve Bulletin* (February 1987).

FISCAL POLICY AND CROWDING OUT

The theoretical discussions in earlier chapters indicated a clear distinction between Monetarist and Keynesian views on the effectiveness of fiscal policy. Monetarists contend that tax and expenditure policies merely displace private spending, leaving little net impact of fiscal policy on GNP. Keynesians, on the other hand, argue that the "crowding out" effects of government policies are incomplete, implying that fiscal policy generates much of the traditional multiplier effect on GNP. It should be clear by now that this dispute can be resolved only by resort to empirical evidence.

Experiments with the Federal Reserve model show that, holding the money supply constant, an increase in government spending by 1 percent of GNP increases the level of real GNP by about 1 percent for at least two years. It takes more than three years for crowding out to reduce the impact on real GNP to zero. An alternative experiment shows that if the money supply varies so that the level of interest rates is held constant, then the multiplier effects on GNP are enormous: even after four years GNP is 4 percent higher than without the expansion in government spending. These results suggest that according to the Federal Reserve's model, fiscal policy has a multiplier of about one without any help from monetary policy, but that an accommodating monetary authority can make fiscal policy even more effective.

The original version of the Monetarist model developed at the Federal Reserve Bank of St. Louis was much more pessimistic about fiscal policy: it reported complete crowding out of fiscal effects within the first year after government spending was increased. One of the problems with this revolutionary result was that the St. Louis model was silent on the specific categories of private spending that were crowded out by the government's expenditure. This agnosticism of the St. Louis model made its results highly suspect, according to most Keynesians. In point of fact, more recent estimates of the Monetarist model are less adamant on the absence of any fiscal effects on GNP.[7]

It seems that the empirical evidence on fiscal policy confirms significant crowding out, but only if the contractionary effects on private spending are given substantial time to work themselves out. This brings us to the question of the role of interest rates within the framework of our models. First let's look at how changes in money supply

[7]See, for example, Benjamin M. Friedman, "Even the St. Louis Model Now Believes in Fiscal Policy," *Journal of Money, Credit, and Banking* (May 1977).

influence the level of rates, and then we can turn to the specific categories of spending that are most sensitive to interest rate movements.

THE IMPACT OF MONEY ON INTEREST RATES

According to both Monetarists and Keynesians, the initial liquidity impact of an expansionary monetary policy reduces the level of interest rates. Similarly, both Monetarists and Keynesians recognize that inflationary expectations generated by excessively expansionary monetary policy will raise interest rates. The key difference of opinion, as we explained back in Chapter 23, focuses on how long it takes for inflationary expectations to counteract the initial liquidity effects.

Chart 2 illustrates that the levels of short-term interest rates have been rather closely related to actual movements in the rate of inflation. Thus a broad sweep of the data clearly shows the impact of inflation on the rate of interest. But the chart also shows substantial intervals of independent movements in the level of interest rates. And to identify the separate role of monetary policy in this area, it is once again necessary to consult the statistical evidence.

Most econometric models, including that of the Fed, report that interest rates decline and remain below their original levels for six months to a year after an expansionary monetary policy and that they are above their original levels for a similar period after a contractionary monetary policy. After a year, however, the initial liquidity effect is reversed, and interest rates move in the opposite direction. In contrast, there are some Monetarist models that show the Treasury bill rate snapping back to its original level and going above it within three months after an expansionary monetary policy.[8]

It should be emphasized that the response of inflationary expectations depends crucially on the initial state of the economy. At levels of economic activity that are very close to full employment, or when saver and investor concerns about inflation are especially strong, an upward jump in inflationary expectations due to expansionary monetary policy can be even quicker than we just indicated. Thus while the formal models show a relatively slow adjustment, their predictions are

[8]For a result showing virtually no reduction in long-term interest rates due to expansionary monetary policy, see Fredrick Mishkin, "Monetary Policy and Long-Term Interest Rates," *Journal of Monetary Economics* (January 1981).

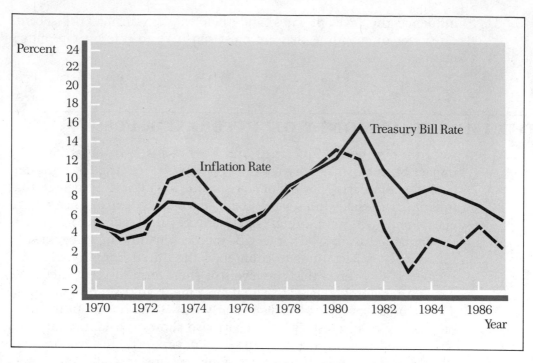

CHART 2 Interest Rates Move with the Rate of Inflation

based on the average historical experience. Any particular historical event can show more sensitivity than the average if the specific conditions are ripe.

At this point it seems useful to go one step further in examining the behavior of interest rates. Rising rates should cut off some spending and falling rates should be stimulative. Let us see which categories of spending are most sensitive to movements in interest rates. In this way we can isolate the channels through which monetary policy operates, as well as identify the categories of private spending that are likely to be crowded out by fiscal actions.

BUSINESS INVESTMENT

One would expect interest rates and all types of investment spending to move in opposite directions: an increase in interest rates, for example, should lower business spending on plant and equipment. If the cost of borrowing rises, so our theory said, business firms should presumably be less willing to incur new debt to build new factories or buy new machines. The simple historical record shows, however, that interest rates and business investment almost always move in the *same* direction. As in most cases where fact contradicts economic theory, one of them must give ground—and it is usually fact.

In the historical record, many things are happening simultaneously, so separate strands of cause and effect are not sorted out. Investment spending on plant and equipment is influenced by a number of factors besides interest rates—sales expectations, changes in anticipated profitability, pressures from competitors, the degree of capacity currently being utilized, and expectations regarding inflation, to name only some. An increase in interest rates may inhibit investment, and yet investment may, in fact, rise if a number of these other elements shift sufficiently to offset its effect.

Econometric methods, such as those used in constructing the Federal Reserve model, permit us to sort out the effects of individual variables. For our particular concern, we can examine the impact of interest rates on investment, holding all other influences constant. The Fed model shows, for example, that an increase of 1 percentage point (say from 8 to 9 percent) in the corporate bond rate lowers business spending on new plant and equipment by about $6 billion after one year, by more than $9 billion after two years, and by about $16 billion after three years.

In this instance, the time delay of interest rate effects is clearly quite substantial. Most investment decisions are not made today and executed tomorrow. Decisions regarding installation of new machinery and construction of new plants are usually made far in advance. Thus an increase in interest rates does not promptly affect investment in plant and equipment. What it does affect is current decisions that will be implemented months or years in the future.

RESIDENTIAL CONSTRUCTION

The impact of monetary policy is felt more promptly and more powerfully on residential construction expenditures. In particular, an increase of 1 percentage point in the interest rate lowers spending on housing by more than $10 billion within a year. In addition to this interest rate effect, residential construction is also affected by monetary policy through credit rationing activities by financial institutions engaged in mortgage lending. In fact, credit availability is often emphasized by modern Keynesians as a significant channel through which monetary policy influences spending. But this specific case of mortgage credit rationing is likely to become less important in the future as financial regulations are relaxed and as institutions become less specialized.

Construction expenditures by state and local governments also appear sensitive to the actions of the monetary authorities. Municipal bond flotations are often reduced, postponed, or canceled during periods of high and rising interest rates. Many municipal governments have self-imposed interest rate ceilings that eliminate them from the market when rates go up. In other instances, when interest costs become too large, local voters are reluctant to approve bond issues for school construction and other projects, since the higher interest burden implies the immediate or eventual imposition of higher property or sales taxes.

CONSUMER SPENDING

The last major item on the monetary policy hit list is consumer spending. In this case the Federal Reserve model includes the wealth effect of modern Keynesians to channel the impact of interest rates to spending. In particular, a lower interest rate raises the value of stocks and bonds, according to the model, and this increases the level of consumer spending.

The importance of the wealth effect in the overall impact of monetary policy is quite substantial, according to the Federal Reserve's formulation. About one third of the impact of monetary policy on GNP after one year stems from the effects of changes in wealth on consumer spending. This is more than four times the response in plant and equipment expenditure and just about equal to the powerful effect of monetary policy on residential construction.

Perhaps the most important message of the entire set of empirical results is that there are significant impacts of monetary policy on spending. While at first glance this seems to bolster the role of the Federal Reserve in the countercyclical efforts of the government, the potentially destabilizing impacts discussed in Chapter 23 become even more threatening. The Federal Reserve model suggests that monetary policy is a force to be reckoned with but might be too powerful to harness for delicate fine-tuning of economic activity.

SUMMARY

1. The historical behavior of GNP relative to M1 rules out the simple notion that velocity is fixed and unchanging. Although M2 velocity and M3 velocity are somewhat more stable historically, it is more important to concentrate on the predictability of velocity, rather than its stability.

2. Most statistical investigations of money demand lend credibility to the position that the demand for money, hence the behavior of velocity, is predictably related to economic activity and interest rates. Although innovations in technology and financial practices have confounded some of the historical regularities, there is reason to believe that a less cumbersome set of government regulations will mitigate the problem.

3. The impact of monetary policy on economic activity, as well as the associated time delays, is best illustrated by the results of econometric models. The main implication of both Monetarist models and the Federal Reserve's model is a rather substantial impact of money on GNP.

4. Fiscal policy has an impact on GNP, according to the models, but there is also evidence of significant crowding out. In particular, if government spending increases when the money supply is held constant, the rising rates of interest will cut off substantial amounts of private spending.

5. Interest rates increase and decrease with the rate of inflation. The relationship is not close enough, however, to negate the fact that increased money supply growth will lower short-term interest rates for a while (perhaps six months) before inflationary expectations take over.

6. Tight monetary policy and rising rates of interest have the most significant contractionary effects on residential construction. Consumer spending is also discouraged through a wealth effect of higher interest rates on stock and bond values. Business plant and equipment spending responds to higher interest rates with a significant delay.

Suggestions for Further Reading

A comprehensive empirical test of the alternative specifications of money demand is found in Stephen M. Goldfeld, "The Demand for Money Revisited," in *Brookings Papers on Economic Activity* (No. 3, 1973). For an overview of the consequences of financial and technological innovations for velocity and money demand, see Thomas D. Simpson and Richard D. Porter, "Some Issues Involving the Definition and Interpretation of Monetary Aggregates," in *Controlling Monetary Aggregates III*, Federal Reserve Bank of Boston (October 1980).

There are four excellent references on the Federal Reserve model: Frank de Leeuw and Edward M. Gramlich, "The Federal Reserve–MIT Econometric Model," *Federal Reserve Bulletin* (January 1968); Robert H. Rasche and Harold T. Shapiro, "The FRB-MIT Econometric Model: Its Special Features," *American Economic Review* (May 1968); Frank de Leeuw and Edward M. Gramlich, "The Channels of Monetary Policy: A Further Report on the Federal Reserve–MIT Model," *Journal of Finance* (May 1969); and Franco Modigliani, "Monetary Policy and Consumption," in *Consumer Spending and Monetary Policy* (Federal Reserve Bank of Boston, 1971). For an analytical update of the Fed model's interest rate picture, see Robert Anderson, Albert Ando, and Jared Enzler, "Interaction Between Fiscal and Monetary Policy and the Real Interest Rate," *American Economic Review* (May 1984). A detailed evaluation of monetary and fiscal policy multipliers in the Fed's model is found in "Structure and Uses of the MPS Quarterly Econometric Model of the United States," *Federal Reserve Bulletin* (February 1987).

The two best expositions of the St. Louis model are Leonall C. Andersen and Jerry Jordan, "Monetary and Fiscal Policy: A Test of Their Relative Importance in Economic Stabilization," Federal Reserve Bank of St. Louis *Review* (November 1968), and Leonall C. Andersen and Keith Carlson, "A Monetarist Model for Economic Stabilization," Federal Reserve Bank of St. Louis *Review* (April 1970). For a discussion of the pros and cons of the St. Louis Monetarist approach, once again see Alan Blinder and Robert Solow, "Analytical Foundations of Fiscal Policy," in *The Economics of Public Finance* (Washington, D.C.: Brookings Institution, 1974), especially pp. 63–78. For some political economy on this, see William L. Silber, "The St. Louis Equation: Democratic and Republican Versions and Other Experiments," *Review of Economics and Statistics* (November 1971).

A formal investigation of how interest rates reflect inflation is found in Eugene Fama, "Short Term Interest Rates as Predictors of Inflation," *American Economic Review* (June 1975). For a critique of that study, see John A. Carlson's "Comment," in *American Economic Review* (June 1977). Finally, for a surprising result on monetary policy and interest rates, see Frederick Mishkin, "Monetary Policy and Long-Term Interest Rates," *Journal of Monetary Economics* (January 1981).

FINANCIAL MARKETS AND INTEREST RATES

CHAPTER 26

Risk and Portfolio Choice

Risk is a double-edged sword: it complicates decision-making but makes things interesting. That is true of life in general and monetary-financial economics in particular. At this point we'll stick to the economic perspective, although the end of our chapter will hint at issues with broader appeal.

Our main concern is setting the framework for decisions regarding the allocation of wealth among alternative assets. This is what is meant by portfolio selection. In accountants' terminology, we will examine the balance sheet decisions of the individual. The most interesting elements concern how to choose among assets with varying degrees of risk. This will set the stage for the discussions in the next few chapters on the structure of credit flows and interest rates on various assets.

Before our foray into risky decision-making, however, it is useful to describe the financial sector without risk. It's certainly not the world as we know it, but it is a good point of departure.

A WORLD OF CERTAINTY

Without risk there are no disappointments. All plans proceed as conceived; all expectations are fulfilled; no promises are broken. Life is perfectly predictable, and so is the financial sector.

One person's promise to repay a loan is as good as anyone else's. No one is a welcher—not even your in-laws. Under such ideal conditions the same interest rate is applicable to each and every loan. Anyone trying to charge more will not succeed in making a loan; anyone charging less will be deluged with requests for funds. All promissory notes are perfect substitutes for each other; hence they must sell for the same price, which means they offer the same yield. Thus the interest rate is the same for all—it is the yield earned by lenders on a riskless loan, one that will be repaid in full by all borrowers, without a shadow of a doubt, at a designated time in the future.

Since this is a rather peculiar world, to say the least, it's worth asking whether there will be any borrowing or lending at all under such mythical conditions. The answer is yes, as long as individuals differ regarding the desired time patterns of their consumption. Those preferring instant gratification (IG) may want to consume more today than their current income, while prudent providers (PP) may want to consume less than their current income. The PPs lend to the IGs at the rate of interest. That rate is determined, in fact, by the balancing of the total demand for funds by the IGs with the total supply of funds from the PPs.

The rate of interest doesn't have anything to do with risk, because there isn't any. Rather, the interest rate influences people's consumption and investment decisions. If more people want to borrow—either to buy a new hat (consumption) or to build a new factory (real investment)—than want to lend, the rate of interest will be pushed up by the unsatisfied (and still-eager) borrowers. The rise in the rate of interest causes some to rethink their borrowing and spending plans, while others may decide to save and lend more; with a higher interest rate it pays to be a prudent provider. Thus the key decisions influenced by the rate of interest are consumption, saving, and investment.[1] There are no portfolio problems, because every financial asset is the same.

SOURCES OF UNCERTAINTY

At the very least, the world as we know it is rife with unanticipated disappointment. Borrowers, however well intentioned, may be simply

[1] The ideas in this discussion underlie the Classical school's interest rate theory described in Chapter 19.

unable to fulfill their promises to repay borrowed funds. Factories built to produce polyester fabrics may become obsolete because of renewed enchantment with natural fibers. The manufacturer who borrowed funds with every intention of repaying out of expected polyester sales cannot pay the promised interest and/or principal on the loan. Either event is called a default, and the lenders' expected return is either reduced or wiped out.

Default risk is associated with all promissory notes of individuals and private corporations. The obligations of the federal government, on the other hand, do not have that problem. Federal taxing power means that payment of interest and principal on federal obligations is never in doubt. There is, however, still another source of uncertainty affecting even the yields of default-free government securities: the risk of fluctuations in the level of the interest rate—sometimes called market risk or capital uncertainty.

A two-year government bond selling for its $1,000 face value and bearing an interest coupon of $60, payable at the end of each year, has an expected yield of 6 percent. There is no question that this bond will yield 6 percent if held to maturity. If you buy it you'll receive $60 per annum plus $1,000 at maturity. That's 6 percent, given the initial $1,000 outlay. But in our world of uncertainty, it's just possible that you will have to sell unexpectedly before maturity—say, at the end of one year. To whom do you sell? To someone else, to someone who wants to lend funds for one year (the original two-year bond now has one year to maturity). At what price? Aha! That's the big question. Can you get $1,000 for the bond, thereby realizing 6 percent, as expected? Not necessarily. It depends on the yield on newly issued one-year government securities. If the going rate of interest on one-year securities is 6 percent, the old bond sells for $1,000 and the yield is as expected. But if, for some reason, yields have risen to 7 percent, so that new bonds bear a coupon of $70 per $1,000, then you'll be offered less. In fact, you'll be offered about $990, or just enough to make the $60 coupon yield 7 percent to the new holder; that, after all, is the going rate of interest.

What has happened to the two-year government bond sold after one year? Instead of 6 percent, the expected yield to maturity, its actual yield turns out to be only 5 percent—the $60 coupon *minus* a capital loss of $10. The *holding-period yield* can be less than the original expected yield to maturity if the level of interest rates rises. Thus bonds that are sold before maturity have uncertain yields, even if all coupon payments are made on time and even if the face value is paid at maturity. And, in our uncertain world, it's not unlikely for bond-holders to need funds before their investments mature.

Still more uncertainty would be evident if we considered real interest rates rather than nominal yields. Government bonds do not promise payments in real goods and services, just nominal payments—a certain number of dollars. But let's ignore real yields for now, since we already have enough confusion, and examine the principles of portfolio choice under uncertainty.

Obviously there are many rates of interest on securities that differ with respect to maturity and issuer. More generally, securities have different expected yields and varying degrees of risk. How can or should these securities be combined under rational decisionmaking? We have already mentioned the principle of diversification in connection with financial intermediaries in Chapter 4. We are also familiar with its usage in everyday discussion. As we will see below, portfolio diversification is desirable under most circumstances and can be optimally designed given specific interrelationships between securities.

RISK AVERSION AND PORTFOLIO ANALYSIS

One of the most important *assumptions* of modern portfolio analysis is risk aversion. People are assumed to dislike risk. That doesn't mean they'll never indulge—they will if the price is right. And in the context of securities in a portfolio, the right price translates into a sufficiently high expected yield.

The simplest example illustrating risk aversion is the preference for a security that is certain to pay 5 percent compared with one having an equal chance of paying either 8 percent or 2 percent. The second security has an average return of 5 percent: about half the time its yield is 8 percent, and about half the time its yield is 2 percent. Its *expected* yield is 5 percent, where the formal definition of expectation is the sum of the possible outcomes multiplied by their respective probabilities: $8\% \times \frac{1}{2}$ plus $2\% \times \frac{1}{2} = 5\%$. Note that the *expected* yield is nothing more than the average yield.

Why does a risk averter prefer the certain return of 5 percent to an equal chance of 8 percent or 2 percent, even though the expected values of the two securities are identical? Simply put, with the risky security, the extra pleasure when the return is 8 percent is less than the additional pain when the return is 2 percent. Sound familiar? It should, because it's nothing more than diminishing marginal utility of money: each additional dollar is worth less (although you always want more!).

Would the risk averter ever be indifferent between a security paying a fixed yield with certainty, such as a 5 percent savings deposit in a commercial bank, and a bond whose return is uncertain? Yes, but only if the bond had a higher expected return to compensate for the undesirable uncertainty. For example, if the bond's equally probable outcomes were either 10 percent or 2 percent, so that the expected return would be 6 percent (10 percent $\times \frac{1}{2}$ plus 2 percent $\times \frac{1}{2} = 6$ percent), then our risk-averting portfolio manager might be indifferent. If the possible outcomes are 12 percent and 2 percent, so that the expected return is 7 percent, the manager might even prefer the risky venture, since the compensation in terms of higher expected yield might be enough to induce risk-taking. The required trade-off of higher return per unit of risk—the degree of risk aversion—is a subjective measure, quite different for every individual.

Does all this mean that someone who is not a risk averter must have deep-seated emotional problems? Not at all—he or she is simply a risk lover (also known as a compulsive-degenerate gambler). We observe that most people in the real world are risk averters, not because they tell us so in any direct way, but because most people hold diversified portfolios—many different securities rather than just one with the highest possible return. Diversification is the salvation of the risk averter, but mere child's play to the risk lover.

Before proceeding to the principles of diversification and portfolio selection, it is useful to note that we have used what is formally called a probability distribution to represent the outcomes of our financial investment. Each of the possible "events" (8 percent and 2 percent) has a probability of occurring ($\frac{1}{2}$ in our case), and the sum of the probabilities is unity (at least one of the possible outcomes must occur). Moreover, we have used a statistic called the arithmetic mean (the common average) to summarize the most likely outcome—the expected value. In this vein, we can try to specify more carefully the meaning of risk.

Uncertain outcomes make for risky investments. While the expected value of our equally probable 8 percent and 2 percent investment is 5 percent, sometimes the return will be 3 percent more than the mean (8 minus 5 is 3) and sometimes the return will be 3 percent less (2 minus 5 is -3). The deviation of actual returns from expected returns is a useful measure of risk. Formal statistical techniques suggest a slightly more complicated approach—just to terrorize the uninitiated. Deviations of actual outcomes from the mean can be either positive or negative. In fact, if one were to add them up, the pluses and minuses would cancel! We could apply either of two arithmetic operations to sum up the deviations and avoid the canceling problem: (1) take absolute values; (2) square the deviations (recalling that a negative number squared is a positive number). The second is used in calculating what is called the standard deviation, which we now describe in somewhat greater detail.

In addition to the magnitude of the deviation around the expected value, risk should also be related to the probability of such events actually occurring. Thus if the 2 percent outcome has only a 1 in 10 chance of actually occurring, this represents less of a risk than if it has a probability of $\frac{1}{2}$. In calculating the standard deviation, the squared deviations around the mean are "weighted" by their probabilities of occurring; that is, they are multiplied by their respective probabilities. This makes the standard deviation a still more intuitive measure of risk. The final step in the calculation is to restore the numbers to their original scale by taking the square root of the entire mess. In our example, we have the following: $(8 - 5)^2 \times \frac{1}{2} + (2 - 5)^2 \times \frac{1}{2} = 9 \times \frac{1}{2} + 9 \times \frac{1}{2} = 9$, the square-root of which is 3. In particular, for this investment the standard deviation of the probability distribution of returns is 3 percent. With a more complicated probability distribution, the numerical results are not quite so simple.

A potential drawback of the standard deviation is the use of both positive and negative deviations around the expected value. Shouldn't risk measure only the disappointments—that is, when actual outcomes are below expectations? That's a reasonable suggestion. But when the probability distribution is symmetrical above and below the mean, it makes no difference (below the mean is just half the total). Since there is evidence suggesting that security returns have this symmetry (they are normally distributed), and since the standard deviation has nice statistical properties (whatever that means), much of portfolio analysis uses the standard deviation to measure risk.

We are now prepared for one of the most fundamental propositions of modern portfolio theory:[2] An asset may seem very risky when viewed in isolation, but when combined with other assets, the risk of the portfolio may be substantially less—even zero! To illustrate this

[2]The original work on modern portfolio theory is Harry Markowitz, *Portfolio Selection* (New York: Wiley, 1959). Major extensions are summarized in William F. Sharpe, *Portfolio Theory and Capital Markets* (New York: McGraw-Hill, 1970).

we also consider the central problem of portfolio analysis: how to choose an efficient portfolio.

PORTFOLIO SELECTION

Take two assets (please). The first we'll call asset A for Adventure Inc. We're not quite sure what business they're in, but it's a good one. In good times it pays 16 percent and in bad times it pays 2 percent— clearly a cyclical industry. An expected return of 9 percent, but with fairly large uncertainty over the actual outcome, which varies directly with the pulse of economic activity. Now consider asset B for Badlands Inc. In good times they lose money, producing a return of minus 2 percent. But in bad times they rake it in, earning 12 percent for the misanthropic investors. The expected return is 5 percent, with substantial variance in the actual results. Note, however, that asset B's outcomes are countercyclical—they are better when the economy is worse.

Could it make sense to buy both of these highly risky investments— apparently exposing oneself to all sorts of disappointment? The answer is definitely yes. In fact, dividing your funds equally between assets A and B yields a return of 7 percent, in both good times and bad; there is no uncertainty at all.[3]

Does that mean I would definitely prefer the half-and-half combination to either A or B by itself? Well, I know I prefer it to B, because B's expected return is only 5 percent and it is uncertain at that, while the half-and-half portfolio gives me 7 percent and no risk. In this case, the risk averter clearly chooses the combination portfolio. Less clear is whether I would choose the fifty-fifty strategy or put all my money in A. While A has uncertainty, it also has a higher expected return (9 percent versus 7 percent). The choice of A versus the combination depends upon the precise nature of the risk averter's preferences— whether the extra 2 percent expected return compensates for the increase in risk.

The principal lesson derived from the example is twofold. First, the

[3]Here's the arithmetic: Start with $200. Put $100 in A and $100 in B. In "good times" A pays $16 (= 16 percent of $100) and B loses $2. The investor earns $14 ($16 minus $2) on $200 invested, or 7 percent ($\frac{14}{200}$). In "bad times" the $100 in A earns $2 while the $100 in B earns $12, for a total of $14, which is once again 7 percent. Note: The standard deviation of the returns on the half-and-half portfolio is zero, even though each security's return had a positive standard deviation.

uncertainty of return of an individual asset is *not* by itself a measure of its riskiness. Rather it is the contribution of the asset's uncertain return to total portfolio risk that matters. Second, a key determinant of the latter is the interrelationship between the variability of the assets' returns. This is so important it has a name of its own—covariance.[4]

In the example just given, assets A and B are perfectly negatively correlated: when asset A's realized yield is low, that of B is high, and vice versa; and the magnitudes are such that there is perfect offset. That's why combining the two reduces risk (in this case to zero). Indeed, this *is* the principal of portfolio diversification: hold a number of assets (rather than one), so that the exposure to risk is reduced. An asset such as B, whose returns are countercyclical (high when everything else is low), is an ideal addition to a risk averter's portfolio.

But assets such as B are relatively hard to come by. If portfolio diversification to reduce risk depended on finding assets with "negative covariance of returns," we'd be in for tough times (and lots of risk). But the magic of portfolio diversification extends to other cases as well. In particular, as long as assets do not have *precisely* the same *pattern* of returns, then holding a group of assets reduces risk.[5]

Take the case where each asset yields either 6 percent or 2 percent, but the outcomes are independent of goods times or bad times, *and of each other*, like the flip of a coin. Does dividing the portfolio between two such assets, X and Y, reduce risk? Well, if I hold both X and Y in equal amounts and *both* happen to yield 6 percent or both happen to yield 2 percent, I'm in the same situation as with holding just one.

[4]Covariance has a simple intuitive definition: comovement. It also has a precise mathematical measurement. In our case, the deviation of each security's return from its mean is derived; the product of the paired observations is then weighted (as in the standard deviation) by the probability of each of the paired observations actually occurring. Positive covariance indicates that when one security's return is above its mean, so is the other. Negative covariance indicates that when one security's return is above its mean, the other is below.

The term "correlation" used in the following sentence of the text also has specific mathematical connotation. It is the covariance divided by the product of the standard deviations. It rescales covariance so that *perfect* comovement is $+1.0$ and perfectly offsetting movement is -1.0, with intermediate relationships between these two extremes. A zero correlation means that the returns of the two securities are independent.

[5]The same pattern of returns translates into a correlation coefficient of $+1.0$ (the returns on all assets are above or below their respective means at the same time and are proportional to their standard deviations).

But it's also possible, in fact *just* as possible, that when X is yielding 6 percent, Y yields 2 percent, or when X yields 2 percent, Y yields 6 percent. In these cases, uncertainty is zero, because half my portfolio is in X and half is in Y, hence the return is the average—4 percent. In fact, if I hold many, many such assets, all with an equal chance of 6 percent or 2 percent, and the outcome of each one is *independent* of every other asset, then I am virtually certain of always earning 4 percent. About half of the outcomes will be 6 percent and half will be 2 percent.

You should recognize that the key condition in this last example is the word "independent." When asset returns are relatively independent (zero covariance), putting many together tends to produce the average return just about all of the time. Risk is thereby reduced to zero. Does that mean that most people who hold diversified portfolios have zero risk? No, it doesn't, because most assets are affected in a systematic way by economic conditions—hence most asset returns are not completely independent of each other. But as long as returns are not perfectly correlated, portfolio diversification reduces risk.

SOME IMPLICATIONS FOR FINANCIAL MARKETS

The examples of portfolio diversification just given permit some refinement in the first principles discussed earlier. The standard deviation of returns is a good measure of risk for analyzing a security by itself. It is also a good measure of risk for an entire portfolio. But it is a relatively poor measure of the risk contribution of a single security to an entire portfolio. That depends much more on the covariance of returns with other securities; more precisely, the *average covariance* of a security's returns with all others. The reason lies in the magic of diversification: the risk contribution to a portfolio of a security's returns that are substantially independent of all other returns is nearly zero. This *nonsystematic* risk is diversified away as the number of securities held increases (as in our coin flipping example). Only the *systematic* movement of the return on a security with all others adds to portfolio risk.

If most asset holders are risk averse, then it also follows that they will demand extra compensation—higher expected returns—in proportion to the systematic risk of a security. Thus investors will pay attention to a risky security only if it also promises to pay a higher expected yield.

This information is just about all the necessary preparation for describing the process of portfolio decision making. The first step is to separate *efficient* from *inefficient portfolios.* In our earlier example, asset B was ruled out because it had the same risk as the half-and-half portfolio (zero) but yielded less (5 percent versus 7 percent). A portfolio consisting only of asset B is inefficient. More generally, efficient portfolios have the following characteristics: greatest possible return for a given risk; lowest risk for a given return.

After calculating the various combinations of assets that produce efficient portfolios, investors choose that portfolio which matches their risk-return preferences. In our earlier example, we could not say whether asset A (yielding 9 percent with risk) dominated the half-and-half combination (yielding 7 percent and no risk). Both of these are efficient portfolios. Which is preferred depends upon the subjective trade-off between risk and return demanded by an individual.

Actually, the final choice of portfolio composition can be separated into two distinct decisions: first, derive the efficient combination of risky securities, and second, determine how much cash to hold versus the risky assets. We have already discussed the second issue in Chapter 20 under the demand for money. In Chapter 28 we discuss the choice among risky assets within the context of the structure of interest rates.

At this point, however, we can anticipate a fundamental fact of life in financial markets. Securities with a greater risk must offer investors higher expected yields. Or, looked at somewhat less charitably: if you want to earn a higher expected yield, you will have to accept greater risk. This result stems directly from risk-averse behavior by individual investors and their search among efficient portfolios for what suits them best. If a security that is more risky does not offer the opportunity to earn a higher expected yield, then investors will simply ignore it in constructing their preferred portfolio. The only way issuers of such securities can entice potential investors is to offer higher yields to compensate for the extra risk.

It is worth emphasizing that all our analysis holds only for risk averters. For risk lovers this has been a classroom exercise, useful primarily in preparation for the final exam. How many of you are really risk lovers? Although it sounds like an enjoyable avocation, fewer people than you think actually meet the standard.

The fact that most investors hold many financial assets supports the assumption of risk aversion. A risk lover would not find it sensible to hold a diversified portfolio. He or she chooses to invest in an asset with large possible capital gains (and losses, although the latter is usually put in parentheses). That doesn't necessarily mean that people won't gamble occasionally; putting down a dollar in a lottery for a one-in-two-million chance of winning a million dollars has some psychic appeal (the mere thought of winning is enough to make you buy two tickets). An occasional trip to Las Vegas—while not an appropriate risk-averter activity—has its other compensations. But when it comes to putting *all* your assets to work, would you take a fifty-fifty chance of doubling your money or losing it all? If your answer is no, you're a risk averter; if the answer is yes, you're a risk lover. If you are the former, then some of the principles of diversification suggested here can help in deciding on the assets you should place in your portfolio. If you are the latter, see you on the next junket to Vegas (bring all of your money and jewelry and clothes and whatever else you can muster up and join the ASCPA—Anonymous Spurner of Conventional Portfolio Analysis).

SUMMARY

1. In a world without risk there is no problem of portfolio choice; one asset is as good as any other. In fact, each and every asset offers the same yield.

2. Risk stems from uncertainty over the payments that will actually be received from investing in an asset. There are two sources of risk: (1) if the debtor defaults on principal or interest, actual payments will be less than promised; and (2) if an asset is sold before maturity, the price received may be less than expected. Both circumstances cause the actual yield on an asset to differ from what was expected.

3. Investors must, in general, be compensated for bearing risk. An investor will prefer an asset that always yields 5 percent to one that yields 5 percent *on average* but at any particular time may yield less or more. This preference is called risk aversion.

4. Risk-averse investors will try to combine securities in a portfolio in order to reduce risk. Such risk reduction through portfolio diversification occurs because the uncertain outcomes on each security can offset each other somewhat.

5. Do not judge the riskiness of a security by its own variability of possible outcomes. More important to a risk averter is whether the security's uncertain outcomes offset some of the risks on other securities in the portfolio.

6. Decisions about how to combine risky assets influence the structure of yields on securities. In particular, investors who want to earn higher yields on average will have to invest in more risky securities.

Suggestions for Further Reading

The seminal book by Harry Markowitz, *Portfolio Selection* (New York: Wiley, 1959), is still the best place to start. A leading text on investments is Edwin J. Elton and Martin J. Gruber, *Modern Portfolio Theory and Investment Analysis*, 3rd edition (New York: Wiley, 1987).

Flow of Funds Accounting: A Framework for Financial Analysis

Accounting gives off bad vibes. It is widely believed to be the world's dullest profession. Kids grow up wanting to be movie or rock stars but never accountants. This is unfortunate, because it is easier to be an accountant than a Diane Keaton or a Michael Jackson. Those jobs are already taken. It is also unfortunate because accounting is often more exciting than it looks (or so they say).

Flow of funds accounting is used to analyze borrowing and lending in financial markets. It traces financial transactions by recording the payments each sector makes to other sectors and the receipts it receives from them—just as a family might keep track of its money by recording all its payments and receipts.

Flow of funds accounting is useful in many ways. It provides a useful framework for analyzing what happens in various financial markets. It can also be thought of as tracing the financial flows that interact with and influence the "real" saving-investment process we discussed in Part 4. It records the maze of financial transactions underlying real saving and investment.

To appreciate all these implications, however, we will first have to learn what flow of funds accounting is all about. Specifically, it is a record of payments between and among various sectors. This is done via sector "sources and uses of funds" statements, which is what most of this chapter is devoted to explaining. You need not commit all the accounting details to memory; it will be sufficient to understand the main concepts that emerge. Let us begin by seeing how a typical sector "sources and uses" statement is constructed.

A GENERALIZED SECTOR INCOME STATEMENT

A sector "sources and uses of funds" statement is nothing more than the integration of its income statement with its balance sheet. Taking first things first, a simplified income statement, general enough to apply to any sector, would look something like the following:

(1) *A Generalized Income Statement for a Single Sector*

USES OF FUNDS (ON CURRENT ACCOUNT)	SOURCES OF FUNDS (ON CURRENT ACCOUNT)
Current Expenditures Saving (Addition to Net Worth)	Current Receipts

$$\Sigma = \Sigma$$

An income statement like the above merely lists a sector's current receipts during a period of time as a source (inflow) of funds, and its current expenditures as a use (outflow) of funds. Current receipts differ depending on which sector is involved; they consist mainly of wages and salaries for the household sector, sales receipts for the business sector, and tax revenues for the government. Similarly, the composition of current expenditures also differs, depending on which sector we are looking at.

In all cases, however, one sector's payments become another sector's receipts; for example, tax payments, a major *use* of funds for households and business firms, become tax receipts, a major *source* of funds for the government. As we shall see, it is this mutual interaction that gives the eventual flow of funds matrix its interlocking nature.

Saving, on the left-hand side, is defined as any excess of current receipts for a sector over and above its current spending. It is the same as our old definition of saving from Chapter 19: saving equals income minus consumer spending. When it involves the government sector it is usually called a budget surplus, and when applied to the business sector it is frequently labeled either retained earnings or addition to net worth. In any case, since it is defined as the difference between current receipts and current expenditures, it is the balancing entry on an income statement. Thus summation equality signs are at the bottom of income statement (1).

A GENERALIZED SECTOR BALANCE SHEET

Let us leave income statements for a moment and move over to balance sheets. Income statements show current receipts and expenditures over a *period* of time (say, during the year 1990), whereas a balance sheet shows not receipts and expenditures but assets and liabilities, and not over a period of time but at an *instant* in time (say, on December 31, 1990). A simplified balance sheet, general enough to apply to any sector, would look something like the following:

(2) *A Generalized Balance Sheet for a Single Sector*

ASSETS	LIABILITIES AND NET WORTH
Financial Assets	Liabilities
a. Money	
b. Other	
Real Assets	Net Worth

$$\Sigma = \Sigma$$

As with income statements, the principal difference between the balance sheets of different sectors is in the characteristic items that appear under each heading; consumer durable goods such as furniture and automobiles are typical real assets for consumers, inventories and capital equipment are typical real assets for business firms, and so on. Also like income statements, balance sheets must balance, in this case because the net worth entry is defined as the difference between total assets and total liabilities. Thus our simplified balance sheet also contains summation equality signs.

On the balance sheet above, assets are divided into two broad categories, real and financial. A *real* asset, like a car or a calculator, appears on only one balance sheet, that of its owner. A *financial* asset, however, like money or bonds, always appears on two balance sheets: that of whoever owns it (as an asset), and that of whoever owes it (as a liability). This is because every financial asset is a *claim* by someone against someone else—an IOU of some sort—like a government bond (an asset to whoever owns it, a liability of the government) or a bank deposit (again an asset to the owner, a liability of the bank).[1]

While only *financial* assets appear on two different balance sheets, *all* liabilities do, because all liabilities—by definition—represent debts owed to others. Thus any time a liability is listed on anyone's balance sheet, a corresponding financial asset must be rung up on some other balance sheet.

CONVERTING BALANCE SHEET STOCKS TO FLOWS: SAVING AND INVESTMENT

To analyze financial trends during a year, we need data on flows over a period of time, not stocks on a balance sheet at an instant in time. But all is not lost. We can convert balance sheet stocks (of goods or of money) into flows by comparing two balance sheets for the same sector, two balance sheets "snapped" at different times. For example, we can take the balance sheet of a household on December 31, 1990, and then again on December 31, 1991. By comparing them, and seeing what *changes* have taken place in each entry, we can translate stocks into flows: we can tell how much furniture was purchased or how much cash was accumulated *during the year* 1991.

Going back to our simplified balance sheet (2), let's take the bottom pair of entries, real assets and net worth—ignoring financial assets and liabilities for the time being—and see how we can convert those stock figures, snapped at a moment in time, into flows covering a period of time. The change (Δ) between two dates could be displayed like this:

---

[1]A complication arises in this connection with respect to corporate equities (corporate stocks), because they are financial assets to whoever holds them but are not, legally, liabilities of the issuing corporation. For most purposes, the simplest way to handle this is to assume that corporate stocks and bonds are roughly the same thing, despite their legal differences, and treat them both as liabilities of the corporation. (In other words, we ignore the problem.)

A related problem, which also remains unresolved, is that both bonds and stocks are traded on organized markets and change in price, so they may be valued differently by the holder and the issuing corporation. For example, a $100 bond issued by a corporation may rise in price to $120; to the holder it is now a $120 financial asset, but to the corporation it is still a $100 liability. The difference is capital gains to the bondholder, although the bondholder receives no funds inflow unless the bond is sold.

(3) *A Partial Sector Sources and Uses of Funds Statement,*
on Capital Account

USES OF FUNDS (ON CAPITAL ACCOUNT)	SOURCES OF FUNDS (ON CAPITAL ACCOUNT)
Δ Real Assets (Investment)	Δ Net Worth (Saving)

Since (3) is derived from only part of the balance sheet, it need not balance, so there are no summation equality signs at the bottom. Notice also that the column headings are different from those in (2): "Assets" and "Liabilities and Net Worth" have been replaced by "Uses of Funds" and "Sources of Funds," the same as in income statement (1). Now, however, they refer to uses and sources of funds on *capital* rather than current account—that is, to long-term uses and sources instead of short term ones.

On the uses side, the change in real assets refers to capital expenditures, as contrasted with an income statement's current expenditures. Capital expenditures involve the purchase of *real* assets with an expected useful life of a year or more; the term is synonymous with real investment spending (or simply *investment* spending), as we have been using that term throughout this book.[2] Such capital expenditures are not included in an income statement; in accordance with conventional accounting practice, income statements are confined to current expenditures—the purchase of assets with an expected useful life of less than a year.

A distinction has to be made between "investment" spending as economists use the word (it always refers to the purchase of *real* assets with a useful life of a year or more, like houses or machine tools), and the use of the word in general conversation, where it often refers to the purchase of *financial* assets, like stocks or bonds. When we say simply investment, we have reference to buying real assets; if we want to refer to the purchase of financial assets, we will say, explicitly, financial investment.

On the sources side, the change in a sector's net worth during the period is exactly the same thing as "saving" on its income statement covering that time interval. This deserves a word of explanation, since it is not immediately obvious (even though the fact that "saving" is frequently labeled "addition to net worth" should provide a clue that they are one and the same). On a balance sheet, net worth is defined as equal to a sector's total assets minus its total liabilities. A change

---

[2]Real investment can be recorded on either a net or gross basis, depending on whether or not depreciation is deducted from original value.

in net worth must therefore equal any change in total assets less any change in total liabilities. On an income statement, in contrast, saving refers to an excess of current receipts over current expenditures. But any excess of current receipts over current expenditures (flows) must imply a resulting buildup of total assets or a reduction of liabilities, or some combination of the two. Conclusion: Saving on a sector's income statement must become an equivalent change in net worth on its balance sheet.

Put somewhat differently, as a "use" of funds on current account (on the income statement), saving means *not* spending. It means retention or accumulation. As such, it represents an addition to one's wealth or net worth and becomes available as a "source" of funds for capital account.[3]

Since statement (3) is derived from only part of the balance sheet and thus does not have to balance, it follows that an individual unit or sector may or may not invest (that is, buy capital goods) just equal to its current saving. It may save more than it invests, or invest more than it saves. If a unit or sector invests an amount equal to its current saving it is called a balanced budget sector. If it saves more than it invests it is called a surplus sector, and if it invests more than it saves it is called a deficit sector.[4] (Read this paragraph again—these will be useful concepts later on.)

How could a sector invest more than it saves? One way is simply by borrowing enough to finance its deficit, which brings us to the other pair of balance sheet entries—liabilities and financial assets.

CONVERTING BALANCE SHEET STOCKS TO FLOWS: BORROWING, LENDING, AND HOARDING

So far we have ignored the possibility of changes in liabilities and financial assets, the remaining entries on (2), our generalized sector balance sheet. Such changes between two balance sheet dates would look like this:

---

[3]As with investment, saving can be measured on a net or a gross basis, depending on whether or not depreciation is deducted. It should be noted that even if depreciation is deducted, so that saving is measured on a net basis, depreciation will still be a source of funds for capital account, since it represents a noncash "expense" rather than an actual current outlay of funds.

[4]Alternatively, a surplus unit is one that spends (on consumption plus real investment) *less* than its current income, and a deficit unit is one that spends *more* than its current income.

(4) *A Partial Sector Sources and Uses of Funds Statement, on Capital Account*

USES OF FUNDS (FINANCIAL, ON CAPITAL ACCOUNT)	SOURCES OF FUNDS (FINANCIAL, ON CAPITAL ACCOUNT)
Δ Financial Assets Other Than Money (Lending) Δ Money (Hoarding)	Δ Liabilities (Borrowing)

Since (4), like (3), is derived from only partial balance sheets, it need not balance and thus contains no summation equality signs. But whereas (3) dealt with nonfinancial or "real" sources and uses of funds, (4) is concerned with *financial* transactions—with *borrowing* (an increase in outstanding liabilities) as a source of funds, and with *lending* (an increase in holdings of financial assets other than money) and *hoarding* (increased money holdings) as uses of funds.

Strictly speaking, we should separate short-term financial transactions from long-term, comparable to our distinction between short- and long-term spending on real assets. However, in flow of funds accounting such distinctions are rarely made with respect to financial transactions, and all borrowing and lending, regardless of duration, are typically considered as on capital account.

The three possibilities in (4)—borrowing, lending, and hoarding—do not exhaust all the potential financial sources or uses of funds open to a sector. For instance, another possible financial *source* of funds, in addition to borrowing, is selling some holdings of financial assets. Still another source of funds is *dis*hoarding. And an additional possible *use* of funds would be to repay one's debts. These alternatives do not appear on (4) because only *net* changes are considered there, and it is implicitly assumed that they are all positive.

By convention, if the net change in any entry turns out to be negative over a period, it is kept on the side where it presently appears in (4) but preceded by a minus sign. If the net change in financial assets for a sector turns out to be minus—for example, as when a person liquidates some government bonds—it would be recorded on the uses side but preceded by a minus sign and referred to as a negative use of funds. But a negative use is actually a source of funds—aha! Another useful concept.

A COMPLETE SECTOR SOURCES AND USES OF FUNDS STATEMENT

Believe it or not, if we string together everything we've done so far we will have before us, in all its pristine glory, a complete sector sources and uses of funds statement. Lo and behold:

(5) = (1) + (3) + (4) *A Complete Sector Sources and Uses of Funds Statement*

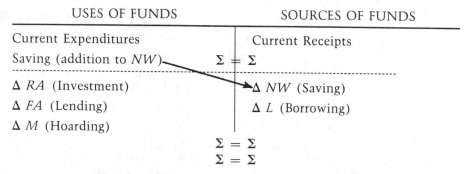

USES OF FUNDS	SOURCES OF FUNDS
Current Expenditures	Current Receipts
Saving (addition to *NW*) $\Sigma = \Sigma$	
$\Delta\ RA$ (Investment)	$\Delta\ NW$ (Saving)
$\Delta\ FA$ (Lending)	$\Delta\ L$ (Borrowing)
$\Delta\ M$ (Hoarding)	
	$\Sigma = \Sigma$
	$\Sigma = \Sigma$

Above the dashed line is the income statement, below the dashed line the changes in the balance sheet. Since the income statement must balance, as must the changes in the balance sheet, the summation of all the sources must equal the summation of all the uses of funds, and therefore we have summation equality signs all over the place.

We are now able to define more precisely what we mean by a sector's sources and uses of funds:

Sources of funds consist of (a) *current receipts;* (b) any *increase in a liability* item (borrowing); or (c) any *decrease in an asset* item (selling off assets, dishoarding).

Uses of funds consist of (a) *current expenditures;* (b) any *increase in an asset* item—increased holdings of real assets (investment), of financial assets (lending), or of money (hoarding); or (c) any *decrease in a liability* item (debt repayment).

We could simplify (5) by eliminating current receipts from sources and current expenditures from uses, taking only the difference between them—saving—as a source of funds (if positive, or as a use if negative). That is what we have, in effect, if we look only below the dashed line (which is the way the flow of funds accounts are published by the Federal Reserve).

The requirement that everything below the dashed line must bal-

"I called in you people from Accounting because I wanted to ask you if you're having fun."

Drawing by Weber; © 1978 The New Yorker Magazine, Inc.

ance means that each sector's investing + lending + hoarding must equal its saving + borrowing. As we know, however, a sector might save more than it invests (a surplus sector) or invest more than it saves (a deficit sector). If it does have a discrepancy between its saving and its investing, this necessarily implies a corresponding differential between its *financial* sources and uses of funds. To be more specific: a surplus sector, with saving greater than investment, *must* dispose of its surplus by lending, repaying debts, or hoarding (building up its cash holdings) in an amount equal to its surplus. And a deficit sector, with investment in excess of its saving, *has to* finance its deficit by borrowing, selling off financial assets, or dishoarding (running down its cash holdings) in an amount equal to its deficit.[5]

These conclusions flow from the fact that below the dashed line, as well as above it, the sum of all a sector's uses of funds must equal the sum of all its sources. Putting the same thing rather formally:

For any one sector:

investment + lending + hoarding = saving + borrowing

So if:

saving > investment, then lending + hoarding > borrowing

[5]A deficit sector might also finance its deficit by issuing new money. However, only two sectors are legally able to exercise that unique option—banks (by creating demand deposits) and the government (by creating dollar bills). If they did so, it would be entered on their statement (5) as an increase in their liabilities (borrowing), because while money is an asset to whoever owns it, it is a liability of whoever issues it.

And if:

investment > saving, then borrowing > lending + hoarding

THE FLOW OF FUNDS MATRIX FOR THE WHOLE ECONOMY

Early in this chapter we said that flow of funds accounting records payments between and among sectors via sector sources and uses of funds statements. Since one sector's payments become another sector's receipts, when we put all these individual sector statements together we get a flow of funds *matrix* for the economy as a whole, an interlocking grid that reveals financial relationships among all the sectors. When the flow of funds matrix was first published by the Federal Reserve in 1955, it contained the complete statements for each sector in the form of statement (5) above. Since 1959, however, it has consisted of only partial sector sources and uses statements, namely that part of (5) below the dashed line. Current receipts and current expenditures are not shown explicitly, but they are implicitly included in that the difference between them—saving (or dissaving)—is there.

Assuming a total of three sectors and omitting some detail, the flow of funds matrix appears essentially as follows:

(6) Flow of Funds Matrix for the Whole Economy

	Sector A		Sector B		Sector C		All Sectors	
	U	S	U	S	U	S	U	S
Saving (ΔNW)		s		s		s		S
Investment (ΔRA)	i		i		i		I	
Borrowing (ΔL)		b		b		b		B
Lending (ΔFA)	l		l		l		L + H	
Hoarding (ΔM)	h		h		h			
	$\Sigma = \Sigma$		$\Sigma = \Sigma$		$\Sigma = \Sigma$		$\Sigma = \Sigma$	

NOTE: The small letters within the matrix represent the data for sector saving (s), investment (i), borrowing (b), lending (l), and hoarding (h), and are placed in the appropriate space where such data would be entered. The capital letters similarly represent the aggregate sum totals for the whole economy. Thus $s + s + s = S$, $i + i + i = I$, etc. (Roman "U" and "S" represent uses and sources of funds.)

This matrix is nothing more than the placing of the sector sources and uses statements side by side, each in the form of that part of (5) below the dashed line. The resulting matrix forms an interlocking self-contained system, showing the balanced sources and uses of funds for each sector, interrelations among the sectors, and the aggregate totals of saving, investment, borrowing, lending, and hoarding for the economy as a whole.

For each individual sector, as we know, its investment + lending + hoarding must equal its saving + borrowing. Since that is true for each individual sector, it is also true in summation for all the sectors taken together, that is, for the economy as a whole.

In addition, something else is true for the economy as a whole which need not be true for any one sector taken by itself: *Saving must equal investment.* (Haven't we met that one somewhere before?) We developed that relationship in "real" terms in Chapters 19 and 20, and now here it is again, emerging this time from the financial side:

For the whole economy:

investment + lending + hoarding = saving + borrowing

But since one sector's financial asset is another sector's liability:

lending + hoarding = borrowing

Therefore:

investment = saving

The conclusion that saving must equal investment applies only to the entire economy taken in the aggregate, not to any single sector taken by itself. As we have seen, any single sector may save more than it invests, or invest more than it saves. But since saving must equal investment for the economy as a whole, it follows that for each sector that saves more than it invests there must, somewhere, be other sectors that invest correspondingly more than they save.[6]

The economic function of financial markets, after all, is to provide channels through which the excess funds of surplus units (whose

[6]This is true not only because the economy-wide total of saving must equal investment, but also because a surplus sector must dispose of its surplus, as we have seen, by lending, repaying debts, or hoarding an amount equal to its surplus. This in turn implies the existence of deficit sectors to borrow, reduce their financial assets, or dishoard.

Similarly, deficit sectors, which invest more than they save, necessarily imply the existence of surplus sectors. A deficit sector must finance its deficit by borrowing, selling off financial assets, or dishoarding. This in turn implies the presence of surplus sectors to do the lending, buying of the securities, or hoarding.

saving exceeds their investment) can be transferred to potential deficit units (who want to invest more than they are saving). The flow of funds matrix enables us to trace these transactions and see how various spending flows are financed.

SUMMARY

1. Flow of funds accounting combines sector income statements and balance sheets to construct sector sources and uses of funds statements.

2. Any one sector can save more or less than it invests and lend more or less than it borrows. One that saves more than it invests is called a surplus sector: it is likely to be a net lender. One that invests more than it saves is called a deficit sector: it is likely to be a net borrower.

3. For the whole economy, however, saving must equal investment and lending plus hoarding must equal borrowing.

4. The flow of funds matrix for the whole economy is an interlocking grid of sector sources and uses statements. It shows borrowing and lending relationships between and among all the sectors. By examining it we can analyze who lent to whom and who borrowed from whom.

Suggestions for Further Reading

The best source of information on the actual construction of the accounts is *Introduction to Flow of Funds* (Board of Governors of the Federal Reserve System, June 1980). Also see A. D. Bain, "Flow of Funds Analysis," *Economic Journal* (December 1973). The usefulness of the flow of funds is exemplified by James S. Earley, Robert J. Parsons, and Fred A. Thompson, *Money, Credit, and Expenditure: A Sources and Uses of Funds Approach* (New York University, Center for the Study of Financial Institutions Monograph, No. 3, 1976).

The Structure of Interest Rates

Burt Reynolds is not easily ruffled. He is hardly ever caught off guard. But once, while he was at one of those swinging dinner parties in Washington (actors campaigning for politicians), he met his one-time economics instructor, Dr. Mark Etz. Reynolds was standing in the corner, surveying the scene, when Etz walked up to him, puffing on his ever-present pipe, and said: "Young man, I've just realized something. There are more interest rates out there than hairs on your chest." Reynolds was dumfounded. He could hardly believe his ears. He had always thought there was only one—*the* interest rate that Etz had talked about all term long.

To make sure you won't be caught in equally embarrassing circumstances, we now take note of the many different interest rates on various types of financial instruments. The structure of yields on different maturities of the *same* class of securities is explored first. We then turn to the relationship between yields on different categories of securities (such as government bonds versus corporate bonds). Along the way, we describe how taxes, marketability, and other "special effects" influence the structure of rates.

THE TERM STRUCTURE OF RATES AND THE YIELD CURVE

The relationship between yields on different maturities of the same type of security is called the *term structure* of interest rates (from "term to maturity"). For government bonds we might compare the yields on three-month Treasury bills, two-year notes, and twenty-year bonds.

The relationship between yield and maturity is sometimes depicted graphically by a *yield curve,* as in Figure 1, where yield is measured on the vertical axis and term to maturity is on the horizontal axis. Often the yield curve is upward sloping—that is, short-term securities yield less than long-term securities (curve *A*). Sometimes it is rather flat—short-term yields equal long-term yields (curve *B*). And sometimes the yield curve is even downward sloping—short-term interest rates are *above* long-term rates (curve *C*).

What determines the shape of the yield curve? A number of analytical explanations have been proposed, ranging from the application of basic supply and demand to more complicated theories based on expectations and preferred maturity ranges of different investors. Each ap-

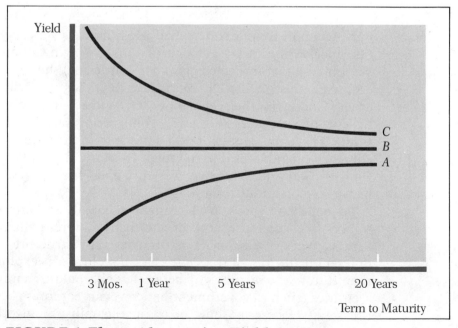

FIGURE 1 Three Alternative Yield Curves

proach is aimed at explaining real world observations, such as why yields on all maturities tend to move together while at the same time there are distinct divergent patterns between movements in short-term and long-term yields. First we will develop the alternative theories of the term structure, and then we will describe how they best explain actual events.

Supply and Demand. Just about everything in economics is determined by supply and demand, and the term structure of interest rates should be no exception. Back in Chapter 6 we showed how the overall level of interest rates was determined by the supply of and demand for loanable funds or, alternatively, by the supply of and demand for securities as a whole. A simple extension of that approach suggests that the interest rates on different maturity categories of securities are determined by the relative supply of and demand for each maturity class. For example, the interest rate on three-month Treasury bills is determined by the supply of and demand for three-month Treasury bills, while the interest rate on twenty-year bonds is determined by the supply of and demand for twenty-year bonds. Thus, when the supply of three-month bills goes up, the yield on bills rises to induce investors to buy the additional supply; when the supply of bills falls, the yield on bills falls to ration the smaller supply among eager investors.[1] If nothing happens to the supply of and demand for twenty-year bonds, these shifts change the relationship between yields on securities of different maturity; that is, the term structure of interest rates changes.

Although there is much to be said in favor of supply and demand in general, there are severe limitations to using that approach by itself to explain the term structure of interest rates. The problem is that supply and demand analysis focuses attention on the particular market in question, such as three-month Treasury bills, and deals with other markets, such as twenty-year securities, as an afterthought. When there is a close relationship between two markets, as there is in the case of different maturities of the same security, it is perhaps more useful to focus on the interrelationships more directly. Thus instead of treating the maturity structure of interest rates from the vantage point of supply and demand in separate markets, we examine the relationships among securities within the framework of a single market.

The Pure Expectations Approach. There are many—and here fi-

---

[1] Do not be confused by the fact that a decrease in supply causes yields to fall; yields decline because the decrease in supply raises security *prices* and prices and yields are inversely related.

nancial analysts and economists often find much common ground—who argue that short-term securities and long-term securities are very good substitutes for each other in investor portfolios, not for every investor but for enough so that their decisions *collectively* make a significant impact on the market. For such investors the important feature of the security they buy is not the maturity date of the final payment, but rather what it yields over the period for which they want to invest (also called the "holding period" yield).[2] This implies that expectations of future short-term rates determine how long-term rates are related to short-term rates. Let's illustrate that with a particular example.

Say you are the portfolio manager of a bank and you want to invest funds for two years. Suppose you could buy a one-year Treasury security today yielding 8 percent, and you expect that next year the rate on one-year securities will be 10 percent. If you buy the one-year security today and reinvest in a one-year security next year, you expect an average return over the two years of about 9 percent. If you had the option of buying a *two-year* Treasury security today that yielded $9\frac{1}{2}$ percent, you'd jump at it (so would everyone else). On the other hand, if two-year Treasury securities were yielding only $8\frac{1}{2}$ percent, you wouldn't touch them (neither would anyone). This means that unless the two-year security yielded exactly 9 percent (the average of the current and expected short-term rate), portfolio managers would try to buy it (if it yielded more) or sell it (if it yielded less). This buying and selling pressure by portfolio managers maintains the long-term rate as an average of the current short-term rate and the expected future short-term rate.[3]

A somewhat more general statement is as follows: the relationship between the yield on a two-year (long-term) security and a one-year (short-term) security depends on the expected future short-term rate. If next year's *expected* short-term rate is above the current short-term rate, then the current long-term rate will be above the current short-term rate and the yield curve will be upward sloping. On the other

[2]See Chapter 5 for a definition of holding period yield that is especially simple, in particular, the case of a zero-coupon bond. Our discussion of term structure theory is, in fact, strictly applicable only to the term structure on zero-coupon bonds. And that is because the maturity of a bond is an unambiguous concept only for zero-coupon securities. For coupon-bearing bonds the proper concept is duration. See the Appendix for a complete discussion.

[3]In Chapter 33 we discuss futures markets for Treasury securities. These institutions provide additional investment opportunities for portfolio managers. It turns out that prices in the futures market mirror the implicit interest rates discussed here.

hand, if next year's expected short-term rate is below the current short-term rate, the yield curve will be downward sloping.[4]

The key to this "expectations" theory of the term structure is that short-term securities and long-term securities are very good substitutes for each other in investor portfolios. In fact, they are perfect substitutes: if expected "holding period" yields are the same, the portfolio manager is indifferent between "shorts" and "longs." Instead of separate markets for short-term and long-term securities, there is a single market. Note in this case that if the supply of long-term securities goes up and the supply of short-term securities goes down, it makes absolutely no difference as far as yields are concerned. Because investors are indifferent among maturity categories of the same security, they will happily exchange long-term securities for short-term securities, with no change in yields, as long as expected future short-term rates are unchanged.

The Liquidity Premium Modification. It is difficult to argue that investors are unconcerned about differences between short-term securities and long-term securities. It is simply a fact of life—embedded in the mathematics of bond prices—that the *prices* of long-term securities are more volatile than those of short-term securities (see Chapter 5). If you have to sell a security before it reaches maturity and interest rates have increased, a long-term security will have fallen in price much more than a short-term one. If you might have to sell to raise cash, you'll prefer short-term securities. They are safer. Commercial banks, for example, prefer short-term securities precisely because their needs for cash are often unpredictable.

Recognition of the greater capital uncertainty of long-term securities leads to the "liquidity premium" modification in the expectations theory of the term structure. If most investors are like commercial banks and prefer the capital certainty of short-term securities, while most bond issuers prefer to issue long-term securities, then investors on balance will demand a premium for holding long-term securities.

---

[4]The story of the downward sloping yield curve is as follows. If the current one-year rate is 8 percent and investors expect next year's one-year rate to be 6 percent, portfolio managers could earn an average return of 7 percent by investing in two successive one-year securities. If the current rate on a two-year security were above 7 percent all investors would buy it, forcing up the price and reducing the yield. If the current two-year rate were below 7 percent, no one would buy it, forcing down the price and raising the yield. Thus the two-year security must yield 7 percent when the current one-year security yields 8 percent and the expected one-year rate is 6 percent. Since the short-term (one-year) rate is 8 percent and the long-term (two-year) rate is 7 percent, we have exactly what we call a downward sloping yield curve.

This is often called a liquidity premium, but it is really a *risk* premium—a reward for exposure to the capital uncertainty of long-term securities. Thus in our previous numerical example a two-year security would have to yield more than the average of the current one-year rate and next year's expected one-year rate. Otherwise investors wouldn't want to hold the riskier two-year security.

The Preferred Habitat Approach. It seems reasonable to suggest that many investors prefer short-term securities. But to leave it at that would be misleading, because some investors actually have a *preference* for long-term securities. Life insurance companies and pension funds, for example, don't worry that much about surprising needs for cash. Their liabilities are actuarially predictable. In fact, they want to make sure they earn at least 8 (or 10 or 12) percent on their assets over the next ten (or twenty or thirty) years. That way they are sure of a profit—because they promise to pay pension holders something less than that. These institutions therefore prefer long-term securities.

Because some institutions prefer long-term securities while others prefer short-term issues (like members of the animal kingdom, they have preferred habitats), it would seem that the supply-demand emphasis in explaining the term structure could make a healthy comeback. For example, when the supply of five-year securities increases relative to other maturities, the yield on such issues will have to increase above the "expectations theory average" in order to induce investors to leave their preferred maturity ranges and to invest in the unfamiliar "five-year" territory. The same would be true for any increased supply of a particular maturity category. Thus the yields on various maturities would seem to have relatively little to do with expectations, and much more to do with relative supply and demand.

Not so fast, say the proponents of the expectations theory. While many institutions have preferred maturity ranges for their investments, they can also be induced rather easily to switch between short-term securities and long-term securities when yields get out of line with expectations. Commercial banks, for example, require only a "liquidity premium" to invest in longer-term securities. A large increase in the supply of five-year bonds may therefore initially push up their yield to a higher level than is warranted by the expectations theory alone. But commercial banks will then be lured away from their preferred one-year securities by the attractive yields on five-year bonds. And pension funds will be enticed as well. Both these actions mitigate the upward pressure on five-year bond yields caused by the increased supply of securities in that maturity category. In the process, the role of expectations is restored.

Real World Observations. Each of the theories outlined above is aimed at explaining the real world. We started with the pure expectations approach and then modified it to make the theory conform more closely to reality. A further step is to recognize that investors do not usually have precise numerical predictions of short-term rates for next year or the year after. More likely, investors form expectations of when the "level" of rates is in general relatively high and when the "level" of rates is in general relatively low. While this is a rather casual version of the expectations theory, it provides a powerful explanation of when the yield curve is likely to be upward sloping (curve *A* in Figure 1) or downward sloping (curve *B*).

When interest rates are high relative to what they have been, investors generally expect them to decline in the future. Falling interest rates mean rising bond prices, and those investors who are holding long-term bonds in their portfolio will reap their just reward—big capital gains. Therefore, when all rates are relatively high, investors will prefer to hold long-term securities rather than short-term securities (because the potential capital gains on short-term securities are relatively low). This additional demand for long-term securities drives their prices up and their yields down, relative to short-term securities. Thus long-term yields are below short-term yields (that is, the yield curve is downward sloping) when the overall level of rates is high.

Similarly, when the general level of rates is low and yields are expected to rise in the future, investors prefer not to hold long-term securities because they are likely to incur large capital losses. This drives the price of long-term securities down (and the yield up), thereby producing long-term rates above short-term rates (an upward sloping yield curve).

Chart 1 illustrates the accuracy of these conjectures with yield curves during the mid-1970s, a particularly illustrative period. The actual yield curve on August 30, 1974, was downward sloping, and that's when the overall "level" of rates was quite high by then-current historical standards. On the other hand, the most sharply upward sloping curve is for January 23, 1976, when the "level" of rates was relatively low.

Chart 1 also emphasizes another empirical regularity: short-term rates fluctuate more than long-term rates over the course of the business cycle. Indeed, over the sixteen-month period covered by the yield curves, short-term rates fluctuated by about five percentage points, while twenty-year bond yields hardly moved at all. The simple expectations theory provides the best explanation for this phenomenon: since long-term rates are averages of current short-term rates and ex-

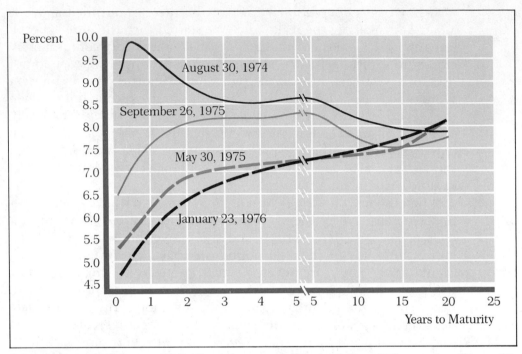

CHART 1 Yields on U.S. Government Securities. When the "Level" of Rates Is High, the Yield Curve Is Likely to Be Downward Sloping

pected future short-term rates, as long as expectations are less volatile than actual short-term rate movements, long-term rates will move less than short-term rates.[5]

There is some empirical evidence lending credibility to the liquidity premium modification to the expectations theory of the term structure. In particular, over long periods of time, the yield curve tends to be upward sloping more often than it is downward sloping. Under the pure expectations theory this should not happen. After all, there is no

[5]Expected future short-term rates move less than current short-term rates as long as people view some of the influences on interest rates as temporary events—for example, a temporary slowdown in economic activity. The arithmetic of the rate movements is as follows: we saw earlier in the chapter that if the one-year rate were 8 percent and the expected one-year rate next year were 10 percent, then two-year rates would be 9 percent. If the one-year rate jumped to 12 percent and the expected one-year rate rose to 11 percent, then the equilibrium long-term rate would be $11\frac{1}{2}$ percent (the average of 12 and 11). Thus, when the short-term rate jumped by 4 percentage points, the long-term rate rose by only $2\frac{1}{2}$ percentage points. And that is what we said in the text: short-term rates fluctuate more than long-term rates.

reason to think that expected future short-term rates are usually above current short-term rates—and that's the only thing that would explain this phenomenon according to the pure expectations approach. But once a liquidity premium is added to the story, long-term rates exceed the average of the current short-term rate and expected future short-term rates. This implies an upward sloping yield curve more of the time.

A final observation comes from market participants. Most practitioners would stress that over the very short run, large supplies in a specific maturity range would raise the interest rate on that particular category of security. Such anecdotal evidence supports the supply/demand or preferred habitat approach to the term structure of interest rates. In point of fact, in the very short run (such as over a week or two), there is little doubt that relative supplies of securities must be brought into the picture. After all, it takes time for the expectations-based substitution between short-term and long-term securities to occur. But after all is said and done, and all portfolio adjustments have been completed, the impact of relative supplies is swamped by expectations of future short-term rates.[6]

To summarize: The best approach to the term structure is ecumenical. The expectations theory forms the foundation; liquidity premiums then enter as a permanent modification to the yield curve; and finally, over short periods of time, even relative supplies of securities have an impact.

THE ROLE OF TAXES AND MARKETABILITY

We could continue with more details on the term structure relationship. But we've gone about as far as we should without recognizing that nicely shaped curves such as those drawn in Figure 1 and Chart 1 hardly ever occur in nature. Not that the yield curve for any of the dates listed in Chart 1 is wrong. It's just that the yield curve depicts the relationship between yield and maturity, and there are other factors that influence yields—even on a relatively homogeneous group of securities such as government bonds.

There are many different issues of government bonds, and each one differs in some respect (besides maturity) from the others. Some have

---

[6]For empirical support for this view, see Michael J. Hamburger and William L. Silber, "Debt Management and Interest Rates: A Reexamination of the Evidence," *The Manchester School of Economic and Social Studies* (December 1971).

coupons of 4 percent, others of 14 percent. Some are accepted at par (face value) in payment of estate taxes, even though they are selling well below par. Let's first review the role of taxes in explaining yield differentials and then turn to marketability, the second part of the story.

Prior to the Tax Reform Act of 1986, capital gains were treated differently from ordinary income as far as taxes were concerned. If you bought a 7 percent–coupon $1,000 bond for $900 (because yields had increased above 7 percent) and held it to maturity, you would pay the regular income tax rate on the $70 coupon payment each year but would pay a lower capital gains tax on the appreciation in the price of the bond (from $900 to $1,000). Thus, part of the yield to maturity on the bond would be subject to favorable capital gains tax treatment. Investors would prefer bonds that were selling at a discount (those with coupons below the current level of interest rates) to bonds selling at par or above par (those with higher coupons than the current level of rates), because after taxes investors were better off with the discount bonds. This meant, of course, that investors would pay a somewhat higher price for discount bonds, thereby reducing their yields compared with bonds selling at or above par. The normal state of affairs prior to 1986, therefore, was for government bonds selling at prices below par to have lower yields to maturity than government bonds with similar maturities that sold at or above par.

A second tax-related factor accounting for yield differentials on government securities with identical maturity is the special estate tax treatment accorded certain government bonds. Until the early 1960s the federal government issued bonds that could be tendered at par to settle estate taxes. Most of these bonds had low coupons compared with subsequent yields in the marketplace. For example, the $3\frac{1}{2}$ per-cent–coupon government bonds due in 1995 can be used at par to settle estate taxes. Since the level of interest rates has been well above $3\frac{1}{2}$ percent, these bonds have sold at a discount from par. Under such circumstances these "flower bonds," as they are irreverently called, are in special demand by elderly wealthy people. Because of this special demand, flower bonds have had lower yields to maturity than bonds of similar maturity.

Differences in yield to maturity on government bonds with the same maturity can also be traced to differences in the marketability of spe-cific issues. The most recently issued government bonds in each matu-rity range, often referred to as the "current coupon" issue, are usually the most actively traded securities in the secondary market. Although we discuss the details of marketability in the next chapter, it is sufficient to recognize that government securities dealers are most willing to buy and sell the most recently issued securities, so that investors can count on finding a ready market for these issues in case they want to alter their existing portfolios. Because these "current coupon" issues are highly marketable, they carry somewhat lower yields to maturity than the older so-called "off the run" issues.

Although the term structure of interest rates is frequently considered the dominant force accounting for yield differentials among government securities, taxes and marketability play a significant role as well. Ignoring these special effects will not only cause confusion but could be quite costly if actual portfolio decisions were at stake.[7]

YIELDS ON CORPORATES, MUNICIPALS, AND MORTGAGES

We've just seen that government securities of the *same* maturity can have different yields because of tax and marketability considerations. Once we step away from the safety of governments, default risk plays an even more important role in explaining yield relationships. Indeed, for lack of a better name, this is often called the risk structure of interest rates, even though other factors besides the relative risk of default come into play. We'll take a look at the relationship between yields on governments, corporates, municipals, and mortgages, staying away from term structure influences by looking at long-term bonds only.

As with term structure theory, a straightforward supply-demand analysis can be tried in explaining yield relationships. For example, as the supply of corporate bonds rises relative to, say, governments, the yield on corporates should increase. But as with the term structure, a simplistic supply-demand approach ignores important relationships between these markets that dominate the yield structure. In particular, because all bonds are substitutes for each other in investor portfolios,

[7]There is an additional complication associated with yield relationships among securities of identical maturity. Although bonds with the same maturity have the same date for the final payment of principal, different coupons alter the "effective maturity" of each bond. For example, a 10 percent–coupon five-year bond returns a larger fraction of the investment before maturity than a 5 percent–coupon five-year bond. The "effective maturity" of a bond is calculated in a special way and is called duration. See the Appendix to this chapter for a more complete discussion.

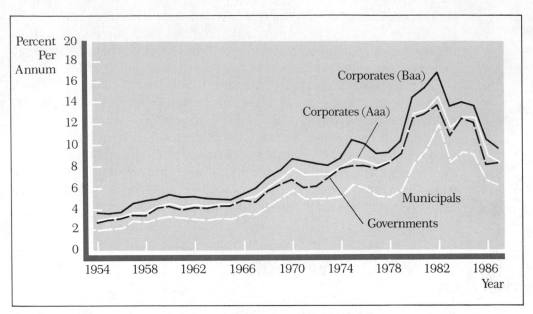

CHART 2 Riskier Securities Carry Higher Yields

as soon as one yield begins to rise relative to others, investors switch into that security. This substitution process holds down the widening yield differentials among securities.

In fact, when you think about it, every security entitles the holder to receive exactly the same thing—a stream of dollar payments in the future. One reason investors pay a different price for each of these contracts is that sometimes people break their promises. They don't wind up doing what they said they'd do. In religion you do penance for such transgressions; in the financial world you go bankrupt. So, bonds are risky—they may not pay either the interest or the principal. Since the federal government has substantial taxing power, and since it can always print money to pay off its bonds, there is no risk of default on government securities.[8] But for corporations, individuals, and even municipal governments, the risk of default is prominent. Since people usually have to be paid to bear more risk, yields on corporate bonds exceed those on governments, as is evident in Chart 2.

In a similar vein, within the corporate sector, firms have differing

---

[8]But there *is* a risk of inflation if the government prints money to pay off its debt. And if the public thinks this is a real possibility, *nominal* yields will be very high even on "risk-free" governments.

degrees of default risk. As we will see in greater detail in Chapter 31, credit-rating agencies, such as Standard & Poor's and Moody's Investors Service, put the bonds of these firms into different risk categories, depending on the strength of the company's balance sheet, cash flows, and management. The highest rating, Aaa in Moody's rating system, goes to companies such as AT&T. The credit rating used by some investors (such as pension funds) as a cut-off for so-called "investment grade issues" is Baa. At the other end of the scale, those bonds that are in default get a C rating. Chart 2 illustrates what we would expect: lower-rated corporate bonds (Baa) have higher yields than bonds in the higher-rated category (Aaa).

Municipal bonds—the debt issued by state and local governments— have a number of interesting features. The default risk of such bonds used to be considered quite low, with the only significant bankruptcies occurring during the Great Depression. The taxing power of state and local governments is the ultimate backing for municipal bonds. But the taxing power of states and cities is limited by people's willingness to stay put and subject themselves to the burden of ever-increasing local taxes. As a result of this and the *de facto* defaults of New York City in 1975 and Cleveland in 1978, default risk considerations exert considerable influence on the yield relationships among municipals and between municipals and other bonds.

The tax-exempt status of interest payments on municipal bonds is, however, the most important influence on municipal yields versus governments and corporates. Assume it's the bad old days and you pay 50 percent of your income in federal income taxes. If the yield on a government bond is 8 percent, you get $80 per $1,000 invested, but after taxes you'll wind up with only $40—or an after-tax yield of 4 percent. But if you own a municipal bond that pays $80 per $1,000 invested, you keep it all, because interest on municipal bonds is immune from the Internal Revenue Service. If the municipal bond had no chance of default and if everyone were in the 50 percent bracket, then investors would refuse to buy government bonds and would buy all the municipals they could lay their hands on if both yielded 8 percent before taxes. This would drive down the price of governments and push up the price of municipals. When would investors be indifferent between these two securities? Clearly, when the municipal bond yielded 4 percent and the government bond yielded 8 percent, they would both pay their owners $40 *after* taxes, and the market would be in equilibrium.

At a lower income tax rate, the yield on municipals would have to be higher—say $5\frac{1}{2}$ percent versus 8 percent on governments.[9] Further-more, municipal bonds ain't what they used to be in terms of their default-free reputation. This tends to push such rates even closer to the yield on fully taxable U.S. government bonds. As can be seen in Chart 2, the yields on municipal bonds have usually stayed well below comparable maturity governments, as dictated by tax considerations. But back in the Great Depression and in more recent times when default risk jitters surfaced and income tax rates were reduced, the yields on municipal bonds were forced toward yields on fully taxable governments.

Let us now turn to the yields on mortgages versus the rest. Compared with corporate bonds, mortgages are probably somewhat more risky because they are liabilities of individuals with unfamiliar credit rat-ings. But this cannot explain the pattern of yields on mortgages in-sured by the Federal Housing Administration (FHA) or the Veterans Administration (VA). Indeed, most of these individual mortgages are now wrapped up in mortgage pools, whose *timely* payment (not just ultimate payment) of interest and principal is insured further by the Government National Mortgage Association (GNMA). Moreover, even with conventional mortgages—that is, mortgages not insured by any federal agency—the assessed value of the property underlying the mortgage far exceeds (by 25 percent or more) the size of the loan granted by the lender. Thus, credit risk by itself can hardly explain the relationship between mortgage yields and the yields on other capital market instruments.

In the good old days (back in the 1960s), mortgages yielded much more than corporate bonds. That was so because mortgages had virtu-ally no marketability. But that's no longer the case. First, government-insured mortgages are now highly marketable, because most are wrapped up in GNMA pools, as we discussed back in Chapter 3. The improved marketability has brought their yields to within one-half of a percentage point of government bonds. Conventional mortgages yield somewhat more than that, because they do not, as yet, have a very active secondary market. But even here, conventional mortgage pools have been formed with default insurance from private compa-nies. This has added marketability to a once-illiquid market and has lowered the yield on such instruments as well.

---

[9]If your tax rate is t, the yield on governments is G, and the yield on municipals is M, then after-tax yields are equal when $G(1 - t) = M$. Hence, the ratio of M to G equals $(1 - t)$. With a marginal tax rate of 30 percent, the equilibrium yield on governments would be 8 percent compared with 5.6 percent on municipals.

Perhaps the most enduring feature of mortgages, causing their yields to be somewhat higher than bonds of comparable risk and marketability, is uncertainty over their cash flows. In Chapter 3 we pointed out that prepayments on mortgages are uncertain, depending in part on actuarially predictable events such as marriages and births, but also a function of the level of interest rates. This makes it especially difficult to specify the precise maturity, much less yield to maturity, of a mortgage. For example, a pool of thirty-year 15 percent–coupon mortgages will not yield 15 percent to maturity if many borrowers pay off those mortgages after two years because the level of interest rates has fallen to only 10 percent. This uncertainty, by itself, makes mortgages undesirable from the standpoint of some institutional investors, such as pension funds, who require fixed cash inflows to match the profile of their liabilities. Thus, mortgages tend to yield somewhat more in order to compensate investors for the volatile cash flow.[10]

To summarize: Our discussion of yield differentials has touched upon many specific features of bonds—so many, in fact, that it's hard to see how anyone can ignore them. How did we talk about interest rates for twenty-seven chapters without mentioning each and every one? How could our analysis of movements in the *level* of interest rates have been accurate when the level is made up of so many very different parts? A quick glance at Chart 2 indicates that while rate differentials can and do change, all rates still move more or less together. Much of the *overall* movement is determined by monetary policy, inflation, and the course of economic activity. Our focus in this chapter has put those overall movements under a microscope, producing a different perspective. Sometimes one approach is preferable and sometimes the other. It depends on what you're looking for.

SUMMARY

1. The relationship between yields on short-term and long-term securities is frequently illustrated graphically by a yield curve. The yield curve can be upward sloping (short-term rates are below long-term rates), downward sloping (short-term rates are above long-term rates), or flat (the yields on shorts and longs are the same).

2. The basic expectations theory maintains that the shape of the yield curve is determined by investors' expectations of future short-term interest

---

[10]In Chapter 31 we will describe how the collateralized mortgage obligation (CMO) was invented to minimize this problem.

rates. In particular, if short-term rates are expected to rise the yield curve will be upward sloping, while if short-term rates are expected to fall the yield curve will be downward sloping. A specific result is that long-term rates are averages of current and expected future short-term rates.

3. There are a number of modifications to the pure expectations theory that reflect other influences on rate structure. For example, since investors are usually considered risk averse, and since long-term securities have greater capital uncertainty than short-term securities, a liquidity premium is likely to be attached to long-term yields. In addition, some investors, such as life insurance companies, prefer long-term securities because they can "lock in" a guaranteed return on funds. This suggests that there are preferred maturity ranges for investors, and changes in supplies of securities will alter yields on different maturities.

4. The fundamental role of expectations in shaping the yield curve is emphasized by the following empirical regularity: when the overall level of rates is high compared with the recent past, the yield curve slopes downward; when the level of rates is low compared with recent experience, the yield curve slopes upward.

5. Default risk helps to explain the excess of corporate bond yields over comparable maturity government bonds. The probability of default also influences the structure of yields within the corporate bond market.

6. Municipal bonds yield less than government bonds because the interest payments on municipals are exempt from federal income taxes. Nevertheless, when default probabilities on municipal debt increase, their tax-free yields can approach taxable yields on governments.

7. The ready marketability of a bond reduces the yield necessary to attract investors. Government bonds have the best marketability of all debt instruments.

8. Mortgages yield somewhat more than bonds of comparable risk, maturity, and marketability because of the cash flow uncertainty associated with a mortgage.

Suggestions for Further Reading

There are many excellent studies of the term structure of interest rates. A good survey as well as advanced material is found in Burton Malkiel, *The Term Structure of Interest Rates* (Princeton, N.J.: Princeton University Press, 1966). A somewhat more difficult study is by Richard Roll, *The Behav-*

ior of Interest Rates (New York: Basic Books, 1970). The hardest one of all is by John Cox, Jonathan Ingersoll, and Stephen Ross, "A Reexamination of Traditional Hypotheses about the Term Structure of Interest Rates," *Journal of Finance* (September 1981).

The risk structure of interest rates has a less organized career. An early article on the subject is Lawrence Fisher, "Determinants of Risk Premiums on Corporate Bonds," *Journal of Political Economy* (June 1959). A somewhat more general analysis is Dwight M. Jaffee, "Cyclical Variations in the Risk Structure of Interest Rates," *Journal of Money, Credit, and Banking* (July 1975). An interesting analysis of risk and term structure together is in Philip Cagan, "A Study of Liquidity Premiums on Federal and Municipal Securities," in Jack Guttentag and Phillip Cagan, ed., *Essays on Interest Rates* (New York: National Bureau of Economic Research, 1969). For an analysis of the impact of marketability on mortgage yields, see Deborah G. Black, Kenneth D. Garbade, and William L. Silber, "The Impact of the GNMA Pass-Through Program on FHA Mortgage Costs," *Journal of Finance* (May 1981).

A survey of rate structure issues is found in James C. Van Horne's excellent paperback *Financial Market Rates and Flows*, 2d ed. (Englewood Cliffs, N.J.: Prentice-Hall, 1984). Finally, for the nitty-gritty on specific features of bonds such as call provisions, intermarket spreads and swap opportunities, loss recovery periods, cushion bonds, perpetuities, and the magic of compounding, see Sidney Homer and Martin Liebowitz, *Inside the Yield Book* (Englewood Cliffs, N.J.: Prentice-Hall, 1970). Don't miss the discussion, on page 101, of the yield pickup swap and the net gains to the swapper.

Bond Price Volatility: Duration Versus Maturity

We have mentioned on a number of occasions that long-term bonds are riskier than short-term bonds—not because we don't like long-term bonds, but because numerical examples show that a one-percentage-point change in the yield to maturity on a long-term bond produces a larger change in the price of the bond than the impact of a one-percentage-point change in yield on the price of a short-term bond. Now, this statement is correct—usually. Which is okay most of the time, but not good enough for mathematicians and bond market professionals, who like things somewhat more precise.

The problem with the relationship between bond price volatility and maturity stems from the rather casual way people define maturity. In particular, we identify the maturity of a bond with the date of final repayment of principal. Thus, a bond with ten years to maturity and an 8 percent coupon makes a series of coupon payments equal to $80 per year and then pays the principal borrowed ($1,000) at the end of the tenth year. Our definition of maturity ignores the fact that the bond makes coupon payments in each of ten years before it repays the principal. This is not necessarily bad; we can define maturity as we wish. In fact, this definition of maturity reminds holders of corporate bonds that they have ten years to worry about potential defaults on promised payments. But by ignoring the coupon payments, we have in a sense overstated the maturity of the bond; lenders get some of their money back before the ten-year maturity date.

A more comprehensive measure of a bond's maturity, called *duration*, takes into account the timing of both coupon and principal payments. We will define duration very precisely below. But first, let us focus on a key relationship: A bond with longer duration has greater price volatility than a bond with shorter duration when yields on both bonds change by the same amount in percentage points. We can even write down a simple formula relating the percentage change in the price of a bond to the bond's duration. Let P stand for price, D for duration, i for yield to maturity, and Δ for "change in." Then, we have:

$$\Delta P/P = -\Delta i/(1+i) \times D$$

This says that the percentage change in the price of a bond is opposite in sign (yields go up and bond prices fall) and equal to the percentage change in yield to maturity times the duration of the bond. Thus, if the duration of a bond is five years, for example, and the yield to maturity falls from 8 percent (.0800) to 7.99 percent (.0799), we can readily calculate the percentage change in the price of the bond as follows:

$$
\begin{aligned}
\Delta P/P &= -[\Delta i/(1+i)] \times D \\
&= -[.0001/(1.08)] \times 5 \\
&= -[.000092] \times 5 \\
&= -.00046
\end{aligned}
$$

In particular, if the price of the bond were 100 and the yield to maturity decreased by one basis point (equal to .01 percent or .0001), from 8 percent to 7.99 percent, then the price of the bond would increase to 100.046 (with $\Delta P/P = .00046$ and $P = 100$, $\Delta P = .046$ and the new price is 100.046). If the duration of the bond were ten years, the price would have increased to 100.09, and so on.

This is obviously a handy formula to have. It lets you calculate precisely how a bond's price varies with changes in the yield to maturity. Note that this relationship has nothing at all to do with economics. It all follows from the definition of the price of a bond (displayed in Chapter 5) and the definition of duration. Although we cannot show you why combining the definitions produces this magic result (we trust the mathematicians), we can move one step in that direction by presenting the formula for duration.

Duration is defined as a weighted average of the time periods when a bond's payments are made. That's the easy part. The more difficult part is the weight applied to each time period. In particular, the weight attached to each time period is the present value of the payment at that time divided by the price of the bond. This is most easily understood by way of specific example. Suppose we have our five-year bond with $80 annual coupon payments and a $1,080 principal-plus-coupon payment at the end. Thus, there are five time periods: years 1, 2, 3, 4, and 5. The formula for duration is:

$$D = \frac{\left[\frac{\$80}{(1+i)}\right](1) + \left[\frac{\$80}{(1+i)^2}\right](2) + \left[\frac{\$80}{(1+i)^3}\right](3) + \left[\frac{\$80}{(1+i)^4}\right](4) + \left[\frac{\$1080}{(1+i)^5}\right](5)}{\frac{\$80}{(1+i)} + \frac{\$80}{(1+i)^2} + \frac{\$80}{(1+i)^3} + \frac{\$80}{(1+i)^4} + \frac{\$1080}{(1+i)^5}}$$

This looks messy, but it's really not that bad. First, the numerator: Each of the time periods—1, 2, 3, 4, and 5—is in parentheses and preceded by a term in brackets. The bracketed terms are either the present value of $80 (for the first four years) or the present value of $1,080 (for the fifth year). These weights are each divided by the price of the bond, which appears, therefore, in the denominator of the formula (see Chapter 5 to convince yourself that the formula in the denominator is equal to the price of the bond).

The duration of a bond clearly depends on more than just the date of the final principal payment (five years). For example, if the yield to maturity (i) were 8 percent, so that the bond were selling at par, the duration of our bond would measure 4.2 years. Duration is less than five years because the earlier time periods in the formula receive some weight in the computation. For example, year 2 receives the weight [$80/(1.08)^2] divided by the denominator. If the yield to maturity increased to 12 percent, the duration of the bond would decrease to 4.1 years, because the especially large weight attached to the last time period (5) would become smaller in present value terms. *Thus, it is generally the case that the higher the yield to maturity, the lower the duration of a bond* (holding everything else constant, of course).

The coupon payment clearly plays an important role in the duration calculation. Returning to our initial case of an 8 percent yield, if the coupon of the bond were $40 rather than $80, the duration would be 4.5 years. It is generally the case that *lower coupons mean longer duration* (everything else the same), because the weights attached to the earlier years in the formula would be smaller.

One special case is worth emphasizing. When the coupon payments

TABLE 1
Duration of Bonds with Different Maturities

Coupon	Yield	Maturity	Duration
8%	8%	5 years	4.2 years
8%	8%	10 years	7.1 years
8%	8%	15 years	9.0 years
8%	8%	20 years	10.3 years
8%	8%	30 years	11.8 years

are zero, the duration of our bond is equal to five years. In fact, *duration always equals maturity for a zero coupon bond (and is less than maturity for bonds with coupons).* To convince yourself of this, simply write out our duration formula without the first four terms in both the numerator and denominator (they are equal to zero for a zero-coupon bond). We then have the same term in the numerator and denominator, except that it is multiplied by 5 in the numerator. Thus, everything cancels except the 5 in the numerator, which is the date of the final payment. This makes considerable sense, of course, since we started our discussion by noting that the date of the final principal payment is an imprecise measure of "true" maturity because it ignores coupon payments. If there are no coupon payments, however, the date of the final principal payment is all that matters.

Finally, to show how duration varies with the conventional definition of maturity, Table 1 lists five bonds with 8 percent coupons, all priced at par and thus yielding 8 percent, but with maturity dates varying between five and thirty years. Obviously, longer maturity means longer duration as long as the bonds have the same yield and same coupon. But duration hardly increases at the same pace as maturity. For example, doubling the maturity of a fifteen-year bond to thirty years increases its duration by less than a third (from 9.0 to 11.8). Moreover, if our thirty-year bond had a 17 percent coupon and yielded the same 8 percent, its duration would be 10.1 years, less than the duration of the twenty-year bond shown in the table.

The moral of the story is keep your eye on duration, not maturity. First, you have a handy little formula that describes how price risk varies with duration. Second, to focus attention on maturity can sometimes be quite misleading.

The Structure and Performance of Securities Markets

Mia Farrow needs a script, Jackson Browne a guitar, Richard Avedon a camera, and Chris Evert a tennis racket. Each performer uses the props appropriate for the medium in question. Performances can be stimulating, comical, pleasurable, disappointing. That's how it is in the world of entertainment.

Well, it's not so different in financial markets. Brokers, dealers, specialists, and traders are the actors. Telephones, ticker tapes, and computer terminals are the props. Stocks, bonds, and mortgages are the media. Performances are described as resilient, deep, broad, thin, liquid. Our task is to describe who goes with what and why. You can then decide whether to applaud or hiss after your next financial transaction.

NATURE AND FUNCTION OF SECURITIES MARKETS

In Chapter 28 we examined the forces that influence the equilibrium prices of different types of securities. For the most part we ignored the structure of these markets, taking for granted that somehow the interested buyers and sellers of the securities would find their way to the marketplace. And that is precisely the main assumption underlying the equilibrium price that emerges from the intersection of supply and demand curves: the price balances the supplies of and demands for the security by *all* potential market participants.

In practice, bringing all buyers and sellers together is not quite so simple. Trading interests are not uncovered costlessly, because buyers and sellers may be in different locations and therefore not aware of each other. Similarly, time may elapse between a buyer's arrival at the marketplace and the appearance of a compatible seller. Such geographical and temporal fragmentation makes the prices at which transactions actually take place differ from the equilibrium price. Real world trading at prices that straddle the true equilibrium is the best we can hope for. In fact, we might think of the ideal situation as actual transactions prices doing a little dance around the theoretical equilibrium price.

Securities markets are organized to help bring buyers and sellers together, so that both parties to the transaction will be satisfied that a fair transactions price, close to the true equilibrium price, has been arranged. There are three main types of market organization that facilitate the actual purchase and sale of securities: an auction market, a brokered market, and a dealer market. In each case, the aim is to match up buyers and sellers.

Auction Market. The main feature of an auction market is that buyers and sellers confront each other directly to bargain over price. There is nothing that stands between buyers and sellers, just an auctioneer who records bids and offers tendered by potential buyers and sellers. The particular rules of the auction determine exactly how buyers and sellers are matched up. For example, there can be a single trade between all buyers and sellers at a single price or a series of trades at different prices. Under all circumstances, the key characteristic of the auction is that orders are centralized, so that the highest bidders and lowest offerers are exposed to each other. The most popular example of an auction market is the New York Stock Exchange, where auctions for individual securities take place at specific locations, called posts, on the floor of the exchange. The auctioneer in this case is the specialist who is designated by the Exchange to represent (as an agent) orders tendered by public customers. A second example of an auction market is the twice daily London gold fixing. Representatives of five London bullion dealers gather together to expose public orders to competitive bidding. One of the dealers is designated by the group as the auctioneer.

Brokered Market. When there are insufficient participants in an auction market, so that potential traders do not always find "reasonable" bids and offers, it may pay traders to employ the services of a broker to search for the other side of a trade. Thus a seller of securities may ask a broker to show the securities to potential buyers or a buyer may ask a broker to uncover potential sellers. Unlike the auctioneer, whose role is completely passive, the broker provides information about potential buyers and sellers and earns a commission in return. Many of us are familiar with real estate brokers who provide information for potential buyers and sellers of homes. Municipal bonds are the best example of securities that trade primarily in a brokered market.

Dealer Market. During the time it takes a broker to uncover a compatible trading partner, the equilibrium price of the security may change. It can be profitable, therefore, for a person to remain in the marketplace, continuously bidding for securities that investors want to sell and offering securities that investors want to buy. This person acts as a dealer, buying securities for his or her own account when the public is selling and selling from her or his own account when the public is buying. Unlike brokers, dealers commit capital to the process of bringing buyers and sellers together and take on the risk of price changes in the securities they hold in inventory. Dealers expect to earn a profit, because they always quote a bid price (at which they buy) that is below their offer price (at which they sell).

Many securities trade in dealer markets, including government bonds, corporate bonds, and equities not traded on the organized exchanges, the so-called over-the-counter (OTC) market. There are usually many dealers in each security. They are linked together either by telephone or by computer hookup. In fact, many over-the-counter stocks trade in a semiautomated system called NASDAQ (National Association of Securities Dealers Automated Quotation System). On the New York Stock Exchange the specialists who are the designated auctioneers also quote bids and offers in their capacity as dealers. Thus, trading on the New York Stock Exchange is a cross between a dealer market and an auction market.

The organizational structure of a market—the existence of brokers, dealers, exchanges—as well as the technological paraphernalia—such as quotation screens, computer terminals, and telegraphic communications—are all mobilized to keep transaction prices as close to true (but unknown) equilibrium prices as is economically feasible. Easy access to a trading forum, with many potential buyers and sellers, means that a security can be bought or sold quickly with little deviation from its equilibrium value. That is what is meant by marketability, a catch-all phrase indicating small deviations of actual transaction prices about the true equilibrium.

Good marketability implies that a security can be sold, liquidated, turned into cash, very quickly without triggering a collapse in price. A highly marketable security is more desirable to investors, so its equilibrium price will be higher, and its yield lower, relative to less marketable securities.

The rest of our discussion is devoted to examining the efficiency of securities markets. First we look at how effective they are in bringing buyers and sellers together, the so-called operating efficiency of securities markets. We then turn to pricing efficiency and related regulatory concerns.

PRIMARY VERSUS SECONDARY MARKETS

Before detailing the nature of trading in securities markets, it is important to distinguish primary markets from secondary markets. Most of the popular markets, such as the New York Stock Exchange, are secondary markets, where existing securities are exchanged between individuals and institutions. The primary markets—markets for newly issued securities—are much less well known.

New issues of stock or bonds to raise funds for General Motors, General Electric, or Colonel Sanders are not sold to saver-lenders on the floor of the New York Stock Exchange, the American Stock Exchange, or even the Midwest Stock Exchange in Chicago. Rather, the matchmaking takes place behind closed doors, aided by Wall Street's investment bankers. The names Morgan Stanley, Goldman Sachs, Salomon Brothers, and Merrill Lynch dominate the list. They often act as brokers and dealers in secondary markets as well. But in their role as investment bankers they help distribute newly issued stocks and bonds to ultimate investors—insurance companies, pension funds, and individuals throughout the country.

These distributions are called underwritings: the investment banker guarantees an issuer of bonds a price (and implicitly a yield) on the new issue. Often a number of investment bankers band together in a syndicate to market a new issue; by sticking together they share the risk of adverse movements in interest rates between the time an issue is bought from the corporation and the time it goes out of the investment bankers' inventory, safely tucked away in some pension fund's portfolio for many years to come. The idea is to get rid of the issue as quickly as possible—within a day or two. That minimizes the risk exposure of the investment banking firm's capital. Announcements of successful underwritings, such as the one reproduced here, appear frequently in the financial press.

This announcement is neither an offer to sell nor a solicitation of offers to buy any of these securities.
The offering is made only by the Prospectus and the related Prospectus Supplement.

NEW ISSUE   January 15, 1988

$100,000,000

Pitney Bowes Inc.

8⅞% Notes Due 1993

Price 99.65%

plus accrued interest, if any, from January 21, 1988

Copies of the Prospectus and the related Prospectus Supplement may be obtained in
any State in which this announcement is circulated only from such of the
undersigned as may legally offer these securities in such State.

The First Boston Corporation

Goldman, Sachs & Co.	Merrill Lynch Capital Markets	Morgan Stanley & Co. Incorporated
Salomon Brothers Inc		Shearson Lehman Brothers Inc.
Bear, Stearns & Co. Inc.	Dillon, Read & Co. Inc.	Donaldson, Lufkin & Jenrette Securities Corporation
Drexel Burnham Lambert Incorporated	Kidder, Peabody & Co. Incorporated	Lazard Frères & Co.
PaineWebber Incorporated	Prudential-Bache Capital Funding	L.F. Rothschild & Co. Incorporated
Smith Barney, Harris Upham & Co. Incorporated	Wertheim Schroder & Co. Incorporated	Dean Witter Capital Markets

Newspaper Advertisement: An Underwriting Syndicate Floats a New Issue.

A number of features of this new-issue market are noteworthy. First, as with many—or most—markets, it is not located in any particular spot. Underwritings of new issues do not take place on the floor of an organized exchange. Rather, the marketplace is the conference rooms of investment banking firms, linked by telephone with each other, with corporations, and with ultimate investors. Second, the most important commodity sold by these market-makers is information—information about the yield required to sell an issue and who the likely buyers are. That's one of the most important functions of markets—

dissemination of price and trading information. To market the new issue, investment bankers also sell the services of their capital, buying the issue outright from the corporation and thereby insuring that the firm pays only the agreed-upon yield. Subsequent adverse or favorable yield movements do not affect the issuing firm, just the vacation prospects of the investment bankers. As compensation for their time and trouble, investment bankers earn a fee, called an underwriting spread, on each newly issued security.

The near-invisibility of primary markets, compared with the immense popular recognition of secondary markets for equities, does not change the fact that both serve essential functions. Moreover, there is a close interrelationship between yields on securities in secondary markets and those in primary markets. One important clue to the required new-issue yield on a corporation's bonds, for example, is the recent yield on the firm's obligations in the secondary market. How useful these yields are depends, in part, upon the "quality" of secondary market yields. Are they close to equilibrium prices, or do they reflect one or two transactions that might not be representative? Only by recognizing the nature of the secondary market can the yields recorded there be evaluated.

EFFICIENCY OF SECONDARY MARKET TRADING

As we indicated at the beginning of the chapter, secondary markets work well if they bring together buyers and sellers of securities so that they transact at prices close to the true equilibrium price. Markets that accomplish this objective have low transactions costs and are considered liquid. One measure of the liquidity costs of a market is the spread between the bid price and the offer (or asked) price quoted by a dealer who "makes a market" in the particular security. In order to understand how the dealer's bid-asked spread measures liquidity costs, let's begin with a market that operates as an auction and then introduce dealers as participants.

The equilibrium price that we identify with the intersection of supply and demand curves emerges from the following type of auction. At a prearranged point in time buyers and sellers interested in a particular security gather before an auctioneer. The auctioneer announces a price for the security (perhaps the price from the previous auction) and asks buyers and sellers to submit quantities they want to buy or sell at that price. If the quantity supplied exceeds what is demanded, the auctioneer announces a lower trial price and asks market participants to resubmit orders to buy or sell. If at the new lower price there are more buyers than sellers the auctioneer tries a slightly higher price and asks for still a new set of orders. This iterative "recontracting" process continues until a price emerges at which buying and selling interest are equal. At that point, the auctioneer instructs buyers to tender cash and sellers to tender the securities, and the exchange takes place at what has been established as the equilibrium price.

This auction is known as a Walrasian auction, after Leon Walras, a nineteenth-century French economist who conceptualized the auction underlying the determination of equilibrium prices in this way. There is, in fact, one very real marketplace that operates as a "Walrasian auction," namely the twice-daily London gold fixing, where the price of gold bullion is determined.

Most markets operate quite differently from the Walrasian auction. Transactions usually occur continuously throughout the day rather than at a single point in time. In most cases, buyers and sellers of securities do not want to wait until a scheduled auction takes place. They prefer to transact immediately in order to eliminate the uncertainty over where the new equilibrium price might be. To provide this service of immediate execution, dealers enter the marketplace to quote a bid price at which they will buy from potential sellers and an offer price at which they will sell to potential buyers.

Figure 1 shows the bid price ($97) at which a dealer will buy from the sellers (on the supply curve) and the asked or offer price ($99) at which the dealer will sell to the buyers (on the demand curve). Unlike the buyers and sellers on the demand and supply curves, the dealer is not interested in the security itself. Rather the dealer's sole objective is to sell whatever inventory has been purchased before the equilibrium price has a chance to change. The dealer's reward is the spread between the bid and offer, in the case of Figure 1, the $2 difference between the $99 asked price and the $97 bid.

Note that if trading in this security were conducted in a Walrasian auction, all transactions would have occurred at the equilibrium price of $98 (that's the price where the quantity people want to sell just matches what others want to buy). But since buyers and sellers were concerned that the equilibrium price might change before the auction took place, they chose to transact at the dealer's bid and offer prices. The cost of transacting immediately, therefore, is measured by the spread between the dealer's bid and offer. Wider bid-asked spreads mean that the cost of transacting is high and that transactions prices differ considerably from equilibrium prices. A market is liquid, there-

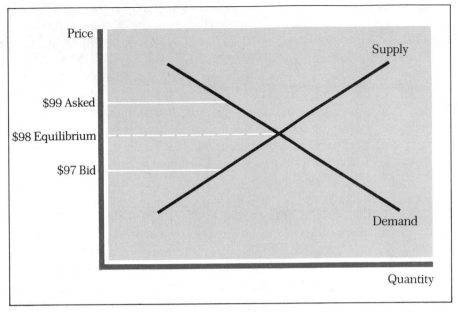

FIGURE 1 Bid-Asked Spreads Cause Actual Transactions Prices to Hover About the True Equilibrium Price

fore, if bid-asked spreads are narrow.[1] A security is considered liquid or marketable if the bid-asked spread is narrow. Let's see what kinds of securities trade in liquid markets versus illiquid markets.

The dealer will quote a narrow bid-asked spread if: (1) the expected volume of transactions is large; and (2) the anticipated risk of large equilibrium price changes is low. Large volume means it's easy to turn over inventory, since there are frequent orders to buy and sell. Low volatility of price changes means that the risk exposure of the dealer's inventory is small. Both mean that the dealer can be forced to quote

---

[1]The original analysis of bid-asked spreads is found in H. Demsetz, "The Cost of Transacting," *Quarterly Journal of Economics* (February 1968). The relationship between transactions prices and equilibrium prices appears in Kenneth Garbade and William L. Silber, "Structural Organization of Secondary Markets: Clearing Frequency, Dealer Activity and Liquidity Risk," *Journal of Finance* (June 1979). One issue that often seems puzzling is: how does a dealer know where the equilibrium price is? The answer is: the information comes from the inventory of securities. For example, if a dealer quotes a very high bid and offer relative to where the equilibrium price is, the dealer will buy a lot more at the bid than he or she sells at the offer, producing an increase in the inventory of securities held. This provides a signal to the dealer to lower the bid and offer. If the bid and offer are too low, the dealer's inventory falls, and that signals the dealer to raise the bid and offer.

narrow bid-asked spreads and still stay in business—committing capital and skill to market-making. Since dealers are no more benevolent than the rest of us, the element forcing dealers to quote narrow spreads is competitive pressure.

Table 1 shows a number of sample bid-asked quotations from March 25, 1987. First some basic explanations of the numbers. All bonds are quoted as a percent of par. Treasury bonds with between one and ten years to maturity are called Notes. Thus, on March 25, 1987, the Treasury 7 percent coupon notes due in June 1988 could be sold at $100\frac{27}{32}$ (the bid price) per $100 face value and could be bought at $100\frac{29}{32}$ (the asked price) per $100 face value. Since minimum denominations of most notes and bonds are $1,000, that means it costs $1,009.06 to buy such a note, while I get $1,008.44 if I sell it. The spread (asked minus bid) recorded in the last column is $\frac{1}{16}$ or 6.25 cents per $100, or 62.5 cents per $1,000 transaction. In other words, if I buy a $1,000 Treasury note and decide to sell immediately because I get a hot stock tip, my schizophrenia will cost me $0.625. A $2,000 round trip, as they call it, costs $1.25, a $3,000 trade, $1.875, and so on. This is a measure of the liquidity costs of the security: the transactions costs of buying and selling.

As can be seen in the first two lines of the table, government notes and bonds have very small bid-asked spreads. The short-term Treasury

TABLE 1
Sample Bid and Asked Quotations on Securities

Name of Market	Particular Issue		Bid	Ask	Spread
	Coupon	Maturity			
1. *Governments and Agencies*					
Treasury Note	7	June 1988	$100^{27}/_{32}$	$100^{29}/_{32}$	$^1/_{16}$
Treasury Bond	12	Feb 2013	$142^{19}/_{32}$	$142^{23}/_{32}$	$^1/_8$
GNMA	13	—	$110^9/_{32}$	$110^{17}/_{32}$	$^1/_4$
Federal Home Loan Bank Bond	7.75	Mar 1991	$101^{30}/_{32}$	$102^6/_{32}$	$^1/_4$
2. *Corporates*					
Sears Roebuck	6	2000	82⅝	83⅛	½
Union Pacific	8½	2017	97¼	97¾	½
3. *OTC Stocks*					
Photon Technology		—	5	5¼	¼
Halsey Drug		—	11	11½	½

SOURCES: *Wall Street Journal, New York Times*

note has the narrowest spread—suggesting correctly that short-term money market instruments have the most liquid market.

The bond of the Federal Home Loan Bank Board and the GNMA security trade on a $\frac{1}{4}$-point spread, or $2.50 per $1,000, compared with the $1.25 per $1,000 round-trip transaction in the Treasury bond. This suggests that federal agency and related securities have somewhat less liquidity than Treasury obligations, which is true.

The corporate bond market in the second section of the table indicates $5 round-trip costs for corporates. The liquidity is less than in either the Treasury market or the agency market.

The explanation for the variation in the spreads lies primarily in the volume of trading in the particular issues. Short-term Treasury bills and notes are more actively traded than Treasury bonds. Treasuries trade more than agencies, while the individual corporate issues trade less frequently.

The last section of Table 1 records the bids and offers for two over-the-counter equities. Photon Technology Corporation trades on a $\frac{1}{4}$-point spread and Halsey Drug on a $\frac{1}{2}$-point spread. Like point spreads in football, these quotations must be scrutinized before you jump to costly conclusions. It would seem, for example, that both securities have liquidity costs that are similar to agency securities. In fact, this is not the case. Quotations in the equity market are *per share*. Thus, to buy 100 shares of Photon Technology costs $525 ($5\frac{1}{4}$ times 100), with an immediate sale netting $500. A 200-share purchase would cost $1,050, and a sale would net $1,000. Thus it costs $50 for a $1,000 round trip in Photon, while a $1,000 round trip in agencies costs only $2.50. The lesson is clear: bid-asked spreads must be related to the price of the security and the implied cost of trading or liquidating a fixed dollar amount. In general, there are higher transaction costs for equities compared with bonds. In part this reflects the greater risk of price fluctuation a dealer is exposed to with equities.[2]

But there's more to the story than bid-asked spreads.[3] For one thing,

---

[2]In addition to these bid-asked spreads, your broker charges a fee, called a commission, for executing your trades. This expense depends more on whether you deal with a discount broker or a full service broker than whether you are buying a stock or bond.
[3]Even the bid-asked spread itself is not as unambiguous as it seems. In competitive dealer markets, bids and offers are quoted by each market-maker. The quotations in Table 1 are averages. Unless all quotes are identical, a potential trader is confronted with price dispersion. It pays to search among dealers for the most favorable quote, but this search adds to the cost of executing a trade. See Kenneth D. Garbade and William L. Silber, "Price Dispersion in the Government Securities Market," *Journal of Political Economy* (August 1976).

we haven't mentioned bid-asked spreads on the organized exchanges. The reason is that they aren't published in the newspapers, even though a specialist on the trading floor will quote a spread. IBM, a very active New York Stock Exchange security, was selling at $152\frac{7}{8}$ on March 25, 1987 and was quoted on a spread of $\frac{1}{8}$. That's $12.50 per $15,000 round trip—not much more than it would cost to trade $15,000 in Treasury notes, and less than the liquidity cost in the agency market. For trades of that size, equities are just about as liquid as Treasury or agency securities, if not more so.

The real difference between liquidity in Treasuries or agencies and liquidity in *any* equity lies in the size of transaction that can be handled without causing either a widening of the bid-asked spread or a shift up (in the case of a buy) or down (for a sale) in the implicit equilibrium price. Quotes in equities must be good for at least a round lot—100 shares. Quotes in the Treasury market must also be good for a round lot—usually $1 million in face value. A $10 million order in Treasuries can also be filled without much trouble. But for equities, there's simply no way to liquidate a $5 million block of stock—or even a $1 million position—without causing dealers to back away after the purchase of 100 or 200 shares. Thus the bid-asked spread measures the liquidity cost of normal-sized transactions, and what's normal in the Treasury and agency markets would be abnormal in any common stock. In fact, blocks of stock are not brought to the auction market on the floor of the New York Stock Exchange unless a trade has been arranged beforehand by dealers. While the public auction of organized exchanges looks good and has distinct advantages, it simply cannot handle the large trades of institutional investors.[4]

This discussion suggests a somewhat more sophisticated measure of market performance, one that focuses on the ability of a market to absorb large trading volume without causing wild gyrations in transactions prices. The qualitative description of such markets is relatively easy: they have depth, breadth, and resiliency. A market is deep if it is easy to uncover buy and sell orders above and below current transactions prices; if these orders exist in large volume, then the market has breadth; if new orders quickly pour in when prices move up or down, the market is called resilient.

All these characteristics imply low transactions price volatility. For

---

[4]Institutional investors sometimes trade among themselves through computerized brokerage services. Trading interests are recorded via computer terminal and then transmitted to other subscribing institutions. When there is a match, the trade is recorded and executed.

example, even if a dealer's bid and asked quotes are good for 100 shares only, if a larger purchase order causes institutions that continuously monitor dealer quotes to call in sell orders, then prices won't gyrate much. Markets that are *not* deep, broad, and resilient are called thin markets; only a small volume of trading can be absorbed without producing wide price swings.

Having said all that, there's not much else to do. There just aren't any good measures of this aspect of liquidity. Simply looking at price volatility is not enough—equilibrium price changes are part of everyday price movements and do not reflect poorly on a market's liquidity.

One important observation can be made, however, concerning the impact of communications technology on the ability of any market to absorb large orders without becoming "disorderly." Traders who can continuously monitor quotation screens like NASDAQ can participate more quickly in buying and selling if prices deviate from their view of equilibrium. When prices fall, they buy; when prices rise, they sell. This very process contributes to price stability and liquidity. Moreover, the reduction in price volatility also leads to narrow bid-asked spreads, since dealer inventories are subject to less risk.[5]

We have extended our discussion of secondary market trading, efficiency, marketability, and liquidity to the point of no return. Price changes should be small when trading is motivated by liquidity needs; that's the characteristic of highly marketable securities. But new information affecting the underlying value of the security should be reflected quickly in equilibrium price changes. Indeed, if prices of financial assets did not reflect news about bankruptcies, earnings trends, lawsuits, and whatever else affects the payments promised by the issuer of the financial instrument, then the market would be inefficient. Some call this aspect of a market allocational efficiency. Up to now we have analyzed the operational efficiency of financial markets. Actually, the popular discussion of "efficient capital markets" focuses on allocational efficiency, without calling it by that name. We discussed some aspects of efficient capital markets in Chapter 26 in the context of portfolio theory and in Chapter 24 when we discussed rational expectations. In the next section we provide an overview of efficient capital markets within the framework of regulation of securities markets.

[5]See Anthony Santomero, "The Economic Effects of NASDAQ: Some Preliminary Results," *Journal of Financial and Quantitative Analyses* (January 1974), for evidence that NASDAQ significantly reduced bid-asked spreads on OTC securities.

EFFICIENT CAPITAL MARKETS AND REGULATION

A vast literature has developed during the past fifteen years based on a relatively straightforward proposition: the current price (hence, expected yield) of a security fully reflects all publicly available information. Put somewhat differently: there is no unexploited publicly available information that would lead to superior investment performance. If securities prices fully reflect all available information, the capital market is called efficient.

It's hard to argue with the statement that markets will be efficient. If securities prices didn't reflect all publicly available information, market pressures would quickly force them to do so. Suppose that dealers ignored a news flash that an OTC-traded company had discovered how to make oil out of used textbooks. Everyone else would find the price of the security relatively cheap in view of the fantastic profits the company will reap. Buy orders would pour into brokerage offices and sell orders would disappear. Dealers would meet their commitment to sell 100 shares at the old price and then would more than double the quoted asking price to avoid selling what they didn't have at ridiculously low prices. As soon as the dealer quoted a price sufficiently high to reflect the rosy profit outlook, buy orders would drop to normal (the security would no longer be such a bargain), sell orders would reappear (let's take some profits), and the new equilibrium price would fully reflect all publicly available information.

There's nothing wrong with that story. It happens all the time, and that's precisely what we mean when we say that capital markets are efficient. The problem arises in the implications for buying and selling securities. The implication is quite simple: don't trade. If prices quickly incorporate all information affecting the fortunes of a company, then you can't earn above-average returns by selling so-called overvalued securities or buying undervalued ones. There aren't any bargains. Moreover, the fancy charts sold by investment advisers, suggesting that you buy when the price of a stock rises by 5 or 10 percent, aren't worth the paper they are printed on.

Needless to say, securities analysts have little use for such academic ranting and raving. How quickly do you think markets absorb new information? Within a day or two is the best estimate of academic researchers.[6] If that's the case, there is little to gain from buying or

---

[6]One of the first articles testing market efficiency is Eugene Fama, Lawrence Fisher, Michael Jensen, and Richard Roll, "The Adjustment of Stock Prices to New Informa-

selling after reading the investment bulletins of your favorite brokerage house. By the time you've finished, there's nothing to do but watch which way the price of your security went.

Allegations that manipulation, deception, and misinformation helped turn the 1929 stock market collapse into a national disaster led Congress to enact the Securities and Exchange Act of 1934. The Act provided for the establishment of the Securities and Exchange Commission to prevent fraud and promote equitable and fair operations in securities markets. The focal point of SEC regulations is the disclosure of information that might be relevant for the pricing of securities. There are two major aspects of disclosure requirements: (1) in the primary markets, corporations issuing new securities must file a registration statement with the SEC, disclosing all information that might be pertinent to investors; (2) in secondary markets, corporate insiders may not trade on nonpublic information.

Our discussion of market efficiency made specific reference to publicly available information. It's quite possible—indeed, quite probable—that nonpublicly available information can be used to make extra profits or avoid undesirable losses. The SEC insists that investors should not be at a disadvantage when purchasing or selling securities. Not only must there be full disclosure of all pertinent information, but misinformation and dissemination of false or misleading reports are specifically prohibited.

The SEC's job is not an easy one. It has enlisted the aid of the various organized exchanges and the National Association of Securities Dealers in supervising brokers, dealers, and transactions in secondary markets. The exchanges and the NASD take these disciplinary and supervising responsibilities seriously. And with good reason. The specter of more detailed SEC involvement in day-to-day operations is more than enough to encourage vigorous self-regulation.

It would be a mistake, however, to assume that manipulation, fraud, misinformation, and deception have disappeared from financial transactions simply because the SEC plays watchdog. Markets are efficient because investors and traders scrutinize and search and screen all information for themselves. *Caveat emptor et venditor* are still the watchwords that ensure market efficiency.

---

tion," *International Economic Review* (February 1969). For a general review see Eugene Fama, "Efficient Capital Markets," *Journal of Finance* (May 1970). A specific example appears in Kenneth Garbade, William L. Silber, and Lawrence White, "Market Reaction to the Filing of Antitrust Suits," *Review of Economics and Statistics* (November 1982).

Insider Trading: Efficiency Versus Equity

A number of insider trading scandals wracked the securities industry during the 1980s. Indictments and jail sentences were handed out to lawyers, traders and even newspaper columnists who fell victim to the temptation to misappropriate privileged information for personal profit. The violations in each case are less important than the legal principle: it is a criminal offense to trade on information that is considered confidential. Although the precise definition of confidential information is subject to legal interpretation, it clearly includes information received by officers, directors, lawyers, and investment advisors working directly or indirectly for a company that might affect the price of the company's stock.

The curious thing about the prohibition against insider trading is that it has nothing to do with promoting the efficiency of stock prices. As we have seen, stock prices are efficient if they fully reflect all available information. Prices will be efficient if either public investors bid up the price of a stock or if insiders bid up the price when favorable information is uncovered. In fact, some have argued that if insiders were allowed to trade on confidential information, prices would be more efficient because insiders with access to such information would force up stock prices instantaneously.

Why then the laws against insider trading? Fairness, not efficiency, is the key. As a matter of public policy, we would like investors to feel that in the stock market they have a fair chance to earn a decent return for their risks. More particularly, public investors should not feel that they are always at a disadvantage relative to insiders who can dump stocks of companies about to disclose unfavorable information or who will snap up bargains prior to the disclosure of favorable information. Without an impression of fairness, investors might be reluctant to participate in securities markets—making it difficult for companies to raise capital.

The problem is, of course, that there are considerable monetary incentives to circumvent the law. Are public investors better off with an impression of fairness when deception is rampant? Or are investors better off following the ancient dictum "let the buyer and seller beware"? Unfortunately, there is no simple answer.

SUMMARY

1. The equilibrium price that emerges from the familiar supply-demand picture assumes that all buyers and sellers have been brought together in the marketplace. Actual transactions prices in real world markets may differ from the theoretical equilibrium price, because it is costly to bring together all potential traders.

2. Markets that trade existing securities are organized as either auction, broker, or dealer markets. In all cases, resources are devoted to uncovering compatible trading interests. The New York Stock Exchange is the best example of an auction market, while government and corporate bonds are traded primarily in dealer markets. Brokers are frequently used in the municipal bond market.

3. It is important to distinguish these secondary markets for securities from the primary market, where newly issued securities are initially placed with investors. Virtually all corporations use investment bankers to help market new issues of stock and bonds.

4. The operating efficiency of secondary markets is measured by how close actual transactions prices conform to theoretical equilibrium prices. A narrow bid-asked spread in a dealer market produces transactions prices that are close to the true equilibrium price. Other dimensions to operating efficiency include the size of order that can be accommodated at a given quotation. In terms of these criteria, the market for Treasury securities is the best secondary market.

5. Securities markets are highly efficient processors of new information. Most evidence suggests that current prices fully reflect all publicly available information. Regulatory supervision by the Securities and Exchange Commission is aimed at preventing fraud and promoting fair and equitable trading.

Suggestions for Further Reading

The classic article on the interrelationship between information and markets is George J. Stigler, "The Economics of Information," *Journal of Political Economy* (June 1961). Bid-asked spreads were brought into the picture by Harold Demsetz in "The Cost of Transacting," *Quarterly Journal of Economics* (February 1968). A broad historical perspective on the impact of technology on financial markets is found in Kenneth D. Garbade and William L. Silber, "Technology, Communication, and Performance of Financial Markets: 1840–1975," *Journal of Finance* (June 1978). An excellent description of the structure of broker, dealer, and auction markets, as well as an analysis of futures contracts, appears in Kenneth D. Garbade, *Securities Markets* (New York: McGraw-Hill, 1982). Finally, a comprehensive discussion of the underwriting process in action can be found in Ernest Bloch, *Inside Investment Banking* (Homewood, Ill.: Dow Jones–Irwin, 1986).

CHAPTER 30

The Government Securities Market

The market for federal government securities is at the center of the money and capital markets. The U.S. Treasury has to sell several hundred billion dollars worth of securities a year in order to pay off maturing issues and finance current government operations. The sheer magnitude of these fund-raising activities makes yields on governments the dominant force influencing the entire structure of interest rates, so that in practice the government securities market serves as a reference point for all other securities markets. In this chapter we examine the nature of the government securities market, how securities are issued and distributed, who buys them, how the market functions, and how the Treasury goes about managing its debt operations.

FEDERAL DEFICITS AND THE NATIONAL DEBT

The federal budget refers to the government's spending and tax receipts and the relationship between them. Since 1930 the budget has been in deficit—that is, government spending has been greater than tax receipts—almost every year. Only rarely has the government had a balanced (or surplus) budget, taking in as much in tax receipts as it spent.

When the U.S. government runs a deficit, it has to get the funds somehow. It usually gets the money not by printing brand new dollar bills but by *borrowing*—which means selling securities to individuals, to banks, to insurance companies, to foreigners, indeed to anyone willing to lend to the Treasury by buying government bonds.

How does the national debt fit into this picture? The national debt is the net result of past and present budgetary policies. Fundamentally, it is the sum of all past deficits, less surpluses, in the federal budget. When the government has a deficit and borrows to finance it, the national debt increases. When a surplus (use your imagination) is used to redeem bonds, the national debt decreases.

For example, assume the national debt is $5,000 billion at the end of 1995 and during 1996 the Treasury runs a $200 billion deficit, which it finances by selling new securities; then the national debt will be $5,200 billion at the end of 1996. If the following year the Treasury has a $50 billion surplus, which it uses to retire outstanding securities, then the national debt will be $5,150 billion at the end of 1997.[1]

TYPES OF SECURITIES

In early 1988, the national debt amounted to $2.5 trillion, or $2,500 billion—that is, there were $2,500 billion worth of government securities outstanding. Of this amount, 70 percent or $1,800 billion was in *marketable* form, consisting of securities that can be bought and sold on financial markets. The remaining $700 billion was *nonmarketable*, such as the familiar U.S. savings bonds, in which no secondary market trading is permitted. If you want to sell some savings bonds, you have to sell them directly back to the Treasury at a fixed price.

Naturally enough, it is only marketable securities that are interesting from the point of view of how financial markets function. The $1,800 billion of marketable government securities consists of Treasury bills ($400 billion), Treasury notes ($1,100 billion), and Treasury bonds ($300 billion).

Treasury *bills* are the shortest-term government securities. As a rule, they are issued with original maturities of three months, six months, or a year. Bills are a kind of zero-coupon security (see Chapter 5), in that they are issued on a discount basis—that is, they are sold

---

[1]Budgets, deficits, and the debt are usually referred to with reference to fiscal years rather than calendar years. Fiscal years start on the previous October 1 instead of January 1. For example, the fiscal year 1990 encompasses from October 1, 1989 through September 30, 1990.

originally at a price below their face value, with face value payable at maturity. The difference between the price and face value constitutes the interest payment.

Treasury *notes* are issued with an original maturity of between one and ten years. Generally, the Treasury issues two-, four-, five-, and seven-year notes on a regular schedule. Unlike bills, which are issued on a discount basis, both notes and bonds are coupon instruments. That is, they have a statement printed on them specifying the rate of interest (as a percent of face value) that they carry, and coupons are traditionally attached to the securities. The holder detaches each coupon at the appropriate time and forwards it to the Treasury in order to receive the interest payment.

A coupon rate of 8 percent, for example, means that each year the holder of the note or bond will get an interest payment, from the Treasury, amounting to 8 percent of the security's face value. Interest is usually paid semiannually, so that with a $1,000 face value note or bond each semiannual coupon would entitle the holder to receive $40 from the Treasury.

Treasury *bonds* may be issued with any maturity longer than ten years. The longest bonds that are currently issued have an original maturity of thirty years.

Although Treasury notes and bonds begin life as coupon securities, government securities dealers often take newly issued notes and bonds and convert them to zero-coupon form by "stripping" the coupons from the body of the security. Dealers then market the coupons and the body of the security separately, as zero-coupon securities.

For example, a newly issued fifteen-year Treasury bond can be "stripped" into thirty-one separate zero-coupon securities. Why thirty-one? Because there are two coupons per year (remember that interest is payable semiannually), and 15 × 2 = 30 plus the corpus or body of the bond = 31 (of course, there are only 30 different maturities, since the corpus and last coupon have the same maturity.) To help market such dealer-manufactured zero-coupon securities, they have been given colorful names, like CATS (Certificates of Accrual on Treasury Securities) and TIGRS (Treasury Investment Growth Receipts).

WHO BUYS THE SECURITIES?

The $1,800 billion of marketable U.S. government securities are widely held not only in this country but throughout the world. In the first place, the Federal Reserve owns $200 billion as a result of current and past open market operations. Virtually all Federal Reserve open market purchases and sales are conducted with government securities, mostly bills. The Fed's portfolio of governments provides the central bank with most of its income; after all, even a modest 5 percent yield on a $200 billion portfolio amounts to a healthy $10 billion a year.

This leaves $1,600 billion of marketable government debt held by the private sector—by commercial banks, individuals, insurance companies, nonfinancial corporations, pension funds, money market mutual funds, and foreign investors.

Commercial banks hold especially large amounts of governments—about $200 billion—most of which are Treasury bills. They use them as one of the means through which they adjust their short-term reserve positions (as discussed in Chapter 8). Banks sell bills when they need more reserves and buy them when they have more reserves than required. Since there is a very active market in bills, making them extremely liquid, they are particularly well suited for this purpose. Banks also buy governments as a residual use of funds during recessions, when there is a slowdown in the demand for loans by creditworthy business and household borrowers.

Individual investors also own large amounts of marketable issues, although government securities are not as important to individuals as they used to be. When Regulation Q was still in the saddle, in the seventies and early eighties, Treasury bills used to be a favorite vehicle for households to shift into when market interest rates periodically rose above Regulation Q's deposit rate ceilings. Unable to obtain market rates on their funds in deposit-type institutions, people transferred their money directly into Treasury bills and notes or did so indirectly via money market mutual funds. Since 1982, when the Garn–St. Germain Depository Institutions Act empowered deposit-type financial institutions to offer ceiling-free money market deposit accounts, such waves of financial disintermediation no longer occur.

Since the late seventies, *foreigners* have been particularly large buyers of Treasury issues. They now own approximately $250 billion, about 15 percent of the marketable national debt (in 1969 they owned less than 5 percent).

Foreigners have acquired hundreds of billions of U.S. dollars by successfully selling automobiles, television sets, computers, and just about everything else to Americans. They have invested many of these dollars in U.S. stocks and bonds, especially government bonds. Money from abroad has been attracted here because of this country's political stability, financial freedom, relatively low inflation rate, and relatively high real interest rates.

In recognition of these substantial foreign investments in Treasury securities, it is often said, quite accurately, that recent U.S. budget deficits have been financed largely by foreigners. If it weren't for foreign purchases of Treasury securities, U.S. interest rates would be much higher than they have been.

HOW THE MARKET WORKS

Most of the trading in governments takes place in the over-the-counter dealer market. At the heart of the market are forty or so government securities dealers. Some of the dealers are departments of major banks, like Citibank and Bankers Trust, while others are departments of large brokerage firms, like Merrill Lynch and Salomon Brothers. Most have their principal offices in New York, but some are headquartered in Chicago, San Francisco, and Los Angeles.

As described in the previous chapter, the dealers stand ready to either buy or sell, at posted "bid" or "asked" prices, all the various maturities of government securities. They do business mainly with institutions, like banks, pension funds, and multinational corporations, rather than with individuals. Individuals have access to the market through their local banks or brokerage houses, which in turn contact dealers.

Trading in governments averages more than $100 billion a day, about twenty times a typical day's trading on the New York Stock Exchange. Normal trading hours are from 9 A.M. to 4 P.M., New York time, but trading often extends beyond those hours when there is a lot of market activity. In fact, U.S. government securities are increasingly traded around the clock on virtually a nonstop basis, with trading following the sun around the globe. After trading stops late in the afternoon in New York, it moves west to San Francisco, then to Tokyo, and still later to Frankfurt and London before returning to New York the next morning. Many dealers have offices or affiliates in all those cities as well as in others.

Dealers get much of their inventory of bonds by bidding at competitive auctions. All marketable government securities are initially issued at auctions held by the Treasury. Three- and six-month Treasury bills, for example, are auctioned weekly (on Mondays), one-year bills monthly, and notes and bonds also on a regularly scheduled basis. Potential buyers at the auctions range from government securities dealers and large banks, with hundreds of millions to invest, to individuals with no more than a few thousand dollars to spare. The large investors wait until the very last minute before submitting their bids, trying to get the best price, while individuals usually submit theirs several days before the auction begins.

The best way to understand what happens at an auction is to be there, so in a moment we'll do the next best thing and report on the details of a typical Treasury bill auction. First, though, let's refresh our memories about the basics of calculating yields on zero-coupon securities in general and on Treasury bills in particular. Treasury bills, as mentioned earlier, are a type of zero-coupon security. They are issued at a price below face value, with face value payable at maturity. The difference between price and face value constitutes the interest payment.

CALCULATING YIELDS ONCE AGAIN

We saw back in Chapter 5 that the *general* formula for annual yield to maturity (r) on a zero-coupon bond with n years until maturity is:

$$Price = \frac{Face\ Value}{(1 + r)^n}$$

We also saw in Chapter 5 that the formula for calculating the annual yield on a Treasury bill with *one year* to maturity is:

$$Price = \frac{Face\ Value}{(1 + r)}$$

The exponent n disappears in the denominator, because it is equal to unity when the maturity of the security is one year. We can solve this formula for an explicit value for r:[2]

$$r = \frac{Face\ Value - Purchase\ Price}{Purchase\ Price}$$

When this expression is multiplied by 100, it generates r in percentage terms. For example, if a $100 face value Treasury bill is purchased for $95, the formula produces a yield of 5.26 percent. In effect, this

[2]Take $P = F/(1 + r)$, multiply both sides by $(1 + r)$, producing $P(1 + r) = F$. Now divide both sides by P, giving $(1 + r) = F/P$. Subtract 1 from both sides, so $r = F/P - 1$. Getting the common denominator for the right-hand side gives $F/P - P/P$, which yields the formula in the text.

formula measures the rate at which an initial sum of money (the purchase price) grows to the final sum (the face value).

But the expression must be modified when the growth takes less than a year, because all yields are commonly understood as per annum. For example, if a six-month Treasury bill costs $95 and grows into $100 in just half a year, the annual yield should be 5.263 × 2 = 10.53 percent.

The general formula for the annual yield on Treasury bills of three, six, or twelve months maturity is:

$$r = \frac{Face\ Value - Purchase\ Price}{Purchase\ Price} \times t$$

where t is the *inverse* of the fraction of a year the bill takes to mature. This entire expression is often called the coupon equivalent yield of a Treasury bill, and we will return to it in the following section.

Thus a six-month bill that costs $95 for $100 face value has a value for $t = 2$ (the inverse of $\frac{1}{2}$ year), implying an annual yield of 5.263 × 2 = 10.53 percent according to the formula. A three-month bill that costs $95 has a value for $t = 4$ (three months is $\frac{1}{4}$ of a year), so the annual yield would be 5.263 × 4 = 21.05 percent. Since a one-year bill that costs $95 has a value of $t = 1$, the yield (as noted above) would be 5.26 percent.[3]

With this background in mind, let's turn to an illustrative Treasury bill auction.

TREASURY BILLS: AUCTIONS AND YIELDS

Table 1 shows the results of the regular weekly auction of three- and six-month bills that was held on Monday, August 17, 1987. Before the auction, the Treasury announced that it would sell $6.6 billion of three-month bills and an equal amount of six-month bills (see the second line of the table). Some potential buyers, fearful of not getting their bills by competitive bidding, submitted noncompetitive tenders (line 3), which guaranteed they would receive bills at the *average* price resulting from the auction. Because $1.0 billion of noncompetitive tenders were submitted for the three-month bill, the Treasury had

[3]In reality, of course, yields on 3-month, 6-month, and 1-year bills are likely to be very similar. If each were to yield 5.26 percent, then the 3-month bill would sell for $98.70 and the 6-month bill would sell for $97.40, compared with $95.00 for the 1-year bill.

to use competitive bidding for only the remaining $5.6 billion; and because $1.0 billion of such orders were also submitted for the six-month bill, the Treasury again had to sell only the remaining $5.6 billion competitively (line 4).

Competitive bids can be submitted at any Federal Reserve Bank or Branch until 1:00 P.M. on the day of the auction. At that time the Treasury closes the books and begins ranking the bids from the highest price on down. Table 1 shows that $25.5 billion of bids (both competitive and noncompetitive) were received for the three-month bill and $27.5 billion for the six-month issue—in both cases close to four times what the Treasury wanted to sell.

The highest bid for the three-month bill was $98.501 for a $100 face value bill. (Actually, $10,000 is the minimum denomination for Treasury bills, so $98.501 really means $9,850.10. However, it is easier to do the calculations on the basis of $100 rather than $10,000.) Everyone bidding at that price was a successful bidder. The Treasury continued to accept bids at lower and lower prices until they aggregated $5.6 billion for three-month bills and the same amount for six-month bills. At that point—the stop-out price—the auction was over, and those who submitted lower bids got nothing.

Because the successful bidders bought their bills at different prices, they will be receiving different yields. Two kinds of yield computa-

TABLE 1
Results of Treasury Bill Auction Held on August 17, 1987

	Three-month bills	Six-month bills
Amount applied for at auction	$25.5 billion	$27.5 billion
Amount scheduled to be sold	$ 6.6 billion	$ 6.6 billion
Noncompetitive tenders	$ 1.0 billion	$ 1.0 billion
Sales by competitive bidding	$ 5.6 billion	$ 5.6 billion
High price paid at auction	$98.501	$96.916
Yield on a discount basis	5.93%	6.10%
Coupon equivalent yield	6.12%	6.40%
Average price paid at auction	$98.491	$96.906
Yield on a discount basis	5.97%	6.12%
Coupon equivalent yield	6.16%	6.42%
Low price paid (stop-out price)	$98.488	$96.901
Yield on a discount basis	5.98%	6.13%
Coupon equivalent yield	6.17%	6.43%

SOURCE: United States Treasury.

tions are used in the Treasury bill market: (1) yield on a discount basis, and (2) coupon equivalent yield (also called bond equivalent yield).

1. *Yield on a discount basis* is calculated as the face value minus the purchase price (let's call this D, for discount) divided by the face value. For example, Table 1 shows that high bidders for the new three-month bill received a $100 face value Treasury bill for $98.501. They paid $98.501, but in three months they'll get back $100. The difference ($D$) is $1.499:

$$\frac{1.499}{100} = 1.499\%$$

However, all yields are commonly understood to be on an *annual* basis. Three-month bills are really 13-week bills; they mature 91 days from issue date. Assuming as a rough approximation that a year has 360 days, a yield of 1.499 percent for 91 days can be annualized by multiplying it by 360/91 or 3.956. Thus the annual yield on a discount basis for the three-month Treasury bill high bidders is 1.499% × 3.956 = 5.93% (see Table 1).

The general formula for calculating yield on a discount basis is:

$$\frac{D}{Face\ Value} \times \frac{360}{Number\ Days\ to\ Maturity}$$

As another illustration, take the low bidders for the *six-month* bill. Six-month Treasury bills are really 26-week bills; they mature 182 days from issue date. Three- and six-month bills are always auctioned on a Monday, issued on Thursday of the same week, and mature on Thursday either 13 or 26 weeks later. Its annual yield on a discount basis would be:

$$\frac{3.099}{100} \times \frac{360}{182} = 6.13\% \text{ (see Table 1)}$$

Yields have been quoted on a discount basis in the money market for generations. They keep being used because custom and tradition are hard to overcome. Nevertheless, the yield on a discount basis is a poor indicator of the *true* yield for two reasons. First of all, an investor doesn't pay the full face value of a bill when buying it, so 100 shouldn't be the denominator in the first term of the expression. Second, there aren't 360 days in a year, so 360 shouldn't be the numerator in the second term of the equation.

2. *The coupon equivalent yield* of a Treasury bill (mentioned in the preceding section) corrects for these two flaws in yield on a discount

Reading the Financial News: Government Bond Market Quotations

(1)			(2)	(3)	(4) Bid	(5)
Rate	Mat.	Date	Bid	Asked	Chg.	Yld.
8¼s,	2000–05	May	105.25	106.1	+.4	7.53
12s,	2005	May	141.12	141.20	+.4	7.72
10¾s,	2005	Aug	129.8	129.16	+.2	7.73
9⅜s,	2006	Feb	117.10	117.18	...	7.61
7⅝s,	2002–07	Feb	100.25	101.1	+.5	7.51
7⅞s,	2002–07	Nov	103.4	103.12	+.2	7.51
8⅜s,	2003–08	Aug	106.26	107.2	+.8	7.62
8¾s,	2003–08	Nov	110.4	110.12	+.3	7.64
9⅛s,	2004–09	May	113.18	113.26	+.7	7.67
10⅜s,	2004–09	Nov	125.6	125.14	+.8	7.77
11¾s,	2005–10	Feb	137.18	137.26	+.6	7.81
10s,	2005–10	May	122.12	122.20	+.11	7.68
12¾s,	2005–10	Nov	147.24	148	+.7	7.83
13⅞s,	2006–11	May	158.30	159.6	+.5	7.87
14s,	2006–11	Nov	160.24	161	+.4	7.87
10⅜s,	2007–12	Nov	126.16	126.24	+.5	7.76
12s,	2008–13	Aug	143	143.4	+.7	7.83
13¼s,	2009–14	May	156	156.8	+.9	7.86
12½s,	2009–14	Aug	148.23	148.27	+.6	7.85
11¾s,	2009–14	Nov	142.8	142.16	+.8	7.75
11¼s,	2015	Feb	140.10	140.14	+.6	7.71
10⅝s,	2015	Aug	133.19	133.27	+.9	7.68
9⅞s,	2015	Nov	125.4	125.12	...	7.68
9¼s,	2016	Feb	119.10	119.18	+.9	7.58
7¼s,	2016	May	97.8	97.12	+.8	7.47
7½s,	2016	Nov	101.11	101.15	+.9	7.38

Column (1) identifies each government bond in terms of its coupon rate and maturity date. For example, the *second* bond in Column (1) carries a 12 percent coupon and will mature in May of the year 2005. (Conversationally, it is referred to as "the twelve*s* of oh five," which explains the *s* following each coupon rate.) The next bond has a $10\frac{3}{4}$ percent coupon and will mature in August of 2005 (the ten and three-quarters of oh five).

Many bonds—like the first one, the eight and a quarters of May 2000–05—have *two* maturity dates. Such bonds mature on the second date but are *callable* by the Treasury starting with the first date. The $8\frac{1}{4}$s of May 2000–05, for example, will mature in May of 2005; however, if it wishes, the Treasury can call them for redemption in May of 2000 or at six-month intervals thereafter until it *has* to redeem them by May of 2005.

Columns (2) and (3) indicate what government securities dealers were "bidding" and "asking" for each bond at the close of trading yesterday—that is, their "buying price" (bid) and "selling price" (asked). Government bonds normally have a face value of $1,000 and, like corporate bonds (see the box in Chapter 31), their price is conventionally expressed as a percentage of face value. Note that the numbers after the period are not decimals but 32nds. Thus, with respect to the last bond on the list, the $7\frac{1}{2}$s of 2016, government securities dealers were willing to buy at $101\frac{11}{32}$ (= $1,013.4375) and willing to sell at a slightly higher price of $101\frac{15}{32}$ (= $1,014.6875).

Column (4) is the change in the dealers' bid price at the close of trading yesterday compared with the previous day's close. It is also in 32nds. For example, the $7\frac{1}{2}$s of 2016 closed at $101\frac{11}{32}$ bid, up $\frac{9}{32}$ from the previous day's close of $101\frac{2}{32}$.

Column (5) is the bond's yield to maturity. For callable bonds, the yield to maturity is calculated in one of two ways: (a) to first call date when the asked price is above par (100), and (b) to maturity date when the asked price is equal to or below par. In Column (5) the period is a true decimal point, so there is an implied percent sign (%) after each yield.

basis. The usual formula for calculating the annual coupon equivalent yield is:

$$\frac{D}{Purchase\ Price} \times \frac{365}{Number\ Days\ to\ Maturity}$$

However, whenever a leap year is involved in the annualizing process, the numerator in the second term becomes 366 instead of 365. For the bills auctioned on August 17, 1987, a leap year is indeed involved in annualizing both yields, since a year from that date includes a February 29th.

For example, low bidders for the six-month bill who paid $96.901 for a $100 face value security received a coupon equivalent yield of:

$$\frac{3.099}{96.901} \times \frac{366}{182} = 6.43 \text{ percent (see Table 1)}$$

As Table 1 shows, coupon equivalent yield is always *larger* than yield on a discount basis, because the denominator of the first term is necessarily smaller (it is the purchase price instead of the face value) and the numerator of the second term is larger (365 or 366 rather than 360).

The details of auctions for other types of Treasury securities differ somewhat from bill auctions, but the basics are still the same. Highest bidders buy first until the supply to be auctioned is exhausted. The yield calculations for the coupon-bearing Treasury issues are straightforward (as described in Chapter 5 and the accompanying illustration), without the discount yield complication. At this point, let's spend some time on a market that is intimately connected with Treasury securities—the market for repurchase agreements.

REPURCHASE AGREEMENTS

With the Treasury auctioning billions of dollars in securities to government securities dealers, it should not be surprising that the dealers have developed repurchase agreements (repos or RPs) as an efficient mechanism for financing such activities. It should also not be surprising that once in place, this financing mechanism has taken on a life of its own. In particular, the market for repurchase agreements is, along with the federal funds market, the focal point of overnight borrowing and lending.

In a typical repurchase agreement, a government securities dealer sells government securities (such as those just purchased at an auction) and agrees to repurchase them at a higher price the next day. The price the dealer agrees to pay for the securities the next day has nothing to do with what those securities sell for in the marketplace the next day. Rather the price is set to reflect the overnight cost of funds. And that's because the repurchase agreement is really a vehicle for borrowing money. In particular, when the owners of securities sell them they take in dollars; when they repurchase the securities the next day at a fixed price they are simply repaying those dollars plus interest. Notice that the other side of the repo transaction is called a reverse RP, and involves lending funds overnight.

The repo market and the federal funds market (discussed in Chapter 17) share a number of common characteristics. First, both markets are sources of overnight funds. Second, both markets settle payments the same day the transaction is completed. For example, in the case of the repo, the same day the dealer sells the securities with an agreement to repurchase them at a fixed priced, the funds are transferred into the dealer's accounts by whoever did the other side of the transaction (the reverse RP). The main difference between a repo and federal funds transaction is that the latter is an unsecured overnight loan between financial institutions, while the former is essentially a collateralized loan, with the securities that are subject to repurchase acting as the collateral. Thus the overnight federal funds rate and the rate on repurchase agreements tend to move closely together. Whenever one rate moves up significantly relative to the other, borrowers borrow in the cheaper market, lenders lend in the more expensive market, and the rates are driven together—except that the federal funds rate is always slightly above the repo rate (about $\frac{1}{4}$ of one percent) to reflect the fact that repos are collateralized.

Although the repo market began as a mechanism for financing government securities on an overnight basis, the transaction has evolved into much broader use. First, repos are now done over a wide variety of maturities, ranging from the traditional one day to three months. Second, although Treasuries are most easily financed via repurchase agreements, other securities such as GNMA pass-throughs are also financed via repos. Third, it is somewhat misleading to view the underlying collateral as what the repo is financing. In a sense, the repurchase agreement is used to raise funds for anything the borrower chooses. The underlying securities are simply acting as collateral for the lender.

Having said all that, it is still true that repos play a major role in helping dealers finance their purchases of Treasury securities. Let's now turn to our final topic, which focuses on the other side of the coin—how the U.S. Treasury conducts its debt management operations.

THE TREASURY'S DEBT MANAGEMENT DECISION

What are the objectives of day-to-day debt management? One goal is to minimize the interest cost of the debt to the taxpayers. But this can hardly be the only objective. If it were, the Treasury could minimize the interest cost—indeed, reduce it to zero—simply by printing money and buying back all the outstanding securities. It could thus replace its interest-bearing debt (bills, notes, and bonds) with its non-interest-bearing debt (money). The Treasury does not "monetize the debt" because to do so would probably result in massive inflation, and the Treasury also has the objective of managing the debt to promote economic stability.

These two objectives—minimizing interest cost and promoting economic stabilization—often dictate opposite policy actions. Minimizing the interest cost suggests that when we are in a recession, and interest rates are low across the board, the Treasury should refund its maturing issues with new long-term bonds, thus insuring low interest payments for itself well into the future. During boom periods, when interest rates are typically high, the Treasury should refinance by selling short-term issues, Treasury bills, so the government does not have to continue paying high rates after yields have fallen to more normal levels.

Stabilization objectives call for just the opposite policies. When we are in a recession, the last thing we want to do is raise long-term interest rates, which is precisely what pushing long-term securities onto the market is likely to accomplish. Boom periods, when we *do* want to raise long rates (to reduce investment spending), are when we should sell long-term bonds.

Thus the objective of minimizing interest costs dictates lengthening the maturity structure of the debt (more long-term bonds relative to short-term bills) during recession periods, and shortening the maturity structure during boom periods. For purposes of economic stabilization we should do the opposite—try to shorten the maturity structure during recessions and lengthen it during prosperity.

Debt management policy must be administered in coordination with monetary and fiscal policy. If minimizing the interest cost is the primary goal of Treasury debt management, then monetary and fiscal policy will have to take appropriate action to offset this counterstabilization debt policy. If economic stabilization is the primary objective of debt management, the monetary and fiscal authorities can take this into account and reduce the forcefulness of their own actions.[4]

Coordination between the monetary and debt management authorities is also essential on a continuing basis because of the vast magnitude of the Treasury's frequent refunding operations. When the Treasury refinances a large volume of maturing issues, it often needs central bank help. If the Federal Reserve is pursuing a tight money policy, for example, it may become somewhat less aggressive and resort to a policy of keeping an "even keel" in the bond markets as the date of a refinancing approaches. In effect, the central bank marks time while the Treasury goes through the mechanics of the refunding operation. It is difficult enough for the Treasury to roll over so much debt without being forced to cope with additional complications resulting from aggressive actions of the monetary authorities.

Monetary policy, fiscal policy, and debt management are often considered the three main tools of stabilization policy. In fact, however, debt management has typically been the runt of the litter. Perhaps that is just as well. Given the power of monetary and fiscal policy to implement national economic goals, perhaps debt management can make its most significant contribution by successfully accomplishing the more limited but not unimportant task of continuously refinancing a very large volume of government securities without unduly disturbing the nation's financial markets.

SUMMARY

1. The federal budget has generally been in deficit since 1930, so that the U.S. Treasury has had to borrow large sums by selling government securities.

2. Seventy percent of the national debt is in the form of marketable government securities, consisting of Treasury bills, notes, and bonds.

3. Although notes and bonds begin life as coupon securities, government securities dealers often take newly issued ones and convert them to zero-coupon form by "stripping" them.

4. Commercial banks hold large amounts of governments, as do foreigners. It is often said that recent U.S. budget deficits have been financed largely by

[4]See "Managing Treasury Debt: Are Changes Needed?," Morgan Guaranty *Survey* (January 1982).

foreigners. Money from abroad has been attracted here because of this country's political stability, financial freedom, low inflation, and relatively high real interest rates.

5. Most trading in governments takes place in the over-the-counter dealer market. Government securities dealers are at the heart of the market. Dealers stand ready to buy or sell all the various maturities at quoted "bid" or "asked" prices. Treasury issues are increasingly traded around the clock on virtually a nonstop basis.

6. Dealers get much of their inventory by bidding at competitive auctions, which is how the Treasury initially issues all marketable government securities. Dealers often use repurchase agreements to finance their holdings of governments.

7. Treasury bill yields are calculated in two different ways: yield on a discount basis and, more accurately, coupon equivalent yield (also called bond equivalent yield).

8. Treasury debt management often faces a conflict of goals: minimizing the interest cost of the debt to the taxpayers versus the promotion of economic stability.

Suggestions for Further Reading

Further information on the functioning of the government securities market is contained in Marcia Stigum, *The Money Market,* rev. ed. (Homewood, Ill.: Dow Jones–Irwin, 1983); in the *Handbook of Securities of the United States Government and Federal Agencies,* which is published every other year by The First Boston Corporation; and in Howard M. Berlin, *The Dow Jones–Irwin Guide to Buying and Selling Treasury Securities* (Homewood, Ill.: Dow Jones–Irwin, 1984).

C H A P T E R   3 1

Other Fixed-Income Markets: Corporate Bonds, Municipals, and Mortgages

Federal government bonds dominate the markets for fixed-income securities, but they are not alone. Business corporations and state and local governments also borrow by selling bonds, and mortgages resemble bonds in many respects as well. In the preceding chapter, we explored in some detail the market for federal government securities. This chapter looks, somewhat more briefly, at the markets for corporate debt, including bonds and commercial paper, at state and local government securities, including specialized short-term issues, and at mortgages.

CORPORATE BONDS

About $900 billion of corporate bonds issued by domestic business firms were outstanding at the end of 1986. We have already examined some of their characteristics in Chapter 3. High-quality corporate bonds attract buyers because they usually yield more than government or municipal bonds and they are considered safer than stocks. Bonds have a prior claim before stocks on a corporation's earnings, and bondholders also have a preferred claim before stockholders on the assets of a company that fails. The major shortcoming of bonds is that they are often fairly long term and therefore subject to interest-rate risk—if interest rates rise, their prices plummet.

All corporate bonds are not identical. Differences among them include *call provisions* and *conversion features.* Some bonds are *callable* after a certain specified date; that is, the issuer (the borrower) has the right to pay off part or all of the bond before the scheduled maturity date. Call provisions are exercised by the borrower when it is in the borrower's interest to do so—for instance, when the level of interest rates has fallen, so that the borrower can re-borrow more cheaply. In partial compensation to the lender, the borrower often has to pay a penalty if a bond is called before maturity; the price at which the bond can be called is usually above par—that is, above 100. Naturally, a borrower will call a bond only if the advantages of doing so outweigh the penalty.

Some corporate bonds are *convertible,* in that they offer holders the right to convert their bonds into shares of the company's common stock at a predetermined price. This feature often attracts lenders and thereby enables a corporation to sell such bonds at a lower interest rate than it would otherwise have to pay.

Corporate (and municipal) bonds also differ from one another in *quality.* Some borrowers are more likely and some are less likely to make their scheduled interest payments on time and to pay back the principal (face value) when the bond comes due (that is, when it matures). There is no question about the ability of the U.S. government to service its debts, but the same cannot always be said about corporate and municipal borrowers. Thus corporate and municipal bonds are rated for quality by three private firms—Moody's, Standard & Poor's, and Fitch's. Table 1 shows the rating measures that are used by Moody's and by S&P and what they mean.

Life insurance companies and pension and retirement funds hold most of the outstanding corporate bonds. Such institutions have a minimum need for liquidity because a large fraction of their expenditures can be scheduled many years in advance on the basis of average life expectancies and similar mortality statistics. Thus they can afford to buy long-term bonds and not worry about interest rates, since they probably won't have to sell prior to maturity in order to meet a sudden need for cash. Foreigners have also become large buyers of American corporate bonds, just as they have become big buyers of U.S. government securities, as we saw in the previous chapter.

While the bonds of some large corporations are listed and traded on the New York Stock Exchange, most corporate bond trading takes

TABLE 1
A Guide to Bond Ratings

Moody's	S&P	Description
Investment Grades		
Aaa	AAA	Highest quality with least risk; strong ability to pay interest and principal
Aa	AA	High quality but with slightly less financial strength than above
A	A	Strong capacity to pay interest and principal, but a bit vulnerable to changes in economic conditions
Baa	BBB	Adequate current financial strength, but could be threatened by changes in the economy
Speculative Grades		
Ba	BB	Currently paying interest but with an uncertain future
B	B	Little assurance that interest and principal will continue to be paid
Caa to C	CCC to C	Highly speculative bonds that may be in or near default
	D	Used only by S&P for bonds in default

NOTE: Bonds rated below Baa by Moody's (below BBB by Standard and Poor's) are often called "junk bonds."

place in the over-the-counter market, through market-making dealers. The telephone is still the dominant mechanism for uncovering the best bids and offers of the numerous bond-dealing firms. A life insurance company portfolio manager, for example, may telephone a number of bond dealers to locate the best bid for a bond the company has decided to sell. There are so many individual corporate debt issues that trades in a particular bond are sometimes days or weeks apart. It does not really pay to invest in highly automated trading facilities when the volume of transactions doesn't warrant the huge outlay.

On the other hand, most dealers do maintain extensive computer-based information systems to record the bond preferences and holdings of ultimate investors (insurance companies, pension funds, and other institutions). This helps the dealer unearth buyers and sellers when needed. More importantly, it helps dealers place the corporate bonds they buy in their capacity as underwriters. Almost all corporate bonds are sold through underwriting syndicates of securities dealers.

Reading the Financial News: Corporate Bond Market Quotations

(1) Bonds	(2) Cur Yld	(3) Vol	(4) High	(5) Low	(6) Close	(7) Net Chg.
AGS 7½11	cv	20	130	130	130	−1
AMR 10¼06	10.1	1	101½	101½	101½	−½
ANR 10⅝95	10.4	1	102	102	102	+1½
ANR 13¼97	12.4	20	107¼	107¼	107¼	+¼
ARX 9⅜05	cv	85	109	108¾	108¾	−1¼
AVX 13½00	12.9	5	105	105	105	...
Advst 9s08	cv	6	109	109	109	...
AlaP 9s2000	8.9	10	101⅜	101⅜	101⅜	+¼

Column (1) shows the name of the company that issued the bond and the particular bond involved as identified by its coupon rate and maturity date. For example, the first bond in the column was issued by AGS Computers, a computer engineering and software company; it carries a $7\frac{1}{2}$ percent coupon and will mature in the year 2011. (Conversationally, it is referred to as "AGS's seven and a halves of eleven.") The next one was issued by the AMR Corporation, which provides services for airlines; it carries a $10\frac{1}{4}$ percent coupon and will mature in the year 2006 (AMR's ten and a quarters of oh six). The last one is an Alabama Power Company bond with a 9 percent coupon that matures in the year 2000 (the nines of two thousand).

Column (2) is the bond's current yield—the coupon interest payment divided by yesterday's closing price (see column 6). Where "cv" appears, the bond is convertible into a specified number of shares of the company's common stock. Although the current yield is just as easy to calculate for convertibles as for ordinary bonds, it is usually omitted for convertibles because the market value of a convertible bond is often determined by the price of the stock for which it is exchangeable.

Column (3) (volume of trading) indicates the number of $1,000 bonds that changed hands yesterday on The New York Stock Exchange. Twenty AGS bonds were traded, only 1 AMR bond, 85 ARX bonds, and so on.

Columns (4), (5), and (6) show the highest, lowest, and closing (last) price at which each bond traded yesterday. Corporate bonds normally have a face value of $1,000 and their price is conventionally expressed as a percentage of face value. AGS's seven and a halves closed yesterday at 130 or $1,300 per bond. AMR's ten and a quarters closed at $101\frac{1}{2}$ or $1,015 per bond. Advest's nines of oh eight closed at 109 or $1,090 per bond. Alabama Power's nines of two thousand closed at $101\frac{3}{8}$ or $1,013.75 per bond. Notice that corporate bonds are quoted in one-eighths of a point (= $1.25 per $1,000 bond).

Column (7) is the change in the closing price from the previous day's close. For example, AGS's seven and a halves closed at 130 ($1,300), down 1 ($10) from the previous day's close of 131 ($1,310).

As we described in Chapter 29, underwriters buy newly issued securities from corporations and then sell them to ultimate investors, earning a fee, called an underwriting spread, in the process.

COMMERCIAL PAPER

Commercial paper is to corporate bonds as Treasury bills are to Treasury bonds. That is, the government can borrow short-term (bills) or long-term (bonds), and corporations can similarly borrow short term (commercial paper) or long term (bonds). Commercial paper is a form of unsecured corporate borrowing that typically has an original maturity of between 5 and 270 days, with 30 days the most common. (It is not the only kind of unsecured business borrowing; many bank loans to business, for example, are also unsecured—that is, no specific collateral is pledged as security that the lender can take if the interest or principal is not paid.)

By convention, issuers of commercial paper are divided into two categories: financial companies (such as sales and personal finance companies and bank holding companies), and nonfinancial companies. The first group—financial companies—issues three-quarters of the dollar volume outstanding. Many finance companies are associated with well-known manufacturing firms, such as General Motors Acceptance Corporation (GMAC), the financing arm of General Motors.

Most commercial paper is bought by institutional investors, especially money market mutual funds, but nonfinancial firms and state and local governments also buy significant amounts. Since institutional investors dominate the market, the most popular denomination is $1 million. Historically, yields on commercial paper are somewhat above yields on Treasury bills of comparable maturity, because there is a greater risk of default with commercial paper than with Treasury bills, even for the highest-quality commercial paper. As can be seen in Chart 1, the commercial paper rate is intertwined with the prime rate at commercial banks (the rate charged by banks on short term loans to their most creditworthy business customers).

In the primary market, new issues of commercial paper are often sold directly from the issuer to the buyer without any intermediary (called directly placed paper) or are sold through commercial paper dealers (dealer-placed paper). Most finance companies, for example, issue their paper directly to investors, but many other corporations go through commercial paper dealers who underwrite the issues.

Many of the investment banks and brokerage firms that act as gov-

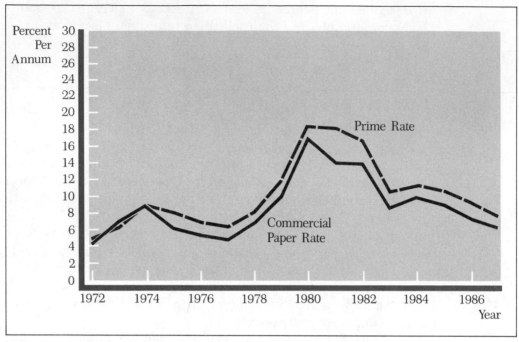

CHART 1 Bank Prime Rate and Yield on Commercial Paper. Since top-rated corporations can borrow short term via either bank loans or commercial paper, the two rates are competitive and move closely together.

SOURCE: Federal Reserve.

ernment securities dealers (see the previous chapter) also act as commercial paper dealers. Until 1980, commercial banks had been barred (by the Glass-Steagall Act) from participating in the market for commercial paper. In 1980, however, the Federal Reserve ruled that banks could "place" commercial paper as an agent for corporate clients although they could not underwrite it directly. An underwriter actually buys and resells an issue, while an agent simply brings buyer and seller together (much as a broker would do—see Chapter 29). After considerable litigation, the legal right of commercial banks to place commercial paper was upheld by the U.S. Supreme Court in 1987, when the Court refused to hear a challenge that would have stopped banks from doing so.

Unlike Treasury bills, commercial paper does not have much of a secondary market. Investors who want to sell their paper before it comes due generally turn to the issuers, who will usually redeem their own obligations before maturity as a gesture of goodwill. Corporations that use dealers to sell their paper needn't be concerned about this nuisance, because the dealers often make a limited secondary market, agreeing to buy back paper from customers only.

MUNICIPAL BONDS

State and local government bonds, usually called municipals, carry the lowest yields of all securities of similar maturity and risk, as we know from Chapter 28. This low yield reflects the fact that their interest is legally exempt from federal income taxation. (Interest on municipal bonds is also usually exempt from state and local income taxes in the state where they are issued.) The federal tax exemption of interest on municipal securities was established by the Supreme Court in the 1895 *Pollock v. Farmers' Loan and Trust Company* case and was reaffirmed in 1913 in the first federal income tax law.[1]

Let's say you earn a 10 percent yield on a municipal bond. What would be the equivalent yield on a fully taxable security? The answer depends on what marginal income tax bracket you are in. Back in the old days, if you were in the 50 percent tax bracket, for example, a 10 percent tax-free yield intuitively was the equivalent of 20 percent fully taxable. Because with taxes taking half of your income, all you'd have left of the 20 percent would be 10 percent. The general formula is:

$$\frac{\text{tax-free yield}}{1 - \text{marginal tax rate}} = \text{taxable yield equivalent}$$

Thus, if the tax-free yield is 10 percent and your marginal tax rate is 30 percent, the municipal has a 14.29 percent taxable yield equivalent.

The tax exemption feature of municipals appeals mainly to high-income individuals and to institutions that are subject to high tax rates, such as commercial banks.

Municipals are usually issued in "serial" maturity form, as contrasted with the single maturity of government and corporate bonds. Serial maturity means that a portion of the total issue matures each year until the entire issue is eventually retired. Each portion carries its own interest rate and is separate from the rest of the issue. Thus when a state issues a ten-year serial bond, it is really issuing a series of one-year, two-year, and so on up to ten-year maturities.

[1]In April 1988 the Supreme Court reversed the *Pollock* decision and ruled that Congress does indeed have the power to tax the interest on municipal bonds.

Denominations of single bonds are usually $5,000, as compared with $1,000 denominations for corporate bonds. Municipal bonds are sold initially through underwriting syndicates, just like corporate bonds, only this time the syndicates include commercial banks. Although Glass-Steagall prohibited banks from underwriting corporate securities and municipal *revenue* bonds, it allowed banks to continue underwriting municipal *general obligation* bonds. The underwriting syndicates buy new issues in large blocks from the borrowing governmental authorities and market the securities to ultimate investors at a slightly higher price, making their profit on the differential, the so-called underwriting spread.

It is important to distinguish between the two kinds of municipal bonds just mentioned: *general obligation bonds,* which are the majority of municipal bonds, and *revenue bonds.* General obligation municipals are issued for a wide variety of reasons, such as borrowing to build schools or to provide social services. They are backed by the general taxing power of the state or local government. Revenue bonds, on the other hand, are issued to finance a specific project—a toll highway, for example—and the interest and principal are paid exclusively out of the receipts that the project generates.

As might be expected, general obligation bonds are usually considered the safer of the two. Revenue bonds are riskier, because the particular project they are tied to might falter financially. A case in point is the 1983 default of the state of Washington on $2.25 billion of Washington Public Power Supply System (WPPSS) bonds, the largest municipal bond failure in U.S. history. The WPPSS (often called Whoops) bonds were originally sold to finance several nuclear power plants in the state of Washington, and the payment of interest and principal depended on the financial success of those specific projects. Two of the plants were plagued by troubles for years; their financial difficulties eventually resulted in defaults and consequent losses to those who had bought the bonds.

Secondary trading in municipals is conducted entirely in the over-the-counter dealer market. There are so many small issues of tiny and virtually unknown municipalities that the secondary market is not particularly active. Although the securities of some large states and cities have above-average liquidity (for a municipal bond, that is), many municipals are traded infrequently or not at all. As a result, the bid-asked spreads on municipal bonds are much wider than they are on either government or corporate bonds. To minimize this problem, when institutional investors want to sell some of their municipal bonds they frequently employ the services of a specialized municipal bond broker. Perhaps the best known broker is J.J. Kenny and Company. The broker disseminates information on the bonds—coupon, maturity, and issuer—to potential investors, namely other institutions. Bids for the bonds are reported back to the seller, who can then decide whether to sell or not.

Most municipal bond prices and yields are not printed in the daily newspapers, but trade papers contain such information. The *Daily Bond Buyer* publishes data on new issues, and the *Blue List of Current Municipal Offerings* specializes in secondary market activity.

SHORT-TERM MUNICIPALS

The two most popular short-term securities issued by state and local governments are tax-anticipation notes (TANs) and bond-anticipation notes (BANs).

Tax receipts flow in intermittently, rather than regularly, so TANs are used to borrow funds in the intervals between tax payment dates. The notes have maturities ranging from a few days to a few months and are paid off when tax receipts come in. BANs similarly provide stopgap financing for large projects, such as sewers or roads, and are paid off when long-term bonds are floated.

Recent innovations in the short-term municipal market include tax-exempt commercial paper and floating-rate issues with the interest rate linked to Treasury bill yields. Tax-exempt commercial paper has maturities between 1 and 270 days. There is no well-developed secondary market, but dealers will generally buy back paper they have sold.

Money market funds that specialize in the purchase of short-term tax exempts have grown rapidly in recent years. Their popularity stems from the fact that they allow people of moderate wealth to diversify their portfolios of such securities. The funds require a minimum investment of only $500 or $1,000, whereas the smallest denomination in which one can buy municipals directly is $5,000 for each security.

MORTGAGE TRADING: POOLS AND PARTICIPATIONS

Mortgages have been around forever, but trading them in a well-developed secondary market is a fairly recent phenomenon. Many of the details of mortgages were discussed in Chapter 3, so let's now focus on trading, which involves the most innovative developments.

Very little secondary trading takes place in individual mortgages. The main difficulty with mortgages is the diversity of individual characteristics and the relatively small size of each issue. These preclude active market-making. A dealer who bought and sold individual mortgage loans would be inundated with unwanted detail.

The major form of secondary market trading in mortgages revolves around mortgage pools. These were introduced in 1970 when the Department of HUD's Government National Mortgage Association (Ginnie Mae) announced that it would insure the timely payment of interest and principal on bundles of FHA-VA insured mortgages. These had to be at least $1 million pools of standardized individual mortgages—government insured, identical coupon, with a servicing fee paid to the originator of the mortgage to collect and "pass through" the interest and principal to the ultimate investor. Dealers viewed these "GNMA pass-through" instruments as quite similar to bonds and began to quote bids and offers on them. The volume outstanding of these neatly wrapped mortgages grew substantially, and trading became extremely active. The underlying mortgages thus gained marketability by disappearing into a package.

Although conventional mortgages (those not federally insured) are less homogeneous than the government-insured variety, they too have entered the pass-through parade. The Federal Home Loan Mortgage Corporation issues participation certificates in conventionals, and a number of private firms, led by major banks and savings and loan associations, have issued pass-throughs backed by conventional mortgages. The once nonexistent secondary market for mortgages now flourishes under the multicolored packaging of pass-throughs and participation certificates.

As pointed out in Chapter 3, one of the unique characteristics of mortgages is the uncertainty that exists for the lender with respect to inflows of cash. Homeowners often prepay their mortgages if they move to a new location or if interest rates fall and they can refinance their loan on better terms. Lenders do not like this uncertainty over cash flows. To make this uncertainty somewhat less of a problem, securities dealers invented the *collateralized mortgage obligation* (CMO). In this case, a number of mortgages are put together into a trust. The interest and principal prepayments are then divided by the trustee (often a bank) into three or four segments, with investors choosing whether they want to receive their payments over the first four or five years, the second four or five years, the third, and so on. In this way the cash flow becomes more predictable for each investor. CMOs now trade alongside pass-throughs in the mortgage market.

SUMMARY

1. Differences exist among bonds with respect to such matters as their call provisions and conversion features. Three private agencies rate corporate and municipal bonds with respect to quality—that is, with respect to the ability of the borrower to pay interest when scheduled and repay principal when due.

2. Life insurance companies and pension funds hold most of the outstanding corporate bonds, because their liquidity needs are minimal. Foreigners have also become large buyers of corporate bonds.

3. Although some corporate bond trading takes place on the New York Stock Exchange, most trading is over-the-counter through market-making dealers. These are the same dealers who act as underwriters when a corporate bond is first issued.

4. Commercial paper is to corporate bonds as Treasury bills are to Treasury bonds. Financial companies issue most of the commercial paper outstanding. In the primary market, some commercial paper is directly placed and some is dealer-placed.

5. Municipal bonds appeal mainly to high-income individuals and to institutions subject to high tax rates, because of their federal income tax exemption. Underwriting syndicates dominate the primary market, and subsequent trading takes place in the over-the-counter market.

6. General obligation municipal bonds are backed by the general taxing power of the state or local government. Revenue bonds are related to a specific project, with interest and principal payments generated by that project's revenues.

7. Short-term municipals include tax-anticipation notes and bond-anticipation notes. Tax-exempt commercial paper and floating rate issues are recent innovations.

8. The major form of secondary market trading in mortgages now revolves around mortgage pools. These "pass-throughs" are collections of individual mortgages that pass the interest and principal on to the ultimate investor. Ginnie Maes are the most popular type of mortgage pool.

Suggestions for Further Reading

The reading suggestions at the end of Chapter 3 are also appropriate for this chapter. In addition, on mortgages see the Federal Trade Commission, *The Mortgage Money Guide* (1986) and Charles M. Sivesand, "Mortgage-Backed Securities: The Revolution in Real Estate Finance," Federal Reserve Bank of New York *Quarterly Review* (Autumn 1979). For developments in the market for state and local government securities, see "Municipals—A Market in Transition," Morgan Guaranty *Economic Quarterly* (June 1987).

CHAPTER 32

Equities, the Stock Market, and Interest Rates

People have been known to make money in the stock market and also to lose some. It is a fact of life that the total number of stocks in existence changes rather slowly. What does change from year to year is not so much the number of shares but rather the price of each.

For example, at the end of 1986 the market value of all the publicly held shares of stock in the United States amounted to something like $3,000 billion. In the early 1960s it was about $500 billion. Yet in the past thirty years or so corporations have raised no more than a couple of hundred billion dollars by issuing new stock. That means that most of the $2,500 billion increase between the 1960s and 1980s must represent price appreciation of existing shares.

Why do stock prices go up and down? Not so much particular stocks, like IBM and Xerox, but why does the entire market, more or less, rise or fall? How important is the money supply in driving stock prices up or down? What about interest rates? We will examine these pricing issues, but first let's take a look at the marketplace itself.

STRUCTURE OF THE STOCK MARKET

According to the New York Stock Exchange, there are now about 35 million individual shareholders in the United States. Nevertheless, in

541

the past decade institutional investors—especially pension funds, mutual funds, and insurance companies—have edged individuals to the side and begun to dominate the stock market.

"The stock market" refers principally to the secondary market for common stocks. The primary market—that is, the original distribution of new stock issues—operates through investment bankers, as we saw in Chapter 29. It is mostly the subsequent trading of securities that constitutes what is generally called the stock market.

The New York Stock Exchange (NYSE)—the Big Board—is the most visible part of the stock market, in part because shares of the largest and best-known corporations are traded there. High visibility also comes from the fact that you can actually see the marketplace. Trading in the shares of about 1,800 corporations takes place on the floor of the exchange at 11 Wall Street. Business is conducted by members of the exchange, and transactions are recorded on an electronic ticker tape flashed on the floor itself as well as in brokerage offices throughout the country. This is a real marketplace, the same as at the county fair, except that it's a lot more hectic.

Individual stocks are traded at particular locations, called posts, on the football-field floor. Traders receiving orders via telephone from brokerage offices throughout the country scurry about placing orders with particular specialists. The job of specialists is to maintain orderly trading for the securities in their charge.

Specialists may simply match publicly tendered buy and sell orders submitted at the same price. Floor traders stand at the post and bid for orders that are not matched on the specialist's order book. When neither of these occur, specialists step in and buy for their own account (at the bid price) or sell from their inventory (at the asked price) in order to prevent excessive gyrations in transactions prices.

In addition to the New York Stock Exchange, another part of the stock market consists of smaller organized exchanges—the American Stock Exchange, the Midwest Stock Exchange, and so on. Each exchange has its own listings—securities that are traded primarily on it. Smaller companies are generally listed on the American Exchange, which is also located in New York, and on the regionals. Shares of large NYSE-listed companies are also frequently traded on regional exchanges, where they have multiple listing.

The various exchanges are linked to each other by electronic communications. Intermarket trading has reached a stage that effectively integrates these geographically separate exchanges. Price discrepancies between General Motors quoted on the NYSE and on the Midwest Exchange are arbitraged away within seconds. This means that if the

Reading the Financial News: Stock Market Quotations

(1)			(2)	(3)	(4)	(5)	(6)	(7)	(8)	(9)
52 Weeks				Yld	P-E	Sales				Net
High	Low	Stock	Div.	%	Ratio	100s	High	Low	Close	Chg.
15⅞	10¾	Huffy	.40	2.9	17	215	14	13½	13⅝	−¼
12¾	6¾	HughTl	.08	.7	...	4366	11¼	10⅞	11⅛	+⅛
30⅜	20⅝	HughSp	.40	1.7	12	94	24	23½	23⅞	+⅛
33⅞	19⅛	Human	.76	3.7	51	1634	20½	20	20⅜	...
36⅜	20½	HuntMf	.44	1.7	26	107	26	25⅝	26	...
54¼	32	HuttEF	.88	2.1	28	4707	41⅞	40	41⅞	+1⅝

Stock market quotations appear on a daily basis in many newspapers. Column (1) lists the high and low price per share for each stock over the past 52 weeks. For example, the common stock of the Huffy Corporation, which makes bicycles and outdoor power equipment, fluctuated between a high of $15.875 a share and a low of $10.75 in the past 52 weeks. Hughes Tool Company fluctuated between $12.75 and $6.75 a share, and Hughes Supply Corporation between $30.375 and $20.625 a share.

Column (2) is the current annual cash dividend being paid by the company. Humana Corporation, a hospital-operating company, is paying its stockholders 76 cents a share annually; Hunt Manufacturing is paying 44 cents a share; and E.F. Hutton (the last stock listed, which has since merged into Shearson Lehman Brothers) 88 cents a share.

Column (3) is the stock's dividend yield, which is the current annual dividend payment divided by yesterday's closing price (Column 8). Hunt, for example, is paying 44 cents and closed at $26: thus $.44 \div 26 = 1.7\%$.

Column (4) is the company's price-earnings ratio—yesterday's closing stock price divided by the company's after-tax earnings per share over the last twelve months. Humana's high P/E multiple of 51 indicates that its stockholders apparently anticipate substantial future earnings growth (or else they wouldn't pay such a high price for the stock relative to the company's current earnings).

Column (5) records the number of shares traded yesterday in terms of hundreds of shares exchanged. Trading in the stock of Hughes Tool Company was quite active—436,600 shares changed hands—while Hughes Supply, which retails electrical and plumbing items, was relatively inactive, with only 9,400 shares traded.

Columns (6), (7), and (8) show the highest, lowest, and closing (last) price at which each stock traded yesterday. For example, Humana Corporation traded as low as $20 a share but closed at $20.375.

Column (9) is the change in the closing price from the previous day's close. E.F. Hutton closed $1.625 a share higher than it closed the previous day, while the Huffy Corporation closed down 25 cents a share.

price of General Motors is $70 on the NYSE but is quoted at $71 on the Midwest, an immediately profitable and riskless transaction (arbitrage) can be executed: buy at $70 in New York and sell at $71 in Chicago. The buying on the NYSE pushes the price up and the selling on the Midwest pushes it down, with the process continuing until prices are equalized.

Actually, such price discrepancies rarely emerge nowadays. The NYSE and the regionals are closely integrated. We have moved toward a national market system as mandated by congressional legislation in 1975, although there are further steps that might still be taken.[1]

Still another part of the stock market is the informal over-the-counter (OTC) market. As compared with the organized exchanges, the OTC market has no single place of business where trading activity takes place. Rather, it is a linkage of many dealers and brokers who communicate with each other via telephone and computer terminals.

OTC-traded securities usually represent smaller companies than the securities traded on organized exchanges. The National Association of Securities Dealers Automated Quotations System (NASDAQ) was instituted in 1971. NASDAQ shows bid and asked prices for thousands of OTC-traded securities on video screens hooked up to a central computer system.

Trading in OTC securities used to be a relatively haphazard operation, especially in comparison with trading on the organized exchanges. Individual broker/dealer firms bought and sold OTC securities for their own accounts, acting as dealers, not brokers. For some of the larger OTC stocks, like Tampax, more than a dozen firms made a market—that is, they quoted bid and asked prices that account executives at brokerage firms could rely on when selling or buying for their customers.

For smaller OTC securities, perhaps only a couple of firms would make a market. If you wanted to buy some shares of Fly-by-Night Air, Inc., your fortune-telling stockbroker would call one or two dealers, get the lowest offer, and execute the trade. But you and your broker could never be sure that it was indeed the best offer—and only you would really care. Moreover, the only record of market-making would appear in the daily pink sheets, which record at the end of the day (on pink paper) bids and offers (not trades).

---

[1]Movement toward a centralized market started back in 1975, when the consolidated ticker tape began reporting trades of NYSE-listed securities no matter where the trades were executed. Among the steps that remain to be taken: automated execution of trades based on most favorable price quotations.

Global Trading

Stock market trading is no longer confined by national boundaries. The shares of many major multi-national companies are multiple-listed in several countries—for example, in New York, London, and Tokyo, where the world's three largest stock exchanges are located. Indeed, in recent years trading has become not only global but around-the-clock as well.

Following the rising and setting sun, Tokyo standard time is nine hours ahead of London standard time and fourteen hours ahead of New York standard time. As a result, the Tokyo stock market opens first, London next, and then New York.

Specifically, when it is 9 A.M. in Tokyo, it is 7 in the evening of the *previous* day in New York—that is, when it is 9 o'clock Wednesday morning in Tokyo (Tokyo time), it is 7 o'clock Tuesday evening in New York (New York time).

By the time 9 A.M. Wednesday morning arrives in London, in Tokyo the hour is 6 P.M. Wednesday evening. But in New York the workday has yet to begin—it is 4 A.M. Wednesday, the middle of the night.

When 9 A.M. Wednesday morning finally comes to New York, it is 2 o'clock Wednesday afternoon in London, 11 P.M. Wednesday night in Tokyo.

Virtual round-the-clock global trading means that national stock exchanges rapidly react to what takes place anywhere in the world. If the Tokyo market drops precipitously, for example, fear of falling prices is soon communicated to London and then to New York. Traders in New York open their day knowing what has already happened in Tokyo and London, which naturally influences their buy/sell decisions. Waves of optimism and pessimism thus race quickly around the world.

Dealers still quote bids and offers on OTC securities, but just about everything else changed for the larger OTC securities when NASDAQ was introduced in 1971. Computer screens replaced telephones as the communications mechanism. Market-makers now enter bids and offers via a terminal linked to the NASDAQ computer, and these quotes are flashed to subscribing brokerage offices throughout the country. The "hunt-and-peck" method of uncovering the best bids and offers has given way to computer search, a far more efficient technique.

A word about stockbrokers is in order. They are formally called account executives at most brokerage firms, and they are usually the closest contact an investor has with the stock market. Yet in the purest sense of the word, they act only as agents, executing orders to buy and sell securities. They charge a commission for filling orders at the best price. They have a fiduciary responsibility to get their customers the best deal. Potential conflicts of interest exist if a stockbroker's firm is also a dealer in an OTC security a customer wants to sell (or buy). Legally and morally, a broker shouldn't sell to his or her own firm unless it's the best bidder. But it is often difficult to monitor such responsibilities.

Customers should also be aware of the possibility that brokers might "churn" their accounts. Brokers make commissions when they buy or sell securities for customers, and they make nothing at all when an account is inactive. Thus some brokers recommend that their customers buy or sell not because it is necessarily a wise move but in order to generate brokerage commissions.

There's a well-known story, possibly apocryphal, about a visitor to New York who is being shown the sights in lower Manhattan, near Wall Street, by a prominent financial executive. The executive points with pride to the Merrill Lynch yacht in the harbor, to the Salomon Brothers yacht, and to the Morgan Stanley yacht. Finally, after four or five more brokerage firms' yachts have been pointed out, the visitor hesitantly asks, "But where are the *customer's* yachts?" Needless to say, there are none.[2]

THE MONEY SUPPLY AND STOCK PRICES

Now that we know something about the marketplace, let's return to our first series of questions. What determines whether stock prices go up or down? We are concerned here not so much with the price of individual shares but with the stock market as a whole.

One fairly popular explanation focuses on monetary policy, more specifically, the money supply. The belief that fluctuations in the money supply provide the key to movements in stock prices is based on a series of cause-and-effect hypotheses. In its simplest form, the reasoning is as follows: when the Federal Reserve increases the money supply at a faster than normal rate, the public, finding itself with more cash than it needs for current transactions, spends some of its excess money buying financial assets, including stocks. Since the supply of

[2]Want another one? A broker calls his customer four months in a row and each time recommends a stock that immediately drops right through the floor. The fifth month the customer calls the broker and says, "Listen, I don't think much of those stocks we've been buying—I think maybe I'd be better off in bonds."

"Yeah, sure," the broker says, "but what do I know about bonds?"

equities is more or less fixed, especially in the short run, this incremental demand raises their price. Some stocks will go up more than others and some may go down, depending on the prospects for particular companies, but overall the *average* of stock prices will rise.

Or the transmission process might be somewhat more complex, but with similar results. The increase in the money supply may first lead the public to step up its *bond* purchases, thereby raising bond prices. Higher bond prices mean lower interest rates. With bonds yielding less, some potential bond purchasers are likely to switch over to the now relatively more attractive stock market. The demand for stocks expands because their substitute, bonds, becomes more expensive— just as the demand for Yamahas will expand when their alternative, Hondas, becomes more expensive.

Or it could be an even more roundabout process. The larger money supply leads to lower interest rates, more investment spending—creating more household income and thereby more consumer spending—a higher level of economic activity, and along with it larger corporate profits. Enlarged corporate profits spur stock purchases, which yield higher stock prices.

In any case, the result is the same. Whether the chain of causation is direct, from the money supply to stock prices, or indirect, through the bond market and interest rates, or through GNP, an increase in the money supply at a faster than normal pace is seen as accelerating the demand for stocks, leading to higher stock prices.

Conversely, decreases in the money supply—or increases at a slower rate than necessary to provide for the transactions needs of a growing economy—leave the public with shortages of funds. The result is, among other things, a cutback in stock purchases—again, either directly or because, with higher interest rates, bonds become more attractive buys, or because corporate profits decline as GNP falls. This reduced demand for stocks lowers their prices.

Conclusion: A rapidly expanding money supply leads to higher stock values; inadequate monetary growth leads to a falling market.

Persuasive as the underlying reasoning seems, all too often the facts simply do not bear it out. Evidently too many other cross-currents simultaneously impinge on the stock market, such as business expectations and political developments. Like so many other single-cause explanations in economics, this simplified view of stock price determination contains too much truth to ignore but not enough to make it very reliable in the clutch.

Consider 1929, and the couple of years before and after. From mid-1927 to mid-1928, the money supply increased by 1.6 percent; from

How Good Is the Dow Jones?

The Dow Jones Industrial Average (DJIA) is the most widely watched measure of what is happening in the stock market. Although it is very popular, the Dow is not nearly as comprehensive as other stock market indicators.

Some other—and in many ways better—market indicators are Standard & Poor's 500 Stock Index and the New York Stock Exchange Composite Index. Others are the NASDAQ Over-the-Counter Composite Index and the American Exchange's AMEX Market Value Index.

The DJIA is an average of the prices of only thirty stocks. Included in the 30 are such blue-chip (that is, high-quality) corporations as General Electric, IBM, and Sears, Roebuck. However, thirty stocks is an extremely small sample to use as a measure of what is happening in the whole stock market.

One reason for the Dow's popularity is that it has been around so long. Charles H. Dow, the first editor of the *Wall Street Journal*, and Edward D. Jones began to calculate it as far back as the 1880s. From 1905 to 1925 the Dow fluctuated mostly between 80 and 100. In the stock market boom of the late twenties, it rose to a peak of 381 on September 3, 1929, and then nose-dived to a low of 41 on July 8, 1932. It took more than two decades for the market to recover from the crash; it was November 1954 before the Dow again reached 381. The average hit 500 in March 1956, 1,000 in November 1972, and peaked at 2,722 on August 25, 1987. A few weeks later, on Black Monday (October 19, 1987) it fell more than 500 points!

The DJIA is expressed in terms of "points," not dollars. It is computed in such a way that higher-priced stocks have a greater influence on the average than lower-priced stocks. This is not the case with the S&P 500 or the NYSE Composite Index, which are calculated so that corporations with a greater *total value* of shares outstanding have more influence on the index than corporations with less total value.

The S&P 500 consists, not surprisingly, of the prices of 500 stocks. The NYSE Composite includes all 2,000 stocks listed on the New York Stock Exchange. Broader than both is the Wilshire 5000 Equity Index, which includes 5,700 stocks—all those listed on the NYSE and the AMEX as well as many actively traded over-the-counter issues. Most financial experts prefer the S&P 500 as their favorite indicator of overall market behavior; it is usually the measure that index funds use as they try to match the market's performance, and mutual fund and trust fund managers are "graded" on whether or not they have done as well as or better than the S&P 500.

As an illustration of how the various measures can differ from each other, here is what happened to six of them over the full calendar year 1986:

Dow Jones Industrials	+ 23 percent
S&P 500	+ 15
NYSE Composite	+ 14
Wilshire 5000	+ 12
NASDAQ Composite	+ 7
AMEX Market Value	+ 7

mid-1928 to mid-1929, it increased by 1.2 percent. The stock market, meanwhile, going its merry way, *doubled.*

In the next two years, from mid-1929 to mid-1931, the money supply contracted by about 5 percent each year. If the stock market was merely reacting to changes in the money supply, it was by all odds the biggest overreaction in history, because the proverbial bottom dropped out and the market promptly lost all the gains it had made in the previous two years and then some.

Furthermore, it is not at all clear precisely what is cause and what is effect. Did the market crash because the money supply contracted? Or did the money supply contract because the market crashed (as banks called speculative margin loans and demand deposits were wiped off the books)? The latter explanation is as logical as the former.

The 1929 stock market collapse, as many see it, was due to many interrelated factors: an unwarranted mood of euphoric optimism prior to the crash, excessive speculative activity, fundamental weakness in underlying business conditions, and so on. The money supply, if it influenced the breakdown at all, did so only as one among many causes.

None of which is meant to imply that the money supply was or is unimportant. If it had been rapidly and forcefully restored to its 1929 level by 1930, or even 1931, the depression initiated by the stock market collapse would probably not have been either as severe or as long as it turned out to be. That the Federal Reserve stood by, wringing its hands, while the money supply declined by 30 percent from 1929 to 1933 undoubtedly intensified and prolonged what we now call the Great Depression. But that is a very different thing from saying that movements in the money supply caused or could have given one even a vague idea of the heights or the depths to which stock prices went from 1927 to 1931. As a matter of fact, most of the drop in the money supply occurred *after* 1931; by that time, however, the market was too weary to do much reacting, either over or under.

To come closer to the present, in 1940 the stock market fell 15 percent even though the money supply was then rising 15 percent (on top of a similar rise the year before). In 1962, again, the market tumbled despite an increasing money supply. In 1973–1974 the stock market fell by more than 40 percent, even though the money supply increased by 11 percent over that two-year period. And, of course, on October 19, 1987 the stock market fell more than 20 percent, without anything at all happening to the money supply!

On other not infrequent occasions, however, it is true that declines in stock prices *were* preceded or accompanied by declines in the rate of growth of the money supply, as in 1957, 1960, 1969, and 1981. And often increases in stock prices were indeed associated with increases in the growth of the money supply, as in 1967, 1968, 1975, and the early and mid-1980s.

In at least some of these instances, however, both stock prices and the money supply might conceivably have been reacting to a third causal force, perhaps an upturn in business conditions stimulated by the outbreak of war () peace ()—check one—a spurt in consumer spending, or something else. An improvement in business conditions, regardless of cause, typically leads to an expansion in bank business loans, a larger money supply, brighter profit prospects, and thereby higher stock prices. As the history of business cycles indicates, such upswings (or downturns) are capable of generating a cumulative push that can work up considerable momentum, carrying *both* the money supply and stock prices along with it.

Chart 1 provides some idea of the pitfalls involved in reading a cause-and-effect relationship into two sets of statistics simply because they move together. The unbroken line indicates the movement of stock prices, annually, from the end of 1960 through the end of 1966, using stock prices at the end of 1960 as the base (= 100).

The thin dashed line, on a similar index basis, is the movement of the money supply annually, also from the end of 1960 through the end of 1966. Over this particular six-year period, changes in the money supply clearly bore little relationship to turning points in stock prices.

Finally, the chart includes a third line (*W*). Its movements are obviously closely related to changes in stock prices. Almost without exception, the line labeled *W* and the line tracing stock prices move up and down together.

Cause and effect? The line labeled *W*, make of it what you will, is an annual index (1960 = 100) of the number of times members of the old Washington Senators baseball team struck out each year, over the period 1960 through 1966. (Source: *The Sporting News's Official Baseball Guide and Record Book,* Annual, 1960–1966.) For at least those years, evidently, an investor trying to forecast turning points in the stock market would have been better off reading *Sports Illustrated* instead of the *Wall Street Journal.*

MONETARY POLICY AND THE STOCK MARKET

Once we expand our horizon to encompass more than the money supply alone, however, there is widespread agreement that monetary

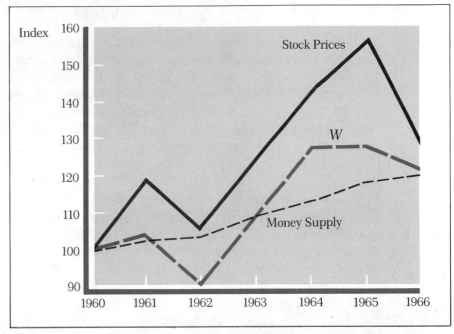

CHART 1 Stock Prices and Other Variables, 1960–1966

SOURCES: For stock prices: Dow Jones Industrials, monthly closing averages for December of each year (December 1960 = 100). For money supply: Demand deposits plus currency, monthly averages for December of each year (December 1960 = 100).

policy *in general* frequently does have considerable influence on the stock market. It is by no means the only influence, and it is often overshadowed by other forces and events, but nevertheless on balance monetary policy is widely believed to have had a substantial impact on stock prices at times in the past, especially since the mid-1960s, and is expected to continue to do so in the foreseeable future.

This is quite aside from the power of the Federal Reserve to set margin requirements on stock purchases. In an attempt to prevent a repetition of the speculative wave, financed heavily with borrowed funds, that carried the market to dizzy heights until the Fall of 1929, Congress in the 1930s authorized the Federal Reserve to impose margin (or minimum down payment) requirements on the purchase of stocks. If the margin requirement is 100 percent, then 100 percent cash must be put up and no borrowing at all is permitted. If the margin requirement is 80 percent, that much of one's own cash must be put up when one buys a security, and only the remaining 20 percent can be financed by borrowing from a bank or a broker. Of course, you could always finance the entire amount by borrowing from your sister-in-law and no one would be the wiser (except perhaps, in the long run, your sister-in-law).

High margin requirements have probably helped restrain speculation in stocks, especially by those who could least afford it. Nevertheless, if the Federal Reserve had only this device to influence the market, it would be relying on a weak reed indeed. Margin requirements are 100 percent at Santa Anita and Hialeah racetracks, but at last report speculative activity by those who could not afford it as well as by those who could appeared unimpaired.

The impact of overall monetary policy on stock prices stems not so much from the Federal Reserve's power to set margin requirements as from its influence over the money supply, the entire spectrum of interest rates and financial markets, current and expected business conditions, and—last but far from least—the expected rate of inflation. It is in the recent past, rather than thirty or forty years ago, that the effects of monetary policy on stock prices are most clearly visible. The credit squeezes of 1966, 1969, 1974, and 1981 are prime examples—stock prices tumbled in each of those episodes. Similarly, easier money sparked major rises in stock prices in the early and mid-eighties.

Indeed, worrying about the stance of monetary policy has become one of the major preoccupations of stock market participants. When the Fed was using M1 as its main policy target, from October 1979 to mid-1982, investors nervously awaited the weekly release of the Fed's money supply figures, fearful of making commitments without this information in hand.

If the Fed's money supply figures showed that M1 was growing faster than the announced target, then Wall Street concluded that the Fed would soon be tightening to get the money supply back on track. Alternatively, if the figures showed that M1 growth was below its target, Wall Street concluded that the central bank would soon be easing to get back on target. In each case, investors acted accordingly, usually assuming that tight money would lower stock prices and easy money would raise them.

Since the Fed abandoned M1 as its main policy target in 1982 and shifted its emphasis to interest rates, especially the federal funds rate, investors have also switched their concentration from the money supply to interest rates in their search for clues regarding the Federal Reserve's intentions. Higher interest rates are generally considered bad for stock prices, because bonds and other fixed-income investments become more attractive, luring money out of stocks and into bonds. On the other hand, lower interest rates are viewed as favorable for stock prices, because stocks then become relatively more attractive than bonds, savings deposits, and similar investments.

In the seventies and eighties, the two greatest enemies of a buoyant stock market were rising interest rates and accelerating inflation, and indeed the two often went hand in hand. Back in the fifties and sixties, stocks used to be considered a good inflation hedge. Pension funds and individuals bought large amounts of stocks in order to safeguard wealth against the ravages of inflation, because it was widely believed that stock prices would keep up with consumer prices.

However, stocks have been a terrible hedge against inflation. Stock prices were no higher in 1981 than they were in 1965, although 1981 consumer prices were *triple* those of 1965. Stock prices did not take off until mid-1982, when inflation finally began to subside.[3]

Most market participants are tuned in to Fed-watching because they want to anticipate—preferably before anyone else—the future course of interest rates and the potential strength of inflation. The Federal Reserve does not fully determine either of these variables, but it certainly exerts a major influence on both. The lesson is that Fed-watching helps to anticipate stock market trends, but it is no quick and easy road to wealth and fame, because too many other things are also impinging on stock prices at the same time.

SUMMARY

1. Individuals used to be the principal owners of common stocks, but institutional investors have become increasingly important.

2. The stock market is mostly a secondary market. It includes the New York Stock Exchange, regional exchanges, and over-the-counter trading.

3. Changes in the money supply alone have been an unreliable guide to predicting fluctuations in the stock market.

4. Monetary policy in general, however, has been more useful. Monetary policy affects interest rates and inflation, both of which have exerted major influences on stock prices.

5. Stocks used to be considered a good hedge against inflation, but that is no longer the case.

[3]Actually, the Great Bull Market of 1982–87 began on Friday the 13th of August, 1982, after the Dow Jones Industrial Average had closed at 777 the previous day. The market peaked at 2722 on August 25, 1987.

Suggestions for Further Reading

For attempts to quantify the relationship between the money supply and stock prices, see Michael W. Keran, "Expectations, Money, and the Stock Market," Federal Reserve Bank of St. Louis *Review* (January 1971); K.E. Homa and Dwight M. Jaffee, "The Supply of Money and Common Stock Prices," *Journal of Finance* (December 1971); and Michael J. Hamburger and Levis A. Kochin, "Money and Stock Prices: The Channels of Influence," *Journal of Finance* (May 1972). For a critical analysis of these efforts, see the discussion by Merton H. Miller in the same May 1972 issue of the *Journal of Finance.* Also see James E. Pesando, "The Supply of Money and Common Stock Prices," *Journal of Finance* (June 1974); Robert D. Auerbach, "Money and Stock Prices," Federal Reserve Bank of Kansas City *Monthly Review* (September–October 1976); and Lawrence S. Davidson and Richard T. Froyen, "Monetary Policy and Stock Returns: Are Stock Markets Efficient?" Federal Reserve Bank of St. Louis *Review* (March 1982). Finally, Douglas K. Pearce has written two excellent articles on the general subject in the Federal Reserve Bank of Kansas City *Economic Review:* "The Impact of Inflation on Stock Prices" (March 1982) and "Stock Prices and the Economy" (November 1983).

One of the early attempts to examine the relationship between money and stock prices was Beryl W. Sprinkel, *Money and Stock Prices* (Homewood, Ill.: Irwin, 1964); this book has since been revised and retitled *Money and Markets: A Monetarist View* (Irwin, 1971). An interesting study of the relationship between stock prices and economic activity is Barry Bosworth, "The Stock Market and the Economy," *Brookings Papers on Economic Activity* (No. 2, 1975).

If this chapter has tempted you to think you can beat the market, before you try to do so read Burton Malkiel's paperback *A Random Walk Down Wall Street,* 4th Ed. (New York: Norton, 1985). Or if you have the notion that other games of chance are more in your line, at least know what the odds are against you. You'll find them all in Edwin Silberstang's *The Winner's Guide to Casino Gambling* (New York: Holt, Rinehart, and Winston, 1980).

CHAPTER 33

Financial Futures and Options

Life was a lot simpler when bonds were bonds, stocks were stocks, and futures were porkbellies. But those days are gone forever. Since the mid-1970s, futures contracts on Treasury securities have grown to the point where the Federal Reserve was asked by Congress to study the effects of Treasury bond futures on the cost of the Federal debt. A similar explosion in options trading on stock indices forced the Securities and Exchange Commission to consider the implications for the liquidity of the capital markets. Although futures and options contracts are complicated instruments, they have found their way into the risk management toolbox of just about every major financial institution. Considering the importance of financial futures and options in the daily operation of our financial markets, it seems like a good idea to understand what they are, how they work, and most importantly, how to avoid losing money in the process.

Futures contracts and options contracts are frequently lumped together, because they share a number of common characteristics. They are both derivative financial instruments in the sense that they derive their economic value from some other underlying asset. In addition, they both trade on organized exchanges and share similar arrangements for finalizing and clearing trades. But the differences between options and futures far outweigh their similarities. It is unfortunate that the only way to understand options and futures contracts fully is to pay attention to the details. Once the specifics are under control, we can turn to the implications. Thus in the next section we describe financial futures contracts and then turn in the following section to how they are priced and how they are used. We do the same for options contracts in the last two sections of the chapter.

AN OVERVIEW OF FINANCIAL FUTURES

A futures contract is a contractual agreement that calls for the delivery of a specific underlying commodity or security at some future date at a currently agreed upon price. Table 1 lists the major types of financial futures contracts currently traded on the various commodity exchanges. As you can see, there are contracts on interest-bearing securi-

TABLE 1
Major Financial Futures Contracts

Contract	Exchange
Interest Rates	
Treasury bonds	Chicago Board of Trade
Treasury notes	Chicago Board of Trade
Municipal bond index	Chicago Board of Trade
Treasury bills	IMM division of Chicago Mercantile Exchange
Eurodollar Time Deposits	IMM division of Chicago Mercantile Exchange
Stock Index	
S&P 500	IMM division of Chicago Mercantile Exchange
New York Stock Exchange Composite	New York Futures Exchange
Major Market Index	Chicago Board of Trade
Value Line	Kansas City Board of Trade
Foreign Currencies	
West German mark	IMM division of Chicago Mercantile Exchange
Japanese yen	IMM division of Chicago Mercantile Exchange
Swiss franc	IMM division of Chicago Mercantile Exchange
British pound	IMM division of Chicago Mercantile Exchange

ties (such as Treasury bonds, Treasury notes, and Eurodollar Time Deposits), on stock indices (such as Standard & Poor's 500 and the New York Stock Exchange Composite Index), and on foreign currencies (such as the West German mark and the Japanese yen). Trading in these contracts is conducted on the various commodity exchanges alongside the conventional agricultural commodities. For example, the most active financial futures contract is Treasury bonds, which trades on the Chicago Board of Trade (CBT) along with futures contracts on wheat, corn, and soybeans. Eurodollar Time Deposits are traded on the Chicago Mercantile Exchange's IMM (International Monetary Market) division alongside the venerable porkbelly and live cattle futures contracts.

Although futures contracts on agricultural commodities have been in existence since the middle of the nineteenth century and financial futures were introduced less than twenty years ago, the volume of trading in financial futures now exceeds the more traditional agricultural commodities. Financial futures have obviously become quite popular in a very short time period. They share a number of common characteristics with all futures contracts that help determine how they are used. The best way to understand these characteristics is by way of specific example.

All futures contracts are standardized agreements to buy or sell a particular asset or commodity at a future date at a currently agreed upon price. The terms of the contract specify the amount and type of asset to be delivered, as well as the location and delivery period. In the case of financial futures, the underlying asset is either a specific security or the cash value of a group of securities. For example, the Treasury bond contract calls for the delivery of $100,000 in Treasury bonds, and the Treasury bill contract calls for the delivery of $1,000,000 in Treasury bills. In the case of stock index futures, the contract calls for the delivery of the cash value of a particular stock index. For example, the popular S&P 500 contract calls for the delivery of $500 times the value of the S&P 500 Stock Index.

The precise terms of each contract are established by the exchange that sponsors trading in the contract. Let's take a closer look at the Treasury bond futures contract. If you buy one December 1990 Treasury bond futures contract, you have the right and obligation to receive $100,000 of 15-year (or more) maturity government bonds during December 1990. The seller of the contract has the right and obligation to deliver those bonds at that time. In futures market terminology the buyer of the contract is called "long" and the seller is called "short." All of the terms of the contract—$100,000 of 15-year government bonds, December delivery, and so on—are established by the Chicago Board of Trade, which sponsors Treasury bond futures trading. The only matter left for negotiation between the buyer and seller of the contract is the price at which the bonds will be delivered. And that is determined by the often frenetic bidding and offering that occurs at the location (called a "pit") on the floor of the Chicago Board of Trade where the auction in Treasury bond futures is conducted.

Note that the standardization of contract terms is designed to promote liquidity, the ability to buy and sell quickly with low transactions costs. Large trading volume promotes narrow bid-asked spreads, as we saw in Chapter 29. Futures exchanges promote large trading volume by standardizing the terms of futures contracts, allowing many individuals to trade the identical commodity.

Of equal importance in promoting the liquidity of futures contracts is the nature of the auction process itself. All orders for a particular contract are directed to a single pit on the exchange floor. The trading pit is circular in shape, with tiered steps where traders stand facing each other. Buying and selling interests must be represented quite literally by open outcry. The scene most closely resembles controlled chaos. But the result is that all orders are exposed to the highest bid and lowest offer, thereby guaranteeing execution at the best possible price.

For example, if you are interested in buying the December 1990 Treasury bond futures contract, you might be told by your account executive that the prevailing bid in the Treasury bond pit is $97\frac{2}{32}$ per $100 face value of bonds, with the best offer at $97\frac{3}{32}$. You may then instruct your account executive to buy one contract from someone in the trading pit who is offering at $97\frac{3}{32}$. You will then be long one December bond future at a price of $97\frac{3}{32}$, and the trader in the crowd will be short one December bond future at $97\frac{3}{32}$.

At this point a number of institutional arrangements in futures markets take over. Although both you—the long—and the short have a contractual agreement to receive and deliver the underlying bonds, respectively, you no longer look to each other to exercise those rights and obligations. Rather the clearing corporation associated with the futures exchange, consisting of well-capitalized members of the exchange, interposes itself between you and the short. In particular, the long looks to the clearing corporation to satisfy the delivery obligation, and the short looks to the clearing corporation to pay the amount due on the delivery date. In this way the clearing corporation reduces the credit risk exposure associated with future deliveries of the underlying securities. Shorts and longs do not have to worry that the other party will not perform their contractual obligations. And that's especially good news if your good-for-nothing cousin happened to have sold the contract to you on the exchange floor.

The clearing corporation, in turn, has a number of special institutional practices to reduce its own credit risk exposure. First, both the short and long must place a deposit, called *margin,* with the clearing corporation. Margin is a performance bond that *both* buyers and sellers must deposit. It is *not* a down payment on the ultimate purchase price, which would be required of the buyer only. Second, the clearing corporation requires that gains and losses be settled each day in what is called *mark-to-market settlement.* Thus, if the price of the December Treasury bond future rises from $97\frac{3}{32}$ to $98\frac{3}{32}$, the value of your (long) position has increased by $1 per $100 face value of bonds. On the $100,000 contract you have a profit of $1,000, and the short has a loss of $1,000. The clearing corporation collects this sum from the short and transfers it to you at the end of the trading day as part of its mark-to-market settlement. In order to facilitate the collection process, the futures exchange imposes *price limits* on the amount that the futures contract can change each day. For example, in the Treasury bond contract, prices cannot change by more than $2 per $100 face value. Thus, a maximum of $2,000 can be transferred out of or into your account each day.[1]

The rights and obligations represented by having a long or short position in Treasury bond futures can be intimidating to say the least. The short must actually deliver $100,000 in Treasury bonds during the delivery month, while the long must come up with the cash when delivery takes place. This can be embarrassing if the long doesn't have the money or the short doesn't have the bonds. Most traders in futures markets, therefore, choose *settlement by offset* rather than delivery. In particular, longs may settle their rights and obligations at any time by making an offsetting sale of the identical December 1990 Treasury bond contract, while shorts may cancel their rights and obligations at any time by making an offsetting purchase. The clearing corporation keeps track of all buyers and sellers and closes out a trader's position when there is both a purchase and a sale of the identical contract on

---

[1]Do not let this give you a false sense of security. In particular, this does not mean that your losses are limited by the futures exchange's price limits. Prices can continue to rise or fall the next day, before you have had a chance to reverse your position. For example, if you are short and the price of the Treasury bond contract rises the limit because there are many buyers and literally no sellers, you must remain short until trading is resumed the following day. If the preponderance of buying interest continues, your losses are extended the following day.

Reading the Financial News: Financial Futures Quotations

(1)	(2)	(3)	(4)	(5)	(6)	(7)	(8)	(9)
(L1)	TREASURY BONDS (CBT)—$100,000; pts. 32nds of 100%							
June	100-13	100-25	100-13	100-23	+ 14	7.928	− .044	192,839
Sept	99-13	99-26	99-13	99-24	+ 15	8.025	− .048	13,051
Dec	98-16	98-26	98-15	98-24	+ 13	8.128	− .041	3,779
Mr88	97-25	97-28	97-23	97-27	+ 13	8.221	− .043	3,680
June	96-26	97-00	96-22	97-00	+ 14	8.310	− .047	3,293
Sept	95-29	96-05	95-29	96-04	+ 13	8.403	− .044	1,744
Dec	...	...	...	95-11	+ 14	8.488	− .047	527
(L2)	Est vol 135,000; vol Wed 125,793; open int 233,373, +1,972.							
	TREASURY NOTES (CBT)—$100,000; pts. 32nds of 100%							
June	103-24	103-30	103-24	103-29	+ 6	7.439	− .027	44,841
Sept	103-02	103-07	103-02	103-06	+ 6	7.540	− .027	5,092
Dec	...	...	...	102-18	+ 7	7.629	− .031	260
	TREASURY BILLS (IMM)—$1 mil.; pts. of 100%							

						Discount		Open
	Open	High	Low	Settle	Chg	Settle	Chg	Interest
June	94.44	94.45	94.39	94.43	+ .02	5.57	− .02	29,938
Sept	94.49	94.50	94.47	94.49	+ .02	5.51	− .02	5,757
Dec	94.53	94.53	94.46	94.49	+ .01	5.51	− .01	1,698
Mr88	94.46	94.46	94.40	94.45	+ .01	5.55	− .01	739
June	94.34	94.37	94.30	94.35	...	5.65	...	293
Sept	9	...	...	94.19	− .02	5.81	+ .02	130

Est vol 5,745; vol Wed 5,814; open int 38,574, +91.

—INDEXES—

(L3)	S&P 500 INDEX (CME) 500 times index							
June	305.50	305.70	302.65	303.40	− .20	305.70	228.90	95,994
Sept	307.20	307.50	304.70	305.35	− .10	307.50	229.90	1,532
Dec	308.00	309.20	306.80	307.30	− .05	309.20	243.20	922

Est vol 70,300; vol Wed 69,149; open int 98,453, +1,129.
Index (prelim.) High 302.72, Low 300.38, Close 300.93 +.55

Futures market quotations appear in a variety of formats in daily newspapers, so you have to read the headings of the columns and rows in each case. In the accompanying example, line (L1) indicates that Treasury bond contracts follow immediately below, that the exchange on which the bond contract is traded is the CBT (Chicago Board of Trade), that the size of the contract is $100,000, and that quotations are in percentage points plus thirty-seconds per 100 face value. Each of the lines listed beneath the Treasury bond heading refers to a specific contract month. At the bottom of the Treasury bond listings, line (L2) records a number of items: the particular day's trading volume in contracts for all months is estimated at 135,000 contracts; the exact volume traded on the previous day (Wednesday) is listed as 125,793 contracts. The last item on line (L2) is open interest. That refers to the total number

its books for the same account. Don't ask what happens when the clearing corporation's computer goes haywire.

Settlement by offset permits hedgers, speculators, and arbitrageurs to make legitimate use of the futures market without getting into the technical details of making or taking delivery of the underlying asset. Now let's see exactly what these legitimate activities by hedgers, speculators, and arbitrageurs actually are.

USING FINANCIAL FUTURES CONTRACTS

The most important activity provided by futures markets is the opportunity to hedge legitimate commercial activities. Hedgers buy or sell futures contracts to reduce their exposure to the risk of future price of long positions outstanding (equal to the total number of short positions outstanding) and is reported at 233,373 contracts, which is an increase of 1,972 contracts over the previous day.

Now let's look at the nine columns of information. Column (1) lists the specific contract month. The first entry is June 1987 and the last entry is for December 1988. In other words, the CBT sponsors trading in seven different contract months for Treasury bond futures. Columns (2), (3), (4), and (5) refer to the opening, high, low, and closing (or settlement) price of the contract. Thus for the June 1987 contract, the closing price is recorded at $100\frac{23}{32}$. Column (6) indicates that the settlement price is $+\frac{14}{32}$ compared with yesterday's settlement. Since each full percentage point in the Treasury bond contract is worth $1,000, column (6) suggests that the futures contract is worth $437.50 more than the previous day ($\frac{14}{32} \times \$1,000$). Column (7) translates

the settlement price into a yield based on an 8 percent–coupon 15-year Treasury bond. Because the settlement price is above par ($\frac{23}{32}$ above par), it is not surprising that the yield is listed as 7.928 percent (less than the 8 percent coupon assumed for the underlying bond). Column (8) shows that the change in yield from the previous close is −.044 (which means that yesterday the yield was 7.972 percent). Column (9) lists the open interest of the particular contract month. The June contract has 192,839 contracts outstanding, which is considerably larger than any other contract month.

Columns (7) and (8) are used to report historical high and low prices for the contracts that do not have interest rate components. For example, in the S&P 500 Stock Index contracts listed under line (L3), the June contract has a historical high price of 305.70 in column (7) and a historical low price of 228.90 in column (8).

movements in the underlying asset. For example, a government securities dealer who has just purchased newly issued government bonds at the Treasury's auction must hold those bonds in inventory until ultimate investors (pension funds, insurance companies, and individuals) place orders to buy the securities. In the meantime, the dealer is exposed to the risk that interest rates will rise and the bonds will fall in price.

Nothing makes dealers more unhappy than losses on their inventory. The dealer can avoid that outcome by taking a short position in Treasury bond futures. Since the price of bond futures moves almost in lockstep with the price of the underlying bonds (thanks to the activities of arbitrageurs, as we will see shortly), a decrease in the value of the dealer's inventory because bond prices decline will be offset by the dealer's short position in Treasury bond futures. For example, if the bonds in the dealer's inventory fall in price from $99 to $98, the dealer loses $1 for each $100 in inventory. If the dealer sold Treasury bond futures short, however, the associated $1 decline in the futures contract will provide an offsetting profit.

Notice that as soon as the dealer's inventory of government bonds has been sold to ultimate investors, the dealer should offset the short position in the futures market by buying back the identical Treasury bond futures. Reversing the position is proper, because once the bonds have been sold there is no need to maintain the short position in bond futures as a hedge against price decreases. The moral of the story is that legitimate hedging use of the futures market occurs with a sale of a futures contract and a subsequent offsetting purchase. Despite contrary propaganda by Russian spies and assorted members of Congress, a hedger does not have to make delivery, or even intend to make delivery, when using futures contracts to offset risk.

Another type of hedge involves taking a long position in a futures contract rather than a short position. For example, a pension fund may anticipate a need to buy bonds one month in the future, after it has accumulated sufficient cash from pension-holder contributions. If the pension fund manager waits until the month is out to buy the bonds and bond prices rise in the interim, then the funds will be invested at lower yields. To hedge the risk that bond prices will rise before the funds are actually invested, the pension fund manager buys Treasury bond futures. If bond prices go up under these circumstances, the long position in Treasury bond futures generates a profit to offset the higher price the pension fund pays for the bonds.

We have just seen that legitimate hedgers in financial futures can be either buyers or sellers of futures contracts. "Short hedgers" offset inventory risk by selling futures, while "long hedgers" offset anticipated purchases of securities by buying futures. Sometimes short hedgers sell contracts to long hedgers. But that would be an accidental occurrence. There is nothing to guarantee that legitimate hedging activities by shorts and longs will coincide in the marketplace. That is where speculators enter the picture.

Unlike hedgers, speculators purposely take on risk when buying or selling futures contracts. For example, if short hedgers depress the price of the Treasury bond contract by their sales, speculators will be induced to buy those contracts in anticipation of a price increase once the hedging pressure has subsided. Similarly, speculators will be induced to sell contracts if the buying activity of long hedgers temporarily drives up the price of the Treasury bond contract. Speculators take on the risk of price movements from hedgers. They expect to earn a profit in the process. If they're good at their craft they earn a return for their time, skill, and invested capital; if they're not so good they go into some other line of business very quickly—with a lot less capital than before.

The buying and selling activities of hedgers and speculators together determine the price of a futures contract. More selling drives the price lower; more buying drives the price higher. Although this sounds trite, it's the best way to describe price determination in the futures market (or any market, for that matter). We can be somewhat more sophisticated, however, when describing the relationship between the price of the futures contract and the price of the assets that underlie the futures contract. The relationship between the price in the so-called "cash market" and the futures market is determined by arbitrageurs. Their activities are crucial for hedgers, because as we saw in our examples above, the price of the futures contract and the price of the underlying securities must move together if hedgers are to be able to reduce their risk by taking offsetting positions in the futures market.

The main reason the price of the futures contract moves closely with the price of the underlying security is that during the delivery period (say, December 1990) there are rights and obligations to deliver the *actual* securities specified in the contract. During the delivery period, in fact, these rights and obligations force the price of the futures contract and the price of the underlying security to be one and the same. Here's why. If the price of the futures contract were higher than the price of the actual securities during the delivery period, then it would pay arbitrageurs to sell the futures at the higher price, buy the securities at the lower price, pocket the price difference, and deliver the securities in satisfaction of their obligations as shorts. This activity drives down the futures price and drives up the price of the underlying securities until they are equal.

On the other hand, if the price of the futures contract were below the price of the underlying security, it would pay the arbitrageur to buy the futures contract and sell the actual security. This time, as the buyer of the futures contract, the arbitrageur would take delivery of the securities and then turn around and deliver them to whoever bought them in the cash market, pocketing the price differential in the process. In this case the arbitrageurs drive up the futures price and drive down the price of the underlying commodity until they are equal.

It doesn't take a genius to make money as an arbitrageur. Just about anyone who can participate in the cash and futures markets simultaneously will recognize the wisdom of instant profits and will undertake these arbitrage activities. Thus, the activities of arbitrageurs will be massive and cause the price of the futures contract and the price of the underlying securities to converge on the delivery date.

A similar arbitrage prior to the final delivery date reinforces the comovement between futures prices and the price of the underlying securities, as long as the securities can be stored by arbitrageurs. The main difference is that prior to the delivery period, the arbitrageur would compare the futures price with the price of the underlying securities plus the cost of carrying those securities to the final delivery date. Price discrepancies will lead to buying and selling in the cash and futures markets until prices are brought into proper alignment. In particular, at any point, the price of the futures contract would be equal to the price of the underlying security plus carrying costs.[2] More importantly for hedgers, whenever the price of the underlying security changes, arbitrageurs will push the price of the futures in the same direction.

The activities of hedgers, speculators, and arbitrageurs combine to make futures markets important risk management arenas for financial institutions. It pays for banks, insurance companies, pension funds, and others to participate in futures markets, because the standardization of the contracts creates a facility for managing risk exposure at low transactions costs. The fact that the futures contract mirrors the cash market, but with lower transactions costs, is the main contribution of futures markets to the financial marketplace. A very different dimension to risk management is offered by options contracts, as we will see in the next two sections.

AN OVERVIEW OF OPTIONS CONTRACTS

Options contracts have both a shorter and a longer history in financial markets than futures contracts. Options on individual stocks have been traded in the over-the-counter market since the nineteenth century. The public visibility of options increased dramatically, however, in 1972 when the Chicago Board Options Exchange (CBOE) standardized the terms of the contracts and introduced futures-type pit trading. As shown in Table 2, in addition to the CBOE, options contracts are now listed on the American Stock Exchange, the Philadelphia Stock

---

[2]The main cost of carrying securities is the interest rate on the funds tied up in the purchase. Thus, in September 1990, the price of the December 1990 Treasury bond futures would equal the price of the underlying Treasury bonds plus the net interest cost of carrying those bonds from September 1990 until they can be delivered in December.

Program Trading: Linking the Futures Market and the Stock Market

Investigations into the stock market collapse of October 19, 1987 focused attention on the practice known as program trading. The main feature of program trading is the simultaneous purchase of stock index futures and sale of the underlying stocks in order to profit from discrepancies in price; or the reverse, the sale of stock index futures and the purchase of the underlying stocks in order to profit from price discrepancies. The term *program* trading emphasizes that the technique requires a program to purchase or sell the 500 individual stocks that underlie the most popular stock index futures contract: the S&P 500. Computers are used to spot price discrepancies and to help execute the purchases or sales of stock on the floor of the New York Stock Exchange.

Since program trading involves *simultaneous* (and opposite) transactions in both the futures market and the underlying cash market to profit from price discrepancies, it is nothing more or less than a form of cash-futures arbitrage. Our accompanying discussion emphasizes that arbitrage between a cash market and the corresponding futures market insures comovement between the prices in these two markets. More importantly, arbitrageurs do not influence the overall level of prices, but only price relationships.

From this perspective it seems inappropriate to blame the more than 20 percent collapse of stock prices on Black Monday on program trading. A more likely scenario is that investors tried to hedge their stock market portfolios by selling stock index futures, thereby driving down the price of futures contracts. Program traders then bought the relatively cheap futures contracts and sold the underlying stocks—pushing down equity prices to reflect investor sentiment. Thus program trading brought the message of lower stock valuation from the futures market to the stock market. Circumscribing program trading because it *precipitated* the stock market collapse is similar to the ancient practice of beheading the messenger who delivered bad news.

Exchange, the Pacific Stock Exchange, and the New York Stock Exchange. In addition, most of the nation's futures exchanges sponsor options on futures contracts. At this point, the options listings in the newspaper rival the stocks themselves for investors' attention.

To appreciate what this options activity is all about, we must examine the contractual obligations of buyers and sellers of options. These contractual obligations are more complicated than futures contracts, so we all have to pay attention (no fooling around this time).

Like futures contracts, options are derivative financial instruments; that is, they derive their value from some underlying asset. In tradi-

TABLE 2
Examples of Options Contracts

Specific Contracts	Exchange
Options on Individual Equities	
IBM, GM, GE	Chicago Board Options Exchange
Disney, GTE, DuPont	American Stock Exchange
Honda, Coleco	Philadelphia Stock Exchange
Genentech, Gannett	Pacific Stock Exchange
NYNEX, Campbells Soup	New York Stock Exchange
Options on Indexes	
S&P 100, S&P 500	Chicago Board Options Exchange
Major Market Index	American Stock Exchange
New York Stock Exchange Index	New York Stock Exchange
Options on Interest Rate Futures	
Treasury bonds, Treasury notes	Chicago Board of Trade
Eurodollar, Treasury bills	Chicago Mercantile Exchange
Options on Foreign Currency Futures	
West German mark, Japanese yen	Chicago Mercantile Exchange

tional stock options, the underlying asset refers to 100 shares of a particular stock, such as General Motors or IBM. In other cases, the underlying asset is a basket of equities represented by some overall stock index, such as the S&P 500 Index or the S&P 100 Index. These are called stock index options, and the contractual obligations are defined by some dollar value of the index, either $500 times the index or $100 times the index. Finally, in options on futures contracts, the contractual obligations call for the delivery of one futures contract. Although the precise value of an option depends upon exactly what the underlying asset is, there are a number of elements common to all options contracts that we can explore.

All types of options come in two varieties: puts and calls. Let's begin our story with calls, because they are somewhat more popular. The buyer of a call option has the right (but not the obligation) to buy a given quantity of the underlying asset at a predetermined price, called the exercise or strike price, at any time prior to the expiration date of the option. For example, you may instruct your account executive at a brokerage firm to place an order at the CBOE to buy a call on IBM with an exercise price of $150 and an expiration date of September 1990. Once your order is executed, you are "long" the IBM $150 call. This option gives you the right to purchase 100 shares of IBM at a price of $150 at any time prior to September 1990. The seller of that option, called the short (or the option writer), has the *obligation* (not the right) to deliver those shares to you at a price of $150.[3]

Note that, unlike futures contracts, the rights and obligations of option buyers and option sellers are not symmetrical. The buyer of the option acquires rights and the seller of the option takes on obligations. The buyer of the call option pays a price to the seller for the rights acquired. This makes considerable sense, because the option seller would be foolish to take on obligations without any compensation. The price paid for the option is often called the value of the option or the option premium. The premium is paid by the long to the short as soon as the option is purchased.[4]

Before examining the determination of option premiums, let's see what rights and obligations are conveyed by put options. The buyer of a put option on IBM with a strike price of $150 and an expiration date of September 1990 has the right (but not the obligation) to *sell* 100 shares of IBM at a price of $150 on or before September 1990. The seller of the put option, called the short or the option writer, has the obligation (but not the right) to receive or buy those shares at a price of $150. In consideration of those rights, the buyer of the put option pays a premium to the seller of the put option.

This has been pretty complicated, so let's summarize: Option buyers have rights; option sellers have obligations. Call buyers have the right to buy the underlying asset; put buyers have the right to sell the underlying asset. In both puts and calls the option buyer pays a premium to the option seller.

Note that in our example of the IBM call and put we used the same strike price and the same expiration date. Although there are a number of different strike prices and expiration dates for each exchange-traded option, the exchange sponsoring the trading establishes rules for determining which strike prices and expiration dates will be traded for each option (see the box for an example with options on Treasury bond futures). This standardization is designed to elicit interest by many potential traders, thereby promoting contract liquidity.

---

[3]The option described here is called an American option, because it gives the right to buy IBM at any time until September 1990. European options (which are also traded in the United States) give the right to buy the underlying asset on (but not before) the expiration date.

[4]Note that in futures contracts both the long and short have rights and obligations, so that there is no premium paid at the time the contractual obligation is struck. In a futures contract only the price at which the future delivery will take place is agreed upon.

As with futures contracts, there is also a clearing corporation that guarantees the performance of contractual obligations, so that buyers and sellers of exchange traded options do not have to be concerned with the credit-worthiness of their trading partners.[5] The only matter up for negotiation on the floor of the exchange is the option premium—the price the option buyer pays to the seller for the rights conferred. Let's turn to the determinants of the option premium and see how options are used by individuals and institutions.

USING AND VALUING OPTIONS

Perhaps the best way to understand why individual investors and financial institutions use options is to look at what an option is worth on the expiration date of the contract. In doing so it is important to remember that investors who buy options, either calls or puts, have rights but no obligations. Therefore option buyers will do whatever is in their best interest on the expiration date. Let's take a look at the value of our IBM call with a $150 exercise price.

Although options are complicated, there are only two possibilities on the expiration date that must be evaluated: the price of IBM can be above $150 or the price can be below $150. If the price of IBM stock is below $150, say $145, the call option to buy IBM at $150 on the expiration date is worthless. The call buyer obviously chooses not to exercise the right to buy IBM at $150. Thus the value of the call is zero. On the other hand, if the price of IBM on the New York Stock Exchange is above $150, say $155, then the option to call (buy) the stock at $150 has value. In fact, if IBM is trading at $155, the call is worth exactly $5 per share of stock on expiration. The call is worth $5 per share because the investor can exercise the option—that is, demand that the option writer deliver IBM at $150—and then immediately sell the shares for $155.

This discussion implies that the payoff on expiration to a long call position is either equal to zero (if the stock is below the exercise price) or equal to the stock price minus the exercise price, called the *intrinsic value* of the option (if the stock price is above the exercise price). A similar argument shows that on expiration, a long put position has a value of zero if the stock price is *above* the exercise price and a value equal to the exercise price minus the stock price (this is just the

[5]Unlike futures contracts, options do not have mark-to-market settlement, nor are there any price limits associated with options.

Reading the Financial News: Options Quotations

(1)	(2)	(3)	(4)	(5)	(6)	(7)

(L1) T-BONDS (CBT) $100,000; points and 64ths of 100%

Strike	Calls—Last			Puts—Last		
Price	Jun-c	Sep-c	Dec-c	Jun-p	Sep-p	Dec-p
96	4–50	4–33	...	0–07	0–56	1–35
98	2–62	3–04	...	0–19	1–27	2–12
100	1–32	1–58	2–00	0–49	2–10	3–10
102	0–36	1–09	1–21	1–52	3–22	...
104	0–12	0–41	...	3–27	...	...
106	0–03	0–22	0–32	...	...	...

(L2) Est. vol. 35,000, Wed vol. 19,189 calls, 17,065 puts

Open interest Wed; 250,647 calls, 186,050 puts

T-NOTES (CBT) $100,000; points and 64ths of 100%

Strike	Calls—Last			Puts—Last		
Price	Jun-c	Sep-c	Dec-c	Jun-p	Sep-p	Dec-p
100	3–60	...	...	0–02	0–18	0–37
102	2–03	1–52	1–41	0–08	0–41	1–07
104	0–36	0–46	0–51	0–42	1–33	...
106	0–05	0–15	0–21	2–08	2–60	...
108	0–01	0–05	...	4–04	...	...
110	0–01	0–02	...	...	...	...

Est. vol. 9,200, Wed vol. 1,508 calls, 1,803 puts

Open interest Wed; 42,402 calls, 25,466 puts

Although options quotations in the daily newspaper differ slightly depending upon whether the underlying asset is a particular stock or a futures contract, they all share a number of common characteristics. In the accompanying example for options on futures, line (L1) indicates that what follows immediately below are options on Treasury bond futures, that these options are traded on the Chicago Board of Trade (CBT), that the size of the underlying futures contract is $100,000, and that the quotations are percentage points plus sixty-fourths (per 100 face value). Immediately beneath the Treasury bond listings, line (L2) records the day's estimated trading volume for both puts and calls as 35,000 contracts and the previous day's volume as 19,189 call contracts and 17,065 put contracts. Beneath that line the open interest as of the previous day is recorded. Open interest is the number of open long (equal to short) positions. The open interest for calls is recorded as 250,647 contracts and the open interest for puts as 186,050 contracts. Since puts and calls are completely separate contracts, there is no need for the open interest on the two types of options to be related.

Now let's look at the columns of information. Column (1) shows the strike (exercise) price for each of the options available for the Treasury bond contract. The first line refers to options with a strike price of 96 and the last line refers to options with a strike price of 106. As you can see, the rules of the CBT call for strike prices that are 2 points apart. Columns (2), (3), and (4) list the closing (settlement) prices for call options with three different expiration dates—June, September, and December. For example, the 100 calls with a September expiration have a closing price of $1\frac{58}{64}$. Since each full percentage point on the Treasury bond contract is worth $1,000, the September 100 call costs $1,906.25. Notice that for some specific options—the 104 calls with a December expiration, for example—no price is listed because there was no trading in that particular contract. Columns (5), (6), and (7) record the closing prices for the June, September, and December put options.

The main difference in the quotation conventions for options on individual stocks is that the closing price of the stock itself is listed (usually in the extreme left-hand column). In addition, open interest and option trading volume are not usually recorded for individual equities.

opposite of the call) if the stock price is below the exercise price. For example, the owner of a $150 put on IBM will not want to exercise the right to sell IBM at $150 if IBM is selling at $155 on the stock exchange; but if IBM is selling for $140, then the put owner's right to sell IBM at $150 is worth exactly $10 on expiration.

One of the main advantages of buying options is the asymmetrical payoff just outlined. Buying a call provides unlimited upside potential, if the underlying asset rises in price, but a maximum downside risk of the premium paid initially if the underlying asset falls in price. Similarly, buying a put provides ever-increasing profit as the underlying asset falls in price but a maximum loss of the initial premium if the asset rises in price. This asymmetrical payoff has the characteristic of insurance, which may be the reason the price paid for an option is called the option premium. As with all insurance policies, if nothing happens (your car does not get hit by a tree), the premium paid is gone and you receive no benefits. For option buyers, the premium paid is a cost and there are no offsetting benefits if the price of the underlying asset does not move up significantly (in the case of a call) or down significantly (in the case of a put).

This analogy with insurance, in fact, provides the best insight into how options are used by hedgers. Let's return to our earlier example of hedging with Treasury bond futures. We showed that securities dealers who have just bought Treasury securities in the auction could protect their inventory by selling Treasury bond futures. As an alternative strategy, a dealer could buy puts on Treasury bond futures. In this case, if bond prices fall, the value of the inventory falls, causing a loss. But as our discussion of puts has just showed, the value of the put increases as the price of the underlying asset falls. This offsets the loss in the dealer's inventory.

The main difference in the two hedging strategies occurs if bond prices rise rather than fall. The dealer who bought puts is clearly better off: rising bond prices increase the value of the inventory, while the worst the puts can do is go out worthless on expiration day. The asymmetrical payoff on the put means that the dealer has protected his or her downside risk by buying the put while retaining upside potential through inventory. The dealer who sold bond futures as a hedge has an offsetting gain on the future if bond prices fall but also has an identical offsetting loss on the future if bond prices rise. Thus, selling futures as a hedge gives downside protection but also eliminates upside potential.

Why, then, doesn't everyone hedge with options rather than futures? The answer, of course, is the premium. The option buyer pays something for the asymmetrical payoff. If prices don't rise or fall, the option expires worthless and the premium is lost. Hedging with futures, on the other hand, does not involve any premium payments. If option premiums are low it may very well pay to hedge with options, while if premiums are high futures may turn out to be more attractive hedging vehicles.

Note that hedging is not the only reason people buy options. Speculating that the price of Treasury bonds will go up is a lot less nerveracking if an investor buys calls rather than the underlying securities (or the futures contract). In particular, buying a call limits your loss to the premium if prices go in the wrong direction (which is usually the case for most of us). Thus, even from the speculator's vantage point, option premiums represent the cost of insurance.

Since option premiums are important to both hedgers and speculators, let's take a look at what determines whether they are large or small. The obvious answer is that option premiums are determined just like any other price—by supply and demand. What we would like, however, is to provide an idea of what underlies the desire to pay a high price for an option (demand) compared with the willingness to sell options (supply). Since this is an extremely complicated subject, our discussion will be brief and intuitive rather than rigorous and mathematical.[6] We'll examine calls first and then extend the discussion to puts.

Let's take our favorite option, the IBM calls with a strike price of $150. The price of such equity options is usually quoted per share, which means that multiplying by 100 (the number of shares the call owner is entitled to buy) gives the dollar price of the option. For example, if this IBM option were quoted at $5, it would cost $500 to buy; if the option were quoted at $15, it would cost $1,500 and so on. What determines whether the price of the IBM 150 calls are priced at $5, $15 or $35? The three main factors are the current price of IBM stock, the volatility of IBM's stock price, and the time to expiration of the option. We will look at each factor in turn.

It should be fairly intuitive that a call option with a given exercise price will be worth more the higher the price of the underlying asset. If IBM stock is selling for $160, the $150 call gives you the right to buy 100 shares at a price which is $10 below the price at which you

[6]For a formal presentation of options theory, see Chapter 5 in John C. Cox and Mark Rubinstein, *Options Markets* (Englewood Cliffs, N.J.: Prentice-Hall, 1985).

could sell the shares. Thus everyone would pay at least $10 for the IBM $150 calls if IBM stock sells for $160, since they could lock in an immediate profit if the call were selling for less. If IBM stock were selling for $180, for example, the $150 call would be worth at least $30. Somewhat more generally, options will sell for at least their intrinsic value at any time, even prior to expiration. And that means that a higher stock price implies a higher call value at all times.

But that can hardly be the entire story. If IBM stock were selling at $140 per share, the intrinsic value of the $150 calls would be less than zero, but the options could still be quite valuable. And that is especially true if the calls have a significant amount of time left before expiration. In particular, if the price of IBM is very volatile, and there is a lot of time before the option expires, then there is always a chance that the price could move up significantly between now and expiration. The greater the volatility of IBM stock, the higher its price can go, hence the more the call could be worth on expiration. Therefore, given the current price of the stock, call buyers will pay more for a call option if the underlying stock is more volatile than otherwise. A similar argument makes option sellers less willing to write options on stock with large price volatility. Thus, for any given price of the underlying asset, call option premiums will be larger for stocks with high price volatility.[7]

The impact of time to expiration on the value of a call is easily seen as an extension of what we have just said. A call option that expires six months from now has more time for the price of the underlying asset to rise above the exercise price than an option with only three months to expiration. Thus call option premiums will be higher, the longer the maturity of the option.

To summarize: Call options will be worth more the higher the price of the underlying asset, the greater the volatility of the underlying asset, and the longer the time to expiration of the option.

A similar discussion would show that premiums on put options will be higher the *lower* the price of the underlying asset, since the put gives the owner the right to sell at the exercise price. In particular, an IBM put with an exercise price of $150 will be worth more if IBM is selling at $140 rather than $150. Higher price volatility of the underlying asset and longer maturity make put options more valuable for the

---

[7]Note that even though high volatility can mean large drops in price as well as high gains, the greater downside risk is less important to the call buyer than the enhanced upside potential because of the asymmetrical payoff to the call. The worst that can occur to the call buyer is that the call goes out worthless, while the upside potential is unlimited.

same reason they make call options more valuable: there is more chance that the option will have higher intrinsic value on the expiration date.[8]

Option pricing comes in much more complicated varieties than we have described here. Mathematical arbitrage arguments produce a more rigorous set of results. But for our purposes we have gone far enough to recognize that options will be an expensive way to hedge portfolio risks if those risks are substantial. There is, after all is said and done, no such thing as a free lunch. In particular, if stock and bond prices are highly volatile, then option premiums will be large. Financial institutions will then have a difficult choice: hedge with options to keep the upside potential while paying a substantial premium, or hedge with futures and forget about premiums and extra profitability. At last glance both options and futures markets had active participants from major financial institutions. Conclusion: Risk reduction takes many forms, depending upon its price (or put somewhat differently, you pay your money and take your chances).

SUMMARY

1. Financial futures contracts include interest rate futures, such as Treasury bonds and Eurodollars; stock index futures, such as the S&P 500; and foreign currency futures, such as the West German mark.

2. The standardization of contract terms on financial futures, together with the centralized auction process, promotes liquidity and low transactions costs in financial futures.

3. Financial futures are used by financial institutions to reduce risk of price changes in the underlying securities. Long hedgers reduce risk by buying futures contracts, short hedgers reduce risk by selling contracts.

4. Futures contracts are priced by the balance of supply of and demand for contracts by hedgers, speculators, and arbitrageurs. The activities of arbitrageurs maintain a close relationship between the price of futures contracts and the underlying financial asset.

5. Options contracts are traded on individual equities, such as IBM and General Motors; on stock indices, such as the S&P 100; and on interest rate futures, such as Treasury bond futures and Eurodollar futures.

[8]As in footnote 7, only the favorable outcome of volatility gets priced in the option; the unfavorable price movements at worst only make the option value go to zero.

6. Options are divided into puts and calls. Buyers of puts have the right to sell at a fixed exercise price, while buyers of calls have the right to buy at a fixed exercise price. The option sellers (or writers) have the obligation to do what the buyers want. In consideration of the rights received, option buyers pay a premium to option sellers.

7. Financial institutions can use options to hedge their risks. The asymmetric payoffs to both puts and calls—unlimited gains with limited losses—can make options especially attractive.

8. The prices of all options—their premiums—are larger the greater the price volatility of the underlying asset and the longer the time to expiration of the option. In addition, puts are worth more when the price of the underlying asset is low, and calls are worth more when the price of the underlying asset is high.

Suggestions for Further Reading

A simple introduction to futures contracts, with a separate section on financial futures, is the *Commodity Trading Manual* (Chicago Board of Trade, 1985). An extensive treatment of the role of financial futures is found in Stephen Figlewski, *Hedging with Financial Futures for Institutional Investors* (Cambridge, Mass.: Ballinger, 1986); and in William L. Silber, "The Economic Role of Financial Futures," in Anne Peck, ed., *Futures Markets: Their Economic Role* (Washington, D.C.: American Enterprise Institute, 1985). The classic article describing how to value options contracts is Fischer Black and Myron Scholes, "The Pricing of Options and Corporate Liabilities," *Journal of Political Economy* (May–June 1973). If you want to understand what's going on, read Chapters 1, 2, and 3 in John Cox and Mark Rubinstein, *Options Markets* (Englewood Cliffs, N.J.: Prentice-Hall, 1985). And if you really want to know what options and futures are all about, rent *Trading Places* at your local video store and watch Eddie Murphy's antics in the trading pit. That's exactly how it happens.

PART VI

INTERNATIONAL FINANCE

CHAPTER 34

Foreign Exchange Rates

In the last thirty or forty years, the growth of multinational corporations, the expansion in world trade, and the explosion of tourism have highlighted the importance of international payments. Big banks and corporations used to do only a small part of their business overseas, but now most of them have branches worldwide. Foreign cars were a novelty in America forty years ago, but now they are giving American automobile manufacturers nightmares. Only the wealthy could afford to vacation in Europe before World War II, but now ten of thousands of college students fly across the Atlantic every summer.

Any time a transaction takes place between the residents of two different countries, one kind of money has to be exchanged for another. What determines whether we will have to pay a little or a lot for a French franc or a German mark? Or, looking at the same thing from the other side of the fence, what determines whether the French or the Germans will have to pay a lot or a little for an American dollar?

Exchanges of one kind of money for another are made on the foreign exchange market, which is worldwide. Many banks throughout the world buy and sell foreign monies, in the form of foreign currencies and deposits in foreign banks. So do foreign exchange dealers, for whom this is their main business. More familiar to most people are currency exchanges, which do most of their transactions with tourists; they are found downtown, at airports, and at railroad stations in all the major tourist centers.

The foreign exchange rate is quoted in either of two ways: the price of 1 Transylvanian franc, for example, is 25 American cents; or 1 American dollar can buy 4 Transylvanian francs. These are obviously equivalent statements.

The price of foreign money, the foreign exchange rate, like the price of anything that is bought and sold, is determined by demand and supply. The only problem is to identify the underlying determinants of the demand for and the supply of foreign money—usually called foreign exchange.

THE EFFECT OF THE BALANCE OF PAYMENTS ON EXCHANGE RATES

Whenever we import foreign goods, buy foreign stocks or bonds, or travel abroad, *we have to make payments to others.* Naturally enough, those others want to get paid in their own money. So we have to get hold of foreign exchange, which we can do by going to a bank or currency exchange and buying some. Our imports thus give rise to a *demand for foreign exchange.* (Notice that when we buy foreign money we do so by offering dollars, so that a demand for foreign money can also be thought of as a supply of dollars on foreign exchange markets.)

On the other hand, whenever we export our goods, sell our securities to others, or are host to foreigners traveling here, *payments have to be made to us.* Naturally, we also want to get paid in our own money. So foreigners have to buy American dollars, which they can do by going to a bank or currency exchange and offering their own money to get dollars. Our exports thus give rise to a *supply of foreign exchange.* (Notice that when they offer or supply foreign money they are trying to buy dollars, so that the supply of foreign money can also be viewed as a demand for dollars on foreign exchange markets.)

These underlying determinants of the demand for and supply of foreign exchange are conveniently summarized in a national *balance of payments,* which is an accounting record of all payments made across national borders. Each country's balance of payments shows the payments made to foreigners and the receipt of funds from them, in

Reading the Financial News: Foreign Exchange Quotations

Foreign Exchange
THURSDAY, JANUARY 15, 1987

Country	$ value per unit of foreign currency	Units of currency per dollar
Argentina (Austral)	.78802	1.269
Australia (Dollar)	.6507	1.5368
Austria (Schilling)	.07752	12.90
Belgium (Franc)		
Commercial rate	.02640	37.88
Financial rate	.02620	38.16
Brazil (Cruzado)	.06596	15.06
Britain (Pound)	1.5055	.6642
30-Day Forward	1.4994	.6669
90-Day Forward	1.4881	.6720
180-Day Forward	1.4720	.6793
Canada (Dollar)	.7344	1.3617
30-Day Forward	.7330	1.3641
90-Day Forward	.7308	1.3683
180-Day Forward	.7273	1.3749
Chile (Official rate)	.004953	201.89
China (Yuan)	.26867	3.722
Colombia (Peso)	.004562	219.21
Denmark (Krone)	.1436	6.9625
Ecuador (Sucre)		
Official rate	.006836	146.28
Floating rate	.006826	146.50
Finland (Markka)	.2174	4.6000
France (Franc)	.1634	6.1200
30-Day Forward	.1629	6.1375
90-Day Forward	.1621	6.1700
180-Day Forward	.1610	6.210
Greece (Drachma)	.00750	133.30
Hong Kong (Dollar)	.1289	7.7570
India (Rupee)	.07651	13.07
Indonesia (Rupiah)	.0006105	1638.00
Ireland (Punt)	1.4490	.6901
Israel (Shekel)	.6761	1.479
Italy (Lira)	.0007669	1304.00
Japan (Yen)	.006523	153.30
30-Day Forward	.006536	152.99
90-Day Forward	.006558	152.49
180-Day Forward	.006591	151.72
Jordan (Dinar)	2.9154	.343
Kuwait (Dinar)	3.4282	.2917
Lebanon (Pound)	.01176	85.00
Malaysia (Ringgit)	.3909	2.5580
Malta (Lira)	2.751	.3635
Mexico (Peso)		
Floating rate	.001059	944.00
Netherland (Guilder)	.4831	2.0700
New Zealand (Dollar)	.5270	1.8975
Norway (Krone)	.1406	7.1100
Pakistan (Rupee)	.05794	17.258
Peru (Inti)	.07168	13.95
Philippines (Peso)	.04883	20.48
Portugal (Escudo)	.007097	140.90
Saudi Arabia (Riyal)	.2666	3.751
Singapore (Dollar)	.4677	2.1380
South Africa (Rand)		
Commercial rate	.4865	2.0555
Financial rate	.2275	4.3956
South Korea (Won)	.001162	860.80
Spain (Peseta)	.007828	127.75
Sweden (Krona)	.1524	6.5600
Switzerland (Franc)	.6498	1.5390
30-Day Forward	.6515	1.5349

Country	$ value per unit of foreign currency	Units of currency per dollar
90-Day Forward	.6541	1.5289
180-Day Forward	.6580	1.5198
Taiwan (Dollar)	.02822	35.43
Thailand (Baht)	.03834	26.08
Turkey (Lira)	.001323	756.04
United Arab (Dirham)	.2723	3.673
Uruguay (New Peso)		
Financial	.005571	179.50
Venezuela (Bolivar)		
Official rate	.1333	7.50
Floating rate	.04	25.00
W. Germany (Mark)	.5451	1.8345
30-Day Forward	.5460	1.8315
90-Day Forward	.5475	1.8266
180-Day Forward	.5496	1.8195

The left-hand column of numbers shows how much U.S. money exchanges for one British pound, one French franc, one West German mark—in other words, it shows how much U.S. money exchanges for *one unit of foreign money*. On January 15, 1987, it took about $1.51 to buy one British pound (look under Britain and ignore the "forward" quotations), 16.3 cents to get a French franc, and almost 55 cents to buy one West German mark (look under W).

The right-hand column shows how much foreign money exchanges for *one U.S. dollar*. On January 15, 1987, $1 would buy 66 British pence, or 6.12 French francs, or 1.83 German marks. Notice that the right-hand column is the reciprocal of the left—that is, 1 ÷ 1.5055 = .6642; 1 ÷ .1634 = 6.1200; 1 ÷ .5451 = 1.8345, and so on.

The various "commercial," "financial," "official," and "floating" rates shown for a few countries are differential

(continued)

rates set by the governments of those countries. Such differentials typically depend on factors like the type and purpose of the transaction, the amount of money involved, whether the parties to the transaction are residents or foreigners, and similar matters.

Major currencies have four different price quotations: the "spot" price, "30-day forward," "90-day forward," and "180-day forward." The spot price is what you pay to buy the money today. Forward prices are what you pay if you sign a contract today to buy the money on a specific future date (30, 90, or 180 days from now).

Check today's paper and see how foreign exchange rates have changed since January of 1987. Has the dollar gotten stronger or weaker?

the same way that a family might keep a record of all its expenditures and receipts.

A deficit in the U.S. balance of payments is similar to a deficit in a household's budget. It means that collectively we are paying out more money abroad than we are taking in, possibly because we are importing more products than we are exporting. A surplus in U.S. the balance of payments is just the opposite. It means we are taking in more money from abroad than we are paying out. Balance of payments deficits and surpluses have an important influence on movements in exchange rates:

1. A *deficit* in our balance of payments means that we are importing more than we are exporting, so that we are paying out more money abroad than we are taking in. This translates into a demand for foreign exchange greater than the supply. As a result, the price of foreign money will rise—foreign exchange will *ap*preciate in value relative to the dollar. The reason is that a deficit in our balance of payments means we are trying to buy more foreign money than foreigners want to sell to us—because they don't need as much of our money as we need of theirs. We can also think of this as a supply of dollars greater than the demand for them on the foreign exchange market, so the dollar will *de*preciate in value relative to other kinds of money.

2. On the other hand, a *surplus* in our balance of payments means that we are exporting more than we are importing, so that we are taking in more money from abroad than we are paying out. This translates into a supply of foreign money (trying to buy dollars) that is greater than the demand, so the price of foreign money will fall. Foreign exchange will depreciate, and the dollar will appreciate.

THE EFFECT OF EXCHANGE RATES ON
THE BALANCE OF PAYMENTS

When exchange rates are free to respond to market forces of demand and supply, as just described, they generate self-correcting changes in imports and exports, and in other types of international transactions, which eliminate balance of payments deficits and surpluses. To see how this works, assume we are importing more goods than we are exporting, so that we are running a payments deficit. The price of foreign exchange will rise because our demand for foreign exchange exceeds supply. As a result, foreign goods and services will become more expensive for us, so we are likely to import less. At the same time, we will probably export more because foreigners will find our products less expensive (they can now get more dollars for the same amount of their money). With fewer imports and more exports, our balance of payments deficit should decline.[1]

The same reasoning applies if we have a payments surplus because we are exporting more goods than we are importing. The price of foreign money will fall, increasing our imports (because foreign goods are now cheaper for us to buy) and decreasing our exports (our products are now more expensive for foreigners), thereby reducing our surplus.

Figure 1 illustrates these principles in the case of Transylvanian francs. The dollar price for one franc is on the vertical axis (for example, 25 cents for one franc), and the number of francs is on the horizontal axis. The demand and supply curves for francs have the conventional shapes: the amount of francs demanded increases as their dollar price falls, because when francs become less expensive, Transylvanian products become cheaper for us, we import more from Transylvania, hence we demand more francs. The amount of francs supplied decreases as their dollar price falls, because when francs become cheaper our goods become more expensive for the Transylvanians, so we export less to them, hence they supply fewer francs on the foreign exchange market.

As drawn, the demand and supply curves for francs imply an equilibrium price of 25 cents for one franc. At that exchange rate, the

[1]Actually, the price elasticities of our exports and imports are important here, but we will ignore this complication. If you want to dig further into such details, see the discussion of the Marshall-Lerner condition in any textbook on international economics. For an advanced treatment see Rudiger Dornbusch, "Currency Depreciation, Hoarding, and Relative Prices," *Journal of Political Economy* (July–August 1973).

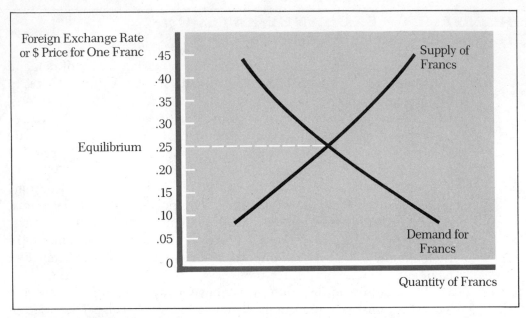

FIGURE 1 Supply of and Demand for Foreign Exchange and Foreign Exchange Rates

demand for francs equals supply and our balance of payments shows neither a deficit nor a surplus (at least with respect to Transylvania).

What would happen if the exchange rate for some reason happened to be at only 20 cents? As Figure 1 shows, at that price, our demand for francs exceeds the available supply. Why might that be the case? With the franc that cheap our imports would grow, increasing our demand for francs, and our exports would shrink, decreasing the supply of francs. But in a free market, such conditions could not last. The excess of demand over supply would push the exchange rate back up to 25 cents once again. At that price the exchange rate would be in equilibrium, and so would our balance of payments. Thus a freely fluctuating exchange rate keeps both supply and demand for foreign money in equilibrium and also balances the record of international payments.

As a final reminder, don't forget that in international transactions of one kind of money for another there is always a reciprocal exchange involved. The demand for foreign money implies a supply of dollars, and the supply of foreign money implies a demand for dollars. We have said that a deficit in our balance of payments means that the demand for foreign money exceeds the supply, so the dollar price of foreign money will *appreciate*. We could just as well say that a deficit in our balance of payments means that the supply of dollars on foreign exchange markets exceeds the demand for them, so the dollar will *depreciate*.

It all follows from the fact that when we have a payments deficit we are paying out more money abroad than we are taking in. American importers are paying out more dollars than foreigners need in order to buy our exports. This produces an excess supply of dollars in world financial markets and depresses the value of the dollar (which is the same thing as saying that it will depreciate).

STILL TO COME

Actually, foreign exchange rates that float freely in response to market forces of demand and supply are fairly new in international finance. From the end of World War II until the early 1970s, exchange rates were fixed by international agreement and were not allowed to react to pressures of the marketplace. The agreed-upon fixed exchange rates were supervised by the International Monetary Fund, an institution established at a monetary conference held in Bretton Woods, New Hampshire, in 1944. This fixed-rate system encountered periodic difficulties, however, and finally fell apart in 1973. In Chapter 35 we will see how fixed exchange rates worked and why they failed.

During the late nineteenth century and the first three decades of the twentieth, the international financial system operated under the gold standard, in which rates of exchange were also fixed. There are always some people who want to go back to the gold standard, so we will examine it in Chapter 37.

SUMMARY

1. Our payments abroad create a demand for foreign exchange (which can also be viewed as a supply of dollars). Payments from foreigners to us create a supply of foreign exchange (or a demand for dollars).

2. An international balance of payments is an accounting record of all payments made across national borders. A deficit in our balance of payments means that collectively we are paying out more money abroad than we are taking in. A surplus means we are taking in more money than we are paying out.

3. A *deficit* in our balance of payments translates into a demand for foreign exchange greater than the supply, leading to *appreciation in the value of foreign exchange* relative to the dollar. Alternatively, we could say that a deficit translates into a supply of dollars on world financial markets greater than the demand for them, leading to *depreciation of the dollar* relative to foreign monies.

4. A *surplus* in our balance of payments translates into a supply of foreign exchange greater than the demand, leading to *depreciation in the value of foreign exchange* relative to the dollar. Alternatively, we could say that a surplus translates into a demand for dollars greater than the supply, leading to *appreciation of the dollar.*

5. When U.S. money *depreciates*, U.S. exports should rise because its goods become cheaper for foreigners, and its imports should fall because foreign goods become more expensive for Americans.

6. When U.S. money *appreciates*, U.S. exports should fall because its goods become more expensive for foreigners, and its imports should rise because foreign goods become less expensive for Americans.

7. If foreign exchange rates are left free to respond to market forces of demand and supply, movements in exchange rates should eliminate both deficits and surpluses. At the equilibrium exchange rate, the demand for and supply of foreign exchange (or the supply of and demand for dollars) are equal, and the balance of payments is in neither deficit nor surplus.

Suggestions for Further Reading

An informative booklet that fleshes out much of the material in this chapter is Roger M. Kubarych, *Foreign Exchange Markets in the United States*, rev. ed. (Federal Reserve Bank of New York, 1983). The New York Fed will send you a copy free if you ask for one; write to the Public Information Department, 33 Liberty Street, New York, N.Y., 10045. See also K. Alec Chrystal, "A Guide to Foreign Exchange Markets," Federal Reserve Bank of St. Louis *Review* (March 1984).

CHAPTER 35

Fixed Versus Floating Exchange Rates

From the end of World War II until 1973, the world's international financial system was based on *fixed* exchange rates. When you spent a weekend in Amsterdam or a spring vacation in Paris, you knew before you started what the price of foreign money would be. Nowadays exchange rates *float,* and you're never sure how much it will cost to buy the money you'll need when you get there.

Fixed exchange rates have undeniable benefits. Within the United States, for example, a dollar costs a dollar no matter where you are. A common currency within a country is a domestic fixed exchange rate system, and it has obvious advantages. It would be a mess if we had domestic floating rates—if dollars were stamped with each state's name on the top and had to be exchanged for a differently stamped dollar, at unpredictable cost, every time you went from one state to another.

Since fixed exchange rates are good at home, why not internationally? On the basis of such thinking, the major countries agreed in 1944 to establish the International Monetary Fund to supervise fixed exchange rates. The fixed exchange rate system worked tolerably well for more than two decades, but then it produced periodic international financial crises that eventually brought the whole system tumbling down.

HOW FIXED RATES WERE MAINTAINED

Remember how *floating* exchange rates work? When a country runs a balance of payments deficit, the supply of its money offered on world financial markets exceeds the demand, so that its money depreciates in value relative to other monies. But with *fixed* exchange rates, as they existed from the end of World War II until 1973, fluctuations in exchange rates were stopped before they could get started. By international agreement, under the supervision of the International Monetary Fund, a deficit country that saw its money start to depreciate had to step in promptly and prevent the decline. How? By buying up its own money in order to absorb the excess of supply over demand at the pegged exchange rate.

As an illustration, say France is initially in a situation where the supply of and demand for francs is equal, so that the foreign exchange rate is in equilibrium. Suddenly the French people decide they no longer like French wine and pastry but prefer American soda pop and Twinkies, which they begin to import in huge quantities.

As Figure 1(a) shows, this change in tastes would shift the entire supply curve of francs to the right, as the French offer more francs (at every exchange rate) to buy the increased number of dollars they need to pay American soda pop and Twinkies exporters. At the old equilibrium exchange rate, France now has a deficit in its balance of payments, which translates into a supply of francs greater than the demand. With exchange rates free to fluctuate, the franc will depreciate and move down toward a new lower equilibrium level.

In Figure 1(b), however, the rate is fixed, or pegged, at an agreed-upon level, called par. Again the shift in the supply curve results in a supply of francs greater than the demand at the old equilibrium exchange rate. This excess of supply over demand is indicated in Figure 1(b) by the cross-hatched line (xxxxxxx). Now, though, the French central bank steps in *and buys up this excess,* thereby preventing the franc from depreciating.

Of course, the French central bank can't buy up its own money by offering more of the same in exchange—which it could simply print—because that's what people are *selling,* not buying. It has to use *other* money to buy up its own, and this other money is called its international reserves.

Traditionally, nations held their international reserves in the form of gold, because of its general acceptability. Since the end of World War II, however, most foreign countries have held a substantial portion of their reserves in the form of U.S. dollars, which generally have

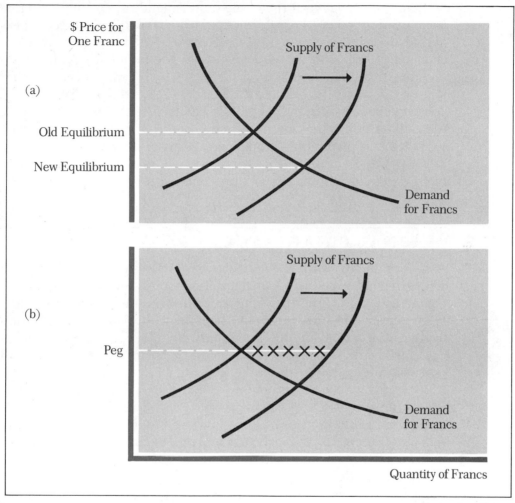

FIGURE 1 In (a), with floating rates, the franc depreciates; in (b), with pegged rates, the French central bank prevents the decline by buying up francs = ✕✕✕✕✕✕. (In effect, the demand curve is shifted to the right by that much, although we haven't drawn the new curve.)

been just about as acceptable as gold in making international payments. They also hold other kinds of "foreign exchange" among their reserves—pounds, yen, marks, and so on—but mostly they hold U.S. dollars. Other nations acquire dollars when we run our deficits and then hold them as their reserves.

In general, countries use their international reserves in the same way individuals and businesses use their cash balances—to bridge temporary gaps between the receipt and expenditure of funds, to tide them over periods when inflows of funds are slack, and to meet unexpected or emergency needs. *In particular,* with a system of fixed exchange rates, countries also used their international reserves to intervene in foreign exchange markets whenever the value of their money threatened to slide away from par (its agreed-upon fixed value). A foreign country generally used U.S. dollars for this purpose, paying out dollars to buy up any excess supply of its own money, thereby preventing its own money from depreciating relative to other monies. Or, if it was a surplus rather than a deficit country, selling its own money to keep it from *ap*preciating relative to others.[1]

INTERNATIONAL FINANCIAL CRISES

A major difficulty with the fixed-rate system was that it contained no self-correcting mechanism to help eliminate a country's balance of payments deficit and bring about an equilibrium in its exchange rate. With floating rates, as we saw in Chapter 34, the Transylvania franc's depreciation would reduce the supply of francs offered on foreign exchange markets, increase the demand for them, and eventually end downward pressure on the franc.

But if no depreciation is allowed, what is there to stop Transylvania from running balance of payments deficits forever? If it does so, then it must continue to pay out its reserves to buy up excess francs, and that's the catch. For Transylvania's foreign exchange reserves are not infinite. Sooner or later, when it starts to run out of reserves, it will have to stop "defending the franc." In international financial terminology, Transylvania will have to *devalue* the franc—that is, lower its agreed-upon par value. At the new lower par value, the deficit will disappear, or so it is hoped. If not, they may have to devalue again—that is, once more lower the international value or price of the franc.

The seeds of the old-fashioned international financial crises that used to erupt periodically, when the world was on fixed exchange rates, sprang from the ever-present threat of devaluation by one country or another.

Once the international financial community senses that devaluation

---

[1]This means, by the way, that since dollars were the reserves of foreign countries, the United States was in the unique position of not having to intervene itself to keep *its* money from changing in value relative to other monies; since all the other countries were intervening to keep their monies from changing in value relative to the dollar, the dollar was automatically prevented from changing relative to them.

is a possibility, no matter how remote, it is likely to take actions that increase the probability of its occurrence. People who own francs, or liquid assets payable in francs, and suspect that the franc may be devalued would be inclined to get out of francs and into some other kind of money—say, West German marks—until the devaluation has been completed. Then, with the marks, they could buy back more francs than they originally had. Such "speculative" sales of francs by private holders must of course be purchased by the Transylvanian monetary authorities, as they try to prevent the franc from depreciating below par. This puts an added strain on their reserves, thereby increasing the likelihood of devaluation—which in turn stimulates renewed "speculative" activity.

International transfers of short-term funds stemming from fears of devaluation can feed on themselves in this fashion and generate massive reserve drains. Since devaluations are an ever-present fact of life under a fixed exchange rate system, countries with balance of payments deficits have traditionally been viewed with some suspicion by those who manage large pools of mobile funds—treasurers of multinational corporations, bankers, oil sheiks, financial consultants to private investors, and others with similar responsibilities. Indeed, fund managers often got nervous about holding a country's money as soon as that country's rate of inflation exceeded that of other countries, since this was taken as an early warning signal of future devaluation (a rise in prices that is more rapid than elsewhere hurts that country's exports, encourages its imports, and thereby invites balance of payments deficits).

DOMESTIC STABILIZATION POLICIES UNDER FIXED AND FLOATING EXCHANGE RATES

To what extent are domestic monetary and fiscal policies influenced or limited by the kind of international exchange rate system that is in effect?

With fixed exchange rates, a country's domestic stabilization policies may be severely constrained by the requirement that it maintain exchange rate stability. With floating rates, on the other hand, it appears—on the surface, at least—that a country can do just about whatever it wants to domestically, because fluctuations in the exchange rate will automatically take care of such external factors as exports and imports.

1. *Let's look at fixed rates first.* Under fixed exchange rates, a country running a balance of payments deficit must use its international reserves to buy up its own money to prevent it from depreciating on the foreign exchange market. A country cannot run a payments deficit forever, because sooner or later it will run out of international reserves. Therefore it has to be concerned about the effects of its domestic policies on its imports and exports, including financial flows that respond to intercountry interest rate differentials.

Under a fixed-rate system, how much freedom do individual nations have to pursue their own independent domestic policies? Not too much, once you think about it. If Great Britain is running a payments deficit, for example, it can hardly ignore that fact and try to live the good life regardless. If it did, its rising prices and higher incomes relative to other countries would stimulate its imports and hamper its exports. Great Britain's balance of payments deficit would worsen, and it would wind up desperately buying pounds to stop the pound from depreciating, in the process using up its scarce international reserves.

Under fixed exchange rate arrangements, with no automatic mechanism to take care of payments imbalances, nations have to take deliberate policy measures to do the job. That means that a chronic-deficit nation sooner or later has no choice but to use monetary and fiscal policies to contract imports, expand exports, and attract financial investments from abroad. Contracting imports and expanding exports requires holding down wages and prices at home, or at least holding the rate of inflation below that of other countries (so that domestic products become relatively less expensive), and quite possibly inducing at least a mild recession. To attract financial flows from abroad requires tight money and higher interest rates at home. If a chronic-deficit nation decides it would rather not take such measures, it will run out of reserves as it tries to prevent its money from depreciating on international financial markets. So under fixed exchange rates, freedom of individual domestic action is severely limited by balance of payments considerations.

There is one exception to this principle, at least for a while: namely, a nation that is in the uniquely fortunate position of having *its* money used as reserves by the rest of the world. Say the United States runs continuous balance of payments deficits. What in any other case would soon be viewed as an excess supply of that country's money on world financial markets is not so promptly thought of as excess in the case of the dollar, since other countries want dollars to hold as part of their reserves. Until other countries start to feel that enough is enough, a reserve money country, such as the United States, can run balance of payments deficits with virtual impunity. In effect, since dollars represent a U.S. liability, everyone else is happily (?) lending to the United States. But eventually this tolerance comes to an end, and when that happens the dollar also starts to depreciate, and then the United States is in the same boat as everyone else. Then our freedom to pursue strictly domestic objectives is also constrained, and ''the discipline imposed by the balance of payments'' becomes universal.

The lesson to be learned from all this is that no central bank can conduct an independent, wholly domestically oriented monetary policy within the framework of fixed exchange rates.

2. *Floating rates are another story.* Flexible foreign exchange rates are generally hailed as the one system that permits a country to pursue domestic policies unhampered by external balance of payments considerations. When a country runs a payments deficit, its money depreciates, reducing imports, stimulating exports, and automatically correcting the deficit.

Under this system, nations have much more freedom to pursue their own independent domestic stabilization policies. A deficit country can continue to use monetary and fiscal policies to maintain a prosperous economy. It does not have to induce a recession at home in order to make its exports more attractive and cut back on its imports; depreciation of its money on world financial markets will automatically take care of that.

All of which sounds too easy. There must be a catch. And sure enough, there is. It is true that deficits (and surpluses) will eventually be taken care of by exchange rate movements. But do *not* leap from that to the further conclusion that the adjustment process will be painless. Because it might be very painful indeed!

Think for a moment of what that adjustment process involves for a deficit country (say Great Britain): it means, for one thing, that its imports will cost more, because the United Kingdom, with its money depreciating, will have to pay more to acquire the marks and francs it needs to pay for imports. If these imports are ''essential''—like food for Britain or oil for the United States—the cost of living will rise and living standards will fall in the deficit country. This is inflation. If you have to pay a lot more for food, or for gasoline, you will have a lot less left over for other things. In addition, there will be fewer ''other things'' available, because England's exports are likely to expand.

Since other countries can obtain pounds cheaply, foreigners will take a larger fraction of Great Britain's output, leaving less for the home folks. On both grounds—more expensive imports and more exports—life will become less comfortable in Great Britain. The U.K. will get rid of its payments deficit, but it will find its standard of living declining in the process.[2]

MANAGED FLOATING

Have freely floating exchange rates been a success? In some respects, yes. Had fixed exchange rates still been in existence throughout the seventies, international financial crises of vast proportions would have erupted every time the Organization of Petroleum Exporting Countries (OPEC) announced large increases in oil prices. Floating rates absorbed those shocks remarkably well.

But floating rates have nevertheless fallen far short of expectations. Most important, they have *not* eliminated this country's chronic balance of trade deficits the way everyone thought they would. If there was anything floating rates were expected to do, it was to wipe out our balance of trade deficits, our huge excess of imports of goods and services over exports of goods and services.

How were floating rates expected to do that? When the United States imports more goods and services than we export, the American demand for foreign money (to pay for U.S. imports) exceeds the foreign demand for dollars (to pay for U.S. exports). Result: foreign money should appreciate and *the dollar should depreciate.* A depreciated dollar should contract our imports (they cost us more) and expand our exports (they become cheaper for foreigners), thereby wiping out our trade deficit.

From 1980 to 1985, however, despite larger and larger U.S. trade deficits, the dollar failed to depreciate the way it was supposed to;

---

[2]Britons *have* to lower their standard of living in the sense that they must consume less, produce fewer capital goods for home use, or accept fewer government services. GNP = $C + I + G$ + exports − imports. Assume that $C + I + G = 110$ and exports = 10 and imports = 20. Thus GNP = 100. Keeping GNP at 100 but forcing exports to equal imports, say at 15 each, requires that $C + I + G$ equal no more than 100, as compared with 110 before. This assumes, however, that the British balance of payments deficit is due to an excess of merchandise imports; if it is due to excessive lending abroad (importing foreign securities), then the British can balance their books by lending less abroad.

instead, the dollar *appreciated* almost sixty percent! The stronger dollar encouraged additional imports into the United States (they cost us less) and discouraged American exports (they cost foreigners more), thereby making our trade deficit *worse* rather than better.

What went wrong? The reason that floating rates failed to function the way they were expected to was the extraordinarily heavy foreign demand for U.S. stocks and bonds. Foreign money was attracted to American stocks and bonds because of this country's political stability, relatively low inflation rate, and relatively high real interest rates.

Foreign purchases of U.S. securities generate a foreign demand for dollars (to pay for them), just as foreign purchases of U.S. goods and services do. The United States was simply exporting stocks and bonds instead of automobiles and computers. The *total* demand for dollars on foreign exchange markets, to pay for U.S. exports of merchandise *and* securities, exceeded the total demand for foreign monies and produced an appreciating dollar.

The higher the American dollar rose, the more it hurt U.S. employment. More imports and less exports means exporting jobs abroad, increasing unemployment at home. Thus in September of 1985 the Group of Five nations—known as G-5 and consisting of the United States, Great Britain, Japan, West Germany, and France—met in New York at the initiative of the United States, which decided it had had its fill of freely floating exchange rates.

With some prodding by Uncle Sam, the G-5 nations agreed in New York that they would act in concert to lower the international value of the dollar in order to help reduce American imports and stimulate American exports. The year 1985 thus witnessed the formal end of the era of freely floating exchange rates, which had begun in 1973, and its replacement by a system that is somewhere midway between fixed and floating exchange rates. Most people call it a "managed floating" system.

Under the present managed floating system, the Treasuries and central banks of the major nations intervene frequently in foreign exchange markets, buying or selling currencies, in order to nudge foreign exchange rates in one direction or another. So far, the managed floating system has been reasonably successful in achieving its aims.

The policies inaugurated in New York in 1985 were reinforced at the Tokyo summit in 1986, where the G-5 nations were joined in their coordinated effort by Canada and Italy. The new Group of Seven agreed to act together in international financial matters in order to "foster greater stability in exchange rates."

Some observers believe that the present managed floating system is just one step on the road back to fixed exchange rates. Many bankers and business executives have never liked floating rates to begin with, because of the uncertainties involved; they hope managed floating is the start of an eventual return to fixed rates.[3] Most economists, on the other hand, like floating rates better than fixed because they prefer market forces to political bargaining. The system of managed floating is an uneasy compromise between the two camps. How long it will last only time will tell.

SUMMARY

1. With fixed exchange rates, a deficit country must intervene and buy up its own money to prevent its depreciation on the foreign exchange market. It uses its international reserves for this purpose, but the process ends when a country runs out of reserves.

2. International financial crises tend to develop under fixed rates when fears of devaluation lead to speculative dumping of a country's money.

3. Nations have more freedom and flexibility in the exercise of independent domestic policies under floating rates than they do under fixed rates, but the "discipline of the balance of payments" exists under floating rates, too.

4. The United States was (and still is) more insulated than other countries with respect to payments deficits and the depreciation of its money, because the dollar is used by many other countries as their international reserve.

5. Fixed exchange rates collapsed in 1973 and were succeeded by freely floating rates, which prevailed until 1985. However, floating rates failed to work as expected; in particular, they did not eliminate this country's chronic balance of trade deficit. Instead of depreciating, the dollar *ap*preciated (because of large-scale foreign purchases of U.S. securities), which made our trade deficit worse than ever.

6. As a result, since 1985 the world has been on a managed floating system, which is midway between fixed and floating exchange rates.

[3]For an expression of views along these lines, see "The Drift Back to Fixed Exchange Rates: Floating Rates Are Being Viewed Worldwide as a Costly, Failed Experiment," *Business Week* (June 2, 1975), pp. 60–63. Also see "Bring Back Bretton Woods," an editorial in the *Wall Street Journal*, June 22, 1982.

Suggestions for Further Reading

For an insider's view of some of the events discussed in this chapter, see Robert Solomon, *The International Monetary System, 1945–1981* (New York: Harper & Row, 1982).

On speculative flows of funds and international financial crises, see Donald L. Kohn, "Capital Flows in a Foreign Exchange Crisis," Federal Reserve Bank of Kansas City *Monthly Review* (February 1973); and Philip Rushing, "Reciprocal Currency Arrangements," Federal Reserve Bank of Boston *New England Economic Review* (November–December 1972).

In more general terms, see Abba P. Lerner, "What Would We Do Without the Speculator?" in his *Everybody's Business* (East Lansing: Michigan State University Press, 1961); and Milton Friedman, "In Defense of Destabilizing Speculation," in his *The Optimum Quantity of Money and Other Essays* (Chicago: Aldine, 1969). Also see the article by Friedman, "The Case for Flexible Exchange Rates," in his *Essays in Positive Economics* (Chicago: University of Chicago Press, 1953).

For more advanced discussions of speculation, see William J. Baumol, "Speculation, Profitability, and Stability," *Review of Economics and Statistics* (August 1957), and Lester G. Telser, "A Theory of Speculation Relating Profitability to Stability," *Review of Economics and Statistics* (August 1959).

Also valuable are Thomas M. Humphrey's articles on international topics in his *Essays on Inflation*, 4th ed. (Federal Reserve Bank of Richmond, 1983).

CHAPTER 36

Balance of Payments Accounting

Questions about the balance of payments are asked so frequently that we feel it would be a service to humanity to correct at least a few of the major misconceptions that abound. For example, the question that arises most often is What color is the balance of payments? Many people think it is purple, but that is wrong. It is generally wrong, anyway, because the balance of payments is purple only when the consumption function is lavender, and, as you recall, that is a special case. In fact, the balance of payments is usually a deep green, except when it has been left out in the rain too long.

And finally: does the balance of payments really balance? The answer to that is definitely yes, unless it is shoved. But since most people seem to remain unconvinced, a further word of explanation is necessary.

SOURCES AND USES ONCE AGAIN

Actually, a country's balance of payments is nothing more than a sector sources and uses of funds statement in disguise. Just as a sources and uses statement (Chapter 27) records a sector's receipts from and payments to other sectors, so a country's balance of international payments shows the country's receipts from and payments to other countries. The main difference is that in flow of funds accounting the sectors are subdivisions within a country (the household sector, the business sector, and so on), while in balance of payments accounting the sectors are divided into "our country" and "the rest of the world."

In principle we could construct a model balance of payments for a country, from the ground up, in exactly the same way we constructed our model sources and uses statement in Chapter 27. All you have to do is think about the United States as a sector, versus the rest of the world, and everything else follows just about the same way. In practice, however, things are a bit more complex, mainly because the entries in our balance of payments—as it is presented by the Department of Commerce—are artfully arranged so as to camouflage the fact that it is really nothing more than a simple sources and uses of funds statement. But lest you be too hard on the economists at the Department of Commerce for making life complicated, don't forget the ancient Buddhist adage: Simplicity is the enemy of Romance.

Without tearing aside the veil of mystery completely, let's return briefly to what we meant by sources and uses of funds when we were doodling with sector sources and uses statements back in Chapter 27.

1. *Sources* of funds consist of (a) *current receipts;* (b) any *increase in a liability* item (borrowing); or (c) any *decrease in an asset* item (selling off assets, dishoarding).

2. *Uses* of funds consist of (a) *current expenditures;* (b) any *decrease in a liability* item (debt repayment); or (c) any *increase in an asset* item—increased holdings of real assets (investment), financial assets (lending), or money (hoarding).

3. We concluded that *the sum of a sector's sources of funds must equal the sum of its uses of funds.* If a sector spends on current and capital goods more than its current receipts (deficit sector), it has to finance its deficit by borrowing, selling off assets, or dishoarding; if its consumption plus investment spending is less than its current income (surplus sector), it has no choice but to repay debts, lend, or hoard an amount equal to its surplus.

Sources and uses of funds have similar meanings and implications in a country's balance of international payments, except that now we have to adapt to the fact that in international transactions we are dealing with *another* country's money. A source or receipt of funds for us as a nation means we get an inflow of foreign money; a use or expenditure of funds for us as a nation means we part with foreign money, an outflow, as we spend abroad. So in international balance of payments accounting, sources and uses of funds become sources and uses of *foreign* monies.

What are some of our main *sources* of foreign money (or foreign exchange, as it is usually called)? Clearly, merchandise exports yield us foreign exchange. When your average Samoan sheepherder subscribes to *Soap Opera Digest,* he mails in some Samoan money which can be taken to our local bank and changed into dollars. But the Samoan money does not disappear; the U.S. bank now owns it. From the point of view of the United States, as a nation, we have acquired foreign exchange. (A unit of Samoan money is called a tala. Remember that. It will probably be on the final.)

The same thing applies if foreign tourists travel across the highways and byways of America in search of Paradise (Montana) or Hell (Michigan). They need American money if they are to get a Big Mac at McDonald's, and to get dollars they have to go to a bank and hand over some sucres, bahts, kyats, or leva—the monies of Ecuador, Thailand, Burma, and Bulgaria respectively.

We similarly receive an inflow of foreign exchange when we export stocks or bonds (borrow from abroad), just as when we export goods—as when an oil sheik in Kuwait buys some U.S. Treasury bills or IBM stock. In all these instances foreigners need to buy dollars, and in the process we as a nation acquire ownership of some of their kind of money.

Uses of funds on our balance of international payments come about when it is Americans who do the spending: when we import voodoo dolls from Haiti or love potions from Xanadu; when American tourists in blue jeans and headbands check in at the Sahara Hilton; and when Americans import stocks or bonds (lend to foreigners), as when we buy some United Kingdom Treasury bills in London. In all these instances we have to pay with foreign money, so we go to a bank or currency exchange and buy pounds or francs or what have you (or else use up some of the foreign exchange we had previously acquired). In the process, of course, foreigners acquire ownership of some of our kind of money.

In other words, the source and uses of foreign exchange for the United States—our balance of international payments—correspond to the standard sources and uses of funds for a sector in domestic trade. Table 1 offers a somewhat formal presentation.

TABLE 1

A Generalized Sources and Uses of Funds Approach to the Balance of Payments for the United States*

Uses of Foreign Exchange	Sources of Foreign Exchange
Current expenditures—as for:	*Current receipts*—as for:
Our merchandise imports	Our merchandise exports
U.S. tourist spending abroad	Foreign tourist spending here
Interest and dividends paid to people abroad	Interest and dividends received from abroad
Services rendered by foreign ships, airlines, etc.	Services rendered by U.S. ships, airlines, etc.
U.S. military spending abroad	Foreign military spending here
Unilateral transfers (gifts, remittances, etc.) from U.S.	Unilateral transfers (gifts, remittances, etc.) to U.S.
Decreases in liabilities (debt repayment)—such as:	*Increases in liabilities* (borrowing)—such as:
Reductions in foreign holdings of U.S. securities	Purchases by foreigners of U.S. securities
Reductions in foreign bank loans to U.S. companies	Increases in foreign bank loans to U.S. companies
Reductions in foreign holdings of U.S. money, in the form of either U.S. currency or demand deposits in U.S. banks	Increases in foreign holdings of U.S. money, in the form of either U.S. currency or demand deposits in U.S. banks
Increases in assets—such as:	*Decreases in assets*—such as:
Direct investment by American firms abroad (ownership interest)	Direct investment by foreign firms in the U.S. (ownership interest)
Our purchases of foreign securities (lending)	Reductions in our holdings of foreign securities
Increases in U.S. bank loans to foreign companies (lending)	Reductions in U.S. bank loans to foreign companies
Increases in our holdings of foreign money, in the form of either foreign currency or demand deposits in foreign banks (hoarding)	Reductions in our holdings of foreign money, in the form of either foreign currency or demand deposits in foreign banks (dishoarding)
And our purchases of gold	And our sales of gold

*In the more traditional presentations of the balance of payments, sources of foreign exchange are usually called credits (or plus items), and uses are called debits (or minus items).

DOES IT REALLY BALANCE?

Does the balance of payments really balance? Of course it does. Just as on a sector sources and uses statement the sum of all a sector's sources of funds must equal the sum of all its uses, so on a nation's balance of international payments all the sources have to equal all the uses. The same logic applies to both.

Like a household, a country cannot incur a deficit by spending on current and capital goods more than its current receipts unless it finances that deficit by borrowing, selling off some assets, or drawing down its cash reserves.[1] It cannot incur a surplus by total spending less than current receipts without disposing of that surplus via debt repayment, lending, or building up its cash reserves (hoarding). In brief, if a country's uses are greater than its sources in some categories, then its sources must be correspondingly greater than its uses on the remainder of the statement.

If all this is so—if the balance of payments always balances—then why all the fuss? How can people keep talking about a deficit in our balance of payments, which implies an inequality, when such an inequality appears to be an impossibility?

Again, as with sector statements, it all depends on precisely what you are measuring. A sector's *total* sources must equal its *total* uses, but within the totals particular pairs may not match up at all: a sector's current expenditures can exceed its current receipts, or vice versa; its saving may exceed its investment, or vice versa; its borrowing may exceed its lending, or vice versa. If you measure the grand totals, they are equal. But if you look behind them, you will find that those grand totals are usually made up of many (eventually offsetting) inequalities.

---

[1]A complication arises in this connection with respect to certain kinds of direct foreign equity investment, similar to the complication regarding corporate equities and bonds mentioned in footnote 1 of Chapter 27. We resolved that problem by assuming that corporate stocks and bonds are roughly the same thing, and we will resolve this difficulty the same way.

Say that Volkswagen ships an entire automobile manufacturing plant, piece by piece, to Ohio. Our imports would rise, but we would *not* be financing this current deficit by borrowing, selling off assets, or dishoarding, since these imports are still owned by Germany. It is handled in the balance of payments accounts as a direct investment by foreigners in the United States (ownership interest). The simplest way to think of this, consistent with footnote 1 in Chapter 27, is to assume that Germany's equity ownership of assets in the United States is roughly the same as if Germany acquired debt claims on this country (our borrowing). In other words, once again stocks and bonds are considered roughly the same thing.

The typical items that adjust to make our balance of payments "balance" are increases or decreases in foreign holdings of U.S. dollars or short-term securities. For example, say we import more than we export: we have to pay for the difference, which we could do by giving a check to the foreign seller's firm. The firm deposits the check in its bank to get francs or pesos, so its bank now has the check, which means that a foreign bank now owns demand deposits in an American bank. Our balance of payments would show more imports than exports, but this would be balanced by an increase in foreign holdings of a U.S. liability (demand deposits are a liability of the U.S. bank). In effect, we have financed our imports by borrowing from abroad—the lender is the foreign bank that now owns a demand deposit in a U.S. bank.

The foreign bank might decide to exchange that demand deposit for U.S. Treasury bills, to earn some interest. But that wouldn't change anything; from the point of view of the balance of payments, that just substitutes one kind of U.S. liability for another. Or prior to August 1971 the foreign bank might, through its government, have used the demand deposit to buy some of our gold: in that case a U.S. gold sale (a source) would balance our imports (a use). No matter how you figure it, in the aggregate sources are always equal to uses.

So what does a balance of payments deficit (or surplus) mean?

MEASURE FOR MEASURE (OR AS YOU LIKE IT)

Economists often talk about the *trade* deficit (or surplus), or the deficit *on current account.* Indeed, reference is frequently made to no less than *six* different balance of payments deficits—or surpluses—each of which results from selecting different categories in the payments accounts. Table 2 illustrates each of the six and their relationships to each other. Although at first glance Table 2 looks rather different from Table 1, way down deep it is the same thing.

Using Table 2 to illustrate the calculations, here are the particulars of each balancing act:

1. The *trade balance* is the most old-fashioned of all, measuring only merchandise exports relative to imports. In Table 2 the merchandise trade balance has a $1 billion surplus, with exports $1 billion greater than imports. In Mercantilist days, in the 1600s and 1700s, this was the exclusive measure. A country with excessive imports would have to settle up by selling off some of its gold, clearly a Bad Thing.

TABLE 2
Illustrative U.S. Balance of Payments* (In billions of dollars)

	Net Balance	Cumulative Net Balance
A. Merchandise Trade:		
1. Exports	+70	
2. Imports	−69	
Merchandise Trade Balance	+1	+1
B. Services:		
1. Military Receipts	+2	
2. Military Payments	−5	
3. Income on U.S. Investments Abroad	+18	
4. Payments for Foreign Investments in U.S.	−9	
5. Receipts from Travel and Transportation	+9	
6. Payments for Travel and Transportation	−11	
7. Other Services (net)	+1	
Balance on Services	+5	
Goods and Services Balance		+6
C. Transfer Payments:		
1. Private	−1	
2. Government	−3	
Balance on Transfer Payments	−4	
Current Account Balance		+2
D. Long-term Capital:		
1. Direct Investment Receipts	+3	
2. Direct Investment Payments	−5	
3. Portfolio Investment Receipts	−4	
4. Portfolio Investment Payments	−1	
5. Government Loans (net)	−2	
6. Other Long-term (net)	−2	
Balance on Long-term Capital	−3	
Basic Balance		−1
E. Short-term Private Capital:		
1. Nonliquid Liabilities	+1	
2. Nonliquid Claims	−5	
Balance on Short-term Private Capital	−4	
F. Miscellaneous:		
1. Allocation of Special Drawing Rights (SDR)	0	

TABLE 2   (*Continued*)

	Net Balance	Cumulative Net Balance
2. Errors and Omissions	2	
Balance on Miscellaneous Items	−2	
Net Liquidity Balance		−7
G. Liquid Private Capital:		
1. Liabilities to Foreigners	+4	
2. Claims on Foreigners	−2	
Balance on Liquid Private Capital	+2	
Official Settlements Balance		−5
The Official Settlements Balance is Financed by Changes in		
U.S. Liabilities to Foreign Official Holders:		
1. Liquid Liabilities	+5	
2. Readily Marketable Liabilities	+1	
3. Special Liabilities	−2	
Balance on Liabilities to Foreign Official Holders	+4	
U.S. Reserve Assets:		
1. Gold	0	
2. Special Drawing Rights	0	
3. Convertible Currencies	+1	
4. IMF Gold Tranche	0	
Balance on Reserve Assets	+1	
Total Financing of Official Settlements Balance		+5

*Pluses are sources of foreign exchange (or credits), and minuses are uses of foreign exchange (or debits). Official data are published monthly in the *Survey of Current Business* (U.S. Department of Commerce).

Adam Smith worked hard in his study in Kirkcaldy, Scotland, for many years and finally emerged with a big book attacking this narrow view of international finance, thereby becoming Famous. He pointed out that it was better to consume more goods than to hoard more gold, but many people are still not convinced to this very day.

2. The *goods and services balance* adds services, including such transactions as military expenditures, tourist spending, and interest and/or dividends paid or received for past investments. In Table 2 services transactions alone show a surplus of $5 billion, so that the surplus of goods and services, which is a cumulative balance, is $6 billion.

3. The *current account balance* adds transfer payments, both private and governmental. Transfer payments are gifts flowing from one country to another. In Table 2 the current account balance has a $2 billion surplus, because the United States made $4 billion more transfer payments to the rest of the world than it received from the rest of the world, thereby shrinking the $6 billion goods and services surplus to only $2 billion on current account.

4. The *basic balance* adds long-term securities transactions to the current account figures.[2] We have a *basic* deficit in our balance of payments when the sum of our current expenditures plus our net purchases of long-term foreign securities exceeds the sum of our current receipts plus foreign net purchases of long-term U.S. securities. In Table 2, for example, our basic deficit is $1 billion.

5. The *net liquidity balance* also incorporates nonliquid short-term private capital movements, allocations of SDRs (see footnote 2 in Chapter 37), and errors and omissions (because many international transactions go unrecorded). Adding these elements brings the net liquidity deficit to $7 billion, as Table 2 shows.

6. Finally, the *official settlements balance* brings in liquid short-term private capital movements. Table 2 indicates that foreigners bought $4 billion of short-term U.S. securities, while we bought $2 billion of theirs, yielding a $2 billion surplus in the liquid private capital accounts. Adding this to the net liquidity balance yields an official settlements deficit of $5 billion.

Why so many different measures of what constitutes a balance of payments deficit (or surplus)? Primarily to confuse the general public, one might surmise. The government can always publicize the measure that currently looks best—the one that shows the smallest deficit. In addition, however, each measure focuses on something a little different from the others.

[2]Securities and bank lending transactions, by the way, whether short- or long-term, are generally called capital movements. Our purchases of foreign securities are a capital outflow from the United States, while foreign purchases of our securities are a capital inflow to the United States. Imports of foreign securities, like imports of foreign goods, are a use of foreign exchange for us; exports of our securities, like exports of our goods, provide us with foreign exchange.

Note that section D of Table 2 includes three kinds of long-term securities transactions: direct investments, portfolio investments, and long-term loans. These distinctions are rather arbitrary. Foreign purchases of U.S. stocks, for instance, are classified as direct investments only if the foreigner acquires 25 percent or more of an enterprise. Otherwise it is considered a portfolio investment. All purchases of U.S. bonds by foreigners are considered portfolio investments.

Today, discussion centers mainly on the relative merits of the basic balance compared with the net liquidity balance and the official settlements balance. The details of these controversies are beyond the scope of this book, and if you are bewildered don't feel you're the only one. In 1976 the Department of Commerce threw up its hands and announced that it would no longer publish figures on any of these three balances. Now it just publishes the numbers on all the transactions and lets people themselves compute whichever balance makes them happiest.

SUMMARY

1. A country's balance of international payments shows its receipts from and payments to other countries.

2. In the aggregate, the balance of payments always balances, because *total* receipts of foreign exchange have to equal *total* payments plus hoarding of foreign exchange.

3. However, subsections of the balance of payments need not balance. For example, merchandise exports can exceed or fall short of merchandise imports. There are six different measures of balance of payments deficits (or surpluses), each of which results from selecting different categories within the total.

Suggestions for Further Reading

One of the most useful articles on balance of payments accounting is Rita M. Maldonado, "Recording and Classifying Transactions in the Balance of Payments," *International Journal of Accounting* (Fall 1979). Also very helpful is Norman S. Fieleke, "Accounting for the Balance of Payments," Federal Reserve Bank of Boston *New England Economic Review* (May–June 1971). An updated version has been published by the Boston Fed titled "What is the Balance of Payments?" Write to the Federal Reserve Bank of Boston, zip code 02106, for a copy. (Remember to say please.)

Also useful is the analysis of alternative balance of payments measures in the 1970 and 1971 editions of the *Economic Report of the President.* If you really want to get down to the nitty-gritty, see the Bernstein Report, more formally titled *The Balance of Payments Statistics of the United States: Review and Appraisal,* Report of the Review Committee for Balance of Payments Statistics to the Bureau of the Budget (Washington, D.C.: U.S. Government Printing Office, 1965).

Another committee has also examined the balance of payments format, and as a result extensive changes have been made in the way the figures are presented. See *Report of the Advisory Committee on the Presentation of Balance of Payments Statistics* in the June 1976 issue of the *Survey of Current Business*, published by the U.S. Department of Commerce.

CHAPTER 37

The Gold Standard

During 1981 and 1982 an official blue-ribbon U.S. Gold Commission deliberated long and hard before deciding against recommending a return to the gold standard. The United States was officially on a full-fledged gold standard from 1900 to 1933, and a lot of people would like to return to those good old days.

What is the gold standard and how is it supposed to work? Well, it's storytelling time.

AN ISLAND PARADISE

Long ago and far away, the natives of a small island in a remote part of the world had a monetary system of which they were extremely proud. Although they lacked commercial banks and had no Federal Reserve, they had something many people consider much more important—a monetary standard. It was not a gold standard, but it was somewhat similar. It was a rock standard. Near the southeastern edge of the island, on a high cliff, sat a handsome and enormous rock, awesome to behold and thrilling to touch, and it was this that they decided should serve as "backing" for their money.

Naturally, the rock was too heavy, and indeed too valuable, to use as an actual means of payment. Instead, for circulating media itself, corresponding to our coins and dollar bills, they used special clam-shells. People had confidence in these because boldly inscribed on them were the words:

> *Will Pay to the Bearer on Demand One Dollar in Rock*

The very fact that this statement was made meant that no one ever demanded any rock. The assurance that it was there was sufficient.

For many years all went well. The economy was simple but prosper-ous, and those from the Great Civilizations across the sea who occa-sionally visited the island marveled at its stability and its thriving commerce. The natives were not reluctant to explain the reasons for their prosperity: hard work, thrift, clean living, and, above all, sound money. Sound as a rock.

Unfortunately, one night a severe storm struck the island. The inhabitants awoke the next morning to find the rock gone, evidently hurled into the sea by the furies of nature. Consternation! Panic! Luckily, however, they were saved from the potential consequences—worthless money and economic collapse—by an accident of fate that took place within the week. One of the younger natives, a child of no more than eight, perched on the very cliff where the rock had once been, was looking at a rainbow arching far out over the horizon. Following it down, the child suddenly saw the rock, fathoms deep, under the water.

After much excitement, it was finally ascertained that on very clear days, when the sea was calm and the sun at a certain angle, some who had especially strong eyes could see it. Those who could not, which included almost everyone, were assured by those who could that the outlines of the boulder were indeed discernible. And so, the backing still there, confidence in the money was restored, and in a short while the island became more prosperous than ever.

Of course, all the outstanding clamshells had to be called in, so that the elders of the community could strike out the words:

> *Will Pay to the Bearer on Demand One Dollar in Rock*

In their place was painstakingly inscribed:

> *Will Pay to the Bearer on Demand One Dollar*
> *in Lawful Money*

Now if anyone brought in a clamshell to be redeemed, it would simply be exchanged for another clamshell. As it turned out, however, no one bothered. After all, with the backing assuredly there, the money obviously was as good as rock.

End of story.

Our own monetary system, of course, has always been much more rational. Until 1933 all our money was redeemable in gold at the United States Treasury. Every dollar bill bore the following inscription:

The United States of America
Will Pay to the Bearer on Demand One Dollar in Gold

Then, overnight, it was declared illegal for anyone in this country to own gold, except for industrial or numismatic purposes. Gold ownership by Americans was made illegal by an Executive Order issued by President Franklin D. Roosevelt on April 5, 1933. The prohibition was formalized by the Gold Reserve Act of 1934. Accordingly, the inscription on the currency was solemnly, officially, and duly altered to:

The United States of America
Will Pay to the Bearer on Demand One Dollar
in Lawful Money

In 1947 a literal-minded citizen of Cleveland, A. F. Davis, sent the Treasury a $10 bill and respectfully requested, in exchange, the promised $10 in "lawful money." He received back, by return mail, two $5 bills.

Seventeen years later, in 1964, the venerable inscription was finally removed from our currency. All that remains is an unpretentious observation: "This note is legal tender for all debts, public and private." Also (in considerably larger print): "In God We Trust."

THE GOLD STANDARD DOMESTICALLY

The main reason for the perennial appeal of the gold standard is that it contains built-in automatic safeguards against inflation. It does this by linking the money supply to gold, making it virtually impossible to increase the money supply enough to support a sustained increase in the price level.

A return to the gold standard could be accomplished overnight by three simple acts:

1. *Impose a fixed legal ratio between gold held by the government and currency in circulation.* For every $1 of gold owned by the U.S. Treasury or the Federal Reserve, for example, print $4 of currency. The ratio need not be 100 percent; a less restrictive ratio, like our 25 percent, serves just as well, for the same reason that banks are not required to hold 100 percent reserves behind their demand deposit liabilities. Fractional gold reserves are based on the same logic as fractional bank reserves: it is unlikely that everyone will want to turn currency into gold at one and the same time, just as it is unlikely that everyone will want to turn demand deposits into currency simultaneously.

2. *Permit unlimited convertibility between currency and gold.* Since bank deposits are interchangeable with currency, in effect deposits would also be freely convertible into gold.

3. *Set an official fixed price of gold for conversions between currency and gold.* Say $400 = 1 troy ounce of gold, as an example. Since this automatically means that $1 is worth 1/400th of an ounce of gold, it is often said that a country thereby "defines" its monetary unit in

"Then it's agreed. Until the dollar firms up, we let the clamshell float."

Drawing by Ed Fisher; © 1971 The New Yorker Magazine, Inc.

terms of a specific physical amount of gold: the dollar is defined as equal to 1/400th of an ounce of gold. *Devaluation*—legally redefining the dollar to be worth *less*, say 1/500th of an ounce of gold, is thus the same as raising the official price of gold to $500 a troy ounce.[1]

Neglecting small handling charges, Americans would then be free to convert $400 into one ounce of gold at the Treasury whenever they wish, or to turn in one ounce of gold and get $400. Of course, the U.S. Treasury must convince people that it will have enough gold to make good on its promise to pay out one ounce to anyone bringing in 400 dollar bills.

This convertibility between currency and gold at a fixed price is the lever that controls the money supply, and through the money supply presumably the price level. Many people are convinced, on the basis of experience, that over the long run gold will retain its value better than paper money. Expectations that prices are going to rise will lead those people to turn in their currency in exchange for gold—and, since bank deposits are freely convertible into currency, also to exchange deposits for currency and then for gold.

With less gold in its vaults, the government will be forced to contract the amount of currency (because of the fixed legal ratio between gold held by the government and currency outstanding). And since banks hold currency as reserves, they will have to call in loans and extinguish demand deposits. Thus the money supply falls when gold flows out of the Treasury. Inflationary expectations thereby automatically generate their own remedy. With a smaller money supply, inflation is aborted before it can really get underway.

Now for the bad news. The gold standard has built-in safeguards against inflation, but not necessarily against recession and unemployment. *Under the gold standard, the money supply is determined by the public, not by the Federal Reserve.* Gold hoarding by the public reduces the money supply, and the central bank, if it abides by the rules, can't do anything about it. This may be effective in minimizing inflation, but it is likely to intensify a recession—especially if fears arise that the government might possibly devalue the dollar—that is,

---

[1] The weight of gold is always expressed in troy ounces. A troy ounce is heavier than the ounce most Americans are used to (the avoirdupois ounce). Specifically, 1 troy ounce = 1.1 avoirdupois ounces. A metric ton contains 32,150 troy ounces, so at $400 an ounce a ton of gold (about 80 standard-size gold bars) is worth a cool $12,860,000.

While we're on the subject, we might as well mention that gold—chemical element 79—melts at 1063° centigrade, boils at 2600° centigrade, and has a specific gravity of 19.3.

raise the official price of gold. Governments are often tempted to devalue during recessions, in order to increase employment by expanding exports. As we will see in the following section, devaluation reduces the foreign exchange value of a country's money, thereby inhibiting its imports and stimulating its exports.

If the public starts to suspect that the government may soon devalue, it will decide that it makes sense to buy as much gold as possible now, before the price rises, and then sell it back to the government after the price has gone up. This is precisely what led the United States to abandon the gold standard in 1933.

In brief, the gold standard provides a powerful barrier against inflation but is far less effective when it comes to recession. It could even turn a mild recession into a major depression.

THE GOLD STANDARD INTERNATIONALLY

Under the international gold standard, each nation similarly agrees to tie its money supply rigidly to its gold stock, decides upon an official fixed price for gold, and then stands ready to buy or sell unlimited quantities at that price.

This necessarily results in fixed rates of exchange between one nation's money and another's: if France establishes 800 francs an ounce as the price it will pay for gold, and the United States decides upon $400 an ounce, then the par rate of exchange will be $1 = 2 francs, since $1 and 2 francs buy equal amounts of gold. (Were the U.S. to devalue the dollar and raise the price of gold to, say, $800 an ounce, then the dollar would depreciate to a new exchange rate of $1 = 1 franc. This should stimulate U.S. exports, because the French can now buy twice as many dollars with the same number of francs.)

This fixed exchange rate of $1 = 2 francs would be quite stable, not varying below or above par by more than the relatively small cost of shipping gold from one country to another. For instance, assume that the United States has a deficit in its balance of payments while France has a surplus. The excess supply of dollars on the foreign exchange market should lead to depreciation of the dollar relative to the franc— the dollar will start to fall in value from $1 = 2 francs to $1 = 1.9 francs and so on.

But it can only depreciate by the cost of shipping gold, which is a fairly modest sum. If an American importer of 800 francs' worth of French perfume is told by the local banker in Topeka that it will cost more than $400 to get the 800 francs, the importer can simply turn

Is Gold a Good Investment?

Gold is probably the favorite asset for hoarding by both governments and individuals around the world, and it has been for centuries. Should you buy some gold, perhaps in the form of a few gold coins? Is gold a good investment?

Because gold earns no interest or dividends, it immediately suffers in comparison with such alternatives as savings accounts, bonds, stocks, and rental property. In this respect it is similar to diamonds, stamps, rare coins, and art objects. Because it yields no current income, the wisdom of buying gold thus depends entirely on the prospect for future price appreciation.

If gold can be expected to rise in price by *more* than 5 to 10 percent annually, which is roughly what one can earn in a savings account or over the long run in bonds or stocks, then it is worth considering seriously as an investment.

The price of gold is determined in the free market just like other commodities, by supply and demand. And in this case, supply and demand factors make the price of gold highly volatile. With respect to supply, new production adds to the existing stockpile at the rate of only about 2 percent a year. This means that the overwhelming element on the supply side is not the amount of current ore production but uncertainty as to how much holders of the existing stockpile might

decide to unload. In other words, sales by large holders are always a threat to break the price.

On the demand side, a significant part of the demand for gold is not for current industrial or artistic use but rather is motivated by psychological elements—in particular, by fear regarding an uncertain social and economic future. Gold has traditionally been thought of as a hedge against inflation and against economic dislocations caused by international tensions and war.

When consumer prices threaten to rise rapidly and/or international tensions increase, the private demand for gold expands. But when inflation subsides and/or international tensions ease, demand often vanishes overnight. This sort of demand typically fluctuates erratically on short notice, and rather small changes in supply or demand can produce wide price swings.

Thus gold is a highly speculative investment. Large gains can occasionally be made, but on the basis of the historical record over the past hundred years large losses are just as likely. Nevertheless, even though it is risky in and of itself, when some gold is added to a conventional portfolio it can often provide diversification that reduces rather than increases the risk exposure of the *total* portfolio.

around and buy $400 worth of gold (1 ounce) from the U.S. Treasury and ship it to France at the importer's own expense, thereby discharging the obligation to the French supplier. Doing this will be cheaper than operating through the foreign exchange office of the local bank.

Thus the dollar can depreciate only to a lower limit, called our gold export point, which is below par by the cost of shipping gold abroad from the U.S.

Or assume that the United States has a balance of payments surplus and France has a deficit. This should lead to appreciation of the dollar relative to the franc—the dollar will start to rise in value from $1 = 2 francs to $1 = 2.1 francs and so on. But the same limit exists at that end, too. If a French importer of $400 worth of American cowboy boots finds that the local banker in Marseilles is charging more than 800 francs for the $400, the importer can simply buy an ounce of gold at the French Treasury for 800 francs and ship it to the U.S. at the importer's own expense. Thus the dollar can appreciate only to an upper limit—called our gold import point—which is above par by the cost of shipping gold from abroad to the United States.

International gold flows thereby produce fairly stable exchange rates under the gold standard. Such gold movements also provide a built-in antidote against inflation, since each country's money supply is supposed to be rigidly tied to its gold stock. Worse inflation here than abroad leads to a U.S. balance of payments deficit, because our goods become more expensive. The result is depreciation of the dollar on foreign exchange markets, followed promptly by *gold outflows* that (a) stop the depreciation of the dollar and (b) force a contraction in our money supply, thereby stifling inflation. As inflation is brought under control, our exports should expand and our imports contract, thus improving our balance of payments position so that the gold outflow gradually ceases. It is a self-correcting system.

If the gold standard functions so smoothly and contains inflation so effectively, why was it abandoned by the leading industrial countries some fifty years ago?

Great Britain, the leader of the international financial system in the late nineteenth century and the early decades of the twentieth, suspended convertibility of the pound into gold—and thereby went off the gold standard—in September of 1931. The United States followed suit in March of 1933. The reasons were the same in both cases: substantial gold drains out of the Treasury, due to unsettled economic conditions and persistent rumors of devaluation.

Under the gold standard, a country losing gold is supposed to contract its money supply and put deliberate downward pressure on its economy. In the early 1930s the governments of both Great Britain and the United States were indeed losing gold (because of private hoarding stemming from fears of devaluation), but understandably neither wanted to impose the tight money called for by the gold

I was born in 1929, when gold was selling for $20.67 an ounce...I married in 1968, in an outwardly happy marriage. That was the year gold began to go up again...For the past few years my wife has been having an affair with another man...

...Six months ago she went off to live with him...If I had bought gold in 1929 I could sell it today at 9 times the price at $180 an ounce, up from $20.67 then...Last week she came back 'To give our marriage another chance,' she says...'To give our marriage another chance?' I tell her, 'until next time you leave, you mean'...

Some say gold stocks yes, gold bars no. I say gold bars yes, gold stocks no...Yesterday she left 'forever'...This morning she's back again...'I want to say something,' she says...

Drawing by Lou Myers; © *1975 The New Yorker Magazine, Inc.*

standard's rules. Both countries were in the midst of major depressions that no one wanted to make worse with monetary tightness.

The United States resumed convertibility of the (devalued) dollar into gold in 1934, for foreign central banks and governments only, and fixed exchange rates were reinstituted after World War II. However, the system collapsed again in the early 1970s, under the weight of persistent U.S. balance of payments deficits, unstable world financial conditions, and recurrent rumors that the United States was once again preparing to devalue the dollar. Since 1973, foreign exchange rates have floated unattached to gold, fluctuating daily with the tides of supply and demand.[2]

WILL THE GOLD STANDARD MAKE A COMEBACK?

What are the probabilities that we will bring back the gold standard in the foreseeable future? Extremely low, for a number of reasons:

1. It is difficult today, perhaps impossible, to establish a fixed relationship between a nation's gold stock and its money supply. The gold standard was the construct of a simpler monetary era. Most of our money now consists of bank deposits, not currency, and there is even considerable controversy about which deposits to include. As a result, we have several different money supplies—M1, M2, M3, and so on— and it is hard to justify why one and not the other should be tied to gold.

2. Just as difficult is the choice of an appropriate official price for gold, given the wide swings in its free market price—between $200 and $875 a troy ounce—in recent years. Too low an official price would encourage wholesale gold flows from government to private hoards, too high a price the reverse.

3. The gold standard has built-in safeguards against inflation but not against recession and unemployment. No democratically elected government could deliberately provoke heavy unemployment simply be-

[2]In 1970 a step toward a substitute for gold in international finance was hesitantly taken with the introduction into the world's monetary system of International Monetary Fund Special Drawing Rights (SDRs), more commonly known as "paper gold." SDRs are a form of international reserve asset, usable only by central banks and governments to settle international debts in much the same way they use gold. But instead of having to be panned, dredged, or mined from the earth, they are created out of thin air—just like demand deposits—by an entry on the books of the International Monetary Fund.

cause of gold outflows and expect to remain long in office. Indeed, even prior to the 1930s the United States "sterilized" the domestic monetary effects of international gold flows by offsetting central bank open market operations—a clear violation of the gold standard's rules—in order to pursue domestic stabilization objectives unhampered by gold constraints.

Fundamentally, the gold standard is based on an illusion, namely, that human judgment in economic life can be replaced by a built-in self-correcting thermostat, so that monetary and financial disturbances are automatically set right without intervention by politicians and central bankers. In fact, human judgment is still involved, even with the gold standard. It is involved in fixing the ratio between the gold stock and the money supply; in selecting the official price of gold; in deciding whether or not to devalue, when, and by how much; and in establishing priorities with respect to national economic goals.

Like it or not, politicians and central bankers will not disappear. In a democracy, our only hope is to try to fill their positions with able and qualified men and women who will do their best to promote the public interest in a world where truth is elusive.

SUMMARY

1. The gold standard involves setting an official price for gold and then permitting unlimited convertibility between currency and gold at that price. The money supply is tied to the stock of gold in the Treasury. As a result, it is the public—not the Federal Reserve—that ultimately determines the country's money supply.

2. The gold standard provides a powerful barrier against inflation, but it is far less effective against recession and unemployment.

3. Internationally, the gold standard results in fixed exchange rates, because flows of gold between countries keep the exchange rate from fluctuating by more than the cost of shipping gold.

4. These same gold flows also provide an automatic self-equilibrating mechanism that controls inflation and corrects balance of payments deficits. A country experiencing more inflation than others will have a balance of payments deficit, as a result of which it will lose gold. This will force a contraction in its money supply. With a smaller money supply, inflation should abate and the country's balance of payments position improve.

5. The gold standard broke down because of fears of devaluation which led to large gold drains out of the Treasury, and the refusal of nations to follow the gold standard's rules, which required that with less gold in the Treasury they should contract their money supplies.

6. It is not likely that the gold standard will be reestablished in the foreseeable future.

Suggestions for Further Reading

The conclusions of the U.S. Gold Commission are contained in its two-volume *Report to the Congress of the Commission on the Role of Gold in the Domestic and International Monetary Systems* (Washington, D.C.: U.S. Government Printing Office, March 1982). Also see Michael David Bordo, "The Classical Gold Standard: Some Lessons for Today," Federal Reserve Bank of St. Louis *Review* (May 1981), and John H. Wood, "The Demise of the Gold Standard," Federal Reserve Bank of Chicago *Economic Perspectives* (November–December 1981).

More required reading: Milton Friedman, "Commodity-Reserve Currency," in *Essays in Positive Economics* (Chicago: University of Chicago Press, 1953), not to mention John Maynard Keynes, *A Treatise on Money* (New York: Harcourt, Brace, 1930), vol. 2, pp. 289 ff. This time Friedman and Keynes are on the same side of the fence.

If you want to learn more about gold as an investment, read Lawrence S. Ritter and Thomas J. Urich, *The Role of Gold in Consumer Investment Portfolios* (New York University, Center for the Study of Financial Institutions *Monograph*, No. 3, 1984).

Actually, you'll probably get a better appreciation of the role of gold in human affairs if you go to the movies and see Alec Guinness in *The Lavender Hill Mob* or Humphrey Bogart in *Treasure of the Sierra Madre.* And don't miss W.C. Fields in the Klondike in *The Fatal Glass of Beer.*

Careers in Banking and Financial Markets

There are lots of jobs at banks having nothing at all to do with banking—like repairing computer terminals and running the executive dining room. Although these are important activities, they are not what we usually think of when banking is mentioned as a career. Our most visible contacts with banks—the teller who takes our money and the branch officer in charge of student loans—are somewhat closer to what banking is all about, but these are only two of the many specialized tasks that fall within a banker's purview.

In the few pages that we have left, we cannot offer a comprehensive review of all career opportunities in banking and financial markets. And even if we could, it would turn out to be more tedious than the discussion of the bank reserve equation in Chapter 16 (if that's possible). Instead we will provide a brief overview of the terrain and then offer some details on specific interesting opportunities. In particular, we will *not* describe what lawyers and accountants who work for banks or other financial institutions actually do; rather we'll focus on the derring-do of bond traders and Fed watchers—after all, that's where the money is (or was).

619

AN OVERVIEW

The first thing to consider with a career in banking and financial markets is whose side you want to be on. Jobs in the private sector with a bank, savings and loan association, or insurance company focus on profits; jobs in the public sector with the Federal Reserve System, FDIC, or state insurance departments focus on safety. Although both public and private sector jobs deal with financial institutions and markets, with people on both sides of the fence often looking at similar things, their perspectives are quite different. A bank examiner with the FDIC or Federal Reserve will review a commercial bank's books to determine whether loans with delinquent payments impair the bank's capital; a commercial loan officer at a bank will examine a prospective borrower's books to determine whether timely repayments of interest and principal will add to the bank's profits. Although both the bank examiner and the loan officer use corporate finance and accounting skills, their objectives and motivations are not the same.

Suppose the profit motive is your favorite pastime. You would then have an array of sub-industries within financial markets to consider, including commercial banking, investment banking, insurance, and pension funds (see Chapters 7, 8, and 9 for a description of these institutions). Although each of these financial institutions has a different overall objective, there are particular skills that are easily transferable among them. For example, both a bank economist and an insurance company economist would forecast interest rates, talk with the institution's corporate customers about their particular industry's outlook, and evaluate the costs and benefits of some internal investment project. Economic and statistical analyses come into play in each and every case. Similarly, an investment officer or portfolio manager for an insurance company, bank, or pension fund will evaluate the merits of putting money into stocks or fixed income securities and, if the latter, whether the investments should be long term or short term.

Once you focus attention on a particular industry, an equally important decision centers on whether to concentrate on the retail or wholesale end of the business. Most financial institutions operate on both levels. A commercial bank has people dedicated to explaining the advantages of different types of certificates of deposit to depositors with as little as $1,000 to invest. Banks also have CD traders and salespeople who specialize in placing large certificates of deposit ($100,000 and up) with institutional investors, such as money market mutual funds and large corporations. Both activities raise funds for the banks, but they require very different skills. Retail CDs are marketed by people with strong interpersonal skills, while wholesale CDs are sold by people who are equally comfortable with interest rate calculations (see Chapter 5), movements in the term structure of interest rates (see Chapter 28), and whether the Federal Open Market Committee is likely to vote yes or no to a tighter or easier monetary policy (for this you must remember all of Part 3). The CD salespeople for commercial banks, savings banks, and S&Ls must be capable of discussing these factors in order to tailor the CDs to the needs of sophisticated corporate treasurers.

A final distinguishing characteristic among institutions, as well as jobs within a particular firm, centers on domestic versus international business. Despite the growing interrelationship between foreign and domestic activities, there are different regulations that apply in each area, as well as foreign exchange rate movements that must be considered when you are dealing with foreign institutions. If you work for an international bank (see Chapter 10) or if you are a foreign exchange trader, you must feel comfortable with the Japanese yen, West German mark, Swiss franc, and whatever else comes along (see Part 6 for some help).

There are, no doubt, many other ways to categorize the opportunities available within banking and financial markets. But once you've decided upon public versus private, banking versus insurance, wholesale versus retail, and domestic versus international, you've come far enough along to focus on exactly what you might want to do. In the next section we outline one or two glamorous opportunities (at least as far as financial markets are concerned).

SPECIFIC OPPORTUNITIES

As financial markets have moved toward deregulation, business has become more transactions-oriented. The increased emphasis on transactions has generated a bonanza for people with skills in sales and trading, as well as for those with the analytical techniques to support these activities. Sales and trading jobs at the major investment banks, commercial banks, and large thrift institutions are exciting, well-paid opportunities; so are the jobs as financial economists, statisticians, and mathematicians that form the underlying brain trust. Let's take a somewhat closer look at what these people do and what it takes to get on the road to financial market stardom.

Trading. We've already encountered the role of a trader in Chapter 29, when we described how a dealer makes a market by quoting a bid and offer for a particular security. Many of the large financial institutions are market-makers in a wide variety of instruments. For example, commercial banks might be market-makers in Treasury securities, mortgage-related instruments, and municipal bonds. Investment banks add corporate bonds to the list, while the major thrift institutions usually restrict their attention to mortgage-backed securities. In addition to buying and selling these investment-type instruments, large banks and thrifts also make markets in CDs and other short-term money market instruments.

The trader's job at these institutions is to quote bids and offers for securities on a continuous basis and to accommodate incoming purchase and sale orders from other banks, thrifts, pension funds, and insurance companies. Recall from Chapter 29 that the dealer earns a profit by buying securities at the bid price ($97) and turning around and selling at the offer price ($99) before the equilibrium price ($98) has changed. A trader has to be extremely sensitive to shifting market conditions; otherwise a profit can quickly turn into a loss. For example, if a trader for the First National Profit Bank buys some government bonds at a price of $97 from an insurance company, and before the trader has a chance to sell the bonds to an incoming purchase order from a regional S&L the government announces a rise in the consumer price index, the equilibrium price of the bonds may drop to $95. With a bid and offer now at $94 and $96, respectively, the dealer winds up selling the securities that were bought at $97 for $96: a one dollar loss instead of a two dollar profit.

Traders must continuously monitor market conditions and alter their quotes so that they don't get stuck with unwanted inventory. In addition to concentrating on the market, traders must have the discipline to take profits when they are there and cut losses before they turn into disasters. It is sometimes said that the three most important characteristics of a successful trader are discipline, discipline, and discipline.

Traders are frequently viewed as interchangeable parts. A person with discipline, concentration, and sensitivity who can trade government bonds successfully can switch to trading municipals, corporates, or CDs. The details of each instrument can be quickly absorbed (see Chapters 28 and 31 first) as long as the trader's intuition is finely tuned.

Traders start their day early—7:30 A.M. on the East Coast, 4:30 A.M. on the West Coast. Much of their time is spent under intense pressure, trying to extract information about likely price movements of the securities they are responsible for from the price movements of related instruments. In trying to gauge market sentiment they work closely with salespeople who deal with their institution's customers. Let's take a closer look at what bond salespeople actually do.

Sales. On the retail level, securities are sold to individuals by people whom we call stockbrokers. They are more formally called account executives by the securities firms that they work for. These investment banks also employ account executives to sell stocks and bonds to institutional investors such as pension funds and insurance companies. Commercial banks and large thrifts similarly employ salespeople to sell government bonds, municipals, and mortgages to institutional investors.

The salesperson's job is twofold: on the one hand, he or she tries to uncover information about the types of securities that institutional investors are most interested in buying and selling; and on the other hand, she or he tries to convince the bank's customers to buy the securities that the bank has already acquired through the activities of its traders. Thus, salespeople provide information to traders about the sentiment within the investment community as well as creating an outlet for the securities that traders have acquired. Obviously these two activities go together. If salespeople report little investor interest in long-term government bonds, the commercial bank's traders will be less aggressive buyers of such securities.

People employed in sales have to be gregarious and people-oriented. They spend considerable time talking on the phone to customers throughout the country and must feel comfortable with simple chitchat. In addition, however, salespeople must bring investment ideas to the party. In order to make a sale, the salesperson must convince the insurance company's portfolio manager, for example, that shifting out of a long-term government bond into a GNMA pass-through security will increase yields without unduly increasing risk exposure. To be effective, therefore, salespeople must have some perspective on the likely movements in interest rates over various investment horizons as well as a working knowledge of how specific bond characteristics, such as particular coupons, call provisions, and tax treatment will influence an investment's performance.

Salespeople obviously benefit considerably, therefore, from a solid course in money, banking, and financial markets. In addition, however, they pay close attention to what the bank's brain trust of professional economists, statisticians, and other fixed-income researchers have to say about markets in general and specific instruments in particular. Let's see what kind of information the research staff provides.

Financial Economist. Most fixed-income divisions within large banks and thrift institutions employ an economist who is designated as a Fed watcher. The primary job of this money market specialist is to alert traders and salespeople to the expected activities of the Federal Reserve. Thus, the Fed watcher pays close attention to the bank reserve equation (see Chapter 14) as well as to the Federal Open Market Committee's most recent policy directive (see Chapter 17). In addition, the Fed watcher examines the financing requirements of the Treasury (see Chapter 18) to determine what pressures that might exert in the marketplace.

Much of the Fed watcher's analysis is communicated to traders and salespeople in brief memos. In addition, when an important news item comes across the news ticker, such as the money supply announcement on Thursday afternoon, the Fed watcher may use the firm's intercom to provide instant analysis to traders and salespeople. All these items provide salespeople with important discussion points for use with customers. However, salespeople have to translate the Fed watcher's general overview of interest rate movements and economic activity into concrete strategies for institutional investors. For this perspective the salesperson turns to the fixed-income group's rocket scientists.

Fixed-Income Research. Swapping a government bond for a GNMA pass-through security has wide-ranging implications for the composition of a pension fund's portfolio, despite the fact that GNMAs and government bonds are both insured by the federal government. Recall from our discussions in Chapters 28 and 32 that the prepayment uncertainty associated with mortgage-related securities makes the maturity of these securities uncertain. The econometricians, statisticians, and mathematicians who work in the fixed income research area provide, among other things, estimates of prepayments on GNMA pass-through securities so that salespeople can help explain the ramifications of GNMA purchases to their customers.

The fixed-income research group also reports on such obscure items as the probability of a particular corporate bond being called by the issuer prior to maturity, the advantages of swapping low-coupon bonds for high-coupons or vice versa, and the price sensitivity of a bond portfolio to a one-percentage-point change in interest rates. Armed with such precision tools, a bond salesperson can back up simple chitchat with hard facts about how to improve portfolio yields without unduly increasing risk. Thus the rocket scientist econometricians, statisticians, and mathematicians earn their way into the hearts and minds of institutional investors even though their native language is one of differential equations, autocorrelated residuals, and lognormal distributions. Salespeople translate these obscure formulae into higher yields for their customers.

Cooperation between traders and salespeople, Fed watchers, and rocket scientists generates clever investment strategies for institutional investors, consistent profits for large banks and thrifts, and high bonuses for all of the fixed-income employees. It sounds as though life after Money, Banking, and Financial Markets can work out pretty well—as long as you know where to look.

Glossary

A

accrued interest Interest accumulated on a bond since the last interest payment. **72**

actuarial probabilities Calculations of life expectancy based on past experience with respect to age, gender, and similar factors. **125**

aggregate demand (supply) The total amount of goods and services demanded (supplied) in the economy. **281**

allocational efficiency The tendency of market prices to reflect all information affecting the underlying value of securities. **509**

amortize To pay off the principal of an indebtedness, along with the interest, during the life of a loan. **32**

annuity A contract to pay an amount of funds in the future, either in a lump sum or in periodic payments. **45**

appreciate To increase in value. **580**

arbitrageur One who engages in **arbitrage**, buying something in one market and simultaneously selling it at a profit in another market. **561–63**

asset (1) An item owned that has value; (2) an item on a balance sheet showing the value of property owned or receivable. **16, 102ff., 227, 467**

assumption method A procedure, used in cases of bank failure, in which the failed bank is merged with a healthy one. **83**

auction market A market where buyers and sellers bargain directly with each other. **499**

automated clearinghouse (ACH) An electronic system for making regular payments or receiving regular credits. **162**

automated teller machine (ATM) A card-operated facility for making bank deposits and withdrawals. **162**

autonomous spending changes Changes in spending that are independent of GNP. **309**

B

balance of payments (national) A record of payments that one country makes to and receives from all other foreign countries. **578**

balance sheet A summary statement of an individual's or a business's financial condition on a given date. **227**

bank See **commercial bank.**

bank failure Situation in which a bank goes out of business because it cannot meet its obligations. See **assumption method** and **payoff method. 81**

bank holding company See **holding company.**

bank (or depository institutions) reserve equation A formal statement of factors affecting bank reserves: Fed assets minus all Fed liabilities and capital accounts, other than those Fed liabilities that constitute bank reserves, plus Treasury currency in bank vaults. **236**

bank reserves See **reserves.**

basis point One-hundredth of a percentage point (.01 percent, or .0001). Yields change by one basis point when interest rates go from 9.00 percent to 9.01 percent. **Ch. 5**

bear market A financial market in which prices are falling. **31**

bid-asked spread The difference between the price a dealer is willing to pay for a security (bid price) and the price at which the dealer is willing to sell the security (asked or offer price). **503**

blue-chip stock Stock of a high-quality corporation with a good record of earnings and stability. **548**

Board of Governors of the Federal Reserve System Seven individuals appointed by the President to help run the central bank. See **Federal Reserve System. 171**

bond A liability issued by a government (government bond) or a business (corporate bond) promising to pay the holder a fixed cash amount at a specified maturity date and (usually) to make regular interest payments in the interim. See also **municipal bond** and **zero-coupon bond. 29**

bond-anticipation notes (BANs) Short-term municipal securities issued to raise stopgap funds and paid off when long-term bonds are issued. **537**

bond equivalent yield See **coupon equivalent yield.**

Bretton Woods The New Hampshire town where fixed exchange rates and the International Monetary Fund were established by international agreement in 1944. See **fixed exchange rates** and **International Monetary Fund. 583**

broker An institution (or individual) who arranges purchases and sales of securities for the account of others and receives a commission on each transaction. **131–132**

brokerage house A financial institution that acts as a broker, dealer, and underwriter of securities. See **broker, dealer, underwriter. 132**

bull market A financial market in which prices are rising. **31**

C

call option An option contract in which the option buyer has the right (but not the obligation) to buy a specified quantity of the underlying asset at a specified price until the expiration date of the option. **566**

call provision A stipulation in a bond that allows the bond issuer to pay off part or all of the bond before the scheduled maturity date. **530**

capital gain The difference between the price paid for an asset and the higher price at which it is sold. If the selling price is lower than the purchase price, there is a **capital loss. 31**

capital market The market for stocks and long-term debt instruments. **36**

cash-balance approach A version of the quantity theory of money that focuses on the demand for money. See also **demand for money equation. 280**

cash items in the process of collection Checks drawn on one bank and deposited in a second bank but not yet cleared. **117**

central bank A governmental "bank for

banks," generally responsible for national monetary policy. See **Federal Reserve System. 7**

Certificates of Accrual on Treasury Securities (CATS) Zero-coupon securities created by stripping Treasury bonds. **516**

certificate of deposit (CD) A time deposit with a specific future maturity date. **5**

checking (checkable) deposits Accounts at a financial institution (checking accounts) that permit the account holder to transfer funds to a third party via a check (an order to pay). **4**

Classical economics A system of economic thought, founded by Adam Smith, that relies on the price system to allocate resources and argues that price flexibility will lead to full employment (Say's Law). **271**

clearinghouse A facility for settling transfers of funds between banks. **160**

Clearing House Interbank Payment System (CHIPS) A telecommunications system that transfers funds between banks internationally. **161–62**

closed-end investment company A mutual fund issuing a limited number of shares that are then traded in the stock market. **130**

collateral Property pledged by a borrower as a guarantee that a loan will be repaid. **107**

collateralized mortgage obligation (CMO) A pool of mortgages placed in a trust with a division of claims designed to give investors a more predictable cash flow than individual mortgages. **538**

commercial bank A financial institution that offers a wide variety of services, including checking accounts and business loans. **42–43**

commercial paper Short-term debt instruments issued by finance companies and large business firms. **533**

common stock Ownership interest in a company; such ownership provides a residual claim to the company's earnings paid in the form of dividends. **31**

compound interest Interest calculated on the sum of the principal and the interest already earned. **51–52**

consols Perpetual bonds, which have no maturity date but pay a fixed cash flow (interest) forever. **29–30**

consumption The using up of goods or services by households; more generally, the purchase of goods for immediate use by households. **11, 301**

consumption function The relationship of consumption spending to the level of income, in its simplest form expressed as $C = a + bY$. See also **marginal propensity to consume. 301–302**

contemporaneous reserves The system of reserve requirements now in effect, which makes required reserves depend on the current level of deposits (but still leaves a small gap between the calculation and the holding of required reserves). **116–123**

conversion feature (of a bond) The right to convert a corporate bond into shares of the company's stock at a predetermined price. **530**

convertible preferred stock Preferred stock that can be converted into common stock at a predetermined price. **31**

correspondent balances Funds kept by one bank in another (a correspondent bank) to facilitate check clearing and other business relationships. **160**

countercyclical monetary policy A policy of the central bank designed to stabilize economic activity, usually by increasing the rate of growth of the money supply **(expansionary monetary policy)** during recessions and decreasing the rate of growth of the money supply **(contractionary monetary policy)** in inflationary periods. **17–18**

coupon equivalent yield (bond equivalent yield) The difference between the face value and the purchase price of a Treasury bill, divided by the purchase price and annualized using 365 days to the year (366 in leap year). **520, 522–24**

coupon rate The interest rate calculated by dividing the annual coupon payment on a bond by the face value of the bond. **53**

coupon securities (coupon-bearing securities) Bonds that make periodic interest payments prior to maturity. In some cases the bonds have actual coupons attached, which bondholders remove and send in at regular intervals to collect interest. **30**

credit union A financial institution organized by a group of people who have some sort of common interest, such as employees of the same firm. Members make deposits by buying shares and may borrow funds. **46, 94**

crowding-out effect A decrease in spending (usually investment) resulting from a rise in interest rates caused by an increase in government spending. **353**

currency Coins and bills used as money. **4**

current yield The annual coupon payment on a bond divided by the current price of the bond. **53**

D

dealer An institution or individual who acts as a marketmaker by continuously quoting bids and offers on a security, with the objective of earning a profit on the bid-asked spread. **131–132**

default To fail to make a payment on schedule. **455**

default risk The chance that the issuer of a security will default. **455**

defensive open market operations. See **open market operations**.

deferred credit items An entry on a bank's balance sheet indicating that at a predetermined time it will receive an addition to its reserve account. **229–30**

deficit nation A nation that imports more than it exports, resulting in a deficit balance of trade. **580**

demand deposit Checking deposit. **183**

demand deposit expansion multiplier The number that when multiplied by the level of reserves determines the maximum amount of demand deposits. In its simplest form, it equals the inverse of the required reserve ratio. **193**

demand for money equation An equation explaining how the demand for money varies with other economic variables, especially income and interest rates. **278**

depository institution An institution that accepts deposits and/or offers services such as checking accounts; includes commercial banks, savings and loan associations, savings banks, and credit unions. **77**

depository institutions reserve equation See **bank reserve equation**.

deposit rate ceilings. See **Regulation Q**.

depreciate To decrease in value. **580**

depression A time span marked by a severe drop in the level of economic activity and very high levels of unemployment. **12**

derivative financial instrument A financial instrument such as an option or futures contract that derives its value from some other, underlying financial asset. **33**

devaluation A lowering of the agreed-upon par value of a country's money, in a system of fixed exchange rates. **588**

discount bond See **zero-coupon bond**.

discount rate The interest rate financial institutions pay to the Federal Reserve to borrow reserves. **210**

discount window The facility that financial institutions are said to use when borrowing reserves from the Federal Reserve. **Ch. 15**

discretionary funds Bank liabilities and assets that are subject to short-term management control. **113**

dishoarding Decreased money holdings. **471**

disintermediation Removal of funds

from financial institutions for direct investment in primary securities. **41**

disposable income Income minus taxes. **311**

dividends Earnings of a corporation that are distributed to stockholders. **31**

dividend yield The current annual dividend of a stock divided by its price. **543**

Dow Jones Industrial Average (DJIA) A measure of the level of stock prices, based on the stock prices of thirty blue-chip industrial companies. **31**

dual banking system The chartering and supervision of commercial banks by both state and federal governments. **78**

duration A measure of the futurity of a bond's payment stream that takes into account coupon size as well as time to maturity. It also measures the price sensitivity of the bond to a change in yield. **495**

dynamic open market operations. See **open market operations**.

E

Edge Act corporation An international banking subsidiary of a U.S. bank. **139**

efficient capital market A financial market in which securities prices reflect all available information. **422**

efficient portfolio A combination of assets that yields the greatest possible return for a given risk and that carries the lowest possible risk for a given return. **462**

electronic funds transfer system (EFTS) A system in which telecommunications replace checks as the means of transferring funds between banks. **162**

equation of exchange $MV = PY$, an expression showing that total spending (the supply of money times velocity) equals the value of what is bought (the price level times the level of real GNP). Sometimes used to relate the price level (P) or nominal GNP (PY) to the money supply. **277**

equilibrium A level or value from which there is no tendency to change. **65**

equilibrium interest rate The interest rate at which the quantity of funds lenders want to lend equals the quantity of funds borrowers want to borrow. At equilibrium, there is no tendency for the interest rate to change. **65**

equilibrium price The price at which the quantity demanded equals the amount supplied, so that there is no tendency for the price to change. **498–99**

equities See **common stock**.

equity capital The difference between total assets and total liabilities on a balance sheet. **107**

Eurodollars Deposits held in dollars in foreign banks. **140**

ex ante Planned or expected (contrast with **ex post**). **62–63**

excess reserves Bank reserves held in excess of what is required. See **reserves** and **required reserves**. **16**

exchange rates See **foreign exchange rate, fixed exchange rates**, and **floating exchange rates**.

exogenous spending Expenditures, such as government spending, that are determined outside of a particular economic model. **326**

expectations hypothesis A theory of the term structure of interest rates stressing that long-term rates will be an average of the current short-term rate and expected future short-term rates. **481**

ex post Actual or realized (contrast with **ex ante**). **62–63**

F

face value The final amount of indebtedness (excluding interest) that must be repaid on a bond. See **principal**. **30**

Fed Federal Reserve System. **15, 171ff.**

Federal Advisory Council A group of commercial bankers that makes recommendations to the Federal Reserve Board of Governors regarding monetary policy. **175**

Federal Deposit Insurance Corporation (FDIC) A federal agency that insures deposits at commercial and savings banks, examines and supervises state-chartered banks not members of the Federal Reserve System, and acts as receiver for banks that declare bankruptcy. **82**

Federal Financial Institutions Examinations Council A group set up to coordinate efforts of the various federal agencies supervising financial institutions. **81**

federal funds An unsecured loan between banks where the funds that are loaned are transferred the same day the loan is made. **106**

federal funds rate The interest rate on federal funds. **111–112**

Federal Home Loan Bank Board (FHLB) An agency that charters, regulates, examines, supervises, and provides credit for federally chartered savings and loan associations and insures deposits through a subsidiary, the Federal Savings and Loan Insurance Corporation (FSLIC). **91**

Federal Home Loan Mortgage Corporation ("Freddie Mac") A subsidiary of the Federal Home Loan Bank that issues debt instruments that provide claims primarily to pools of conventional mortgages. **93**

Federal National Mortgage Association ("Fannie Mae") A private corporation with certain ties to the government that issues debt instruments that provide claims primarily to pools of government-insured mortgages. **93**

Federal Open Market Committee (FOMC) A policy-making group within the Federal Reserve System that directs the open-market operations of the system. **175**

Federal Reserve System ("the Fed") The central banking system and monetary authority of the United States, made up of regional Federal Reserve Banks and the Federal Reserve Board of Governors, which supervises and examines state-chartered member banks, regulates bank holding companies, and is responsible for the conduct of monetary policy. **171ff**.

Federal Savings and Loan Insur-ance Corporation (FSLIC) See **Federal Home Loan Bank Board**.

Fed Wire A telecommunications system, operated by the Federal Reserve, that transfers funds between banks. **161**

FHA-VA mortgage A mortgage insured either by the Federal Housing Authority (FHA) or by the Veteran's Administration (VA). **32**

financial assets See **real assets**.

financial futures Futures contracts whose underlying assets are securities or, in index futures, the cash value of a group of securities. **556**

financial intermediaries Institutions (such as banks or pension funds) that borrow funds from savers by issuing claims (such as deposits or insurance contracts) and lend to others by buying securities (such as corporate bonds) or making loans. **40**

financial intermediation Indirect finance, in which savers place funds with financial intermediaries that in turn lend to ultimate borrowers. **41**

fiscal policy Government policy concerning spending and taxation. **313, 352**

fixed exchange rates An international financial system in which rates of exchange between the values of different countries' currencies are maintained at agreed-upon levels. **585**

fixed-rate loan A loan that carries an unchanging interest rate throughout the life of the loan. **113**

float The total value of checks that have been credited by the Fed to the banks in which they have been deposited but have not yet been collected from the banks on which they are drawn. **230**

floating exchange rates An international financial system in which rates of exchange between the values of different countries' currencies fluctuate according to supply and demand in the marketplace. **585**

floating-rate (variable-rate) loan A loan that carries an interest rate that is adjusted periodically to reflect changes in market interest rates in general. **113**

flower bonds Government bonds that can be used at par value to settle federal estate taxes. **486**

flow of funds accounting A record of payments and receipts among the different sectors of the economy. **465**

foreign exchange rate The value of a unit of one nation's money in terms of another nation's money. **578**

funding (of pension benefits) Setting aside funds now to cover future pension liabilities. **126–27**

futures contract A standardized agreement, traded on an organized futures exchange, for delivery of a specific commodity or security at a specified future date and at a specified price. **556**

G

general obligation bonds Municipal bonds backed by the overall taxing power of the state or local government. **536**

GNMA ("Ginnie Mae") pass-through securities Claims to a pool of FHA-VA mortgages insured by the Government National Mortgage Association (GNMA). **33**

gold export point Under an international gold standard, the limit to which a deficit nation's currency can depreciate before it becomes cheaper to export gold than to purchase foreign currency. **614**

gold import point Under an international gold standard, the limit to which a surplus nation's currency can appreciate before it becomes cheaper for other nations to pay their trade deficits to it in gold than to purchase its currency. **614**

gold standard A monetary system in which currency is redeemable in gold at a fixed price. **609–610**

Government National Mortgage Association (GNMA, "Ginnie Mae") A division of the U.S. Department of Housing and Urban Development that insures pools of FHA and VA mortgages. **33**

Gresham's Law "Bad money drives good money out of circulation." **79**

gross national product (GNP) The total value of goods and services produced in the economy in a given year. **271**

group insurance Insurance made available to members of a group, such as employees of a corporation, usually at favorable rates. **125**

H

hedger One who tries to reduce the risk of loss resulting from a change in the price of a particular asset. In futures markets, it is someone who sells a futures contract while holding the underlying asset **(short hedger)** or purchases such a contract in anticipation of purchasing the underlying asset **(long hedger)**. **560–61**

high powered money See **monetary base**.

hoarding Increased money holdings. **471**

holding company A corporation set up to hold a controlling interest in one or more other corporations. A **bank holding company** owns one or more banks. **90**

holding period yield The rate of discount that will make the sum of the present values of the coupon payments and the price at which the security is sold equal to the purchase price of the security. **57**

hyperinflation A rapid increase in general price levels, e.g., above 100 percent per year. **21**

I

IMF Special Drawing Rights (SDRs) International reserves created on the books of the International Monetary Fund (IMF) and used to settle international debts. **616**

impact lag of monetary policy

The time between the use of a monetary strategy and its effect on the economy. **440**

index fund A mutual fund whose goal is to mimic the performance of one of the financial market indexes, usually the S&P 500. **548**

Individual Retirement Account (IRA) A tax-benefited pension plan for workers. **127, 152–53**

inflation Generally rising price levels. **21, 384**

insider trading Illegal use of knowledge not available to the general public, to gain advantage in buying and selling securities. **511**

insurance company A financial institution providing protection against loss (of life or property) or costs (such as medical or legal costs) by accepting payments (premiums) in return for a guarantee of compensation. **45–46**

Inter-District Settlement Fund A facility for transferring funds among banks located in different Federal Reserve Districts. **187**

interest A charge paid by a borrower to a lender for the use of the lender's money. **11**

interest rate The cost of borrowing expressed as a percent of principal per annum. See **yield** and **yield to maturity**. **50**

internal rate of return See **yield to maturity**.

International Banking Facility (IBF) A domestic branch bank established for international banking and treated for regulatory purposes as a foreign branch. **142**

International Monetary Fund (IMF) An international organization set up in 1944 to supervise exchange rates and to promote orderly international financial conditions. **585**

international reserves Reserves held by one country usually in the form of gold or in the money of another country. **586**

investment bank A financial institution specializing in designing and marketing new issues of stocks and bonds. **501**

investment portfolio The collection of securities, such as stocks and bonds, held by an individual or a corporation. **453**

investment spending The purchase of plant, equipment, and inventories by a business. **469**

IOU See **promissory note**.

IS curve Graph of points showing combinations of level of income and interest rate at which savings equals investment. **341**

ISLM analysis A model of the economy that shows the interaction of monetary policy and fiscal policy and partially integrates the Classical and Keynesian systems. **333ff**.

K

Keogh Plan A tax-benefited pension plan designed for self-employed individuals. **127, 152–53**

Keynesian Derived from the theories of John Maynard Keynes, advocating government spending and taxation to maintain full employment and a stable economy. **298**

L

lagged reserves The former system of bank reserve requirements, which left a gap of two weeks between the calculation of required reserves and the time when the reserves had to be held. **123**

laissez faire "Let (people) do (as they wish)," a policy of government nonintervention in the economy. **272**

legal tender Money that the government requires a creditor to accept in discharge of debts. If it is not accepted, interest need not accrue thereafter. **609**

lender of last resort The Federal Reserve, which acts as the ultimate source of funds to banks and other financial institutions by providing reserves to prevent bank failures. **213**

liability A financial obligation. **185, 227**

liquid asset Cash or an asset that can be quickly converted into cash without risk of substantial loss. **4**

liquidity Ability to convert an asset into cash quickly with little loss in value. **18**

liquidity preference Keynes's term for the demand for money, often used in connection with the rate of interest. **315**

liquidity premium (risk premium) The higher yield on longer-term securities compared with short-term securities, to compensate for the additional risk of long term issues. Associated with the liquidity premium theory of the term structure of interest rates. **481**

liquidity trap In Keynesian theory, the point beyond which an increase in the money supply will no longer cause interest rates to drop. **360**

LM curve Graph of points showing combinations of level of GNP and interest rates at which liquidity preference equals the money supply. **335**

loanable funds Funds that lenders are willing to make available to borrowers. Can be used as a framework for determining the equilibrium level of interest rates. **64**

loan/deposit ratio The ratio of a bank's total loans to its total deposits, a measure of the bank's liquidity. **110**

loaned up Said of a bank that has no excess reserves against which it can make loans. **17**

long The buyer of a financial asset, usually an options or futures contract, who is also said to "take a long position." **557**

M

M1 See **money supply**.

M2 A definition of money supply that adds to M1 such assets as savings accounts, small-denomination time deposits, money market deposit accounts, and money market mutual fund shares. **5**

M3 A definition of money supply that adds to M1 and M2 such assets as large-denomination time deposits. **5**

macroeconomics The study of whole systems of the economy, such as total income and output, the price level and interest rates, and the interrelationships among them. **330**

Magnetic Ink Character Recognition (MICR) A system of imprints on checks that allows for machine sorting. **161**

managed floating system The international financial system currently in use, in which major nations intervene to influence foreign exchange rates by buying and selling currencies. **593**

margin (1) A minimum down payment required by law for the purchase of stock; (2) a deposit placed with a clearing corporation by both the buyer and the seller of a futures contract. **551, 559**

marginal propensity to consume The amount that a person spends out of each dollar of incremental income. **302**

marginal propensity to save The amount that a person saves out of each dollar of incremental income. **304**

marketability The ease of buying and selling an asset, associated with narrow bid-asked spreads. **500**

market risk (capital uncertainty) The risk of price fluctuations for a security. For bonds, it is associated with variations in the level of the interest rate. **455**

mark-to-market settlement Daily adjustments made in balances at a clearing corporation to reflect price changes in futures contracts. **559**

matched sale-purchase agreement Open market operation (sale), sometimes called a "reverse repo," in which the Federal Reserve sells securities and agrees to buy them back in the near future. **223**

maturity date The due date for the final payment on a financial instrument such as a bond or a certificate of deposit. **29**

medium of exchange Something used to finalize payments for goods and services (M1, or currency and checking accounts). **4**

Monetarism The position, based in Classical economics, that an "invisible hand" pushes the economy toward a full employment level of production at which it is inherently stable and that government efforts to affect economic activity through countercyclical policies are unnecessary and potentially damaging. Also associated with the quantity theory of money. **271ff.**

monetary authority An institution responsible for executing national monetary policy, such as the central bank. **7**

monetary base Total bank reserves plus currency held by the nonbank public. **241**

monetary policy Government policy concerning money and credit conditions, especially the rate of growth in the money supply and the level of interest rates. **17**

monetizing the debt The government's creation of money with which to buy back interest-bearing government securities. **526**

money Whatever is used as a medium of exchange, unit of account, and store of value. See **legal tender, money supply. 4**

money market The financial market for short-term securities. **36**

money market deposit account A type of account offered by depository institutions that gives limited check-writing privileges and carries market interest rates. **99**

money multiplier See **demand deposit expansion multiplier.**

money supply (M1) The total of currency outside banks and demand deposits. **5**

mortgage A (usually long-term) loan for the purchase of a home or other building, where the home or building serves as collateral in case of default. **32**

mortgage pool A package of mortgages that is sold as a unit. **33**

multiplier The ratio of the change in GNP to a change in exogenous spending; sometimes called expenditure multiplier to distinguish it from the money multiplier. **307**

municipal bond A bond issued by a state or local government, called a tax-exempt because the interest is exempt from federal income tax. **30**

mutual fund A fund that pools the investments of a large number of shareholders and purchases securities such as stocks or, in a money market mutual fund, money market instruments. **46**

N

National Association of Securities Dealers Automated Quotation System (NASDAQ) A computerized system for displaying bid and asked prices for over-the-counter stocks. **500**

National Credit Union Administration (NCUA) An agency that charters, regulates, examines, and supervises federal credit unions. **81**

natural rate of interest The rate of interest at which savings equals investment at full employment. **382–83**

negotiable order of withdrawal (NOW) account An interest-bearing checking account. **99**

net asset value (NAV) The value of a share of a mutual fund, based on the market value of the assets owned by the fund and the number of shares outstanding. **130**

net worth The difference between an individual's or business's assets and liabilities. **184**

New York Stock Exchange Composite Index A measure of the level of stock prices, based on all the stocks listed on the New York Stock Exchange. **31**

nominal GNP The gross national product measured in current prices. **279**

nominal interest rate Interest rate measured in money terms, as distinct from the real interest rate, which is corrected for changes in purchasing power. **62**

nonbank bank A bank that limits its commercial services (dropping either demand deposits or business loans) in order to bypass various legal restrictions. **133–34**

nondiscretionary funds Bank liabilities and assets not subject to short-term management control. **113**

O

open-end mutual fund A mutual fund that offers to the public shares that are redeemable at net asset value. **130**

open interest The number of open long (equal to short) positions for a given option or futures contract. **569**

open market operations The purchase and sale of government securities by the Federal Reserve in order to control levels of bank reserves. Those aimed at defending a target level of reserves from outside influences are **defensive open market operations;** those aimed at changing the level of reserves are **dynamic open market operations. 216, 238–39.**

operating efficiency (of securities markets) The effectiveness with which markets bring together buyers and sellers. **501**

operating target One of two intermediate objectives of an open market operation, usually either the level of reserves or the federal funds rate. **241**

option contract See **call option** and **put option.**

option premium The price paid by an option buyer to the option seller for the rights acquired. **570**

over-the-counter market (OTC) Trading in stocks, usually of smaller companies, that are not listed on one of the stock exchanges. Also refers to how government and corporate bonds are traded, that is, through dealers who quote bids and offers to buy and sell "over the counter." **500**

P

par (1) the fixed value of a monetary unit of one country in terms of the money of another country (used in a system of fixed exchange rates); (2) the face value of a financial asset, such as a bond. **486, 586**

passbook savings account Bank account which carries a specified rate of interest and from which funds can be drawn at any time without penalty. **106**

pass-through securities See **GNMA pass-through securities.**

payments system The institutional arrangements for settling transactions in the economy. **159ff.**

payoff method A procedure, used in cases of bank failure, in which the bank goes into receivership and the FDIC pays depositors directly. **83**

peg To hold to a fixed level, as in pegging the foreign exchange rate. **586**

Pension Benefit Guaranty Corporation (Penny Benny) An agency that insures pension benefits against company bankruptcy. **127**

pension (retirement) fund A fund, set up for a group of working people, that invests the contributions made by or for the workers and makes regular payments (annuities) to them when they retire. **45**

petrodollars Revenue, in dollars, from sales of oil to other countries. **144**

Phillips Curve The relationship between inflation and unemployment, suggesting that lower unemployment is usually accompanied by higher rates of inflation. Originally presented by Professor A. W. Phillips. **408**

point of sale (POS) terminal An electronic device that automatically debits a buyer's checking account and credits the seller's checking account at the time of sale. **162**

preferred habitat theory The theory of the term structure of interest rates that combines supply and demand forces with expectations. **482**

preferred stock Ownership interest in a company that carries a fixed promised dividend payment. **31**

prepayment Payment of an obligation before the payment is due. **32–33**

price-earnings (P/E) ratio The price of a stock divided by its earnings per share. **543**

primary securities Stocks and bonds issued by ultimate borrower-spenders. **27**

primary securities market The financial market for the purchase and sale of stocks or bonds when they are first issued. **131**

prime rate The interest rate a bank charges on loans to its business customers with the best credit rating. **534**

principal (of a bond) The amount borrowed, excluding interest. Frequently used interchangeably with the face value of a bond, although they are equal only for a coupon-bearing security that is sold at par. **30, 50**

promissory note A written promise to pay a specified sum of money at a specified time or on demand; sometimes called an IOU. **16**

put option An option contract in which the option buyer has the right (but not the obligation) to sell a specified quantity of the underlying asset at a specified price until the expiration date of the option. **567**

Q

quantity theory of money The theory that a proportional increase in the supply of money leads to a proportional increase in the price level. **277–279**

R

rational expectations Expectations of economic variables that reflect all currently available information. According to some, rational expectations may lead individuals to anticipate monetary policy and neutralize its effects. **420ff.**

real assets Property such as land or equipment, as distinguished from financial assets, such as stocks and bonds. **467**

real GNP Gross national product, adjusted for the effects of inflation. **279**

real interest rate The interest rate in terms of goods and services; approximated by subtracting the rate of inflation from the nominal interest rate. **62**

recession A time span marked by a drop in the level of economic activity and increased unemployment.

Regulation Q A provision in the Banking Act of 1933 that imposed ceilings on interest rates on savings and time deposits. No longer in effect. **96**

repurchase agreement (RP or "repo") The sale of securities with a commitment to buy them back at a specified date and at a specified price. Repos are used by the Federal Reserve as a type of open market operation and by government securities dealers to finance their inventories of bonds. **524–25**

required reserves Funds that a bank *must* hold in the form of vault cash or deposits at the Federal Reserve to meet its required reserve ratio. **16**

required reserve ratio The proportion of bank reserves to deposits that a bank must hold according to law. **193**

reserves Funds that a bank holds in the form of vault cash or deposits at the Federal Reserve. **16**

retained earnings Profits of a corporation that are not distributed as dividends to shareholders. **108**

return (rate of return) See **yield to maturity (internal rate of return)**

revenue bond A bond issued to finance a particular project, such as a toll road, the receipts from which are used to pay the interest and principal on the bond. **536**

risk structure of interest rates The relationship between yields on different types of securities, especially those with different credit ratings. **487**

round lot The unit in which securities are usually traded (100 shares of an equity, $1 million of face value in Treasury bills). **508**

S

saving function The relationship between saving and level of income, in its simplest form expressed as $S = -a + (1$

— *b*)*Y*. See also **marginal propensity to save. 301**

savings and loan association (S&L) A financial institution that traditionally was limited to accepting savings deposits, usually as shares, and making home mortgage loans. **43–44**

savings bank A financial institution that traditionally was limited to accepting savings deposits and making home mortgage loans. **44–45**

Say's Law "Supply creates its own demand," hence total spending (demand) will always be sufficient to justify production at full employment (supply). **272**

secondary securities market A financial market in which previously issued securities are traded, such as the New York Stock Exchange. **131**

securities Financial instruments representing ownership or debt, such as stocks and bonds, that provide claims to future expected cash flows. **26**

Securities and Exchange Commission A federal agency that regulates securities brokers and dealers and securities markets. **95**

securitization The sale of shares in a pool of assets (usually mortgages but also car loans, credit card loans, and others). **107**

serial maturity Scheduled retirement of a portion of a bond issue each year until the entire issue has matured. **535**

settlement by offset The cancellation of rights and obligations in the options and futures market through purchases and sales of identical contracts. **559**

share A unit of ownership in the capital stock of a corporation. **31**

shell branch A banking facility set up abroad to avoid domestic regulation and taxation. **142**

short The seller of a financial asset who still has an outstanding obligation to buy back the asset, especially an options or futures contract. Also phrased as "take a short position." **557**

simple interest Interest calculated by multiplying the principal by the interest rate and the time in years. See also **compound interest. 50–51**

Society for Worldwide Interbank Financial Telecommunications (SWIFT) A telecommunications system that transfers funds between banks internationally. **162**

sources and uses of funds statement A financial statement integrating the income statement and balance sheet of a unit or a sector of the economy. **466**

specialist A dealer who makes a market in stocks traded on an organized exchange (such as the New York Stock Exchange) and who is also responsible for matching public buy and sell orders in an auction format. **499**

spot market The market in which an asset is traded for immediate delivery, also called the cash market, as opposed to a market for forward or future delivery.

Standard & Poor's 500 Stock Index A measure of the level of stock prices based on the prices of 500 stocks selected by Standard & Poor's Corporation. **31**

sterilization A central bank policy of offsetting the effects of changes in international reserves on the money supply. **617**

stock flotation The sale of a new stock issue, to raise capital for a corporation. **108**

stocks (equities) Shares of ownership in corporations. See **common stock. 30–31**

store of value The extent to which assets maintain their purchasing power over time. Money must be a good store of value to function well. **4**

stripping Removing the interest coupons from bonds and reselling them as separate (zero-coupon) securities. **516**

supply-side economics The theory that reduction in tax rates increases production incentives and encourages expansion of economic activity, resulting ultimately in increased tax revenues. **330**

T

T-account A simple accounting statement that records only changes in balance sheet items from a starting point. **184**

tax and loan accounts Deposits of U.S. government funds, generated by tax receipts and bond sales, in commercial banks. **233**

tax-anticipation notes (TANs) Short-term municipal securities issued to raise stopgap funds and paid off from tax receipts. **537**

tax-exempts See **municipal bonds.**

term structure of interest rates The relationship between yields on different maturities of the same type of security. **478**

thrift institutions ("thrifts") Savings banks, savings and loan associations, and credit unions. **44**

time deposit A deposit (with a bank or thrift institution) that has a scheduled maturity date. If funds are withdrawn prior to the maturity date, some interest is lost as a penalty. **5**

transactions costs Costs, such as commissions and the bid-asked spread, of buying and selling securities. See **marketability. 506**

transactions demand for money The demand for money associated with the level of economic activity. **322**

Treasury bill A zero-coupon obligation of the U.S. government issued with a maturity of one year or less. **37**

Treasury bond A coupon-bearing obligation of the U.S. government issued with a maturity of over ten years. **516**

Treasury Investment Growth Receipts (TIGRs) Zero-coupon securities created by stripping Treasury bonds. **516**

Treasury note A coupon-bearing obligation of the U.S. government issued with a maturity of one to ten years. **516**

U

underwriting The process by which a newly issued security is sold to the public. **501**

underwriting spread The fee earned by an investment bank or other financial institution for marketing a newly issued security. **503**

unit of account Something used to measure relative values of goods and services. Money is usually a unit of account. **4**

V

variable-rate loan See **floating-rate loan.**

vault cash Currency held in a bank's vault. **16**

velocity The rate of turnover of the money supply; the average number of times per year each dollar is used to purchase goods and services (often measured as GNP divided by the money supply). **20**

vesting Rights in a pension fund that are not lost if the employee leaves the job before retirement. **126**

W

wealth The total value of the assets owned by an individual or business at a particular point in time. **219**

wealth effect The tendency for an increase in wealth to cause consumption to rise. **350, 362**

World Bank (International Bank for Reconstruction and Development) An organization funded by developed countries to lend money to developing countries.

Y

yield The effective rate of return for holding a debt instrument, as distinguished from its coupon rate of interest. See also **current yield, yield to maturity, holding period yield. 53–60**

yield curve A graphic representation of the relationship between yield and maturity of securities. **478**

yield on a discount basis The difference between the face value and the purchase price of a Treasury bill, divided by the face value and annualized using 360 days to the year. **522**

yield to maturity (internal rate of return) The rate of discount that makes the sum of the present values of all future payments of a security equal to its purchase price. **54**

Z

zaibatsu A large Japanese financial-industrial combine. **90**

zero-coupon bond. A bond issued without interest-bearing coupons, at a discount below face value. **30**

Index

D

E

N

Q

R

T